THE RISE OF THE VALUE-ADDED TAX

This book explores one of the most significant trends in the evolution of global tax systems by asking how, within less than half a century, the value-added tax (VAT) has risen from relative obscurity to become one of the world's most dominant revenue instruments. Despite its significance, very little is known about why so many countries have adopted the VAT and, in particular, why different countries adopt the types of VAT that they do. The popular mythology provides that the merits of the VAT have underpinned its global spread; however, this book contends that much scholarship on the VAT confuses the question of why the VAT has risen to dominance with the issue of what makes a good VAT. This book combines policy and legal analysis to propose a new way of understanding the rise of this important revenue instrument so as to better reflect the realities of the VATs that are actually implemented.

Kathryn James is a lecturer in the Faculty of Law at Monash University. She researches in the field of comparative tax law and policy, with particular emphasis on the value-added tax. She has published in a number of leading journals, including the *British Tax Review* and *Theoretical Inquiries in the Law*.

The Rise of the Value-Added Tax

KATHRYN JAMES
Monash University, Faculty of Law

CAMBRIDGE
UNIVERSITY PRESS

CAMBRIDGE
UNIVERSITY PRESS

32 Avenue of the Americas, New York, NY 10013-2473, USA

Cambridge University Press is part of the University of Cambridge.

It furthers the University's mission by disseminating knowledge in the pursuit of education, learning and research at the highest international levels of excellence.

www.cambridge.org
Information on this title: www.cambridge.org/9781107044128

First published 2015

A catalog record for this publication is available from the British Library.

Library of Congress Cataloging in Publication Data
James, Kathryn (College teacher)
The rise of the value-added tax / Kathryn James, Monash University, Faculty of Law.
pages cm. – (Cambridge tax law series)
ISBN 978-1-107-04412-8 (Hardback)
1. Value-added tax. 2. Value-added tax–Law and legislation. 3. Value-added tax–Australia–Case studies. 4. Value-added tax–United States–Case studies. I. Title.
HJ5711.J36 2015
336.2'714–dc23
2014021010

ISBN 978-1-107-04412-8 Hardback

To Colin and Christine James
And for Ms Billie Winsome

Contents

List of figures

List of tables

Preface

Little known outside a handful of jurisdictions in the 1950s, the VAT has now been adopted by more than 150 countries and accounts for approximately 20 per cent of global taxation revenues. Interestingly, despite its significance, very little is known about why so many countries have adopted VATs and, in particular, why different countries adopt the types of VAT they do. This book identifies the source of this myopia and provides an independent, critical and scholarly account of the rise of the VAT so as to better understand this important revenue instrument.

Although the task of research and writing can be a solitary one at times, there are many people to whom I owe a debt of gratitude for helping make this book a reality. This book arose from a doctoral dissertation completed through the Faculty of Law, Monash University. I must therefore express my sincere thanks to the handful of supervisors who steered me through the dissertation: Jeff Waincymer, Rick Krever, Graeme Hodge, Stephen Barkozcy and Patrick Emerton. The latter I owe a special debt for his curiosity, integrity and boundless generosity toward this project and toward my development as a researcher. I am also grateful to the examiners of the dissertation for their enthusiastic and useful feedback and for encouraging me to take the bold next step of converting the dissertation into a monograph.

I am the lucky beneficiary of many wonderful colleagues who lent invaluable support at various stages, from IT support to proofreading. I am sure I have left important names off this list, but thanks to Kay Tucker, Rebecca Giblin, Annegret Kaempf, Ronli Sifris, Melissa Castan and Peter Mellor – who brought my attention to early VAT-like proposals in the United States. Thanks to Sandra Pyke for creating the index. I have presented various parts of this research in a number of different fora and am grateful to colleagues in Australia and overseas for their valuable comments and feedback.

Thanks to John Berger for backing this project and providing steady guidance throughout. Thanks also to the wonderful staff at Cambridge who have helped make this book a reality – Dave Morris, Britto Fleming Joe, Ezhil Sugu Maran and Marianne Tatom deserve special mention.

Although a paragraph is entirely insufficient to do it justice, I would like to express my enormous gratitude to my partner, Melanie Hodge, whose efforts went well beyond the usual struggles that accompany the unwieldy task of partnering a doctoral candidate and then first-time book author. Not only did you, unlike most others, think this project interesting, but you provided me with the intellectual, emotional and practical support to see it through. I am forever grateful to you for that and for so much more.

Thanks to my wonderful parents, Christine and Colin James. All my achievements are a product of the opportunities provided for me by both my parents – opportunities which they were not able to access themselves. My greatest sorrow is that my dad is not here to share these victories that are as much his as they are mine.

This book has had a long gestation that now spans the birth of my own daughter, Billie Winsome. My hope is that, just as my parents did for me, I can enable Billie to find her own place in this world from which to grow, thrive and shake things up just a little.

The law is current at 28 February 2014.

List of commonly used abbreviations and key terms

ATO	Australian Taxation Office
BoT	Board of Taxation
B2B	Business-to-business supply
B2C	Business-to-consumer supply
GATT	General Agreement on Tariffs and Trade
GDP	Gross domestic product
GNP	Gross national product
EU	European Union
IMF	International Monetary Fund
OECD	Organisation for Economic Cooperation and Development
RST	Retail sales tax
UK	United Kingdom
US	United States
VAT	Value-added tax
WST	Wholesale sales tax
WTO	World Trade Organization
§	This symbol is used to denote sections within the chapters of this book.

All cross-references to section numbers are made to sections within a chapter unless indicated otherwise.

1

The rise of the value-added tax

Within less than half a century, the value-added tax (VAT) has become one of the most dominant revenue instruments across the world. From relatively inauspicious beginnings in the early twentieth century, the VAT has been adopted by more than 150 countries and accounts for approximately 20 per cent of worldwide tax revenue.[1] In population terms, it is estimated that more than 4 billion people, or 70 per cent of the world's population, live in countries with a VAT.[2]

If considered as a variant of a sales tax (or specifically, a turnover tax), the origins of the VAT run deep;[3] however, the VAT is generally perceived as a thoroughly modern fiscal innovation. Attribution is variously to one of two sources. The first suggests that German businessman Dr Wilhelm von Siemens proposed the VAT in 1918 as a 'refinement' or improvement to the German cascading turnover tax.[4] The second suggests that the American economist T. S. Adams, writing between 1910 and 1921, proposed an invoice-credit method VAT as an alternative to business income taxation.[5]

1 OECD, *Consumption Tax Trends 2012: VAT/GST and Excise Rates, Trends and Administration Issues* (OECD Publishing, Paris, 2012), 58, 211–19; Michael Keen and Ben Lockwood, 'The Value Added Tax: Its Causes and Consequences', *Journal of Development Economics* 92 (2) (2010), 138.

2 Liam Ebrill et al., *The Modern VAT* (IMF, Washington, DC, 2001), xi.

3 The origins of the turnover tax as a form of percentage charge on trading transactions have been traced to Ancient Greece, Hellenistic Egypt and throughout the Roman Empire: Günter Schmölders, *Turnover Taxes* (International Bureau of Fiscal Documentation, Amsterdam, 1966), 7; Robert F. van Brederode, *Systems of General Sales Taxation: Theory, Policy and Practice* (Kluwer Law International Alphen aan den Rijn, 2009), 5.

4 The attribution to von Siemens was by younger brother Carl Friedrich von Siemens, who assumed leadership of the von Siemens' company following the deaths of his older brothers: C. F. von Siemens, *Veredelte Umsatzsteuer* (translated as 'improving sales tax' or 'the improvement of the concept of sales tax') (Siemensstadt 1921), see especially 14–18.

5 T. S. Adams, 'Fundamental Problems of Federal Income Taxation' (1921), *Quarterly Journal of Economics* 35(4), 527, 553. Given that Adams was a German speaker and there were frequent

Irrespective of attribution, however, the rapidity of the VAT's ascendancy is remarkable. Before the 1967 decision to adopt the VAT as the common form of sales tax in the European Economic Community (EEC),[6] less than a handful of countries had experimented with the tax, and almost none in the form by which the VAT is known today.[7] Now, in terms of revenue collection, the VAT ranks among

interactions between German and US tax policy-makers at the time, it was likely there was some cross-pollination: Holger Nehring, 'The Paradoxes of State-Building: Transnational Expertise and the Income Tax Debates in the United States and Germany, c. 1880–1914' in H. Nehring and F. Schui (eds.), *Global Debates About Taxation* (Palgrave Macmillan, Basingstoke, UK; New York, 2007), 97. Due contends that it 'was likely that Adams was familiar with the German discussion': John F. Due, *Sales Taxation* (University of Illinois Press, Urbana, 1957), 138–39. Lindholm claims that 'Adams had previously supported the basic concept of VAT in 1911': Richard W. Lindholm, *Value-Added Tax and Other Tax Reforms* (Nelson-Hall, Chicago, 1976), 42. Sullivan suggests that the 'credit method was first suggested by Thomas S. Adams': Clara K. Sullivan, *The Tax on Value Added* (New York, 1965), 12, 17; Liam Ebrill et al., *The Modern VAT* (IMF, Washington, DC, 2001), 4; Dan Throop Smith, James Webber and Carol Cerf, *What You Should Know About the Value Added Tax* (Dow Jones-Irwin, Homewood, IL, 1973), 12; Alan Schenk and Oliver Oldman, *Value Added Tax: A Comparative Approach* (rev. edn., Cambridge University Press, 2007), 4.

6 Article 99 (ex. 93) of the EEC Treaty instructed the European Commission to 'consider how the legislation of the various Member States concerning turnover taxes, excise duties and other forms of indirect taxation...can be harmonised in the interest of the common market': *The Treaty Establishing the European Economic Community*, as revised ('EEC Treaty') (*Official Journal of the European Union*, 2006/C321/E1). *Revision of the Treaty Establishing the European Economic Community*, opened for signature 25 March 1957, 298 UNTS 11 (entered into force 1 January 1958). The First Council Directive outlined the definition and aims of the proposed VAT: *First Council Directive 67/227/EEC of 11 April 1967 on the Harmonisation of Legislation of Member States Concerning Turnover Taxes* [1967] OJ L 1/14; [1967] OJ Spec Ed 14. The Second Council Directive of 11 April 1967 provided the details for the new system (by, for example, outlining concepts such as taxable transaction and place of supply) but gave Member States considerable scope to determine the content of their domestic VATs with freedom to determine their own VAT rate structure and exemptions: *Second Council Directive 67/228/EEC of 11 April 1967 on the Harmonisation of Legislation of Member States Concerning Turnover Taxes – Structure and Procedures for Application of the Common System of Value Added Tax* [1967] OJ 1/14; [1967] OJ Spec Ed 16. The passage of the Sixth Directive in May 1977 provided greater guidance on the operation of the common VAT: *Sixth Council Directive 77/388/EEC of 17 May 1977 on the Harmonization of the Laws of the Member States Relating to Turnover Taxes – Common System of Value Added Tax: Uniform Basis of Assessment* [1977] OJ L 145/1. The current Directive is a recast of the Sixth Directive: *Council Directive 2006/112/EC of 28 November 2006 on the Common System of Value Added Tax* [2006] OJ L 347/1 (referred to hereafter as the '*Recast VAT Directive 2006/112/EEC*'). See generally: Ben Terra and Julie Kajus, IBFD, *A Guide to the European VAT Directives* [online] (15 April 2011); Rita de la Feria, *The EU VAT System and the Internal Market* (IBFD, Amsterdam, 2009); Walter van der Corput and Fabiola Annacondia (eds.), *EU VAT Compass* (IBFD Publications, Amsterdam, 2007).

7 Although France is often regarded as the first jurisdiction to introduce a national VAT, France phased in the introduction of a VAT over a two-decade period. Disputes as to the actual date of introduction can therefore arise based on the definition one might adopt of the VAT. In 1948 France introduced a fractional payment system, which meant that rather than suspending tax on physical goods acquired by manufacturers, purchasers were able to offset tax already paid on the goods against their total tax liability. In 1954 the ability to offset was extended to tax paid on capital goods. However, even then the tax was a very limited coverage tax and did not move to a full VAT extending to the retail sector until 1968. Maurice Lauré is credited with

the income tax and social security tax in 32 of the 33 member countries of the Organisation for Economic Cooperation and Development (OECD) that have adopted VATs. From 1965 to 2009, VAT revenue as a share of total tax revenue rose from an unweighted average of 1.8 per cent to 19.2 per cent across the OECD.[8]

However, it is among developing and transitional economies that the growth of the VAT has been truly ascendant. Approximately three-quarters of countries with VAT are low- to middle-income countries,[9] and two-thirds of the least developed countries in the world have VATs.[10] As Table 1.1[11] shows, the vast bulk of VAT

developing the French tax on value-add: Maurice Lauré, *La taxe sur law valeur ajoutée* (Paris, 1952); Liam Ebrill et al., *The Modern VAT* (IMF, Washington, DC, 2001), 4; Schenk and Oldman list the date as either 1948 or 1968: Alan Schenk and Oliver Oldman, *Value Added Tax: A Comparative Approach* (rev. edn., Cambridge University Press, 2007); Alan A. Tait, *Value Added Tax: International Practice and Problems* (IMF, Washington, DC, 1988), 7–8. The first full VAT in Europe was introduced in Denmark in 1967, although it did not join the EEC until 1973. The tax replaced the Danish gross receipts tax. However, the initial VAT did not tax services in a comprehensive manner: Sijbren Cnossen, *Value Added Taxes in Central and Eastern Europe: A Survey and Evaluation* (European Commission, OECD, Paris, 1998), 424; Robert F. van Brederode, *Systems of General Sales Taxation: Theory, Policy and Practice* (Kluwer Law International Alphen aan den Rijn, 2009), 7. A number of variations and false starts preceded the introduction of these VATs. Perhaps the most infamous is the abandoned VAT reform in postwar Japan, undertaken at the suggestion of the Shoup Mission headed by Professor Carl Shoup who, upon the invitation of General Douglas MacArthur to review the Japanese tax system, recommended the introduction of a VAT at the prefectural level to replace existing turnover taxes. Although a law implementing the tax was enacted in 1950, intense opposition from the business community resulted in the introduction of the tax being postponed several times until its eventual repeal in 1954: Shoup Mission, *Report on Japanese Taxation* (SCAP, Tokyo, 1949); Shoup Mission, *Second Report on Japanese Taxation* (Japan Tax Association, Tokyo, 1950); Hiromitsu Ishi, *The Japanese Tax System* (2nd ed., Oxford University Press, 1993), 315.

8 OECD, *Consumption Tax Trends 2012: VAT/GST and Excise Rates, Trends and Administration Issues* (OECD Publishing, Paris, 2012), 65.

9 Approximately 109 of the more than 150 countries with a VAT are classified as low-, low-to-middle- or upper-middle-income countries. These income indicators are generally adopted as a rough proxy for developing countries. More than half of the 150 countries with VAT are low-income or low-to-middle-income economies. Estimates based on: Fabiola Annacondia and Walter van der Corput, 'Overview of General Turnover Taxes and Tax Rates' (2012), March/April *International VAT Monitor* 2, 2–10; World Bank, *Country and Lending Groups* (2012), http://go.worldbank.org/D7SN0B8YU0.

10 The UN classification of least developed countries (LDCs) includes countries that are 'highly disadvantaged in their development process' and are facing the risk of failing to come out of poverty more than other countries. The 48 countries currently on the list of LDCs are therefore 'considered to be in need of the highest degree of attention on the part of the international community': United Nations Conference on Trade and Development, *The Least Developed Countries Report 2009: The State and Development Governance*, UNCTAD/LDC/2009, iii.

11 Country classifications based on Liam Ebrill et al., *The Modern VAT* (IMF, Washington, DC, 2001), 6, 206–7, Table AI.1. Variations to classifications and additions are noted below nn a–f. Results reflect the author's own calculations based on data assembled from: International Tax Dialogue (ITD), 'The Value Added Tax: Experience and Issues' (Background Paper Prepared for the International Tax Dialogue Conference on the VAT, Rome, March 15–16, 2005, ITD), 9, 4–6; OECD, *Consumption Tax Trends 2012: VAT/GST and Excise Rates, Trends and*

TABLE 1.1 – *VAT uptake by region as of 2013*

	Sub-Saharan Africa[a]	Asia and the Pacific[b]	EU15 plus[c]	Central Europe and the former Soviet Union[d]	North Africa and the Middle East[e]	Americas	Small islands (population < 1 million)[f]
Countries with VAT*	39(44)	19(25)	21(23)	28(28)	9(21)	25(26)	14(24)
2006–2013	6	1	0	1	2	2	9
1996–2005	18	7	0	6	1	1	3
1986–1995	13	9	9	21	4	6	2
1976–1985	1	2	0	0	2	6	0
1966–1975	0	0	11	0	0	10	0
Before 1965	1	0	1	0	0	0	0

[a] Including South Sudan: Deloitte, Taxation and Investment: South Sudan – Highlights 2014 ; IBFD, *Country Surveys* (31 January 2014), 'South Sudan'. Gambia introduced a VAT taking effect 1 January 2013: Fabiola Annacondia and Walter van der Corput, 'Overview of General Turnover Taxes and Tax Rates' (2013), March/April *International VAT Monitor* 2, 5.

[b] Modified to include Timor-Leste, which does not have a VAT but levies a separate sales tax and services tax. India has sub-national VATs in most states but no federal VAT, but is counted as a country with VAT: OECD, *Consumption Tax Trends 2012: VAT/GST and Excise Rates, Trends and Administration Issues* (OECD Publishing, Paris, 2012), 215.

[c] EU 15 include: Austria, Belgium, Denmark, Finland, France, Germany, Greece, Ireland, Italy, Luxembourg, Netherlands, Portugal, Spain, Sweden and the United Kingdom: Liam Ebrill et al., *The Modern VAT* (IMF, Washington, DC, 2001), 6, 206–07, Table AI.1. Additions include the micro-states, sovereign and semi-sovereign states within the European geographic zone: Andorra, Republic of Cyprus (EU member state as of 2004), Iceland, Liechtenstein, Malta (EU member state as of 2004), Monaco (applies the French VAT and is included with France), Norway, San Marino and Switzerland. Andorra and San Marino have no VAT. Liechtenstein, Iceland, Norway and Switzerland are not in the EU, but all are members of the European Free Trade Association (EFTA) and all levy VATs: Ernst & Young, *Worldwide VAT, GST and Sales Tax Guide* (Ernst & Young, 2014), 746–53; OECD, *Consumption Tax Trends 2012: VAT/GST and Excise Rates, Trends and Administration Issues* (OECD Publishing, Paris, 2012), 211.

[d] Many of the states within this classification have joined the EU, including the Czech Republic, Estonia, Hungary, Latvia, Lithuania, Poland, Slovak Republic and Slovenia in 2004; and Bulgaria and Romania in 2007. The regional classification is carried over from Ebrill et al. because it demonstrates the VAT uptake in this general geographic region following the end of the Soviet Union. Serbia (VAT introduced in 2005) and Montenegro (VAT introduced in 2003) have also been included: ibid.

[e] Bahrain, Oman, Qatar, Saudi Arabia, Syria and United Arab Emirates were expected to introduce VAT systems in 2013: OECD, *Consumption Tax Trends 2012: VAT/GST and Excise Rates, Trends and Administration Issues* (OECD Publishing, Paris, 2012), 219. This did not occur. Annacondia and van der Corput now estimate that VATs will be introduced in these jurisdictions (as well as Kuwait) 'in the near future': Fabiola Annacondia and Walter van der Corput, 'Overview of General Turnover Taxes and Tax Rates' (2013), March/April *International VAT Monitor* 2, 3, 9.

[f] Countries include Tuvalu but exclude the Republic of Cyprus and Malta (which have subsequently joined the EU), Iceland (which is included in the EU Plus category as it is in the EFTA) and San Marino (which is in the EU Plus category as it is a member of the Council of Europe). After much delay,

difficulty and IMF intervention, a VAT in the Republic of Seychelles took effect on 1 January 2013. A VAT is proposed to take effect in the Bahamas on 1 July 2014: Robert F. van Brederode, 'VAT News: Bahamas – Introduction of VAT' (July/August 2013), *International VAT Monitor* 24(4), 209, 237.
* (out of total number of countries in region)

uptake, particularly in the developing world, occurred in the final two decades of the twentieth century.

There are now far fewer countries in the world without a VAT than with a VAT. The most prominent exception in the developed world is the United States (US).[12] The pace and breadth of VAT reform means that the VAT rivals the income tax as an exemplar of twentieth-century tax policy convergence, so much so that one leading VAT commentator, Sijbren Cnossen, claims that '[t]he nearly universal introduction of the value added tax should be considered the most important event in the evolution of tax structure in the last half of the twentieth century'.[13]

1 WHAT LIES BEHIND THE REMARKABLE RISE OF THE VAT?

One might think that the rapid rise and growing significance of the VAT have promoted much research on what has contributed to its remarkable rise. However, very little is known about why so many countries have adopted VATs and, in particular, why different countries adopt the types of VAT they do. This state of affairs persists despite the rise of the VAT having spawned a veritable growth industry of technocrats to variously analyse, prescribe and promote it.[14]

Administration Issues (OECD Publishing, Paris, 2012), 211–19; Fabiola Annacondia and Walter van der Corput, 'Overview of General Turnover Taxes and Tax Rates' (2013), March/April *International VAT Monitor* 2, 2–10; Fabiola Annacondia and Walter van der Corput, 'Overview of General Turnover Taxes and Tax Rates' (2012), March/April *International VAT Monitor* 2, 2–10; Alan Schenk and Oliver Oldman, *Value Added Tax: A Comparative Approach* (rev. edn., Cambridge University Press, 2007), 459–62; Ernst & Young, *Worldwide VAT, GST and Sales Tax Guide* (Ernst & Young, 2014). The caveats that inform these sources also inform this table – the accuracy of the information varies according to the reliability of the data, which has been compiled from a number of sources over a period of time.

12 As Table 1.1 indicates, VATs are less common across the Middle East and in smaller islands, but recent VAT reforms and proposed VAT reforms continue to address this gap: Richard Bird and Pierre-Pascal Gendron, *The VAT in Developing and Transitional Countries* (Cambridge University Press, 2007), 17.

13 Sijbren Cnossen, 'Global Trends and Issues in Value Added Taxation', *International Tax and Public Finance* 5(3) (1998), 399.

14 The use of this term is intended as descriptive only. For a similarly benign use of the descriptor in relation to tax reform, see, e.g., Robert Bates, 'A Political Scientist Looks at Tax Reform,' in M. Gillis (ed.), *Tax Reform in Developing Countries* (Duke University Press, Durham, NC, 1989), 473. For a more pejorative use see Joseph E. Stiglitz, 'Don't Trust Technocrats,' *The Guardian* (online), 16 July 2003, www.theguardian.com/politics/2003/jul/16/globalisation.economy.

Most writing on the global rise of the VAT subscribes to what this book describes as the *conventional approach*. This term denotes a general body of work by authors, often with shared organisational affiliations, who are united in their support for the VAT, are frequently active in VAT reform and share conceptions of what constitutes best-practice VAT design.[15] Nearly all authors within the conventional approach are directly or indirectly associated with organisations at the forefront of worldwide VAT reform, such as the International Monetary Fund (IMF),[16] the OECD[17] and the World Bank.[18]

The core of the conventional approach is a body of work published by these organisations or written by employees of these organisations.[19] As the references within this book demonstrate, most authoritative VAT texts are published by these

[15] Bird and Gendron, for example, refer to the 'conventional wisdom' on VAT: Richard Bird and Pierre-Pascal Gendron, *The VAT in Developing and Transitional* Countries (Cambridge University Press, 2007), 2, 8; Ebrill et al. refer to the 'conventional wisdom' regarding the advantages of a VAT over a retail sales tax: Liam Ebrill et al., *The Modern VAT* (IMF, Washington, DC, 2001), 23; Bogetic and Hassan in 1993 referred to 'the emerging conventional wisdom' on VAT design: Zeljko Bogetic and Fareed Hassan, 'Determinants of Value-Added Tax Revenue: A Cross-Section Analysis' (Policy Research Working Paper No. WPS 1203, Washington, DC, 1993), 2; Keen makes repeated reference to the 'conventional wisdom' on the VAT: Michael Keen, 'What Do (and Don't) We Know about the Value Added Tax? A Review of Richard M. Bird and Pierre-Pascal Gendron's *The VAT in Developing and Transitional Countries*', *Journal of Economic Literature* 47(1) (2009), 159, 161, 165, 169.

[16] See, e.g., Liam Ebrill et al., *The Modern VAT* (IMF, Washington, DC, 2001); Michael Keen, 'VAT Attacks!' (Working Paper No. WP/07/142, IMF, 2007); Graham Harrison and Russell Krelove, 'VAT Refunds: A Review of Country Experience' (Working Paper No. WP/05/218, IMF, 2005); Michael Keen and Ben Lockwood, 'The Value Added Tax: Its Causes and Consequences' (2010), *Journal of Development Economics* 92(2), 138; David Williams, 'Value-Added Tax,' in V. Thuronyi (ed.), *Tax Law Design and Drafting* (IMF, Washington, DC, 1996), vol. 1, 164; Jean-Paul Bodin and Vincent Koukpaizan, 'The Rise of VAT in Africa – Impact and Challenges' (2009), *International VAT Monitor*, 178; Parthasarathi Shome (ed.), *Tax Policy Handbook* (Tax Policy Division, Fiscal Affairs Department, IMF, Washington, DC, 1995), especially Part III.

[17] See, e.g., the OECD Consumption Tax Trends series, of which the latest is OECD, *Consumption Tax Trends 2012: VAT/GST and Excise Rates, Trends and Administration Issues* (OECD Publishing, Paris, 2012); OECD, 'Consumption Taxes: The Way of the Future? (Policy Brief)' (2007), *OECD Observer*, 1; Erik Jørgensen and Jeffrey Owens, 'The Move to VAT', *OECD Observer* (August/September 1995), 21; OECD, *International VAT/GST Guidelines* (OECD Publishing, Paris, 2014); OECD, *Forum on Tax Administration: Compliance Sub-Group, Information Note, Developments in VAT Compliance Management in Selected Countries* (OECD, Centre for Tax Policy and Administration, Paris, 2009); OECD, Global Forum on VAT (2015) www.oecd.org/ctp/consumption/vat-global-forum.htm.

[18] See, e.g., Malcolm Gillis, Carl S. Shoup and Gerardo P. Sicat (eds.), *Value Added Taxation in Developing Countries* (World Bank, Washington, DC, 1990); Zeljko Bogetic and Fareed Hassan, 'Determinants of Value-Added Tax Revenue: A Cross-Section Analysis' (Policy Research Working Paper No. WPS 1203, Washington, DC, 1993); Farid Tadros, 'Introducing the Value-Added Tax: Considerations for Implementation' (The Investment Climate In Practice Note Series. No. 4, World Bank, 2009); Z. Shalizi and World Bank Group, *Lessons of Tax Reform* (World Bank, Washington, DC, 1991), 24–25, 29–33.

[19] See the references quoted above in notes 16 to 18. Current or former staff members of these organisations include Bodin, Cnossen, Smith, Keen and Tait.

organisations or are written by authors with affiliated links.[20] The leading text to which most analyses refer is a 2001 IMF publication titled *The Modern VAT*.[21] Such is the dominance of the conventional approach to global VAT analysis that one is hard pressed to find accounts that, if not made from within the conventional approach, will not at least reference one or more of the main works or dominant ideas within it.[22]

At the periphery of the conventional approach exists a larger body of work written predominantly by scholars who share a commitment to the VAT as well as a shared view of what constitutes best-practice VAT design. These scholars also generally have practical experience in VAT reform, with many having acted in some consultative capacity for the IMF, World Bank or OECD.[23]

20 See the references quoted above in notes 16 to 18. Keen notes the dominance of the IMF in particular when he equates the "Fund view" to the conventional wisdom on the VAT: Michael Keen, 'What Do (and Don't) We Know about the Value Added Tax? A Review of Richard M. Bird and Pierre-Pascal Gendron's *The VAT in Developing and Transitional Countries*', *Journal of Economic Literature* 47(1) (2009), 159, 160–61. See also: The International Tax Dialogue (ITD), which defines itself as a 'collaborative arrangement involving the EC [European Community], IDB [International Development Bank], IMF, OECD, World Bank Group and CIAT [Inter-American Center of Tax Administrations] to encourage and facilitate discussion of tax matters among national tax officials, international organisations, and a range of other key stakeholders'. ITD, *ITD Web*, www.itdweb.org/Pages/Home.aspx.

21 Liam Ebrill et al., *The Modern VAT* (IMF, Washington, DC, 2001). Bird and Gendron state that:

> The most comprehensive of these [VAT] studies remains Ebrill et al. (2001) which is more subtle and restrained in its analysis than the practical application of the advice contained therein seems to have been in some instances.

Richard Bird and Pierre-Pascal Gendron, *The VAT in Developing and Transitional Countries* (Cambridge University Press, 2007), 2.

22 For rare criticisms of the *conventional approach*, see, e.g., Scott Riswold, 'VAT in Sub-Saharan Africa – A Critique of IMF VAT Policy' (March/April 2004), *International VAT Monitor* 97; M. Shahe Emran and Joseph E. Stiglitz, 'On selective indirect tax reform in developing countries' (2005), *Journal of Public Economics* 89, 599.

23 Texts in this category include Richard Bird and Pierre-Pascal Gendron, *The VAT in Developing and Transitional Countries* (Cambridge University Press, 2007); Alan Schenk and Oliver Oldman, *Value Added Tax: A Comparative Approach* (rev. edn., Cambridge University Press, 2007); Robert F. van Brederode, *Systems of General Sales Taxation: Theory, Policy and Practice* (Kluwer Law International Alphen aan den Rijn, 2009). See further the authors referred to in the footnotes to this chapter. They include authors who have acted as consultants of the IMF, World Bank or OECD (Bodin, Koukpaizan, Gillis, Bird, Schenk, Shoup). Shoup has been labelled the 'intellectual father of the value-added tax': Wayne Thirsk, 'Intellectual Foundations of the VAT in North America and Japan,' in L. Eden (ed.), *Retrospectives on Public Finance* (Duke University Press, Durham, NC and London, 1991), 133. The dominance of the conventional approach is sometimes acknowledged by those within it. Keen, for example, notes that one of the 'great potential advantages' of the Bird and Gendron text is that the authors 'are not full-time employees of the IMF': Michael Keen, 'What Do (and Don't) We Know about the Value Added Tax? A Review of Richard M. Bird and Pierre-Pascal Gendron's *The VAT in Developing and Transitional Countries*', *Journal of Economic Literature* 47(1) (2009), 159, 160.

Whereas the conventional approach devotes enormous attention to questions of how best to design a VAT and to articulating the associated merits that ensue from a well-designed VAT, very little attention has been paid to explaining its rise. When attention is paid to this question, the conventional approach explains the introduction of VAT in more than 150 countries by reference to the merits of a well-designed VAT. The book demonstrates that this explanation generally rests on the merits of an ideal or *good VAT* that is rarely, if ever, realised in practice by *real VATs*. While this book does not dispute the merits claimed of the good VAT, or real VATs for that matter, the negative component of the book contends that an explanation of the rise of the VAT by reference to its merits does not withstand scrutiny at both a theoretical and an empirical level. In light of the insufficiency of existing explanations for the rise of real VATs, the positive component of the book suggests better ways to explain the rise of this increasingly important revenue instrument.

2 OVERVIEW OF THE BOOK

This book proposes a new approach to explaining the rise of the VAT and adopts a tripartite structure to do so.

2.1 *Part I – The rise of the value-added tax – Exploring the gap between expectation and delivery*

Part I traces the trajectory of the VAT's rise and explores the gap between the promise of the good VAT supported by the conventional approach and the reality of the more than 150 real VATs in existence.

Chapter 2 explores the type of VAT the conventional approach promotes, labelled the *good VAT*. The *good VAT* does not refer to a theoretically pure VAT but rather represents the consensus position within the conventional approach on what a best-practice VAT should look like based on certain shared normative preferences and common experiences in real-world VAT implementation. The term *good VAT* is not intended to endorse or pass judgment on the conventional approach's preference for this best-practice VAT but simply to describe it in the terms used by the conventional approach. The good VAT is, in essence, achieved through three design norms that require the VAT be levied: (1) on a broad consumption base at a single rate; (2) through the invoice-credit method; and (3) on a destination basis. The chapter discusses these design norms and highlights the associated merits they are said to facilitate. These merits include those traditionally related to the evaluation of revenue instruments such as revenue generation, efficiency, neutrality, simplicity and equity. The chapter also introduces some problematic aspects in the design of the good VAT – *frontier issues* which test the limits of the good

VAT,[24] such as the application of the VAT to real property and cross-border supplies, as well as the increasingly problematic issue of VAT fraud. The remainder of the book focuses on one frontier issue – the taxation of financial supplies – to illustrate the types of issues that arise when the limits of the good VAT are reached.

Chapter 3 assesses how the many real VATs in existence fare against the three design norms of the good VAT. The term *real VATs* is deployed to encompass the variety of VATs which actually exist in practice. The analysis shows that even by the conventional approach's own assessment few, if any, real VATs resemble the prescriptions or promises of the good VAT. That is, they infrequently apply to a broad base at a single rate and there are various difficulties in levying the VAT through the invoice-credit method and on a destination basis. As a result, these real VATs fail, in various ways, to realise the promised merits of the good VAT.

2.2 *Part II – Explaining the rise of the VAT*

Part II focuses on the much-neglected question of explaining the rise of the VAT. It identifies that more than mere neglect contributes to a poor understanding of the rise of the VAT and proposes an alternative to the dominant and insufficient explanations provided by the conventional approach.

Chapter 4 examines the various attempts to explain the rise of the VAT. It reveals that the dominant explanation provided by the conventional approach attributes the VAT's rise to the merits of the good VAT despite the conventional approach's own acknowledgement that few, if any, countries actually have a good VAT. Such is the confidence in the belief of the merits of the good VAT by the conventional approach that many of its proponents treat the history of VAT reform as irrelevant or unproblematic. Whereas the histories of VAT reform are treated as having little or no bearing on the VAT's design and operation, the design of the VAT is presented as having ultimate bearing in explaining the history of the VAT's rise.

The book contends that an explanation of the rise of the VAT by reference to its merits cannot hold. First, at a basic level, the good is not self-realising – 'good' ideas might never get adopted, while 'bad' ideas often are.[25] Second, in light of the discrepancy between the good VAT and real VATs, an explanation that attributes the VAT's rise to the merits of the good VAT falters when confronted by the fact that no one in practice has a good VAT. When it is acknowledged that no one has a good VAT, or that the merits of real VATs operate in different and sometimes contradictory ways, the empirical account of the conventional approach fails. In essence, the conventional approach is explaining the rise of something that does not exist – there

[24] For this notion of a frontier issue, see Richard Bird and Pierre-Pascal Gendron, *The VAT in Developing and Transitional Countries* (Cambridge University Press, 2007), 2, 97.

[25] Raymond Geuss, *Philosophy and Real Politics* (Princeton University Press, Princeton, NJ, 2008), 28.

is no one good VAT in practice, just as there is no one meritorious real VAT that appeals to all people in all places at all times. Instead, there are a number of real VATs that appeal for overlapping, different and sometimes contradictory reasons dependent on local context. However, right at the point when the merits matter the most, at the point of a country deciding whether to introduce a VAT, rather than examining this context and deriving some useful insights into how merits are actually perceived and how real VATs come about, the conventional approach circumvents the analysis by simply attributing the VAT's rise back to its general merits.

Chapter 4 demonstrates that one major problem with the explanations provided by the conventional approach of the rise of the VAT is a failure to adequately take account of the policy-making processes that result in real VATs. Some authors treat the merits of the VAT as solely determinative of its rise. The promise of more sophisticated explanations which begin to take account of mediating factors, such as the role of transnational actors, the impact of fashionable trends, or yardstick competition, is cut short by the authors treating these factors as mere consequences of the merits of the VAT, good or real. So, international government actors, such as the IMF and World Bank, simply become mere messengers of the virtues of the good VAT, and countries converge on fashionable trends not because it is the fashion but because the fashion is virtuous or good. There is little discussion, for example, of what deeper forces, if any, underpin the fashionable trend toward VAT reform, or of how key intergovernmental actors have shaped VAT reform or of what might have prompted their actions. Moreover, there is virtually no discussion of the role of other transnational actors, such as consultants, private firms and aid and development agencies, in promoting VAT reform. These omissions are particularly striking given that it is those within the conventional approach who have been at the forefront of VAT reform.

In light of the many deficiencies in the explanations for the VAT's rise provided by the conventional approach, Chapter 5 proposes refocusing the inquiry from a general one into how the VAT has risen to one that better reflects the empirical reality and therefore examines how *real VATs* have risen. Chapter 5 brings to light those aspects of the policy process ignored or downplayed by the conventional approach. It considers two prominent yet divergent approaches to policy analysis, public choice and historical institutionalism, for an alternative means by which to explain the rise of the VAT. Both approaches highlight the manner in which policy outcomes are constrained by a combination of factors that challenge the very perceptions of merits, let alone the realisation of those merits. Public choice, for example, shows how the constraints on, and choices of, actors in the tax-policy-making process can result in policy outcomes that might be considered politically optimal but decidedly unmeritorious from the perspective of the conventional approach.[26] So, the much-derided

[26] See, e.g., Walter Hettich and Stanley L. Winer, *Democratic Choice and Taxation: A Theoretical and Empirical Analysis* (Cambridge University Press, 1999).

features of real VATs, such as their multiple rates or exclusions to the base, might be the politically efficient, if not economically efficient, outcome of the political constraints of the policy-making process. Historical institutionalism emphasises how history and the institutionalisation of past choices influence both the perception of merits and the capacity of actors to realise policy outcomes, whether or not motivated by merits or otherwise.[27] The chapter explains the overlap between historical institutionalism and fiscal sociology and the benefits of applying such context-driven analysis toward the task of explaining the rise of the many real VATs in existence. However, as well as demonstrating the theoretical inadequacy of the explanations provided by the conventional approach, Chapter 5 also highlights a significant gap in existing public policy accounts of the VAT's rise. Many public policy analyses of the VAT to date unwittingly reinforce the merits-based accounts of the conventional approach, in part because they defer to the technical expertise of the conventional approach on questions relating to the VAT. That is, because analyses of VAT reform outside the conventional approach do not take account of the important distinction made in this book between the good VAT and real VATs, these accounts fall victim to the same flawed assumption of the conventional approach – that the VAT's rise is attributable to its merits.

To demonstrate the benefit of an alternative approach which does not fall victim to the same flawed merits-based explanations, Chapter 5 proposes an alternative approach for explaining the rise of the VAT so as to better account for the rise of *real VATs*. The book adopts an historical case-study approach, which is commonly employed in historical institutionalism, so as to examine two case studies, the adoption of the VAT in Australia and the non-adoption of the VAT in the US. The purpose of the case studies is not to show how all real VATs in all circumstances come about, but rather to reveal that merits are unable to account for both the decision to adopt a VAT and the real VATs that get adopted. Although informed by historical institutionalism, in addition to focusing on how history shaped the decision to introduce or not introduce a VAT, the book continues where most public policy accounts end. It draws on the distinction made in Chapters 2 and 3 between the good VAT and real VATs to examine how considerations relating to the legal design and implementation of VATs impact both the decision to adopt a VAT and the shape of the real VATs that get adopted. The use of legal analysis is crucial here, as it permits an exploration of the ways in which real VATs depart from the good VAT, and the often overlooked political processes that lead to these departures, which is missing not only from the conventional approach but from the public policy studies of the VAT undertaken to date.

[27] See, e.g., Evan S. Lieberman, *Race and Regionalism in the Politics of Taxation in Brazil and South Africa* (Cambridge University Press, 2003); Paul Pierson, *Politics in Time: History, Institutions, and Social Analysis* (Princeton University Press, Princeton, NJ, 2004).

2.3 *Part III – Case studies on the real-world challenges of VAT reform*

Part III explores the VAT reform debate in Australia and the US from 1960 to 2010. During this half-century period, global VAT uptake peaked but VAT reform in both jurisdictions remained controversial. Given that real VATs are the product of domestic political contests and VAT reform has remained controversial in both jurisdictions, these are both useful cases. Despite sharing relatively similar fiscal histories, the outcome of each case study is very different. Australia offers an example of a country that introduced a 'modern VAT',[28] which is a VAT viewed by the conventional approach as more closely resembling the good VAT than, for example, European VATs. The US offers a particularly useful case. In many respects, the US is yet another frontier issue, since it remains the 'final frontier'[29] as the only developed country without a national VAT, despite having long pioneered the VAT and long considered VAT reform. It is also the one developed jurisdiction where the debate on merits as a basis for the introduction of the tax is still a live issue.

Chapter 6 outlines the history of VAT reform in Australia from 1960 to 2010. The case study reveals that, like most other jurisdictions, the Australian VAT, which commenced operation in 2000 and is known as the goods and services tax (GST), is a real VAT. In showing how Australia came to introduce this real VAT, the limits of the merits-based account of the VAT's rise put forward by the conventional approach become apparent. The GST is the product of the actions of real political actors whose preferences and actions have been shaped by their historical and institutional context, which the historical-case-study method is well suited to capturing but which merits-based explanations ignore. Unlike most public policy accounts of the VAT, which end at the point of the VAT's introduction, the analysis focuses on the impact of law on shaping real VAT outcomes in Australia. This includes a detailed analysis of the frontier issue of the application of the GST to financial supplies. The extension of the historical analysis to a high degree of legal detail highlights key political contests that shape the operation of real VATs but which are absent from most public policy accounts of the VAT's rise and exposes the inadequacy of the merits-based explanations for the VAT's rise put forward by the conventional approach.

The US, as the only OECD country without a VAT, presents one of the most potent challenges to the conventional approach's explanation that the VAT has arisen by virtue of its merits. In short, the US resistance to VAT reform challenges the underlying presumption in the conventional approach, that the good is self-actualising. Chapter 7 examines the history of the VAT reform debate in the US

[28] Liam Ebrill et al., *The Modern VAT* (IMF, Washington, DC, 2001).

[29] Michael Keen, 'What Do (and Don't) We Know about the Value Added Tax? A Review of Richard M. Bird and Pierre-Pascal Gendron's *The VAT in Developing and Transitional Countries*', *Journal of Economic Literature* 47(1) (2009), 159, 168.

from 1960 to 2010. The chapter outlines the major stumbling blocks to US VAT reform and considers how the same institutionalised factors that have blocked VAT reform might in turn shape a VAT in the event that one is ever enacted in the US. It also identifies some distinctive features of any likely US approach to the frontier issue of subjecting financial supplies to a VAT. The chapter shows that, should the US enact a VAT, it will undoubtedly be a real VAT, the final shape of which will be explained less by merits than by real actors whose perceptions of the VAT's merits and actions in response to these perceptions are profoundly shaped by the history and institutions of the US policy-making process.

Chapter 8 serves as the conclusion for the book and draws out the major themes from the case studies. It considers what the insights from the case studies might contribute to better explaining the rise of real VATs. Importantly, the book reminds us that the task of explaining real-world outcomes needs to be taken seriously, so as to move beyond explanations which, in acting as much to promote the VAT as to explain its rise, impede understanding of the rise of this important revenue instrument.

PART I

The rise of the value-added tax – Exploring the gap between expectation and delivery

2

An introduction to the good VAT

This chapter explores the type of VAT that the conventional approach promotes, labelled the good VAT. It outlines the three design norms that are necessary components of the good VAT and highlights the associated merits these design norms are said to facilitate. Chapter 3 explores how the VATs that have actually been introduced worldwide, labelled real VATs, depart from the design norms of the good VAT. Part II of the book explores the consequences of this departure for the merits-based explanation of the VAT's rise put forward by the conventional approach.

1 DEFINING THE GOOD VAT

As §3.1 will later demonstrate, there are in fact many ways by which to conceive of and levy a VAT.[1] However, the conventional approach is committed to promoting one particular type of VAT, labelled by this book as the good VAT.

The *good VAT* is regarded by those within the conventional approach as constituting best-practice design. *Best practice* in this sense does not refer to a theoretically pure ideal, as might be the case under optimal tax theory.[2]

[1] See, e.g., 'The concept of value added is not clearcut or easily defined': John F. Due quoted in David Williams, 'Value-Added Tax', in V. Thuronyi (ed.), *Tax Law Design and Drafting* (IMF, Washington, DC, 1996), vol. 1, 164. See also the comprehensive discussion of the VAT design options in Clara K. Sullivan, *The Tax on Value Added* (New York, 1965), ch. 5; Carl S. Shoup, *The Value-Added Tax* (Center of Planning and Economic Research, Athens, Greece, 1973); Carl S. Shoup, 'Choosing among Types of VATs', in M. Gillis, C. S. Shoup and G. P. Sicat (eds.), *Value Added Taxation in Developing Countries (A World Bank Symposium)* (World Bank, Washington, DC, 1990), 3; Liam Ebrill et al., *The Modern VAT* (IMF, Washington, DC, 2001), ch. 2; Richard Bird and Pierre-Pascal Gendron, *The VAT in Developing and Transitional Countries* (Cambridge University Press, New York, 2007), 15.

[2] Optimal tax theory contains a set of normative tax policy prescriptions, which have been particularly influential. Slemrod describes it as the 'reigning normative approach to taxation': Joel Slemrod, 'Optimal Taxation and Tax Systems', *Journal of Economic Perspectives* 4(1)

Rather, it represents the consensus position within the conventional approach on principles for VAT design. These principles are based on certain shared normative preferences (see §2) and on administrative considerations arising from shared experiences in real-world VAT implementation.[3] The use of the term *good VAT* in this book is not intended to endorse or pass judgment on the conventional approach's preference for this best-practice VAT, but simply to describe it in the language used by the conventional approach. The book deploys the term *good VAT* because the degree of consensus is so strong that authors within the conventional approach almost universally describe as *good* all the basic elements that constitute a *good* VAT and label any deviations from these prescriptions as *bad*.[4] Cnossen provides an example:[5]

(1990), 157. The theory is highly formalised and subject to a number of common assumptions. Slemrod contends that most optimal tax theoretical models share three common features: (1) Models specify individual preferences and how individual and firms will act based on market constraints (many assume perfect competition); (2) Each model identifies a set range of taxes available to governments to raise a fixed amount of revenue (lump sum taxes unrelated to economic decisions are ruled out); (3) The models propose criteria by which to rank outcomes and choose the best or 'optimal' option from the limited range available: at 158. See generally William M. Gentry, 'Optimal Taxation', in J. J. Cordes, R. D. Ebel and J. Gravelle (eds.), *Encyclopedia of Taxation and Tax Policy* (2nd ed., Urban Institute Press, Washington, DC, 1999), 281–83; Peter Birch Sørensen, 'The Theory of Optimal Taxation: What Is the Policy Relevance?' (2007), *International Tax and Public Finance* 14(4), 383; Peter Diamond and Jim Mirrlees, 'Optimal Taxation and Public Production I: Production Efficiency', *American Economic Review* 61(1) (1971), 8; Peter Diamond and Jim Mirrlees, 'Optimal Taxation and Public Production II: Tax Rules', *American Economic Review* 61(3) (Part 1 of 2) (1971), 261. Although authors within the conventional approach are clearly influenced by the insights of optimal taxation, they do not slavishly adhere to it. *Contra* Keen, who claims that 'the remarkable spread of the VAT can be seen as the greatest triumph, and vindication, of optimal tax theory': Michael Keen, 'VAT Attacks!' (Working Paper No. WP/07/142, IMF, 2007), 6. This book highlights points at which optimal tax theory influences the conventional approach on good VAT design.

3 OECD, *Consumption Tax Trends 2012: VAT/GST and Excise Rates, Trends and Administration Issues* (OECD Publishing, Paris, 2012), 32–33.

4 Sijbren Cnossen, 'Global Trends and Issues in Value Added Taxation', *International Tax and Public Finance* 5(3) (1998), 399–400 (emphasis added); Carl S. Shoup, 'Choosing among Types of VATs', in M. Gillis, C. S. Shoup and G. P. Sicat (eds.), *Value Added Taxation in Developing Countries (A World Bank Symposium)* (World Bank, Washington, DC, 1990), 3, 4–5; Bird and Gendron state that '[n]onetheless, though one may regret it later, some *bad* initial VAT features may be an essential element in getting the tax accepted in the first place': Richard Bird and Pierre-Pascal Gendron, *The VAT in Developing and Transitional Countries* (Cambridge University Press, New York, 2007), 4 (emphasis added); Ebrill et al. contend that when it comes to 'best practices' in VAT design, 'many issues in the design of the tax are not contentious': Liam Ebrill et al., 'The Allure of the Value Added Tax' (2002), *Finance and Development* 39(2), 44, 46, 66; Ebrill et al. contend elsewhere that 'there is widespread agreement on what constitutes "best practice"': Liam Ebrill et al., *The Modern VAT* (IMF, Washington, DC, 2001), 15; Gillis et al. summarise 'consensus issues' agreed to by experts participating in a World Bank symposium on VAT for developing countries: Malcolm Gillis, Carl S. Shoup and Gerardo P. Sicat, 'Lessons for Developing Countries', in M. Gillis, C. S. Shoup and G. P. Sicat (eds.), *Value Added Taxation in Developing Countries (A World Bank*

> It is widely agreed that a *good VAT* extends through the retail stage, is as broadly based as possible, permits registered firms a full and immediate deduction (tax credit) of the VAT on inputs (including capital goods) from the VAT on output, limits the extent of rate differentiation, and is imposed on the destination principle.

The *good VAT* is narrowly defined by the conventional approach. For example, in an influential background paper to an International Tax Dialogue (ITD) conference on VAT (the '*ITD VAT Paper*'), staff from the IMF, OECD and World Bank offered the following definition of the *good VAT*:[6]

> The key features of the VAT are that it is a broad-based tax levied at multiple stages of production, with – crucially – taxes on inputs credited against taxes on output. That is, while sellers are required to charge the tax on all their sales, they can also claim a credit for taxes that they have been charged on their inputs. The advantages of this is that revenue is secured by being collected throughout the process of production (unlike a retail sales tax) but without distorting production decisions (as a turnover tax does).

In defining the VAT through reference to its advantages, the definition serves as much as a promotion for the good VAT as it does a definition. This good VAT is

Symposium) (World Bank, Washington, DC, 1990), 219, 220; Zee states that there exists 'a broad consensus among VAT experts on almost all significant. . .aspects of its design', save for the treatment of financial services: Howell H. Zee, 'VAT Treatment of Financial Services: A Primer on Conceptual Issues and Country Practices', *INTERTAX* 34(10) (2006), 458; Z. Shalizi and World Bank Group, *Lessons of Tax Reform* (World Bank, Washington, DC, 1991), 57; IMF, *Fiscal Monitor (November 2010) – Fiscal Exit: From Strategy to Implementation* (IMF Publication Services, Washington, DC, 2010), 79. Messere et al. claim that:

> It is rare that there is unanimity in the tax world. . .[but] there now appears to be universal agreement that in its greater neutrality, greater ability to tax services and not to tax producer goods, and greater defences against tax evasion VAT is superior to any other general consumption tax. Its remaining opponents worry that it provides governments with too much temptation to increase taxation.

Ken Messere, Flip de Kam and Christopher Heady, *Tax Policy: Theory and Practice in OECD Countries* (Oxford University Press, Oxford, 2003), 22. The major multinational accountancy firms also refer to, and support, these 'best practice' design principles: Ine Lejeune, Jeanine Daou-Azzi and Mark Powell (of PricewaterhouseCoopers), 'The Balance Has Shifted to Consumption Taxes – Lessons Learned and Best Practices for VAT', in M. Lang, P. Melz and E. Kristoffersson (eds.), *Value Added Tax and Direct Taxation: Similarities and Differences* (IBFD, Vienna, 2009), 3.

5 Sijbren Cnossen, 'Global Trends and Issues in Value Added Taxation', *International Tax and Public Finance* 5(3) (1998), 399, 400 (emphasis added).

6 International Tax Dialogue (ITD), 'The Value Added Tax: Experience and Issues' (Background Paper Prepared for the International Tax Dialogue Conference on the VAT, Rome, March 15–16, 2005, ITD), 8, www.itdweb.org/VATConference/Documents/VAT%20-%20EXPERIENCE%20AND%20ISSUES.pdf (hereafter referred to as the '*ITD VAT Paper*').

also reflected in Article 1(2) of the European *Recast VAT Directive 2006/112/EC*, which provides that a VAT:[7]

> entails the application to goods and services of a general tax on consumption exactly proportional to the price of the goods and services, however many transactions take place in the production and distribution process before the stage at which the tax is charged.
>
> On each transaction, VAT, calculated on the price of the goods or services at the rate applicable to such goods or services, shall be chargeable after deduction of the amount of VAT borne directly by the various cost components.

These definitions highlight three key elements, labelled by this book as the *three design norms*, of the *good VAT*: it is (1) levied on a consumption base; (2) collected incrementally through all stages of the production and distribution chain through the invoice-credit method; and (3) imposed on a destination basis. These three design norms for the good VAT will be explained in §3 to §6 of this chapter. Before examining these design norms, §2 outlines the merits that a good VAT is said to achieve.

2 MEASURING THE MERITS OF THE GOOD VAT

The conventional approach contends that a good VAT has merits when measured against the public finance norms traditionally employed to evaluate tax instruments such as revenue generation, efficiency, neutrality, equity and simplicity. Before outlining the claims made of the good VAT against these criteria, it must be noted that the preference within the conventional approach for the good VAT stems from a number of broad economic assumptions and theoretical preferences, which include:

(1) Consumption is the preferred tax base (see §2.1);
(2) Tax instruments are best when they interfere least with the operations of the market. Therefore, neutrality is best in tax design (see §2.2.2); and
(3) Efficiency trumps in the efficiency-equity trade-off when designing taxes (see §2.2.3).[8]

The first key preference will be introduced here as it goes to the heart of the conventional approach's enthusiasm for the VAT. The remaining two preferences

7 *European Council Directive 2006/112/EC of 28 November 2008 on the Common System of Value Added Tax* [2006] OJ L 347/1, art. 1(2) (referred to hereafter as '*Recast VAT Directive 2006/112/EC*'). See also Schenk and Oldman, who define VAT as 'a type of multistage sales tax imposed on goods and services that is collected in chunks at each stage of production and distribution of goods or the rendition of services in proportion to the value added by each taxpaying firm': Alan Schenk and Oliver Oldman, *Value Added Tax: A Comparative Approach* (rev. edn., Cambridge University Press, Cambridge; New York, 2007), 23.

8 Jonathon Gruber, *Public Finance and Public Policy* (3rd ed., Worth Publishers, New York, 2011), 593, 616.

will be discussed under the relevant public finance criteria of efficiency and neutrality and throughout the discussion of the design norms.

Although all of these preferences or assumptions are contestable, it is not the purpose of this book to endorse or defend them but rather to note that they motivate the support for the good VAT within the conventional approach.

2.1 *Consumption is the preferred tax base*

The conventional approach has a strong preference for a consumption base over an income base.[9] This preference is informed by the following ideas:

(1) Consumption is a less mobile base and therefore a more efficient and reliable base than income, especially highly mobile capital income;[10]
(2) Consumption is a less volatile and more stable revenue source because it is less susceptible to fluctuations in the economic cycle;[11]
(3) Consumption is a fairer and more reliable measure of welfare than income;[12]

[9] See, e.g., Michael Keen, 'VAT Attacks!' (Working Paper No. WP/07/142, IMF, 2007), 3; David Williams, 'Value-Added Tax', in V. Thuronyi (ed.), *Tax Law Design and Drafting* (IMF, Washington, DC, 1996), vol. 1, 164, 167; Z. Shalizi and World Bank Group, *Lessons of Tax Reform* (World Bank, Washington, DC, 1991), 8; Richard Bird and Pierre-Pascal Gendron, *The VAT in Developing and Transitional Countries* (Cambridge University Press, New York, 2007), 6, 20, 48; International Tax Dialogue (ITD), 'The Value Added Tax: Experience and Issues' (Background Paper Prepared for the International Tax Dialogue Conference on the VAT, Rome, March 15–16, 2005, ITD), 2; OECD, *Consumption Tax Trends 2012: VAT/GST and Excise Rates, Trends and Administration Issues* (OECD Publishing, Paris, 2012), 31.

[10] John Norregaard and Tehmina S. Khan, 'Tax Policy: Recent Trends and Coming Challenges' (Working Paper No. WP/07/274, IMF, 2007), 36; Junko Kato, *Regressive Taxation and the Welfare State: Path Dependence and Policy Diffusion* (Cambridge University Press, Cambridge, 2003), 36–37; Reuven Avi-Yonah, 'Globalization, Tax Competition, and the Fiscal Crisis of the Welfare State' (2000), *Harvard Law Review* 113(7), 1573, 1575–1576. This is said to be consistent with the dictates of optimal tax theory that tax should be levied where elasticity is lowest according to the general understanding that parties with inelastic supply or demand bear taxes, while parties with elastic supply or demand avoid them: Jonathon Gruber, *Public Finance and Public Policy* (3rd ed., Worth Publishers, New York, 2011), 564. *Contra* others contend that the mobility arguments are relevant only to a particular type of income from capital – returns from mobile investments – but less so to location-specific rents such as mineral resources or location-specific features that mitigate the mobility of capital such as appropriate infrastructure, security and access to a skilled and healthy workforce: Commonwealth of Australia Treasury, Australia's Future Tax System Review Panel, *Australia's Future Tax System: Report to the Treasurer* (Australia's Future Tax System Review Panel: The Treasury, Canberra, 2009), 154.

[11] Ben Terra and Julie Kajus, IBFD, A *Guide to the European VAT Directives* [online] (15 April 2011), 7.6.1–7.6.2.

[12] Liam Ebrill et al., *The Modern VAT* (IMF, Washington, DC, 2001), 106–7. This fairness largely derives from point (5). *Contra* Reuven Avi-Yonah, 'Risk, Rents and Regressivity Revisited' (2009), *Australian Tax Forum* 24, 41, 57; Alvin C. Warren, 'Fairness and a Consumption-Type or Cash Flow Personal Income Tax', *Harvard Law Review* 88(5) (1975),

(4) Consumption taxes are simpler to administer because they do not rely on complex realisation and timing rules;[13]

(5) Consumption taxes are to be preferred for their relative neutrality in relation to: savings and investment decisions (because the returns from savings are not taxed or are taxed less or later under a consumption tax);[14] consumption decisions (the exclusion of savings means that no

931, 946; Barbara H. Fried, 'Fairness and the Consumption Tax', *Stanford Law Review* 44 (1991–1992), 961, 962–67.

[13] For example, they dispose of tricky measurement difficulties such as depreciation (because everything is expensed) and measuring capital gains (because they are excluded): see, e.g., Richard Bird and Pierre-Pascal Gendron, *The VAT in Developing and Transitional Countries* (Cambridge University Press, New York, 2007), 28, 81; Carl S. Shoup, 'Choosing among Types of VATs', in M. Gillis, C. S. Shoup and G. P. Sicat (eds.), *Value Added Taxation in Developing Countries (A World Bank Symposium)* (The World Bank, Washington, DC, 1990), 3, 6; Howell H. Zee, 'World Trends in Tax Policy: An Economic Perspective' (2004), *INTERTAX* 32(8/9), 352, 359; Gilbert E. Metcalf, 'Consumption Taxation', in J. Cordes et al. (eds.), *Encyclopedia of Taxation and Tax Policy* (Urban Institute Press, Washington, DC, 1999), 62, 63–64; Robert F. van Brederode, *Systems of General Sales Taxation: Theory, Policy and Practice* (Kluwer Law International Alphen aan den Rijn, 2009), 333. *Contra* Gruber contends that '[i]n principle, it is much more straightforward to simply tax individuals on their purchases than on a complicated definition of income' (at 756), but later claims that it 'is much harder to track consumption expenditures than it is to track income earned, where withholding from paychecks can solve compliance problems for the vast majority of the population': Jonathon Gruber, *Public Finance and Public Policy* (3rd ed., Worth Publishers, New York, 2011), 759. See also Brooks, who claims that '[i]t seems disingenuous for business and rich individuals to lobby for all sorts of concessionary treatment for income from capital under the income tax and then announce that the rules have become so complex that income from capital should not be taxed at all': Neil Brooks, 'An Overview of the Role of the VAT, Fundamental Tax Reform, and a Defence of the Income Tax', in R. Krever and D. White (eds.), *GST in Retrospect and Prospect* (Brookers, Wellington, 2007), 597, 626.

[14] Based on the Shanz Haig-Simons definition, the income tax base is equal to consumption + savings (increases in net wealth) over a period of time, and therefore consumption is equal to income minus savings: John R. King, 'The Concept of Income', in P. Shome (ed.), *Tax Policy Handbook* (IMF, Washington, DC, 1995), 117. This definition of consumption is disputed: Harry Grubert and Richard Krever, 'VAT and Financial Services: Competing Perspectives on What Should Be Taxed?' (2012), *Tax Law Review* 65(2), 199–204. The objection to the income tax is based on the view that the income tax discourages savings by allegedly double taxing the returns from savings (as the tax applies first to income earned and then to the rewards (interest and profits) for saving). See, e.g., John Stuart Mill, *Principles of Political Economy with Some of Their Applications to Social Philosophy* (Longmans, Green and Co., London, 1848, 1909 ed.), book V, Chapter 2, §4, at v.2.22 (note that Mill also argues for wealth taxation at §5, V2.27–2.29); Carl S. Shoup, 'Choosing among Types of VATs', in M. Gillis, C. S. Shoup and G. P. Sicat (eds.), *Value Added Taxation in Developing Countries (A World Bank Symposium)* (World Bank, Washington, DC, 1990), 3, 6. McCaffery highlights how it was precisely the double taxation of savings argument that led to support for the income tax in the US: Edward McCaffery, 'A New Understanding of Tax' (2004), *Michigan Law Review* 58, 807, 809–810. Reasonable minds differ as to whether the double taxation of savings is a good or bad thing. For those who favour the income tax on this point: Neil Brooks, 'An Overview of the Role of the VAT, Fundamental Tax Reform, and a Defence of the Income Tax', in R. Krever and D. White (eds.), *GST in Retrospect and Prospect* (Brookers, Wellington, 2007), 597, 619; Reuven Avi-Yonah, 'Risk, Rents and Regressivity Revisited' (2009), *Australian Tax Forum* 24, 41, 55. For

penalty is applied for choosing to consume now or later);[15] production decisions (business is free to make decisions under market-based conditions without tax-induced distortions, such as those that would occur if capital was taxed);[16] and decisions on labour supply (decreased reliance on progressive income taxes that apply high marginal rates increase incentives to work);[17] and

those who contend that the difference in the taxation of savings is not as great as contended: David Weisbach, 'The (Non-)Taxation of Risk' (2004), *Tax Law Review* 58, 1; Joseph Bankman and Thomas Griffith, 'Is the Debate Between an Income Tax and a Consumption Tax a Debate About Risk? Does It Matter?', *Tax Law Review* 47 (1992), 377; Joseph Bankman and David A. Weisbach, 'The Superiority of an Ideal Consumption Tax over an Ideal Income Tax' (2006), *Stanford Law Review* 58, 1413. Ebrill et al. claim that the VAT is effectively a superior form of income tax (because it excludes taxation of the return to savings and avoids the distortions of the corporate income tax): Liam Ebrill et al., *The Modern VAT* (IMF, Washington, DC, 2001), 198.

15 A World Bank publication repeats the familiar refrain when it claims that the 'use of income as a tax base...tends to favour current consumption at the expense of future consumption or saving': Z. Shalizi and World Bank Group, *Lessons of Tax Reform* (World Bank, Washington, DC, 1991), 24; Gillis et al. claim that 'the consumption type of VAT does not distort the choice between consuming now and consuming later, in favour of the former, as does the income tax. In this way the VAT does not penalize, as does the income tax, capital accumulation and economic growth': Malcolm Gillis, Carl S. Shoup and Gerardo P. Sicat, 'Lessons for Developing Countries', in M. Gillis, C. S. Shoup and G. P. Sicat (eds.), *Value Added Taxation in Developing Countries (A World Bank Symposium)* (World Bank, Washington, DC, 1990), 219, 230. This is based on the highly contestable assumption that savings is simply the deferment of consumption. *Contra* Avi-Yonah, who offers an example contesting the claim when he contends that money can be used for other things than consumption and notes that the power of the rich lies primarily in their ability to invest, not consume: Reuven Avi-Yonah, 'Risk, Rents and Regressivity Revisited' (2009), *Australian Tax Forum* 24, 41, 55. See also Neil Brooks, 'An Overview of the Role of the VAT, Fundamental Tax Reform, and a Defence of the Income Tax', in R. Krever and D. White (eds.), *GST in Retrospect and Prospect* (Brookers, Wellington, 2007), 597, 619–23.

16 Liam Ebrill et al., *The Modern VAT* (IMF, Washington, DC, 2001), 17; Richard Krever, 'Designing and Drafting VAT Laws for Africa', in R. Krever (ed.), *VAT in Africa* (Pretoria University Law Press, Pretoria, 2008), 9, 10; Ben Terra and Julie Kajus, IBFD, A *Guide to the European VAT Directives* [online] (15 April 2011), 7.5.2.1; Sijbren Cnossen, 'Global Trends and Issues in Value Added Taxation', *International Tax and Public Finance* 5(3) (1998), 399, 404–5; International Tax Dialogue (ITD), 'The Value Added Tax: Experience and Issues' (Background Paper Prepared for the International Tax Dialogue Conference on the VAT, Rome, March 15–16, 2005, ITD), 7.

17 An OECD Policy Brief contends that:

> ...a 'revenue-neutral' shift from taxes on income – particularly personal income tax – to taxes on consumption will not have much effect on the total taxes paid by typical workers and so is unlikely to affect their decisions as to whether or not to work. However, it will reduce their marginal tax rate...and thus increase the incentive for them to work additional hours. This is because taxes on income are generally progressive – taxing additional income at higher rates – while taxes on consumption are broadly proportional to income and expenditure. The shift towards taxes on consumption will therefore increase hours worked and thus economic growth.

OECD, 'Consumption Taxes: The Way of the Future? (Policy Brief)' (2007), *OECD Observer* 1, 4–5; *Cf* Ian Crawford, Michael Keen and Stephen Smith, 'Value Added Tax and Excises', in

(6) The neutrality of consumption taxes leaves decisions to be made according to market conditions, and this should enhance investment, efficiency and economic growth.[18]

The debate on the relative merits of income and consumption taxes is well established, and it is not necessary for the purposes of this book to recreate it.[19] Needless to

Stuart Adam et al. (eds.) for the Institute for Fiscal Studies, *Dimensions of Tax Design: The Mirrlees Review* (Oxford University Press, Oxford, 2010), 275, 281–82.

[18] In large part, the claims for VATs' facilitation of economic growth rest on a series of interlinked assumptions that arise from a shift in the tax mix from an income tax to an ideal consumption tax: Jonathon Gruber, *Public Finance and Public Policy* (3rd ed., Worth Publishers, New York, 2011), 754–56; OECD, 'Consumption Taxes: The Way of the Future? (Policy Brief)' (2007), *OECD Observer* 1, 4–5; Reuven Avi-Yonah, 'Risk, Rents and Regressivity Revisited' (2009), *Australian Tax Forum* 24, 41, 43; Peter H. Lindert, *Growing Public: Social Spending and Economic Growth since the Eighteenth Century* (Cambridge UK; New York, Cambridge University Press, 2004), 241. The IMF contends that '[t]axing consumption is equivalent to taxing accumulated assets and labor income: thus it falls partly on a completely inelastic base – previously existing assets – and partly on a base less internationally mobile than capital income. Broad-based consumption taxes are therefore considered less harmful to growth than income taxes': IMF, *Fiscal Monitor (November 2010) – Fiscal Exit: From Strategy to Implementation* (IMF Publication Services, Washington, DC, 2010), 80. See also John Norregaard and Tehmina S. Khan, 'Tax Policy: Recent Trends and Coming Challenges' (Working Paper No. WP/07/274, IMF, 2007), 37–38; Liam Ebrill et al., *The Modern VAT* (IMF, Washington, DC, 2001), 17, 198; Carl S. Shoup, 'Choosing among Types of VATs', in M. Gillis, C. S. Shoup and G. P. Sicat (eds.), *Value Added Taxation in Developing Countries (A World Bank Symposium)* (World Bank, Washington, DC, 1990), 3, 6; Robert F. van Brederode, *Systems of General Sales Taxation: Theory, Policy and Practice* (Kluwer Law International Alphen aan den Rijn, 2009), 333; Ben Terra and Julie Kajus, IBFD, *A Guide to the European VAT Directives* [online] (15 April 2011), 7.5.2.1; Sijbren Cnossen, 'Global Trends and Issues in Value Added Taxation', *International Tax and Public Finance* 5(3) (1998), 399, 404–5; International Tax Dialogue (ITD), 'The Value Added Tax: Experience and Issues' (Background Paper Prepared for the International Tax Dialogue Conference on the VAT, Rome, March 15–16, 2005, ITD), 7. *Contra* Scott Riswold, 'VAT in Sub-Saharan Africa – A Critique of IMF VAT Policy' (March/April 2004), *International VAT Monitor* 97, 103; Neil Brooks, 'An Overview of the Role of the VAT, Fundamental Tax Reform, and a Defence of the Income Tax', in R. Krever and D. White (eds.), *GST in Retrospect and Prospect* (Brookers, Wellington, 2007), 597, 610, 623–24; Reuven Avi-Yonah, 'Risk, Rents and Regressivity Revisited' (2009), *Australian Tax Forum* 24, 41, 43. Others highlight that the progressive income tax might also have a positive impact on growth depending on the income and substitution effect of the tax. For example, Gruber suggests that the taxation of capital income can improve work effort in high-ability individuals who, in light of capital taxation, may work harder to increase their savings: at 758; see also Joel Slemrod, 'The Economic Consequences of Taxing the Rich', in Joel Slemrod (ed.), *Does Atlas Shrug? The Economic Consequences of Taxing the Rich* (Russell Sage Foundation; Harvard University Press, New York, 2000), 3–28.

[19] For those on the consumption side, see, e.g., William D. Andrews, 'A Consumption-Type or Cash Flow Personal Income Tax', *Harvard Law Review* 87(6) (1974), 1113; Edward McCaffrey, 'A New Understanding of Tax' (2005), *Michigan Law Review* 103(5), 807; Joseph Bankman and David A. Weisbach, 'The Superiority of an Ideal Consumption Tax over the Ideal Income Tax' (2006), *Stanford Law Review* 44(5), 163; Daniel Shaviro, 'Replacing the Income Tax with a Progressive Consumption Tax' (2004), *Tax Notes*, 91; OECD, 'Consumption Taxes: The Way of the Future? (Policy Brief)' (2007), *OECD Observer* 1, 4; Z. Shalizi and World Bank Group, *Lessons of Tax Reform* (World Bank, Washington, DC, 1991), 24. Mill and Hobbes are

say, each of the perceived advantages listed is fiercely contested.[20] It does not matter to this book who is right or wrong as to whether an income or consumption base is in fact preferable, but rather that the perceived advantages of consumption taxation underlie the conventional approach's support for the good VAT.

2.2 *The good VAT measured against public finance criteria*

The good VAT is said to be virtuous according to traditional public finance criteria.[21] Some of these virtues are a product of the good VAT's status as the preferred method to tax consumption; other merits derive from the unique features of the good VAT such as the invoice-credit mechanism.

2.2.1 Revenue generation

The revenue-raising capacity of the good VAT is considered so impressive that it has a reputation as a 'money machine'.[22] As Cnossen contends:[23]

generally cited in support of consumption taxes: John Stuart Mill, *Principles of Political Economy with Some of Their Applications to Social Philosophy* (Longmans, Green and Co., London, 1848, 1909 ed.), book V, ch. 2, §4; Thomas Hobbes, *Leviathan* (Cambridge University Press, Cambridge, first published 1651, 1991 ed.), 238–39. See also the influential report of the Meade Committee: Institute for Fiscal Studies, *The Structure and Reform of Direct Taxation (Report of a Committee Chaired by Profesor J. E. Meade* (Allen and Unwin, London, 1978); United States Dept. of the Treasury, *Blueprints for Basic Tax Reform* (Dept. of the Treasury, Washington, DC, 1977), 2, 3, ch. 2. Many now acknowledge the role for both an income tax and a consumption tax such as a VAT; see, e.g., Ian Crawford, Michael Keen and Stephen Smith, 'Value Added Tax and Excises', in Stuart Adam et al. (eds.) for the Institute for Fiscal Studies, *Dimensions of Tax Design: The Mirrlees Review* (Oxford University Press, Oxford, 2010), 275, 280–83. For those who also defend the income tax, see Neil Brooks, 'An Overview of the Role of the VAT, Fundamental Tax Reform, and a Defence of the Income Tax', in R. Krever and D. White (eds.), *GST in Retrospect and Prospect* (Brookers, Wellington, 2007), 597; Barbara H. Fried, 'Fairness and the Consumption Tax', *Stanford Law Review* 44 (1991–1992), 961, 962, 1016; Alvin C. Warren, 'Fairness and a Consumption-Type or Cash Flow Personal Income Tax', *Harvard Law Review* 88(5) (1975), 931; Thomas Piketty and Emmanuel Saez, 'Income Inequality in the United States, 1913–1998', *Quarterly Journal of Economics* 118(1) (2003), 1, 37; Peter Diamond and Emmanuel Saez, "The Case for a Progressive Tax: From Basic Research to Policy Recommendations" (2011), *Journal of Economic Perspectives* 25(4), 165; Reuven Avi-Yonah, 'Risk, Rents and Regressivity Revisited' (2009), *Australian Tax Forum* 24, 41.

[20] See the references cited in the footnotes for each of the six advantages listed above.

[21] See, e.g., OECD, *Consumption Tax Trends 2010: VAT/GST and Excise Rates, Trends and Administration Issues* (OECD Publishing, Paris, 2011) 11–13. See the references in § 2.2 of this chapter generally.

[22] US President's Advisory Panel on Federal Tax Reform, *Simple, Fair, and Pro-Growth: Proposals to Fix America's Tax System* (2005), 192; Michael Keen and Ben Lockwood, 'Is the VAT a Money Machine?' (2006), *National Tax Journal* 59(4), 905, 905; Michael Keen and Ben Lockwood, 'The Value Added Tax: Its Causes and Consequences' (2010), *Journal of Development Economics* 92(2), 138, 139.

[23] Sijbren Cnossen, 'Global Trends and Issues in Value Added Taxation', *International Tax and Public Finance* 5(3) (1998), 399, 413.

> Basically, the VAT is a revenue workhorse. Properly designed and administered, it can raise more revenue with lower operational and economic costs than can other broadly based consumption taxes.

Estimates suggest that each one per cent increase in the rate of the good VAT would raise an additional 0.5 per cent of GDP in revenue.[24] There are a number of reasons cited for the VAT's impressive revenue-generating capacity. But in essence the claim rests on the good VAT's ability to tax a broad consumption base (norm 1: see §4) and the advantages of the invoice-credit method as a collection mechanism (norm 2: see §5). In addition, the low visibility of the good VAT is said to reduce incentives to avoid or evade, as well as more readily facilitating rate and base increases by reducing awareness of, and therefore resistance to, efforts to expand the reach of the VAT.[25]

2.2.2 Neutrality

A key assumption underlying the conventional approach's enthusiasm for the VAT is that tax instruments work best when they interfere least with production and consumption decisions in a properly functioning market.[26] As Brederode explains, consumption, labour and investment decisions 'should be made based on their economic merits and not for tax reasons'.[27] Although this idea is highly controversial,[28] the purpose of

[24] IMF, *Fiscal Monitor (November 2010) – Fiscal Exit: From Strategy to Implementation* (IMF Publication Services, Washington, DC, 2010), 79; Cnossen estimates that 0.4 per cent of GDP is raised with every percentage increase in the good VAT rate: Sijbren Cnossen, 'Global Trends and Issues in Value Added Taxation', *International Tax and Public Finance* 5(3) (1998), 399. An attempt and explanation of the modelling used to estimate potential VAT revenues based on the good VAT in developing countries is provided by Glenn P. Jenkins and Chun-Yan Kuo, 'A VAT Revenue Simulation Model for Tax Reform in Developing Countries' (2000), *World Development* 28(4), 763, 764.

[25] Ben Terra and Julie Kajus, IBFD, *A Guide to the European VAT Directives* [online] (15 April 2011), 7.6.1–7.6.2.

[26] See, e.g., Liam Ebrill et al., *The Modern VAT* (IMF, Washington, DC, 2001), 17; International Tax Dialogue (ITD), 'The Value Added Tax: Experience and Issues' (Background Paper Prepared for the International Tax Dialogue Conference on the VAT, Rome, March 15–16, 2005, ITD), 7; Ben Terra and Julie Kajus, IBFD, *A Guide to the European VAT Directives* [online] (15 April 2011), 7.3.1.3; Robert F. van Brederode, *Systems of General Sales Taxation: Theory, Policy and Practice* (Kluwer Law International Alphen aan den Rijn, 2009), 46.

[27] Robert F. van Brederode, *Systems of General Sales Taxation: Theory, Policy and Practice* (Kluwer Law International Alphen aan den Rijn, 2009), 45.

[28] For opposing views see, e.g., Liam Murphy and Thomas Nagel, *The Myth of Ownership: Taxes and Justice* (Oxford University Press, New York, 2002); Secretariat – United Nations Conference on Trade and Development, *Trade and Development Report, 2012* (UNCTAD/TDR/2012) (United Nations Publications, Geneva, 2012), 118; Stiglitz provides a forceful critique of the claim that neutrality necessarily facilitates growth because it is based on the dubious assumption of perfect markets and ignores the corrective role of taxation in addressing market failures: Joseph E. Stiglitz, 'Development-Oriented Tax Policy' in R. H. Gordon (ed.), *Taxation in Developing Countries: Six Case Studies and Policy Implications* (Columbia University Press, New York, 2010), 11, 14.

this book is not to dispute the premise but simply to show that it informs the conventional approach's analysis and support of the good VAT.[29]

The good VAT is considered neutral because it does not interfere, or interferes less than other taxes, with market decisions relating to consumption, production or saving.[30] Neutrality is rated highly in evaluation of tax instruments because, as the US Advisory Commission on Intergovernmental Relations explains:[31]

> Although there are many considerations to be evaluated in judging a particular tax instrument, neutrality is particularly important in that it can be dealt with best by means of structural tax policy – as is the case with equity considerations. Other indirect consequences of the tax, such as its effect on the balance of payments, economic growth, etc., relate to objectives that can also be achieved by "non-tax" mechanisms; tax neutrality and the burden of tax distributions cannot.

By contrast, others have queried the appropriateness of neutrality as a policy objective at all in relation to developing countries where market failure is common.[32]

29 Robert F. van Brederode, *Systems of General Sales Taxation: Theory, Policy and Practice* (Kluwer Law International Alphen aan den Rijn, 2009), 46.

30 US Department of the Treasury, *Tax Reform for Fairness, Simplicity, and Economic Growth* (Office of the Secretary, Department of the Treasury, Washington, DC, 1984), vol. 3, ch. 3, 17–19; Liam Ebrill et al., *The Modern VAT* (IMF, Washington, DC, 2001), 15–16; Robert F. van Brederode, *Systems of General Sales Taxation: Theory, Policy and Practice* (Kluwer Law International Alphen aan den Rijn, 2009), 46; Alan Schenk and Oliver Oldman, *Value Added Tax: A Comparative Approach* (rev. edn., Cambridge University Press, Cambridge; New York, 2007), 33; Ben Terra and Julie Kajus, IBFD, *A Guide to the European VAT Directives* [online] (15 April 2011), 7.3; United States Advisory Commission on Intergovernmental Relations, *The Value-Added Tax and Alternative Sources of Federal Revenue: An Information Report* (Washington, DC, 1973), 9.

31 United States Advisory Commission on Intergovernmental Relations, *The Value-Added Tax and Alternative Sources of Federal Revenue: An Information Report* (Washington, DC, 1973), 8.

32 Stiglitz claims that taxation plays a key role in compensating for market imperfections in developing countries: Joseph E. Stiglitz, 'Development-Oriented Tax Policy', in R. H. Gordon (ed.), *Taxation in Developing Countries: Six Case Studies and Policy Implications* (Columbia University Press, New York, 2010), 11. Stiglitz lists as examples taxes on capital flows in Chile that reduced the instability caused by short-term influx of capital: at 15; taxes which target monopolies and oligopolies, such as the corporate income tax, which are more likely to enhance growth (by reducing the market dominance of the monopoly or oligopoly); and taxation of imported products (as could be achieved through excises or increased VAT rates), which are more likely to enhance productivity because imported goods might be used in both the formal and informal sectors and thus provide a de facto tax on the informal sector. In addition, because many imported goods are also luxury goods, taxing imports will introduce an element of progressivity in the system: at 20–23. Stiglitz contends that tariffs played a key role in the early stages of development in the economies of Western Europe and the US because the ease of collection and monitoring of tariffs played a key role in generating revenue: at 16. Given the structure of developing economies, Stiglitz contends that the VAT can be 'distortionary [and] may impede development and growth': at 19. See also Scott Riswold, 'VAT in Sub-Saharan Africa – A Critique of IMF VAT Policy' (March/April 2004), *International VAT Monitor* 97, 107.

Favourable measures of the good VAT's neutrality include: (1) the forms or methods of doing business are not influenced (the good VAT is not a tax intended to fall on business because the tax is forward shifted to consumers: norm 2, §5);[33] (2) choices to consume or save are not influenced (the returns from savings are not taxed as such – or at least not taxed until consumed) (norm 1: §4); (3) choices relating to which products and services to consume are not impacted (because all are taxed alike and the VAT burden is measured as a percentage of the retail price) (norm 1: §4);[34] and (4) the good VAT levied on a destination basis is neutral toward international trade (see norm 3: §6).[35]

2.2.3 Efficiency

As Ebrill et al. explain, 'The case for the value-added tax rests upon the view that a well designed and implemented VAT is a particularly efficient tax.'[36] The good VAT is said to raise revenue with the least cost and the least economic distortions relative to other comparable taxes.[37] The reasons for the latter measure derive from the good VAT's neutrality, as discussed above. The conventional view is that a good VAT that falls only on final consumption and not intermediate business

33 Sijbren Cnossen, 'Global Trends and Issues in Value Added Taxation', *International Tax and Public Finance* 5(3) (1998), 399. As the discussion of norm 2 explains, the separate identification of the VAT component on VAT invoices is said to facilitate forward shifting to consumers, making it more likely that the economic incidence of the tax is as intended: Ben Terra and Julie Kajus, IBFD, A *Guide to the European VAT Directives* [online] (15 April 2011), 7.3.1.1–7.3.1.3. Cnossen notes that '[i]mportantly, the VAT is not a cost to business': Sijbren Cnossen, 'A VAT Primer for Lawyers, Economists, and Accountants' (2009), *Tax Notes International* 55(4), 319 and 320.

34 Sijbren Cnossen, 'VAT and RST: A Comparison', *Canadian Tax Journal* 35(3) (1987), 559, 567; Ben Terra and Julie Kajus, IBFD, A *Guide to the European VAT Directives* [online] (15 April 2011), 7.3.1.1.

35 As the OECD explains, the VAT's 'neutrality principle towards international trade has also made it the preferred alternative to customs duties in the context of trade liberalization': OECD, Consumption Tax Trends 2012: VAT/GST and Excise Rates, Trends and Administration Issues (OECD Publishing, Paris, 2012), 44. There is a long debate on the relative merits of the VAT and tariffs: see, e.g., Michael Keen, 'What Do (and Don't) We Know about the Value Added Tax? A Review of Richard M. Bird and Pierre-Pascal Gendron's *The VAT in Developing and Transitional Countries*', *Journal of Economic Literature* 47(1) (2009), 159, 163–65.

36 Liam Ebrill et al., *The Modern VAT* (IMF, Washington, DC, 2001), 27; John Norregaard and Tehmina S. Khan, 'Tax Policy: Recent Trends and Coming Challenges' (Working Paper No. WP/07/274, IMF, 2007), 38; Alan Schenk and Oliver Oldman, *Value Added Tax: A Comparative Approach* (rev. edn., Cambridge University Press, Cambridge; New York, 2007), 33; The IMF contends that 'a "pure" VAT with a single rate and minimal exemptions is an efficient way to raise revenue': IMF, *Fiscal Monitor (November 2010) – Fiscal Exit: From Strategy to Implementation* (IMF Publication Services, Washington, DC, 2010), 79. *Contra* Scott Riswold, 'VAT in Sub-Saharan Africa – A Critique of IMF VAT Policy' (March/April 2004), *International VAT Monitor* 97, 103.

37 Robert F. van Brederode, *Systems of General Sales Taxation: Theory, Policy and Practice* (Kluwer Law International Alphen aan den Rijn, 2009), 47.

transactions is attractive for its neutrality regarding production decisions, which in turn facilitates production efficiency.[38]

Of greater significance here are the reasons why the VAT itself is considered an efficient tax beyond its status as a neutral consumption tax. The good VAT is thought of as a particularly efficient tax instrument because its incremental and self-enforcing collection mechanism is said to be administratively efficient and reduces the cost of compliance (norm 2: §5).[39] Ancillary benefits that contribute to efficiency in the context of transitional and developing countries include the opportunity that VAT reform offers to improve tax administration, such as through moving to a system of self-assessment,[40] and to replace inefficient taxes (such as turnover and trade taxes) with the good VAT, which might also facilitate economic growth.[41]

38 The Diamond-Mirrlees theorem provides that it is economically rational to pursue production efficiency as a policy goal (achieved when the economy is on its production possibility frontier, where one more good cannot be produced without producing less of some other good). Ebrill et al. explain that while the absence of tax on intermediate inputs does not guarantee production efficiency (because imperfect competition can result in firms facing differing marginal costs in equilibrium, resulting in production inefficiency), it is still generally desirable as a policy goal: Liam Ebrill et al., *The Modern VAT* (IMF, Washington, DC, 2001), 16–17; *Contra* Joseph E. Stiglitz, 'Development-Oriented Tax Policy', in R. H. Gordon (ed.), *Taxation in Developing Countries: Six Case Studies and Policy Implications* (Columbia University Press, New York, 2010), 11, n 17, 32.

39 International Tax Dialogue (ITD), 'The Value Added Tax: Experience and Issues' (Background Paper Prepared for the International Tax Dialogue Conference on the VAT, Rome, March 15–16, 2005, ITD), 12.

40 John Norregaard and Tehmina S. Khan, 'Tax Policy: Recent Trends and Coming Challenges' (Working Paper No. WP/07/274, IMF, 2007), 38; Liam Ebrill et al., *The Modern VAT* (IMF, Washington, DC, 2001), 138.

41 Michael Keen and Ben Lockwood, 'The Value Added Tax: Its Causes and Consequences' (2010), *Journal of Development Economics* 92(2), 138, 139; Richard Bird and Pierre-Pascal Gendron, *The VAT in Developing and Transitional Countries* (Cambridge University Press, New York, 2007), 50; The *ITD VAT Paper* predicts that '[l]ooking forward, the VAT is likely to have a key role to play, in many parts of the world, in dealing with the revenue consequences of trade liberalization': International Tax Dialogue (ITD), 'The Value Added Tax: Experience and Issues' (Background Paper Prepared for the International Tax Dialogue Conference on the VAT, Rome, March 15–16, 2005, ITD), 10; Ebrill et al. contend that '[i]n many developing countries, adoption of the VAT has been given additional impetus by the long-run revenue implications of trade reform – the economic efficiency arguments favouring the VAT have been bolstered as trade tax revenues have come under pressure with deepening trade liberalization commitments': Liam Ebrill et al., *The Modern VAT* (IMF, Washington, DC, 2001), 6. *Contra* Emran and Stiglitz, who question the 'current consensus that favors a reduction and eventual elimination of trade taxes, and almost exclusively relies on VAT as the instrument of indirect taxation in developing countries': M. Shahe Emran and Joseph E. Stiglitz, 'On Selective Indirect Tax Reform in Developing Countries' (2005), *Journal of Public Economics* 89, 599, 618. The authors claim the argument takes insufficient account of the impact of the informal economy and that, as a result, the revenue generating potential of broad-based VAT reform is undermined because the VAT increases the distortions between the formal and informal sector (in favour of the informal economy) and the large informal sector escapes the VAT net: at 600. See above, n 32. For the reply from the conventional approach, see Michael Keen, 'VAT, Tariffs, and Withholding: Border Taxes and Informality in Developing

2.2.4 Growth

At their most ebullient, authors within the conventional approach claim that the good VAT is a growth tax not simply because VAT revenues will increase with economic growth but because the VAT *facilitates* economic growth.[42] The latter claim again rests on the perceived superiority of consumption over other tax bases. For example, Johannson et al. conclude that taxes on immoveable property are best for growth, followed by consumption taxes and personal income taxes, with the worst tax being taxes on business such as the corporate income tax.[43] Some go so far as to contend that countries with a greater reliance on indirect taxes are at a greater competitive advantage than those without because, unlike direct taxes like the corporate income tax, indirect taxes such as the VAT are able to be refunded under international trade rules.[44] The argument has been prominent in the US, but is not taken seriously by US policy-makers or most within the conventional approach on the basis that trade theory holds that destination-based VATs should have a neutral impact on trade because exchange rate adjustments and domestic price settings can counteract any relative advantage (or disadvantage).[45] By contrast, there is

Countries', *Journal of Public Economics* 92 (2008), 1892, summarised in Chapter 3, §4.1 of this book. Gruber also highlights research showing that targeted redistribution from high- to low-income earners that is affected through taxing capital is in fact an efficient way to redistribute: Jonathon Gruber, *Public Finance and Public Policy* (3rd ed., Worth Publishers, New York, 2011), 758.

42 See, e.g., Terra and Kajus, who contend that 'VAT is believed to be superior to an income tax in fostering capital formation (and economic growth)': Ben Terra and Julie Kajus, IBFD, *A Guide to the European VAT Directives* [online] (15 April 2011), 7.6.1.3; Robert F. van Brederode, *Systems of General Sales Taxation: Theory, Policy and Practice* (Kluwer Law International Alphen aan den Rijn, 2009), 333; OECD, 'Consumption Taxes: The Way of the Future? (Policy Brief)' (2007) *OECD Observer* 1, 4–5; IMF, *Fiscal Monitor (November 2010) – Fiscal Exit: From Strategy to Implementation* (IMF Publication Services, Washington, DC, 2010), 80; *Contra* Secretariat – United Nations Conference on Trade and Development, *Trade and Development Report 2012* (UNCTAD/TDR/2012) (United Nations Publications, Geneva, 2012), 118–19.

43 Johansson et al. order tax instruments along a 'tax and growth ranking', with recurrent taxes on immovable property being the preferred tax instrument in terms of long-run GDP per capita, followed by consumption taxes (and other property taxes), personal income taxes and corporate income taxes. Asa Johansson et al., 'Taxes and Firm Performance: Evidence from the OECD', in I. Claus et al. (eds.), *Tax Reform in Open Economies: International and Country Perspectives* (Edward Elgar, Chletneham, UK, 2010), 15, 32. For a summary of recent studies and their limitations, see, e.g., International Monetary Fund (IMF), *Fiscal Monitor (October 2013) – Taxing Times* (IMF, Washington, DC, 2013), 31–32.

44 Richard Bird and Pierre-Pascal Gendron, *The VAT in Developing and Transitional Countries* (Cambridge University Press, New York, 2007), 49. See § 6 of this chapter.

45 Mihir A. Desai and James R. Hines Jr., 'Value-Added Taxes and International Trade: The Evidence' (Workshop in Law and Economics Working Paper, University of Chicago, Law School, 2002), 1–2. The *ITD VAT paper* concludes that '[f]or these reasons, improved export performance is rarely used as an argument for adoption of the VAT'. International Tax Dialogue (ITD), 'The Value Added Tax: Experience and Issues' (Background Paper Prepared for the International Tax Dialogue Conference on the VAT, Rome, March 15–16, 2005, ITD),

significant debate as to whether the move to the informal sector that the introduction of a VAT entails actually constrains growth.[46] Leaving aside these criticisms, ancillary growth benefits of the good VAT are said to include the VAT's ability to be used as a countercyclical tool through using cuts in VAT rates to stimulate demand (and thereby increase economic growth) and by using increases in VAT rates to suppress demand.[47]

2.2.5 Simplicity

Simplicity is not considered to be the good VAT's greatest virtue.[48] The VAT's complexity has caused some to question its appropriateness for developing countries with limited administrative and compliance capacity.[49] Nevertheless, the

11; Richard Bird and Pierre-Pascal Gendron, *The VAT in Developing and Transitional Countries* (Cambridge University Press, New York, 2007), 49–55, ch. 4; Ben Terra and Julie Kajus, IBFD, *A Guide to the European VAT Directives* [online] (15 April 2011), 7.6.1.3; Auerbach contends that '[s]ome of the key advantages seen by some in adopting some form of consumption tax don't stand simple scrutiny, notably its purported ability to improve the trade balance through border adjustments and to reach economic activities that escape the income tax:' Alan J. Auerbach, 'The Choice Between Income and Consumption Taxes: A Primer' (Conference paper for Key Issues in Public Finance, New York University) (New York, 2006), 38. However, the argument is more of a riposte to the US claim that the VAT offers an unfair subsidy to countries that are able to refund indirect taxes to exporters over countries that rely more heavily on direct taxes (which cannot be refunded without offending trading rules). Ironically, those within the conventional approach who challenge the argument that VAT is a trade advantage critique the claim on the basis that it assumes conditions that are not met in reality (such as broadly based VATs or, in other words, that the good VAT exists in reality when in fact it does not): Richard Bird and Pierre-Pascal Gendron, *The VAT in Developing and Transitional Countries* (Cambridge University Press, New York, 2007), 51.

46 M. Shahe Emran and Joseph E. Stiglitz, 'On Selective Indirect Tax Reform in Developing Countries', *Journal of Public Economics* 89 (2005), 599, 619–623; Richard Bird and Pierre-Pascal Gendron, *The VAT in Developing and Transitional Countries* (Cambridge University Press, New York, 2007), 78–80. *Contra* Michael Keen, 'VAT, Tariffs, and Withholding: Border Taxes and Informality in Developing Countries' (2008), *Journal of Public Economics* 92, 1892. See Chapter 3, §4.1 of this book.

47 Gillis et al. claimed in 1990 that this 'issue has received almost no attention': Malcolm Gillis, Carl S. Shoup and Gerardo P. Sicat, 'Lessons for Developing Countries', in M. Gillis, C. S. Shoup and G. P. Sicat (eds.), *Value Added Taxation in Developing Countries (A World Bank Symposium)* (World Bank, Washington, DC, 1990), 219, 225.

48 Richard Bird and Pierre-Pascal Gendron, *The VAT in Developing and Transitional Countries* (Cambridge University Press, New York, 2007), 20; Liam Ebrill et al., *The Modern VAT* (IMF, Washington, DC, 2001), 54–61; International Tax Dialogue (ITD), 'The Value Added Tax: Experience and Issues' (Background Paper Prepared for the International Tax Dialogue Conference on the VAT, Rome, March 15–16, 2005, ITD), 12; John F. Due contends that '[o]n the whole, the value-added tax is not nearly a simple levy as is sometimes argued', quoted in David Williams, 'Value-Added Tax', in V. Thuronyi (ed.), *Tax Law Design and Drafting* (IMF, Washington, DC, 1996), vol. 1, 164, 229–30.

49 Scott Riswold, 'VAT in Sub-Saharan Africa – A Critique of IMF VAT Policy' (March/April 2004), *International VAT Monitor* 97, 109; Joseph E. Stiglitz, 'Development-Oriented Tax Policy', in R. H. Gordon (ed.), *Taxation in Developing Countries: Six Case Studies and Policy Implications* (Columbia University Press, New York, 2010), 11, 12–13.

conventional approach contends that the more closely one adheres to the three design norms of the good VAT, the greater chance of achieving simplicity. The case for simplicity depends on the comparator used. Against the income tax, the good VAT is considered superior because of the professed ease of taxing consumption over income (see §2.1); the VAT involving fewer taxpayers (registered entities as opposed to all income earners);[50] and the levying of the VAT on a destination basis, which avoids the complex and costly distinctions of source/residence under the income tax.[51] However, when compared to the retail sales tax, it is generally agreed that simplicity is not a strong point for the VAT (see §5).

2.2.6 Equity

On traditional measures of equity, the good VAT rates favourably on horizontal equity because it taxes the consumption of most goods alike and is neutral in its application to business.[52] However, most within the conventional approach acknowledge that the good VAT is perceived to rate poorly on the measure of vertical equity,[53] which requires that the burden of taxation should fall heaviest on those with most and lightest on those with least.[54] The failing on this measure

[50] Junko Kato, *Regressive Taxation and the Welfare State: Path Dependence and Policy Diffusion* (Cambridge University Press, Cambridge, 2003), 27, 41–42.

[51] That is, whether to tax income at source (where it is earned) or according to the taxpayer's residence. But see the difficulties in levying VAT on a destination basis, discussed in Chapter 3, §6 of this book.

[52] Ben Terra and Julie Kajus, IBFD, *A Guide to the European VAT Directives* [online] (15 April 2011), 7.2.1. Horizontal equity might also be furthered by the base broadening that the VAT offers because, when used in conjunction with the income tax, the tax base expands to tax those who might otherwise escape the income tax, such as the self-employed: Ian Crawford, Michael Keen and Stephen Smith, 'Value Added Tax and Excises', in Stuart Adam et al. (eds.) for the Institute for Fiscal Studies, *Dimensions of Tax Design: The Mirrlees Review* (Oxford University Press, Oxford, 2010), 275, 282.

[53] The OECD confirms that the 'VAT is not a progressive but a proportional tax. In its origins, it was not designed to meet social or redistributive objectives': OECD, *Consumption Tax Trends 2010: VAT/GST and Excise Rates, Trends and Administration Issues* (OECD Publishing, Paris, 2011), 106. The 2012 edition makes a similar point: 'At its origin, it was designed not to meet social or redistributive objectives, but to raise revenues from the taxation of goods and services without distorting international trade': OECD, *Consumption Tax Trends 2012: VAT/GST and Excise Rates, Trends and Administration Issues* (OECD Publishing, Paris, 2012), 104; Richard Bird and Pierre-Pascal Gendron, *The VAT in Developing and Transitional Countries* (Cambridge University Press, New York, 2007), 70, ch. 5; Liam Ebrill et al., *The Modern VAT* (IMF, Washington, DC, 2001), 105–7; Van Brederode states that '[b]y my knowledge, there exists no VAT system in the world designed to be progressive. The only way to make an indirect consumption tax progressive is by rate variation': Robert F. van Brederode, *Systems of General Sales Taxation: Theory, Policy and Practice* (Kluwer Law International Alphen aan den Rijn, 2009), 33.

[54] Vertical equity is traditionally justified according to the measure of ability to pay (that those with more should pay more) and/or from the benefit principle (that those who benefit from the state should pay accordingly for those benefits). Some separate the two rationales, while

derives almost entirely from the good VAT being a broadly based indirect consumption tax. Although the highest absolute burden of the good VAT would be borne by those who spend the most on consumption (i.e., the rich), the good VAT nevertheless places a significant absolute burden on the poor because the purchases made by the poor would constitute a significant part of the tax base by virtue of the good VAT's broad base and flat rate.[55] Whereas a direct tax, such as the income tax, can exclude individuals based on their means, an indirect tax such as the good VAT precludes adjustments for individual circumstances.[56] The good VAT also places a higher *relative* burden on the poor, given that the ratio of spending on current consumption decreases as incomes rise (while savings increase as income rises). Therefore, given that the poor spend more as a portion of their incomes than the rich, the relative burden of the VAT falls most heavily on those with least, thus making the good VAT a regressive tax.[57]

The conventional approach has developed a number of defences of the good VAT against the inequity charge.[58] These include conceding the good VAT's vertical inequity but contending that because efficiency trumps equity in tax design, equity issues are generally best addressed elsewhere, either by spending or by variations to other taxes such as the income tax or estate and gift duties: see norm 1 (§4).[59] Of these measures, however, only spending will address the absolute

others see ability as being linked to benefits: Edward McCaffery, 'A New Understanding of Tax' (2004), *Michigan Law Review* 58, 807, 831.

55 US Department of the Treasury, *Tax Reform for Fairness, Simplicity, and Economic Growth* (Office of the Secretary, Department of the Treasury, Washington, DC, 1984), vol. 3, ch. 5, 43.

56 See § 4 of this chapter. The retail sales tax (RST) is susceptible to the same critique.

57 Richard Krever, 'Designing and Drafting VAT Laws for Africa', in R. Krever (ed.), *VAT in Africa* (Pretoria University Law Press, Pretoria, 2008), 9, 18. If a consumption tax increases the price of essential or non-discretionary items of consumption, this further exacerbates the impact on the poor who, by virtue of the fact that they have less resources, may be forced to consume less of these essential items of consumption.

58 Another response is to attempt to reclaim or repackage the notion of equity. For example, van Brederode contends that:

> Since moral values change over time, the concept of fairness is not carved in stone. The statement that a progressive income tax is fair and just is merely a statement of political correctness; it is not a statement of fact. In this same sense is the rejection of, for instance, a VAT on the grounds of its presumed regressive nature, a statement of political correctness.

Robert F. van Brederode, *Systems of General Sales Taxation: Theory, Policy and Practice* (Kluwer Law International Alphen aan den Rijn, 2009), 33. The notion that a proper conception of fairness is a matter of changing fashion rather than a deep moral obligation is highly controversial at best; see, e.g., John Rawls, *A Theory of Justice* (Clarendon Press, Oxford, 1972).

59 Ebrill et al. state that 'the amount of redistribution that can be achieved through any indirect tax alone is quite limited': Liam Ebrill et al., *The Modern VAT* (IMF, Washington, DC, 2001), 75, ch. 10; OECD, *Consumption Tax Trends 2012: VAT/GST and Excise Rates, Trends and Administration Issues* (OECD Publishing, Paris, 2012), 104; Richard Bird and Pierre-Pascal Gendron, *The VAT in Developing and Transitional Countries* (Cambridge University Press, New York, 2007), 70; Sijbren Cnossen, 'A VAT Primer for Lawyers, Economists, and Accountants' (2009), *Tax Notes International* 55(4), 319, 331. The IMF states that:

burden the VAT imposes on the poor, as adjustments to the income tax (unless they take the form of tax credits) will be of little use for individuals below the tax threshold.[60] Alternatively, the conventional approach lodges a theoretical defence to claim that the measure of inequity is wrong. So, for example, when the VAT is measured as a proportion of expenditure rather than income or when measured over a lifetime rather than on an annual basis, the effective incidence of the good VAT is less regressive (meaning the poor still pay relatively more, but less so than when measured against annual income) or proportionate (meaning the relative tax burden is constant across all income categories).[61]

> Policymakers should focus on developing a broadly based, efficient, and easily administered tax system with moderate marginal rates. Although the primary goal of the tax system should be to promote efficiency, policymakers also need to consider how to distribute the burden of taxation so the system is seen as fair and just. The expenditure side of the budget offers better opportunities than the tax side for redistributing income.

IMF Fiscal Affairs Department, 'Should Equity Be a Goal of Economic Policy?', *Finance and Development* (September 1998), 2, 4. See also Peter H. Lindert, *Growing Public: Social Spending and Economic Growth since the Eighteenth Century* (Cambridge UK; New York, Cambridge University Press, 2004), 235–45; Joseph E. Stiglitz, 'Development-Oriented Tax Policy', in R. H. Gordon (ed.), *Taxation in Developing Countries: Six Case Studies and Policy Implications* (Columbia University Press, New York, 2010), 11, 25.

60 US Department of the Treasury, *Tax Reform for Fairness, Simplicity, and Economic Growth* (Office of the Secretary, Department of the Treasury, Washington, DC, 1984), vol. 3, ch. 5, 43.

61 Liam Ebrill et al., *The Modern VAT* (IMF, Washington, DC, 2001), 106–7; Richard Bird and Pierre-Pascal Gendron, *The VAT in Developing and Transitional Countries* (Cambridge University Press, New York, 2007), ch. 5; IMF, *Fiscal Monitor (November 2010) – Fiscal Exit: From Strategy to Implementation* (IMF Publication Services, Washington, DC, 2010), 81; International Tax Dialogue (ITD), 'The Value Added Tax: Experience and Issues' (Background Paper Prepared for the International Tax Dialogue Conference on the VAT, Rome, March 15–16, 2005, ITD), 15; Erik Caspersen and Gilbert Metcalf, 'Is a Value Added Tax Regressive? Annual versus Lifetime Incidence Measures', *National Tax Journal* 47(4) (1998), 731; John Creedy, 'Are Consumption Taxes Regressive?' *Australian Economic Review* 31(2) (1998), 107, 113. Arguments in support of this claim include the contention that savings is simply the deferral of consumption and that, because most people consume what they earn in a lifetime, the incidence of the good VAT and the income tax is effectively the same; see Alan Schenk and Oliver Oldman, *Value Added Tax: A Comparative Approach* (rev. edn., Cambridge University Press, Cambridge; New York, 2007), 8; Ebrill et al. at 19, 198; Robert F. van Brederode, *Systems of General Sales Taxation: Theory, Policy and Practice* (Kluwer Law International Alphen aan den Rijn, 2009), 33–45. Although the existence of gifts and bequests poses some difficulty for the equivalence argument, as this clearly indicates that not all income (or wealth) is consumed in a lifetime but rather passed down intergenerationally, the conventional approach contends that intergenerational equity is best addressed through effective estate and gift taxation rather than the good VAT: Ebrill et al., at 107. *Contra* Zee who highlights the generally accepted contention that the equivalence between income and consumption taxes holds only if one compares the consumption tax to a tax on labour income only (the arguments do not hold when compared to a comprehensive income tax [the aggregate of labour and capital income]). Therefore, the equity considerations that a shift from income to consumption might entail are not alone addressed by lifetime incidence: Howell H. Zee, 'World Trends in Tax Policy: An Economic Perspective' (2004), *INTERTAX* 32(8/9), 352, 358–59; John Norregaard and Tehmina S. Khan, 'Tax Policy: Recent Trends and Coming Challenges' (Working Paper No. WP/07/274, IMF, 2007), 37; Reuven Avi-Yonah,

Of all the public finance norms, it is perhaps the vertical equity measure that has been the most fiercely contested. However, this book is prepared to accept all the merits claimed of the good VAT by the conventional approach, because even when one accepts the merits of the good VAT they still fail to provide an adequate explanation for the outcomes achieved by real VATs.

3 PRESCRIBING THE GOOD VAT – A COMPARISON WITH OTHER VAT ALTERNATIVES

In theory, there are many ways to levy a VAT. However, one form of VAT, labelled by this book as the good VAT, is dominant. Such is the dominance of the good VAT that it has become synonymous with the definition of a VAT. However, this section reminds us that the good VAT is the product of a number of deliberate design choices. A brief introduction to the design options is provided to introduce the discussion of the three design norms favoured by the conventional approach for the good VAT.

'Value-add' is the value that a producer contributes to raw materials and can be calculated in a number of ways. One can calculate value-add through adding up all component parts that add value to the raw materials or, in more technical terms, the payments made to these factors of production (the 'addition method'):[62]

'Risk, Rents and Regressivity Revisited' (2009), *Australian Tax Forum* 24, 41, 42, 51, 54–55; Barbara H. Fried, 'Fairness and the Consumption Tax', *Stanford Law Review* 44 (1991–1992), 961, 1016; Neil Brooks, 'An Overview of the Role of the VAT, Fundamental Tax Reform, and a Defence of the Income Tax', in R. Krever and D. White (eds.), *GST in Retrospect and Prospect* (Brookers, Wellington, 2007), 597, 621. Alternative versions in support of consumption taxes contend that higher lifetime incomes do not suggest higher lifetime savings, because saving rates are invariant to income, but simply a method to smooth out consumption over a lifetime. This means that an individual with high current income will save more, so as to consume when their income falls as, for example, with retirement; while a low-income individual will save less in anticipation of earning more: Ebrill et al., at 106–7. *Contra* Dynan et al., who find strong evidence that the 'rich do, indeed, save more': Karen E. Dynan, Jonathon Skinner and Stephen P. Zeldes, 'Do the Rich Save More?' (2004), *Journal of Political Economy* 112(2), 397, 437–38. The US Treasury highlighted that '[s]till, it is the current year's income that in large part determines the current living standard and the sum out of which most taxes are paid. Moreover, the current year's income is usually regarded as the most practical basis for the comparison of value-added tax burdens at various income levels'. US Department of the Treasury, *Tax Reform for Fairness, Simplicity, and Economic Growth* (Office of the Secretary, Department of the Treasury, Washington, DC, 1984), vol. 3, ch. 8, 90.

62 Liam Ebrill et al., *The Modern VAT* (IMF, Washington, DC, 2001), 20; Ken Messere, Flip de Kam and Christopher Heady, *Tax Policy: Theory and Practice in OECD Countries* (Oxford University Press, Oxford, 2003), 141; Alan A. Tait, *Value Added Tax: International Practice and Problems* (IMF, Washington, DC, 1988), 4; Alan Schenk and Oliver Oldman, *Value Added Tax: A Comparative Approach* (rev. edn., Cambridge University Press, Cambridge; New York, 2007), 42–43; Clara K. Sullivan, *The Tax on Value Added* (New York, 1965), 7; US Department of the Treasury, *Tax Reform for Fairness, Simplicity, and Economic Growth* (Office of the Secretary, Department of the Treasury, Washington, DC, 1984), vol. 3, ch. 2, 8.

$$\text{Value-add} = \text{wages} + \text{net profit}$$[63]

Alternatively, the value added by a business to raw materials can be calculated by subtracting the difference between the business's outputs (sales) from its inputs (purchases) (the 'subtraction method'):

$$\text{Value-add} = \text{outputs} - \text{inputs}$$

The two methods for calculating value-add are equivalent so that

$$\text{Value-add} = \text{wages} + \text{net profit} = \text{outputs} - \text{inputs.}$$[64]

The value-added method can in theory apply to a number of potential tax bases: consumption, income or gross product.[65] A major difference between each base as it applies to the private sector is the manner in which capital goods are treated. Table 2.1 details which components of the value-add are included, depending on the choice of base.[66]

As has already been foreshadowed and as the next section explains in greater detail, much of the conventional approach's enthusiasm for the good VAT is because it applies to a consumption base (norm 1).[67] A consumption VAT is

63 This equation may be more accurately represented to account for payments made to all factors of production, so that Value-add = wages + net profit + rents + interest. However, this book uses the simplified equation of wages + profits to illustrate the general design issues: Alan A. Tait, *Value Added Tax: International Practice and Problems* (IMF, Washington, DC, 1988), 4.

64 Ibid.

65 Clara K. Sullivan, *The Tax on Value Added* (New York, 1965), ch. 1, 5; Carl S. Shoup, *The Value-Added Tax* (Center of Planning and Economic Research, Athens, 1973), 17–26; US Department of the Treasury, *Tax Reform for Fairness, Simplicity, and Economic Growth* (Office of the Secretary, Department of the Treasury, Washington, DC, 1984), vol. 3, ch. 2, 6–7; Zee refers to the VATs applied to different bases as the 'P-VAT' (gross product base), 'I-VAT' (income base) and 'C-VAT' (consumption base): Howell Zee, 'Value-Added Tax', in P. Shome (ed.), *Tax Policy Handbook* (Fiscal Affairs Department, IMF, Washington, DC, 1995), 86.

66 There will also be differences in the treatment of government purchases and imports and exports: see, e.g., US Department of the Treasury, *Tax Reform for Fairness, Simplicity, and Economic Growth* (Office of the Secretary, Department of the Treasury, Washington, DC, 1984), vol. 3, ch. 2, 5–6.

67 The *ITD VAT Paper* states that 'the consensus favors ensuring the final base of the tax is consumption': ITD International Tax Dialogue (ITD), 'The Value Added Tax: Experience and Issues' (Background Paper Prepared for the International Tax Dialogue Conference on the VAT, Rome, March 15–16, 2005, ITD), 7; Alan Schenk and Oliver Oldman, *Value Added Tax: A Comparative Approach* (rev. edn., Cambridge University Press, Cambridge; New York, 2007), 17; Malcolm Gillis, Carl S. Shoup and Gerardo P. Sicat, 'Lessons for Developing Countries', in M. Gillis, C. S. Shoup and G. P. Sicat (eds.), *Value Added Taxation in Developing Countries (A World Bank Symposium)* (World Bank, Washington, DC, 1990), 219, 223; OECD, *Consumption Tax Trends 2012: VAT/GST and Excise Rates, Trends and Administration Issues* (OECD Publishing, Paris, 2012), 31, 45; Terra and Kajus contend that '[s]ince the consumption version is the type of value added tax used in Europe, there is a tendency to regard this type of VAT as the only type. . .we believe it is far superior to the other types': Ben Terra and Julie Kajus, IBFD, *A Guide to the European VAT Directives* [online] (15 April 2011), 7.5.2.1.

TABLE 2.1 – *The choice of VAT base*[a]

Norm 1 – Design options for the choice of base	The good VAT – Net consumption base	Design alternative – Income base	Design alternative – Gross product base
Means to achieve the chosen base	Tax all sales with full and immediate deductions/credits available for all purchases/inputs, including capital goods	Tax all sales with deductions/credits for purchases/inputs of raw materials but with credit for capital goods limited to the depreciation value of such goods	Tax all sales with credits available only for the purchase of raw materials but no deductions/credits for capital goods

[a] Based on Alan A. Tait, *Value Added Tax: International Practice and Problems* (IMF, Washington, DC, 1988), 4; Ken Messere, Flip de Kam and Christopher Heady, *Tax Policy: Theory and Practice in OECD Countries* (Oxford University Press, Oxford, 2003), 141.

designed to tax the goods and services that are acquired by individuals for their personal use or enjoyment, but generally not the goods and services used in the production or distribution of those goods or services rendered; that is, business inputs.[68] As Table 2.1 shows, for a consumption-based VAT, all consumption is taxed but business receives credits for tax paid on inputs. On the assumption that the retail price paid for a good or service is equal to the sum of the value added by all the businesses in the production process, a value-added tax that extends through all stages of the production process, including the retail stage (with credits allowed for business inputs), will amount to a tax on final private consumption.[69]

When the choice for a consumption base is made, the conventional approach favours methods of VAT collection that best complement consumption. The preference within the conventional approach is to calculate VAT liability through an indirect subtraction method (referred to in this book as the 'invoice-credit method' (see §5)).[70]

As Table 2.2 shows, the method is labelled *indirect* because it taxes the transaction by subtracting the VAT paid on a business's inputs/purchases from the VAT charged on its outputs/sales. Adoption of the invoice-credit method, therefore,

68 Ben Terra and Julie Kajus, IBFD, *A Guide to the European VAT Directives* [online] (15 April 2011), 7.2.2; Alan Schenk and Oliver Oldman, *Value Added Tax: A Comparative Approach* (rev. edn., Cambridge University Press, Cambridge; New York, 2007), 1.

69 US Department of the Treasury, *Tax Reform for Fairness, Simplicity, and Economic Growth* (Office of the Secretary, Department of the Treasury, Washington, DC, 1984), vol. 3, ch. 2, 5.

70 The need to assess VAT on total purchases and sales (or on inputs for the addition method) on an accounts basis means the subtraction VAT is more akin to an entity-based tax, rather than a transactional one: Liam Ebrill et al., *The Modern VAT* (IMF, Washington, DC, 2001), 21.

TABLE 2.2 – *Mechanisms to levy VAT*[a]

Norm 2 – Design options for levying VAT	The good VAT – Invoice-credit method (indirect subtraction method)[b]	Design alternative – Direct subtraction accounts method[c]	Design alternative – Indirect addition method	Design alternative – Direct addition method
Means to calculate and collect VAT	Subtract tax paid on outputs/ sales from tax paid on inputs/ purchases on a transactional basis; i.e., t (sales) – t (purchases)[d]	Tax the difference between total outputs/sales from inputs/ purchases over an accounting period; i.e., t (total sales – total purchases)	Tax the value-add of each component part that contributes to the value-add rather than the total value-add; i.e., t (wages) + t (profits). Ill suited for a consumption base[e]	Tax the total value-add by all factors of production; i.e., t (wages + profits). Ill suited for a consumption base

[a] Carl S. Shoup, 'Choosing among Types of VATs', in M. Gillis, C. S. Shoup and G. P. Sicat (eds.), *Value Added Taxation in Developing Countries (A World Bank Symposium)* (World Bank, Washington, DC, 1990), 3, 4; Alan A. Tait, *Value Added Tax: International Practice and Problems* (IMF, Washington, DC, 1988), 4.

[b] While the adoption of the invoice-credit method fits well with a consumption VAT, it is considered less compatible with an income VAT, as invoices issued on a transactional basis are ill suited to distinguishing between capital and current use goods and taking into account depreciation: Carl S. Shoup, 'Choosing among Types of VATs', in M. Gillis, C. S. Shoup and G. P. Sicat (eds.), *Value Added Taxation in Developing Countries (A World Bank Symposium)* (World Bank, Washington, DC, 1990), 3, 9.

[c] The accounts-based subtraction method calculates a firm's VAT liability by subtracting total purchases from total sales for a specified period. The balance, equivalent to the value added by the firm, is then subject to the VAT rate: Carl S. Shoup, 'Choosing among Types of VATs', in M. Gillis, C. S. Shoup and G. P. Sicat (eds.), *Value Added Taxation in Developing Countries (A World Bank Symposium)* (World Bank, Washington, DC, 1990), 3, 7–8; Liam Ebrill et al., *The Modern VAT* (IMF, Washington, DC, 2001), 20. The invoice-credit method reaches the same result as the subtraction method by subtracting tax paid on purchases from tax charged on sales, as evidenced by invoices: Carl S. Shoup, *Public Finance* (Aldine Publishing Company, Chicago, 1969), 258. Although the accounts-based subtraction method offers intuitive simplicity and possibly lower compliance costs, consensus favours the invoice-credit mechanism. The accounts-based subtraction or addition methods generally require longer reporting periods, usually on an annual basis, in order to accurately calculate VAT liability. By contrast, the invoice-credit mechanism levied on a transactional basis enables more frequent reporting, such as on a monthly basis, which in turn increases revenue flows: Liam Ebrill et al., *The Modern VAT* (IMF, Washington, DC, 2001), 20–22; Alan A. Tait, *Value Added Tax: International Practice and Problems* (IMF, Washington, DC, 1988), 5.

[d] 't' = tax, or the application of the tax rate to the relevant base: Alan A. Tait, *Value Added Tax: International Practice and Problems* (IMF, Washington, DC, 1988), 4.

[e] The addition method is more suited to income VATs because it includes in the tax base the rewards to all factors, including interest and profits. Where a consumption VAT is intended to be borne by consumers, the identification of VAT with wages and profits is considered inappropriate. It is assumed that because VAT liability under the addition method is based on profits and wages and not the sale price of goods, it is therefore unlikely that the exact VAT will be shifted to consumers: Carl S. Shoup, 'Choosing among Types of VATs', in M. Gillis, C. S. Shoup and G. P. Sicat (eds.), *Value Added Taxation in Developing Countries (A World Bank Symposium)* (World Bank, Washington, DC, 1990), 3, 8; Alan Schenk and Oliver Oldman, *Value Added Tax: A Comparative Approach* (rev. edn., Cambridge University Press, Cambridge; New York, 2007), 42–46.

makes the good VAT a transaction-based consumption tax whereby VAT liability is calculated on the sale of goods and services (taxable supplies), as evidenced by an invoice.[71] This is in contrast to an accounts-based method, such as the direct subtraction accounts-based method, which subtracts a business's purchases from its sales over an accounting period and then applies the VAT rate to the balance.[72] Table 2.2 explains the other methods available to compute VAT liability.

The VAT is a general *indirect* consumption tax because the consumer ultimately bears the burden of the tax in the form of increased prices rather than the retailer or service provider who collects and remits the tax.[73] The personal consumption of an individual is taxed (measured as a percentage of the price paid for goods and services) rather than directly assessed against an individual's consumption expenditure.[74] This is in contrast to a *direct* tax, such as the income tax or a personal expenditure tax, which is assessed directly on the income or expenditure of the individual taxpayer.[75]

71 Liam Ebrill et al., *The Modern VAT* (IMF, Washington, DC, 2001), 21; Alan Schenk and Oliver Oldman, *Value Added Tax: A Comparative Approach* (rev. edn., Cambridge University Press, Cambridge; New York, 2007), 40.

72 Clara K. Sullivan, *The Tax on Value Added* (New York, 1965), 17; International Tax Dialogue (ITD), 'The Value Added Tax: Experience and Issues' (Background Paper Prepared for the International Tax Dialogue Conference on the VAT, Rome, March 15–16, 2005, ITD), 7; Liam Ebrill et al., *The Modern VAT* (IMF, Washington, DC, 2001), 20; Alan Schenk and Oliver Oldman, *Value Added Tax: A Comparative Approach* (rev. edn., Cambridge University Press, Cambridge; New York, 2007), 38–39; Sijbren Cnossen, 'Global Trends and Issues in Value Added Taxation', *International Tax and Public Finance* 5(3) (1998), 399–400; Alan A. Tait, *Value Added Tax: International Practice and Problems* (IMF, Washington, DC, 1988), 4–6.

73 Ben Terra and Julie Kajus, IBFD, A *Guide to the European VAT Directives* [online] (15 April 2011), 7.2. See also § 6 of this chapter for the WTO classification.

74 As the OECD explains, '[a]s the final consumer is unable to recover the tax, the amount of tax actually collected through the staged collection process should be equal to the amount of VAT charged by the last vendor in the supply chain': OECD, *Consumption Tax Trends 2012: VAT/GST and Excise Rates, Trends and Administration Issues* (OECD Publishing, Paris, 2012), 31. There are forms of direct consumption/expenditure tax levied at the individual, with many models a variation on requiring some calculation of income over a period and then the deduction of savings with the balance being the individual's consumption base on which the tax is levied: see, e.g., Nicholas Kaldor, *An Expenditure Tax* (Allen & Unwin, London, 1955); William Andrews, 'A Consumption-Type or Cash Flow Personal Income Tax', *Harvard Law Review* 87 (1974), 1113. The idea has been especially prominent in the US in recent times – see Chapter 7 of this book.

75 The direct/indirect distinction has a long intellectual lineage and can be found in the work of John Stuart Mill, who based the distinction on whether both the impact and incidence of the tax was on the same person (direct) or on different people (indirect); that is, when the burden is shifted away from the taxpayer and borne by someone else, the tax is indirect: John Stuart Mill, *Principles of Political Economy with Some of Their Applications to Social Philosophy* (1909 ed., Longmans, Green and Co., London, 1848), book 5, Chapter 6 – 'Comparison between Direct and Indirect Taxation'. The distinction is also captured through labelling the VAT an *in rem* tax (levied against the taxable supplies of goods and services), as opposed to an *in personam* tax (levied against the person): Sijbren Cnossen, 'A VAT Primer for Lawyers, Economists, and Accountants' (2009), *Tax Notes International* 55(4), 319, 322.

TABLE 2.3 – *Jurisdictional reach of VAT*

Norm 3 – Design options for jurisdictional reach of VAT	The good VAT – Destination based	Design alternative – Origin based
Means to achieve	Tax according to the place of consumption – Imports are taxed and exports are tax free	Tax according to the place of production/origin – Imports are tax free and exports are taxed

Table 2.3 shows how the destination method is also thought to complement the choice of a domestic consumption base because the tax is levied at the place of consumption rather than production. The jurisdictional reach of the good VAT might therefore be regarded as another aspect of the choice of a consumption base.

The following sections outline the three design norms that reflect the consensus within the conventional approach on what is necessary to constitute the good VAT. Each of these design norms give effect to choices relating to the base, mechanism to levy and jurisdictional reach of the VAT, outlined in Tables 2.1–2.3:[76]

- Norm 1 – A single-rate VAT levied on a broad consumption base with minimal exclusions

[76] Ebrill et al. refer to these 'core features' on which there is 'widespread agreement on what constitutes "best practice"': Liam Ebrill et al., *The Modern VAT* (IMF, Washington, DC, 2001), 15, 23. The *ITD VAT Paper* provides that '[w]hile there are many variations on the structure of the VAT and how it is implemented, there is wide agreement on some core issues': International Tax Dialogue (ITD), 'The Value Added Tax: Experience and Issues' (Background Paper Prepared for the International Tax Dialogue Conference on the VAT, Rome, March 15–16, 2005, ITD), 7; Bogetic and Hassan in 1993 summarised the 'emerging conventional wisdom' on a best-practice VAT as 'a single rate VAT (with the rate between 10 and 20 percent), with very few exemptions and, therefore, a broad base': Zeljko Bogetic and Fareed Hassan, 'Determinants of Value-Added Tax Revenue: A Cross-Section Analysis' (Policy Research Working Paper No. WPS 1203, Washington, DC, 1993), 2; Michael Keen, 'What Do (and Don't) We Know about the Value Added Tax? A Review of Richard M. Bird and Pierre-Pascal Gendron's *The VAT in Developing and Transitional Countries*', *Journal of Economic Literature* 47(1) (2009), 159, 160–61. Other key VAT design issues are not dealt with here because the design issues are more peripheral and the consensus is less secure. These include decisions as to whether to calculate VAT on a price-exclusive or price-inclusive basis. Either option is available under a transaction-based VAT, and neither impacts on overall revenue yields, but the choice to disclose VAT paid separate from price can have important political ramifications in reminding consumers of the tax paid on the goods they purchase: Alan Schenk and Oliver Oldman, *Value Added Tax: A Comparative Approach* (rev. edn., Cambridge University Press, Cambridge; New York, 2007), 35–6; Alan A. Tait, *Value Added Tax: International Practice and Problems* (IMF, Washington, DC, 1988), 8; US Government Accountability Office, *Value-Added Taxes: Lessons Learned from Other Countries on Compliance Risks, Administrative Costs, Compliance Burden, and Transition (GAO-08-566)* (Washington, DC, 2008), 12–13.

- Norm 2 – Calculation of VAT liability using the invoice-credit mechanism
- Norm 3 – Levying VAT on a destination basis (i.e., on a base of domestic consumption)

Although norms 1 and 3 both relate to the base of the VAT and norm 2 more to its administration, it is customary within the conventional approach to separate the discussion of each norm. This book adopts this convention, as norms 1 and 2 give rise to overlapping but discrete issues. The discussion of each norm covers economic concepts that, in turn, require translation into legal terminology. The chapter adopts a common example to show the manner in which this translation occurs; the example is a draft bill for a hypothetical VAT labelled the 'Value Added Tax Act of the New Commonwealth of Vatopia' (hereafter the '*New Vatopia Model*'), drafted by Alan Schenk and members of the IMF Legal Department as one of four 'off-the-shelf' models for use in developing countries.[77]

4 NORM 1 – A BROAD CONSUMPTION BASE AT A SINGLE RATE WITH MINIMAL EXCLUSIONS

The first design norm prescribed by the conventional approach to achieve the good VAT is intended to ensure that the VAT taxes final consumption in a neutral manner.

The good VAT uses expenditure on consumption as a proxy for consumption.[78] As an indirect consumption tax, the good VAT is levied on transactions, giving rise to expenditure on consumption rather than directly levied on the actual

[77] Although the draft VAT bill has not received official endorsement from the IMF Executive and has the status of a working paper, it is a useful summary of the types of prescriptions recommended by the conventional approach: Alan Schenk and Members of the IMF Legal Department, *Value Added Tax Act of the Commonwealth of New Vatopia* (IMF, 2006). The *New Vatopia Model* is chosen as illustrative of the manner in which the design norms are translated into legal language. The model replaces an earlier model (one of the three other hypothetical VATs) and is chosen over the two remaining models, as it most closely resembles the good VAT (a VAT law for Fantasia is directed at countries of the former Soviet Union; a VAT Law of Republica is based on advisory work in Uganda, Tonga and Lesotho and has a narrower base): IMF Legal Department, *Tax Law Drafting Samples VAT* (24 January 2006) (www.imf.org/external/np/leg/tlaw/2003/eng/tlvat.htm).

[78] Using expenditure as a proxy for consumption generally avoids the difficulties in defining consumption, such as in determining immediate consumption, as occurs with the eating of a meat pie, or continuous consumption, as might occur through the purchase of a work of art. Although these distinctions do enter the design debate, for example with the treatment of real property, VATs are generally predictive in that they tax consumption before consumption occurs, as opposed to the income tax, which is generally reactive, intending to be levied only on a person's actual income: Ben Terra and Julie Kajus, IBFD, *A Guide to the European VAT Directives* [online] (15 April 2011), 7.2.2; Alan Schenk and Oliver Oldman, *Value Added Tax: A Comparative Approach* (rev. edn., Cambridge University Press, Cambridge; New York, 2007), 1.

expenditure accounts of consumers themselves. Expenditure is the price paid, or in legal terms the 'consideration', for the good or service acquired.[79] In legislating for the good VAT, it is generally necessary to identify some taxable transaction (referred to for the purposes of this book as a 'taxable supply'), such as the supply of a good or service, that triggers the expenditure on consumption and therefore the liability to pay VAT.[80] As §5 further explains, in order for the good VAT to be borne by the consumer and not by business, the good VAT also requires eligible entities such as businesses to be able to register so as to receive credit for the tax paid on these taxable supplies (referred to as 'input tax credits').[81]

Table 2.4 shows how the good VAT works in a world of perfect competition in which business can fully shift the VAT forward to consumers. The example assumes that there are three businesses in the production and distribution chain, each of which adds $100 worth of value. The VAT applies at a rate of 10 per cent.

The example demonstrates several features of the good VAT. The row indicating the VAT payable per transaction illustrates the strong revenue cash flow that the good VAT is said to generate. The row indicating net tax payable illustrates that the $30 paid by the final consumer represents the total of the tax imposed on the value-add for each transaction in the production and distribution chain. Other than the cost of collecting and remitting the VAT, the refunds available to the non-end consumers ensure that no cost is borne by any of the businesses in the supply chain. Instead, the VAT is borne by the end consumer.

As already noted, the good VAT is an indirect consumption tax. The direct/indirect dichotomy turns on assumptions of shifting, so that an indirect tax on consumption can be fully shifted forward to consumers in the form of increased prices. The appeal of the good VAT similarly turns on the assumption that the tax is fully shifted from producers to consumers in the form of higher sales prices.[82] Just as some challenge the distinction between direct and indirect taxes,[83] some dispute that the economic incidence of the good VAT is on final consumption. This is

[79] See, e.g., §13 of the *New Vatopia Model*: Alan Schenk and Members of the IMF Legal Department, *Value Added Tax Act of the Commonwealth of New Vatopia* (IMF, 2006).

[80] §9 of the *New Vatopia Model* requires a 'taxable supply' or import of a good or services by a 'taxable person': ibid.

[81] §27 of the *New Vatopia Model* refers to this as an 'input tax deduction': ibid.

[82] See, e.g., Sijbren Cnossen, 'A VAT Primer for Lawyers, Economists, and Accountants' (2009), *Tax Notes International* 55(4), 319, 320; Commonwealth of Australia Treasury, Australia's Future Tax System Review Panel, *Architecture of Australia's Tax and Transfer System* (Commonwealth of Australia Treasury, Canberra, 2008), §3.3.

[83] The distinction between indirect and direct taxes is challenged by modern economic theorists who argue that, from an economic perspective, an indirect tax might not be fully shifted and direct taxes might be shifted. So, the income tax can in certain circumstances be shifted to different degrees, while in some cases the true incidence of a tax may be unknown, as with the corporate income tax: Victor Thuronyi, *Comparative Tax Law* (Kluwer Law International, The Hague, 2003), 54–55; Ben Terra and Julie Kajus, IBFD, *A Guide to the European VAT Directives* [online] (15 April 2011), 7.2.3.

TABLE 2.4 – *The application of the good VAT*[a]

Stage in the production/ distribution chain	Manufacturer (Assuming no material inputs for the supply – No input credits for the manufacturer)	→ Supply 1 – $110: $100 (pre-VAT price) $10 output tax borne by wholesaler but payable by manufacturer ⇒	Wholesaler ⇐ Input tax credit for wholesaler ($10)	→ Supply 2 – $220: $200 (pre-VAT price) $20 output tax borne by retailer but payable by wholesaler ⇒	Retailer ⇐ Input tax credit for retailer ($20)	→ Supply 3 –$330: ($300 pre-VAT price) $30 output tax borne by consumer but payable by retailer ⇒	Consumer No input tax credit (because end consumer)
VAT payable per transaction		$10		$20		$30	
Net tax payable			$0		$0		$30

[a] See also Graeme Cooperand Richard Vann, 'Implementing the Goods and Services Tax', *Sydney Law Review* 23 (1999), 337, 348; Howell Zee, 'Value-Added Tax' in P. Shome (ed.), *Tax Policy Handbook* (Fiscal Affairs Department, IMF, Washington, DC, 1995), 86, 92–96.

because the extent to which the VAT component can be shifted forward depends on other factors, such as market conditions determining the elasticity of supply and demand for goods and services and the degree of competition in the marketplace.[84] If the elasticity of demand for a consumer good is high, for example, and competition in the provision of that good is strong, then the retailer might absorb the VAT component in order to attract consumers. Therefore, whereas the 10 per cent VAT in the above example should increase the price of the $300 consumer good to $330, the retailer might be tempted to maintain the total purchase price at $300 by reducing the net price to $272.73 and charging VAT (of $27.27) on the net amount. In doing so, the retailer absorbs the VAT and the incidence of the tax is, in turn, borne by the business (and by the factors of production such as labour or capital).[85]

Rather than dispute whether the VAT is fully shifted forward to the consumer, the preference within the conventional approach is to prescribe design features to facilitate forward shifting to the end consumer.[86] Measures to encourage the good VAT to fall on a consumption base include the following:

(1) Extension through all stages of the production and distribution chain up to the retail stage: see §4.1; and

[84] In technical terms, elasticity is the percentage change in the quantity of a product, or factor of production (labour, capital, land, etc.) supplied or demanded, divided by the percentage change in its price: Robert F. van Brederode, *Systems of General Sales Taxation: Theory, Policy and Practice* (Kluwer Law International Alphen aan den Rijn, 2009), 29–30. Van Brederode states that (at 32):

> . . .the assumption, generally postulated in legal literature on consumption taxation, that the tax is always and fully shifted forward to the final consumer is obviously an inaccurate simplification. For the tax burden to be fully borne by private consumers and to be correctly characterized as a mere wash through for traders would require supply to be perfectly elastic and demand to be perfectly inelastic. In reality, the tax burden will fall on those who are the least able to shift the burden to someone else. In this sense, the tax burden is on the shoulders of consumers, labor factor and capital factor to the extent of their respective elasticities.

Cooper states that '[i]f the firm cannot raise its prices by the amount needed to recover the VAT, the burden of the tax will have to be absorbed by the firm in the form of a reduction of its profits. So the tax will in the short run at least be borne by the firm's owners': Graeme Cooper, 'The Discrete Charm of the VAT' (University of Sydney Law School Legal Studies Research Paper No. 07/65, University of Sydney, 2007), 30. Incidence will also depend on other factors, such as whether monetary policy allows prices to rise with the introduction of VAT; if not, the tax falls on production: Peggy Musgrave, 'Consumption Tax Proposals in an International Setting' (2001[March/April]), *International VAT Monitor*, 56, 61; Liam Ebrill et al., *The Modern VAT* (IMF, Washington, DC, 2001), 15.

[85] Ibid.

[86] Liam Ebrill et al., *The Modern VAT* (IMF, Washington, DC, 2001), 18; Carl S. Shoup, *Public Finance* (Aldine Publishing Company, Chicago, 1969), 253; International Tax Dialogue (ITD), 'The Value Added Tax: Experience and Issues' (Background Paper Prepared for the International Tax Dialogue Conference on the VAT, Rome, March 15–16, 2005, ITD), 7; Alan A. Tait, *Value Added Tax* (McGraw-Hill, London, New York, 1972), 11.

(2) Full and immediate crediting of goods (including capital goods) used in the production of goods and services: see the discussion in §5 of norm 2.

To further ensure that consumption is taxed on as broad a base as possible in a neutral manner, the conventional approach also recommends that the good VAT is

(3) Applied to a broad base with minimal exclusions and distortions: see §4.2;
   (a) Minimising equity-based exclusions: see §4.2.4;
   (b) Accepting pragmatically based exclusions, including financial services: see §4.2.5.1; and
(4) Levied at a single rate: see §4.3.

4.1 *Extend the good VAT through all stages of the production and distribution chain*

There are many ways to indirectly tax consumption, such as through pre-retail single-stage sales taxes[87] or through turnover taxes.[88] The deficiencies of these taxes

[87] Single-stage taxes levied at the pre-retail level offer the advantage of a relatively low number of taxpayers, which is outweighed by a number of disadvantages. Chief among the disadvantages of these pre-retail taxes is that the base of the tax is not the retail price. The imposition of a sales tax as close to the final point of consumption and on all firms involved in the production of the good (from manufacture, to wholesale and retail) eliminates the need for complex discount and uplift mechanisms and removes the imprecise art of estimating taxable values. For example, both Manufacturing Sales Taxes (MSTs) and Wholesale Sales Taxes (WSTs) carry a high potential for cascading, as taxes on input products cannot be easily measured, meaning that like products may not be taxed alike. Both MSTs and WSTs involve complex definitional issues (for example in distinguishing manufacturing from distribution) and valuation problems (as is triggered when manufacturers or wholesalers sell directly to consumers). These issues also mean that it is difficult to accurately refund the tax on exports and might therefore disadvantage exporters who are unable to recover the tax actually incurred. The narrow base of these taxes means that their revenue-raising capacity is limited without significant rate increases: Alan A. Tait, *Value Added Tax: International Practice and Problems* (IMF, Washington, DC, 1988), 7–8; Sijbren Cnossen, 'Global Trends and Issues in Value Added Taxation', *International Tax and Public Finance* 5(3) (1998), 399, 401–2; Ben Terra and Julie Kajus, IBFD, *A Guide to the European VAT Directives* [online] (15 April 2011), 7.4; US Department of the Treasury, *Tax Reform for Fairness, Simplicity, and Economic Growth* (Office of the Secretary, Department of the Treasury, Washington, DC, 1984), vol. 3, ch. 4, 33–35; Ken Messere, Flip de Kam and Christopher Heady, *Tax Policy: Theory and Practice in OECD Countries* (Oxford University Press, Oxford, 2003), 143–44.

[88] Although, like the VAT, the turnover tax is levied at all stages of the production and consumption chain, unlike the VAT, business is denied credits for tax paid on their inputs, meaning that the tax liability cascades with each transaction and represents a cost to business. As a result, the base of the turnover tax is more like a gross product base: Robert F. van Brederode, *Systems of General Sales Taxation: Theory, Policy and Practice* (Kluwer Law International Alphen aan den Rijn, 2009), 54; Ken Messere, Flip de Kam and Christopher Heady, *Tax Policy: Theory and Practice in OECD Countries* (Oxford University Press, Oxford, 2003), 143–44.

are well documented and will not be revisited here, other than to note that the VAT's main competitor as a preferred indirect broad-based consumption tax is the retail sales tax (RST). In theory, the economic incidence of the good VAT and the good RST are exactly the same, as Table 2.5 shows.

When Table 2.5 is compared with the good VAT in Table 2.4, it shows that the difference between the two taxes lies in the manner in which the tax is collected. Whereas the VAT taxes everyone but allows registered entities to receive credit for tax paid on eligible inputs through the invoice-credit mechanism, the RST suspends the collection of tax (by not requiring registered entities to pay the tax) until goods or services are sold to the end consumer. Table 2.5 also shows that an RST does not have the same self-enforcing features of the good VAT, nor does it offer the same benefits in revenue cash flow for government that derive from the incremental collection of the VAT.

Further differences between the two taxes will be explored in §5. At this stage, it is sufficient to note that in order for the economic equivalence between the two taxes to be maintained, it is necessary to apply the VAT at all stages in the production and distribution chain up until the retail stage.[89] Failure to do so introduces the issues common to pre-retail sales taxes that arise by virtue of the fact that the tax is not reflected in the retail price.[90] In addition, it is necessary to allow business to receive full and immediate credits for VAT paid on any inputs in the production process, including on capital goods (see norm 2, §5). Failure to allow all entities in the chain to claim credits on their inputs moves the VAT away from a consumption base toward more of a gross product or income base, as it means that the VAT will fall to some degree on business inputs.[91]

4.2 *Maintain a broad VAT base with minimal exclusions*

The conventional approach recommends that the good VAT apply to a broad consumption base to maximise revenue, maintain neutrality and simplify administration.[92]

[89] 'There is general agreement that a "good" VAT should make all entities liable to tax that produce goods and services which are used by or benefit other entities or individuals': Sijbren Cnossen, 'Global Trends and Issues in Value Added Taxation', *International Tax and Public Finance* 5(3) (1998), 399, 401–2; Alan A. Tait, *Value Added Tax: International Practice and Problems* (IMF, Washington, DC, 1988), 6–8; Alan Schenk and Oliver Oldman, *Value Added Tax: A Comparative Approach* (rev. edn., Cambridge University Press, Cambridge; New York, 2007), 33.

[90] See above, n 87.

[91] Liam Ebrill et al., *The Modern VAT* (IMF, Washington, DC, 2001), 16–18.

[92] Ibid., 16, ch. 8; Sijbren Cnossen, 'Global Trends and Issues in Value Added Taxation', *International Tax and Public Finance* 5(3) (1998), 399–400; International Tax Dialogue (ITD), 'The Value Added Tax: Experience and Issues' (Background Paper Prepared for the International Tax Dialogue Conference on the VAT, Rome, March 15–16, 2005, ITD), 15–16;

TABLE 2.5 – *Retail sales tax*[a]

Stage in the production/distribution chain	Manufacturer (Assuming no material inputs for the supply)	→ Supply 1 – $100: No tax paid by wholesaler because a registered business	Wholesaler	→ Supply 2 – $200: No tax paid by retailer because a registered business	Retailer	→ Supply 3 – $330: ($300 pre-RST price) $30 tax paid by final consumer because not a registered business	Consumer
Tax payable per transaction		$0		$0		$30	
Net tax payable			$0		$0		$30

[a] The example adopts the same assumptions as for the good VAT example – three firms in the production and distribution chain each adding $100 of value and the RST levied at 10 per cent.

Although in its purest form the VAT should theoretically apply to the consumption of all goods and services, the good VAT does not extend this far.[93] There are three methods to introduce exclusions to the VAT base: (1) exempting; (2) zero-rating specific goods and services; or (3) removing certain entities from the VAT system.[94] Each method is examined in turn. §4.2.4 and §4.2.5 explain how the conventional approach cautions that the content of the items excluded from the VAT base should be kept as short as possible, in effect being limited to only those transactions or entities that are too difficult to tax effectively under the good VAT.[95]

4.2.1 Methods to exclude – Exemption of select goods and services

When the supply of a good or service is exempt, no VAT is payable but equally no input tax credit can be recovered by the supplier for the VAT paid on their inputs. Jurisdictions within the European Union (EU) label this exclusion an 'exemption'; other jurisdictions, such as Australia and New Zealand, prefer to label these exemptions 'input taxed supplies'.[96]

Depending on the stage in the production and distribution chain at which exemption occurs, an exemption can either add to, or reduce, revenue. If the exemption occurs at the initial stage in the production chain (such as in the provision of raw materials) or at the final retail stage, the VAT chain is not broken but there is a loss of revenue. Table 2.6 illustrates this in the case of an exemption at the retail stage.[97] In addition, Table 2.6 shows how the exemption of a business-to-consumer supply (B2C)) results in the consumer bearing a lower VAT burden than if the supply was fully taxed, as was the case in Table 2.4. In this example, when the retailer makes an exempt supply to an end consumer and is able to shift the VAT forward in the price, the final consumer pays the $20 of the embedded VAT in the

OECD, *Consumption Tax Trends 2012: VAT/GST and Excise Rates, Trends and Administration Issues* (OECD Publishing, Paris, 2012), 31.

93 For example, non-market one-off transactions are excluded by registration provisions: see § 4.2.3 of this chapter. Alan Schenk and Oliver Oldman, *Value Added Tax: A Comparative Approach* (rev. edn., Cambridge University Press, Cambridge; New York, 2007), 48.

94 Ibid., 3.

95 Paul van den Noord and Christopher Heady, 'Surveillance of Tax Policies: A Synthesis of Findings in Economic Surveys' (Economics Department Working Paper No. 303, OECD, 2001), 31; David Williams, 'Value-Added Tax', in V. Thuronyi (ed.), *Tax Law Design and Drafting* (IMF, Washington, DC, 1996), vol. 1, 164, 203; OECD, *Consumption Tax Trends 2012: VAT/GST and Excise Rates, Trends and Administration Issues* (OECD Publishing, Paris, 2012), 53; Alan A. Tait, *Value Added Tax* (McGraw-Hill, London, New York, 1972), 20.

96 This chapter will use the term 'exempt' supply. §16 of the *New Vatopia Model* refers to 'exempt supplies': Alan Schenk and Members of the IMF Legal Department, *Value Added Tax Act of the Commonwealth of New Vatopia* (IMF, 2006).

97 This is subject to the assumption that the supplier can pass on any embedded VAT: Michael Keen and Ben Lockwood, 'Is the VAT a Money Machine?' (2006), *National Tax Journal* 59(4), 905, 908; Graeme Cooper and Richard Vann, 'Implementing the Goods and Services Tax', *Sydney Law Review* 23 (1999), 337, 350.

TABLE 2.6 – *Exemption at the retail stage*[a]

Stage in the production/distribution chain	Manufacturer (Assuming no material inputs for the supply – No input credits for the manufacturer)	→ Supply 1 – $110: ($100 pre-VAT price) $10 – Output tax borne by wholesaler but payable by manufacturer ⇒	Wholesaler ⇐ Input tax credit for wholesaler ($10)	→ Supply 2 – $220: ($200 pre-VAT price) ⇒	Retailer No input tax credit for retailer because the retailer makes an exempt supply	→ Supply 3 - 'exempt supply' – $320: $220 purchase price (Assuming retailer passes forward embedded VAT in retail price) plus $100 in value added by the retailer	Consumer No output tax paid by consumer, but $20 of VAT payable by retailer embedded in price
VAT payable per transaction		$10		$20		$0	
Net tax payable			$0		$20 (passed on by retailer to consumer)		

[a] The example assumes that there are three businesses in the production and distribution chain, of which each adds $100 worth of value. The VAT applies at a rate of 10 per cent.

price paid for the good. This $20 represents the tax payable on the total of the $200 in value added by the manufacturer (of $100) and by the wholesaler (of $100). This is $10 less than the $30 burden the consumer would bear if the final supply to the consumer was a taxable rather than exempt supply (which would represent the tax payable on the total of the $300 in combined value added by the manufacturer ($100), wholesaler ($100) and retailer ($100)).[98]

If the exemption occurs at an intermediate stage in the production process, in a business-to-business (B2B) supply, the exemption either adds to revenue (if the VAT cost that cannot be credited is forward shifted in the price paid by the consumer) or becomes a cost to business (if the business is unable to shift the VAT component forward in the price). Where the VAT is a cost to business, there is an incentive to self-supply to avoid the tax.[99] Table 2.7 shows what occurs when exemption occurs at the wholesale stage and assumes the embedded VAT can be shifted forward in price.

The total revenue collected of $41 exceeds by $11 the 10 per cent, or $30, that would be collected on the base of the good VAT of $300 ($100 for the value added by each of the manufacturer, wholesaler and retailer), as was shown in Table 2.4. Of this $11, $1 is due to the tax on a tax (10 per cent of the $10 in VAT paid by the exempt wholesaler on their inputs) and the remaining $10 results from taxing the value of the inputs acquired by the exempt wholesaler twice (once at the wholesale stage and again at the retail stage).[100] The inability to recover the embedded VAT breaks the VAT chain because the $10 VAT paid by the wholesaler is not refunded. This breaking of the chain can also lead to cascading tax liability because if, as this example assumes, the wholesaler can shift the $10 unrecoverable VAT forward in the price, then double taxation might occur.[101] The example shows the revenue impact of this double taxation.

The conventional approach therefore strongly discourages the use of exemptions for the following reasons:[102]

[98] Graeme Cooper and Richard Vann, 'Implementing the Goods and Services Tax', *Sydney Law Review* 23 (1999), 337, 350; Michael Keen, Russell Krelove and John Norregaard, 'The Financial Activities Tax', in Stijn Claessens, Michael Keen and C. Pazarbasioglu (eds.), *Financial Sector Taxation: The IMF's Report to the G-20 and Background Material* (IMF, 2010), 118, 120.

[99] See the discussion of financial supplies at § 4.2.5.1 of this chapter.

[100] See generally Howell H. Zee, 'VAT Treatment of Financial Services: A Primer on Conceptual Issues and Country Practices', *INTERTAX* 34(10) (2006), 458, 462–63.

[101] Ibid.; Alan Schenk and Oliver Oldman, *Value Added Tax: A Comparative Approach* (rev. edn., Cambridge University Press, Cambridge; New York, 2007), 53; Carl S. Shoup, *Public Finance* (Aldine Publishing Company, Chicago, 1969), 259–60; Michael Keen and Ben Lockwood, 'Is the VAT a Money Machine?' (2006), *National Tax Journal* 59(4), 905, 908; Liam Ebrill et al., *The Modern VAT* (IMF, Washington, DC, 2001), 85–86.

[102] David Williams, 'Value-Added Tax', in V. Thuronyi (ed.), *Tax Law Design and Drafting* (IMF, Washington, DC, 1996), vol. 1, 164, 203; Alan A. Tait, *Value Added Tax: International Practice and Problems* (IMF, Washington, DC, 1988), 50; Crawford, Keen and Smith state that '[a]ny exemption is anathema to the logic of the VAT, since it inherently breaks the chain of

TABLE 2.7 – *Exemption at an intermediate (wholesale) stage*[a]

Stage in the production/ distribution chain	**Manufacturer** (Assuming no material inputs for the supply – No input credits for the manufacturer)	Supply 1 – $110: $100 (pre-VAT price) $10 – Output tax borne by wholesaler but payable by manufacturer	**Wholesaler** No input tax credit for wholesaler because the wholesaler makes an exempt supply	Supply 2 – 'the exempt supply' – $210: Price consists of $10 of VAT (assuming the $10 VAT for which no credit is available can be shifted forward in the price) plus $100 each in value added by manufacturer and wholesaler	**Retailer** No input tax credit for retailer because no VAT charged on exempt supply	Supply 3 – $341: ($310 pre-VAT price plus VAT) $31 output tax borne by consumer but payable by retailer $31	**Consumer** No input tax credit (because end consumer)
VAT payable per transaction		$10		$0		$31	
Net tax payable			$10		$0		$31

[a] The example assumes that there are three businesses in the production and distribution chain, of which each adds $100 worth of value. The VAT applies at a rate of 10 per cent.

- Exemptions increase administrative and compliance costs in requiring exempt goods and services to be defined or in allocating inputs when a business produces both exempt and taxable supplies;
- Exemptions result in either a loss of revenue (when products are exempted at the retail stage) or an increase in revenue through the non-neutral effect of the tax falling on business inputs or through double taxation;
- The associated economic distortions that arise when businesses attempt to rearrange their affairs to avoid the VAT being a cost to business, for example by self-supplying rather than incurring unrecoverable VAT on acquisitions;
- The potential for exemption to undermine the destination principle (see norm 3, §6). This might occur if an exporter uses exempt goods or services in the production of goods or services for export and cannot recover the VAT paid on these exempt inputs. As a result, the price of the exported good or service will carry the unrecoverable VAT, which might compromise an exporter's competitiveness if a comparable producer in the importing jurisdiction does receive credit on the same input.[103]

credit and refund, leading to an element of production taxation': Ian Crawford, Michael Keen and Stephen Smith, 'Value Added Tax and Excises', in Stuart Adam et al. (eds.) for the Institute for Fiscal Studies, *Dimensions of Tax Design: The Mirrlees Review* (Oxford University Press, Oxford, 2010), 275, 305; Ebrill et al. claim that '[e]xemptions are abhorrent to both the logic and functioning of the VAT': Liam Ebrill et al., *The Modern VAT* (IMF, Washington, DC, 2001), 100; OECD, *Consumption Tax Trends 2012: VAT/GST and Excise Rates, Trends and Administration Issues* (OECD Publishing, Paris, 2012), 75; LeJeune et al. note that '[b]est practices suggest that...[the use of exemptions] should be restricted wherever possible': Ine Lejeune, Jeanine Daou-Azzi and Mark Powell (of PricewaterhouseCoopers), 'The Balance Has Shifted to Consumption Taxes – Lessons Learned and Best Practices for VAT', in M. Lang, P. Melz and E. Kristoffersson (eds.), *Value Added Tax and Direct Taxation: Similarities and Differences* (IBFD, Amsterdam, 2009), 59, 78; Alan Schenk and Oliver Oldman, *Value Added Tax: A Comparative Approach* (rev. edn., Cambridge University Press, Cambridge; New York, 2007), 52; International Tax Dialogue (ITD), 'The Value Added Tax: Experience and Issues' (Background Paper Prepared for the International Tax Dialogue Conference on the VAT, Rome, March 15–16, 2005, ITD), 16; Ben Terra and Julie Kajus, IBFD, *A Guide to the European VAT Directives* [online] (15 April 2011), 7.6.3.4.

[103] Alan Schenk and Oliver Oldman, *Value Added Tax: A Comparative Approach* (rev. edn., Cambridge University Press, Cambridge; New York, 2007), 52; International Tax Dialogue (ITD), 'The Value Added Tax: Experience and Issues' (Background Paper Prepared for the International Tax Dialogue Conference on the VAT, Rome, March 15–16, 2005, ITD), 16; Ben Terra and Julie Kajus, IBFD, *A Guide to the European VAT Directives* [online] (15 April 2011), 7.6.3.4; Richard Bird and Pierre-Pascal Gendron, *The VAT in Developing and Transitional Countries* (Cambridge University Press, New York, 2007), 121; OECD, *Consumption Tax Trends 2012: VAT/GST and Excise Rates, Trends and Administration Issues* (OECD Publishing, Paris, 2012), 74; Liam Ebrill et al., *The Modern VAT* (IMF, Washington, DC, 2001), 88.

Exemptions are also discouraged for triggering 'exemption creep', whereby traders who supply to exempt entities lobby for the further exemption of their supplies in order to avoid the purchaser of their product or service seeking to avoid the unrecoverable VAT liability by self-supplying.[104] Table 2.8 demonstrates the incentive to lobby for exemptions. It shows that the effect of extending exemptions upstream makes the VAT neutral on the businesses involved but makes the VAT work like an RST (see Table 2.5) by effectively suspending the collection of tax until the final retail stage.

For all the reasons outlined in this section, the conventional approach recommends exemptions only when absolutely necessary, such as when it is not possible to effectively levy the VAT on particular transactions (see §4.2.5).

4.2.2 Methods to exclude – Zero-rating of goods and services

Zero-rating of a good or service means that no VAT is charged on the supply of the good or service but, unlike under an exemption, registered entities *can* recover VAT paid on the inputs to that supply. Some jurisdictions, such as those within the EU, label this zero-rating; others, such as Australia and New Zealand, refer to this as a 'GST-free supply'.[105] Table 2.9 shows how the application of zero-rating at the final retail stage results in an effective tax burden on final consumption of zero.

Conventional advice recommends the zero-rating of exports (in accordance with the destination principle)[106] but discourages zero-rating on domestic supplies.[107]

[104] Liam Ebrill et al., *The Modern VAT* (IMF, Washington, DC, 2001), 89. See the discussion of financial supplies in this chapter at § 4.2.5.1.

[105] This chapter will use the term 'zero-rating'.

[106] International Tax Dialogue (ITD), 'The Value Added Tax: Experience and Issues' (Background Paper Prepared for the International Tax Dialogue Conference on the VAT, Rome, March 15–16, 2005, ITD), 14; Liam Ebrill et al., *The Modern VAT* (IMF, Washington, DC, 2001), 3; Alan Schenk and Oliver Oldman, *Value Added Tax: A Comparative Approach* (rev. edn., Cambridge University Press, Cambridge; New York, 2007), 50–51. See the discussion of norm 3 in § 6 of this chapter.

[107] Williams notes that a 'few states have distorted the VAT framework by allowing the zero rating of internal supplies': David Williams, 'Value-Added Tax', in V. Thuronyi (ed.), *Tax Law Design and Drafting* (IMF, Washington, DC, 1996), vol. 1, 164, 203; Alan Schenk and Oliver Oldman, *Value Added Tax: A Comparative Approach* (rev. edn., Cambridge University Press, Cambridge; New York, 2007), 50–51; International Tax Dialogue (ITD), 'The Value Added Tax: Experience and Issues' (Background Paper Prepared for the International Tax Dialogue Conference on the VAT, Rome, March 15–16, 2005, ITD), 14; Alan A. Tait, *Value Added Tax: International Practice and Problems* (IMF, Washington, DC, 1988), 51; Malcolm Gillis, Carl S. Shoup and Gerardo P. Sicat, 'Lessons for Developing Countries', in M. Gillis, C. S. Shoup and G. P. Sicat (eds.), *Value Added Taxation in Developing Countries (A World Bank Symposium)* (World Bank, Washington, DC, 1990), 219, 222; The IMF contends that reduced and zero-rate VATs 'are an expensive and poorly targeted means of addressing distributional concerns': IMF, *Fiscal Monitor (November 2010) – Fiscal Exit: From Strategy to Implementation* (IMF Publication Services, Washington, DC, 2010), 81; Bird and Gendron declare that '[z]ero zero-rating should be the goal': Richard Bird and Pierre-Pascal Gendron, *The VAT in Developing and Transitional Countries* (Cambridge University Press, New York, 2007), 133.

TABLE 2.8 – *The incentive and effect of exemption creep – Exemption extended to manufacturing stage*[a]

Stage in the production/ distribution chain	Manufacturer (Assuming no material inputs for the supply – No input credits for the manufacturer)	→ Supply 1 (exempt supply) – \$100: No output tax charged because manufacturer lobbied for an exemption	Wholesaler No input tax credit for wholesaler because the wholesaler makes an exempt supply	→ Supply 2 (exempt supply) – \$200:	Retailer No input tax credit for retailer because no VAT charged on exempt supply	→ Supply 3 – \$330: \$300 pre-VAT price plus \$30 VAT borne by the consumer but payable by the retailer ⇨	Consumer No input tax credit (because end consumer)
VAT payable per transaction		\$0		\$0		\$30	
Net tax payable			\$0		\$0		\$30

[a] The example assumes that there are three businesses in the production and distribution chain, of which each adds \$100 worth of value. The VAT applies at a rate of 10 per cent.

TABLE 2.9 – *A zero-rated supply at the retail stage*[a]

Stage in the production/ distribution chain	**Manufacturer** (Assuming no material inputs for the supply – No input credits for the manufacturer)	→ Supply 1 – \$110: \$100 (pre-VAT price) \$10 – Output tax borne by wholesaler but payable by manufacturer ⇨	**Wholesaler** Input tax credit for wholesaler (\$10) ⇦	→ Supply 2 – \$220: \$200 (pre-VAT price) \$20 output tax borne by retailer but payable by wholesaler ⇨	**Retailer** Input tax credit for retailer (\$20) ⇦	→ Supply 3 – Zero-rated supply: \$300 VAT-free price	**Consumer** No VAT paid because a zero-rated supply
VAT payable per transaction		\$10		\$20		\$0	
Net tax payable			\$0		\$0		\$0

[a] The example assumes that there are three businesses in the production and distribution chain, each of which adds \$100 worth of value. The VAT applies at a rate of 10 per cent. See also Graeme Cooper and Richard Vann, 'Implementing the Goods and Services Tax', *Sydney Law Review* 23 (1999), 337, 348; Howell Zee, 'Value-Added Tax', in P. Shome (ed.), *Tax Policy Handbook* (Fiscal Affairs Department, IMF, Washington, DC, 1995), 86, 92–96.

The rationale for opposing the use of zero-rating outside exports is that efficiency should trump equity in VAT design; see §4.2.4. The conventional consensus is that while zero-rating does not result in the breaking of the VAT chain like an exemption does, the cost to revenue can be significant. Zero-rating also gives rise to potentially sizeable claims for VAT refunds or potentially negative VAT liability, and therefore incentivises avoidance and evasion activity or lobbying to extend similar treatment to other goods and services.[108]

4.2.3 Methods to exclude – Removal or exemption of certain entities from VAT registration

The good VAT should ideally apply to all entities engaged in the regular supply of goods and services. This is achieved through requiring entities to register in order to collect VAT on their supplies and by making access to input credits dependent on registration. Entities eligible for registration should, in theory, include all business, non-profit organisations and government bodies engaged in making regular supplies.[109] However, the good VAT does not extend this far. Certain entities can be excluded based on their size or function. This feature of the good VAT is informed more by administrative concerns than by theoretical purity, because exemption means that some entities bear input tax, which can lead to distortions and inefficiencies similar to those outlined in §4.2.1.

4.2.3.1 EXEMPTING BY SIZE – VAT THRESHOLD The setting of registration thresholds enables small entities to be excluded from the VAT system.[110] The exemption of these entities is in recognition of the fact that the VAT can be administered effectively only if the tax is limited to a band of larger entities capable of complying with the VAT. Any negative consequences that arise from keeping these entities out of the VAT system are therefore a consequence of these administrative concerns.

[108] Richard Bird and Pierre-Pascal Gendron, *The VAT in Developing and Transitional Countries* (Cambridge University Press, New York, 2007), 133.

[109] §20(1) of the *New Vatopia Model* makes registration dependent on a business undertaking 'taxable activity' defined positively in §5(1) as an activity that is carried on regularly or continuously (mostly or partly in Vatopia), 'whether or not for profit, that involves or is intended to involve, in whole or in part, the supply of taxable goods or services to any other person for consideration'. Taxable activity does not include private or recreational supplies carried on by a natural person or exempt supplies (the negative limb – §5(2)): Alan Schenk and Members of the IMF Legal Department, *Value Added Tax Act of the Commonwealth of New Vatopia* (IMF, 2006).

[110] Malcolm Gillis, Carl S. Shoup and Gerardo P. Sicat, 'Lessons for Developing Countries', in M. Gillis, C. S. Shoup and G. P. Sicat (eds.), *Value Added Taxation in Developing Countries (A World Bank Symposium)* (World Bank, Washington, DC, 1990), 219, 224; Alan A. Tait, *Value Added Tax: International Practice and Problems* (IMF, Washington, DC, 1988), 132. §20 of the *New Vatopia Model* leaves the setting of thresholds to be included in a schedule – Schedule V: Alan Schenk and Members of the IMF Legal Department, *Value Added Tax Act of the Commonwealth of New Vatopia* (IMF, 2006).

Exemption via this means generally takes two forms: first, through the setting of registration thresholds that relieve suppliers from requirements to register and collect VAT; second, through the setting of collection thresholds that require entities to register for VAT (even when below the registration threshold) but exempt the entities from collecting VAT until a minimum threshold is exceeded.[111] Thresholds are usually based on turnover for a specified period. Entities exempted under the first method do not report taxable sales and do not claim credit for tax paid on inputs, and their customers are also denied credit for tax paid on their products.[112] This latter feature means that even entities below compulsory thresholds may elect to register so that their purchasers are able to claim input credits.

The setting of thresholds involves striking a balance between revenue foregone and administration and compliance costs.[113] In attempting to strike the right balance,[114] the conventional approach recommends setting relatively high registration thresholds for developing and transitional economies, where the size of the informal sector may be large and the administrative capacity of the state and compliance capacity of the taxpayer is weak.[115] By contrast, when administration and compliance are strong, the conventional approach prefers developed countries to set lower thresholds to broaden the VAT base (especially once the VAT is established).[116]

4.2.3.2 EXEMPTION BY FUNCTION It is also possible to exempt certain entities based on their function (as distinct from the specific goods or services they supply).[117] This might apply to financial institutions,[118] farms, non-profit

[111] OECD, *Consumption Tax Trends 2012: VAT/GST and Excise Rates, Trends and Administration Issues* (OECD Publishing, Paris, 2012), 76.

[112] Alan Schenk and Oliver Oldman, *Value Added Tax: A Comparative Approach* (rev. edn., Cambridge University Press, Cambridge; New York, 2007), 49.

[113] OECD, *Consumption Tax Trends 2012: VAT/GST and Excise Rates, Trends and Administration Issues* (OECD Publishing, Paris, 2012), 77; Richard Bird and Pierre-Pascal Gendron, *The VAT in Developing and Transitional Countries* (Cambridge University Press, New York, 2007), 115.

[114] Liam Ebrill et al., *The Modern VAT* (IMF, Washington, DC, 2001), 65. For an attempt to capture the trade-off between revenue and collection costs, see Michael Keen and J. Mintz, 'The Optimal Threshold for a Value-Added Tax' (2004), *Journal of Public Economics* 88, 559.

[115] Bird and Gendron identify the setting of compulsory registration thresholds as 'one of the most critical VAT design decisions' for developing and transitional countries: Richard Bird and Pierre-Pascal Gendron, *The VAT in Developing and Transitional Countries* (Cambridge University Press, New York, 2007), 3; Liam Ebrill et al., *The Modern VAT* (IMF, Washington, DC, 2001), 66; Sijbren Cnossen, 'A VAT Primer for Lawyers, Economists, and Accountants' (2009), *Tax Notes International* 55(4), 319, 331.

[116] OECD, *Consumption Tax Trends 2012: VAT/GST and Excise Rates, Trends and Administration Issues* (OECD Publishing, Paris, 2012), 77.

[117] Liam Ebrill et al., *The Modern VAT* (IMF, Washington, DC, 2001), 83; Alan Schenk and Oliver Oldman, *Value Added Tax: A Comparative Approach* (rev. edn., Cambridge University Press, Cambridge; New York, 2007), 48–50.

[118] See § 4.2.5.1 of this chapter.

organisations and government entities.[119] Exempt entities would not be required to register and file returns but equally would receive no tax credits for any VAT paid. There is much debate and little consensus on the merits of excluding whole entities or sectors, and on the relative merits of which types of entity or sectors to exempt. However, the preference within the conventional approach is generally to tax these entities when feasible to do so. This is therefore one of a number of those frontier issues mentioned in Chapter 1, which tests the limits of the good VAT.[120] This book does not explore the issues surrounding the exemption of entire entities or sectors, but the discussion of financial supplies at §4.2.5.1 further illustrates the impact of exemptions generally and the nature of the difficulties that arise when the limits of the good VAT are reached.

4.2.4 Avoid or minimise equity-based exclusions

Although the conventional approach acknowledges that there might exist compelling motives to exclude domestic supplies from the VAT base, exclusions are strongly discouraged unless absolutely necessary. Calculations of necessity generally fall within one of two broad categories: first, the exclusion of basic goods and essential services on equity grounds; and second, the exclusion of 'hard-to-tax' goods and services on pragmatic grounds (see §4.2.5).[121]

As §2.2.6 explained, the broad base of the good VAT and the indirect manner in which it is levied (on transactions rather than individuals) means that the good

[119] See generally Howell Zee, 'Value-Added Tax', in P. Shome (ed.), *Tax Policy Handbook* (Fiscal Affairs Department, IMF, Washington, DC, 1995), 86, 98; John F. Due, 'VAT Treatment of Farmers and Small Firms', in M. Gillis, C. S. Shoup and G. P. Sicat (eds.), *Value Added Taxation in Developing Countries* (World Bank, Washington, DC, 1990), 58; Liam Ebrill et al., *The Modern VAT* (IMF, Washington, DC, 2001), ch. 9; Alan A. Tait, *Value Added Tax: International Practice and Problems* (IMF, Washington, DC, 1988), ch. 7.

[120] Richard Bird and Pierre-Pascal Gendron, *The VAT in Developing and Transitional Countries* (Cambridge University Press, New York, 2007), 2. See generally Sijbren Cnossen, 'Global Trends and Issues in Value Added Taxation', *International Tax and Public Finance* 5(3) (1998), 399, 402–3; Alan Schenk and Oliver Oldman, *Value Added Tax: A Comparative Approach* (rev. edn., Cambridge University Press, Cambridge; New York, 2007), 49–50; Ian Crawford, Michael Keen and Stephen Smith, 'Value Added Tax and Excises', in Stuart Adam et al. (eds.) for the Institute for Fiscal Studies, *Dimensions of Tax Design: The Mirrlees Review* (Oxford University Press, Oxford, 2010), 275, 306; Liam Ebrill et al., *The Modern VAT* (IMF, Washington, DC, 2001), 65, 91–93; US Department of the Treasury, *Tax Reform for Fairness, Simplicity, and Economic Growth* (Office of the Secretary, Department of the Treasury, Washington, DC, 1984), vol. 3, ch. 5, 40.

[121] Krever and de la Feria contend that some broad categories of exclusion, such as those based on equity grounds, have been offered as *ex post facto* rationales when in fact the initial exclusions were based on the design of existing turnover taxes and the political need to appease groups who benefited from these pre-existing concessions: Richard Krever and Rita de la Feria, 'Ending VAT Exemptions: Towards a Post-Modern VAT', in R. de la Feria (ed.), *VAT Exemptions: Consequences and Design Alternatives* (Volume 37, EUCOTAX Series on European Taxation, Kluwer Law International, Alphen aan den Rijn, 2013), 3, 22. For a fuller discussion of this phenomenon of path dependence, see Chapter 5, §3.1.

VAT rates poorly on the measure of vertical equity. One method of compensating for this is through excluding the supply of essential goods and services from the VAT base. This might include items such as basic food; health and medical supplies; educational supplies; essential services such as electricity, gas and water; public services such as public transport, public broadcasting and postal services; and charitable, cultural, sporting and recreational activities.[122]

The conventional approach generally discourages the exclusion of basic goods and services on equity grounds because efficiency trumps equity in good VAT design.[123] However, because the conventional approach would prefer that a country muddy a good VAT with some exclusions rather than introduce no VAT at all, some acknowledge the need to exclude certain essential supplies. However, they stress that the list of exclusions should be as short as possible.[124] The *New Vatopia Model*, for example, incorporates this political reality into its design by providing for the option of a general regulation-making power to provide for exemptions to the VAT base, which avoids the need for parliament to amend the Act.[125]

The equity gains achieved by excluding goods or services are said to be outweighed by revenue loss, administrative complexity and efficiency losses. Deadweight loss is said to occur through firms diverting resources to reclassify goods in order to receive preferential status and the consequent diversion of firm and taxpayer resources in disputing these classifications.[126] Equity is also said to be poorly served through excluding these goods and services.[127] For example, the exclusion of items such as basic food is said to provide greater absolute value to rich taxpayers (as this group spends a higher absolute amount on these items) even though the poor spend a greater relative proportion of their income on these items.

[122] Tait refers to these as 'merit goods': Alan A. Tait, *Value Added Tax: International Practice and Problems* (IMF, Washington, DC, 1988), ch. 4; OECD, *Consumption Tax Trends 2012: VAT/GST and Excise Rates, Trends and Administration Issues* (OECD Publishing, Paris, 2012), 71.

[123] Liam Ebrill et al., *The Modern VAT* (IMF, Washington, DC, 2001), 65, 108; International Tax Dialogue (ITD), 'The Value Added Tax: Experience and Issues' (Background Paper Prepared for the International Tax Dialogue Conference on the VAT, Rome, March 15–16, 2005, ITD), 15; Alan A. Tait, *Value Added Tax: International Practice and Problems* (IMF, Washington, DC, 1988), 58–69; David Williams, 'Value-Added Tax', in V. Thuronyi (ed.), *Tax Law Design and Drafting* (IMF, Washington, DC, 1996), vol. 1, 164, 203; Ian Crawford, Michael Keen and Stephen Smith, 'Value Added Tax and Excises', in Stuart Adam et al. (eds.) for the Institute for Fiscal Studies, *Dimensions of Tax Design: The Mirrlees Review* (Oxford University Press, Oxford, 2010), 275, 277; Sijbren Cnossen, 'A VAT Primer for Lawyers, Economists, and Accountants' (2009), *Tax Notes International* 55(4), 319, 331.

[124] Ibid. (all citations above).

[125] Schedule II, n 21 of the *New Vatopia Model*: Alan Schenk and Members of the IMF Legal Department, *Value Added Tax Act of the Commonwealth of New Vatopia* (IMF, 2006), 58.

[126] Richard Krever, 'Designing and Drafting VAT Laws for Africa', in R. Krever (ed.), *VAT in Africa* (Pretoria University Law Press, Pretoria, 2008), 9, 17.

[127] Some point out that concessional treatment may exacerbate rather than ameliorate regressivity. For example, Krever argues that the increased compliance costs of distinguishing preferentially from non-preferentially treated goods and services falls disproportionately on small businesses, which are more likely to pass these costs on to the poor: ibid., 19.

The preference is therefore for equity issues to be addressed via other taxes, such as the income tax, or through spending.[128] Given the greater ability of developed economies to deal with distributional issues through other policy instruments (such as through spending and/or adjusting income tax settings), the conventional approach contends that equity objectives are better pursued through these alternative means rather than through the blunt tools of exclusions to the base and rate variation.[129]

4.2.5 Introduce exclusions into the good VAT base only when it is necessary to do so

Despite the resistance to excluding or altering the VAT base, there has traditionally been a degree of resignation by the conventional approach to the fact that certain supplies remain too hard to tax under the good VAT. These most frequently include supplies made of real property,[130] financial services and agriculture.[131] Whereas the non-taxation of agricultural supplies is more the product of the political difficulty in effectively taxing this sector, the non-taxation of real property and financial supplies derives primarily, or at least partly, from the technical difficulty of taxing these supplies. The preference within the conventional approach to tax these supplies is demonstrated by the voluminous literature that

[128] International Tax Dialogue (ITD), 'The Value Added Tax: Experience and Issues' (Background Paper Prepared for the International Tax Dialogue Conference on the VAT, Rome, March 15–16, 2005, ITD), 14; Richard Krever, 'Designing and Drafting VAT Laws for Africa', in R. Krever (ed.), *VAT in Africa* (Pretoria University Law Press, Pretoria, 2008), 9, 19; Liam Ebrill et al., *The Modern VAT* (IMF, Washington, DC, 2001), 112.

[129] Ian Crawford, Michael Keen and Stephen Smith, 'Value Added Tax and Excises', in Stuart Adam et al. (eds.) for the Institute for Fiscal Studies, *Dimensions of Tax Design: The Mirrlees Review* (Oxford University Press, Oxford, 2010), 275, 284; Michael Keen, 'The Anatomy of VAT' (Working Paper No. WP/13/111, International Monetary Fund, 2013), 11.

[130] For a discussion of the issues relating to the application of VAT to real property see, e.g., Robert Conrad and Anca Grozav, 'Real Property and VAT', in R. Krever (ed.), *VAT in Africa* (Pretoria University Law Press, Pretoria, 2008), 81; Sijbren Cnossen, 'VAT Treatment of Immovable Property', in V. Thuronyi (ed.), *Tax Law Design and Drafting: Volume 1* (IMF, Washington, DC, 1996), 231; Alan Schenk and Oliver Oldman, *Value Added Tax: A Comparative Approach* (rev. edn., Cambridge University Press, Cambridge; New York, 2007), ch. 13; Liam Ebrill et al., *The Modern VAT* (IMF, Washington, DC, 2001), 98–99.

[131] Cnossen states that '[w]hile VATs should have the broadest possible coverage and bases, some sectors are nonetheless difficult to include on administrative grounds. Thus, it does not seem feasible to tax residential housing services, financial services, and agricultural activities': Sijbren Cnossen, 'Global Trends and Issues in Value Added Taxation', *International Tax and Public Finance* 5(3) (1998), 399, 405, and at 405–9; the OECD identifies the exclusion of real property as based on 'historical reasons' and the exclusion of financial services as based on 'practical reasons': OECD, *Consumption Tax Trends 2012: VAT/GST and Excise Rates, Trends and Administration Issues* (OECD Publishing, Paris, 2012), 74; Tait classifies these exclusions as 'difficult to tax' goods and services: Alan A. Tait, *Value Added Tax: International Practice and Problems* (IMF, Washington, DC, 1988), 80; Erik Jørgensen and Jeffrey Owens, 'The Move to VAT', *OECD Observer* (August/September 1995), 21, 22–23.

seeks to find effective ways to do so.[132] Nevertheless, absent an effective means to do so, the traditional approach was to suggest exemption of these hard-to-tax supplies. This book focuses specifically on one hard-to-tax area, the taxation of financial supplies, to explore what occurs in response to these frontier issues that test the limits of the good VAT.

4.2.5.1 FINANCIAL SERVICES Most within the conventional approach agree that, in principle, supplies of financial services, such as banking and insurance, should be taxable under the good VAT just like any other service.[133] However, these supplies have historically been exempted from the VAT base because of the difficulty in isolating and attributing the value of these services on a transactional basis, as is required under the good VAT.[134] To illustrate the issues, the analysis will

[132] IMF, *Fiscal Monitor (November 2010) – Fiscal Exit: From Strategy to Implementation* (IMF Publication Services, Washington, DC, 2010), 82. See the sources referenced in § 4.2.5.1 of this chapter.

[133] Alan A. Tait, *Value Added Tax: International Practice and Problems* (IMF, Washington, DC, 1988), 92. Depending on different understandings of what constitutes final consumption, some dispute the proposition that financial services should form part of the VAT base. Instead, they contend that financial supplies, such as a consumer loan, facilitate the consumption of other goods (such as a car) or services, but are not themselves the product of end consumption and, as a result, should not be included in the VAT base: Harry Grubert and James Mackie, 'Must Financial Services Be Taxed Under a Consumption Tax?', *National Tax Journal* 53(1) (2000), 23, 39; *Cf* William Jack, 'The Treatment of Financial Services under a Broad-Based Consumption Tax' (2000), *National Tax Journal* 53(4), 841, 842. The argument has not attracted broad support within the conventional approach. Boadway and Keen describe it as a 'fallacy' because the VAT applies to many goods and services that are not the end product of consumption but rather facilitate consumption, such as pet food (fed to a dog) and cutlery: Robin Boadway and Michael Keen, 'Theoretical Perspectives on the Taxation of Capital Income and Financial Services', in P. Honohan (ed.), *Taxation of Financial Intermediation: Theory and Practice for Emerging Economies* (World Bank; Oxford University Press, Washington, DC, 2003), 31, 60–61; Howell H. Zee, 'VAT Treatment of Financial Services: A Primer on Conceptual Issues and Country Practices', *INTERTAX* 34(10) (2006), 458, 459–60; Howell H. Zee, 'Further Thoughts on Reforming the VAT: Treatment of Financial Intermediation Services', in R. de la Feria (ed.), *VAT Exemptions: Consequences and Design Alternatives* (vol. 37, EUCOTAX Series on European Taxation, Kluwer Law International, Alphen aan den Rijn, 2013), 345, 348–51; Alan J. Auerbach and Roger H. Gordon, 'Taxation of Financial Services under a VAT' (2002), *American Economic Review* 92(2), 411. The theoretical issues are complex and beyond the scope of this book. For a comprehensive overview, see, e.g., Harry Grubert and Richard Krever, 'VAT and Financial Services: Competing Perspectives on What Should Be Taxed?' (2012), *Tax Law Review* 65(2), 199; Ben Lockwood, 'How Should Financial Intermediation Services Be Taxed?' (Centre for Economic Policy Research (CEPR) Discussion Paper 8122, University of Warwick – Department of Economics, CEPR, revised 30 September 2013).

[134] Liam Ebrill et al., *The Modern VAT* (IMF, Washington, DC, 2001) 94; Tim Edgar, 'Exempt Treatment of Financial Intermediation Services Under a Value-Added Tax: An Assessment of Alternatives' (2001), *Canadian Tax Journal* 49(5), 1137, 1144–45; Richard Bird and Pierre-Pascal Gendron, *The VAT in Developing and Transitional Countries* (Cambridge University Press, New York, 2007), 98; David Williams, 'Value-Added Tax', in V. Thuronyi (ed.), *Tax Law Design and Drafting* (IMF, Washington, DC, 1996), vol. 1, 164, 205; International Tax Dialogue (ITD), 'The Value Added Tax: Experience and Issues' (Background Paper Prepared

focus on one canonical example – that of the deposit-taking and lending services provided by a financial institution such as a bank.[135]

If a bank charges an explicit fee to provide a service, such as a fee to set up a deposit account, then, in theory, there is no problem in identifying the value of the service (the fee charged) and therefore no problem in applying the good VAT to that supply.[136] However, many financial services are intermediary in nature, meaning that banks connect (or mediate) the funds deposited by investors with the funds required by borrowers. The cost of these services is not generally charged for by an explicit fee, but rather in a margin spread across a range of the bank's activities.[137] The problems relating to the taxation of financial supplies under the good VAT arise because of both its transactional nature and its consumption base, which seeks to tax only the value of the financial intermediation service but not the value of other amounts that constitute the margin, such as returns from savings.[138] Depositors/

for the International Tax Dialogue Conference on the VAT, Rome, March 15–16, 2005, ITD), 15; Commonwealth of Australia Treasury, Australia's Future Tax System Review Panel, *Australia's Future Tax System: Report to the Treasurer* (Australia's Future Tax System Review Panel: The Treasury, Canberra, 2009), 306–7.

135 Similar but discrete issues apply to other financial supplies, such as pooling intermediary services such as insurance (the difference between premiums received and claims paid – 'the pure insurance coverage') and gambling/lotteries (broadly the difference between wagers and prizes paid), as well as brokerage services (when fees are charged implicitly as the spread between bid and ask prices): see generally Tim Edgar, 'Exempt Treatment of Financial Intermediation Services Under a Value-Added Tax: An Assessment of Alternatives' (2001), *Canadian Tax Journal* 49(5), 1137, 1148, 1158; Howell H. Zee, 'VAT Treatment of Financial Services: A Primer on Conceptual Issues and Country Practices', *INTERTAX* 34(10) (2006), 458, 460; Harry Grubert and Richard Krever, 'VAT and Financial Services: Competing Perspectives on What Should Be Taxed?' *Tax Law Review* 65(2) (2012), 199, 212–27. Additional issues arise in relation to a third category of financial supply being the supply of intangible ownership rights such as shares, interests in unit trusts and mutual funds, and interests in pension and superannuation funds. While such supplies should not form part of a consumption base, their treatment as exempt supplies means embedded tax is levied on such supplies. However, resolving this issue through an invoice-credit method transactional VAT (either through requiring all investors to register to receive input credits or through zero-rating such supplies) is administratively unworkable, see generally Richard Krever and Rita de la Feria, 'Ending VAT Exemptions: Towards a Post-Modern VAT', in R. de la Feria (ed.), *VAT Exemptions: Consequences and Design Alternatives* (vol. 37, EUCOTAX Series on European Taxation, Kluwer Law International, Alphen aan den Rijn, 2013), 3, 29.

136 Howell H. Zee, 'VAT Treatment of Financial Services: A Primer on Conceptual Issues and Country Practices', *INTERTAX* 34(10) (2006), 458, 463; Robin Boadway and Michael Keen, 'Theoretical Perspectives on the Taxation of Capital Income and Financial Services', in P. Honohan (ed.), *Taxation of Financial Intermediation: Theory and Practice for Emerging Economies* (World Bank; Oxford University Press, Washington, DC, 2003), 31, 33.

137 Commonwealth of Australia Treasury, Australia's Future Tax System Review Panel, *Australia's Future Tax System: Report to the Treasurer* (Australia's Future Tax System Review Panel: The Treasury, Canberra, 2009), 306–7.

138 Ine Lejeune, Jeanine Daou-Azzi and Mark Powell (of PricewaterhouseCoopers), 'The Balance Has Shifted to Consumption Taxes – Lessons Learned and Best Practices for VAT', in M. Lang, P. Melz and E. Kristoffersson (eds.), *Value Added Tax and Direct Taxation: Similarities and Differences* (IBFD, Amsterdam, 2009), 59, 90. For deeper objections to the

lenders, for example, should not bear tax on their investments under a consumption tax, nor arguably should borrowers be taxed for merely taking out a loan, as this is simply shifting funds forward in time. However, the conventional approach supports the good VAT taxing the *charge for facilitating* these financial transactions.

The margin might be able to be calculated on an aggregate basis as the difference between the interest received by borrowers and the interest paid to depositors/lenders over an accounting period (the interest rate margin).[139] However, the difficulty lies in identifying the value of the bank's intermediation services on a transactional basis.[140] For example, if a consumer borrows $100,000 at a rate of 5 per cent, the retail interest rate does not necessarily represent the cost of the service provided to the consumer by the bank but is influenced by a variety of factors that spread risk across a range of transactions and are influenced by short-term and long-term investment positions.[141] In simple terms, there is no clear supply chain linking a specific depositor to a specific borrower and no reliable way for identifying the value added by the bank. Further difficulties arise in allocating the value of the service between, for example, personal consumers (who should bear VAT) and business consumers (who should not).[142]

application of VAT to financial services stemming from different theoretical views of consumption, see generally Harry Grubert and Richard Krever, 'VAT and Financial Services: Competing Perspectives on What Should Be Taxed?' (2012), *Tax Law Review* 65(2), 199.

[139] Edgar explains that this can be calculated on a cash-flow basis where [revenue from sales of goods and services + dividends received, interest income, and capital gains] is subtracted from [current non-wage expenses = capital expenditures + purchases of financial assets + dividends paid, interest expenses, and capital losses]: Tim Edgar, 'Exempt Treatment of Financial Intermediation Services Under a Value-Added Tax: An Assessment of Alternatives' (2001), *Canadian Tax Journal* 49(5), 1133, 1148.

[140] It is highly artificial, for example, to match a specific depositor with a specific lender to complete the supply chain: Arthur Kerrigan, 'The Elusiveness of Neutrality – Why Is It So Difficult to Apply VAT to Financial Services?' (2010[March/April]) *International VAT Monitor*, 103, 104; *Contra* the US Treasury in its *Treasury* I report did not think this issue fatal, as the relevant supply chains could be broken up from the depositor to the bank, and then from the bank to the borrower. If the depositors/suppliers were registered businesses, the banks could be charged VAT on the interest paid to depositors (and receive credit for the tax paid in relation to these suppliers/depositors) and in turn charge VAT on their 'sales'; that is, on the interest received on their loans: US Department of the Treasury, *Tax Reform for Fairness, Simplicity, and Economic Growth* (Office of the Secretary, Department of the Treasury, Washington, DC, 1984), vol. 3, ch. 6, 49. As Chapter 7, §3.2, explains, the Treasury identified problems with this model for other reasons.

[141] Arthur Kerrigan, 'The Elusiveness of Neutrality – Why Is It So Difficult to Apply VAT to Financial Services?' (2010[March/April) *International VAT Monitor*, 103–104. See also Alan Schenk, 'Taxation of Financial Services Under a US Value-Added Tax' (2010), *Tax Law Review* 63(2), 409, 412; Harry Huizinga, 'A European VAT on Financial Services?' (2002), *Economic Policy* 17(35), 497, 500; Commonwealth of Australia Treasury, Australia's Future Tax System Review Panel, *Australia's Future Tax System: Report to the Treasurer* (Australia's Future Tax System Review Panel: The Treasury, Canberra, 2009), 306–7.

[142] As Edgar explains, margins can be extremely fluid; they can change on an hourly basis and involve cross-subsidisation of margins of other products. The invoice-credit mechanism VAT requires allocation of some portion of the aggregate charge of the financial service provider to

These valuation problems arise because of the transactional nature of the good VAT and are therefore not a feature of accounts-based VATs (using the addition or subtraction method).[143] The subtraction-method VAT can calculate the value of interest margins (calculated as the difference between aggregate interest revenue and expenditure [i.e., borrowing costs] over a set period) on an accounts rather than a transactional basis.[144] The addition-method accounts-based VAT can tax financial services by computing the sum of wages and profits, which equate to the value-add provided by the financial institution. However, because both approaches rely on accounts-based rather than transaction-based methods, they sit awkwardly with the invoice-credit mechanism VAT.[145] For example, the calculation of interest margins under the subtraction approach can occur only over a period of time and not by reference to individual transactions, meaning that the VAT chain is broken and a business cannot shift the VAT forward to consumers on a transactional basis.

Exempting financial supplies avoids the need to identify the value of the services provided by a bank on a transactional basis because no VAT is charged on the transaction. However, as §4.2.1 explained, exemption causes a number of problems, arising mostly from the fact that financial service providers cannot claim input tax credits for any of the inputs used in making these supplies and that financial supplies are the subject of many B2B transactions.[146]

It is commonly claimed by the conventional approach that the exemption of financial supplies leads to the over-taxation of business and the under-taxation of consumers.[147] A simple basis for the claim is that banks cannot claim back credits

particular consumers, but for each consumer the amount of the charge will differ: Tim Edgar, 'Exempt Treatment of Financial Intermediation Services Under a Value-Added Tax: An Assessment of Alternatives' (2001), *Canadian Tax Journal* 49(5), 1133, 1148; Robin Boadway and Michael Keen, 'Theoretical Perspectives on the Taxation of Capital Income and Financial Services', in P. Honohan (ed.), *Taxation of Financial Intermediation: Theory and Practice for Emerging Economies* (World Bank; Oxford University Press, Washington DC, 2003), 31, 33.

143 Howell H. Zee, 'VAT Treatment of Financial Services: A Primer on Conceptual Issues and Country Practices', *INTERTAX* 34(10) (2006), 458, 461; Sijbren Cnossen, 'Global Trends and Issues in Value Added Taxation', *International Tax and Public Finance* 5(3) (1998), 399, 406.

144 Sijbren Cnossen, 'Global Trends and Issues in Value Added Taxation', *International Tax and Public Finance* 5(3) (1998), 399, 407.

145 Howell H. Zee, 'VAT Treatment of Financial Services: A Primer on Conceptual Issues and Country Practices', *INTERTAX* 34(10) (2006), 458, 461.

146 Ibid., 461–63; Alan Schenk, 'Taxation of Financial Services Under a US Value-Added Tax', *Tax Law Review* 63(2) (2010), 409, 410; Harry Huizinga, 'A European VAT on Financial Services?' *Economic Policy* 17(35) (2002), 497, 505–10; Arthur Kerrigan, 'The Elusiveness of Neutrality – Why Is It So Difficult to Apply VAT to Financial Services?' *International VAT Monitor* (March/April 2010), 103, 104–5; Robert F. van Brederode, *Systems of General Sales Taxation: Theory, Policy and Practice* (Kluwer Law International Alphen aan den Rijn, 2009), 138–63; Liam Ebrill et al., *The Modern VAT* (IMF, Washington, DC, 2001), 94–100.

147 Howell H. Zee, 'VAT Treatment of Financial Services: A Primer on Conceptual Issues and Country Practices', *INTERTAX* 34(10) (2006), 458, 462–63; Harry Huizinga, 'A European VAT on Financial Services?' *Economic Policy* 17(35) (2002), 497, 505–9; Alan Schenk, 'Taxation of Financial Services Under a US Value-Added Tax', *Tax Law Review* 63(2) (2010), 409, 418.

for their inputs and are therefore over-taxed. However, the basis for the claim is more complex.[148] For this it is instructive to return to the examples in Tables 2.6 to 2.8. Although the supply of a financial intermediation service does not follow the linear supply chains shown in these cases, the examples are sufficient to show the *consequences* of exempting financial services under a VAT.

Table 2.6[149] shows what occurs in a business-to-consumer (B2C) supply, where the bank (in this case represented by the retailer) supplies directly to an end consumer and is able to shift the VAT forward in the price for its service to a final consumer. The final consumer pays $20 of the embedded tax in the price for the service. The potential VAT base (consisting of the value added by the manufacturer, wholesaler and bank) is $300, but the consumer bears a tax burden of only $20 (representing only the value added by the manufacturer and wholesaler but excluding the value added by the bank). This is $10 less than the $30 burden the consumer would have borne if the supply by the bank was a taxable supply.[150]

Table 2.7 shows what occurs when the bank (in this case represented by the wholesaler) supplies to a business (a B2B supply). This example shows that the total revenue is $41 – which exceeds by $11 the 10 per cent of the correct VAT base of $300 (the total of the value added of $100 each by the manufacturer, the bank and the retailer). Of this $11, $1 is due to the tax on a tax (10 per cent of the $10 VAT paid by the exempt bank on its inputs) and the remaining $10 results from taxing the value of the inputs acquired by the bank twice.[151] The inability to recover the embedded VAT breaks the VAT chain (because the $10 VAT paid on the bank's input cannot be recovered by the bank). This breaking of the chain also leads to cascading tax liability because if the bank can shift the $10 embedded VAT forward in the price, then this amount is taxed twice.

Although these examples support the claim that the exemption of financial supplies leads to the over-taxation of business and the under-taxation of consumers, the claim holds only if it is assumed that the VAT-registered business is itself unable to shift the cascading tax liability on to the end consumer. As Table 2.7 shows, it is not the VAT-registered business that pays the VAT, but rather the end consumer.[152] This may offset the under-taxation that occurs when a financial supply is made directly to the consumer, as was shown in Table 2.6. Ultimately, this will be

[148] Howell H. Zee, 'VAT Treatment of Financial Services: A Primer on Conceptual Issues and Country Practices', *INTERTAX* 34(10) (2006), 458, 462–63.

[149] Howell H. Zee, 'VAT Treatment of Financial Services: A Primer on Conceptual Issues and Country Practices', *INTERTAX* 34(10) (2006), 458, 462–63.

[150] Ibid.; Michael Keen, Russell Krelove and John Norregaard, 'The Financial Activities Tax', in Stijn Claessens, Michael Keen and C. Pazarbasioglu (eds.), *Financial Sector Taxation: The IMF's Report to the G-20 and Background Material* (IMF, 2010), 118, 120.

[151] Howell H. Zee, 'VAT Treatment of Financial Services: A Primer on Conceptual Issues and Country Practices', *INTERTAX* 34(10) (2006), 458, 462–63.

[152] Alan Schenk, 'Taxation of Financial Services Under a US Value-Added Tax', *Tax Law Review* 63(2) (2010), 409, 417.

determined by market conditions and other factors determining the ability of banks and businesses to both identify and shift forward embedded tax in their prices.[153]

However, irrespective of who bears the final incidence of the VAT arising from the exemption, it can be seen from this example that the exemption of financial supplies goes against the principle that the VAT should have a neutral impact on the price paid by businesses for their inputs.[154] The potential for the exemption to impact business profits provides an incentive for businesses to avoid the impact of the exemption as much as possible. The exemption, for example, creates an incentive or bias for financial service providers to self-supply inputs used in the making of their supplies in order to avoid VAT liability.[155] This in turn leads to pressure from the suppliers to financial service providers to have exemptions extended upstream. As Table 2.8 in this chapter demonstrated, this eliminates the adverse impact on these businesses but renders the VAT more of an RST. In addition, because financial supplies are exempt (as opposed to the financial

[153] If the embedded VAT cannot be shifted forward, it will then affect the profits of the banks and businesses involved: OECD, *Consumption Tax Trends 2012: VAT/GST and Excise Rates, Trends and Administration Issues* (OECD Publishing, Paris, 2012), 75. See also Rita de la Feria and Ben Lockwood, 'Opting for Opting-In? An Evaluation of the European Commission's Proposals for Reforming VAT on Financial Services' (2010), *Fiscal Studies* 31(2), 171, 185; Howell H. Zee, 'Further Thoughts on Reforming the VAT: Treatment of Financial Intermediation Services', in R. de la Feria (ed.), *VAT Exemptions: Consequences and Design Alternatives* (vol. 37, EUCOTAX Series on European Taxation, Kluwer Law International, Alphen aan den Rijn, 2013), 345, 354; Tim Edgar, 'Comment: Is the Comprehensive Application of Cash-Flow Taxation Necessary to Integrate Financial Services into an Invoice/Credit VAT?', in R. de la Feria, *VAT Exemptions: Consequences and Design Alternatives* (vol. 37, EUCOTAX Series on European Taxation, Kluwer Law International, Alphen aan den Rijn, 2013), 357, 360–62.

[154] As Keen et al. explain:

> Normally, the credit mechanism of the VAT ensures that prices paid by registered businesses on their purchases are not affected by the VAT; exemption means that this is not so either for financial institutions themselves or their customers (and, through further pass-throughs, the customers of their customers...). This effect – 'cascading' of the tax – runs counter to the principle, underlying the VAT, that transactions between businesses should not be taxed unless doing so addresses some clear market failure.

Michael Keen, Russell Krelove and John Norregaard, 'The Financial Activities Tax', in Stijn Claessens, Michael Keen and C. Pazarbasioglu (eds.), *Financial Sector Taxation: The IMF's Report to the G-20 and Background Material* (IMF, 2010), 118, 119.

[155] Avoiding the incentive to self-supply or vertically integrate was one of the principal reasons for the support of VATs over turnover taxes: Günter Schmölders, *Turnover Taxes* (International Bureau of Fiscal Documentation, Amsterdam, 1966), 56–58; OECD, *Consumption Tax Trends 2012: VAT/GST and Excise Rates, Trends and Administration Issues* (OECD Publishing, Paris, 2012), 74. *Contra* Edgar, who contends that the self-supply rationale 'rests on shaky grounds', as the ability to self-supply is affected by other tax and non-tax factors, and given these additional constraints the evidence of 'the extent to which financial intermediaries are free to substitute insourced for outsourced services in response to a tax bias in favour of the former' is unsystematic and anecdotal at best: Tim Edgar, 'Exempt Treatment of Financial Intermediation Services Under a Value-Added Tax: An Assessment of Alternatives' (2001), *Canadian Tax Journal* 49(5), 1133, 1181.

supplier), if the financial supplier provides both taxable and exempt supplies, this can lead to complex definitional and apportionment difficulties in allocating inputs between taxable and exempt supplies.[156] Further difficulties arise when financial services provided domestically are exempt but financial services provided overseas are zero-rated, as this creates an incentive to acquire supplies offshore, to the disadvantage of domestic suppliers.[157]

These problems, combined with the significance of the financial services industry, estimated to constitute up to 30 per cent of global GDP,[158] have led to a concerted effort to improve the taxation of financial services. Zee sums up the requirements needed for a potentially successful reform option:[159]

> ...the successful approach would impose no VAT burden on business users, impose an appropriate VAT burden on consumer users, and accomplish both of these objectives by means of a transaction-based VAT.

Although there are a number of proposals to tax financial services under a VAT,[160] none has gained sufficient consensus within the conventional approach to warrant

[156] OECD, *Consumption Tax Trends 2012: VAT/GST and Excise Rates, Trends and Administration Issues* (OECD Publishing, Paris, 2012), 75; Howell H. Zee, 'VAT Treatment of Financial Services: A Primer on Conceptual Issues and Country Practices', *INTERTAX* 34(10) (2006), 458, 463.

[157] OECD, *Consumption Tax Trends 2012: VAT/GST and Excise Rates, Trends and Administration Issues* (OECD Publishing, Paris, 2012), 75; Michael Keen, Russell Krelove and John Norregaard, 'The Financial Activities Tax', in Stijn Claessens, Michael Keen and C. Pazarbasioglu (eds.), *Financial Sector Taxation: The IMF's Report to the G-20 and Background Material* (IMF, 2010), 118, 119.

[158] Ian Crawford, Michael Keen and Stephen Smith, 'Value Added Tax and Excises' in Stuart Adam et al. (eds.) for the Institute for Fiscal Studies, *Dimensions of Tax Design: The Mirrlees Review* (Oxford University Press, Oxford, 2010), 275, 305.

[159] Howell H. Zee, 'VAT Treatment of Financial Services: A Primer on Conceptual Issues and Country Practices', *INTERTAX* 34(10) (2006), 458, 462.

[160] Poddar and English suggest adopting a modified cash-flow approach so that VAT is imposed on total cash inflows (including loan repayments, deposits and interest receipts) and a tax credit is granted for all cash outflows (including lending, deposit withdrawals and interest payments): Satya Poddar and Morley English, 'Taxation of Financial Services under a Value-Added Tax: Applying the Cash-Flow Approach', *National Tax Journal* 50(1) (1997), 89. The method was trialled without success in the EU. For criticisms, see Howell H. Zee, 'VAT Treatment of Financial Services: A Primer on Conceptual Issues and Country Practices', *INTERTAX* 34(10) (2006), 458, 467–68. Others suggest a combination of two approaches, with the zero-rating of business-to-business transactions and the adoption of a modified cash-flow approach to transactions with final consumers: Ian Crawford, Michael Keen and Stephen Smith, 'Value Added Tax and Excises' in Stuart Adam et al. (eds.) for the Institute for Fiscal Studies, *Dimensions of Tax Design: The Mirrlees Review* (Oxford University Press, Oxford, 2010), 275, 306–9. Zee proposes a modified reverse-charge mechanism – which combines the practice of reverse charging (i.e., the bank pays VAT, and issues a VAT invoice to itself for the tax paid on its inputs [i.e., the interest paid to depositors]). Rather than credit this against the output tax paid (i.e., the VAT on the interest paid by borrowers), which Zee argues would result in an over-taxing of consumers who borrow because it would include the value added by the depositor as well as the bank (at 470), the bank operates a form of franking account that uses the VAT credits received on deposits to reduce the VAT paid by borrowers: Howell H.

change.[161] As a result, the taxation of financial supplies remains a key frontier issue that tests the limits of the good VAT.

4.3 *Levy the VAT at a single rate*

There is a clear consensus within the conventional approach that the VAT should be levied at a uniform rate (save for the zero-rating of exports).[162]

Zee, 'VAT Treatment of Financial Services: A Primer on Conceptual Issues and Country Practices', *INTERTAX* 34(10) (2006), 458, 468–73; Howell H. Zee, 'Further Thoughts on Reforming the VAT: Treatment of Financial Intermediation Services', in R. de la Feria (ed.), *VAT Exemptions: Consequences and Design Alternatives* (vol. 37, EUCOTAX Series on European Taxation, Kluwer Law International, Alphen aan den Rijn, 2013), 345, 352–54; *Contra* the approach in *Treasury I* (see Chapter 7, §3.2). See also Harry Huizinga, 'A European VAT on Financial Services?' *Economic Policy* 17(35) (2002), 497; Tim Edgar, 'The Search for Alternatives to the Exempt Treatment of Financial Services under a Value Added Tax', in R. Krever and D. White (eds.), *GST in Retrospect and Prospect* (Brookers, Wellington, 2007), 131; Satya Poddar, 'VAT on Financial Services – Searching for a Workable Compromise', in R. Krever and D. White (eds.), *GST in Retrospect and Prospect* (Thomson Brookers, Wellington, 2007), 179. For one of the earliest contributions to options for taxing financial supplies under a VAT, see Carl Bakker and Phil Chronican, 'Financial Services and the GST: A Discussion Paper' (Victoria University Press for the Institute of Policy Studies, Victoria University of Wellington, 1985).

161 OECD, *Consumption Tax Trends 2012: VAT/GST and Excise Rates, Trends and Administration Issues* (OECD Publishing, Paris, 2012), 76; Bird and Gendron conclude that '[n]o convincing conceptually correct *and* practical solution for capturing the bulk of financial services under the VAT has yet been developed': Richard Bird and Pierre-Pascal Gendron, *The VAT in Developing and Transitional Countries* (Cambridge University Press, New York, 2007), 97 (emphasis in original); Satya Poddar, 'VAT on Financial Services – Searching for a Workable Compromise', in R. Krever and D. White (eds.), *GST in Retrospect and Prospect* (Thomson Brookers, Wellington, 2007), 179, 180. Cnossen contends that '[m]ost economists and lawyers, therefore, probably still share his conclusion that "while unsatisfactory, the exemption of financial services from VAT, and the subsequent cascade effect, look to be the best solution for the time being."' Sijbren Cnossen, 'Global Trends and Issues in Value Added Taxation', *International Tax and Public Finance* 5(3) (1998), 399, 408. Richard Krever and Rita de la Feria, 'Ending VAT Exemptions: Towards a Post-Modern VAT', in R. de la Feria (ed.), *VAT Exemptions: Consequences and Design Alternatives* (vol. 37, EUCOTAX Series on European Taxation, Kluwer Law International, Alphen aan den Rijn, 2013), 3, 32.

162 OECD, *Consumption Tax Trends 2012: VAT/GST and Excise Rates, Trends and Administration Issues* (OECD Publishing, Paris, 2012), 73; Carl S. Shoup, 'Choosing among Types of VATs', in M. Gillis, C. S. Shoup and G. P. Sicat (eds.), *Value Added Taxation in Developing Countries (A World Bank Symposium)* (World Bank, Washington, DC, 1990), 3, 4; Malcolm Gillis, Carl S. Shoup and Gerardo P. Sicat, 'Lessons for Developing Countries', in M. Gillis, C. S. Shoup and G. P. Sicat (eds.), *Value Added Taxation in Developing Countries (A World Bank Symposium)* (World Bank, Washington, DC, 1990), 219, 222; Erik Jørgensen and Jeffrey Owens, 'The Move to VAT', *OECD Observer* (August/September 1995), 21, 22; Ebrill surveyed IMF advice to 37 countries and found the advice was for a single positive VAT rate in all countries bar two: Liam Ebrill et al., *The Modern VAT* (IMF, Washington, DC, 2001), 64; Bird and Gendron capture the sentiment when they state that '[e]xpert advice on VAT rates is simple: there should be only one rate': Richard Bird and Pierre-Pascal Gendron, *The VAT in Developing and Transitional Countries* (Cambridge University Press, New York, 2007), 108; the *ITD VAT Paper* provides that '[s]tandard advice has been for a single-rate VAT (other than

The conventional approach prefers policy-makers not to be tempted to alter rates on the basis of equity or other policy concerns.[163] So, for example, rather than addressing equity concerns through setting higher rates on luxury goods and lower rates on essential goods and services, the conventional approach prefers, in line with the equity-efficiency trade-off, that these issues be addressed, if at all, by other revenue instruments such as the income tax and by government transfers.[164] This approach, in turn, is said to avoid pressure to extend favourable rate treatment to other goods and services.[165] Moreover, the conventional approach prefers a single rate to multiple rates based on taxing goods according to their own price elasticity of demand, on the basis that it is ultimately more administratively efficient to tax goods at a single rate.[166]

a zero rate for exports only)': International Tax Dialogue (ITD), 'The Value Added Tax: Experience and Issues' (Background Paper Prepared for the International Tax Dialogue Conference on the VAT, Rome, March 15–16, 2005, ITD), 14; Ken Messere, Flip de Kam and Christopher Heady, *Tax Policy: Theory and Practice in OECD Countries* (Oxford University Press, Oxford, 2003), 22; Richard Goode, 'Tax Advice to Developing Countries: An Historical Survey', *World Development* 21(1) (1993), 37, 44. *Contra* Cnossen, who favours a single rate for developed countries but dual rates for developing countries: Sijbren Cnossen, 'Global Trends and Issues in Value Added Taxation', *International Tax and Public Finance* 5 (3) (1998), 399, 409–11.

[163] International Tax Dialogue (ITD), 'The Value Added Tax: Experience and Issues' (Background Paper Prepared for the International Tax Dialogue Conference on the VAT, Rome, March 15–16, 2005, ITD), 14; Richard Bird and Pierre-Pascal Gendron, *The VAT in Developing and Transitional Countries* (Cambridge University Press, New York, 2007), 108; Richard Goode, 'Tax Advice to Developing Countries: An Historical Survey', *World Development* 21(1) (1993), 37, 44; Robert F. van Brederode, *Systems of General Sales Taxation: Theory, Policy and Practice* (Kluwer Law International Alphen aan den Rijn, 2009), 38.

[164] Liam Ebrill et al., *The Modern VAT* (IMF, Washington, DC, 2001), 74–82.

[165] The OECD states that '[a]bolishing a wide range of reduced rates prevents the "me too" syndrome. By granting a reduced rate to one sector, other sectors will inevitably lobby hard for inclusion': OECD, *Consumption Tax Trends 2012: VAT/GST and Excise Rates, Trends and Administration Issues* (OECD Publishing, Paris, 2012), 73. See also Liam Ebrill et al., *The Modern VAT* (IMF, Washington, DC, 2001), 79–80.

[166] The degree to which this recommendation is supported by optimal tax theory is debated. Ramsey showed that a uniform commodity tax rate is not optimal, and that under certain conditions tax rates should vary according to the demand of a good, meaning that goods with inelastic demand (e.g., bread) should attract higher taxes than goods with elastic demand (e.g., fairy floss): F. P. Ramsey, 'A Contribution to the Theory of Taxation', *Economic Journal* 37(1) (1927), 47–61. *Contra* Anthony B. Atkinson and Joseph E. Stiglitz, 'The Design of Tax Structure: Direct versus Indirect Taxation"', *Journal of Public Economics* 6 (1976), 55; Ian Crawford, Michael Keen and Stephen Smith, 'Value Added Tax and Excises' in Stuart Adam et al. (eds.) for the Institute for Fiscal Studies, *Dimensions of Tax Design: The Mirrlees Review* (Oxford University Press, Oxford, 2010), 275, 284–91; William M. Gentry, 'Optimal Taxation', in J. J. Cordes, R. D. Ebel and J. Gravelle (eds.), *Encyclopedia of Taxation and Tax Policy* (2nd ed., Urban Institute Press, Washington, DC, 1999), 281–83. Corlett and Hague interpret the Ramsay model according to cross-price elasticity of demand or the substitutability of goods (which are taxed) with leisure (which is untaxed). Therefore, tax rates should be higher on leisure goods because they are a complement to leisure and therefore an indirect means by which to tax leisure, whereas commodities relating to activities that substitute for leisure (i.e., work) should be taxed more lightly (e.g., uniforms): W. J. Corlett and D. C. Hague,

5 NORM 2 – CALCULATION OF VAT LIABILITY USING THE INVOICE-CREDIT MECHANISM

As §3.1 explained, the consensus within the conventional approach is to levy the good VAT through the invoice-credit mechanism.[167] It is this collection mechanism that distinguishes the VAT from other consumption taxes, including its main competitor – the RST.[168]

5.1 *Operation of the invoice-credit mechanism*

As a transaction-based tax, the good VAT requires laws to stipulate how and when the transaction, the 'taxable supply', occurs.[169] The invoice-credit mechanism requires each entity to charge VAT on all 'taxable supplies' and provide the purchaser with an invoice showing the amount of VAT charged.[170] If the purchaser is a registered entity, the VAT charge incurred on their purchases can be credited/ deducted against the VAT charged on their supplies.[171] Registered entities submit

'Complemetarity and the Excess Burden of Taxation', *Review of Economic Studies* (1953), 21–30. See further Joel Slemrod, 'Optimal Taxation and Tax Systems' *Journal of Economic Perspectives* 4(1) (1990), 157, 159; Gentry at 281–83. Nevertheless, a general preference is expressed by the conventional approach for other taxes, such as excise taxes, to address varying demand elasticities: Liam Ebrill et al., *The Modern VAT* (IMF, Washington, DC, 2001), 69, 72.

[167] Ben Terra and Julie Kajus, IBFD, *A Guide to the European VAT Directives* [online] (15 April 2011), 7.5.3; 'Practice and consensus heavily favours the invoice credit method': Liam Ebrill et al., *The Modern VAT* (IMF, Washington, DC, 2001), 20; International Tax Dialogue (ITD), 'The Value Added Tax: Experience and Issues' (Background Paper Prepared for the International Tax Dialogue Conference on the VAT, Rome, March 15–16, 2005, ITD), 7; Sijbren Cnossen, 'Global Trends and Issues in Value Added Taxation' (1998), *International Tax and Public Finance* 5(3), 399–400; Alan Schenk and Oliver Oldman, *Value Added Tax: A Comparative Approach* (rev. edn., Cambridge University Press, Cambridge; New York, 2007), 38; Carl S. Shoup, 'Choosing among Types of VATs', in M. Gillis, C. S. Shoup and G. P. Sicat (eds.), *Value Added Taxation in Developing Countries (A World Bank Symposium)* (World Bank, Washington, DC, 1990), 3, 8–11; David Williams, 'Value-Added Tax', in V. Thuronyi (ed.), *Tax Law Design and Drafting* (IMF, Washington, DC, 1996), vol. 1, 164, 167.

[168] Michael Keen and Ben Lockwood, 'The Value Added Tax: Its Causes and Consequences', *Journal of Development Economics* 92(2) (2010), 138, 139. See § 4.1 of this chapter.

[169] See, e.g., §10 of the *New Vatopia Model*, which provides that a supply occurs on the earliest of: (1)(a)when the goods are delivered or made available or the performance of services is completed; (1)(b) an invoice for the supply is issued by the supplier; or (1)(c) any consideration for the supply is received. There are also a number of rules for specific supplies. Time of import rules are contained in §11: Alan Schenk and Members of the IMF Legal Department, *Value Added Tax Act of the Commonwealth of New Vatopia* (IMF, 2006).

[170] See, e.g., §32(1) of the *New Vatopia Model*, which places the onus on the 'registered supplier' to provide an 'original tax invoice' to the 'recipient' of the supply: ibid.

[171] E.g., under the *New Vatopia Model*, input tax credits or 'input tax deductions' are generally available when the input tax was payable in 'respect of taxable supplies' 'for use in a taxable activity carried on by the person' during the relevant tax period: §27(1)(a): ibid.

'tax returns'[172] for a 'tax period' (which can be monthly, quarterly or annually).[173] The net tax liability for the tax period will be the difference between the output tax charged on taxable sales and the input tax credits available for the tax paid on inputs/purchases.[174] Timing rules are necessary to assign sales and purchases to a relevant 'tax period'.[175] If a registered entity receives more VAT than it pays, then it remits the difference (between the VAT charged and the VAT paid) to the revenue authorities.[176] If the entity pays more VAT than it receives (for example, if an entity is an exporter), then the entity is entitled to a refund.[177] Timing rules and valuation rules are also necessary to identify the value (or consideration) of the goods or services supplied.[178] Timing and place of supply rules are also necessary to identify the relevant location of the supply for the purposes of assessing the appropriate jurisdiction to tax (see norm 3, §6).[179] It can therefore be seen that rather than ridding tax collection from the timing and valuation requirements of the income tax, the good VAT simply replaces one set of timing rules with another.[180]

In addition to requiring laws to indicate when and how a taxable supply occurs, it is also necessary to have laws that specify what the relevant documentary trail requires, such as what is required on an invoice.[181] Furthermore, given that the good VAT is a self-assessed tax, it is necessary to have laws that allow for auditing of the documentary trail.[182]

[172] See, e.g., §24 of the *New Vatopia Model*: ibid.

[173] See, e.g., §23 of the *New Vatopia Model*, which adopts a monthly tax period with the option of regulating for different tax periods for different classes of taxpayers: ibid.

[174] Alan Schenk and Oliver Oldman, *Value Added Tax: A Comparative Approach* (rev. edn., Cambridge University Press, Cambridge; New York, 2007), 39.

[175] See, e.g., §26 of the *New Vatopia Model*: Alan Schenk and Members of the IMF Legal Department, *Value Added Tax Act of the Commonwealth of New Vatopia* (IMF, 2006).

[176] Ibid.

[177] But see §26(2) and §45 of the *New Vatopia Model*, which provide for the 'excess amount' of deductions/input tax credits over output tax charged on sales to be carried forward for a three-month period after which the taxpayer may claim a refund. This reflects the fact that the model is geared toward advising developing countries with limited administrative capacity and pressing revenue needs: ibid.

[178] See, e.g., §13(1) of the *New Vatopia Model*, which specifies that the value of a supply of goods or services is the amount of the consideration for the supply. It then details a further 16 alternative rules for when this is not applicable, as for example in §13(3) for related party transactions made for no or little consideration, where the value will be 'fair market value' (defined in §3). Value of imports is governed by §14: ibid.

[179] Graeme Cooper and Richard Vann, 'Implementing the Goods and Services Tax', *Sydney Law Review* 23 (1999), 337, 396.

[180] E.g., the *New Vatopia Model* has an additional 12 timing rules developed for specific supplies in addition to the standard rule in §10: §§10(2)–(13): Alan Schenk and Members of the IMF Legal Department, *Value Added Tax Act of the Commonwealth of New Vatopia* (IMF, 2006).

[181] See, e.g., §32(1) of the *New Vatopia Model*; see also §24(2) for the requirements for 'tax returns': ibid.

[182] See, e.g., 'Part XI – Records and Investigation Powers' of the *New Vatopia Model*: ibid.; Richard Krever, 'Designing and Drafting VAT Laws for Africa', in R. Krever (ed.), *VAT in Africa* (Pretoria University Law Press, Pretoria, 2008), 9, 10–11.

As §4 highlighted, in order to facilitate the good VAT falling on a consumption base, full and immediate refunding of VAT paid on all business inputs should be provided. The delaying of that crediting can make the base more akin to an income base (as it more closely resembles depreciation), and the denial of the crediting of capital expenses makes the VAT more akin to a gross product base.[183] However, the need to provide prompt refunds must be balanced against the need to verify refund claims made by registered entities because, as the next section demonstrates, the refund mechanism is susceptible to abuse.[184]

5.2 *The advantages of the invoice-credit method over other methods*

A number of factors are cited by the conventional approach to explain the overwhelming preference for the levying of VAT through the invoice-credit mechanism. Some factors derive explicitly from the invoice-credit method itself, and others from the incremental collection technique that the method facilitates.

The invoice-credit mechanism is said to facilitate the forward shifting of VAT to more readily reach a consumption base by separately identifying the VAT component on each transaction throughout the production and distribution chain, which in turn increases the likelihood that the VAT is borne by consumers through a corresponding increase in prices.[185] As Tait explains, the 'tax is *supposed* to be passed on to the consumer and should be seen to be passed on as a separate item on invoices right through to the final retail sales'.[186]

The prevention of cascading tax liabilities is another perceived advantage of the invoice-credit mechanism. All agree that the good VAT is superior to the turnover tax[187] because the refund mechanism prevents cascading of the tax and is therefore

[183] Graham Harrison and Russell Krelove, 'VAT Refunds: A Review of Country Experience ' (Working Paper No. WP/05/218, IMF, 2005), 5; Alan Schenk and Oliver Oldman, *Value Added Tax: A Comparative Approach* (rev. edn., Cambridge University Press, Cambridge; New York, 2007), 38; Victor Thuronyi, *Comparative Tax Law* (Kluwer Law International, The Hague, 2003), 315; Carl S. Shoup, *The Value-Added Tax* (Center of Planning and Economic Research, Athens, Greece, 1973), 26; Ben Terra and Julie Kajus, IBFD, A *Guide to the European VAT Directives* [online] (15 April 2011), n 298.

[184] Michael Keen and Stephen Smith, 'VAT Fraud and Evasion: What Do We Know and What Can Be Done?' *National Tax Journal* 59(4) (2006), 861, 879.

[185] Clara K. Sullivan, *The Tax on Value Added* (New York, 1965), 11, 17; Robert F. van Brederode, *Systems of General Sales Taxation: Theory, Policy and Practice* (Kluwer Law International Alphen aan den Rijn, 2009), 32.

[186] Alan A. Tait, *Value Added Tax* (McGraw-Hill, London, New York, 1972), 11 (emphasis in original).

[187] Liam Ebrill et al., *The Modern VAT* (IMF, Washington, DC, 2001), 3; F. Neumark, *Neumark Committee, 'Report of the Fiscal and Financial Committee on Tax Harmonization'* (IBFD, Amsterdam, 1963), 46; Alan Schenk and Oliver Oldman, *Value Added Tax: A Comparative Approach* (rev. edn., Cambridge University Press, Cambridge; New York, 2007), 3; Van Brederode argues that there is no present-day economic justification for the use of turnover taxes but highlights a rise in the popularity of gross receipts taxes by US states: Robert F. van

neutral toward business. In part, the preference for the VAT over the RST might stem from the VAT's European origins, where the VAT was perceived as clearly superior to the cascading turnover tax, which did not allow for the recovery of tax paid on business inputs. The RST also prevents cascading by effectively suspending collection of the tax (when the vendor is satisfied that the purchaser is a registered business that can prove the purchase is used for business purposes) until the final retail sale.[188] The VAT limits an entity's tax liability to the value added by the firm at each turnover (rather than the entire amount of the turnover).[189] The good VAT's credit mechanism ensures that the tax does not fall on business inputs because all purchasers are treated as end consumers but businesses can obtain a refund. The absence of this mechanism in an RST places the onus on sellers to verify the taxable status of the consumer and makes it more difficult to make sure the tax does not fall on business inputs for businesses that sell products to both other businesses and consumers.[190] For this reason, the good VAT is thought to be better at reaching services, although there is no reason, in theory, why an RST cannot extend to an equally broad base.[191]

The RST offers the advantages of simplicity, neutrality and cash-flow benefits for business (in not requiring businesses to pay tax and then wait for credits, which if delayed or denied can transform the VAT into a tax on business). Nevertheless, consensus favours the good VAT over the RST.[192] The conventional approach

Brederode, *Systems of General Sales Taxation: Theory, Policy and Practice* (Kluwer Law International Alphen aan den Rijn, 2009), 70, and at 52, 54.

188 Richard Krever, 'Designing and Drafting VAT Laws for Africa', in R. Krever (ed.), *VAT in Africa* (Pretoria University Law Press, Pretoria, 2008), 9, 10–11.

189 Clara K. Sullivan, *The Tax on Value Added* (New York, 1965), 6–7.

190 Liam Ebrill et al., *The Modern VAT* (IMF, Washington, DC, 2001), 23.

191 The exclusion of services from the RST base is an historic one. Services are traditionally difficult to tax because they occur at the final stage (or the weakest link) of the distribution chain, have a high labour component and are often provided by small-scale entities. As many services are provided for business and personal use, it is considered administratively difficult to require service providers to ascertain the taxable status of the recipient, as is required under an RST. The good VAT is thought to be better at taxing services because of its self-enforcing properties. Service providers that provide services to business and private consumers have a greater incentive to register so that their business consumers can claim input credits on the services. In addition, because the VAT treats all purchasers the same, but allows registered entities to receive inputs, there is no onus on the provider of the services to ascertain the taxable status of the purchaser, therefore making it administratively simpler for the service provider and reducing the incentive for the service provider and recipient to evade VAT: Ronald T. McMorran, 'A Comparison between the Sales Tax and a VAT', in P. Shome (ed.), *Tax Policy Handbook* (IMF, Washington, DC, 1995), 82, 85. However, as the section indicates, the advantages of the VAT can be overstated.

192 George R. Zodrow, 'The Sales Tax, the VAT, and Taxes in Between – Or, Is the Only Good NRST a "VAT in Drag"?' *National Tax Journal* 52(3) (1999), 429, 430; Neil Brooks, 'An Overview of the Role of the VAT, Fundamental Tax Reform, and a Defence of the Income Tax', in R. Krever and D. White (eds.), *GST in Retrospect and Prospect* (Brookers, Wellington, 2007), 597, 633; Liam Ebrill et al., *The Modern VAT* (IMF, Washington, DC, 2001), 24; Krever describes the debate about the relative merits of each tax as 'purely academic', given the

claims that the cash-flow benefits of an RST are not necessarily significant, given that most purchasers are vendors who have cash coming in to match the cash going out, provided that VAT refunds are processed in a timely manner.[193] The conventional approach considers the good VAT to have administrative benefits over the RST.[194] A 1994 study by Cnossen estimated the costs to administer the good VAT in the OECD at approximately $100 per taxpayer per annum, with a corresponding figure for compliance costs of $500.[195]

The good VAT is lauded for its purported resistance to fraud because of the self-enforcing nature of the invoice-credit mechanism, which links the purchaser's tax credit to the tax remitted by the seller, as evidenced by an invoice.[196] It is to the buyer's advantage to overstate the transaction value to maximise credits, but to the seller's advantage to understate it so as to reduce VAT payable. Although the accounts-based subtraction method also carries this feature, the credit mechanism links this incentive to the issuing of a tax invoice, thus encouraging purchasers to ensure that sellers appropriately charge and document VAT, and in the process leading to a useful documentary trail for enforcement purposes.[197] Although both the good VAT and the income tax are self-assessed, the good VAT is said to offer further advantages because the matching of inputs with outputs to obtain refunds is facilitated by business inventories. Because the documentary trail extends throughout the production and distribution chain, as opposed to one stage, the VAT is said to offer a better audit trail than the RST.[198] By contrast, because the onus rests with the seller to accurately account for RST, purchasers have an incentive to misrepresent their

strength of support for VAT: Richard Krever, 'Designing and Drafting VAT Laws for Africa', in R. Krever (ed.), *VAT in Africa* (Pretoria University Law Press, Pretoria, 2008), 9, 13; Bird and Gendron state that 'in most circumstances a VAT is the most sensible form of general consumption tax': Richard Bird and Pierre-Pascal Gendron, *The VAT in Developing and Transitional Countries* (Cambridge University Press, New York, 2007), 28; Erik Jørgensen and Jeffrey Owens, 'The Move to VAT', *OECD Observer* (August/September 1995), 21.

193 Richard Krever, 'Designing and Drafting VAT Laws for Africa', in R. Krever (ed.), *VAT in Africa* (Pretoria University Law Press, Pretoria, 2008), 9, 11–13.

194 *Contra* a pure theoretical comparison of the VAT against the RST, absent concerns about administration, can favour the RST: see, e.g., Commonwealth of Australia Treasury, *Reform of the Australian Tax System: Draft White Paper* (Australian Govt Pub Service, Canberra, 1985); George R. Zodrow, 'The Sales Tax, the VAT, and Taxes in Between – Or, Is the Only Good NRST a "VAT in Drag"?' *National Tax Journal* 52(3) (1999), 429, 431.

195 Study quoted in Liam Ebrill et al., *The Modern VAT* (IMF, Washington, DC, 2001), 53.

196 OECD, *Consumption Tax Trends 2012: VAT/GST and Excise Rates, Trends and Administration Issues* (OECD Publishing, Paris, 2012), 32.

197 International Tax Dialogue (ITD), 'The Value Added Tax: Experience and Issues' (Background Paper Prepared for the International Tax Dialogue Conference on the VAT, Rome, March 15–16, 2005, ITD), 7; Liam Ebrill et al., *The Modern VAT* (IMF, Washington, DC, 2001), 21, 23. *Contra* Shoup, who contends that the accounts-based direct subtraction method can achieve the same result: Carl S. Shoup, 'Choosing among Types of VATs', in M. Gillis, C. S. Shoup and G. P. Sicat (eds.), *Value Added Taxation in Developing Countries (A World Bank Symposium)* (World Bank, Washington, DC, 1990), 3, 9.

198 Ronald T. McMorran, 'A Comparison between the Sales Tax and a VAT', in P. Shome (ed.), *Tax Policy Handbook* (IMF, Washington, DC, 1995), 82, 85.

status as final consumers or reselling businesses. The susceptibility of the RST to avoidance and evasion leads most commentators to argue that the RST is administratively viable only if set at low rates of between 5 and 10 per cent.[199]

However the claims in relation to the VAT's self-enforcement have been criticised for being overstated,[200] the extent to which this has been borne out in practice will be examined in Chapter 3. For now, it suffices to note the theoretical susceptibility of the good VAT to avoidance and evasion. The VAT's self-enforcement mechanism can be undermined by the fact that a purchaser's interest lies not necessarily in ensuring that a seller has appropriately paid VAT, but in simply obtaining an acceptable invoice for processing by the tax authorities. A fraudulently produced invoice may still enable credits to be obtained.[201] Dishonest merchants might register to claim credit on inputs but record only a fraction of their final sales (or ignore cash sales) to minimise VAT liability on output. This presents a threat to VAT revenue collections when the final consumer requires no invoice, and therefore the VAT is likely to fare no better than the RST at taxing the cash economy.[202]

Keen and Smith identify points of susceptibility to fraud common to both RSTs and VATs. These include under-reporting of sales; failure to register; misclassification of commodities; omission of self-deliveries (where an entity supplies directly to its proprietor or employees but does not declare the transaction for taxation purposes); tax collected but not remitted; and imported goods not brought to tax.[203]

Although the invoice-credit mechanism at once distinguishes the good VAT from other similar broad-based consumption taxes, it is also regarded as the 'Achilles heel' of the VAT because a VAT invoice can be a cheque written on the government.[204] Bird and Gendron note that 'VAT is the only tax that requires the government not only to collect substantial money from the private sector but

[199] Liam Ebrill et al., *The Modern VAT* (IMF, Washington, DC, 2001), 23.

[200] Commonwealth of Australia Treasury, Australia's Future Tax System Review Panel, *Australia's Future Tax System: Report to the Treasurer* (Australia's Future Tax System Review Panel: The Treasury, Canberra, 2009), 287; George R. Zodrow, 'The Sales Tax, the VAT, and Taxes in Between – Or, Is the Only Good NRST a "VAT in Drag"?' *National Tax Journal* 52(3) (1999), 429, 434.

[201] Liam Ebrill et al., *The Modern VAT* (IMF, Washington, DC, 2001), 23.

[202] Richard Krever, 'Designing and Drafting VAT Laws for Africa', in R. Krever (ed.), *VAT in Africa* (Pretoria University Law Press, Pretoria, 2008), 9, 12–13.

[203] Michael Keen and Stephen Smith, 'VAT Fraud and Evasion: What Do We Know and What Can Be Done?' *National Tax Journal* 59(4) (2006), 861, 866–67. See also Alan A. Tait, *Value Added Tax: International Practice and Problems* (IMF, Washington, DC, 1988), ch. 14.

[204] Richard Bird and Pierre-Pascal Gendron, *The VAT in Developing and Transitional Countries* (Cambridge University Press, New York, 2007), 20, 133; Richard Krever, 'Designing and Drafting VAT Laws for Africa', in R. Krever (ed.), *VAT in Africa* (Pretoria University Law Press, Pretoria, 2008), 9, 13; International Tax Dialogue (ITD), 'The Value Added Tax: Experience and Issues' (Background Paper Prepared for the International Tax Dialogue Conference on the VAT, Rome, March 15–16, 2005, ITD), 27; Graham Harrison and Russell Krelove, 'VAT Refunds: A Review of Country Experience ' (Working Paper No. WP/05/218, IMF, 2005), 4.

also to pay much of it back to the same people in the form of input tax credits.'[205] The vulnerability is such that some suggest the VAT may be more prone to fraud than the RST because in offering the possibility of a refund cheque from the government if a fraudulent tax credit is claimed, the VAT might further incentivise fraud.[206] Keen and Smith point to three specific fraudulent activities unique to the invoice-credit VAT: first, the false claiming of refunds; second, the claiming of credits or refunds for items that are not eligible; and third, the establishment of bogus traders whose sole purpose is to generate invoices and refunds without paying VAT.[207] Chapter 3 later confirms that these activities have indeed occurred to the point where the susceptibility of the good VAT to fraud might constitute another frontier issue that tests its limits. All these risks underscore the importance of audits in a self-assessed good VAT system.

Despite these problems, another perceived advantage of the good VAT is that the invoice-credit mechanism enables the incremental collection of VAT across multiple stages of the production and distribution process. Therefore, in the event that the tax is evaded at the point of sale by a non-registered entity, the loss to revenue under a VAT is said to be less than under an RST because some tax would have been collected on intermediate transactions (for which the non-registered entity could not claim input credits). By contrast, if tax is evaded at the point of sale under the RST, which is the 'weakest link'[208] in the distribution chain, then there is a corresponding absolute loss to revenue.[209] Although this perceived advantage rests on the taxation of

[205] Richard Bird and Pierre-Pascal Gendron, *The VAT in Developing and Transitional Countries* (Cambridge University Press, New York, 2007), 185; Michael Keen and Stephen Smith, 'VAT Fraud and Evasion: What Do We Know and What Can Be Done?' *National Tax Journal* 59(4) (2006), 861.

[206] US Government Accountability Office, *Value-Added Taxes: Lessons Learned from Other Countries on Compliance Risks, Administrative Costs, Compliance Burden, and Transition (GAO-08-566)* (Washington, DC, 2008), 14; Cooper and Vann note the specific risks:

> The GST [Goods and Services Tax, i.e.; VAT], on the other hand, involves two cash flows – the refund of input tax credits, as well as the charging of tax on sales. This makes GST vulnerable to a further kind of evasion – the claiming of input credits for tax on fictitious acquisitions. The analogy with the income tax is evident – income tax taxpayers, like GST taxpayers, but unlike WST or RST taxpayers, can cheat by overstating their deductions as well as underreporting their sales income. And, again unlike the WST or RST, the GST puts this temptation in the face of every commercial firm and for every transaction they undertake (or do not undertake), not just a few.

Graeme Cooper and Richard Vann, 'Implementing the Goods and Services Tax', *Sydney Law Review* 23 (1999), 337, 356.

[207] Michael Keen and Stephen Smith, 'VAT Fraud and Evasion: What Do We Know and What Can Be Done?' *National Tax Journal* 59(4) (2006), 861, 866–68. See also Alan A. Tait, *Value Added Tax: International Practice and Problems* (IMF, Washington, DC, 1988), ch. 14.

[208] Ronald T. McMorran, 'A Comparison between the Sales Tax and a VAT', in P. Shome (ed.), *Tax Policy Handbook* (IMF, Washington, DC, 1995), 82, 85.

[209] Ian Crawford, Michael Keen and Stephen Smith, 'Value Added Tax and Excises' in Stuart Adam et al. (eds.) for the Institute for Fiscal Studies, *Dimensions of Tax Design: The Mirrlees Review* (Oxford University Press, Oxford, 2010), 275, 294–95.

intermediate transactions,[210] Crawford, Keen and Smith contend that input taxation in the absence of a final tax on sales may be justified because where final sales cannot be taxed, it might be desirable to tax inputs as a surrogate for the missing output tax.[211] However, it is also important to note that if the VAT is evaded by a registered entity who manages to get credit on their inputs but does not report or remit tax on their sales, then no revenue is obtained and the outcome under the good VAT is much the same as under the RST.[212] Moreover, there is the distinct possibility that 'bad' VAT chains can emerge when those supplying to a non-registered entity have a similar incentive not to register (because their customer is unable to obtain credit for VAT the entity would otherwise have to charge).[213]

A final perceived advantage of the good VAT is that the invoice-credit mechanism is better suited to VATs levied at differentiated rates because differences can be reflected in invoices rather than in business accounting for differentiated rates on an annual basis.[214] This feature makes the invoice-credit mechanism ideal for destination-based VATs because it allows for the zero-rating of exports (see norm 3, §6).[215] However, it also facilitates the use of exemptions and variable rates which, as §4 explained, are discouraged by the conventional approach.

6 NORM 3 – LEVYING VAT ON A DESTINATION BASIS

A destination-based VAT taxes goods and services at the place of *consumption*. This ensures that all products and services that share the same destination are taxed equally,

210 Ibid.; Michael Keen, 'VAT Attacks!' (Working Paper No. WP/07/142, IMF, 2007), 6; Neil Brooks, 'An Overview of the Role of the VAT, Fundamental Tax Reform, and a Defence of the Income Tax', in R. Krever and D. White (eds.), *GST in Retrospect and Prospect* (Brookers, Wellington, 2007), 597, 630. For a fuller account of the relative advantages and disadvantages of both methods of taxation, see generally Sijbren Cnossen, 'VAT and RST: A Comparison', *Canadian Tax Journal* 35(3) (1987), 559; Arindam Das-Gupta and Ira N. Gang, 'A Comparison of Sales Taxes', *Public Finance* 51(2) (1996), 217; George R. Zodrow, 'The Sales Tax, the VAT, and Taxes in Between – Or, Is the Only Good NRST a "VAT in Drag"?' *National Tax Journal* 52(3) (1999), 429.

211 Ian Crawford, Michael Keen and Stephen Smith, 'Value Added Tax and Excises' in Stuart Adam et al. (eds.) for the Institute for Fiscal Studies, *Dimensions of Tax Design: The Mirrlees Review* (Oxford University Press, Oxford, 2010), 275, 295.

212 Ronald T. McMorran, 'A Comparison between the Sales Tax and a VAT', in P. Shome (ed.), *Tax Policy Handbook* (IMF, Washington, DC, 1995), 82, 85.

213 Michael Keen, 'What Do (and Don't) We Know about the Value Added Tax? A Review of Richard M. Bird and Pierre-Pascal Gendron's *The VAT in Developing and Transitional Countries*', *Journal of Economic Literature* 47(1) (2009), 159, 162.

214 Carl S. Shoup, *Public Finance* (Aldine Publishing Company, Chicago, 1969), 259. *Contra* Ebrill et al., who note that Oldman and Schenk see the ill fit between the accounts-based subtraction-type VAT and differential rates as being a reason to favour subtraction-type VATs to minimise multiple rates: Liam Ebrill et al., *The Modern VAT* (IMF, Washington, DC, 2001), 21.

215 Liam Ebrill et al., *The Modern VAT* (IMF, Washington, DC, 2001), 22; Clara K. Sullivan, *The Tax on Value Added* (New York, 1965), 32.

regardless of their place of production. This differs from taxing goods and services at their *origin*, namely the jurisdiction where the goods or services are produced.[216]

The destination method is favoured by the conventional approach because it is viewed as more readily compatible with taxing domestic consumption[217] and is said to preserve production efficiency by taxing the supply of both foreign and domestic producers equally.[218] In addition, the destination principle is said to facilitate international trade by removing VAT from exports and treating imports on par with domestically produced goods.[219] This is, in turn, consistent with international

216 The origin principle taxes equally all products that share the same origin, regardless of where they are consumed: Clara K. Sullivan, *The Tax on Value Added* (New York, 1965), 30; Liam Ebrill et al., *The Modern VAT* (IMF, Washington, DC, 2001), 176–77. The result is that exports are taxed and imports are not taxed, thus obviating the need for border tax adjustments: Alan Schenk and Oliver Oldman, *Value Added Tax: A Comparative Approach* (rev. edn., Cambridge University Press, Cambridge; New York, 2007), 183. Although the destination principle is thought more suitable to the invoice-credit mechanism, the difference in compatibility between the various methods and the jurisdictional reach of the tax might not necessarily be as great as it might first seem. However, this technical debate goes beyond the scope of this book. See generally Carl S. Shoup, *Public Finance* (Aldine Publishing Company, Chicago, 1969), 9, 263–64; Carl S. Shoup, 'Choosing among Types of VATs', in M. Gillis, C. S. Shoup and G. P. Sicat (eds.), *Value Added Taxation in Developing Countries (A World Bank Symposium)* (World Bank, Washington, DC, 1990), 3, 7; Liam Ebrill et al., *The Modern VAT* (IMF, Washington, DC, 2001), 179–81; Sullivan at 35–36; Richard Bird and Pierre-Pascal Gendron, *The VAT in Developing and Transitional Countries* (Cambridge University Press, New York, 2007), 52.

217 Crawford et al. note that '[t]he international norm is for commodities to be taxed where they are consumed: the destination principle': Ian Crawford, Michael Keen and Stephen Smith, 'Value Added Tax and Excises', in Stuart Adam et al. (eds.) for the Institute for Fiscal Studies, *Dimensions of Tax Design: The Mirrlees Review* (Oxford University Press, Oxford, 2010), 275, 331; Sijbren Cnossen, 'Global Trends and Issues in Value Added Taxation', *International Tax and Public Finance* 5(3) (1998), 399–400; Liam Ebrill et al., *The Modern VAT* (IMF, Washington, DC, 2001), 176; International Tax Dialogue (ITD), 'The Value Added Tax: Experience and Issues' (Background Paper Prepared for the International Tax Dialogue Conference on the VAT, Rome, March 15–16, 2005, ITD), 19; OECD, *Consumption Tax Trends 2012: VAT/GST and Excise Rates, Trends and Administration Issues* (OECD Publishing, Paris, 2012), 34–35; LeJeune et al. note that '[t]he application of the destination principle for international trade in services is certainly not questioned and should always be the base for VAT design in order to remove trade distortions or discrimination': Ine Lejeune, Jeanine Daou-Azzi and Mark Powell (of PricewaterhouseCoopers), 'The Balance Has Shifted to Consumption Taxes – Lessons Learned and Best Practices for VAT', in M. Lang, P. Melz and E. Kristoffersson (eds.), *Value Added Tax and Direct Taxation: Similarities and Differences* (IBFD, Amsterdam, 2009), 59, 86.

218 International Tax Dialogue (ITD), 'The Value Added Tax: Experience and Issues' (Background Paper Prepared for the International Tax Dialogue Conference on the VAT, Rome, March 15–16, 2005, ITD), 19. A consumption VAT in an open economy (where imports are taxed and exports are not) should equate with total domestic retail sales. It will not equate to value added in the economy (unless exports equal imports): Carl S. Shoup, 'Choosing among Types of VATs', in M. Gillis, C. S. Shoup and G. P. Sicat (eds.), *Value Added Taxation in Developing Countries (A World Bank Symposium)* (World Bank, Washington, DC, 1990), 3, 5.

219 Liam Ebrill et al., *The Modern VAT* (IMF, Washington, DC, 2001), 177; Alan A. Tait, *Value Added Tax: International Practice and Problems* (IMF, Washington, DC, 1988), 33. Some

trading rules developed under the General Agreement on Tariffs and Trade (GATT) and later through the World Trade Organization (WTO). Those rules accept the classification of the VAT as an 'indirect' tax and therefore enable signatory countries to refund VAT to exporters without offending rules prohibiting export subsidies – an option not available for 'direct' taxes such as the corporate income tax.[220] This treatment, developed under GATT, suited trade-active European countries heavily reliant on indirect taxes and was justified on the basis that the VAT component on goods for export is able to be more accurately identified and therefore refunded because it is reflected in the price of the goods or services (unlike a direct tax).[221] The treatment of VAT under these rules also reflects a perception of the VAT as a consumption tax and thereby implicitly accepts the contention that VAT is forward shifted to consumers.[222]

The practical result of a destination VAT is that exports remain tax free but imports attract VAT, which is achieved practically through zero-rating exports. The invoice-credit mechanism, which allows for zero-rating on a transaction-by-transaction basis, enables the accurate identification of tax already paid (to facilitate refunds on exports and the appropriate taxation of imports). Exporters can thus claim credit for VAT paid on inputs, meaning that exporters would usually be entitled to VAT refunds. An RST can achieve the same result through suspending the tax on exports.[223]

The destination principle requires effective rules governing the place of supply to effectively determine the place of consumption.[224] Destination-based VATs have traditionally been administratively dependent on borders, and more specifically

contend that this provides VAT jurisdictions with an advantage over non-VAT jurisdictions; however, the basis for the claim is not strong: see above, n 45.

[220] WTO rules restrict a contracting party's ability to grant subsidies to exports or to impose more burdensome taxes on imports than domestic goods. However, border tax adjustments for indirect taxes do not constitute subsidies for exports, nor do they disadvantage imports under WTO rules (provided that the refund does not exceed the rate of VAT imposed on imported and domestic goods). According to the WTO classification, indirect taxes include VAT, while direct taxes include all forms of income taxation, including taxes on wages, profits, interests, rents, royalties, and taxes on the ownership of real property: *Marrakesh Agreement Establishing the World Trade Organization*, opened for signature 15 April 1994, 1867 UNTS 3 (entered into force 1 January 1995), Annex 1A 'Agreement on Subsidies and Countervailing Measures', Annex I (Illustrative list of Export Subsidies, item (e), n 58 and 'General Agreement on Tariffs and Trade 1994' Article 16(4).

[221] OECD, *Consumption Tax Trends 2012: VAT/GST and Excise Rates, Trends and Administration Issues* (OECD Publishing, Paris, 2012), 34.

[222] See §4 of this chapter.

[223] Richard Krever, 'Designing and Drafting VAT Laws for Africa', in R. Krever (ed.), *VAT in Africa* (Pretoria University Law Press, Pretoria, 2008), 9, 12.

[224] See, e.g., §12 of the *New Vatopia Model*, which provides that 'a supply of goods takes place where the goods are delivered or made available by the supplier or, if the delivery or making available involves the goods being transported, the place where the goods are when the transportation commences': Alan Schenk and Members of the IMF Legal Department, *Value Added Tax Act of the Commonwealth of New Vatopia* (IMF, 2006).

effective VAT-adjustment facilities at borders (to refund VAT on exports and collect VAT on imports). Chapter 3 demonstrates how many real-world changes that postdate the inception of the good VAT, such as the rapid expansion in the trade of intangible goods and cross-border services, have severely undermined the effectiveness of these border controls. As a result, the application of the destination principle presents another frontier issue that tests the limits of the good VAT.

7 CONCLUSION

This chapter detailed the preference within the conventional approach for the good VAT. The conventional approach rates the good VAT highly against traditional public finance criteria on the basis of a strong preference for consumption taxation (over income taxation) and a belief that the good VAT is the most neutral and efficient method by which to tax consumption. The good VAT is rated most highly for its revenue-generation capability, neutrality and efficiency. Although rated less highly on the measures of simplicity and vertical equity, the consensus position within the conventional approach is that the good VAT's perceived advantages strongly outweigh its weaknesses. This chapter outlined the three interdependent design norms posited by the conventional approach which, if met, should combine to produce the good VAT – that is, the good VAT should tax a broad consumption base at a single rate through the invoice-credit method on a destination basis. The next chapter explores the extent to which the good VAT is realised in practice.

3

An introduction to the many real VATs in existence

Chapter 2 revealed how the *conventional approach* is committed to a narrow definition of the *good VAT* and to the three design norms that underpin it. By contrast, a review of the conventional approach's own assessment of *real VATs* against the prescriptions and promised merits of the *good VAT* reveals an entirely different approach – one where the conventional approach is forced to broaden definitions and design criteria to accommodate the reality of *real VATs*. The deliberately plural term *real VATs* is intended to encompass the variety of VATs that exist in practice.[1] As this chapter shows, though it is possible to speak of one *good VAT*, it is only possible to speak of many *real VATs*. The analysis demonstrates that, even on the conventional approach's own assessment, few *real VATs* resemble the prescriptions or promises of the *good VAT*. The implications of this finding for the *conventional approach*'s merits-based explanation of the VAT's rise are explored in Chapter 4.

1 DEFINING REAL VATS

Chapter 2 demonstrated that the *conventional approach* is committed to a narrow definition of the *good VAT*, which is defined by reference to the three design norms, so that the *good VAT* is a broad-based consumption tax levied incrementally at each stage of the production and distribution chain through the invoice-credit method and imposed on a destination basis. However, in order to provide a definition able to encompass the diversity of *real VATs* that have actually been implemented, the *conventional approach* is forced to offer a much broader definition.

[1] Bird and Gendron state that the 'real tax system is that which is administered, not that which appears in formal law': Richard Bird and Pierre-Pascal Gendron, *The VAT in Developing and Transitional Countries* (Cambridge University Press, New York, 2007), 8.

In an effort to reflect the reality that the label of VAT 'may cover a variety of taxes in different countries',[2] the *ITD VAT Paper* offers an alternative definition of the VAT:[3]

> ...the VATs observed in practice exhibit considerable diversity as regards, inter alia, the base of the tax and the range of economic activity to which the tax applies. As a result, there can be room for disagreement as to whether a given tax is properly called a VAT or not. This paper takes a VAT to be: a broad-based tax levied on sales up to and including, at least, the *manufacturing stage*, with *systematic offsetting* of tax charged on inputs—*except perhaps on capital goods*—against that due on outputs.

The attempt to provide a definition broad enough to encompass *real VATs* includes VATs that depart from all three of the design norms of the *good VAT*. It introduces VATs levied on bases other than consumption, as seen by the possible exclusion of capital goods and the acknowledgement that VATs can be levied below the retail stage. The inclusion of VATs levied below the retail level may also include VATs that depart from the third design norm of levying the VAT on a destination basis. For example, a VAT levied below the retail level is not necessarily accurately reflected in the price of a good, and therefore may not be able to be accurately refunded to the exporter of that good.[4] Moreover, the definition is also broad enough to include VATs levied other than through the invoice-credit method (for example, a subtraction accounts-based VAT can satisfy the systematic offsetting of VAT charged on inputs), therefore including VATs that depart from the second design norm.

The inability to articulate a consistent definition that encompasses both the *good VAT* and *real VATs* reveals a profound tension in the *conventional approach*: on the

[2] Ibid., 10. The authors go on to state that 'Like the personal income tax, a VAT is not so much a single tax as a set of taxes that share certain characteristics. To put the point in zoological terms, VAT is neither a gorilla nor a chimpanzee but rather a genus of like "primates".'

[3] International Tax Dialogue (ITD), 'The Value Added Tax: Experience and Issues' (Background Paper Prepared for the International Tax Dialogue Conference on the VAT, Rome, March 15–16, 2005, ITD) (hereafter referred to as the *ITD VAT Paper*), 7 (emphasis altered). The definition is adopted elsewhere within the conventional approach and is almost identical to that adopted by Ebrill et al.:

> A broad-based tax levied on commodity sales up to and including, at least, the manufacturing stage, with systematic offsetting of tax charged on commodities purchased as inputs – except perhaps on capital goods – against that due on outputs.

Liam Ebrill et al., *The Modern VAT* (IMF, Washington, DC, 2001), 2. This definition is adopted by the OECD: OECD, *Consumption Tax Trends 2008 – VAT/GST and Excise Rates, Trends and Administration Issues* (OECD, Paris, 2008), 23; see also OECD, *Consumption Tax Trends 2012: VAT/GST and Excise Rates, Trends and Administration Issues* (OECD Publishing, Paris, 2012), 31; Michael Keen and Ben Lockwood, 'The Value Added Tax: Its Causes and Consequences', *Journal of Development Economics* 92(2) (2010), 138, 139; Michael Keen, 'What Do (and Don't) We Know about the Value Added Tax? A Review of Richard M. Bird and Pierre-Pascal Gendron's *The VAT in Developing and Transitional Countries*', *Journal of Economic Literature* 47(1) (2009), 159, 162.

[4] See Chapter 2, §4.1, n 87, for an explanation of why sales taxes levied at below the retail stage make it difficult to accurately refund VAT incurred on exports.

one hand, the VAT has spread everywhere because it is good; on the other hand, very few jurisdictions adopt the *good VAT*. In accounting for the VAT's success, commentators are forced to include VATs that do not meet their own criteria of the *good VAT*. This complicates the accurate measurement of the rise of the VAT, because as the *ITD VAT Paper* acknowledges there is controversy in relation to whether a tax is properly characterized as a VAT.[5] Krever contends that:[6]

> There is undoubtedly some exaggeration of the numbers. Many so-called VAT systems are in reality turnover taxes without full credits for tax on inputs or are really mislabeled manufacturers or wholesale sales taxes.

Defining *real VATs* is not merely of academic interest; for example, access to IMF assistance can be conditional on the adoption of a VAT.[7]

The next section considers how the *conventional approach* assesses whether these *real VATs* realise the promised merits of the *good VAT*.

2 MEASURING THE MERITS OF REAL VATS

Chapter 2 detailed the favourable assessment of the merits of the good VAT by the conventional approach against public finance criteria. This favourable assessment was informed by some key preferences that, when combined, amounted to a strong preference for a neutral and efficient consumption tax base.[8]

The extent to which real VATs have realised the merits promised of the good VAT has not been subject to much investigation by the conventional approach. Keen nonetheless acknowledges the need to examine real VATs:[9]

> If it functions as it should, any VAT is indeed simply a uniform tax on final consumption, to which all our simple textbook models in principle apply. But a less than perfectly functioning VAT is an analytical mess, with particularities of production relationships and compliance behavior immediately becoming key. And it is imperfectly functioning VATs that we observe in practice and need to understand better.

Those within the conventional approach who have considered the manner in which real VATs measure against traditional public finance criteria generally present a fairly negative assessment. This negative assessment is a product of the

[5] Liam Ebrill et al., *The Modern VAT* (IMF, Washington, DC, 2001), 2; OECD, *Consumption Tax Trends 2012: VAT/GST and Excise Rates, Trends and Administration Issues* (OECD Publishing, Paris, 2012), 31.

[6] Richard Krever, 'Understanding Chinese VAT Law: Lessons from Abroad', in X. Yang (ed.), *China VAT Law: Reform and Justice* (China Taxation Publishing House, Beijing, 2007), 19.

[7] Liam Ebrill et al., *The Modern VAT* (IMF, Washington, DC, 2001), 2; Richard Krever, 'Designing and Drafting VAT Laws for Africa', in R. Krever (ed.), *VAT in Africa* (Pretoria University Law Press, Pretoria, 2008), 9, 13.

[8] See Chapter 2, §2 of this book.

[9] Michael Keen, 'VAT Attacks!' (Working Paper No. WP/07/142, IMF, 2007), 18.

departures in real VATs from the three design norms of the good VAT. This section introduces these assessment of the merits of real VATs by the conventional approach against these public finance criteria. The sources of the departures from these ideals are canvassed in the discussion of the three design norms in §3 to §6.

2.1 *Preference for consumption*

Chapter 2 outlined the strong preference within the conventional approach for consumption taxes over income taxes. As this chapter reveals, many of the putative theoretical benefits of consumption taxes that underlie support within the conventional approach for the good VAT are undermined in practice by real VATs. For example, §6 of this chapter demonstrates how the difficulties with levying VAT on an increasing number of cross-border supplies undermine the strength of the proposition that consumption taxes offer a less mobile and more stable base than the income tax. The professed simplicity of consumption taxes relative to the income tax is undermined not just by the complexity of real VATs in practice but by the fact that attempts to find solutions to frontier issues such as the taxation of financial supplies repeatedly turn on complex conceptual issues over what constitutes consumption.[10] In addition, this chapter provides numerous instances (introduced at §2.3) of how the perceived neutrality of the VAT is undermined in practice.

In addition, many of the benefits of the good VAT are in effect indirect benefits said to derive from replacing 'inferior' taxes such as tariffs, single-stage sales taxes or cascading turnover taxes.[11] The data for OECD countries in Table 3.1 show that VAT revenue as a share of total tax revenue has risen from 2 per cent in 1965 to 19 per cent in 2010. However, the data do not reveal any clear and sustained tax mix trends, with the revenue share of income and consumption taxes remaining relatively stable over the period. Despite a small drop in revenue from the personal income tax, the figures more clearly reveal that, at this stage, increasing VAT revenue has replaced revenue from specific consumption taxes, which has fallen dramatically over the period.[12] More recent reform discussion in the EU has focused on 'fiscal devaluation' through increasing reliance on VAT revenue and decreasing reliance on taxes on labour, namely social security taxes, as a short-term measure to stimulate economic growth (on the assumption that the former is less

[10] Richard Krever and Rita de la Feria, 'Ending VAT Exemptions: Towards a Post-Modern VAT', in R. de la Feria (ed.), *VAT Exemptions: Consequences and Design Alternatives* (vol. 37, EUCOTAX Series on European Taxation, Kluwer Law International, Alphen aan den Rijn, 2013), 3, 35.

[11] See Chapter 2, §2 of this book. OECD, *Consumption Tax Trends 2012: VAT/GST and Excise Rates, Trends and Administration Issues* (OECD Publishing, Paris, 2012), 70.

[12] *Contra* a UN Report finds a decline in the ratio of income taxes to VAT in developed countries from 2.42 in the period from 1981 to 1985 to 1.70 in the period from 2006 to 2010: Secretariat – United Nations Conference on Trade and Development, *Trade and Development Report, 2012* (UNCTAD/TDR/2012) (United Nations Publications, Geneva, 2012), 116, Table 5.1.

TABLE 3.1 – *Major taxes as a percentage of tax revenue share in the OECD (unweighted average)*

	1965	1975	1985	1995	2005	2010
Personal income tax	26	30	30	26	24	24
Corporate income tax	9	8	8	8	10	9
Social security contributions	18	22	22	25	25	26
Payroll taxes	1	1	1	1	1	1
Property taxes	8	6	5	5	6	5
General consumption taxes	12	13	16	20	20	20
VAT component of general consumption taxes	2	9	11	17	19	19
Specific consumption taxes	24	18	16	13	11	11
Other taxes	2	2	2	3	3	3

harmful to growth than the latter). Although some reforms have occurred in this direction, no major shifts are detectible.[13,14]

Although results vary, data in relation to developing countries tend to show increasing reliance on general consumption taxes, such as the VAT, but also an increasing reliance on the income tax, albeit from a much lower base than in most developed economies.[15] Therefore, the extent to which the VAT has facilitated a significant change in the tax mix among developing countries is also unclear.[16]

[13] European Commission (EC), Directorate-General for Economic and Financial Affairs, Directorate General for Taxation and Customs Union, *Tax Reforms in EU Member States: Tax Policy Challenges for Economic Growth and Fiscal Sustainability – 2013 Report* (EC, Brussels, 2013), 11, 17–20. See generally Michael Keen and Ruud de Mooij, '"Fiscal Devaluation" and Fiscal Consolidation: The VAT in Troubled Times', in Alberto Alesina and Francesco Giavazzi (eds.), *Fiscal Policy After the Financial Crisis* (University of Chicago Press, 2013), 443, 444.

[14] OECD, *Consumption Tax Trends 2012: VAT/GST and Excise Rates, Trends and Administration Issues* (OECD Publishing, Paris, 2012), Table 3.7, 67; OECD, *Revenue Statistics: 1965–2011* (OECD, Paris, 2012), Table C, 23. 'Other taxes' includes certain taxes on goods and services as well as stamp taxes. Reproduced with permission: OECD (2012), *Consumption Tax Trends 2012: VAT/GST and Excise Rates, Trends and Administration Issues*, OECD Publishing, dx.doi.org/10.1787/ctt-2012-en; OECD (2012), *Revenue Statistics 2012*, OECD Publishing,

[15] Richard Bird and Pierre-Pascal Gendron, *The VAT in Developing and Transitional Countries* (Cambridge University Press, New York, 2007), 18. UNCTAD reports that the ratio of income tax to VAT has varied according to different regions for the period 1991–2010. The ratio remained relatively low but variable in Latin America (at 0.64 for 2006–2010, which reversed a decline from 0.60 to 0.56 from 1991 to 2005) and in East, South and South East Asia (at 1.11 for 2006–2010). The ratio declined in West Asia from 0.56 for 1996–2000 to 0.48 for 2006–2010. The ratio has risen steadily in African economies (from 0.91 from 1991 to 1995 to 1.15 for 2006–2010): Secretariat – United Nations Conference on Trade and Development, *Trade and Development Report, 2012* (UNCTAD/TDR/2012) (United Nations Publications, Geneva, 2012), Table 5.2, 117, 120–121.

[16] Richard Bird and Pierre-Pascal Gendron, *The VAT in Developing and Transitional Countries* (Cambridge University Press, New York, 2007), 19.

2.2 *Revenue generation*

Despite the VAT's reputation as a 'money machine',[17] there is surprisingly little empirical evidence in support of the claim.[18] While this might result in part from the difficulty of reliably measuring the VAT's revenue impact,[19] some of those who have attempted to do so express surprise at the lack of empirical attention to the issue, given that there exist a 'relatively rich data on the VAT revenue performance' in the form of government finance statistics and the wealth of data collected by organisations such as the IMF, the World Bank and the OECD.[20]

The results of the research from those who have assessed the revenue-generating capacity of real VATs are mixed at best. Most find that real VATs have a slightly positive effect on revenue but different measurements yield different results.[21] Keen

[17] United States. President's Advisory Panel on Federal Tax Reform, *Simple, Fair, and Pro-Growth: Proposals to Fix America's Tax System* (2005), 192; Michael Keen and Ben Lockwood, 'Is the VAT a Money Machine?' *National Tax Journal* 69(4) (2006), 905.

[18] Ebrill et al. observe that the question as to whether countries with VATs raise more revenue has been little studied: Liam Ebrill et al., *The Modern VAT* (IMF, Washington, DC, 2001), 29; Bogetic and Hassan note that 'very few studies have empirically tested some basic hypotheses about key features and the performance of VAT as a revenue-raising instrument': Zeljko Bogetic and Fareed Hassan, 'Determinants of Value-Added Tax Revenue: A Cross-Section Analysis' (Policy Research Working Paper No. WPS 1203, Washington, DC, 1993), 1; David Nellor, 'The Effect of Value-Added Tax on the Tax Ratio' (IMF Working Paper No. 87/47, Washington, DC, 1987). Riswold provides a critical account:

> Even as recent as 1998, the IMF noted that the revenue raising potential of VAT has proven to be substantial for economies at all levels of economic development. Yet, in the same report, it notes that determining the revenue performance of VAT is subject to difficulties in assessing the quality of a particular VAT from available data and only over the medium to long term might revenue be expected to grow given the greater revenue buoyancy built into well-designed tax reforms.

Scott Riswold, 'VAT in Sub-Saharan Africa – A Critique of IMF VAT Policy', *International VAT Monitor* (March/April 2004), 97, 101, and at 103.

[19] Measurement can be complicated by the fact that some countries, such as Australia, introduce VAT as part of a revenue-neutral or even revenue-negative reform package. In addition, it is difficult to find a reliable comparator by which to measure the VAT's revenue performance. Options might range from the revenue performance of the tax system prior to VAT (which may be influenced by a range of factors including any other reforms introduced alongside VAT) to measuring the revenue performance of countries with a VAT to countries without a VAT – which are so few they offer an unreliable measure: Liam Ebrill et al., *The Modern VAT* (IMF, Washington, DC, 2001), 25–29; Michael Keen and Ben Lockwood, 'The Value Added Tax: Its Causes and Consequences', *Journal of Development Economics* 92(2) (2010), 138, 141.

[20] Zeljko Bogetic and Fareed Hassan, 'Determinants of Value-Added Tax Revenue: A Cross-Section Analysis' (Policy Research Working Paper No. WPS 1203, Washington, DC, 1993), 1–2.

[21] Bird and Gendron contend that 'the effects on revenue of VAT remain open to interpretation': Richard Bird and Pierre-Pascal Gendron, *The VAT in Developing and Transitional Countries* (Cambridge University Press, New York, 2007), 55–56; Ebeke and Ehrhart find a positive effect on revenue stability: Christian Ebeke and Helene Ehrhart, 'Does VAT reduce the Instability of Tax Revenues?' (online paper – E 2011.24, Centre for Studies and Research on

and Lockwood survey 143 countries and find that the introduction of a VAT generally (but not always) results in 'significantly positive but fairly modest' revenue gains.[22] Ebrill et al. find 'mixed evidence'[23] as to whether the VAT increases revenues in a study of 183 countries.[24] A more recent study by Keen notes that average VAT revenues have increased in countries with a VAT across all income groups from 1993 to 2012, with the most significant gains in low income (from 3 to 5 per cent of GDP), lower-middle income (from 3 to 6 per cent of GDP) and upper-middle income countries (from 4 to 7 per cent of GDP). VAT revenues in high-income countries remainedrelatively stable (from 6.5 to 7.5 GDP).[25]

All agree that the extent of the revenue gain varies with a country's circumstances.[26] Keen and Lockwood, for example, find that the VAT has a negative

International Development, 2011), 15. Kloeden finds that VATs in Anglophone Africa have 'proven to be an important revenue source for all countries that have adopted it, often being generated from a relatively small pool of taxpayers': David Kloeden, 'Revenue Administration Reforms in Anglophone Africa Since the Early 1990s' (Working Paper WP/11/162, IMF, 2011), 44. Riswold criticises the 'rather inadequate attempts to support the revenue-raising potential of VAT' for failing to specify the time period over which the study occurred and 'the weakness of cross-country regression models': Scott Riswold, 'VAT in Sub-Saharan Africa – A Critique of IMF VAT Policy', *International VAT Monitor* (March/April 2004), 97, 102.

22 Michael Keen and Ben Lockwood, 'The Value Added Tax: Its Causes and Consequences', *Journal of Development Economics* 92(2) (2010), 138, 148. The authors note that usable panel data do not exist to encompass the variety of real VATs to control for variances in rates, exemptions, thresholds, extension through the production and distribution chain and refund facilities: 142. *Contra* Ebrill et al. find impressive revenue gains for select countries when measured against predecessor sales taxes (excluding Baltic states, Russia and other countries of the former Soviet Union): Liam Ebrill et al., *The Modern VAT* (IMF, Washington, DC, 2001), 26–27. *Contra* Riswold, who labels this measure 'very misleading' because the comparison is made only between the VAT and previous sales taxes rather than all the taxes (including trade taxes) VAT has replaced: Scott Riswold, 'VAT in Sub-Saharan Africa – A Critique of IMF VAT Policy', *International VAT Monitor* (March/April 2004), 97, 101. Across other measures, Ebrill et al. find the results mixed: at 27–38.

23 Liam Ebrill et al., *The Modern VAT* (IMF, Washington, DC, 2001), 33.

24 Ibid., 37–39, ch. 3. Bogetic and Hassan find that one percentage point of VAT raises an average of 0.35 per cent of GDP revenue across 49 countries: Zeljko Bogetic and Fareed Hassan, 'Determinants of Value-Added Tax Revenue: A Cross-Section Analysis' (Policy Research Working Paper No. WPS 1203, Washington, DC, 1993), 2–3. For more up-to-date estimates, see the '*Collecting Taxes Data System*' provided by the 'Fiscal Reform and Economic Governance' – a joint project funded by USAID (United States Agency for International Development): USAID, Fiscal Reform and Economic Governance, Collecting Taxes Data System (2010) (www.fiscalreform.net/index.php?option=com_wrapper&Itemid=132)

25 Michael Keen, 'The Anatomy of VAT' (Working Paper No. WP/13/111, International Monetary Fund, 2013), 4. The author attributes the increases to improvements in the C-efficiency ratio (see §4.1) rather than an increase in VAT rates over the period: at 8.

26 Ibid., 4; Michael Keen and Ben Lockwood, 'The Value Added Tax: Its Causes and Consequences', *Journal of Development Economics* 92(2) (2010), 138, 148. Ebrill et al. find that revenue performance increases with a number of different factors that include increases in the standard VAT rate (with a 1 per cent increase in VAT rate resulting in a 0.6 per cent rise in the ratio of VAT revenues to private consumption); the importance of trade to the economy (because it offers a collection point on imports); the age of the VAT; literacy (as a rough indicator of the administrative capacity of a country): Liam Ebrill et al., *The Modern VAT*

impact on closed and low-income economies,[27] but a positive effect on high-income and open economies.[28] Among OECD countries, Keen and Lockwood find some signs that the VAT is a money machine (in the weak sense that countries with a VAT tend to raise more revenue than those without)[29] but add that the evidence is not overpowering and the impact of a VAT is subject to country-specific characteristics.[30] The authors find no 'strong evidence' in 'a purely statistical sense' of the VAT being a money machine in the strong sense. That is, they do not find 'that the VAT has in itself *caused* the growth of government'.[31]

(IMF, Washington, DC, 2001), 47–48; International Tax Dialogue (ITD), 'The Value Added Tax: Experience and Issues' (Background Paper Prepared for the International Tax Dialogue Conference on the VAT, Rome, March 15–16, 2005, ITD), 11–12.

27 Michael Keen and Ben Lockwood, 'The Value Added Tax: Its Causes and Consequences', *Journal of Development Economics* 92(2) (2010), 138, 148. This is supported by studies that have found that the adoption of VATs across Latin America has led to a decrease rather than increase in revenues over the past few decades: Richard Bird and Pierre-Pascal Gendron, *The VAT in Developing and Transitional Countries* (Cambridge University Press, New York, 2007), 195; Eduardo Lora, Inter-American Development Bank (IDB) 'Decade of Structural Reforms in Latin America: What Has Been Reformed and How to Measure It' (Working Paper Green Series No 348, IDB, 1997), 6. *Contra* Keen and Lockwood, who predict strong VAT revenue gains in the Americas: at 147. This is not true of all countries; for example, Bird and Gendron cite studies that show the Colombian VAT resulted in a real increase in taxation revenue: at 199.

28 This result is also supported by Ebrill et al., *The Modern VAT* (IMF, Washington, DC, 2001), 32. Keen and Lockwood predict that, on the basis of their future revenue projections, VAT should improve revenues for most countries (with the exception of sub-Saharan Africa): Michael Keen and Ben Lockwood, 'The Value Added Tax: Its Causes and Consequences', *Journal of Development Economics* 92(2) (2010), 138, 147–48. *Contra* Christian Ebeke and Helene Ehrhart, 'Does VAT Reduce the Instability of Tax Revenues?' (online paper – E 2011.24, Centre for Studies and Research on International Development, 2011), 14.

29 Michael Keen and Ben Lockwood, 'Is the VAT a Money Machine?' *National Tax Journal* 69 (4) (2006), 905, 910.

30 Ibid., 911, 917, 924. The authors conjecture that the weakness of the evidence for the weak hypothesis is because gains in VAT revenue are offset by reductions in other 'less effective' tax instruments: at 925. Despite the underwhelming nature of the findings, this study is frequently cited by those within the conventional approach as evidence for the claim as to the VAT's revenue-generating capability: see, e.g., Michael Keen and Ruud de Mooij, '"Fiscal Devaluation" and Fiscal Consolidation: The VAT in Troubled Times', in Alberto Alesina and Francesco Giavazzi (eds.), *Fiscal Policy After the Financial Crisis* (University of Chicago Press, 2013), 443, 466.

31 Ibid., 917, 925. The authors find some preliminary support for this thesis because the share of taxes and social security contributions to GDP has increased across the OECD by an average of six points between the years prior to the introduction of VAT and the year 2003. However, the authors find that the increase in the overall tax ratio is less than the increased revenues raised by VAT because around two-thirds of VAT revenue is used to offset reductions in other taxes rather than fund an increase in government: at 910–11. This trend is identified by Sullivan: Martin A. Sullivan, 'Was the VAT a Money Machine for Europe?' *Tax Notes* (2012), 143. Presumably referring to the Keen and Lockwood research, the *ITD VAT Paper* tentatively concludes that 'there is some evidence that the presence of a VAT has been associated with a higher ratio of general government revenue and grants to GDP:' International Tax Dialogue (ITD), 'The Value Added Tax: Experience and Issues' (Background Paper Prepared for the International Tax Dialogue Conference on the VAT, Rome, March 15–16, 2005, ITD), 11. A more recent study of 21 OECD economies over the period 1960–1997

The surprisingly underwhelming effect of real VATs on revenue generation is attributed to departures from the three design norms of the good VAT. Ebrill et al. find that the mixed results on revenue performance 'naturally reflect the fact that they [the studies] are based on VATs that have been implemented in practice, rather than some ideal VAT'.[32] Bogetic and Hassan find that the VAT's revenue generation is both a product of the extent of compliance with design norms and a strong tax administration.[33] The departures that undermine the performance of real VATs are detailed in §4 to §6 and include widespread exclusions to the VAT base (norm 1); the high rather than low visibility of the VAT (norm 2);[34] the practical difficulties in administering real VATs, including the susceptibility of VAT to avoidance and evasion (norm 2); and the difficulties of levying a VAT on cross-border supplies of intangible goods and tradable services (norms 2 and 3).

Perhaps in response to the inconclusive evidence of the VAT's capacity to generate revenue, Ebrill et al. contend:[35]

> The performance of a tax must be gauged by more than the revenue it raises. It must also be assessed in terms of the efficiency and fairness with which it raises that revenue, and the cost incurred by government and taxpayer in doing so.

However, the conventional approach's assessment suggests that real VATs fare not much better against these other measures.

2.3 *Neutrality*

Whereas the good VAT rates highly on neutrality in the sense of interfering least with market-based production and consumption decisions (see Chapter 2, §2.2.2), real VATs rank less favourably against this measure. As the discussion of norm 1 reveals, exclusions to the base do impact on production and consumption choices because different supplies are taxed differently (see §4). Delays in, or denials of,

found no evidence that a VAT contributed to the rate of government growth but rather found that the rate of government growth decelerates when the share of the VAT revenues in total tax revenues rises (and rises when the share of the general turnover tax revenues in total tax revenues rises): Ali Riza Ozdemir, 'The Effects of Value Added Tax on the Rate of Government Growth: An OECD Panel Study', *World Tax Journal* 4(3) (2012), 259, 271 (and the studies cited at 260 further supporting the finding).

32 Liam Ebrill et al., *The Modern VAT* (IMF, Washington, DC, 2001), 33.

33 Zeljko Bogetic and Fareed Hassan, 'Determinants of Value-Added Tax Revenue: A Cross-Section Analysis' (Policy Research Working Paper No. WPS 1203, Washington, DC, 1993), 10. See also Glenn P. Jenkins and Chun-Yan Kuo, 'A VAT Revenue Simulation Model for Tax Reform in Developing Countries', *World Development* 28(4) (2000), 763–764.

34 The claims that VAT is hidden in prices is described by Keen and Lockwood as 'simply wrong', as there is no reason that the VAT cannot be separately identified in the price charged to customers, as is done in Canada and Italy: Michael Keen and Ben Lockwood, 'Is the VAT a Money Machine?' *National Tax Journal* 69(4) (2006), 905, 911.

35 Liam Ebrill et al., *The Modern VAT* (IMF, Washington, DC, 2001), 25.

VAT refunds impact business (see §5), while difficulties relating to imposing real VATs on a destination basis undermine the VAT's trade neutrality (see §6).

2.4 *Efficiency*

As Chapter 2 explained, much of the conventional approach's support for the good VAT rests on favourable evaluations of the good VAT's efficiency.[36] Measuring the broader efficiency gains within the economy that result from the introduction of a VAT is difficult, and there is very little evidence to suggest that the introduction of real VATs translates into broader macro-economic efficiencies.[37] LeJeuene, Daou-Azzi and Powell highlight the issues:[38]

> Macroeconomic analysis of the benefits and impairments of tax reform are useful in terms of analysis of economic tax theory; however, in practice it is often difficult to obtain precise conclusions without extensive caveats or severely restricting inputs. In large part this is due to the wide variety of tax structures, rules, exemptions and actual practices adopted in each country, on top of more general issues of causation and relevance when it comes to broader economic analysis.

[36] See Chapter 2, §2.2.3 of this book.

[37] Ebrill et al. state that '[i]t is difficult to quantify the impact on economic efficiency of adopting a VAT': Liam Ebrill et al., *The Modern VAT* (IMF, Washington, DC, 2001), 27. In response, the authors look for indirect evidence in support of the claim by assuming that increases in revenue will imply efficiency gains based on the 'common presumption' that because the adoption of a VAT makes it easier to obtain revenue, an increase in VAT revenue would provide an increase in the efficiency of the overall tax system: at 33, 37. Both assumptions might be criticised for doing no more than attributing features of the good VAT to real VATs without showing that these features are realised by real VATs. However, given the modest finding on the revenue measure (see §2.2), the authors find that there is 'only mixed evidence that the adoption of VAT has been associated with higher revenues, and hence of an underlying efficiency gain from its use': at 33. See also Michael Keen and Ben Lockwood, 'The Value Added Tax: Its Causes and Consequences', *Journal of Development Economics* 92 (2) (2010), 138, 139–40. Riswold criticises measuring efficiency through revenue gains, as it is:

> a very weak measure of efficiency. The simple fact that tax revenues increase with the presence of a VAT, does in no way imply increased efficiency...The revenue and efficiency arguments are linked by the notion that revenue gains result in efficiency gains. Without a strong revenue argument, the efficiency argument becomes very weak.

Scott Riswold, 'VAT in Sub-Saharan Africa – A Critique of IMF VAT Policy', *International VAT Monitor* 97 (March/April 2004), 103, 108. Such criticisms have prompted some within the conventional approach to insert some caveats on the efficiency claims that acknowledge that potential efficiency gains might vary with the quality of the VAT in place: see, e.g., Michael Keen and Ben Lockwood, 'The Value Added Tax: Its Causes and Consequences', *Journal of Development Economics* 92(2) (2010), 138, 142–43.

[38] Ine Lejeune, Jeanine Daou-Azzi and Mark Powell (of PricewaterhouseCoopers), 'The Balance Has Shifted to Consumption Taxes – Lessons Learned and Best Practices for VAT ', in M. Lang, P. Melz and E. Kristoffersson (eds.), *Value Added Tax and Direct Taxation: Similarities and Differences* (IBFD, Vienna, 2009), 3 (emphasis added).

This is possibly true of VAT *more than other taxes*, given the large variance in factors such as the breadth of exemptions, multiple rates, tax base and general complexity of the model. Other factors relate to more practical matters such as the level of sophistication of the tax administration and businesses collecting the tax and economic circumstances prevailing at the time of introduction.

Given that the evidence in support of the broader macroeconomic claims made of the VAT is unreliable, a more reliable measure might be to assess the efficiency of the VAT itself. However, Edmiston and Fox highlight that many analyses do so by reference to the good VAT rather than real VATs:[39]

> Expected efficiency gains (reduction in efficiency losses) have been an important argument for replacing other taxes, and particularly sales taxes, with the VAT. However, the defense of these gains is often drawn from theoretical analysis of an optimal VAT and from indirect evidence but not from actual VAT practices. For example, Ebrill et al. (2001, p. 27) partly defend the efficiency gains from replacing a sales tax with a VAT by comparing the gains from sales taxes as they are actually imposed with a uniform consumption tax. But, VATs, like every other tax, are legislated in political environments where the resulting structure contains a series of warts as viewed from the economist's perspective. Analysis of both the gains and the consequences of imposing VATs is most usefully accomplished in the context of the taxes as they are actually levied. Then, the efficiency gains that would result from a more efficient structure can also be evaluated, but as the difference between actual practice and the economist's ideal.

Nevertheless, the conventional approach has employed some real-world measures of efficiency, for example through assessing the extent to which real VATs reach a consumption base (see §4.1) and through estimates of administration and compliance costs (see §5.3).[40] The assessment by the conventional approach against these measures is not necessarily positive.[41] Nevertheless, the response of the

[39] Kelly D. Edmiston and William F. Fox, 'A Fresh Look at the VAT', in J. Alm, J. Martínez-Vázquez and M. Rider (eds.), *The Challenges of Tax Reform in a Global Economy* (Springer, New York, 2006), 249.

[40] See, e.g., Ali Agha and Jonathan Haughton, 'Designing VAT Systems: Some Efficiency Considerations', *The Review of Economics and Statistics* 78(2) (1996), 303.

[41] Van Brederode concludes that '[o]verall, the efficiency of VAT systems. . .is not impressive': Robert F. van Brederode, *Systems of General Sales Taxation: Theory, Policy and Practice* (Kluwer Law International Alphen aan den Rijn, 2009), 50. Terra and Kajus contend that the 'efficiency of the value added tax above other tax instruments to influence consumption and production is not at all clear': Ben Terra and Julie Kajus, IBFD, *A Guide to the European VAT Directives* [online] (15 April 2011), 7.6.1.3; Aizenman and Jinjarak conclude that their paper does 'not negate the possibility of efficiency gains associated with greater reliance on a VAT. . . [but] points out that these gains are not automatic, and may depend on structural factors' (i.e., domestic circumstances): Joshua Aizenman and Yothin Jinjarak, 'The Collection Efficiency of the Value Added Tax: Theory and International Evidence', *Journal of International Trade and Economic Development* 17(3) (2008), 391, 406.

conventional approach to these less than favourable assessments is to urge that compliance with the design norms will produce the promised merits of the good VAT.

2.5 *Growth*

As Chapter 2 demonstrated, the argument that the good VAT is a growth tax extends beyond claims that the VAT grows with gross domestic product (GDP) (as does the income tax) but rather that the good VAT contributes to economic growth. Although increased economic growth should be reflected in an increase in GDP figures following the introduction of a VAT, given the number of factors that contribute to GDP, reliably measuring the impact of real VATs on economic growth is difficult.[42]

As Chapter 2, §2.2.4 explained, the claims as to the VAT's positive impact on economic growth generally rest on the perceived theoretical superiority of consumption taxes over other tax bases such as the income tax. The empirical evidence has been less forthcoming despite an intensity of effort to provide it. When an account is made of the reality of VATs in practice, the growth claims of the VAT become more difficult to sustain. For those who have attempted it, the empirical evidence in support of the claim that real VATs increase economic growth is inconclusive.[43] The postwar economic growth of the US is also an obvious

[42] Ebrill et al. observe that the magnitude of the VAT's impact on improved production efficiency (and therefore economic growth) is 'hard to gauge': Liam Ebrill et al., *The Modern VAT* (IMF, Washington, DC, 2001), 27; Peter H. Lindert, *Growing Public: Social Spending and Economic Growth since the Eighteenth Century* (Cambridge UK; New York, Cambridge University Press, 2004), 235.

[43] A UN report found that the introduction of a VAT along with other measures designed to reduce progressivity in the tax system resulted in neither greater overall efficiency nor higher growth: Secretariat – United Nations Conference on Trade and Development, *Trade and Development Report, 2012* (UNCTAD/TDR/2012) (United Nations Publications, Geneva, 2012), 118–19. *Contra* Richard Kneller, Michael F. Bleaney, Norman Gemmell, 'Fiscal Policy and Growth: Evidence from OECD Countries', *Journal of Public Economics* 74 (1999), 171 – the authors find in an empirical study of 22 OECD countries from 1970 to 1995 that non-distortive taxation (of which only taxes on domestic goods and services satisfy the criteria) has a positive effect on growth, but this is subject to a significant caveat that the result was sensitive to five-year averaging (so as to take out short-run factors), and the authors therefore recommend that 'considerable caution should be exercised in predicting the precise growth effects of fiscal changes': at 188. The results also suggest that the impact of tax structure on growth cannot be divorced from the impact of spending policies. The authors conclude by stating that their lowest estimates suggest that a 1 per cent per GDP reduction in distortionary taxes can increase growth 0.1–0.2 per cent per year: at 188. A recent study found that the long-term growth effects of a shift to VAT and sales taxes have a more pronounced effect in developed than in developing economies. The authors find a shift to property taxes (from income taxes) to be more beneficial than a shift to consumption taxes: Santiago Acosta-Ormaechea and Jiae Yoo, 'Tax Composition and Growth: A Broad Cross- Country Perspective' (Working Paper No. WP/12/257, International Monetary Fund, 2012), 17–18. For a summary of more recent studies: International Monetary Fund (IMF), *Fiscal Monitor (October 2013) – Taxing Times*

additional challenge, at least in a conceptual sense, to the thesis that the VAT increases growth.[44] Evidence does suggest that, consistent with economic theory, the VAT does not offer a trade advantage.[45] Furthermore, it is unclear whether, as is frequently claimed by the conventional approach, trade benefits accrue from the VAT replacing trade-retarding taxes, such as tariffs or inferior sales taxes.[46]

(IMF, Washington, DC, 2013), 31–32. Some single-country studies have suggested a small gain: Smart and Bird find that replacement of RST with VAT in some Canadian provinces led to a short-run increase in machinery and equipment investment: Michael Smart and Richard M. Bird, 'The Impact on Investment of Replacing a Retail Sales Tax with a Value-Added Tax: Evidence from Canadian Experience', *National Tax Journal* 62 (2009), 591. Lindert finds that European welfare states have achieved impressive postwar growth through relying on a larger share of regressive but pro-growth taxes (such as VAT) to fund universalist welfare states: Peter H. Lindert, *Growing Public: Social Spending and Economic Growth since the Eighteenth Century* (Cambridge UK; New York, Cambridge University Press, 2004), 235–45. However, his claim rests on attributing to real VATs the merits of the good VAT (at 302), as explained in Chapter 5, §4 of this book.

44 See Chapter 7 of this book.

45 Desai and Hines find no discernible link between a VAT and improved trade performance, and indeed find a negative link between a VAT and trade flows for developing countries, which result from the problems of real VATs. The authors conclude that:

> The proposition that value-added taxes encourage exports by rebating taxes at the border appears to have no empirical foundation. Indeed, countries that rely heavily on VATs export and import less as a fraction of GDP than do other countries. . .The negative effects of VATs on international trade are most pronounced among lower-income countries, though they are present in high-income countries.

Mihir A. Desai and James R. Hines Jr, 'Value-Added Taxes and International Trade: The Evidence' (Workshop in Law and Economics Working Paper, University of Chicago, Law School, 2002), 20–21; Michael Keen, 'VAT, Tariffs, and Withholding: Border Taxes and Informality in Developing Countries', *Journal of Public Economics* 92 (2008), 1892, 1901–2. See also International Tax Dialogue (ITD), 'The Value Added Tax: Experience and Issues' (Background Paper Prepared for the International Tax Dialogue Conference on the VAT, Rome, March 15–16, 2005, ITD), 11; Richard Bird and Pierre-Pascal Gendron, *The VAT in Developing and Transitional Countries* (Cambridge University Press, New York, 2007), 49, 51–55.

46 In part, this is because it is not clear what taxes have been replaced by a VAT: see §2.1 above. Richard Bird and Pierre-Pascal Gendron, *The VAT in Developing and Transitional Countries* (Cambridge University Press, New York, 2007), 54. Desai and Hines conclude that, while 'it is difficult to rule out the possibility that countries using VATs would have even worse export performance if they were forced to rely on corporate income taxes or other methods of raising the same tax revenues, none of the evidence appears to point in this direction': Mihir A. Desai and James R. Hines Jr, 'Value-Added Taxes and International Trade: The Evidence' (Workshop in Law and Economics Working Paper, University of Chicago, Law School, 2002), 20. Norregaard and Khan note that some empirical studies have found that low-income countries have been less able to recover revenue lost from trade taxes than middle-high-income countries, with estimates suggesting that low-income countries recover only approximately 30 per cent of the lost revenue. The studies attribute this to the limited administrative capacity in low-income countries and the absence of reliable alternative sources of revenue like the income tax. That is, many countries have relied on direct taxes to recover lost revenue from trade taxes (despite the assumption that direct taxes such as the income tax adversely impact trade performance). Studies have also found that the presence of VAT itself does not enhance the ability to recover revenue, but rather the presence of a good VAT (or countries that come

The inconclusive evidence as to the growth benefits of real VATs might be the result of the departures from the three design norms of the good VAT, such as delays or denials in VAT refunds on exports (see §5 and §6), and exclusions to the VAT base (see §4). Alternatively, it may arise from more fundamental criticisms, such as the ineffectiveness of VAT as a countercyclical tool,[47] or the inappropriateness of VAT for developing countries.[48] Whatever the reason for the disparity, it is clear that, once again, real VATs do not necessarily deliver on the gains promised of the good VAT.

2.6 *Simplicity*

As Chapter 2 demonstrated, simplicity is not considered to be the good VAT's greatest virtue. The conventional approach acknowledges that real VATs are far more complex than the good VAT.[49] Complexities result from various sources that include exclusions to the VAT base (see §4); rules relating to the time and place of taxable supplies (see §5); and imposition of VAT on a destination basis absent effective border controls (see §6).

2.7 *Equity*

Given that the high rating of the good VAT against horizontal equity depends on the VAT being levied on a broad base, the many exclusions to the base of real VATs undermine the realisation of this key merit (see §4). Others contend that horizontal equity is further undermined by the shift to the informal economy that the introduction of a VAT entails, which is a particular issue in developing economies.[50] Of course, many of the exclusions to the VAT base that undermine

closer to the good VAT) enhances the ability to recover revenue: John Norregaard and Tehmina S. Khan, 'Tax Policy: Recent Trends and Coming Challenges' (Working Paper No. WP/07/274, IMF, 2007), 45.

47 Terra and Kajus query the effectiveness of VAT as a countercyclical tool because anecdotal observations on the use of VAT reductions as a countercyclical tool in the 2007 global economic downturn suggest the measure was no more effective for countries that chose to reduce VAT rates than for those countries that retained their VAT rates: Ben Terra and Julie Kajus, IBFD, *A Guide to the European VAT Directives* [online] (15 April 2011), 7.6.13.

48 See Chapter 2, §2.2.2 of this book.

49 International Tax Dialogue (ITD), 'The Value Added Tax: Experience and Issues' (Background Paper Prepared for the International Tax Dialogue Conference on the VAT, Rome, March 15–16, 2005, ITD), 12; European Commission, *Green Paper on the Future of VAT: Towards a Simpler, More Robust and Efficient VAT System* [2010] COM (2010), 695, 4–5.

50 M. Shahe Emran and Joseph E. Stiglitz, 'On Selective Indirect Tax Reform in Developing Countries', *Journal of Public Economics* 89 (2005), 599, 600; Richard Bird and Pierre-Pascal Gendron, *The VAT in Developing and Transitional Countries* (Cambridge University Press, New York, 2007), 77–80. *Contra* Michael Keen, 'VAT, Tariffs, and Withholding: Border Taxes and Informality in Developing Countries', *Journal of Public Economics* 92 (2008), 1892.

horizontal equity are motivated by addressing the good VAT's perceived vertical inequity.

Although there are many studies on the distributional impact of all taxes, there have been very few attempts to quantify the distributional impact of the VAT, which, in part, results from disagreement over the best measure to assess the incidence of consumption taxes and on the availability of reliable data.[51] Warren concludes that, for developed countries, 'all studies agree that consumption taxes have a significant regressive impact on the distribution of household disposable income'.[52] By contrast, nearly all studies find that the personal income tax has a progressive impact.[53] Reliable data on the incidence of VAT in developing countries are scarce, and the results are mixed.[54] Studies that have found the VAT to be less regressive generally do so as a result of exclusions to the base of real VATs or through measuring the incidence of the VAT as a proportion of expenditure rather than income.[55]

[51] Neil Warren, 'A Review of Studies on the Distributional Impact of Consumption Taxes in OECD Countries' (Social, Employment and Migration Working Paper No. 64, OECD, 2008), 8. See also Liam Ebrill et al., *The Modern VAT* (IMF, Washington, DC, 2001), 108–10.

[52] This includes studies that take into account spending in measuring distributional impact: Neil Warren, 'A Review of Studies on the Distributional Impact of Consumption Taxes in OECD Countries' (Social, Employment and Migration Working Paper No. 64, OECD, 2008), 4, 28–49. See also OECD, *Growing Unequal: Income Distribution and Poverty in OECD Countries* (OECD, Paris, 2008), 18.

[53] Neil Warren, 'A Review of Studies on the Distributional Impact of Consumption Taxes in OECD Countries' (Social, Employment and Migration Working Paper No. 64, OECD, 2008), 57–58; Liam Ebrill et al., *The Modern VAT* (IMF, Washington, DC, 2001), 110; Richard Bird and Pierre-Pascal Gendron, *The VAT in Developing and Transitional Countries* (Cambridge University Press, New York, 2007), 72. These studies typically adopt annual measures because of the difficulty of effectively measuring the lifetime incidence of taxes. Thomas Piketty and Emmanuel Saez, 'Income Inequality in the United States, 1913–1998', *Quarterly Journal of Economics* 118(1) (2003), 1, 37.

[54] See a summary of these studies in Richard Bird and Pierre-Pascal Gendron, *The VAT in Developing and Transitional Countries* (Cambridge University Press, New York, 2007), 73. The authors note that studies tend to find the VAT slightly more progressive than excise taxes but note that there is no convincing evidence that a VAT is preferable to trade taxes: at 20, 28. Some point out that the failure of the VAT to tax the informal sector (which is frequently the rural sector) may indirectly benefit the poor (effectively providing them with tax-free goods): Jenkins et al., 'Is the Value-Added Tax Naturally Progressive?' (ssrn.com/abstract=897677, Queens University, 2006), 4, 7, 15. However, this clearly can only be a feature of real VATs and might cause greater difficulties in the long run: see Joseph E. Stiglitz, 'Development-Oriented Tax Policy', in R. H. Gordon (ed.), *Taxation in Developing Countries: Six Case Studies and Policy Implications* (Columbia University Press, New York, 2010), 11, 18.

[55] Liam Ebrill et al., *The Modern VAT* (IMF, Washington, DC, 2001), 108–10. For example, Jenkins et al. find a progressive VAT incidence in the Dominican Republic, but only when measuring against expenditure and only by assuming the presence of a real VAT; i.e., one that fails to tax the consumption of the poor because such consumption occurs largely in the informal market: Jenkins et al., 'Is the Value-Added Tax Naturally Progressive?' (ssrn.com/abstract=897677, Queens University, 2006), 4, 7, 15; *Contra* Sarker and Faridy, who find a highly regressive VAT incidence in Bangladesh: Nahida Sarker and Tapan Faridy, 'Who Really Pays Value Added Tax (VAT) in Developing Countries? Empirical Evidence from

Although the conventional approach generally acknowledges that exclusions to the base and variations to VAT rates reduce the absolute and relative burden of the VAT on the poor,[56] most generally insist that other taxes and spending measures are the best way to address inequity.[57] The point is made most strongly in relation to developed economies, on the basis that such countries have a greater capacity to address distributional concerns through other policy options such as spending.[58] However, the extent to which these compensating measures have been introduced varies according to country circumstances. Developing countries often have not done so because of the absence of an effective income tax or because the poor generally pay no income tax and do not benefit from transfer payments because of a lack of resources to fund them.[59] Developed countries, on the other hand, have varied widely on instituting compensating measures. On the expenditure side, studies find that spending offsets the impact of VAT,[60] but the capacity and enthusiasm to spend varies with a country's circumstances. Although early VAT adopters tended to use VAT revenue to fund universal welfare provision, this is less a feature of countries that adopted VAT later.[61] On the revenue side, virtually no

Bangladesh', *International Proceedings of Economics Development and Research* 11 (2011), 191, 194.

56 Robert F. van Brederode, *Systems of General Sales Taxation: Theory, Policy and Practice* (Kluwer Law International Alphen aan den Rijn, 2009), 33; Richard Bird and Pierre-Pascal Gendron, *The VAT in Developing and Transitional Countries* (Cambridge University Press, New York, 2007), 73, 76–77.

57 Liam Ebrill et al., *The Modern VAT* (IMF, Washington, DC, 2001), 112. *Contra* Bird and Gendron, who contend that 'in view of the relatively heavy burden of such taxes on the poor and the apparent inability or unwillingness of governments in many countries to provide offsets to such tax burdens through other fiscal adjustments, building some relief into VAT design may often be justifiable': Richard Bird and Pierre-Pascal Gendron, *The VAT in Developing and Transitional Countries* (Cambridge University Press, New York, 2007), 76–77. See also Neil Warren, 'A Review of Studies on the Distributional Impact of Consumption Taxes in OECD Countries' (Social, Employment and Migration Working Paper No. 64, OECD, 2008), 29, 38.

58 Michael Keen and Ruud de Mooij, '"Fiscal Devaluation" and Fiscal Consolidation: The VAT in Troubled Times', in Alberto Alesina and Francesco Giavazzi (eds.), *Fiscal Policy After the Financial Crisis* (University of Chicago Press, 2013), 443, 470.

59 Joseph E. Stiglitz, 'Development-Oriented Tax Policy', in R. H. Gordon (ed.), *Taxation in Developing Countries: Six Case Studies and Policy Implications* (Columbia University Press, New York, 2010), 11, 22, 25; Scott Riswold, 'VAT in Sub-Saharan Africa – A Critique of IMF VAT Policy', *International VAT Monitor* (March/April 2004), 97, 108; Richard Bird and Pierre-Pascal Gendron, *The VAT in Developing and Transitional Countries* (Cambridge University Press, New York, 2007), 76; Liam Ebrill et al., *The Modern VAT* (IMF, Washington, DC, 2001), 112.

60 The OECD Growing Unequal Report finds that '[t]aking into account consumption taxes widens inequality, though not by as much as the narrowing due to taking into account public services': OECD, *Growing Unequal: Income Distribution and Poverty in OECD Countries* (OECD, Paris, 2008), 18.

61 See Chapter 5, §§3–4 for Lindert and Kato's contention that countries that introduced VATs earlier, such as Sweden and Finland, were more than able to offset these regressive taxes through spending on universal welfare provision, whereas countries that introduced VATs

nation that has introduced a VAT has complemented its introduction with reforms to achieve or strengthen the effective taxation of gifts and bequests.[62] Instead, the introduction of VATs has often occurred alongside moves to flatten marginal income taxes and to exempt or grant preferential treatment of capital income – moves generally encouraged by the conventional approach on efficiency and growth grounds, but which exacerbate rather than alleviate regressivity.[63]

3 ASSESSING REAL VATS AGAINST THE THREE DESIGN NORMS OF THE GOOD VAT

The broad degree of consensus within the conventional approach as to what constitutes a good VAT is matched by a consensus that these 'normative requirements' for what makes a good VAT 'are often met only in the breach'.[64] The conventional approach identifies *policy* gaps as the main source of departure among developed countries and *compliance* gaps as the main issue in developing countries. The IMF therefore recommends that:[65]

later, such as Australia, New Zealand and Canada, have not necessarily directed VAT revenue to funding greater social transfers but have utilised VAT revenues to reduce other taxes. An OECD *Policy Brief* concludes that, despite 'the possibilities of offsetting the effects of inequality, it is difficult to ensure that there are no poor people who lose out': OECD, 'Consumption Taxes: the Way of the Future? (Policy Brief)', *OECD Observer* (2007), 1, 5.

62 Gruber notes that 'no developed nations that have consumption taxes include bequests in the measure of consumption, and consumption taxes are regressive in practice relative to income taxes': Jonathon Gruber, *Public Finance and Public Policy* (3rd ed., Worth Publishers, New York, 2011), 757. See also David Duff, 'The Abolition of Wealth Transfer Taxes: Lessons from Canada, Australia, and New Zealand', *Pittsburgh Tax Review* 3(1) (2005), 1.

63 Reuven Avi-Yonah, 'Globalization, Tax Competition, and the Fiscal Crisis of the Welfare State', *Harvard Law Review* 113(7) (2000), 1573, 1575–76. Reducing spending and decreasing reliance on income taxation has been a feature of advice from the conventional approach itself. See, e.g., John Norregaard and Tehmina S. Khan, 'Tax Policy: Recent Trends and Coming Challenges' (Working Paper No. WP/07/274, IMF, 2007), 4; A PricewaterhouseCoopers publication refers to 'moving towards flatter taxes': PricewaterhouseCoopers, *Shifting the Balance: The Evolution of Indirect Taxes* (PricewaterhouseCoopers, 2007), 14; Secretariat – United Nations Conference on Trade and Development, *Trade and Development Report, 2012* (UNCTAD/TDR/2012) (United Nations Publications, Geneva, 2012), 115–19.

64 Sijbren Cnossen, 'Global Trends and Issues in Value Added Taxation', *International Tax and Public Finance* 5(3) (1998), 399, 400; International Tax Dialogue (ITD), 'The Value Added Tax: Experience and Issues' (Background Paper Prepared for the International Tax Dialogue Conference on the VAT, Rome, March 15–16, 2005, ITD), 11; Michael Keen and Ben Lockwood, 'The Value Added Tax: Its Causes and Consequences', *Journal of Development Economics* 92(2) (2010), 138, 142–43; Richard Bird and Pierre-Pascal Gendron, *The VAT in Developing and Transitional Countries* (Cambridge University Press, New York, 2007), 4, 8, 15, 22, 55–56; OECD, *Consumption Tax Trends 2012: VAT/GST and Excise Rates, Trends and Administration Issues* (OECD Publishing, Paris, 2012), 15; Liam Ebrill et al., *The Modern VAT* (IMF, Washington, DC, 2001), 66–67.

65 IMF, *Fiscal Monitor (November 2010) – Fiscal Exit: From Strategy to Implementation* (IMF Publication Services, Washington, DC, 2010), 84; International Monetary Fund (IMF), *Fiscal*

> With some exceptions, VAT reform should concentrate on closing the policy gap in advanced economies, while emerging countries should focus on cutting compliance gaps.

In other words, whereas developed countries depart more explicitly in the design prescriptions for the good VAT, developing and transitional economies depart more in relation to their capacity to effectively administer the good VAT. There can, of course, be exceptions to these general trends,[66] but §4 to §6 of this chapter provide an overview of the nature of these policy and compliance gaps.

4 NORM 1 – A BROAD CONSUMPTION BASE AT A SINGLE RATE WITH MINIMAL EXCLUSIONS

Of all the design norms, real VATs depart from the first norm most decisively. Chapter 2 outlined the prescriptions put forward by the conventional approach so as to achieve the good VAT on this measure:

(1) Extension through all stages of the production and distribution chain up to the retail stage;
(2) Full and immediate crediting of goods (including capital goods) used in the production of goods and services: norm 2, see §5;
(3) Application to a broad base with minimal exclusions:
  (a) Minimising equity-based exclusions: see §4.2.3;
  (b) Accepting pragmatic-based exclusions where necessary, including financial services: see §4.2.4; and
(4) Levied at a single rate: see §4.3.

As this section demonstrates, the departure of real VATs is not so much in the choice to adopt a consumption base, as most countries with some exceptions have done so,[67] nor is it in failing to extend the VAT through all phases of the

Monitor (October 2013) – Taxing Times (IMF, Washington, DC, 2013), 30–31; Scott Riswold, 'VAT in Sub-Saharan Africa – A Critique of IMF VAT Policy', *International VAT Monitor* (March/April 2004), 97; a PricewaterhouseCoopers publication notes that a 'tension between theory and practice is a feature of much of the problems with VAT in Africa': PricewaterhouseCoopers, *Shifting the Balance: The Evolution of Indirect Taxes* (PricewaterhouseCoopers, 2007) 24.

66 International Monetary Fund (IMF), *Fiscal Monitor (October 2013) – Taxing Times* (IMF, Washington, DC, 2013), 30.

67 VATs explicitly levied on an income base are rare, having previously been used by Argentina, Peru and in the US state of Michigan. In 2001, Ebrill et al. noted eight counties that denied input credits on capital goods: Liam Ebrill et al., *The Modern VAT* (IMF, Washington, DC, 2001), 64; Sijbren Cnossen, 'Global Trends and Issues in Value Added Taxation', *International Tax and Public Finance* 5(3) (1998), 399, 405, 415–20. Only a handful of VATs deliberately exclude capital inputs in this manner, and the list is contracting – it includes state-based Brazilian VATs. France employed a gross product VAT from 1936 to 1953: Alan Schenk and Oliver Oldman, *Value Added Tax: A Comparative Approach* (rev. edn., Cambridge University Press, Cambridge; New York, 2007), 21, 38; OECD, *Consumption Tax Trends 2012: VAT/GST*

production and distribution chain, which most, but not all, countries have done.[68] Instead, the main source of departure is in relation to points 3 and 4 – the significant exclusions made to the base and the variations in VAT rates. These departures will therefore be the primary focus of this section.

4.1 *Most real VATs do not reach a broad consumption base*

The extent to which real VATs actually tax a consumption base is most commonly assessed by one of two measures that compare actual VAT revenues against the revenue that would be collected by a standard rate VAT levied on a full base of final consumption.[69] The VAT Revenue Ratio (VRR) excludes VAT in the calculation

and Excise Rates, Trends and Administration Issues (OECD Publishing, Paris, 2012), 11–12; Carl S. Shoup, 'Choosing among Types of VATs', in M. Gillis, C. S. Shoup and G. P. Sicat (eds.), *Value Added Taxation in Developing Countries (A World Bank Symposium)* (World Bank, Washington, DC, 1990), 3, 5–7; Malcolm Gillis, Carl S. Shoup and Gerardo P. Sicat, 'Lessons for Developing Countries', in M. Gillis, C. S. Shoup and G. P. Sicat (eds.), *Value Added Taxation in Developing Countries (A World Bank Symposium)* (World Bank, Washington, DC, 1990), 219, 221; Richard Bird and Pierre-Pascal Gendron, *The VAT in Developing and Transitional Countries* (Cambridge University Press, New York, 2007), 15. Indonesia exempts supplies of capital inputs: D. Kaur, *Indonesia – Corporate Taxation*, IBFD, *Country Surveys* (1 June 2014). China is in the process of introducing a multistage, credit-offset, invoice-based VAT system to replace the existing VAT and Business Tax (a turnover tax). In 2010, China converted its indirect tax base to allow for the refund of select capital goods, thereby moving its VAT toward a consumption base. However, VAT refunds are still selectively applied to different industries, in line with the shifting emphasis of the Chinese government's industrial policies: PricewaterhouseCoopers, *Shifting the Balance: The Evolution of Indirect Taxes* (PricewaterhouseCoopers, 2007), 46; Wei Cui and Alan Wu, 'China', in Thomas Ecker, Michael Lang and I. Lejeune (eds.), *The Future of Indirect Taxation: Recent Trends in VAT and GST Systems Around the World* (Kluwer Law International, Netherlands, 2012), 159, Wei Cui, 'Learning to Keep the Consumption Tax Base Broad: Australian and Chinese VAT Design for the Housing Sector', in C. Peacock (ed.), *GST in Australia: Looking Forward from the First Decade* (Lawbook Company, Pyrmont, 2011), 367–69; Ernst & Young, *Worldwide VAT, GST and Sales Tax Guide* (Ernst & Young, 2014), 126–141.

68 For example, Bangladesh, Algeria, Benin, Ivory Coast adopted pre-retail VATs. In 1998, Cnossen identified at least ten countries with VATs that extended only to the wholesale or manufacturing stage. Most have since reformed their VATs to extend through to the retail stage. These countries include the Dominican Republic (now levied at all stages on consumption); Bangladesh (tax is levied on manufacturing and wholesale supplies of goods, services and importations, while select retail sales are also subject to tax); Mongolia (recent reforms extended VAT to the retail stage); Pakistan (extends to the retail stage but has only selective application to services depending on the approach of individual provinces); Sri Lanka (amended its VAT in 2002 to extend to the retail stage); Algeria (largely wholesale base), Benin (variable base primarily up to the wholesale stage); Guinea (now extends to retail stage); Kenya (extends to the retail stage but with a long list of exemptions); and Nigeria (still retains some targeted exemptions of certain items of capital equipment in specific industries): Sijbren Cnossen, 'Global Trends and Issues in Value Added Taxation', *International Tax and Public Finance* 5(3) (1998), 399, 400; IBFD, *Country Surveys* (2014).

69 The conventional approach prefers measuring VAT against a consumption base, as opposed to measuring VAT revenue as a proportion of GDP, because most VATs are intended to apply to a consumption base (rather than an income or gross product base): OECD, *Consumption Tax Trends 2012: VAT/GST and Excise Rates, Trends and Administration Issues* (OECD

of the potential consumption base and is increasingly preferred over the C-efficiency ratio (CER), which includes VAT in the base (by measuring consumption as measured by national accounts at market prices that include VAT).[70] As a result of the exclusion, ratios tend to be higher under VRR than CER. The closer a country is to a good VAT system, the closer the value is to 1 for the VRR and 100 for the CER.[71] The lower the value, the more likely the VAT base has been eroded, while the higher the value, the broader the VAT base. However, the measures have limitations.[72] High values can alternatively indicate that the VAT is falling on more than a consumption base (as might occur in a VAT system that has many exempt supplies: see Chapter 2, §4.2.1). Values in excess of 1 for the VRR or 100 for the CER are a strong indicator of cascading VAT liabilities.[73] Even the good VAT would not necessarily reach a perfect ratio, given the administrative need to set registration thresholds or the difficulties in reaching hard-to-tax supplies such as financial services.[74]

Publishing, Paris, 2012), 104. However, VAT productivity figures can be useful as a means to assess the revenue-generation capabilities of the VAT, especially against the income tax, which can also be measured this way, and also to establish whether real VATs are in fact taxing more than just domestic consumption because of, for example, exemptions to the base. As the focus here is on assessing the breadth of the consumption base, the VRR and CER measures are referred to. For VAT productivity figures for the years 1998–2000, see Richard Bird and Pierre-Pascal Gendron, *The VAT in Developing and Transitional Countries* (Cambridge University Press, New York, 2007), 228–31.

70 Michael Keen and Ben Lockwood, 'Is the VAT a Money Machine?' *National Tax Journal* 69(4) (2006), 905, 908. The OECD developed the C-efficiency ratio but has now adopted the VRR: OECD, *Consumption Tax Trends 2012: VAT/GST and Excise Rates, Trends and Administration Issues* (OECD Publishing, Paris, 2012), 106, 104–11. The VRR can be represented by the following equation: VAT Revenue Ratio = (VAT revenue)/([consumption base – VAT revenue] x standard rate). The equation for the CER is CER = VAT Revenue/Consumption x standard rate: OECD, *Consumption Tax Trends 2008 – VAT/GST and Excise Rates, Trends and Administration Issues* (OECD, Paris, 2008), 67; OECD, *Consumption Tax Trends 2012: VAT/GST and Excise Rates, Trends and Administration Issues* (OECD Publishing, Paris, 2012), 105.

71 OECD, *Consumption Tax Trends 2008 – VAT/GST and Excise Rates, Trends and Administration Issues* (OECD, Paris, 2008), 67–68; OECD, *Consumption Tax Trends 2012: VAT/GST and Excise Rates, Trends and Administration Issues* (OECD Publishing, Paris, 2012), 110.

72 Michael Keen, 'The Anatomy of VAT' (Working Paper No. WP/13/111, International Monetary Fund, 2013), 8–22; OECD, *Consumption Tax Trends 2012: VAT/GST and Excise Rates, Trends and Administration Issues* (OECD Publishing, Paris, 2012), 110–11; US Government Accountability Office, *Value-Added Taxes: Lessons Learned from Other Countries on Compliance Risks, Administrative Costs, Compliance Burden, and Transition (GAO-08–566)* (Washington, DC, 2008), 27.

73 OECD, Consumption Tax Trends 2012: VAT/GST and Excise Rates, Trends and Administration Issues (OECD Publishing, Paris, 2012), 110; Robert F. van Brederode, *Systems of General Sales Taxation: Theory, Policy and Practice* (Kluwer Law International Alphen aan den Rijn, 2009), 47.

74 The OECD is developing new measures of VAT performance that distinguish between revenue lost from policy departures from an ideal VAT base (the 'policy efficiency ratio') and revenue lost from poor compliance (the 'compliance efficiency ratio'): OECD, *Consumption Tax Trends 2012: VAT/GST and Excise Rates, Trends and Administration Issues* (OECD

However, despite the limitations, the conventional approach adopts these measures, as they provide one of the few means to judge the efficiency of real VATs in reaching a consumption base.[75]

The results from various attempts to measure VRR and CER tend to show a number of patterns. Ratios are lower in developing economies and indicate that some of the VATs in these jurisdictions are reaching little more than 30 per cent of the potential consumption base.[76] An early study by Ebrill et al., for example, showed a CER of 38 for sub-Saharan Africa in 2001,[77] while a more recent assessment by the IMF of a select group of emerging economies found an average CER of 50.[78] Although, at a formal level, the real VATs in developing countries might more closely resemble the prescriptions of the good VAT when measured by the law on the statute books, the gap between the potential good VAT base and the base actually achieved by real VATs in these jurisdictions is attributed to weak administrative capacity and compliance issues.[79] These include issues that result from the large presence of the informal economy – estimated to be between 30 and 60 per cent of GDP in these economies.[80] Keen and Lockwood also highlight that the VAT seems to have marked difficulty relative to other taxes in reaching the agricultural sector.[81]

Publishing, Paris, 2012), 110–11. See also Michael Keen, 'The Anatomy of VAT' (Working Paper No. WP/13/111, International Monetary Fund, 2013), 8–22.

75 OECD, *Consumption Tax Trends 2012: VAT/GST and Excise Rates, Trends and Administration Issues* (OECD Publishing, Paris, 2012), 110–11.

76 Richard Bird and Pierre-Pascal Gendron, *The VAT in Developing and Transitional Countries* (Cambridge University Press, New York, 2007), 121–22.

77 Other results were CER rates of 58 in the Asia-Pacific; 57 in the Americas and North Africa and the Middle East; 64 in the EU, 62 in Central Europe and the Baltic, Russian and former Soviet states, and 83 in small islands (reflecting the large role of imports in these countries): Liam Ebrill et al., *The Modern VAT* (IMF, Washington, DC, 2001), 41, 51. Kloeden provides more recent measures but through VAT productivity ratios: David Kloeden, 'Revenue Administration Reforms in Anglophone Africa Since the Early 1990s' (Working Paper WP/11/162, IMF, 2011), 38.

78 IMF, *Fiscal Monitor (November 2010) – Fiscal Exit: From Strategy to Implementation* (IMF Publication Services, Washington, DC, 2010), 83.

79 International Monetary Fund (IMF), *Fiscal Monitor (October 2013) – Taxing Times* (IMF, Washington, DC, 2013), 30–31.

80 Richard Bird and Pierre-Pascal Gendron, *The VAT in Developing and Transitional Countries* (Cambridge University Press, New York, 2007), 74. A survey of VATs in Anglophone African countries found relatively good compliance on rate setting – with most countries adopting or moving to a single rate. However, most countries had a low VAT productivity ratio, resulting from the introduction of exemptions to the base, low registration thresholds and a lack of administrative capacity, particularly in terms of administering refunds and VAT enforcement. Countries studied included (1) Southern Africa: Botswana, Lesotho, Mauritius, Namibia, Seychelles, South Africa, Swaziland and Zimbabwe; (2) Eastern Africa: Kenya, Malawi, Rwanda, Tanzania, Uganda and Zambia; and (3) Western Africa: Gambia, Ghana, Liberia, Nigeria and Sierra Leone: David Kloeden, 'Revenue Administration Reforms in Anglophone Africa Since the Early 1990s' (Working Paper WP/11/162, IMF, 2011), 4, 36–46.

81 Michael Keen and Ben Lockwood, 'The Value Added Tax: Its Causes and Consequences' *Journal of Development Economics* 92(2) (20100, 138, 143.

Some contend that the weak performance of real VATs in developing countries is because the VAT is ill suited to the structure of developing economies. Stiglitz, for example, contends that the large presence of the informal economy in developing countries makes the VAT inefficient (because it fails to reach a broad base) and transfers resources away from the more productive formal sector to the informal sector because the VAT taxes only the formal sector. This leads to an inefficient allocation of resources and therefore interferes with production efficiency.[82] Stiglitz contends that this is but one way in which VATs operate as a distortive tax on development that can lower incomes, impede growth and increase unemployment in developing countries.[83] In reply, Keen claims that the criticism fails to account for the way 'real'[84] VATs in practice manage to tax the informal sector in developing economies. Given that informal sector firms (who are not registered in the VAT system and are therefore not entitled to refunds on inputs supplied by the formal sector, either domestically or through imports) pay unrecoverable VAT on inputs, the VAT acts in part as a tax on the informal sector.[85] As the vast bulk of VAT collections in developing and transitional economies are on imports,[86] Keen suggests that the implicit tax on the informal sector might be significant. In addition, Keen contends that many developing economies respond to the presence of the informal sector by applying withholding taxes to various high-risk transactions. For example, withholding taxes might be levied on imports that, when VAT is paid by formal sector firms on their imports, will be credited against VAT or income tax liability but not for informal sector firms.[87] Thus, withholding taxes in turn strengthen the VAT's reach into the informal sector. Keen admits that there are limitations to his defence of the VAT, not least of which is the assumption that informal sector firms pay VAT on their inputs (which can be avoided through adopting informal supply chains or registering for VAT credits but not remitting VAT) and the less-than-optimal result that informal sector inputs are taxed at the same (rather than a greater) rate as final sales, which is only partly addressed by withholding taxes.[88] However, the more interesting point for the purposes of this

[82] Support for this contention is found in J. R. Hines, 'Might Fundamental Tax Reform Increase Criminal Activity?' *Economica* 71(283) (2004), 483. Stiglitz further contends that where the informal sector is concentrated in the rural sector, this shift has a demographic impact because the VAT effectively becomes a tax on urban wages. This in turn encourages labour to move to the less productive rural sector and consequently lowers overall productive output: Joseph E. Stiglitz, 'Development-Oriented Tax Policy', in R. H. Gordon (ed.), *Taxation in Developing Countries: Six Case Studies and Policy Implications* (Columbia University Press, New York, 2010), 11, 22.

[83] Joseph E. Stiglitz, 'Development-Oriented Tax Policy', in R. H. Gordon (ed.), *Taxation in Developing Countries: Six Case Studies and Policy Implications* (Columbia University Press, New York, 2010), 11, 19, 21–22.

[84] Michael Keen, 'VAT, Tariffs, and Withholding: Border Taxes and Informality in Developing Countries', *Journal of Public Economics* 92 (2008), 1892, 1894.

[85] Ibid., 1893. [86] Ibid., 1894. [87] Ibid., 1895, 1897.

[88] In addition, there is the limited administrative capacity of developing countries to, for example, credit withholding payments to compliant taxpayers: Ibid., 1895, 1902–1903.

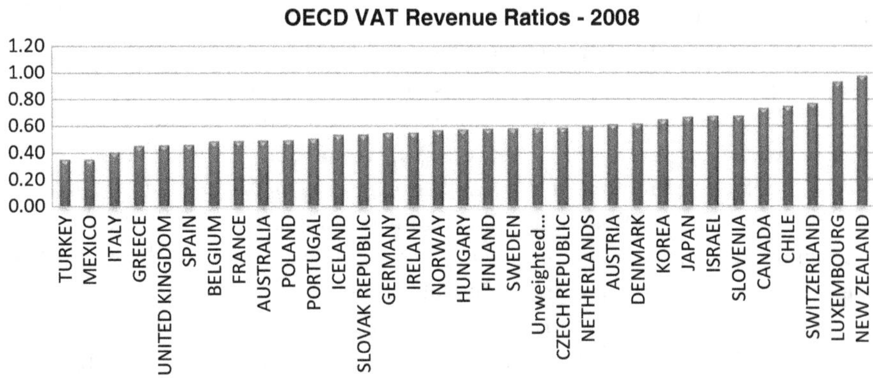

FIGURE 3.1 – OECD VAT revenue ratios – 2008[89]

book is that the defence of the VAT in this instance rests on 'real' VATs (that is, a VAT that admits of a particular susceptibility to non-compliance) rather than a good VAT (for more on this, see Chapter 4, §2.1).[90] Beyond this defence, the response of the conventional approach to the Stiglitz critique is to encourage developing economies to improve VAT compliance and administration rather than abandon the VAT.[91] The administrative and compliance issues in real VATs are discussed under norm 2 (see §5).

As Figure 3.1 shows, developed countries do not necessarily fare all that much better than developing countries in reaching a consumption base.

Figure 3.1 shows that VRR rates range from 0.35, in Mexico and Turkey, to 0.98 in New Zealand. OECD data from 2012 show that the majority of OECD countries (26 of 33) have a VRR of less than 0.65, while approximately half of OECD countries (14 of 33) have a VRR of less than 0.50.[92] An indicator that demonstrates the impact of exemptions on VAT revenues is that countries with large financial sectors, such as Luxembourg and Switzerland, have high VRRs, in part due to the

[89] OECD, *Consumption Tax Trends 2010: VAT/GST and Excise Rates, Trends and Administration Issues* (OECD Publishing, Paris, 2011), figure 4.1, 112. Reproduced with permission: OECD (2011), *Consumption Tax Trends 2010: VAT/GST and Excise Rates, Trends and Administration Issues*, OECD Publishing (dx.doi.org/10.1787/ctt-2010-en).

[90] Michael Keen, 'VAT, Tariffs, and Withholding: Border Taxes and Informality in Developing Countries', *Journal of Public Economics* 92 (2008), 1892, 1894, 1903.

[91] For further replies to Stiglitz, see Jean-Paul Bodin and Vincent Koukpaizan, 'The Rise of VAT in Africa – Impact and Challenges' (2009), *International VAT Monitor*, 178. See also IMF, *Fiscal Monitor (November 2010) – Fiscal Exit: From Strategy to Implementation* (IMF Publication Services, Washington, DC, 2010), 84; International Tax Dialogue (ITD), 'The Value Added Tax: Experience and Issues' (Background Paper Prepared for the International Tax Dialogue Conference on the VAT, Rome, March 15–16, 2005, ITD), 31; Liam Ebrill et al., *The Modern VAT* (IMF, Washington, DC, 2001), 61, ch. 5.

[92] OECD, *Consumption Tax Trends 2012: VAT/GST and Excise Rates, Trends and Administration Issues* (OECD Publishing, Paris, 2012), 112.

revenue gained from the exemption of financial services from the VAT base.[93] The European Commission noted that recent VAT reforms following the global financial crisis in the EU have tended to increase rates rather than expand the VAT base.[94] Despite claims that the ratios have increased over recent years,[95] these figures reveal that, even on the more expansive measure of the VRR, most real VATs in OECD economies reach less than two-thirds of final consumption.

Given that a large proportion of the claims relating to the VAT's efficiency and neutrality rest on it reaching a broad base, these figures are a sobering reflection of the capacity of real VATs to realise the benefits of the good VAT. As noted earlier, the conventional approach tends to attribute the difficulties that real VATs in developed countries have in reaching a broad consumption base to 'policy gaps' that introduce exclusions to the base and multiple rates.[96] The IMF claims that '[a]dvanced economies appear to enjoy higher rates of compliance but with VAT systems that make greater use of exemptions and zero rates' than do the VATs of developing countries.[97] A 2010 evaluation of the EU VAT system identifies exemptions to the VAT base, rate variations and evasion as the major weaknesses in VATs across the EU.[98] Keen and de Mooij note that with recent increases in VAT rates across the EU pushing VAT rates close to the maximum limit of 25 percent informally agreed to by member states, reform will need to address expanding the VAT base.[99] The next section discusses the exclusions that figure most prominently in the base of most real VATs

[93] Ibid., 112; Michael Keen, 'The Anatomy of VAT' (Working Paper No. WP/13/111, International Monetary Fund, 2013), 20.

[94] European Commission (EC), Directorate-General for Economic and Financial Affairs, Directorate General for Taxation and Customs Union, *Tax Reforms in EU Member States: Tax Policy Challenges for Economic Growth and Fiscal Sustainability – 2013 Report* (EC, Brussels, 2013), 10.

[95] Michael Keen, 'The Anatomy of VAT' (Working Paper No. WP/13/111, International Monetary Fund, 2013), 8.

[96] Keen and de Mooij reinforce this observation for a selection of European counties: Michael Keen and Ruud de Mooij, '"Fiscal Devaluation" and Fiscal Consolidation: The VAT in Troubled Times', in Alberto Alesina and Francesco Giavazzi (eds.), *Fiscal Policy After the Financial Crisis* (University of Chicago Press, 2013), 443, 468–70.

[97] IMF, *Fiscal Monitor (November 2010) – Fiscal Exit: From Strategy to Implementation* (IMF Publication Services, Washington, DC, 2010), 84. The OECD's response is to note that VAT performance depends on the structural features of the tax, the capacity of tax administration and degree of taxpayer compliance and that 'more work is needed to identify the specific factors that influence the performance of VAT and how they interact': OECD, *Consumption Tax Trends 2012: VAT/GST and Excise Rates, Trends and Administration Issues* (OECD Publishing, Paris, 2012), 114. The use of mandatory exemptions in the EU leads Keen to propose (but not adopt) VAT collection ratios against a reduced consumption benchmark that takes account of these exclusions: Michael Keen, 'The Anatomy of VAT' (Working Paper No. WP/13/111, International Monetary Fund, 2013), 13.

[98] Institute for Fiscal Studies (IFS), *A Retrospective Evaluation of Elements of the EU VAT System: Final Report for the European Commission* (IFS, London, 2011), 14–16.

[99] Michael Keen and Ruud de Mooij, '"Fiscal Devaluation" and Fiscal Consolidation: The VAT in Troubled Times', in Alberto Alesina and Francesco Giavazzi (eds.), *Fiscal Policy After the Financial Crisis* (University of Chicago Press, 2013), 443, 476.

4.2 *Most real VATs have multiple exclusions to their base*

The conventional approach acknowledges that, in direct contravention to the first design norm, exclusions from the VAT base are commonplace and are usually introduced through the zero-rating and exemption of domestic supplies.[100] Even those jurisdictions that have implemented 'modern VATs', known for their broader base and more limited exclusions, have still introduced a number of exclusions into the VAT base.[101] The main exception is New Zealand, which has adopted one of the broadest VAT bases (although the New Zealand GST is still subject to some exclusions).[102]

4.2.1 Form of exclusion

About half of real VATs zero-rate some domestic supplies.[103] This occurs even within the European Union (EU) which, despite prohibiting the levying of VAT at

[100] Liam Ebrill et al., 'The Allure of the Value-Added Tax', *Finance & Development* 39(2) (2002), 44. The authors highlight the departures that occur from conventional advice for the good VAT (at 46):

> Zero rating—under which sales are not taxed, but tax paid on inputs can nevertheless be reclaimed—is recommended only for exports, but, in practice, is used more widely. . .Exemptions—situations under which tax is not charged on output but also cannot be recovered on input—are more common than advised, undoing the VAT's good work in avoiding distortions of input decisions and compromising its transparency.

See also International Tax Dialogue (ITD), 'The Value Added Tax: Experience and Issues' (Background Paper Prepared for the International Tax Dialogue Conference on the VAT, Rome, March 15–16, 2005, , 2005), 15; OECD, *Consumption Tax Trends 2012: VAT/GST and Excise Rates, Trends and Administration Issues* (OECD Publishing, Paris, 2012), 66; David Williams, 'Value-Added Tax', in V. Thuronyi (ed.), *Tax Law Design and Drafting* (IMF, Washington, DC, 1996), vol. 1, 164, 203. As was explained in Chapter 2, in jurisdictions such as Australia and New Zealand, zero-rated supplies are called GST-free supplies and exempt supplies are called input-taxed supplies.

[101] Liam Ebrill et al., *The Modern VAT* (IMF, Washington, DC, 2001), 68, 83; Richard Krever, 'Designing and Drafting VAT Laws for Africa', in R. Krever (ed.), *VAT in Africa* (Pretoria University Law Press, Pretoria, 2008), 9, 13–18.

[102] Paul van den Noord and Christopher Heady, 'Surveillance of Tax Policies: A Synthesis of Findings in Economic Surveys' (Economics Department Working Paper No. 303, OECD, 2001), 31.

[103] Approximately 67 jurisdictions apply a zero rate to domestic supplies based on the list by Annacondia and van der Corput: Fabiola Annacondia and Walter van der Corput, 'Overview of General Turnover Taxes and Tax Rates' (2009 [March/April]), *International VAT Monitor*, 1, 3–9; Ine Lejeune, Jeanine Daou-Azzi and Mark Powell (of PricewaterhouseCoopers), 'The Balance Has Shifted to Consumption Taxes – Lessons Learned and Best Practices for VAT ', in M. Lang, P. Melz and E. Kristoffersson (eds.), *Value Added Tax and Direct Taxation: Similarities and Differences* (IBFD, Vienna, 2009), 59, 79–83; David Williams, 'Value-Added Tax', in V. Thuronyi (ed.), *Tax Law Design and Drafting* (IMF, Washington, DC, 1996), vol. 1, 164, 203; Liam Ebrill et al., *The Modern VAT* (IMF, Washington, DC, 2001), 66–67.

rates lower than the minimum rate of 5 percent, allows for the zero-rating of domestic supplies through derogations.[104]

The use of exemptions in real VATs is so widespread, and the categories of exempt supplies so variable from country to country, that it is difficult to collate all the exemptions in summary form. The number of exemptions range from the 'best practice' approach of New Zealand, which exempts only a handful of supplies,[105] to well over a dozen exemptions in jurisdictions such as Kenya, Egypt, Algeria and Laos.[106] The *ITD VAT Paper* reflects the conventional approach's disapproval of the extensive use of exemptions when it concludes that 'the rolling back of exemptions is likely to be a recurrent theme in VAT reform over the coming years'.[107] However, 'there is little firm evidence on the quantitative importance of these distortions'.[108]

Practical experience with the implementation of VATs reveals another category broadly termed 'out-of-scope' supplies, which can mirror the effect of direct exemptions, albeit through different means. A supply might fall outside the scope of VAT legislation either because of the particular design of the legislative scheme or because of its narrow interpretation by the judiciary. Examples include supplies of inaction, such as restrictive covenants, and involuntary supplies, such as when property is compulsorily acquired. The effect of such out-of-scope supplies depends on the overall legislative scheme. In EU member states, the requirement that input tax credits be available only when an acquisition is linked to a taxable supply means such out-of-scope supplies are in essence treated as an explicitly exempt supply – no VAT is charged on the supply, but the supplier is not entitled to input tax credits.

104 A derogation allows states to depart from or vary a particular provision in EU law: *Council Directive 2006/112/EC of 28 November 2006 on the Common System of Value Added Tax* [2006] OJ L 347/1 (referred to hereafter as the '*Recast VAT Directive* (2006/112/EC)', art. 395.

105 The limited categories of exemption include: financial supplies to consumers (but the zero-rating of business-to-business supplies [see §4.2.4]); supplies of residential accommodation in a dwelling; supplies of fine metal; and supplies by non-profit organisations of goods and services: *Goods and Services Tax Act 1985* (NZ), s14.

106 IBFD *Country Surveys* (2014); Ernst & Young, *Worldwide VAT, GST and Sales Tax Guide* (Ernst & Young, 2014).

107 International Tax Dialogue (ITD), 'The Value Added Tax: Experience and Issues' (Background Paper Prepared for the International Tax Dialogue Conference on the VAT, Rome, March 15–16, 2005, ITD), 16; see also Liam Ebrill et al., *The Modern VAT* (IMF, Washington, DC, 2001), 66–67. Institute for Fiscal Studies (IFS), *A Retrospective Evaluation of Elements of the EU VAT System: Final Report for the European Commission* (IFS, London, 2011), 18–19.

108 Ian Crawford, Michael Keen and Stephen Smith, 'Value Added Tax and Excises', in Stuart Adam et al. (eds.) for the Institute for Fiscal Studies, *Dimensions of Tax Design: The Mirrlees Review* (Oxford University Press, Oxford, 2010), 275, 305, and at 352; Richard Bird and Pierre-Pascal Gendron, *The VAT in Developing and Transitional Countries* (Cambridge University Press, New York, 2007), 100; David Williams, 'Value-Added Tax', in V. Thuronyi (ed.), *Tax Law Design and Drafting* (IMF, Washington, DC, 1996), vol. 1, 164, 203; International Tax Dialogue (ITD), 'The Value Added Tax: Experience and Issues' (Background Paper Prepared for the International Tax Dialogue Conference on the VAT, Rome, March 15–16, 2005, ITD), 15–16.

By contrast, in jurisdictions such as Australia, where entitlement to input tax credits is not directly connected to the use of the acquisition in making a taxable supply, the result is the equivalent of a zero-rated supply, as the supplier is entitled to input tax credits and no VAT is charged on the supply.[109]

The general assessment by the conventional approach on the setting of VAT thresholds is that they are often set too low in developing countries, which is said to contribute to the resistance to, evasion of, and even the failing of VATs – the latter occurring in the initial aborted attempts to introduce VATs in Ghana and Malta.[110] By contrast, although the setting of thresholds varies greatly in developed countries,[111] thresholds are sometimes identified as too high.[112] In many developed countries, entities often choose to opt in for registration so as to enable them and their customers to claim input credits, but this is not necessarily the case in Japan, which allows full payment of input credits for entities purchasing from small exempt suppliers.[113] As with out-of-scope supplies, different VAT regimes can also create out-of-scope suppliers either explicitly (such as through setting registration thresholds or through the use of specific exclusions in the relevant legislative scheme) or implicitly through narrow judicial interpretation of the concept of a taxable enterprise.[114]

[109] Richard Krever and Rita de la Feria, 'Ending VAT Exemptions: Towards a Post-Modern VAT', in R. de la Feria (ed.), *VAT Exemptions: Consequences and Design Alternatives* (vol. 37, EUCOTAX Series on European Taxation, Kluwer Law International, Alphen aan den Rijn, 2013), 3, 12–13.

[110] Both countries have reintroduced the VAT. International Tax Dialogue (ITD), 'The Value Added Tax: Experience and Issues' (Background Paper Prepared for the International Tax Dialogue Conference on the VAT, Rome, March 15–16, 2005, ITD), 16; Liam Ebrill et al., *The Modern VAT* (IMF, Washington, DC, 2001), 66–67.

[111] The OECD detects no consistent pattern with the setting of thresholds in OECD countries. An OECD report identifies 15 countries with relatively high exemption thresholds above $US30,000 (Australia, Austria, the Czech Republic, Estonia, France, Hungary, Ireland, Italy, Japan, New Zealand, Poland, the Slovak Republic, Slovenia, Switzerland and the United Kingdom); 14 with a relatively low threshold of between $US1,500 and $30,000 (Belgium, Canada, Denmark, Finland, Germany, Greece, Iceland, Israel, Korea, Luxembourg, Netherlands, Norway, Portugal and Sweden); and, four countries with no threshold (Chile, Mexico, Spain and Turkey): OECD, *Consumption Tax Trends 2012: VAT/GST and Excise Rates, Trends and Administration Issues* (OECD Publishing, Paris, 2012), 76–77.

[112] Van den Noord and Heady contend that the setting of lower registration thresholds better promotes compliance: Paul van den Noord and Christopher Heady, 'Surveillance of Tax Policies: A Synthesis of Findings in Economic Surveys' (Economics Department Working Paper No. 303, OECD, 2001), 32.

[113] Alan Schenk and Oliver Oldman, *Value Added Tax: A Comparative Approach* (rev. edn., Cambridge University Press, Cambridge; New York, 2007), 54.

[114] Richard Krever and Rita de la Feria, 'Ending VAT Exemptions: Towards a Post-Modern VAT', in R. de la Feria (ed.), *VAT Exemptions: Consequences and Design Alternatives* (vol. 37, EUCOTAX Series on European Taxation, Kluwer Law International, Alphen aan den Rijn, 2013), 3, 12, 14–22.

4.2.2 Content of exclusions

The content of exclusions from the base of real VATs is a long and varied list that reflects a mix of measures to address equity concerns over the VAT; the success of, and importance of, specific sectors in lobbying for preferential treatment;[115] and pragmatic exclusions such as financial supplies.[116] The following quote from the OECD identifies five categories of exclusion to the base of real VATs that are common across the OECD:[117]

(a) Essentials – medical and hospital, food and water supplies;
(b) Utilities such as public transport, post, public television;
(c) Socially desirable activities – charities, culture, sport or activities that support employment;
(d) Geographic areas deserving preferential treatment such as islands, remote areas and border areas; and
(e) Sectors that are exempt from VAT for 'historical or practical' reasons and may be subject to specific taxes such as property and financial services (including insurance).

The list applies equally to non-OECD VAT economies but reflects only some of the many exclusions to the base of real VATs in these jurisdictions.[118]

4.2.3 Equity-based exclusions are common in real VATs

Exclusions from the base of real VATs are commonly motivated by an apparent concern for equity. Common exclusions include supplies of food, health, education, clothes and books.[119] Although justified on grounds of equity, exclusions to the supply of goods and services commonly provided by government, such as education and health, can often be measures to preserve neutrality between public and private providers, when the government provision of such services is excluded from the VAT base.[120]

[115] In fact, exclusions to the base often give an insight into the relative importance of various industries in a domestic economy; for example, Iceland zero-rates shipbuilding, while Australia provides generous treatment of supplies of precious metals: OECD, *Consumption Tax Trends 2012: VAT/GST and Excise Rates, Trends and Administration Issues* (OECD Publishing, Paris, 2012), 80–81.

[116] Ernst & Young, *Worldwide VAT, GST and Sales Tax Guide* (Ernst & Young, 2014); IBFD, *Country Surveys* (2014).

[117] OECD, *Consumption Tax Trends 2008 – VAT/GST and Excise Rates, Trends and Administration Issues* (OECD, Paris, 2008), 51.

[118] IBFD, *Country Surveys* (2014).

[119] Ernst & Young, *Worldwide VAT, GST and Sales Tax Guide* (Ernst & Young, 2014); IBFD *Country Surveys* (2014).

[120] IMF, Fiscal Monitor (November 2010) – *Fiscal Exit: From Strategy to Implementation* (IMF Publication Services, Washington, DC, 2010), 82.

In addition to exclusions to the base, some jurisdictions follow the conventional approach and alleviate the perceived inequity of the VAT through other means. Canada, for example, introduced a refundable sales tax credit for low-income families; however, this was in addition to exclusions to the Goods and Services Tax (GST) base.[121] By contrast, New Zealand most closely followed the conventional approach and employed some limited tax credits and rebates for low-income earners while resisting the introduction of equity-based exclusions to the GST base.[122] The success of these measures varies. Some studies found a significant reduction in the regressivity of the incidence of the Canadian GST, through taking into account the GST credit.[123] However, despite being hailed as the leading exponent of the good VAT, a study by Stephens of the incidence of the New Zealand GST reforms found that the tax reforms that included the introduction of the GST in New Zealand contributed to one of the largest increases in income inequality in the OECD.[124] Stephens attributes this to inadequate direct assistance to the poor and to the fact that the benefits of most cuts in the personal income tax went to upper-income groups that also bore the smallest incidence of net GST.[125]

Inequality is clearly influenced by more than the mere presence of a VAT, and a VAT need not have a negative impact on inequality if adequate provision is made for social spending. The presence of VAT in countries with low inequality, such as Denmark and Sweden, and the absence of VAT in countries with high inequality, such as the US, confirm this.[126] However, the patterns suggested by Stephens in relation to New Zealand lend support to Ganghof's observation, quoted in Chapter 5 of this book, that although a VAT might fund greater spending, it need not necessarily do so for those states that choose low spending for the same reason they choose regressive taxes.[127]

[121] Neil Warren, 'A Review of Studies on the Distributional Impact of Consumption Taxes in OECD Countries' (Social, Employment and Migration Working Paper No. 64, OECD, 2008), 37.

[122] Robert Stephens, 'The Economic and Equity Effects of GST in New Zealand', in R. Krever and D. White (eds.), *GST in Retrospect and Prospect* (Thomson Brookers, Wellington, 2007), 65, 72.

[123] Neil Warren, 'A Review of Studies on the Distributional Impact of Consumption Taxes in OECD Countries' (Social, Employment and Migration Working Paper No. 64, OECD, 2008), 38.

[124] Robert Stephens, 'The Economic and Equity Effects of GST in New Zealand', in R. Krever and D. White (eds.), *GST in Retrospect and Prospect* (Thomson Brookers, Wellington, 2007), 65, 66.

[125] Ibid., 87.

[126] Denmark and Sweden rank highest among OECD countries on equality, while the US rates relatively poorly: OECD, *Growing Unequal: Income Distribution and Poverty in OECD Countries* (OECD, Paris, 2008), 25.

[127] Steffen Ganghof, 'Tax Mixes and the Size of the Welfare State: Causal Mechanisms and Policy Implications', *European Journal of Social Policy* 16(4) (2006), 360, 371. See Chapter 5, §4 of this book.

4.2.4 Most real VATs exempt financial supplies, although the responses vary

Three main approaches are discernible in the varied responses of real VATs to the frontier issue of the taxation of financial supplies.[128]

The first follows the traditional European approach of exempting financial supplies.[129] Zee notes that a common response among developing countries is to exempt the financial sector altogether.[130] Chapter 2 outlined the potential consequences that result from the exemption of financial supplies.[131] Some contend that there is little empirical evidence of the actual impact of the exemption of financial supplies in practice.[132] Edgar, for example, claims that the presumed distortions arising from the exemption of financial supplies have not been subject to any systematic empirical inquiry.[133] Gillis et al. contend that in developing countries with a nascent financial sector, the exemption of the financial sector can

[128] For an overview of country practices, see Alan Schenk, 'Taxation of Financial Services Under a U.S. Value-Added Tax', *Tax Law Review* 63(2) (2010), 409, 419–30; Howell H. Zee, 'VAT Treatment of Financial Services: A Primer on Conceptual Issues and Country Practices', *INTERTAX* 34(10) (2006), 458, 462–66; Alan Schenk, 'Financial Services', in R. Krever (ed.), *VAT in Africa* (Pretoria University Press, Pretoria, 2010), 31; Richard Bird and Pierre-Pascal Gendron, *The VAT in Developing and Transitional Countries* (Cambridge University Press, New York, 2007), 100–104; OECD, *Indirect Tax Treatment of Financial Services and Instruments* (OECD, Paris, 1998). The most commonly stated rationale for the European exemption is the difficulty in appropriately valuing and attributing value-add on a transactional basis, as was explained in Chapter 2, 4.2.5.1. Wersand and Cazes also attribute the approach to the existing practice of France and Germany to exempt financial services under the predecessor sales taxes in place: Frédéric Wersand and Samuel Cazes, 'EU VAT and the Conundrum of Financial Investments' *International VAT Monitor* 24(2) (March/April 2013), 83, 84. For a comprehensive analysis of the EU approach, including proposed reforms, see Claus Bohn Jespersen, *Intermediation of Insurance and Financial Services in European VAT* (Kluwer Law International, Alphen aan den Rijn, The Netherlands, 2011).

[129] The EU *Recast VAT Directive* requires member states to exempt a range of financial services other than equipment leasing and specific fee-based services like financial advice: *Recast VAT Directive (2006/112/EC)*, art. 135; Alan Schenk, 'Taxation of Financial Services Under a U.S. Value-Added Tax', *Tax Law Review* 63(2) (2010), 409, 421–42.

[130] Howell H. Zee, 'VAT Treatment of Financial Services: A Primer on Conceptual Issues and Country Practices', *INTERTAX* 34(10) (2006), 458, 463.

[131] See Chapter 2, §4.2.1 and §4.2.5.1 of this book.

[132] Arthur Kerrigan, 'The Elusiveness of Neutrality –Why Is It So Difficult To Apply VAT to Financial Services?' *International VAT Monitor* (March/April 2010), 103; Ian Crawford, Michael Keen and Stephen Smith, 'Value Added Tax and Excises', in Stuart Adam et al. (eds.) for the Institute for Fiscal Studies, *Dimensions of Tax Design: The Mirrlees Review* (Oxford University Press, Oxford, 2010), 275, 305; Richard Bird and Pierre-Pascal Gendron, *The VAT in Developing and Transitional Countries* (Cambridge University Press, New York, 2007), 100.

[133] Tim Edgar, 'The Search for Alternatives to the Exempt Treatment of Financial Services under a Value Added Tax', in R. Krever and D. White (eds.), *GST in Retrospect and Prospect* (Brookers, Wellington, 2007), 131, 133; Alan Schenk, 'Taxation of Financial Services Under a US Value-Added Tax', *Tax Law Review* 63(2) (2010), 409, 417; Michael Keen, Russell Krelove and John Norregaard, 'The Financial Activities Tax', in Stijn Claessens, Michael

significantly impede development.[134] Some predict that there could be significant revenue gains in taxing business-to-consumer financial supplies (at least for countries with large markets for the purchase of financial services by consumers).[135] Others consider that the exemption of financial supplies produces a net revenue gain (because of the inability of business to recover input credits).[136] This latter

Keen and C. Pazarbasioglu (eds.), *Financial Sector Taxation: The IMF's Report to the G-20 and Background Material* (IMF, 2010), 118, 120.

134 Malcolm Gillis, Carl S. Shoup and Gerardo P. Sicat, 'Lessons for Developing Countries', in M. Gillis, C. S. Shoup and G. P. Sicat (eds.), *Value Added Taxation in Developing Countries (A World Bank Symposium)* (World Bank, Washington, DC, 1990), 219, 222.

135 The European Commission has estimated that the exemption of financial supplies results in a net revenue loss of €18 billion per annum in the EU: European Commission, 'Financial Transaction Tax: Making the Financial Sector Pay Its Fair Share' (Press Release, IP/11/1085, 28 September 2011). A study by the European Commission estimates that the inclusion of financial intermediation services into the VAT base and taxation of those services at the standard rate would potentially increase revenue by approximately €14–22 billion (based on 2008 data): European Commission, 'Staff Working Paper Accompanying the Document Proposal for a Council Directive on a Common System of Financial Transaction Tax and Amending Directive 2008/7/EC – Impact Assessment: Instruments for the Taxation of the Financial Sector' (SEC 2011) 1102 final, vol. 1, European Commission, 2011), Annex 5 – Is the Financial Sector Under-Taxed? Empirical Part. In 2002, Huizinga suggested that the €12 billion to be gained from taxing household consumption of financial services in 15 member states of the EU would considerably exceed the revenue lost from the taxation of business through the exemption of financial supplies: Harry Huizinga, 'A European VAT on Financial Services?' *Economic Policy* 17(35) (2002), 497, 501. De la Faeria and Lockwood estimate that irrecoverable VAT constitutes approximately 1 per cent of total tax revenue in a selection of EU countries (France, Germany, Italy, the Netherlands, Spain), but more for the UK (at 1.48 per cent of total tax revenue), which reflects the substantial size of the financial sector in that country: Rita de la Feria and Ben Lockwood 'Opting for Opting-In? An Evaluation of the European Commission's Proposals for Reforming VAT on Financial Services', *Fiscal Studies* 31(2) (2010), 171, 177, Appendix A, 195–96. The IMF estimates that the exemption of financial services results in a net revenue loss: International Monetary Fund (IMF), *A Fair and Substantial Contribution by the Financial Sector – Final Report for the G-20* (IMF, Washington, DC, 2010), 65; Crawford, Keen and Smith predict a likely revenue gain from the taxation of B2C financial services: Ian Crawford, Michael Keen and Stephen Smith, 'Value Added Tax and Excises', in Stuart Adam et al. (eds.) for the Institute for Fiscal Studies, *Dimensions of Tax Design: The Mirrlees Review* (Oxford University Press, Oxford, 2010), 275, 308–9. Buettner and Erbe use German data to conclude that the revenue gains from ending the exemption depend on the extent to which financial institutions can already recover VAT on their inputs (which is possible in Germany). To the extent that they cannot recover VAT on acquisitions, the ending of the exemption would amount to a revenue loss (of 0.80 per cent of VAT revenues); to the extent that most financial institutions currently recover VAT, the authors predict a slight revenue gain (of 1.3 per cent of VAT revenues): Thiess Buettner and Katherine Erbe, 'Revenue and Welfare Effects of Financial Sector VAT Exemption' *International Tax and Public Finance* 21 (6) (2014), 1028.

136 Estimates tend to substitute for empirical analysis of this question: Robin Boadway and Michael Keen, 'Theoretical Perspectives on the Taxation of Capital Income and Financial Services', in P. Honohan (ed.), *Taxation of Financial Intermediation: Theory and Practice for Emerging Economies* (World Bank; Oxford University Press, Washington, DC, 2003), 31, 36. A study commissioned by a number of large European banks in response to the finding by the European Commission that banks are under-taxed as a result of the financial supply exemption found that the removal of the exemption of financial supplies might result in net revenue

point has been identified as contributing to the inertia around reform of the taxation of financial supplies.[137] European experience suggests, however, that the exemption, in combination with the proliferation of new forms of financial products, novel supply chains and aggressive tax planning, generates a significant proportion of VAT litigation.[138] The confusion over the exact impact of the VAT exemption, and a concern to develop effective measures to effectively tax the financial sector in the wake of the 2008 global financial crisis, have led to much reform debate but little progress on this issue in the EU.[139]

Often the exemption of financial supplies is accompanied by a variety of ad hoc measures to reduce the impact of the exemption on business, which constitutes the second response to the treatment of financial supplies. The European *Recast VAT Directive*, for example, provides member states with an option to tax certain

losses: PriceWaterhouseCoopers, *How the EU VAT Exemptions Impact the Banking Sector: Study to Assess Whether Banks Enjoy a Tax Advantage as a Result of the EU VAT Exemption System* (PWC, 2011), 6. Bird and Gendron state that it is not clear whether taxing financial services would result in more or less revenue for developing countries: Richard Bird and Pierre-Pascal Gendron, *The VAT in Developing and Transitional Countries* (Cambridge University Press, New York, 2007), 97. See also Richard Krever and Rita de la Feria, 'Ending VAT Exemptions: Towards a Post-Modern VAT', in R. de la Feria (ed.), *VAT Exemptions: Consequences and Design Alternatives* (vol. 37, EUCOTAX Series on European Taxation, Kluwer Law International, Alphen aan den Rijn, 2013), 3, 30–31.

137 Arthur Kerrigan, 'The Elusiveness of Neutrality – Why Is It So Difficult to Apply VAT to Financial Services?' *International VAT Monitor* (March/April 2010), 103, 110.

138 Rita de la Feria and Ben Lockwood, 'Opting for Opting-In? An Evaluation of the European Commission's Proposals for Reforming VAT on Financial Services', *Fiscal Studies* 31(2) (2010), 171, 178; Frédéric Wersand and Samuel Cazes, 'EU VAT and the Conundrum of Financial Investments', *International VAT Monitor* 24(2) (March/April 2013), 83.

139 Some claim that the means to include financial services in the VAT base exist, but are yet to be realised in practice. However, this results from the fact that no one solution fits neatly into the traditional invoice-credit mechanism: International Monetary Fund (IMF), *A Fair and Substantial Contribution by the Financial Sector – Final Report for the G-20* (IMF, Washington, DC, 2010), 65; Michael Keen and Ruud de Mooij, ' "Fiscal Devaluation" and Fiscal Consolidation: The VAT in Troubled Times', in Alberto Alesina and Francesco Giavazzi (eds.), *Fiscal Policy After the Financial Crisis* (University of Chicago Press, 2013), 443, 475–76; see Chapter 2, n 160. The European Commission adopted a proposal for reforms of the VAT treatment of financial supplies, including redefining and clarifying the scope of exempt services so as to better accord with current market and industry conditions. Agreement by member states on this limited aspect of reform has not been forthcoming: European Commission, *Proposal for a Council Directive Amending Directive 2006/112/EC on the Common System of Value Added Tax, as Regards the Treatment of Insurance and Financial Services* (COM/2007/747, European Commission, 2007); European Commission, *Proposal for a Council Regulation Laying Down Implementing Measures for Directive 2006/112/EC on the Common System of Value Added Tax, As Regards the Treatment of Insurance and Financial Services* COM (2007), 746 final. For a summary of the full suite of proposals, see Rita de la Feria and Ben Lockwood, 'Opting for Opting-In? An Evaluation of the European Commission's Proposals for Reforming VAT on Financial Services', *Fiscal Studies* 31(2) (2010), 171. For a survey of a broader range of reform options, see European Commission, 'Background Paper Requested by the Council Presidency; Subject: Financial and Insurance Services' (TAXUD/2414/08); European Commission, *Value Added Tax: A Study of Methods of Taxing Financial and Insurance Services* (EC, Brussels, 1996).

financial supplies.[140] Member states that choose to do so allow business to elect to treat certain exempt financial supplies as taxable; for example, Germany, France and Belgium allow for the recovery of input credits on specific financial supplies.[141] The European Commission proposed amending the *Recast VAT Directive* to extend the opt-in treatment to charge and recover VAT on fee-based financial supplies.[142] Australia and Singapore exempt many financial supplies but allow for the partial recovery of VAT incurred on certain inputs.[143] New Zealand adopts a zero-rating of business-to-business supplies where the recipient is VAT registered and more than 75 per cent of its supplies are taxable, but exempts business-to-consumer financial supplies.[144] None of these measures completely overcome all

[140] *Recast VAT Directive* (2006/112/EC), art. 137 (1)(a).

[141] Only Austria, Belgium, Bulgaria, Germany, Estonia, France and Lithuania have legislated for this option, but approaches vary: European Commission and PricewaterhouseCoopers, 'Review of Current Practices for Taxation of Financial Instruments, Profits and Remuneration of the Financial Sector' (Working Paper No. 11/09/12, European Commission, 28 June 2012), 30–31; Rita de la Feria and Ben Lockwood, 'Opting for Opting-In? An Evaluation of the European Commission's Proposals for Reforming VAT on Financial Services', *Fiscal Studies* 31(2) (2010), 171, 182–91, 196–98, Appendix B. Proposed reforms adopted by the European Commission would allow banks and insurance companies the ability to opt in to apply VAT on certain supplies (without the need for specific member state legislation allowing this, as all member states would be required to legislate for the option): European Commission, 'Proposal for a Council Directive Amending Directive 2006/112/EC on the Common System of Value Added Tax, as Regards the Treatment of Insurance and Financial Services ' (COM/2007/747, European Commission, 2007).

[142] European Commission, *Proposal for a Council Directive Amending Directive 2006/112/EC on the Common System of Value Added Tax, as Regards the Treatment of Insurance and Financial Services* [2007] Commission of the European Communities COM (2007), 747. This proposal has not been approved by member states. Public consultation has revealed that stakeholders have been divided on the best way to reform the treatment of financial supplies in the EU: see Directorate General Customs and Taxation Union European Commission, Indirect Taxation and Tax Administration, VAT and Other Turnover Taxes, *Summary of Results: Public Consultation on Financial and Insurance Services* (European Commission, 2006). For an analysis of the proposals, see Rita de la Feria and Ben Lockwood, 'Opting for Opting-In? An Evaluation of the European Commission's Proposals for Reforming VAT on Financial Services', *Fiscal Studies* 31(2) (2010), 171. See Chapter 6, §4.3.4 of this book for a similar muted response to proposals to reform financial supply provisions in Australia.

[143] For the Australian approach, see Chapter 6, §4.3.3.4 of this book. For an overview of both approaches, see Zee, who criticises both approaches for failing to completely eliminate cascading; aggravating the problem of under-taxation of consumers of financial supplies; and for its differential impact on financial service providers: Howell H. Zee, 'VAT Treatment of Financial Services: A Primer on Conceptual Issues and Country Practices', *INTERTAX* 34 (10) (2006), 458, 463–64.

[144] Although the approach addresses the cascading issues caused by exemptions, it is criticised for under-taxing financial supplies to consumers and for its administrative complexity arising from the 75 per cent taxable supplies eligibility requirement. Zero-rating also results in a potentially significant loss of revenue and raises equity issues in that it appears to prioritise financial supplies over other categories of goods and services: Ine Lejeune, Jeanine Daou-Azzi and Mark Powell (of PricewaterhouseCoopers), 'The Balance Has Shifted to Consumption Taxes – Lessons Learned and Best Practices for VAT', in M. Lang, P. Melz and E. Kristoffersson (eds.), *Value Added Tax and Direct Taxation: Similarities and Differences* (IBFD,

the difficulties that arise in relation to the application of the VAT to financial supplies and, although intended to reduce the impact on business, these measures can be costly, complex and distortive in and of themselves.[145]

The third response is to tax financial supplies. The approaches are varied, and few have prompted many others to follow. Some jurisdictions, such as South Africa, tax fee-based financial services, but many other jurisdictions are reluctant to follow suit because of the fear that the taxation of these fee-based services would provide an incentive for explicit fees to be transformed to implicit fees.[146] Few have explored the opportunity that might be provided by the ready substitutability between explicit and implicit fees in valuing financial services on a transactional basis.[147] Morocco is unique in applying the VAT to a range of financial services at a reduced rate, but few refer to the Moroccan approach in the extensive literature on financial supplies.[148] Israel applies an accounts-based addition-method VAT (separate from its invoice-credit VAT) to select financial services such as insurers and deposit-taking institutions. However, as Chapter 2 showed, this approach fails to prevent the breaking of the VAT chain that results from exemption (as the accounts-based approach means that the VAT component cannot be passed forward on a transactional basis) and has been criticised for over-taxing financial supplies.[149] Despite being best placed to tax financial supplies because of its

Vienna, 2009), 59, 92; Howell H. Zee, 'VAT Treatment of Financial Services: A Primer on Conceptual Issues and Country Practices', *INTERTAX* 34(10) (2006), 458, 465–66. Pallot highlights that these issues were tempered by the small size of the financial service sector in New Zealand, which is dominated largely by Australian banks: Marie Pallot, 'GST and Financial Services in New Zealand', in C. Peacock (ed.), *GST in Australia: Looking Forward from the First Decade* (Thomson Reuters, Pyrmont, 2011), 161, 163–64.

145 See Chapter 6, §4.3.3.4 of this book.

146 Howell H. Zee, 'VAT Treatment of Financial Services: A Primer on Conceptual Issues and Country Practices', *INTERTAX* 34(10) (2006), 458, 463; IBFD, *Country Surveys* (2014), 'South Africa' – '8.3 – 8.6'.

147 Marie Pallot, 'GST and Financial Services in New Zealand', in C. Peacock (ed.), *GST in Australia: Looking Forward from the First Decade* (Thomson Reuters, Pyrmont, 2011), 161, 163.

148 Arthur Kerrigan, 'The Elusiveness of Neutrality –Why Is It So Difficult to Apply VAT to Financial Services?' *International VAT Monitor* (March/April 2010), 103; IBFD, *Country Surveys* (1 March 2014) – 'Morocco' – '8.3, 8.5'. De La Feria and Lockwood observe of the German experience with the option to tax financial services that the method to value financial services on a transactional basis appears to be a 'closely-held secret amongst most German financial institutions'. The comment of course implies that the method is possible, just not widely known: Rita de la Feria and Ben Lockwood, 'Opting for Opting-In? An Evaluation of the European Commission's Proposals for Reforming VAT on Financial Services', *Fiscal Studies* 31(2) (2010), 171, 184–85.

149 As was explained in Chapter 2, the value-add is measured by the sum of wages and profits: Howell H. Zee, 'VAT Treatment of Financial Services: A Primer on Conceptual Issues and Country Practices', *INTERTAX* 34(10) (2006), 458, 461; Alan Schenk, 'Taxation of Financial Services Under a U.S. Value-Added Tax', *Tax Law Review* 63(2) (2010), 409, 420; Alan Schenk and Oliver Oldman, 'Analysis of Tax Treatment of Financial Services under a Consumption Style VAT: A Report of the American Bar Association Section of Taxation Committee on Value Added Tax', *Tax Lawyer* 44(1) (1990–1991), 181, 191; Sijbren Cnossen, 'Global Trends

accounts-based subtraction VAT (see §5), Japan exempts banking and insurance supplies.[150] Some jurisdictions, such as New Zealand, Australia and Singapore, tax non-life insurance products.[151]

The difficulty in developing workable solutions to the taxation of financial supplies has led to a number of suggestions that a new tax, or series of taxes, might be needed to effectively tax the financial sector to fill the gap left by the good VAT.[152] This discussion of financial supplies highlights how the frontier issues that test the limits of the good VAT, such as the taxation of financial supplies, result in real VAT responses that fail, in varying ways, to live up to the promises of the good VAT. When the conventional approach itself is divided as to the appropriate VAT treatment of specific supplies, the diversity that follows in VAT practice is amplified.

and Issues in Value Added Taxation', *International Tax and Public Finance* 5(3) (1998), 399, 406.

[150] IBFD, *Country Surveys* (2014), 'Japan' – '8.6 – Exemptions'.

[151] Howell H. Zee, 'VAT Treatment of Financial Services: A Primer on Conceptual Issues and Country Practices', *INTERTAX* 34(10) (2006), 458, 474.

[152] The 'IMF has proposed a 'Financial Activities Tax' as an alternative to "fix" the VAT and raise revenue from the financial services sector'. This is essentially an addition method VAT: IMF, *Fiscal Monitor (November 2010) – Fiscal Exit: From Strategy to Implementation* (IMF Publication Services, Washington, DC, 2010), 76–77, 82. The Financial Activities Tax is a 'family of possible taxes' to tax the financial services sector; see further Michael Keen, Russell Krelove and John Norregaard, 'The Financial Activities Tax', in Stijn Claessens, Michael Keen and C. Pazarbasioglu (eds.), *Financial Sector Taxation: The IMF's Report to the G-20 and Background Material* (IMF, 2010), 118; International Monetary Fund (IMF), *A Fair and Substantial Contribution by the Financial Sector – Final Report for the G-20* (IMF, Washington, DC, 2010). Attention has also been paid to a suite of financial transaction taxes (FTTs) as a means to generate revenue and an attempt to regulate financial markets (through, for example, attempting to reducing the volume of speculative financial transactions). The IMF recommends a FAT over FTTs for the same reasons it opposes cascading transaction taxes: Thornton Matheson, 'Taxing Financial Transactions: Issues and Evidence', in Michael Keen, Russell Krelove and John Norregaard, 'The Financial Activities Tax', in Stijn Claessens, Michael Keen and C. Pazarbasioglu (eds.), *Financial Sector Taxation: The IMF's Report to the G-20 and Background Material* (IMF, 2010), 144, 176–78. The European Commission used the estimated revenue loss from exempting financial supplies to justify its proposed Financial Transactions Tax (FTT) – the FTT does not, however, attempt to tax the same base; for example, deposits and loans are exempt from the FTT: European Commission: 'Financial Transaction Tax: Making the Financial Sector Pay Its Fair Share' (Press Release, IP/11/1085, 28 September 2011). The FTT remains on the reform agenda but not yet realised: European Commission, 'Commission Proposes Green Light for Enhanced Cooperation on Financial Transactions Tax' (Press Release, IP/12/1138, 23 October 2012). As agreement from all member states has not been forthcoming, moves are under way to enable 11 member states to implement FTT reforms. However, there remain a number of unresolved issues, including a legal challenge by the UK to the enhanced cooperation procedure necessary to allow the 11 member states to proceed with the reforms: European Commission, *Taxation of the Financial Sector* (9 December 2013) (ec.europa.eu/taxation_customs/taxation/other_taxes/financial_sector/; Laurent De La Mettrie and Donald Murre, 'The European Financial Transaction Tax: Update', *Derivatives & Financial Instruments* (November/December 2013), 218–219.

4.3 *Many real VATs are levied at multiple rates*

The conventional approach acknowledges that the recommendation for VATs to be levied at a single rate is often not observed in real VATs.[153] Bird and Gendron, for example, note that not 'for the first time, however, the world does not seem to agree with the experts' and that despite 'the preponderance of expert advice favouring a single standard rate applied to all taxable transactions, most countries do not seem to be listening'.[154]

The average (unweighted) VAT rate in the OECD has risen in recent years to around 19 per cent. In part, this reflects increases in VAT rates across many EU member states to respond to the revenue pressures that resulted from the global financial crisis. However, there is significant variation in VAT rates across and within jurisdictions.[155] It is perhaps significant that Japan is both the only OECD country to levy a single-rate VAT (currently at 8 per cent) and the only one to adopt an accounts-based mechanism (see §5).[156] Four OECD countries apply a single rate but zero-rate certain domestic supplies (Australia, Denmark, Korea and New Zealand).[157] Within the EU, the *Recast VAT Directive* allows for up to two reduced

[153] Liam Ebrill et al., 'The Allure of the Value Added Tax', *Finance and Development* 39(2) (2002), 44–47; International Tax Dialogue (ITD), 'The Value Added Tax: Experience and Issues' (Background Paper Prepared for the International Tax Dialogue Conference on the VAT, Rome, March 15–16, 2005, ITD), 14; Liam Ebrill et al., *The Modern VAT* (IMF, Washington, DC, 2001), 66–68; OECD, *Consumption Tax Trends 2012: VAT/GST and Excise Rates, Trends and Administration Issues* (OECD Publishing, Paris, 2012), 67; Ken Messere, Flip de Kam and Christopher Heady, *Tax Policy: Theory and Practice in OECD Countries* (Oxford University Press, Oxford, 2003), 22. *Contra* Zee, who quite incredulously remarks that '[m]ost countries, except those in Western Europe, have now moved to a single-rate VAT, largely on account of administrative considerations': Howell H. Zee, 'VAT Treatment of Financial Services: A Primer on Conceptual Issues and Country Practices', *INTERTAX* 34 (10) (2006), 458, 461.

[154] Richard Bird and Pierre-Pascal Gendron, *The VAT in Developing and Transitional Countries* (Cambridge University Press, New York, 2007), 109.

[155] OECD, *Consumption Tax Trends 2012: VAT/GST and Excise Rates, Trends and Administration Issues* (OECD Publishing, Paris, 2012), 67.

[156] The Japanese Diet passed legislation for a staged increase in the rate of the consumption tax to 8 per cent (effective 1 April 2014) and then to 10 per cent (effective 1 October 2015). The proposals are subject to a number of restrictions and escape clauses. In addition, pressure is being applied from a member of the current coalition government to introduce reduced rates on certain essential items such as basic food items in response to the proposed rate increase: Atsuhi Shibata, 'VAT News – Japan' (2012) *International VAT Monitor* 23(5), 248, 365; Reiji Yoshida, 'Showdown over Sales Tax Breaks on the Horizon', *Japan Times* (online), 17 January 2013,japantimes.co.jp/text/nb20130117a5.html; IBFD, *Country Surveys* (2014) – 'Japan', '8.5 – Rates'. The OECD incorrectly lists the Slovak Republic as having no reduced rates when it has reduced rates and zero-rating (although the latter is not labelled zero-rating in the relevant laws): IBFD, *Country Surveys* (1 September 2014) – 'Slovak Republic', '8.5 – Rates' ; Fabiola Annacondia and Walter van der Corput, 'Overview of General Turnover Taxes and Tax Rates', *International VAT Monitor* (March/April 2009), 1, 3–10.

[157] Although Canada levies VAT at a single rate at a federal level, the interaction of the VAT with provincial sales taxes (not all of which are harmonized with the federal VAT) causes some

rates (of not less than 5 per cent). Efforts to formally set maximum rates have been stymied by resistance from member states. As a result, even with these restrictions on rates, EU member states continue to vary in their VAT rate structures. Among EU countries, rates range from a 1 per cent super reduced VAT rate on certain supplies in France to a standard rate of 27 per cent in Hungary.[158]

Rate variation tends to be justified by the need to alleviate vertical inequity, so that many real VATs apply higher rates on luxury items and lower rates on essential goods and services.[159] However, Van den Noord and Heady observe that rate differentiation is also used as a means of ad hoc revenue raising or to achieve industrial policy objectives such as promoting the tourism industry. The conventional approach criticises such measures as constituting non-transparent indirect subsidies.[160]

Developing countries tend to be more compliant on the measure of rate setting. More than 80 per cent of the 39 jurisdictions reported as levying VAT at a single rate rank as least developed or low- to middle-income countries on the UN development index. More than 60 per cent of the 32 jurisdictions that levy a single rate alongside zero-rating for domestic supplies are least developed and low- to middle-income jurisdictions.[161]

additional rate variation: OECD, *Consumption Tax Trends 2012: VAT/GST and Excise Rates, Trends and Administration Issues* (OECD Publishing, Paris, 2012), 67. See Chapter 6, §4.1 for why the classification of Australia as a country with a single-rate VAT is in itself questionable.

158 Member states must adopt a general VAT rate of at least 15 per cent on supplies of goods and services and may apply up to two reduced rates of not less than 5 per cent to a range of restricted goods (such as basic necessities). Further provision is made to apply a reduced rate, for example, in relation to labour-intensive services: *Recast VAT Directive 2006/112/EC*, art. 93–130 and Annex III and IV. For a list of the varied rates, see European Commission, *VAT Rates Applied in Member States of the European Union (situation as at 1 July 2013)* (Brussels, 2013); Richard Bird and Pierre-Pascal Gendron, *The VAT in Developing and Transitional Countries* (Cambridge University Press, New York, 2007), 11. States have also continued to vary from common VAT standards through the use of derogations, which allow a member state to depart from or vary a particular provision in EU law. This has facilitated further rate reductions for otherwise non-eligible categories, super-reduced rates and the zero-rating of domestic supplies: *Recast VAT Directive 2006/112/EC*, art. 395.

159 Annacondia and van der Corput report that 17 jurisdictions impose VAT at increased rates primarily on luxury goods and services. Many more have reduced rates: Fabiola Annacondia and Walter van der Corput, 'Overview of General Turnover Taxes and Tax Rates', *International VAT Monitor* (March/April 2009), 1, 3–10.

160 Paul van den Noord and Christopher Heady, 'Surveillance of Tax Policies: A Synthesis of Findings in Economic Surveys' (Economics Department Working Paper No. 303, OECD, 2001), 31. China employs different rates in line with industry policy objectives: OECD, *Consumption Tax Trends 2008 – VAT/GST and Excise Rates, Trends and Administration Issues* (OECD, Paris, 2008), 107.

161 Out of these countries, 32 of 39 have a single rate (and no zero-rating of domestic supplies), and 19 out of 32 of these countries adopt a single-rate VAT and zero-rate domestic supplies. Figures based on Fabiola Annacondia and Walter van der Corput, 'Overview of General Turnover Taxes and Tax Rates', *International VAT Monitor* (March/April 2009), 1, 3–10; United Nations Conference on Trade and Development, *The Least Developed Countries Report 2009: The State and Development Governance* (United Nations, Geneva, 2009), iii.

The greater compliance of developing countries on the measure of rate setting is notable in light of the fact that developing countries might have a stronger case for rate differentiation than developed countries, given the greater availability to the latter of other tax and expenditure tools to compensate for the VAT's potential vertical inequity.[162] Not much attention has been devoted to why developing and transitional economies fare better on the measure of rates when, on many other aspects of good VAT design and implementation, they generally fare much worse.[163] It might, for example, suggest a shared conviction among policy-makers in these jurisdictions to levy VAT at a single rate, or a political process more impervious to the political accretion of special rates. Alternatively, the compliance could reflect the fact that VAT rates are one of the most readily identifiable and measurable elements of VAT systems. As a result, it might be especially important for countries seeking, or in receipt of, funds to be seen to comply with IMF or World Bank advice.[164]

Others within the conventional approach prefer to view the issue along evolutionary lines, by emphasising how the real VATs that have been more recently introduced tend to more closely adhere to the single-rate recommendation. Although this might simply reflect the fact that most late VAT adopters are developing countries, Ebrill et al. prefer to conclude that this 'presumably reflects, in large part, the perceived success of existing single-rate VATs'.[165] The claim to perceived success is made despite the authors' later acknowledgement that some empirical evidence suggests that multiple-rate VATs might fare better on revenue generation,[166] which may, in turn, do no more than reflect that most multiple-rated VATs are in developed countries.

4.4 *The impact of departures from norm 1 on the incidence of real VATs*

Although most jurisdictions choose a consumption base and levy the VAT across all stages of the production and distribution chain, the major departure of real VATs

[162] Liam Ebrill et al., *The Modern VAT* (IMF, Washington, DC, 2001), 75.

[163] Richard Bird and Pierre-Pascal Gendron, *The VAT in Developing and Transitional Countries* (Cambridge University Press, New York, 2007), 22.

[164] See Chapter 4, §4.1 of this book.

[165] Liam Ebrill et al., *The Modern VAT* (IMF, Washington, DC, 2001), 47–48, 69; International Tax Dialogue (ITD), 'The Value Added Tax: Experience and Issues' (Background Paper Prepared for the International Tax Dialogue Conference on the VAT, Rome, March 15–16, 2005, ITD), 11–12. *Contra* Bogetic and Hassan, who find weak evidence that single-rate VATs generate higher revenues but caution that revenue performance is influenced by more than just rates, but by other factors such as the base and administration: Zeljko Bogetic and Fareed Hassan, 'Determinants of Value-Added Tax Revenue: A Cross-Section Analysis' (Policy Research Working Paper No. WPS 1203, Washington, DC, 1993), 9; Richard Bird and Pierre-Pascal Gendron, *The VAT in Developing and Transitional Countries* (Cambridge University Press, New York, 2007), 135.

[166] Liam Ebrill et al., *The Modern VAT* (IMF, Washington, DC, 2001), 79.

from the good VAT is in the widespread exclusions to the base and the significant rate variation of real VATs.

Chapter 2, §4 highlighted how the assumption that the economic incidence of the good VAT is on final consumption is disputed by some, who contend that the extent to which the VAT component can be forward shifted depends on other factors, such as market conditions determining the elasticity of supply and demand for goods and services and the degree of competition in the marketplace. Van Brederode, for example, cites a German study estimating that the business sector bore about 37 per cent of the VAT burden in Germany.[167] Although not going directly to incidence, a 2012 KPMG business survey confirms the potentially negative impact of VAT on business cash flow, with 61 per cent of survey respondents reporting that the VAT had a negative effect on their business's cash flow.[168] The conventional approach responds by stating that compliance with design norms 1 and 2 will more readily ensure that the final base is consumption. Therefore, the more real VATs depart from these design norms, the more likely it is that the VAT might not be fully borne by consumers, but by business as well. The widespread exclusions to the base, especially through the use of exemptions, contribute to real VATs not falling on a consumption base, as do departures from norm 2.

5 NORM 2 – CALCULATION OF VAT LIABILITY USING THE INVOICE-CREDIT MECHANISM

Most real VATs employ the invoice-credit mechanism.[169] Japan is the most notable exception, as it employs an accounts-based subtraction method to levy VAT.[170] The

[167] Robert F. van Brederode, *Systems of General Sales Taxation: Theory, Policy and Practice* (Kluwer Law International Alphen aan den Rijn, 2009), 33.

[168] Only 22 per cent reported the VAT as having a neutral impact, and 23 per cent reported a positive impact: KPMG, *The 2012 Benchmark Survey on VAT/GST* (KPMG International, 2012), 5–6.

[169] Howell H. Zee, 'VAT Treatment of Financial Services: A Primer on Conceptual Issues and Country Practices' (2006), *INTERTAX* 34(10), 458, 461. Perhaps reflecting the perception of the VAT in the US as a business tax, two US states have enacted variants of addition-method VATs. The Michigan Single Business Tax was a modified version of an addition-method VAT. New Hampshire has also employed an addition VAT. Israel employs an addition method for the calculation of VAT for financial and insurance supplies calculated by the sum of a firm's wages and profits: Carl S. Shoup, *Public Finance* (Aldine Publishing Company, Chicago, 1969), 258; Alan Schenk and Oliver Oldman, *Value Added Tax: A Comparative Approach* (rev. edn., Cambridge University Press, Cambridge; New York, 2007), 43; Alan A. Tait, *Value Added Tax* (McGraw-Hill, London, New York, 1972), 9–11; Liam Ebrill et al., *The Modern VAT* (IMF, Washington, DC, 2001), 20; Richard Bird and Pierre-Pascal Gendron, *The VAT in Developing and Transitional Countries* (Cambridge University Press, New York, 2007), 15.

[170] *Contra* Zee, who contends that the label of the Japanese VAT as an accounts-based subtraction-method VAT is erroneous and instead describes the Japanese consumption tax as a VAT levied through the credit method but without invoices (with some limited exceptions requiring invoices to substantiate credit refund claims on large transactions): Howell H. Zee, 'Further Thoughts on Reforming the VAT: Treatment of Financial Intermediation Services',

decision was largely politically motivated to appease a small business community notorious for its non-compliance with record-keeping and tax-paying obligations.[171] Despite the fact that administrative and compliance capabilities are even more limited in developing economies, these countries have tended to comply with conventional advice to implement the invoice-credit method VAT. The reasons for this compliance are not subject to much scrutiny within the conventional approach beyond referring to the merits of compliance with this design norm. Perhaps, as with VAT rates, it is because the norm is easily measured by outside organisations that provide assistance and funding. Whatever the reason for the greater formal compliance, significant problems affect the implementation of this norm across both developing and developed economies. This section will examine three prominent issues. The first – delay in, or denial of, the payment of refunds – is of particular concern in relation to developing countries. The remaining two – avoidance and fraud, administrative and compliance costs – are issues in both developed and developing economies.

5.1 *Denials and delays in the payment of refunds*

Chapter 2 demonstrated that in order for the VAT to apply to a consumption base, full and immediate crediting of the VAT paid on business inputs, including capital items, is required.[172] The conventional approach has highlighted that delays and denials of refunds, particularly in transitional and developing economies, are an area of concern in the administration of real VATs.[173]

Based on a study of 36 developing and developed economies, Harrison and Krelove find general compliance with the requirement of timely VAT refunds among developed countries, with the authors finding that refunds are generally paid within four weeks of a refund claim.[174] The joint World Bank/PricewaterhouseCoopers *Paying Taxes Report* (the '*Paying Taxes Report*') found that 65 per cent of businesses in the OECD that responded to their survey on VAT compliance reported the typical time taken to process VAT refunds as less than three months.[175] Although these refund times might be more than the 30-day statutory deadlines

in R. de la Feria (ed.), *VAT Exemptions: Consequences and Design Alternatives* (vol. 37, EUCOTAX Series on European Taxation, Kluwer Law International, Alphen aan den Rijn, 2013), 345, 346.

[171] Tatsuo Hatta, 'The Nakasone-Takeshita Tax Reform: A Critical Evaluation', *AEA Papers and Proceedings* 82(2) (1992), 231, 233.

[172] Chapter 2, §4 and §5 of this book.

[173] Liam Ebrill et al., *The Modern VAT* (IMF, Washington, DC, 2001), 66–67.

[174] Graham Harrison and Russell Krelove, 'VAT Refunds: A Review of Country Experience' (Working Paper No. WP/05/218, IMF, 2005), 5.

[175] PricewaterhouseCoopers, *The Impact of VAT Compliance on Business* (PricewaterhouseCoopers, 2012), 12.

legislated for in many jurisdictions,[176] the refund times are far better than in transitional and developing countries.

Harrison and Krelove identify refund times in developing countries as generally taking several months and sometimes more than a year.[177] These findings are supported by the *Paying Taxes Report*, which found that in Latin America, the Caribbean and African Union countries, around 19 per cent of business reported typical refund times of less than three months for the processing of refunds, while more than 30 per cent indicated times of more than a year.[178] In some cases, refunds are denied altogether. An indirect indicator of this phenomenon is the low levels of VAT refunds as a percentage of gross collections in developing countries. As Table 3.2 shows, refund levels are generally less than 20 per cent in low-income and developing countries, and often below 10 per cent in Africa, Asia and Latin America. Cambodia, for example, recorded a refund level of just 2.8 percent. This compares to an average refund level of 40 per cent within the EU, which is broadly in line with refund levels in developed countries and might be seen as something of a benchmark for developing and transitional economies.[179]

These results suggest a failure of governments in many developing and emerging economies to provide VAT refunds at all, let alone to provide them in a timely manner. The conventional approach notes that the delay or denial of refunds is a particular issue in relation to refunds made to exporters and other zero-rated providers, as well as to capital-intensive industries, because of a common practice of delaying or denying refunds for capital inputs.[180] The practice is a major cause of concern for the conventional approach because, as Cnossen explains:[181]

[176] Harrison and Krelove explain that '90 percent of the countries that responded to the IMF survey reported that their tax authorities are bound by law to making refunds within a prescribed timeframe, generally 30 days': Graham Harrison and Russell Krelove, 'VAT Refunds: A Review of Country Experience' (Working Paper No. WP/05/218, IMF, 2005) ,14, and at 6.

[177] Ibid., 5. Some jurisdictions provide for interest to be paid on late refunds: at 14.

[178] PricewaterhouseCoopers, *The Impact of VAT Compliance on Business* (PricewaterhouseCoopers, 2012), 12–13.

[179] The measure is indirect, as refund levels can be determined by a number of factors, including the extent to which investment generates excess VAT credits; the value added by export industries; the proportion of taxable and zero-rated sales in the economy; taxpayer behaviour; the extent of VAT fraud; and the number of VAT rates: Graham Harrison and Russell Krelove, 'VAT Refunds: A Review of Country Experience' (Working Paper No. WP/05/218, IMF, 2005), 8–9. Table 3.2 shows Tables 1 and 2 from the same source. Reproduced with permission.

[180] Ebrill et al. note that 'the processing of refunds in relation to exports is one of the most problematic features of the VAT in developing countries': Liam Ebrill et al., *The Modern VAT* (IMF, Washington, DC, 2001), 195 and at 66–67; International Tax Dialogue (ITD), 'The Value Added Tax: Experience and Issues' (Background Paper Prepared for the International Tax Dialogue Conference on the VAT, Rome, March 15–16, 2005, ITD), 31.

[181] Sijbren Cnossen, 'Global Trends and Issues in Value Added Taxation', *International Tax and Public Finance* 5(3) (1998), 399, 404–5.

> [D]isallowing the tax credit on capital goods.. . .violates the neutrality of VAT. . .deters investment, which hampers technological change. . .and acts as a disincentive to exports, because exporters facing world prices will have to absorb the tax.

Measuring the economic impact of the delay or denial of refunds is complicated by the fact that the delay and denial are often a product of VAT administration rather than the actual tax laws of the relevant jurisdictions.[182] Analysing the extent of the

TABLE 3.2 – *Value of VAT refunds as a percentage of gross VAT collections in advanced, transitional and emerging economies (1998–2001)*

Advanced economies	Refund amount (as % of gross VAT collections)	Transitional economies	Refund amount (as % of gross VAT collections)
Canada	50.3	Former Soviet Union countries	29.6
EU	38.1	Eastern Europe	36.8
New Zealand	35.5	Bulgaria	21.5
France	21.2	Hungary	48.2
Sweden	48.6	Latvia	49.1
United Kingdom (UK)	40.9	Romania	24.7
Ireland	24.9	Slovak Republic	53.9

Emerging economies	Refund amount (as % of gross VAT collections)	Other – Developing economies	Refund amount (as % of gross VAT collections)
Chile	28.8	Algeria	24.3
Colombia	4.1	Bolivia	10. 4
Indonesia	12.4	Cambodia	2.8
Asia (excluding Singapore)	7.0	Cameroon	8.8
Latin America	17.4	El Salvador	9.6
Morocco	5.1	Kenya	7.2
South Africa	39.5	Mozambique	2.7

[182] Michael Keen and Ben Lockwood, 'The Value Added Tax: Its Causes and Consequences', *Journal of Development Economics* 92(2) (2010), 138, 142.

problem therefore depends as much on accessing reliable information on refund claims from national VAT administrators.

A review of the documented reasons for the delays and denials of VAT refunds suggests a variety of reasons for the practices. These range from the inherent vulnerabilities in the invoice-credit method[183] to the poor administrative capacity of developing and emerging economies.[184] Keen and Smith identify the specific administrative difficulties that the invoice-credit method poses:[185]

> [R]efunds open up particular revenue risks, placing the tax authorities in an intrinsically awkward situation: too lax an attitude towards the payment of refunds invites fraud, while too miserly an attitude transforms the VAT into exactly what it is not supposed to be—a tax on production, and on exports in particular. Striking an appropriate balance between these two has proved one of the most difficult aspects of VAT administration.

It is therefore of no surprise that countries with weak tax administrations perform poorly on this measure. Harrison and Krelove report that two African countries enacted legislation to deny payment of all refund claims 'in an effort to wipe the slate clean of large backlogs of refund claims'.[186] In addition to administrative limitations, cash-flow difficulties and budget pressures in developing countries mean that refunds are delayed and denied. For example, Bird and Gendron report that Jamaica has been slow to pay refunds (and interest owing) because of cash-flow problems.[187] A final problem for developing and transitional countries is the corruption risk in the administration of refunds under the invoice-credit method:[188]

> For the scheme to work effectively, it requires a high-integrity (noncorrupt) accounting profession, together with a sufficiently strong tax administration and sound judicial system to enforce sanctions if required.

This problem is compounded by the risk of fraud inherent in the invoice-credit method of collection, as the next section explains.

183 Richard Bird and Pierre-Pascal Gendron, *The VAT in Developing and Transitional Countries* (Cambridge University Press, New York, 2007), 20.

184 Many VAT administrations, such as the Ukraine, struggle to clear a backlog of refund claims: Ibid., 177–78.

185 Michael Keen and Stephen Smith, 'VAT Fraud and Evasion: What Do We Know and What Can Be Done?' *National Tax Journal* 69(4) (2006), 861, 879. Graham Harrison and Russell Krelove, 'VAT Refunds: A Review of Country Experience' (Working Paper No. WP/05/218, IMF, 2005), 4.

186 Graham Harrison and Russell Krelove, 'VAT Refunds: A Review of Country Experience' (Working Paper No. WP/05/218, IMF, 2005), 16.

187 Richard Bird and Pierre-Pascal Gendron, *The VAT in Developing and Transitional Countries* (Cambridge University Press, New York, 2007), 177.

188 Graham Harrison and Russell Krelove, 'VAT Refunds: A Review of Country Experience' (Working Paper No. WP/05/218, IMF, 2005), 28.

5.2 VAT Fraud and Avoidance

The conventional approach acknowledges that experience shows that real VATs are less resistant to fraud and avoidance than might be suggested by the good VAT.[189] Although the specific issues vary, VAT avoidance and evasion are a significant issue across all jurisdictions.[190] VAT avoidance is an increasingly significant issue, with particularly elaborate schemes occurring in developed countries.[191] This is perhaps reflected by the tendency of more recently introduced VATs to contain general anti-avoidance provisions.[192]

The 'VAT gap' is yet another measure designed at estimating the performance of the VAT, albeit on a narrower range than the CER and VRR tests discussed at §4.1. The VAT gap reflects the difference between VAT actually collected and the VAT that should theoretically be collected if all taxpayers fully complied with the law. Although similar to the VRR in its calculation, unlike the VRR the theoretical VAT liability factors in actual tax rates, exclusions to the base and thresholds. As a result, it is a better measure for estimating revenue losses arising from compliance gaps such as VAT fraud, avoidance and unpaid VAT debts, rather than policy gaps. While not a direct measure of VAT fraud, the VAT gap provides one of the best measures currently available to estimate revenue losses that arise from evasion and avoidance activities.[193] The Reckon Report estimated that the 'VAT gap' across the

[189] Richard Bird and Pierre-Pascal Gendron, *The VAT in Developing and Transitional Countries* (Cambridge University Press, New York, 2007), 20; Michael Keen and Stephen Smith, 'VAT Fraud and Evasion: What Do We Know and What Can Be Done?' *National Tax Journal* 69(4) (2006), 861, 878–79.

[190] Richard Bird and Pierre-Pascal Gendron, *The VAT in Developing and Transitional Countries* (Cambridge University Press, New York, 2007), 25.

[191] Kent Matthews, 'VAT Evasion and VAT Avoidance: Is There a European Laffer Curve for VAT?' *International Review of Applied Economics* 17(1) (2003), 105. See also Chapter 6 of this book for a discussion of some of the issues in relation to Australia.

[192] This includes Australia (*A New Tax System (Goods and Services Tax) Act 1999* (Cth, div. 165), Canada (*Excise Tax Act*, RSC 1985, c E-15, s274) and New Zealand (*Goods and Services Tax Act 1985* (NZ), s 76). This is in direct contrast to the European approach, which is typically averse to such provisions: see generally Kerstin Alvesson, 'Anti-Avoidance Rules in the European Union and a Comparison with Canada and Australia', in M. Lang, P. Melz and E. Kristoffersson (eds.), *Value Added Tax and Direct Taxation: Similarities and Differences* (IBFD, Amsterdam, 2009), 517.

[193] A number of different methods exist to calculate the VAT gap – see Michael Keen, 'The Anatomy of VAT' (Working Paper No. WP/13/111, International Monetary Fund, 2013), 14–21; Central Planning Bureau (CPB), Netherlands Bureau for Economic Policy Analysis, *Study to Quantify and Analyse the VAT Gap in the EU-27 Member States – Final Report (TAXUD/2012/DE/316; FWC No. TAXUD/2010/CC/104)* (Study Commission by the European Commission, CPB Netherlands Bureau for Economic Policy Analysis, The Hague, 2013), 18–26. One commonly employed method employed by the latter study calculates the VAT gap on a top-down basis using national accounts data on household spending. Findings are constrained by the reliability of data and the relevant assumptions that are applied to estimate the VAT gap. For a further explanation, see Reckon Report, *Study to Quantify and Analyse the VAT Gap in the EU-25 Member States* (Reckon LLP, London, 2009), 5–10; OECD, *Consumption*

EU for the years 2000–2006 ranged from 12 to 14 per cent of theoretical VAT revenues, which in 2006 equated to approximately €106.7 billion.[194] A more recent report commissioned by the European Commission identified an increase in the VAT gap for the period 2000–2011. Across 26 member states, the average VAT gap was 17 per cent of theoretical VAT revenues, which in 2011 amounted to a loss of €193 billion (or 1.5 per cent of GDP).[195]

Studies have also shown VAT fraud to be a significant problem elsewhere.[196] For example, the US Government Accountability Office (GAO) studied VAT administration and compliance costs for Australia, New Zealand, Canada, France and the UK and noted that:[197]

> A VAT's reliance on credits and refunds makes the tax more susceptible than an income tax or RST to the compliance risks of fraudulent refund claims. Fraudulent refund claims could exist under a conceptually simple VAT [i.e., the good VAT] and are a particular concern for all our study countries.

VAT evasion has occurred with varying degrees of sophistication. Simple techniques include the falsification of invoices or the false claiming of refunds. More elaborate schemes include 'missing trader' fraud, whereby a bogus company is established to falsely claim VAT credits (with or without false invoices) and then disappears before VAT liabilities fall due (see Figure 3.2). This can occur in any jurisdiction.[198] The removal in 1993 of customs borders for intra-community trade in the EU also led to a number of schemes in the EU, such as 'carousel fraud'. A common type of carousel fraud exploits the VAT's incremental collection mechanism, the zero-rating of exports and the deferred payment of VAT on imports, which does not require VAT to be payable at the border for intra-

Tax Trends 2012: VAT/GST and Excise Rates, Trends and Administration Issues (OECD Publishing, Paris, 2012), 111; Michael Keen and Stephen Smith, 'VAT Fraud and Evasion: What Do We Know and What Can Be Done?' *National Tax Journal* 69(4) (2006), 861, 873.

194 Reckon Report, *Study to Quantify and Analyse the VAT Gap in the EU-25 Member States* (Reckon LLP, London, 2009), 8–9; European Commission, *Green Paper on the Future of VAT: Towards a Simpler, More Robust and Efficient VAT System* [2010] COM (2010) 695, 5.

195 There is great variation in results across member states. The median VAT gap across the EU-26 for 2000–2011 was 13 percent. The results show the VAT gap increased with the economic recession and with an increase in VAT rates: Central Planning Bureau (CPB), Netherlands Bureau for Economic Policy Analysis, *Study to Quantify and Analyse the VAT Gap in the EU-27 Member States – Final Report (TAXUD/2012/DE/316; FWC No TAXUD/2010/CC/104)* (Study Commission by the European Commission, CPB Netherlands Bureau for Economic Policy Analysis, The Hague, 2013), 10, 28.

196 Michael Keen and Stephen Smith, 'VAT Fraud and Evasion: What Do We Know and What Can Be Done?' *National Tax Journal* 69(4) (2006), 861, 873.

197 US Government Accountability Office, *Value-Added Taxes: Lessons Learned from Other Countries on Compliance Risks, Administrative Costs, Compliance Burden, and Transition (GAO-08-566)* (Washington, DC, 2008), 14.

198 Michael Keen and Stephen Smith, 'VAT Fraud and Evasion: What Do We Know and What Can Be Done?' *National Tax Journal* 69(4) (2006), 861, 865–68.

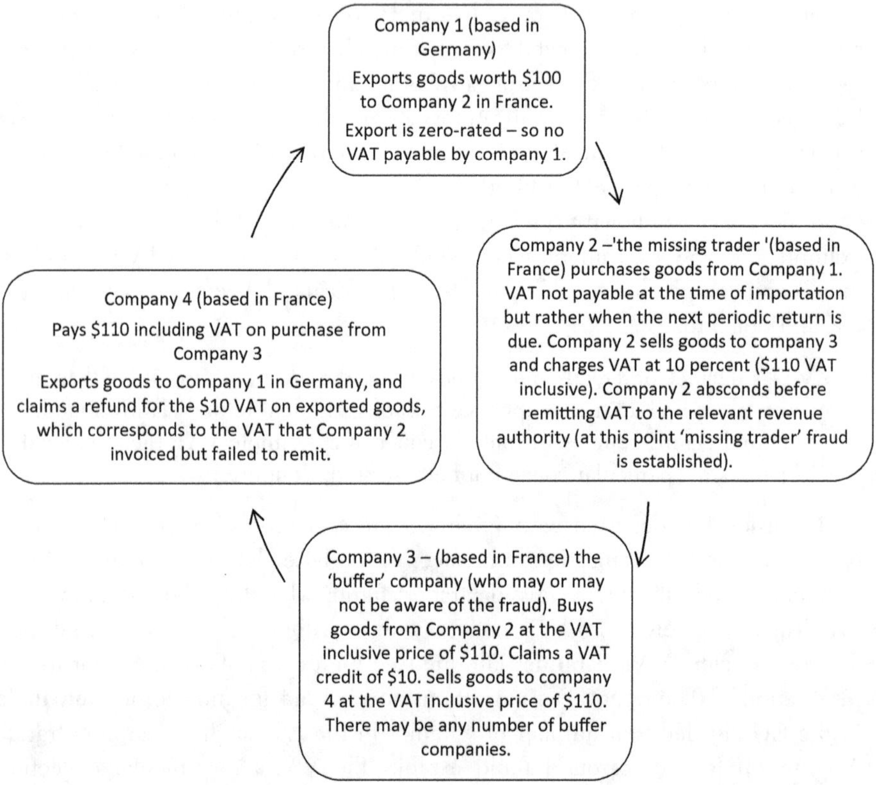

FIGURE 3.2 – Missing-trader fraud and carousel fraud[199]

community supplies but payable at the next periodic return.[200] Put very simply, these schemes exploit the time lag between incurring VAT liabilities and being required to remit VAT and involve at least one entity charging VAT and absconding before being required to remit the VAT to revenue authorities. Figure 3.2 provides a simplified example – the example assumes that there is no price markup for each transaction.

As Figure 3.2 shows, there is a total loss of revenue of $10 – which consists of the $10 VAT not remitted by Company 2. The carousel fraud is complete when the goods return to the country of origin of Company 1.[201] In practice, the schemes are

[199] Institute for Fiscal Studies, *Dimensions of Tax Design: The Mirrlees Review* (Oxford University Press, Oxford, 2010), Figure 4.3 from p. 312 – reproduced and adapted by permission of Oxford University Press. See also Michael Keen and Stephen Smith, 'VAT Fraud and Evasion: What Do We Know and What Can Be Done?' *National Tax Journal* 69(4) (2006), 861, 870–72.

[200] See generally Stephen Smith, 'VAT Fraud and Evasion', in Robert Chote et al. (eds.), *The IFS Green Budget* (Institute for Fiscal Studies, London, 2007), 167, 170.

[201] Michael Keen and Stephen Smith, 'VAT Fraud and Evasion: What Do We Know and What Can Be Done?' *National Tax Journal* 69(4) (2006), 861, 870–72.

far more complex and have developed apace with new technologies and markets, so much so that revenue authorities have struggled to keep pace with the various evasion techniques.[202]

A number of measures have been suggested to try to address this problem, as well as other evasion schemes. The measures include:

- Efforts to enhance information exchange, cooperation and coordination between the revenue authorities of EU member states,[203] such as the establishment of Eurofisc, a network of national officials charged with the detection and response to cross-border VAT evasion schemes such as carousel fraud. Moves to enhance cooperation and information exchange have extended beyond the EU and across the OECD;[204]
- Law reform options, including proposed reforms to the place of supply rules (see §6),[205] the introduction by some member states of joint and

[202] As Ainsworth explains, the schemes are not limited simply to goods, provided that the requisite elements of the fraud are present: VAT-free supply (purchase by the missing trader) + Taxable supply (collection of VAT by missing trader on an onward sale) + an entity (the missing trader) that disappears before VAT liability is due. The schemes have been as numerous, as there are available opportunities with notable schemes involving high-value and low-volume goods (supplies of computer chips, mobile phones) as well as services (emissions trading permits, VOIP/cell-phone minutes). Ainsworth labels these 'tradable services' (which can be bought and on-sold like goods), unlike consumable services (which are consumed on purchase, such as a restaurant meal) (see §6 of this chapter): Richard Ainsworth, 'VAT Fraud: MTIC & MTEC – The Tradable Services Problem' (Working Paper No. 10–39, Boston University School of Law, 2010), 3–4; Richard Ainsworth, 'VAT Fraud and Technological Solutions' in C. Philips (ed.), *The VAT Reader: What a Federal Consumption Tax Would Mean for America* (Tax Analysts, Arlington, VA, 2011), 204–6.

[203] The European Commission has responded to carousel fraud by adopting proposals to amend the *Recast VAT Directive (2006/112/EC)* and associated regulations to enhance collection and exchange of information on intra-communities supplies from 1 January 2010: Commission of the European Communities, *Communication from the Commission to the Council, the European Parliament, the European Economic and Social Committee, 'On a Coordinated Strategy to Improve the Fight against VAT fraud in the European Union'* COM (2008), 807; European Commission, *Green Paper on the Future of VAT: Towards a Simpler, More Robust and Efficient VAT System* [2010] COM(2010), 695, 5. See also Ine Lejeune, Jeanine Daou-Azzi and Mark Powell (of PricewaterhouseCoopers), 'The Balance Has Shifted to Consumption Taxes – Lessons Learned and Best Practices for VAT', in M. Lang, P. Melz and E. Kristoffersson (eds.), *Value Added Tax and Direct Taxation: Similarities and Differences* (IBFD, Vienna, 2009), 59, 87; Michael Keen and Stephen Smith, 'VAT Fraud and Evasion: What Do We Know and What Can Be Done?' *National Tax Journal* 69(4) (2006), 861–87; Sijbren Cnossen, 'VAT Coordination in Common Markets and Federations: Lessons from the European Experience', *Tax Law Review* 63(3) (2010), 583, 603–4.

[204] Council Regulation 904/2010 of 7 October 2010 on Administrative Cooperation and Combating Fraud in the Field of Value Added Tax (Recast) [2010] OJ L268 of 12/10/2010/1, art 18; OECD, *Consumption Tax Trends 2012: VAT/GST and Excise Rates, Trends and Administration Issues* (OECD Publishing, Paris, 2012), 54.

[205] The European Commission has acknowledged that the response to VAT fraud also requires a more coherent policy approach to non-member states: European Commission, *Communication from the Commission to the European Parliament and the Council on Concrete Ways to*

several liability provisions[206] and the introduction of a reverse-charge mechanism on selected vulnerable intra-community business-to-business (B2B) supplies. A reverse-charge mechanism means that the recipient of a supply remits the VAT rather than the supplier. If the recipient is a registered business, it self-assesses and applies for credit without collecting or paying VAT. While this addresses the missing trader issue (because Company 2 no longer has an incentive to go missing), it means that the VAT operates much like an RST. So, for example, the seller needs to ascertain the status of the recipient to determine whether to charge the VAT, and all the tax is collected at the final stage of the distribution chain (i.e., the sale to the final consumer), which therefore gives rise to all the fraud risks that such an approach entails.[207] The selective application of the reverse-charge mechanism to problematic supplies, such as the temporary option available to EU member states of applying the reverse-charge mechanism to supplies in carbon emissions trading permits, has thus far not been sufficient to stem abuse and has therefore prompted the European Commission to call for a more widespread application of the mechanism.[208] Reforms to date have

Reinforce the Fight against Tax Fraud and Tax Evasion Including in Relation to Third Countries COM(2012), 351, pp. 9–13; European Commission, *Communication from the Commission to the European Parliament and the Council on an Action Plan to Strengthen the Fight against Tax Fraud and Tax Evasion* COM(2012) 722, p. 11 (4.2.1.6). This is, in part, an acknowledgement of the growing problem of VAT fraud involving extra-community supplies. Particular issues have arisen in relation to growing missing-trader schemes involving extra-community supplies (Missing Trader Extra-Community Supply (MTEC)), which involve tradable services (such as VOIP minutes or emissions trading permits). The schemes exploit the fact that, unlike goods, the importation of a tradable service from a non-member state does not trigger VAT collection upon importation. Instead, place-of-supply rules dictate that the place of supply is the buyer's location, and if the buyer is a business, the business will apply the reverse-charge mechanism. This enables the requisite elements necessary to achieve missing-trader fraud: a VAT-free supply of a tradable service + collection of VAT on an onward supply + disappearing before VAT liabilities fall due: Richard Ainsworth, 'VAT Fraud: MTIC & MTEC – The Tradable Services Problem' (Working Paper No. 10-39, Boston University School of Law, 2010), 4–17.

[206] Under such provisions, a taxpayer may be jointly and severally liable if, at the time of the transaction, the taxpayer knew or should reasonably have known that some or all of the VAT payable in relation to the transaction would not in fact be paid: *Recast VAT Directive (2006/112/EC)*, art. 205; Sijbren Cnossen, 'VAT Coordination in Common Markets and Federations: Lessons from the European Experience' *Tax Law Review* 63(3) (2010), 583, 603.

[207] Lee Shepard, 'Addressing VAT Fraud Problems', *Tax Notes International* 46 (2007), 225. The recent Henry Review of taxation in Australia highlighted the same point: '[r]everse charging would be similar in effect to a retail sales tax, as some transactions within the supply chain would be excluded from GST, provided that the recipient is registered for GST': Commonwealth of Australia Treasury, Australia's Future Tax System Review Panel, *Australia's Future Tax System: Report to the Treasurer* (Australia's Future Tax System Review Panel: The Treasury, Canberra, 2009), 290.

[208] Council Directive 2010/23/EU of 16 March 2010 amending Directive 2006/112/EC on the Common System of Value Added Tax, as Regards an Optional and Temporary Application of

extended the reverse charge-mechanism to other vulnerable supplies[209] and introduced a Quick Reaction Mechanism to allow member states an expedited procedure to apply the reverse-charge mechanism to transactions suspected of sudden and massive VAT fraud;[210] and

- Efforts to strengthen VAT collection techniques ranging from proposals for real-time VAT collection and/or verification measures for B2B supplies to the certification of taxpayers' VAT processing systems.[211]

To date, despite numerous reviews and proposals, VAT fraud continues to outpace the response of EU revenue authorities.[212]

the Reverse-Charge Mechanism in Relation to Supplies of Certain Services Susceptible to Fraud [2010] OJ L72/1, art. 1. Although not recommending the application of a generalised reverse-charge mechanism for all intra-community B2B supplies, the EC has proposed extending the temporary mechanism to a wider range of problematic supplies. The measure would enable member states to apply the reverse-charge mechanism to certain problematic sectors rather than needing to rely on an individual derogation to do so: European Commission, *Communication from the Commission to the European Parliament and the Council on An Action Plan to Strengthen the Fight against Tax Fraud and Tax Evasion* COM(2012) 722, pp. 4–5; OECD, *Consumption Tax Trends 2012: VAT/GST and Excise Rates, Trends and Administration Issues* (OECD Publishing, Paris, 2012), 54.

209 The list of supplies include those of mobile telephones, certain gas and electricity supplies, telecommunication services, game consoles, tablet PCs and laptops and cereals and industrial crops: Council Directive 2013/43/EU of 22 July 2013 amending Directive 2006/112/EC on the Common System of Value Added Tax, as Regards an Optional and Temporary Application of the Reverse-Charge Mechanism in Relation to Supplies of Certain Goods and Services Susceptible to Fraud [2013] OJ L201/4.

210 Council Directive 2013/42/EU of 22 July 2013 amending Directive 2006/112/EC on the Common System of Value Added Tax, as Regards a Quick Reaction Mechanism against VAT Fraud [2013] OJ L201/1.

211 For example, under the real-time collection model, VAT would be charged and remitted to revenue authorities at the time of the settlement of a transaction (rather than VAT withheld and remitted later). Although such a proposal would address the exploitation of the time lag between the receipt of VAT by the missing trader and the remittance of VAT common to such missing-trader schemes, stakeholders have opposed such suggestions because of concerns over the cost and complexity of introducing such a system, as well as the significant cash-flow implications: European Commission, *Green Paper on the Future of VAT: Towards a Simpler, More Robust and Efficient VAT System* [2010] COM(2010) 695, 5.4; European Commission, Directorate-General Taxation and Customs Union, Indirect Taxation and Tax Administration, VAT and Other Turnover Taxes, *Summary Report of the Outcome of the Public Consultation on the Green Paper on the Future of VAT Towards a Simpler, More Robust and Efficient VAT System (1 December 2010 – 31 May 2011)*, taxud.c.1 (2011) 1417007, 5.4. For an overview of the technology-based options, see Richard Ainsworth, 'VAT Fraud and Technological Solutions', in C. Philips (ed.) *The VAT Reader: What a Federal Consumption Tax Would Mean for America* (Tax Analysts, Arlington VA, 2011), 204, 210–23.

212 OECD, *Consumption Tax Trends 2012: VAT/GST and Excise Rates, Trends and Administration Issues* (OECD Publishing, Paris, 2012), 54. For a summary of judicial responses to the issue, see Redmar Wolf, 'Mecsek-Gabona: The Final Step of the ECJ's Doctrine on Reliance on EU Law for Abusive or Fraudulent Ends in the Context of Intra-Community Transactions' (September/October 2013), *International VAT Monitor*, 280.

Developing countries are even more susceptible to the fraudulent schemes present in developed countries by virtue of their weaker administrative capacity. As the *ITD VAT Paper* highlights:[213]

> In addition to the reluctance of financially weak governments to pay refunds, it has become increasingly apparent that many tax administrations are incapable of policing the issuance of cash refunds to taxpayers without inviting abuse.

In some cases, the delays in refunds discussed at §5.1 are a product of attempts to guard against fraud.[214] In addition, the significant size of the informal economy means that the VAT chain can be bypassed altogether, and therefore the VAT is no more effective at reaching the cash economy than the retail sales tax.[215] Official fraud and corruption are also a major source of concern in developing countries. Stiglitz contends that:[216]

> ...one developing country after another has had problems in its rebate system. Sometimes rebates are paid only after a long lag. For firms facing a shortage of capital, this can be crippling. Even worse, the rebates have become a source of corruption, as fake documents have been used to secure large payments to corporations.

Stiglitz cites the example of Kenya, where corruption in relation to the issuing of VAT refunds prompted the introduction of a requirement that large refund claims be verified by a certified public accountant, which has reduced refund claims by 40 per cent – a figure that suggests the magnitude of the fraud.[217]

[213] International Tax Dialogue (ITD), 'The Value Added Tax: Experience and Issues' (Background Paper Prepared for the International Tax Dialogue Conference on the VAT, Rome, March 15–16, 2005, ITD), 31.

[214] Many countries, for example, have carry-forward provisions for non-exporters with excess VAT credits, whereby excess VAT credits, rather than being refunded, are carried forward from one tax period to the next on the assumption that subsequent tax periods should produce net VAT liabilities. The provisions attempt to improve revenue balance sheets while guarding against fraud. These carry-forward periods vary from 30 days to more than a year. The practice is common across Latin America: Graham Harrison and Russell Krelove, 'VAT Refunds: A Review of Country Experience' (Working Paper No. WP/05/218, IMF, 2005), 14; Victor Thuronyi, *Comparative Tax Law* (Kluwer Law International, The Hague, 2003), 315.

[215] Scott Riswold, 'VAT in Sub-Saharan Africa – A Critique of IMF VAT Policy', *International VAT Monitor* (March/April 2004), 97, 109; Joseph E. Stiglitz, 'Development-Oriented Tax Policy', in R. H. Gordon (ed.), *Taxation in Developing Countries: Six Case Studies and Policy Implications* (Columbia University Press, New York, 2010), 11, 15. Interestingly, PricewaterhouseCoopers contends that lessons learned from VAT fraud reinforce the need for a broad base and low rate, with a VAT rate of more than 25 per cent increasing the incentive for fraud compared with an 8–12 per cent VAT rate reducing the incentive. This reflects advice that used to be made in relation to the RST to keep rates low: PricewaterhouseCoopers, *Shifting the Balance: The Evolution of Indirect Taxes* (PricewaterhouseCoopers, 2007), 14.

[216] Joseph E. Stiglitz, 'Development-Oriented Tax Policy', in R. H. Gordon (ed.), *Taxation in Developing Countries: Six Case Studies and Policy Implications* (Columbia University Press, New York, 2010), 11, 13.

[217] Ibid., 11, 13.

Many resources have been devoted to stemming VAT fraud, with limited success.[218] Country-specific measures have included selectively matching invoices to verify refund claims (Pakistan); large-scale cross-checking of invoices (Korea, China); VAT withholding regimes that combine a reverse-charge mechanism with the requirement that VAT withheld be remitted to revenue authorities (common in Latin American jurisdictions such as Argentina and Ecuador);[219] and the establishment of special VAT bank accounts (Bulgaria).[220]

Beyond country-specific measures, the extent of the compliance issues in relation to cross-border supplies globally has led to a growing emphasis on the need for an internationally coordinated approach on VAT (see §6). These issues show that, as with the implementation of any other tax instrument, real VATs present points of weakness that are open to exploitation in practice.

5.3 *Administrative and compliance costs*

The conventional approach generally acknowledges that real VATs are not particularly simple or cheap to administer and comply with. Norregard and Khan refer to arguments that the claimed 'efficiency gains [of a VAT] can be offset by substantial administrative and compliance costs'.[221] Cnossen notes that administrative 'and compliance costs are not as low as is often believed'.[222] The *ITD VAT Paper* refers to the claim that the VAT is a 'particularly complex and costly tax to comply with and administer' and refers to indirect evidence in support of the claim, such as the fact that VAT revenues as a percentage of private consumption are generally higher

218 See, e.g., the efforts in Germany to make the buyer legally liable for the VAT not paid by the seller, which in practice has had little effect because of the difficulty in showing that the buyer knew of the seller's intention not to pay VAT. See further Richard Bird and Pierre-Pascal Gendron, *The VAT in Developing and Transitional Countries* (Cambridge University Press, New York, 2007), 179; Michael Keen and Stephen Smith, 'VAT Fraud and Evasion: What Do We Know and What Can Be Done?' *National Tax Journal* 69(4) (2006), 861, 880–84.

219 As with the real-time VAT collection mechanism, withholding regimes can have a significantly negative impact on business cash flow: Richard Ainsworth, 'VAT Fraud as a Policy Stimulus – Is the US Watching? VAT Withholding, RTVAT, and the Mittler Model' (Working Paper No. 11-08, Boston University School of Law, 2011), 2–5. The effectiveness of such withholding regimes depends on informal sector firms entering the VAT chain at some point (rather than completely circumventing it) as well as the willingness and capacity of tax administrations to credit withheld payments for compliant taxpayers: Michael Keen, 'VAT, Tariffs, and Withholding: Border Taxes and Informality in Developing Countries', *Journal of Public Economics* 92 (2008), 1892, 1894–95.

220 Graham Harrison and Russell Krelove, 'VAT Refunds: A Review of Country Experience' (Working Paper No. WP/05/218, IMF, 2005), 27–33.

221 John Norregaard and Tehmina S. Khan, 'Tax Policy: Recent Trends and Coming Challenges' (Working Paper No. WP/07/274, IMF, 2007), 38.

222 Sijbren Cnossen, 'Global Trends and Issues in Value Added Taxation' (1998), *International Tax and Public Finance* 5(3), 399, 426, n 39; Richard Bird and Pierre-Pascal Gendron, *The VAT in Developing and Transitional Countries* (Cambridge University Press, New York, 2007), 20.

with higher literacy rates.[223] Although the conventional approach acknowledges that 'there is little hard evidence on the costs of administering and complying with the VAT in developing countries',[224] this section demonstrates that the cost of VAT administration and compliance is indeed much greater in developing and transitional economies than in developed economies.

There is very little data on the administration costs of a VAT. Many within the conventional approach simply refer to Cnossen's estimation of administrative costs based on a good VAT in an OECD country.[225] HM Revenue and Customs in the UK estimate collection costs for the VAT at 0.55 per cent of revenue (compared to 1.278 per cent for the income tax), while in Europe estimates are between 0.5 and 1 per cent of revenue.[226] Chapter 6, §3.1.3 reveals that administrative costs are highest for the Australian VAT than any other federal tax.

Much of the evidence on compliance costs suggests that the VAT is relatively costly to comply with and that the impact of compliance falls heaviest on smaller business and on taxpayers in developing and transitional economies.[227] The *Paying Taxes Report* notes that worldwide, it 'takes longer to comply with VAT than it does with corporate income tax' with a model company requiring an average of 123 hours to comply with the VAT compared to an average of 74 hours to comply with the corporate income tax.[228] Indeed, the Paying Taxes Report estimates that across a world average, consumption taxes take longer to comply with than both labour taxes and the corporate income tax.[229] However, results are split along

[223] Literacy is treated as a de facto marker of administrative capacity: International Tax Dialogue (ITD), 'The Value Added Tax: Experience and Issues' (Background Paper Prepared for the International Tax Dialogue Conference on the VAT, Rome, March 15–16, 2005, ITD), 12; Liam Ebrill et al., *The Modern VAT* (IMF, Washington, DC, 2001), 47.

[224] Liam Ebrill et al., *The Modern VAT* (IMF, Washington, DC, 2001), 60.

[225] See Chapter 2, §5.2. There are virtually no publicly available data comparing administrative costs across countries and virtually no data on administrative costs in developing countries: Richard Bird and Pierre-Pascal Gendron, *The VAT in Developing and Transitional Countries* (Cambridge University Press, New York, 2007), 111.

[226] US Government Accountability Office, *Value-Added Taxes: Lessons Learned from Other Countries on Compliance Risks, Administrative Costs, Compliance Burden, and Transition (GAO-08-566)* (Washington, DC, 2008), 4–5, 15–16; Liam Ebrill et al., *The Modern VAT* (IMF, Washington, DC, 2001), 53.

[227] Richard Bird and Pierre-Pascal Gendron, *The VAT in Developing and Transitional Countries* (Cambridge University Press, New York, 2007), 20.

[228] Although the report does not say so, presumably this is an annual estimate: World Bank Group and PricewaterhouseCoopers, *Paying Taxes 2012: The Global Picture* (World Bank, 2012), 41. The lower compliance burden of the corporate income tax is consistent with the findings of Burgess and Stern, who contend that the corporate income tax is an effective revenue raiser because of the sizeable profits of corporations and the fact that they are bound to comply with statutory accounting requirements, unlike small traders and the agricultural sector. However, the finding of a higher compliance burden in relation to the VAT is not necessarily consistent with the authors' favourable assessment of the VAT: Robin Burgess and Nicholas Stern, 'Taxation and Development', *Journal of Economic Literature* 31(2) (1993), 762, 777, 812–15.

[229] The results were 108 hours for the consumption tax, 99 hours for labour taxes and 70 hours for the corporate income tax: World Bank Group and PricewaterhouseCoopers, *Paying Taxes*

developmental lines. The level of development, in essence, reverses the results, with high-income countries showing lower compliance times for consumption taxes than for labour taxes and the corporate income tax (although the difference between consumption tax compliance and corporate income tax compliance is marginal).[230] Nevertheless, these figures challenge the assumption within the conventional approach that the VAT compliance burden is less than the income tax, and cast some doubt on the claim that the merit of the VAT's inherent efficiency (as measured by compliance costs) has necessarily underpinned its rise.[231]

Other studies in developed countries suggest that VAT compliance costs are high, but perhaps not as high as the income tax in some jurisdictions.[232] Estimates of compliance burdens for Canada, New Zealand and the UK range from approximately 2 per cent of annual sales for small businesses (with less than $50,000 in sales) to 0.04 per cent for larger businesses (with more than $1,000,000 in sales).[233] Most studies confirm that VAT compliance costs are higher for small traders when measured as a percentage of sales.[234]

The cost of compliance is influenced by a number of factors, including the required frequency of filing VAT returns (with more time required for monthly returns than annual returns); documentary requirements such as the need to provide invoices; and technological factors, with compliance times reduced by 52 per cent in countries with online VAT filing systems (further assisted if VAT filings are coordinated with the filing requirements of other taxes).[235] As an indirect indication of the link between compliance and administration costs,

2012: The Global Picture (World Bank, 2012), 30. Consumption taxes include the VAT as well as other forms of sales tax: at 45.

[230] For high-income countries, the result is 69 hours for labour taxes, 51 hours for 'profits taxes', primarily the corporate income tax, and 48 hours for consumption taxes. For low-income countries, they were 115 hours for consumption taxes, 91 for labour taxes and 65 for the corporate income tax: World Bank Group and PricewaterhouseCoopers, *Paying Taxes 2012: The Global Picture* (World Bank, 2012), 30.

[231] Liam Ebrill et al., *The Modern VAT* (IMF, Washington, DC, 2001), 54, 60–61; but see above n 227.

[232] Ibid., 54.

[233] US Government Accountability Office, *Value-Added Taxes: Lessons Learned from Other Countries on Compliance Risks, Administrative Costs, Compliance Burden, and Transition (GAO-08-566)* (Washington, DC, 2008), 16; International Tax Dialogue (ITD), 'The Value Added Tax: Experience and Issues' (Background Paper Prepared for the International Tax Dialogue Conference on the VAT, Rome, March 15–16, 2005, ITD), 12.

[234] Cnossen describes the 'exceptional severity' of the VAT compliance burden on small business: Sijbren Cnossen, 'Administrative and Compliance Costs of the VAT: A Review of the Evidence' (1994) *Tax Notes International* 8, 1649, 1665–66; Liam Ebrill et al., *The Modern VAT* (IMF, Washington, DC, 2001), 53.

[235] World Bank Group and PricewaterhouseCoopers, *Paying Taxes 2012: The Global Picture* (World Bank, 2012), 41, 47; World Bank and the International Finance Corporation, *Doing Business 2013: Smarter Regulations for Small and Medium-Size Enterprises* (World Bank; International Finance Corporation, Washington, DC, 2013), 81.

PricewaterhouseCoopers note that 'there is a correlation between the time to receive a refund and the time to comply. On average it takes twice as long, or more, to comply with VAT in Africa and in Latin America and the Caribbean, where refunds are slower, than in the OECD and EU countries.'[236]

The higher relative cost of VAT compliance in developing countries[237] leads Stiglitz to question the appropriateness of VAT for developing counties:[238]

> Even the VAT's alleged administrative advantages (low compliance costs) may not be true for developing countries . . .[because t]he so-called self-enforcing property of the VAT can easily unravel – and it often does in developing countries where farmers and small producers sell directly to consumers.

One response of the conventional approach to this critique is to emphasise how the VAT can positively transform tax administration and taxpayer compliance by, for example, introducing requirements to keep records and to self-assess.[239] The claim, however, seems overstated. Ebrill et al. note that some transitional economies departed from the advice to self-assess VAT, and other developing jurisdictions have struggled to successfully implement effective self-assessment procedures.[240] While the self-enforcing mechanism of the VAT should be compatible with self-assessment, Ebrill et al. note that 'experience indicates the positive impact of self-checking on VAT compliance can be over-estimated'.[241] The strength of the connection might more accurately be described as those who were already able to keep appropriate accounts and invoices are also those who are able to self-assess. It is therefore not entirely clear why the VAT fares any better than the self-assessing

[236] PricewaterhouseCoopers, *The Impact of VAT Compliance on Business* (PricewaterhouseCoopers, 2012), 12. The European Commission Green Paper on the future of the VAT lists improving the VAT compliance burden as a major priority for reform: European Commission, *Green Paper on the Future of VAT: Towards a Simpler, More Robust and Efficient VAT system* [2010] COM(2010) 695, 4.

[237] See also Joshua Aizenman and Yothin Jinjarak, 'The Collection Efficiency of the Value Added Tax: Theory and International Evidence', *Journal of International Trade and Economic Development* 17(3) (2008), 391.

[238] Joseph E. Stiglitz, 'Development-Oriented Tax Policy', in R. H. Gordon (ed.), *Taxation in Developing Countries: Six Case Studies and Policy Implications* (Columbia University Press, New York, 2010), 11, 12–13.

[239] Michael Keen, 'VAT, Tariffs, and Withholding: Border Taxes and Informality in Developing Countries', *Journal of Public Economics* 92 (2008), 1892, 1903; John Norregaard and Tehmina S. Khan, 'Tax Policy: Recent Trends and Coming Challenges' (Working Paper No. WP/07/274, IMF, 2007), 38; Liam Ebrill et al., *The Modern VAT* (IMF, Washington, DC, 2001), 138; International Tax Dialogue (ITD), 'The Value Added Tax: Experience and Issues' (Background Paper Prepared for the International Tax Dialogue Conference on the VAT, Rome, March 15–16, 2005, ITD), 12; Michael Keen and Ben Lockwood, 'The Value Added Tax: Its Causes and Consequences', *Journal of Development Economics* 92(2) (2010), 138, 147; Robin Burgess and Nicholas Stern, 'Taxation and Development', *Journal of Economic Literature* 31 (2) (1993), 762, 814.

[240] In 2001, 16 transitional economies did not adopt the self-assessment basis: Liam Ebrill et al., *The Modern VAT* (IMF, Washington, DC, 2001), 139.

[241] Ibid., 140.

income tax does in promoting improved tax administration and taxpayer compliance.[242] Moreover, the rush to introduce VAT in these jurisdictions has often been at the expense of adequate preparation to improve administrative capacity, thereby undermining the operation of real VATs. Ebrill et al. identify that in many transitional economies in the former Soviet Union, the conditions for self-assessment were not met because of inadequate preparation.[243] The failure to make adequate administrative preparation before the introduction of the VAT, often as a result of external pressure from the IMF to introduce a VAT, has also undermined VAT administration in a number of other countries, such as Ethiopia, Kenya and Mozambique.[244]

An alternative response of the conventional approach is to attribute complexity in administration and compliance to departures from the three design norms for the good VAT, and therefore to make the case for the reform of real VATs along the lines of the three design norms for the good VAT. A US Government Accountability Office report on compliance summarises the issues:[245]

> Although we were not able to find any direct quantitative evidence of how VAT complexity impacts administrative costs, tax officials and VAT experts said that complexity increases administrative costs and compliance burden and creates opportunities for noncompliance. VAT preferences introduce rules that apply only to a specific set of goods or services. Such preferences create the need to define the boundaries between goods and services getting different tax treatments, and may result in businesses misclassifying certain goods or services purchased or sold and reducing VAT revenue. Preferences that add complexity to the tax code also increase the time and resources needed for audits and education activities. Exemptions, reduced rates, and zero-rating also add to compliance burden by increasing the time and resources businesses must spend on accounting and record-keeping activities, in order to categorize their sales and purchases as fully taxable, reduced rated, zero-rated, or exempt. In the case of a business making both taxable and

[242] See also Riswold, who argues that 'it is certainly possible that these [administrative and compliance benefits] can all happen without the introduction of VAT': Scott Riswold, 'VAT in Sub-Saharan Africa – A Critique of IMF VAT Policy', *International VAT Monitor* (March/April 2004), 97, 108.

[243] Liam Ebrill et al., *The Modern VAT* (IMF, Washington, DC, 2001), 143.

[244] Scott Riswold, 'VAT in Sub-Saharan Africa – A Critique of IMF VAT Policy', *International VAT Monitor* (March/April 2004), 97, 109; Wollela Abehodie Yesegat, 'Value Added Tax Administration in Ethiopia: A Reflection of Problems', *eJournal of Tax Research* 6(2) (2008), 145.

[245] US Government Accountability Office, *Value-Added Taxes: Lessons Learned from Other Countries on Compliance Risks, Administrative Costs, Compliance Burden, and Transition (GAO-08-566)* (Washington, DC, 2008), 27. The *ITD VAT Paper* states that '[i]t is widely agreed that collection costs are significantly lower where the VAT is simple, with a single rate and high threshold are [sic] conducive to relatively low collection costs': International Tax Dialogue (ITD), 'The Value Added Tax: Experience and Issues' (Background Paper Prepared for the International Tax Dialogue Conference on the VAT, Rome, March 15–16, 2005, ITD), 12.

exempt sales, the business must also apportion its use of inputs and claim input tax credits only for inputs in taxable sales.

Chapter 2, §5.2 outlined a number of advantages that lead the conventional approach to prefer the invoice-credit method VAT over its main rival, the RST. As this section demonstrated, these promised gains are undermined by repeated failings to implement both the first and second design norm in real VATs. These real-world failings in turn increase the complexity and costs of real VATs.

6 NORM 3 – LEVYING REAL VATS ON A DESTINATION BASIS

Most real VATs are designed to be levied on a destination basis so as to tax at the point of final consumption.[246] As was explained in Chapter 2, this should have the practical effect that exports attract no VAT, while imports are taxed the same as domestically produced goods. However, problems with the implementation of this design norm mean that this is not always the case.

As Chapter 2 explained, a destination VAT has traditionally been administratively dependent on borders, and more specifically on the effective administration of those borders to allow for VAT refunds on exports and to impose VAT on imports.[247] As a result, weak borders therefore make the destination principle harder to achieve. Specific practical challenges are therefore posed by the removal of border controls (as for intra-community trade in the EU and sub-national VATs);[248] weak border controls (as for developing countries); and technological advances that have facilitated a massive shift toward trade in intangible goods and cross-border services that do not respect traditional borders (such as global telecommunications and international transport).[249] These challenges mean that the application of the destination principle in a world of porous borders is one of the frontier issues that, like the taxation of financial services, test the limits of the good VAT and result in a number of complexities in real VATs. This book uses the example of financial services to demonstrate the types of problems that arise in

[246] The discrete exceptions include French Polynesia, Netherlands Antilles, Palestine Autonomous Areas, Suriname, Turkmenistan and Western Samoa: Fabiola Annacondia and Walter van der Corput, 'Overview of General Turnover Taxes and Tax Rates', *International VAT Monitor* (March/April 2009), 1, 3–10. Russia taxes oil and gas supplies according to the origin principle. Until July 2001, Russia and other jurisdictions in the Commonwealth of Independent States (CIS) taxed all cross-border trade of goods within the Commonwealth of Independent States according to the origin principle: OECD, *Consumption Tax Trends 2008 – VAT/GST and Excise Rates, Trends and Administration Issues* (OECD, Paris, 2008), 110; Richard Bird and Pierre-Pascal Gendron, *The VAT in Developing and Transitional Countries* (Cambridge University Press, New York, 2007), 15.

[247] Peggy Musgrave, 'Consumption Tax Proposals in an International Setting', *International VAT Monitor* (March/April 2001), 56, 61.

[248] For an overview of the issues, see Rita de la Feria, *The EU VAT System and the Internal Market* (IBFD, Amsterdam, 2009).

[249] Liam Ebrill et al., *The Modern VAT* (IMF, Washington, DC, 2001), 184–88.

relation to these frontier issues, but a brief overview of some of the key practical and technological issues experienced in applying real VATs on a destination basis further demonstrates the difficulties that arise in practice when the limits of the good VAT are tested.[250]

Ebrill et al. note that levying the VAT on imports has proven to be an effective means of collecting revenue, amounting to more than two-thirds of collections in some jurisdictions.[251] Keen claims that, consistent with the expectations of the good VAT, the large share of VAT collections on imports makes the VAT well suited to replace revenue from tariffs in developing and transitional economies. However, empirical evidence suggests that practical experience has not necessarily lived up to the good VAT's promise, with many low-income economies failing to fully recover lost trade tax revenue.[252] Further, as discussed in §5.1, the practice of delaying and denying VAT refunds to exporters means that often real VATs in developing countries operate as a de facto tax on exports and therefore as an implicit tax on domestic production, given that the VAT paid by an exporter might not be recovered from revenue-needy and/or corrupt and/or weak administrations.[253] This practice leads to a number of non-neutralities. It might, for example, disadvantage exporters in absolute terms (by subjecting them to unrecoverable tax) and in relative terms vis-à-vis businesses supplying to the domestic market because goods produced for the domestic market might escape taxation because of the large informal economy.[254] These outcomes of real VATs lead Desai and Hines to find

[250] For more comprehensive accounts, see Michael Keen and Walter Hellerstein, 'Interjurisdictional Issues in the Design of a VAT', *Tax Law Review* 63(2) (2010), 359; Rebecca Millar, 'Cross-Border Services', in R. Krever (ed.), *VAT in Africa* (Pretoria University Law Press, Pretoria, 2008), 175; Rebecca Millar, 'Cross-Border Services: A Survey of the Issues', in R. Krever and D. White (eds.), *GST in Retrospect and Prospect* (Thomson Brookers, Wellington, NZ, 2007), 317; OECD, *Report on Consumption Tax Obstacles to Cross-Border Trade in International Services and Intangibles* (OECD, Paris, 2004); OECD, *The Application of Consumption Taxes to the International Trade in Services and Intangibles* (OECD, Paris, 2005). See also M. Lang, P. Melz and E. Kristoffersson (eds.), *Value Added Tax and Direct Taxation: Similarities and Differences – Online Books IBFD* (IBFD, Amsterdam, 2009) – the extent of the issue is indicated by the fact that most contributions address jurisdictional issues relating to cross-border supplies.

[251] Liam Ebrill et al., *The Modern VAT* (IMF, Washington, DC, 2001), 49–50; Michael Keen, 'VAT, Tariffs, and Withholding: Border Taxes and Informality in Developing Countries', *Journal of Public Economics* 92 (2008), 1892, 1894.

[252] Michael Keen, 'VAT, Tariffs, and Withholding: Border Taxes and Informality in Developing Countries', *Journal of Public Economics* 92 (2008), 1892, 1894, 1901–3.

[253] Michael Keen and Ben Lockwood, 'The Value Added Tax: Its Causes and Consequences', *Journal of Development Economics* 92(2) (2010), 138, 139, 145. For a critique, see M. Shahe Emran and Joseph E. Stiglitz, 'On Selective Indirect Tax Reform in Developing Countries', *Journal of Public Economics* 89 (2005), 599, 619.

[254] M. Shahe Emran and Joseph E. Stiglitz, 'On Selective Indirect Tax Reform in Developing Countries', *Journal of Public Economics* 89 (2005), 599, 619; *Contra* Keen, who claims that the collection of VAT on imports together with appropriate withholding regimes enables the VAT to reach the inputs of the informal sector. However, this argument does not address the specific problems arising from the failure to refund VAT to exporters: Michael Keen, 'VAT,

a negative link between the presence of a VAT and trade flows for developing countries. They conclude that the 'results suggest that VAT practice differs markedly from VAT theory, and point to the potential salutary effects of reforming VAT administrations in countries around the world'.[255]

The Chinese VAT provides an interesting example of divergence from this design norm. Initially, the Chinese government selectively denied VAT refunds to exporters for the familiar reasons adopted by developing and transitional economies, such as the desire to retain revenue and concerns about VAT fraud.[256] However, despite an improved fiscal position, the Chinese government still selectively applies different VAT rebate rates on exports to different industries in line with the shifting emphasis of the Chinese government's industrial policies. Cui notes that the Chinese administration views the zero-rating of exports as a 'merely aspirational objective', and he claims that 'whether exports should receive a full VAT rebate has become deeply entangled with hugely controversial issues relating to China's exchange rate and trade policy'.[257] In the use of VAT refunds as an 'intentionally non-neutral. . .instrument of trade policy',[258] China has reduced the rate at which the VAT is refunded to carbon-intensive exports (to zero on selected items) but increased rates of refund to promote high-technology industries.[259]

Increasingly for developed countries, the biggest challenge to the destination principle is a technological one. Many VAT rules were drafted, or influenced by rules that were drafted, at a time when most supplies were of tangible goods and most services were consumed at the place they were supplied.[260] As the OECD has highlighted, these VAT rules have struggled to keep pace with technological advances, such as the Internet, that have among other things facilitated the rapid expansion of global trading markets; the emergence of large multinational corporations able to supply services across a range of jurisdictions through complex and

Tariffs, and Withholding: Border Taxes and Informality in Developing Countries', *Journal of Public Economics* 92 (2008), 1892, 1893–95.

255 Mihir A. Desai and James R. Hines Jr, 'Value-Added Taxes and International Trade: The Evidence' (Workshop in Law and Economics Working Paper, University of Chicago, Law School, 2002), 21; *Contra* Keen and Lockwood, who caution that it is premature to attribute a *causal* link between the VAT and poor trade performance: Michael Keen and Ben Lockwood, 'The Value Added Tax: Its Causes and Consequences', *Journal of Development Economics* 92 (2) (2010), 138, 145.

256 Wei Cui, 'Indirect Taxation of Cross-Border Services in China: (Partial) Switch to Destination-Based Taxation', in M. Lang, P. Melz and E. Kristoffersson (eds.), *Value Added Tax and Direct Taxation: Similarities and Differences* (online book, IBFD, Amsterdam, 2009), I, Introduction.

257 Ibid. 258 Ibid.

259 OECD, Consumption Tax Trends 2008 – VAT/GST and Excise Rates, Trends and Administration Issues (OECD, Paris, 2008), 107–8; PricewaterhouseCoopers, *Shifting the Balance: The Evolution of Indirect Taxes* (PricewaterhouseCoopers, 2007), 46.

260 OECD, *Consumption Tax Trends 2012: VAT/GST and Excise Rates, Trends and Administration Issues* (OECD Publishing, Paris, 2012), 49; Richard Krever, 'Designing and Drafting VAT Laws for Africa', in R. Krever (ed.), *VAT in Africa* (Pretoria University Law Press, Pretoria, 2008), 9, 27.

often opaque corporate structures; and new forms of products and services that defy the traditional categories of goods and services, as well as new and complex supply chain processes which give rise to them.[261] For example, now it is possible not only to speak of tangible and intangible goods but to distinguish between 'consumable services' (which are consumed immediately on or after supply, such as a restaurant meal) and 'tradable services' (which can be bought and on-sold like goods and which can be consumed in a jurisdiction [or across multiple jurisdictions] other than where the service was provided, such as the provision of VOIP services).[262] However, unlike tangible goods, tradable services do not respect traditional customs borders, are incapable of being physically traced and are therefore much more difficult to tax according to traditional criteria and much more susceptible to fraud (see §5.2).

As Chapter 2 explained, a VAT levied on a destination basis requires place and time of supply rules to effectively determine where and when consumption occurs in order to establish which jurisdiction to tax.[263] Although identifying the place of supply for tangible goods or consumable services might be relatively straightforward, determining when and where a tradable service has been consumed is a far more complex proposition.[264] Rendahl provides an example that outlines some of the issues and approaches involved:[265]

[261] OECD, *Consumption Tax Trends 2012: VAT/GST and Excise Rates, Trends and Administration Issues* (OECD Publishing, Paris, 2012), 49.

[262] Richard Ainsworth, 'VAT Fraud: MTIC & MTEC – The Tradable Services Problem' (Working Paper No. 10-39, Boston University School of Law, 2010), 3–4. The terminology used to classify different supplies based on the nature of the service varies. The OECD adopts the terminology of 'tangible services' as an attempt to include those services for which the identification of the place of consumption might be regarded as fairly straightforward. This might be the case where a service is performed in the immediate presence of the supplier and customer, such as with the purchase of a restaurant meal (this meets Ainsworth's consumable service definition). Or the term 'tangible service' might also refer to a supply where consumption of the service might be more readily ascertained because it relates to a more readily identifiable thing such as immovable property or goods. By contrast, 'intangible services' is used to describe services capable of being delivered in a remote location and capable of being used in more than one jurisdiction, which more readily resembles Ainsworth's tradable service category. Given the brevity of the discussion here, these terminological issues will not be explored further and the term 'tradable service' will be used for the purposes of this discussion: OECD, *Consumption Tax Trends 2012: VAT/GST and Excise Rates, Trends and Administration Issues* (OECD Publishing, Paris, 2012), 49; Michael Keen and Walter Hellerstein, 'Interjurisdictional Issues in the Design of a VAT', *Tax Law Review* 63(2) (2010), 359, 371–74; Rebecca Millar, 'Cross-Border Services: A Survey of the Issues', in R. Krever and D. White, (eds.), *GST in Retrospect and Prospect* (Thomson Brookers, Wellington, NZ, 2007), 317.

[263] See Chapter 2, §6 of this book.

[264] Of course, there are problems in identifying the consumption of tangible or consumable services: see Rebecca Millar, 'Cross-Border Services: A Survey of the Issues', in R. Krever and D. White (eds.), *GST in Retrospect and Prospect* (Thomson Brookers, Wellington, NZ, 2007), 317, 318–21; Richard Krever, 'Designing and Drafting VAT Laws for Africa', in R. Krever (ed.), *VAT in Africa* (Pretoria University Law Press, Pretoria, 2008), 9, 27; Liam Ebrill et al., *The Modern VAT* (IMF, Washington, DC, 2001), 187.

[265] Pernilla Rendahl, *Cross-Border Consumption Taxation of Digital Supplies* (online ed., IBFD, Amsterdam, 2009), §1.1.

> Consumer X resident in Sweden but currently on vacation in Canada downloads a standard contract from a Canadian webpage. Consumer Y resident in Australia downloads music files from a British webpage. Consumer Z resident in Canada uses an IP-telephone phoning a friend in Australia; later on she watches a soccer game streamed to her computer. In order to decide where these transactions should be consumption taxed it is vital to establish where these three consumers usually reside, and from which state these services are supplied. The consumers' place of residence and the place where the supplier has established her business is, however, less important than access to the different supplies, considering that they can be obtained and supplied from a distance. The access to the services is instead limited by the technical equipment used by the consumer and the supplier as well as available networks. Furthermore, the classification of these supplies affects whether they are considered as taxable transactions and, if so, the applicable tax rate.

Although the ultimate aim is to tax where the service is consumed, the impossibility of effectively tracing the physical flow of such services across borders means that place-of-supply rules use a series of proxies such as taxing according to the location of the consumer or the supplier.[266] Complicating the issue is the fact that jurisdictions may have differing responses to these technological challenges and might therefore classify the same supply differently.[267] For example, a digital supply might be classified as the supply of a service in one jurisdiction, but may be classified as the supply of an intangible good in another.[268] These different classifications can in turn trigger the application of different rules, which may result in the unintended consequences of double or non-taxation that are outlined below.

Discrete problems can arise in taxing business-to-consumer (B2C) supplies and business-to-business (B2B) supplies.[269] For example, additional enforcement problems can arise in relation to remote B2C supplies of tradable services where, for example, the supply is made by a business based in a different jurisdiction from the customer and there is no power within the customer's jurisdiction to compel the remote supplier to levy VAT. Whereas with a B2B supply this obligation can be transferred to the business purchaser through mechanisms such as the reverse charge, the same option is not available for end consumers.[270]

[266] OECD, *Consumption Tax Trends 2012: VAT/GST and Excise Rates, Trends and Administration Issues* (OECD Publishing, Paris, 2012), 36.

[267] OECD, *Consumption Tax Trends 2012: VAT/GST and Excise Rates, Trends and Administration Issues* (OECD Publishing, Paris, 2012), 45.

[268] Pernilla Rendahl, *Cross-Border Consumption Taxation of Digital Supplies* (online ed., IBFD, Amsterdam, 2009), §4.2.4.

[269] For an overview of business to consumer issues, see Pernilla Rendahl, *Cross-Border Consumption Taxation of Digital Supplies* (online ed., IBFD, Amsterdam, 2009). See above, n 250.

[270] As noted in Chapter 2, the good VAT seeks to tax final consumption and is levied incrementally through each stage of the production and distribution chain. It might seem anathema to define consumption as occurring when a business acquires a service (as this should have no necessary bearing on the taxation of the end consumer). However, as the OECD identifies, pragmatics might dictate drafting place-of-supply rules to redefine 'consumption' as occurring when a business acquires or even supplies a tradable service, so as to facilitate the implementation of the destination principle. This might be to address the enforcement concerns relating

Even if different jurisdictions can agree on how to categorise the thing supplied and the appropriate tax treatment of B2B and B2C supplies, they may have different place-of-supply rules for the same supply, which can produce different and sometimes conflicting outcomes. Reforms have been proposed to address problems that have arisen in the EU as a result of discrepancies between place-of-supply rules that depend on, among other things, the nature of the thing supplied and the status of the customer (business or consumer).[271] For example, in relation to extra-community supplies, a B2B supply of a service will, in general terms and subject to a number of exceptions, be taxed according to the location of the customer; a B2C supply of a service will be taxed according to the location of the supplier, although with exceptions.[272] Among the most significant of these exceptions is that certain electronic supplies (such as the electronic provision of websites, software, music, film, or games, and broadcast services) provided by a supplier from a non-member state to an end consumer in a member state will be taxed according to the location of the end consumer.[273] In contrast to the EU framework, the New Zealand approach starts from a focus on the residence of the supplier subject to a

to remote B2C supplies or to ensure that business can recover VAT paid on inputs: OECD, *Consumption Tax Trends 2012: VAT/GST and Excise Rates, Trends and Administration Issues* (OECD Publishing, Paris, 2012), 33–34; Keen, Michael and Hellerstein, Walter, 'Interjurisdictional Issues in the Design of a VAT', *Tax Law Review* 63(2) (2010), 359, 376.

[271] The EU has its own unique set of problems in determining appropriate place-of-supply rules for intra-community trade. Reforms have been directed at redrafting place-of-supply rules for both intra-community and extra-community trade in services. Place-of-supply rules in relation to services have changed from a focus on the supplier's location (be it place of business, permanent establishment or residence) to different rules depending on the nature of the thing supplied and the status of the purchaser. Although taxing according to the supplier's location might more closely resemble an origin-based approach, for traditional supplies of consumable services where the service provider and consumer were usually in the same location, the rules were generally aligned with the destination approach. However, the proliferation of tradable services has called for a change of approach, so as to better meet the general goal of taxing services at the place of consumption. The new rules for intra-community trade are similar to those for extra-community trade. Subject to a number of exceptions, an intra-community B2B supply of a service will be taxed in the jurisdiction of the customer and a B2C supply will be taxed according to the location of the supplier. As of 2015, certain intra-community B2C supplies (such as telecommunications, radio and television and electronically supplied services) will be taxed according to the customer's location through a one-stop-shop mechanism (and therefore more closely align with the rules for extra-community supplies): VAT Directive note 7, art. 58 (effective 1 January 2015); *Council Directive 2008/8/EC of 12 February 2008 amending Directive 2006/112/EC as Regards the Place of Supply of Services* [2008] OJ L 44/11; *Council Implementing Regulation (EU) 282/2011 of 15 March 2011 Laying Down Implementing Measures for Directive 2006/112/EC on the Common System of Value Added Tax (recast)*, OJ L77/1 (2011). For an analysis of some of the complexities the new place-of-supply rules entail, see Hans-Martin Grambeck, 'B2C Supplies of Electronic Services from 1 January 2015 from a German Perspective' (July/August 2013), *International VAT Monitor*, 215; Madeline Merkx, 'New Implementing Measures for the EU Place-of-Supply Change 2015', *International VAT Monitor* (July/August 2013), 222.

[272] *Recast VAT Directive (2006/112/EC)*, art 44, 45. For exceptions to the general rules, see arts. 46–59b.

[273] *Recast VAT Directive* (2006/112/EC), art. 58, annex II. See above, n 271.

number of qualifications;[274] the Australian approach starts from a focus on whether the supply is connected with Australia, subject to a number of qualifications and exceptions.[275]

In the absence of a globally coordinated or harmonised approach, the different place-of-supply rules between jurisdictions can sometimes result in either double taxation (where more than one jurisdiction's place of supply rules tax the same supply) or involuntary non-taxation (where the place-of-supply rules of more than one jurisdiction fail to tax the supply at all).[276] For example, if business A purchases telecommunications services from business B, but business A resides in a jurisdiction that deems the place of supply to be where the purchaser (business A) is established, while business B resides in a jurisdiction that deems the place of supply to be where the supplier (business B) is established, business A may face paying VAT twice (but may not necessarily be able to recover the VAT twice).[277] Similar outcomes may also arise even with consistent legal rules if different tax administrations and/or courts adopt differing characterisations of the facts giving rise to the supply.[278]

The issues raised by the effective application of the destination principle have resulted in a range of reform proposals, including moving to the origin principle, but consensus still favours the destination approach.[279] In response to the recognition that inconsistent place-of-supply rules were 'creating obstacles to business activity, hindering economic growth and distorting competition',[280] much attention has been devoted by organisations such as the EU[281] and the OECD to

[274] *Goods and Services Tax Act 1985* (NZ), s8, 8A.

[275] *A New Tax System (Goods and Services Tax) Act 1999* (Cth), div. subdiv. 38-E.

[276] OECD, *Consumption Tax Trends 2012: VAT/GST and Excise Rates, Trends and Administration Issues* (OECD Publishing, Paris, 2012), 38.

[277] Where the situation above is reversed, unintentional non-taxation can occur: OECD, *International VAT/GST Guidelines* (OECD Publishing, Paris, 2006), points 7 and 8. For the latest version of the Guidelines see: OECD, *International VAT/GST Guidelines* (OECD Publishing, Paris, 2014), 1.12, 3.111.

[278] Robert F. van Brederode, 'VAT Has Come of Age – Review of Thomas Ecker, A VAT/GST Model Convention', *International VAT Monitor* (November/December 2013), 360.

[279] The European Commission has made it clear that a move to the origin principle for intra-community supplies is not feasible: European Commission, *Communication from the Commission to the European Parliament, the Council, and the European Economic and Social Committee on the Future of VAT – Towards a Simpler, More Robust and Efficient VAT System Tailored to the Single Market* COM (2011) 851, 4.1. For a discussion of the various proposals, see Liam Ebrill et al., *The Modern VAT* (IMF, Washington, DC, 2001), ch. 17, and at 189–96; Ine Lejeune, Jeanine Daou-Azzi and Mark Powell (of Price WaterhouseCoopers), 'The Balance Has Shifted to Consumption Taxes – Lessons Learned and Best Practices for VAT', in M. Lang, P. Melz and E. Kristoffersson (eds.), *Value Added Tax and Direct Taxation: Similarities and Differences* (IBFD, Vienna, 2009), 59, 87; Rita de la Feria, *The EU VAT System and the Internal Market* (IBFD, Amsterdam, 2009), ch. 2.

[280] OECD, *Consumption Tax Trends 2012: VAT/GST and Excise Rates, Trends and Administration Issues* (OECD Publishing, Paris, 2012), 46.

[281] The EU has recognised the need to coordinate better with non-member states: European Commission, Communication from the Commission to the European Parliament and the Council on concrete ways to reinforce the fight against tax fraud and tax evasion, including in

developing appropriate and consistent 'place-of-supply' rules to ensure that goods and services are taxed appropriately. That is, so that they are taxed once but not twice.[282] The efforts reflect a growing recognition among policy-makers that if the VAT is to be effective in meeting the revenue needs of states and the interests of business in rapidly changing global markets, a significantly greater degree of coordination and harmonisation of the place-of-supply rules of different jurisdictions is required. While the OECD approach is aimed at encouraging (rather than directing) member states to harmonise their VAT laws regarding cross-border supplies, another option developed by Ecker proposes a model convention to form the basis of treaty negotiations.[283] Both approaches obviously entail challenging coordination issues that go beyond the scope of this book.[284] For the purposes of this book, it is sufficient to note that the difficulties in levying real VATs on a destination basis highlight a key limit of the good VAT: that, in a world of customs and border controls, the good VAT applied on a destination basis was hailed as a revenue instrument to facilitate trade. However, the expansion of that trade and the subsequent undermining of those borders now provide enormous challenges to the effective administration of real VATs. As a result, the merits of today's VATs (good or real) may not be at the level hoped for historically.

7 CONCLUSION

This chapter has examined the extent to which real VATs measure up against the good VAT, as assessed by the conventional approach. The discussion has shown that in practice, not one country has a good VAT. Instead, countries have enacted a variety of real VATs, which depart from the three design norms of the good VAT in different ways that vary according to the circumstances of each. The departures in developed countries generally tend to be formal departures from the design norms, whereas the departures in developing countries tend to lie more in effective administration and compliance.

These departures from the good VAT are rarely fatal – they leave real VATs intact enough to still bear the name VAT. However, the departures frequently reveal a pressure to depart at the exact points at which the merits of the good VAT

relation to third countries COM(2012), 351, pp. 9–13; Recast VAT Directive (2006/112/EC), art. 59a–b.

[282] The OECD recently endorsed new guidelines to encourage the harmonisation of VAT regimes in relation to cross-border supplies: OECD, *International VAT/GST Guidelines* (April 2014) www.oecd.org/ctp/consumption/international-vat-gst-guidelines.pdf. The Guidelines are a product of the 'Global Forum on VAT' – an OECD initiative to establish a platform for more than 100 countries to discuss and take action on issues of shared concern in relation to VAT design and operation: OECD, *Global Forum* on VAT (2015) www.oecd.org/ctp/consumption/vat-global-forum.htm.

[283] Thomas Ecker, *A VAT/GST Model Convention* (Doctoral Series 25)(IBFD, Amsterdam, 2013).

[284] For a summary of the issues, see ibid., ch. 3–4.

seem to be most compelling for the conventional approach. So, the good VAT is celebrated for its broad base, but real VATs undermine this by containing numerous exclusions to the base. The good VAT is celebrated for the self-enforcing nature of the invoice-credit method, but real VATs have proven quite complex, costly to administer and comply with, and susceptible to avoidance and evasion. The good VAT is praised for facilitating international trade, but this is undermined by real VATs struggling to tax certain cross-border supplies or refund VAT credits where the administration of borders is weak.

The general response of the conventional approach to the perceived failings of real VATs is to sometimes downplay the issues or defend real VATs against other tax alternatives. For example, Thuronyi contends that 'while there are differences in VAT from one country to another, compared with the income tax VAT laws are remarkably similar'.[285] Whether the VAT exhibits more or less variation than taxes given the label of the income tax is not relevant to the inquiry of this book, because the conventional approach does not explain the rise of the income tax by reference to the merits of that tax, but does do so in relation to the VAT. A constant defence to the perceived failing of real VATs by the conventional approach is to encourage countries to reform real VATs in line with the three design norms of the good VAT.[286] This may well be necessary to achieve the outcomes desired by the conventional approach. However, Part II of this book contends that, given the significant departures of real VATs from the good VAT, an explanation that attributes the VAT's rise to its merits cannot hold.

[285] Victor Thuronyi, *Comparative Tax Law* (Kluwer Law International, The Hague, 2003), 312. After acknowledging the wide 'home-grown' variations in real VATs, Bird and Gendron also state that '[n]o one VAT is identical to any other VAT: each has its special features. Nonetheless, compared to the income tax, most VATs found around the world are essentially cut from the same mould, reflecting their relatively recent, and related, origins': Richard Bird and Pierre-Pascal Gendron, *The VAT in Developing and Transitional Countries* (Cambridge University Press, New York, 2007), 10, 16.

[286] The *ITD VAT Paper* quickly defers to the consensus design issues for the good VAT after acknowledging the diversity of real VATs: International Tax Dialogue (ITD), 'The Value Added Tax: Experience and Issues' (Background Paper Prepared for the International Tax Dialogue Conference on the VAT, Rome, March 15–16, 2005, ITD), 7, 19. *Contra* Bird and Gendron, whose examination of VAT in developing countries causes them to contend that 'in most cases there are excellent reasons for the prevailing conventional wisdom' in relation to the three design norms but also note that 'there is surprisingly little evidence supporting much of that wisdom and that there are plausible reasons for diverging from its prescriptions in at least some instances': Richard Bird and Pierre-Pascal Gendron, *The VAT in Developing and Transitional Countries* (Cambridge University Press, New York, 2007), 8.

PART II

Explaining the rise of the VAT

4

The conventional approach to explaining the rise of the VAT

Part I of this book demonstrated the growing significance of the value-added tax (VAT), as well as the disparity between the claims made in relation to the merits of the good VAT and the capacity of real VATs to realise these merits. Part II undertakes the substantial task of explaining the rise of the VAT. This chapter explains how the significance of the VAT is not met by the quality of the explanations that currently exist for its rise, which means that, despite the VAT's growing importance, little is known about the factors shaping its rise. The dominant received explanation for the VAT's rise as provided by the conventional approach attributes the rise of the VAT to the merits of the tax. The tension in an account that answers the empirical question of why the VAT has risen by reference to the normative appeal of the VAT is immediately apparent in light of the gap between the good VAT and real VATs outlined in Chapters 2 and 3 of this book. On the one hand, the VAT has spread everywhere because it is good; on the other hand, very few jurisdictions implement a good VAT. The gap between the good VAT and real VATs suggests that, at a minimum, an appeal to the normative merits of the good VAT is insufficient to explain the rise of real VATs.

This chapter identifies both 'strong' and 'weak' versions of the conventional approach's merits-based explanation for the VAT's rise. Under the 'strong' version, the merits of the good VAT are presented as the sole explanatory factor behind the VAT's rise. This account persists despite repeated acknowledgements within the conventional approach that the good VAT is rarely, if ever, realised by real VATs. 'Weak' versions of the merits-based explanation identify other factors behind the rise of the VAT, such as the role of transnational actors like the International Monetary Fund (IMF), and the impact of fashionable trends or yardstick competition, but then attribute these factors back to the merits of the VAT itself. Both 'strong' and 'weak' versions of the explanation either attribute the VAT's rise to the merits of the good VAT or, when forced to address the fact that real VATs do not resemble the good VAT, fall back on identifying different, and at times conflicting, merits of real VATs to support their explanatory account. In general, most accounts rest on the technical superiority of the good VAT to other alternatives and on the good VAT's perceived economic fit (with domestic and international markets).[1]

This chapter identifies the deficiencies in this account of the VAT's rise. Chapter 5 will go on to assess how alternative conceptions of the VAT's rise might help address the many gaps in the merits-based explanations offered by the conventional approach and develops a new approach to explaining the rise of this significant revenue instrument.

1 CELEBRATION OVER EXPLANATION – EXPLAINING THE VAT'S RISE BY REFERENCE TO ITS MERITS

Most within the conventional approach celebrate the 'remarkable' rise of the VAT.[2] Bird and Gendron typify the refrain:[3]

> VAT has been an enormous success. It has swept away other contending sales taxes in most of the world. Only five countries have ever repealed a VAT, and all either have since reintroduced one or reportedly plan to do so soon. In many countries VAT has come to rival and even dominate the income tax as the mainstay of national finances. No fiscal innovation has ever spread so widely so rapidly or been so successfully adopted in such a wide variety of countries.

Schenk and Oldman remark that:[4]

> The VAT has been the most pervasive tax reform throughout the world during the second half of the twentieth century and into the twenty-first century, and has proved to be a major source of government revenue.

Alan Tait enlists metaphor to capture the VAT's ascendancy:[5]

> The rise of the value-added tax (VAT) is an unparalleled tax phenomenon. The history of taxation reveals no other tax that has swept the world in some thirty years, from theory to practice, and has carried along with it academics who were once dismissive and countries that once rejected it. . .VAT may be thought of as the Mata Hari of the tax world – many are tempted, many succumb, some tremble on the brink, while others leave only to return, eventually the attraction appears irresistible.

[1] See Chapter 2 of this book.

[2] Cedric Sandford, *Successful Tax Reform: Lessons from an Analysis of Tax Reform in Six Countries* (Fiscal, Bath, 1993), 10.

[3] Richard Bird and Pierre-Pascal Gendron, *The VAT in Developing and Transitional Countries* (Cambridge University Press, New York, 2007), 20 (citations omitted).

[4] Alan Schenk and Oliver Oldman, *Value Added Tax: A Comparative Approach* (rev. edn., Cambridge University Press, Cambridge; New York, 2007), 33.

[5] Alan A. Tait, *Value Added Tax: International Practice and Problems* (IMF, Washington, DC, 1988), 3.

Ebrill et al. state that:[6]

> The rapid and seemingly irresistible rise of the value-added tax (VAT) is probably the most important tax development of the latter twentieth century, and certainly the most breathtaking.

Keen and Lockwood declare that:[7]

> By any standards, the rise of the VAT has been the most significant development in tax policy and administration of recent decades. And it is not over.

The *ITD VAT Paper* states that:[8]

> The spread of the VAT has been the most important development in taxation over the last half-century...
>
> It is suggestive of the perceived success of the tax that only five countries have ever removed an existing VAT...Three of these countries have since reintroduced the tax.

Despite the celebratory tone, very little attention is paid by the conventional approach to examining the reasons behind the VAT's rise and, on the few occasions when it is addressed, it is rarely as anything more than a footnote or the preface to an analysis of the VAT's design or operation. Most texts devote less than a chapter to exploring the VAT's rise. Ebrill et al. and Tait both devote less than one chapter (of a total of 18 in each text) to considering the reasons behind the VAT's rise.[9] Most articles expend little more than a few paragraphs to explain the VAT's rise, if they do so at all.[10]

6 Liam Ebrill, et al., *The Modern VAT* (IMF, Washington, DC, 2001), xi.

7 Michael Keen and Ben Lockwood, 'The Value Added Tax: Its Causes and Consequences', *Journal of Development Economics* 92(2) (2010), 138.

8 International Tax Dialogue (ITD), 'The Value Added Tax: Experience and Issues' (Background Paper Prepared for the International Tax Dialogue Conference on the VAT, Rome, March 15–16, 2005, ITD), 3, 10 (hereafter referred to as the *ITD VAT Paper*).

9 Liam Ebrill et al., *The Modern VAT* (IMF, Washington, DC, 2001), 4–14, ch. 1; Alan A. Tait, *Value Added Tax: International Practice and Problems* (IMF, Washington, DC, 1988), ch. 1; Schenk and Oldman devote only a small portion of their comprehensive tome on the VAT to its politics and make very little attempt to link the histories to the design and application of the tax (outside the debate in the US): Alan Schenk and Oliver Oldman, *Value Added Tax: A Comparative Approach* (rev. edn., Cambridge University Press, Cambridge; New York, 2007), 17–19; Robert F. van Brederode, *Systems of General Sales Taxation: Theory, Policy and Practice* (Kluwer Law International Alphen aan den Rijn, 2009), ch. 2; Gillis et al. devote only a handful of pages, primarily one page in each of the introduction and conclusion, to explore the reasons behind the VAT's rise out of a total of 19 chapters (237 pages): Malcolm Gillis, Carl S. Shoup and Gerardo P. Sicat (eds.), *Value Added Taxation in Developing Countries* (World Bank, Washington, DC, 1990), 4, 219.

10 Cnossen bookends his article with a handful of paragraphs examining the VAT's rise: Sijbren Cnossen, 'Global Trends and Issues in Value Added Taxation', *International Tax and Public Finance* 5(3) (1998), 399, 413–14; Jørgensen and Owens devote approximately two paragraphs to explaining the VAT's rise: Erik Jørgensen and Jeffrey Owens, 'The Move to VAT', *OECD Observer* (August/September 1995), 21; The *ITD VAT Paper* notes the VAT's rise without

Instead, most accounts are keen to emphasise the extent of the VAT's apparent success – first, to highlight the extensive uptake of the VAT, and second, to point to indicators of its success. On the first front, at the same time as extolling the VAT's various virtues as the reasons behind its rise, the conventional approach also acknowledges that the good VAT is rarely realised in practice. In demonstrating the success of the VAT through pointing to its uptake, the conventional approach must count VATs that do not meet their own criteria of good. As this book has shown, while committed to a narrow definition of the good VAT in Chapter 2 to address the normative question of what a good VAT is, they are committed to a broad definition of real VATs to emphasise the extent of the VAT's rise. On the second front, the measures relied upon within the conventional approach to indicate the VAT's success are either reliable but weak, such as the claim that few countries have repealed a VAT once introduced (an extremely low measure of success),[11] or they are strong but difficult to verify, such as the claim that VATs lead to economic growth (despite the absence of empirical evidence linking the VAT to economic growth).[12] Even though the ongoing discrepancy between the good VAT and real VATs has prompted a greater degree of circumspection in some more recent VAT analyses, this has prompted calls for a greater understanding of how to overcome the deficiencies in the design of real VATs rather than a revision of the explanations for the VAT's rise that dominate the conventional approach.[13]

There exist two exceptions to this general neglect toward exploring the VAT's rise within the conventional approach. First, Bird and Gendron's examination of the VAT in developing and transitional economies, although largely prescriptive, devotes more attention than usual (two chapters of 12) to examining why the VAT has spread and to exploring the political economy of the VAT.[14] Second is an article by Keen and Lockwood examining the 'causes and consequences' of the VAT. After surveying the literature, the authors conclude that, despite the VAT

explaining it: International Tax Dialogue (ITD), 'The Value Added Tax: Experience and Issues' (Background Paper Prepared for the International Tax Dialogue Conference on the VAT, Rome, March 15–16, 2005, ITD), 3; A 2007 OECD policy brief devotes approximately one paragraph of a seven-page brief to the reasons behind the VAT's rise: OECD, 'Consumption Taxes: The Way of the Future? (Policy Brief)' (2007), *OECD Observer*, 1.

11 International Tax Dialogue (ITD), 'The Value Added Tax: Experience and Issues' (Background Paper Prepared for the International Tax Dialogue Conference on the VAT, Rome, March 15–16, 2005, ITD), 10; Liam Ebrill et al., *The Modern VAT* (IMF, Washington, DC, 2001), 15; Richard Bird and Pierre-Pascal Gendron, *The VAT in Developing and Transitional Countries* (Cambridge University Press, New York, 2007), 20.

12 See Chapter 3, §2.5 of this book.

13 Michael Keen and Ruud de Mooij, '"Fiscal Devaluation" and Fiscal Consolidation: The VAT in Troubled Times', in Alberto Alesina and Francesco Giavazzi (eds.), *Fiscal Policy After the Financial Crisis* (University of Chicago Press, 2013), 443, 476.

14 Richard Bird and Pierre-Pascal Gendron, *The VAT in Developing and Transitional Countries* (Cambridge University Press, New York, 2007), ch. 2 and 11. The analysis, although a step forward, occurs without any substantive application of established public policy frameworks such as those outlined in Chapter 5 of this book.

being the 'most significant tax development in tax policy and administration of recent decades', its 'causes and consequences...have received virtually no attention, either theoretical or empirical'.[15] The authors go on to state that:[16]

> The literature on the VAT is surprisingly sparse. On theoretical aspects, while there is of course a large literature on the optimal design of taxes on final consumption, few contributions concern themselves with the crediting and refund mechanisms (and their potential imperfections) that make the critical difference between a VAT and, for example, a retail sales tax—and which are therefore the distinctive source of any efficiency gain or loss associated with the VAT. The literature establishing conditions under which uniform commodity taxation is optimal, for instance, is just as applicable to any other form of consumption tax as it is to the VAT. Empirical work on the VAT is also scant.

There may be a number of reasons behind the inattention to the factors shaping the VAT's rapid rise. This neglect may stem from the dominantly prescriptive purpose of the conventional approach, which means the focus of analysis is on promoting or refining the three design norms of the good VAT outlined in Chapter 2, rather than on exploring how the VAT rose to prominence. Whatever the reason for the neglect, however, Keen and Lockwood highlight the impact of this inattention:[17]

> Essentially nothing is known about the two most basic questions of all: Are there any signs that the VAT has lived up, in practice, to the claims made for it by its advocates (and feared by some of its opponents)? And what exactly is it that has driven its remarkable spread around the world?

Under the conventional approach, the answers to these two questions are intimately connected because the conventional approach finds that the merits of the VAT suffice to explain its spread. That is, the answer to the first question is assumed and then deployed as the answer to the second question.

In this chapter, §2 to §4 will demonstrate that the dominant mode of explanation adopted by the conventional approach is to explain the rise of the VAT by reference to its merits. §2 will explore the 'strong' version of this explanation, while §3 and §4 will consider two prominent contentions under the weak version that identify the impact of other factors on the VAT's rise, but attribute these factors back to the VAT's merits. The conventional approach's assessment of the influence of evolutionary or fashionable trends and/or yardstick competition on the VAT's rise will be considered at §3. The conventional approach's

[15] Michael Keen and Ben Lockwood, 'The Value Added Tax: Its Causes and Consequences', *Journal of Development Economics* 92(2) (2010), 138; Ebrill et al. state that 'there has been surprisingly – shockingly – little serious research effort devoted to the VAT': Liam Ebrill et al., *The Modern VAT* (IMF, Washington, DC, 2001), xii.

[16] Michael Keen and Ben Lockwood, 'The Value Added Tax: Its Causes and Consequences', *Journal of Development Economics* 92(2) (2010), 138, 139.

[17] Ibid., 138.

assessment (or lack thereof) of the role of transnational actors in promoting VAT reform will be considered at §4 and §5.

2 THE STRONG ARTICULATION – MERITS AS THE REASON FOR THE VAT'S RISE

The strong articulation of the merits-based explanation attributes the rise of the VAT to its merits without identifying any of the intermediating factors usually considered necessary to implement policy change, such as the actors or institutions through which reforms are introduced.

Cnossen captures the essence of the 'strong' articulation of the conventional approach's explanation of the VAT's rise:[18]

> Although the specific *reasons for adopting* the VAT differ from one country to another, the *main argument* has been that a *properly designed VAT* raises more revenue with lower administrative and economic costs than other broadly based consumption taxes.

Here, the causal explanation quickly merges into a discussion of policy merits, where merits become *the* causal explanation for the VAT's rise. Cnossen's 'properly designed VAT' reflects the prescriptions for the good VAT outlined in Chapter 2. According to this account, the VAT has risen because the good VAT raises more revenue at less cost than other consumption taxes. The approach of attributing the VAT's rise to the putative merits of the good VAT prevails despite the explicit and repeated acknowledgement from within the conventional approach, outlined in Chapter 3, that few of the normative requirements of the good VAT are ever realised by real VATs in practice. For example, Cnossen offers this merits-based explanation despite acknowledging less than a few paragraphs later that 'these normative requirements are often met only in the breach'.[19]

Whereas Cnossen identifies the specific merits of the good VAT that underlie the VAT's rise, others simply assume that the merits of the VAT are self-evident enough to explain its rise. Bodin and Koukpaizan, for example, claim that '[l]ike a vast majority of countries in the world, African countries have not been able to resist the attraction of VAT in the past 20 years'.[20]

Other accounts emphasise different aspects of the good VAT. Norregard and Khan, for example, attribute the tendency of developing countries to levy single-rate VATs to a preference for the merits of doing so without considering

18 Sijbren Cnossen, 'Global Trends and Issues in Value Added Taxation', *International Tax and Public Finance* 5(3) (1998), 399 (emphasis added).

19 Ibid., 400.

20 Jean-Paul Bodin and Vincent Koukpaizan, 'The Rise of VAT in Africa – Impact and Challenges', *International VAT Monitor* (2009), 178.

or substantiating the actual motives of policy-makers or the context of the decisions made:[21]

> Developing countries have generally chosen to adopt single-rate VAT systems while more developed OECD countries largely favored multi-rate systems. The preference among developing countries for single-rate VAT systems stems in large measure from their relatively weak administrative capabilities.

Key elements missing from this account are, beyond the administrative constraints, what has in fact informed the choices of policy-makers in these developing countries and what is the capacity of these policy-makers to implement those choices. As Chapter 3 outlined, developing countries may also have good reason to levy multi-rate VATs, which might include introducing rate variation to appease opponents of VAT reform. Indeed, as Chapter 3, §4.3 revealed, there exists a stronger motive for rate variation in developing countries, given that they have less capacity to address distributional issues through other policy options such as spending or variations to the personal income tax. The fact that instead developing countries tend not to engage in rate variation may be the product of a number of explanations beyond simply a choice based on the merits of a single-rate VAT in light of perceived administrative constraints. It might be due to the influence of external advice in these countries, which itself might be a product of the limited capacity of policy-makers in these countries (see §4.2.1). It might also be due to access to funding, which might reward real VATs that more closely resemble the good VAT (see §4.2.2). Bird and Gendron are alive to these alternative explanations:[22]

> Indeed, it is striking that the conventional 'expert' opinion that the fewer VAT rates and exemptions the better seems to have had less influence in some EU countries than in some of the recent VAT adopters in the developing world who are more susceptible to expert (usually FAD [IMF Fiscal Affairs Department]) guidance.

In general, however, the 'strong' articulation of the merits argument tends to rest on the general technical superiority of the good VAT over other alternatives and the good VAT's perceived economic fit (with domestic and international markets).[23] Indeed, many explain the VAT's rise by reference to the perception that it serves a particular economic need. Ebrill et al. attribute specific phases of VAT adoption to the VAT's technical superiority and economic fit. In Europe, the VAT's rise is explained by reference to the 'drive for greater economic integration among

[21] John Norregaard and Tehmina S. Khan, 'Tax Policy: Recent Trends and Coming Challenges' (Working Paper No. WP/07/274, IMF, 2007), 38.

[22] Richard Bird and Pierre-Pascal Gendron, *The VAT in Developing and Transitional Countries* (Cambridge University Press, New York, 2007), 24.

[23] OECD, 'Consumption Taxes: the Way of the Future? (Policy Brief)', *OECD Observer* (2007), 1, 1; Erik Jørgensen and Jeffrey Owens, 'The Move to VAT', *OECD Observer* (August/September 1995), 21.

member states'[24] of the European Union (EU) and the VAT's avoidance of the trade distortions of pre-existing turnover taxes.[25] Similarly, in developing and transitional economies, the VAT's rise is explained by reference to the VAT being 'a more efficient revenue-raising tax'[26] that would be consistent with the needs of increasing trade liberalisation and the needs of emerging market economies.[27] Overall, Ebrill et al. attribute the rise of the VAT primarily to its suitability for market-based economies, which leads the authors to conclude that the 'VAT has been seen as a key instrument for securing *macro-economic stability and growth* by placing *domestic revenue mobilization on a sounder basis*'.[28] Although the object of comparison is not identified by the authors, the basis for their assessment of the VAT's superiority is primarily against other sales taxes, tariffs and, to a lesser extent, against the income tax. Here, the VAT appeals from a broader fiscal perspective and offers much more than revenue generation, but also economic stability and growth. These causal explanations are proposed despite the repeated acknowledgements that these benefits are (1) hard to verify; and (2) difficult to achieve in practice, given the departures of real VATs from the three design norms of the good VAT.[29]

The underlying inference in the explanations provided by the conventional approach appears to be that the history behind the VAT's rise is relatively straightforward because the VAT's rise is simply explained by its virtues. Gillis, for example, concludes that, owing to the superior design of the VAT over other consumption taxes, '[the] reasons for the rapid spread of the VAT across developing nations are fairly straightforward'.[30] In a similar vein, Gillis, Shoup and Sicat reflect upon the outcomes from a World Bank symposium on the VAT in developing countries and consider the question of '[w]hy the VAT?' and conclude that:[31]

[24] Liam Ebrill, et al., *The Modern VAT* (IMF, Washington, DC, 2001), 6.

[25] Ibid. [26] Ibid. [27] Ibid. [28] Ibid., xi (emphasis added).

[29] Ibid., 15. See Chapter 3 of this book.

[30] Malcolm Gillis, 'Historical and Contemporary Debate on Consumption Taxes', in G. Zodrow and P. Mieszkowski (eds.), *United States Tax Reform in the 21st Century* (Cambridge University Press, Cambridge, 2002), 284, 288. This conclusion contradicts an earlier observation by Gillis elsewhere that the:

> [R]ationales for adopting the VAT have of course varied greatly among countries. . .Four widely perceived, and often overstated, advantages of the tax seem to have been particularly significant in influencing policy makers in LDCs [least developed countries] to opt for the VAT: revenue-generating capability, administrative advantages, and the implications of the tax for economic neutrality and export promotion.

Michael J. Boskin and Charles E. McLure, *World Tax Reform: Case Studies of Developed and Developing Countries* (ICS Press, San Francisco, 1990), 229.

[31] Malcolm Gillis, Carl S. Shoup and Gerardo P. Sicat, 'Lessons for Developing Countries', in M. Gillis, C. S. Shoup and G. P. Sicat (eds.), *Value Added Taxation in Developing Countries (A World Bank Symposium)* (World Bank, Washington, DC, 1990), 219, 230.

> The value added tax has been applied ever more widely because it avoids some of the negative features of other forms of taxation, particularly the turnover ("cascade") tax.

The authors then devote the remaining seven paragraphs to explaining the VAT's rise through a series of favourable comparisons of the good VAT with other taxes,[32] despite the acknowledgements elsewhere that real VATs lack many of the features of the good VAT.

Despite the uncertain basis that underlies their causal accounts for the VAT's rise, some within the conventional approach are so confident of the VAT's merits that they predict its future development. Thuronyi, for example, claims that '[i]t can be expected that virtually all countries will adopt the VAT before too long'.[33] Keen and Lockwood claim that the rise of VAT 'is not over'.[34] Bird and Gendron predict that '[n]o doubt still more jurisdictions have leaped, or soon will leap, onto the VAT bandwagon'.[35] Ebrill et al., in considering the future of the VAT, conclude that 'the safest prediction is that the spread of the VAT will continue' and later state that the '*power of its inner logic* is likely to be felt even more strongly'.[36] In another context, the same authors speak of 'the allure of VAT',[37] a theme taken further by Tait's earlier Mata Hari analogy.[38]

2.1 *Deficiencies in the strong articulation of the merits explanation*

There is a fundamental objection to the strong version of the merits-based explanation of the VAT's rise. The political philosopher, Raymond Geuss, reminds us that 'neither the good nor the true is self-realising'.[39] The merits of a particular policy alone do not explain its adoption: some good policies do not get adopted (such as

[32] Key factors cited include those listed in Chapter 2 of this book: the incremental multistage levying of the tax (making it preferable to single-stage taxes); the credit mechanism to prevent cascading (making it preferable to the cascading turnover tax); the VAT's neutrality and consequent contribution to production efficiency (making it preferable to the cascading turnover tax, single-stage sales taxes and the income tax); the VAT's neutrality between consuming now and consuming later (making it preferable to the income tax); and the VAT's impressive revenue-raising capacity: ibid.

[33] Victor Thuronyi, *Comparative Tax Law* (Kluwer Law International, The Hague, 2003), 305.

[34] Michael Keen and Ben Lockwood, 'The Value Added Tax: Its Causes and Consequences', *Journal of Development Economics* 92(2) (2010), 138.

[35] Richard Bird and Pierre-Pascal Gendron, *The VAT in Developing and Transitional Countries* (Cambridge University Press, New York, 2007), 16.

[36] Liam Ebrill et al., *The Modern VAT* (IMF, Washington, DC, 2001), 199 (emphasis added).

[37] Liam Ebrill et al., 'The Allure of the Value Added Tax', *Finance and Development* 39(2) (2002), 44. See also Jean-Paul Bodin and Vincent Koukpaizan, 'The Rise of VAT in Africa – Impact and Challenges', *International VAT Monitor* (2009), 178.

[38] Alan A. Tait, *Value Added Tax: International Practice and Problems* (IMF, Washington, DC, 1988), 3. See above, §1.

[39] Raymond Geuss, *Philosophy and Real Politics* (Princeton University Press, Princeton, 2008), 28.

providing universal access to clean drinking water), while poor policies can be widely adopted (such as subsidies for the tobacco industry). If the merits of the good VAT explained its rise, we would expect to see the good VAT introduced in the more than 150 jurisdictions that have adopted the VAT to date. The fact that these jurisdictions have adopted more than 150 different real VATs suggests that, at best, the 'strong' merits-based explanations of the VAT's rise require supplementation.

Another fundamental objection to the strong articulation of the merits-based account is the underlying assumption that (imputed) rational motivations (i.e., the belief that it is desirable to introduce the good VAT) are sufficient causal explanations for the rise of VATs. This assumption holds absent an account of whether those rational motivations were actually held by the actors involved and, even assuming they were, absent an account of the policy process to show how those rational motivations might produce specific outcomes (i.e., real VATs). Although directed at a different target (a certain mode of rational choice explanation), Elster's insights can provide a potent critique of the strong merits-based account of the VAT's rise:[40]

> But to explain social behaviour by intentions and beliefs that are imputed rather than documented is acceptable only if (1) the sources do not permit us to establish intentions and beliefs directly, (2) the observed empirical fit is very good, (3) other implications of the imputed intentions and beliefs are deduced and verified, and (4) plausible alternative explanations are given a good run for their money and then rejected.

A defender of the conventional approach might argue that condition (3) is satisfied, in so far as it might be seen that other fiscal reforms reflect a belief in the merits of VAT, such as a shift in the tax mix from income to consumption or the repeal of 'inferior' sales tax alternatives. However, as Chapter 3, §2.1 noted, discernible shifts in the tax mix have not necessarily been detected. In any event, Elster's other criteria are clearly not satisfied: (1) Information would exist about the intentions and beliefs of the actors involved in the introduction of VAT for most of the jurisdictions that have enacted one (even though it may require a significant research effort to acquire it). Even if this information was not available, however, the remaining conditions are not met; (2) As Chapter 3 explained, the empirical fit between the good VAT and real VATs is not a 'very good' one; and in relation to (4) due to the dominance of the merits-based accounts of the conventional approach, other plausible alternative explanations for the VAT's rise have barely been articulated, let alone 'given a good run for their money'.

The suggestion that the VAT has risen because it fulfils some unmet need might have the potential to explain the VAT's rise. However, the version proposed by the conventional approach is undermined by the insistence that the history behind the

[40] Jon Elster, 'Rational Choice History: A Case of Excessive Ambition', *American Political Science Review* 94(3) (2000), 685, 693.

VAT's rise is relatively straightforward due to the VAT's merits. The political scientist, Paul Pierson, contends that:[41]

> Functionalist arguments take the following form: Outcome X (e.g., an institution, policy, or organization) exists because it serves the function Y. In a world of purposive actors, it may indeed be the case that the effects of... [a policy] have something to do with an explanation for its emergence and persistence...[However,] there are large dangers in any assumption that a [policy] arose because it serves some particularly useful purpose. Thinking in functionalist terms about an institution, policy, or social organization may be a good way to derive causal hypotheses, but functional accounts are far from being the only plausible ones. Many alternatives to the outcome in question might have been possible, and a dynamic of increasing returns may have locked in a particular option even though it originated by accident, or the factors that gave it an original advantage may have long since passed away. Rather than assume relative efficiency as an explanation, we have to go back and look. Thus, recognizing the possibility of path dependence necessarily draws social scientists to an investigation of history, if only to evaluate the validity of functionalist assertions.

Given the tendency by the conventional approach to explain the VAT's rise by reference to the perceived need it fills, whether that be the need to generate revenue in the most neutral manner available or the need to reform outdated taxes, these explanations are susceptible to Pierson's critique. Chapter 5, §3.1 further develops the notion of path dependence and increasing returns.

The work undertaken by Keen and Lockwood highlights another flaw in the 'strong' articulation of the merits explanation. The authors survey panel data from 143 countries from 1975 to 2000, so as to explore what has driven the VAT's rise.[42] They test a number of standard variables used in the modelling of tax revenues to see what factors affect VAT uptake, including income per capita; the share of agriculture in gross domestic product (GDP); the openness of the economy; demographic variables, including age distribution; the impact of a federal state; the extent of regional adoption; the level of natural resource wealth; and the role of international financial institutions by measuring participation in IMF programs.[43] Some of the authors' results in relation to the reasons shaping VAT uptake are not surprising. This includes the finding that the likelihood of VAT adoption is lower the greater the revenue capacity of the

[41] Paul Pierson, 'Increasing Returns, Path Dependence, and the Study of Politics', *American Political Science Review* 94(2) (2000), 251, 263–64.

[42] The authors exclude former Soviet Union and Central and Eastern European countries on the basis that VAT reforms accompanied broader transitional reforms that aimed to result in a reduction in state capacity and revenue: Michael Keen and Ben Lockwood, 'The Value Added Tax: Its Causes and Consequences', *Journal of Development Economics* 92(2) (2010), 138, 143.

[43] Ibid., 143.

country and the larger the agricultural sector (notoriously difficult to tax especially under a VAT).[44]

One key finding by Keen and Lockwood that challenges the 'strong' articulation of the merits explanation is that '[m]ost strikingly, and intriguingly, it. . .emerges strongly that, all else equal, more open economies are less likely to adopt a VAT'.[45] The finding challenges explanations that rely on the VAT's merits, in this case the VAT's economic fit with international trading conditions, to explain the VAT's rise. Keen and Lockwood are surprised by this finding in light of a further finding that VAT adoption is more likely to be advantageous for increasing revenues in these more open economies.[46]

Keen and Lockwood offer some conjectures to try to reconcile the fact that those countries for whom the VAT might be perceived to be most meritorious (i.e., those with the most to gain from a VAT) are less likely to introduce a VAT. The authors point to some factors that might make the VAT more attractive to less open economies. For example, they argue that the VAT, contrary to its intended effect, acts as a de facto export tax in many developing countries because VAT credits due to exporters are frequently retained by revenue-hungry governments rather than refunded.[47] Beyond this, they are able to suggest only that 'for some reason' more open economies might be less likely to adopt the VAT.[48] The sole reason later provided is to suggest that the VAT might be perceived to be especially costly in more open developing countries, which might prefer to retain a comparatively easy-to-administer tariff system even in the face of the promised revenue gains associated with introducing a VAT because the difficulty of instituting significant change deters governments from doing so.[49]

Emran and Stiglitz dismiss the defence made by the conventional approach that the VAT appeals to developing countries because it is 'essentially a trade tax in the guise of VAT' as 'difficult to reconcile' with the overall commitment by the conventional approach to reducing the distortions of trade taxes.[50] Irrespective of

[44] Ibid., 143–44. Although an earlier working paper version of the article found that a federal state structure was a statistically significant barrier to VAT adoption, this finding was not repeated in the published article: Michael Keen and Ben Lockwood, 'The Value-Added Tax: Its Causes and Consequences' (Working Paper No. WP/07/183, IMF, 2007), 18, 27.

[45] Ibid., 148.

[46] Ibid., 147. [47] Ibid., 145. See Chapter 3, §5.1 and §6 of this book. [48] Ibid.

[49] Ibid., 145. Although Keen and Lockwood speculate as to why more open developing economies might be less likely to adopt a VAT, they are silent as to the position of developed countries (beyond noting that the adoption is no more likely in higher-income countries) and, in particular, the assessment of the political costs of VAT adoption in these countries: ibid., 143–45, 147.

[50] 'The goal of eliminating trade taxes implies that the part of VAT that is collected at the border should also be eliminated, especially when the corresponding domestic production can not be equally taxed under VAT due to its informal character': M. Shahe Emran and Joseph E. Stiglitz, 'On Selective Indirect Tax Reform in Developing Countries', *Journal of Public Economics* 89 (2005), 599, 619.

this critique, the idea that the VAT can act as a de facto trade tax may have weight as an explanation for the VAT's rise in developing countries. However, given that the explanation relies on a less than good VAT, it clearly indicates that the merits of the good VAT alone do not explain the rise of real VATs. The same can be said of the defence made by the conventional approach to the Emran and Stiglitz critique that the VAT is distortive because it fails to reach the informal sector of developing economies (see Chapter 3, §4.1). Keen's claim that the informal sector is taxed because the VAT applies to the inputs of non-registered (i.e., informal sector) firms and because of the practice of many developing countries of applying withholding regimes to high-risk transactions directly appeals to features of 'real'[51] VATs. That is, VATs that admit a particular susceptibility to non-compliance and that require various ad-hoc mechanisms to support their implementation (as is the case with any real-world tax). Again, the substantive defence of the VAT as a policy instrument might be a sound one, but because it relies on real VATs as opposed to the good VAT, the good VAT alone cannot explain these outcomes.

Even if we take the 'strong' articulation as expressing the contention that the merits of real VATs explain the VAT's rise because, in a second-best sense, VATs outperform other tax instruments, this acknowledgement means that the 'strong' merits argument is untenable. Once it is acknowledged that different aspects of the VAT's merits might appeal to different jurisdictions in ways in which certain features (i.e., the VAT not applying to exports) considered meritorious in one country (i.e., a developed country) might be considered undesirable in another (i.e., a developing country), it becomes impossible to fully account for the VAT's rise without considering the local context within which VAT reform takes place because it is this context that determines what features of a VAT will be considered meritorious in each case.

3 THE WEAK ARTICULATIONS – MERITS AS UNDERPINNING EVOLUTIONARY OR FASHIONABLE GROWTH AND YARDSTICK COMPETITION

Tait attributes the rise of the VAT to an evolutionary imperative. Among the four reasons Tait identifies behind the VAT's rise is the 'evolution of the tax system',[52] whereby countries 'are supposed to move from [1] simple to [2] complex tax structures that distort allocation to [3] those that are more neutral'.[53] Tait defers to the

[51] Michael Keen, 'VAT, Tariffs, and Withholding: Border Taxes and Informality in Developing Countries', *Journal of Public Economics* 92 (2008), 1892, 1894.

[52] Alan A. Tait, *Value Added Tax: International Practice and Problems* (IMF, Washington, DC, 1988), 9.

[53] Ibid., 24. The three other factors Tait attributes the VAT's rise to are (1) a dissatisfaction with pre-existing sales taxes; (2) the move to form regional economic groupings (as in Europe and Latin America); and (3) a desire to reduce other taxes (such as corporate profits taxes and the income tax) or to increase revenues: at 9.

merits of the good VAT to explain its evolutionary appeal.[54] Tait also attributes the VAT's rise to a type of 'fashionable growth', where 'the more VAT systems there are, the more likely it is that a country. . .will adopt a VAT'.[55] There are various rephrasings of Tait's 'fashionable growth' rationale. Shoup points to the influence of comparative trends when he states that '[i]n the history of public finance, so rapid a growth is unique, unmatched even by the income tax. Countries that have not adopted the VAT are therefore *naturally* inclined to consider it'.[56] Bird and Gendron identify the fiscal status quo that '[i]n general, however, the normal thing these days is to have a VAT'.[57] Although not strictly part of the conventional approach, Lejuene, Daou-Azzi and Powell of PricewaterhouseCoopers are obviously sympathetic to the account given by the conventional approach when they predict that VAT adoption will spearhead a continued shift to indirect taxes:[58]

> The shift is likely to continue, with the Gulf Cooperation Council nations, following IMF advice, having reached broad agreement to introduce a VAT in each country by 2012. The remaining 'blank spots' in the Middle East, Asia and Africa are likely to adopt VAT in the near future: in response to international trade reform measures; and as a *natural conclusion* to the ongoing modification and increasing sophistication of their excise, general sales and related tax regimes, which will eventually evolve to 'fully fledged' VAT systems.

A slightly more sophisticated articulation of the 'everyone else is doing it' rationale is to attribute the VAT to 'yardstick competition'. In noting the VAT's tendency to spread in regional bursts, Keen and Lockwood hypothesise that:[59]

> What remains unclear, however, is quite what it is that is driving these regional bursts. Since direct international spillovers from the VAT and its adoption are relatively limited the answer seems likely to lie in some form of yardstick competition, with countries noting the stronger performance of neighbors with a VAT in place.

In their attempt to attribute a rational explanation for these regional bursts of VAT reform, Keen and Lockwood rest on assumptions of the VAT's virtues – the contention being that the adoption of the VAT leads to stronger performance, which impresses one's neighbours to the extent that they feel compelled to get one.

54 Ibid., 34. 55 Ibid., 25.

56 Carl S. Shoup, 'Choosing among Types of VATs', in M. Gillis, C. S. Shoup and G. P. Sicat (eds.), *Value Added Taxation in Developing Countries (A World Bank Symposium)* (World Bank, Washington, DC, 1990), 3 (emphasis added).

57 Richard Bird and Pierre-Pascal Gendron, *The VAT in Developing and Transitional Countries* (Cambridge University Press, New York, 2007), 17.

58 Ine Lejeune, Jeanine Daou-Azzi and Mark Powell (of PricewaterhouseCoopers), 'The Balance Has Shifted to Consumption Taxes – Lessons Learned and Best Practices for VAT', in M. Lang, P. Melz and E. Kristoffersson (eds.), *Value Added Tax and Direct Taxation: Similarities and Differences* (IBFD, Amsterdam, 2009), 59, 65 (emphasis added).

59 Michael Keen and Ben Lockwood, 'The Value Added Tax: Its Causes and Consequences', *Journal of Development Economics* 92(2) (2010), 138, 144.

This is despite the authors' own less than conclusive findings as to the extent to which real VATs deliver on these claims.[60] To then assume that these uncertain merits are perceived by neighbours that are then able to introduce VATs relies on many leaps that the authors do not establish, but rather defer to the VAT's merits (good or real) to explain.

3.1 *Deficiencies in the account of evolutionary or fashionable growth and yardstick competition*

The mimicry of fashionable policy trends and the impact of global competition on domestic policy outcomes may be factors that have the potential to explain policy outcomes such as the rise of the VAT.[61] However, the explanatory potential of the fashionable growth/yardstick competition rationales is limited by the conventional approach's repeated attribution of these trends to the VAT's merits.

History shows that fashionable trends need not be meritorious in order to be popular, as the popularity of eugenics in Western nations at the start of the twentieth century suggests. Nor need competitive pressures result in meritorious responses – the rise of neo-nationalism in response to the pressures of globalisation is but one demonstration of this basic point.

Fashion and competition can influence outcomes independently of merit, including in non-rational ways. While fashionable trends can occur absent merit, the assumption underlying the fashionable trend explanation in the conventional approach is that the VAT is fashionable *because* of its merits. Given the discrepancy between the good VAT and real VATs, and given the fierce resistance to VAT reform across many jurisdictions, reframing the rise of the VAT by reference to a shared appreciation of the good VAT's merits (or even the merits of real VATs) does little more than revise history in light of the author's own projected conception of what *should* rationally influence policy outcomes.

4 THE WEAK ARTICULATIONS – MERITS AS THE BASIS FOR THE PROMOTION OF VAT BY TRANSNATIONAL ACTORS

Although the conventional approach occasionally identifies a role for transnational actors in bringing about VAT reform, often the role of these actors is overlooked, downplayed or simply treated as another outcome of the VAT's merits.

60 See Chapter 3, §2 of this book.

61 See, e.g., B. Guy Peters, *The Politics of Taxation: A Comparative Perspective* (Blackwell, Cambridge Massachusetts, 1991), 19–20; Ann Shola Orloff, *The Politics of Pensions: A Comparative Analysis of Britain, Canada, and the United States, 1880–1940* (University of Wisconsin Press, Madison, 1993), 27; Jonathan M. Miller, 'A Typology of Legal Transplants: Using Sociology, Legal History and Argentine Examples to Explain the Transplant Process', *American Journal of Comparative Law* 51(4) (2003), 839, 871.

The term 'transnational actor' is deployed here to refer to the various actors that operate across national borders in the promotion and development of the VAT. These actors can include international intergovernmental organisations, such as the IMF, World Bank and the OECD, as well as regional intergovernmental organisations, such as the EU and the Asian Development Bank.[62] The actors can also include individuals, such as consultants, who might operate in conjunction with these organisations or alone; aid and development agencies that are based nationally (or regionally) but operate internationally, such as the US Agency for International Development (USAID); and non-government organisations, such as global accountancy firms.

Proponents of the conventional approach acknowledge the pivotal role of the EU, and its predecessor organisations, in promoting VAT reform both directly within the European continent and indirectly by the example set by Europe to other jurisdictions.[63] However, despite being closely involved with many of the other intergovernmental organisations that have promoted the VAT, many within the conventional approach give limited or no account of the role of these organisations in facilitating VAT reform, as §4.2 and §4.3 explain. Once the treatment of these intergovernmental actors by the conventional approach has been set out, §5 focuses on other transnational actors, such as individual consultants, non-government organisations and aid and development agencies, that are completely disregarded in the accounts of the conventional approach.

In light of the gaps left by the conventional approach in relation to transnational actors, it is necessary to supplement the analysis of the conventional approach's account of the VAT's rise with additional sources which are referred to in the following sub-sections.

4.1 *Intergovernmental organisations*

Despite authoring an IMF publication that is still arguably the leading comparative text on VAT, Ebrill et al. devote only one line in the text's introduction to examining the IMF's own role in the VAT's rise by acknowledging that 'well over half of all countries that have introduced a VAT during the last twenty years made

[62] While mindful of the artificiality of treating organisations as individual actors, Elster indicates that there may be collective actors who, for practical purposes, can be treated as individuals: Jon Elster, 'Rational Choice History: A Case of Excessive Ambition', *American Political Science Review* 94(3) (2000), 685, 693. This could include organisations, such as the IMF and World Bank, that adopt procedural rules that mean the organisations adopt a common policy position that then becomes the publicly stated position of the organisation. Where the views are those of individuals associated with these organisations, but not necessarily the officially endorsed position of the organisation, the name of the individual is used.

[63] Richard Bird and Pierre-Pascal Gendron, *The VAT in Developing and Transitional Countries* (Cambridge University Press, New York, 2007), 19–20.

use of FAD [the IMF's Fiscal Affairs Department] advice in doing so...'[64] But even this limited acknowledgement is simply treated as yet another *outcome* of the VAT's merits:[65]

> The VAT has been seen as a key instrument for securing macroeconomic stability and growth by placing domestic revenue mobilization on a sounder basis, *so that* the International Monetary Fund (IMF) has attached considerable importance to its proper design and implementation.

Similarly, a World Bank publication explains that:[66]

> The Bank's advice on taxation *generally reflects the prevailing best practices*. For example, the Bank's current emphasis on broadening the base by recommending the VAT is clearly consistent with the professional consensus.

In 2012, the OECD claimed that, among its members:[67]

> [T]he *recognised* capacity of VAT to raise revenue in a *neutral* and *transparent* manner has drawn all OECD member countries (except the United States) to adopt this *broad-based consumption tax*. Its neutrality towards cross-border trade has also made it the preferred alternative to customs duties in the context of trade liberalisation.

Although the statement recognises the agency of member states to introduce the VAT, the recognition is itself attributable to the merits of the good VAT – in this instance, the good VAT's neutrality and transparency.

These explanations reduce the promotion of VAT by these influential actors simply to consequences of the merits of the VAT. Beyond resting on the merits of the VAT as the intuitive motivation behind the IMF and World Bank's promotion of the VAT, little is said about *how* these organisations have specifically contributed to the VAT's rise. This is explored further in §4.2 and §4.3. First, however, the role of three particularly influential intergovernmental organisations, the World Trade Organization (WTO), World Bank and IMF, will be introduced.

4.1.1 World Trade Organization (WTO)

With more than 150 members, the reach of the WTO is widespread. However, the WTO (and the General Agreement on Tariffs and Trade [GATT] before it) has done less to directly promote VAT reform than it has to indirectly facilitate

64 Liam Ebrill et al., *The Modern VAT* (IMF, Washington, DC, 2001), xi.
65 Ibid. (emphasis added).
66 Z. Shalizi and World Bank Group, *Lessons of Tax Reform* (World Bank, Washington, DC, 1991), 8 (emphasis added).
67 OECD, *Consumption Tax Trends 2012: VAT/GST and Excise Rates, Trends and Administration Issues* (OECD Publishing, Paris, 2012), 31 (emphasis added).

VAT adoption through the framing of international trade rules in a manner that encouraged it.[68]

Chapter 2 highlighted how the rules developed under the GATT and, later through the WTO, have provided an international trading framework favourable to the adoption of VATs. First, the classification of the VAT as an indirect tax has enabled signatory countries to refund VAT for exporters without offending rules prohibiting export subsidies – an option not available for direct taxes.[69] Second, the VAT has been proposed, especially to developing and transitional economies, as an ideal vehicle to replace revenue lost from the removal or reduction of other revenue instruments, such as specific consumption taxes and trade-related taxes such as tariffs, levies and customs duties in accordance with GATT/WTO trading rules.[70] Chapter 3 discussed the limited success of real VATs on this latter measure.[71]

4.1.2 The Bretton Woods organisations – The IMF and World Bank[72]

The IMF has been identified as playing a key role in facilitating the VAT's rise.[73] Bird and Gendron are more forthcoming than most within the conventional approach when they identify the Fiscal Affairs Department (FAD) of the IMF as the 'leading change agent'[74] driving VAT reform in transitional and developing countries. In addition to the FAD, the IMF Legal Department offers technical legal assistance relevant to VAT reform.

The FAD was established in 1964 to provide technical assistance on taxation and government budgets. The FAD has two divisions – Tax Policy and Tax Administration. The FAD uses four primary means to undertake these activities: (1) collection, measurement and dissemination of revenue data; (2) analysis and publication

[68] Alan Schenk and Oliver Oldman, *Value Added Tax: A Comparative Approach* (rev. edn., Cambridge University Press, Cambridge; New York, 2007), 18.

[69] See Chapter 2, §6 of this book.

[70] See Chapter 2, §2.2.3 of this book.

[71] Chapter 3, §2.1 of this book highlighted that the evidence is unclear as to what taxes the VAT has replaced, and §5.1 and §6 of Chapter 3 identified the manner in which real VATs themselves have acted as de facto export taxes.

[72] Formerly the International Bank for Reconstruction and Development.

[73] Neil Brooks, 'An Overview of the Role of the VAT, Fundamental Tax Reform, and a Defence of the Income Tax', in R. Krever and D. White (eds.), *GST in Retrospect and Prospect* (Brookers, Wellington, 2007), 597, 604; Lauren Damme, Tiffany Misrahi and Stephanie Orel, 'Taxation Policy in Developing Countries: What Is the IMF's Involvement?' (Consultancy Project No. DV406 for the Bretton Woods Project, 2008), 23 (visar.csustan.edu/aaba/LaurenDamme2008.pdf).

[74] Richard Bird and Pierre-Pascal Gendron, *The VAT in Developing and Transitional Countries* (Cambridge University Press, New York, 2007), 16. For a rare display of frankness from within the conventional approach, see also Michael Keen, 'What Do (and Don't) We Know about the Value Added Tax? A Review of Richard M. Bird and Pierre-Pascal Gendron's *The VAT in Developing and Transitional Countries*', *Journal of Economic Literature* 47(1) (2009), 159, 160.

on fiscal policy; (3) provision of technical assistance on tax policy; and (4) provision of funding contingent on meeting certain tax reform outcomes – such as the introduction of a VAT.[75] To a lesser but related extent, the World Bank also utilises these methods to influence fiscal policy.[76] The first two means enable these organisations to indirectly influence VAT uptake, while the latter two allow the organisations to exert direct influence. Although the conventional approach can more readily identify direct influence on VAT reform outcomes, few consider how the dominance of the IMF and World Bank in VAT research and publication may have indirectly influenced VAT reform.[77]

4.2 *A limited account of direct influence*

Where acknowledgement by the conventional approach of the promotion of VAT by intergovernmental organisation does occur, it is most commonly done when the involvement is direct. Therefore, it occurs most frequently in relation to the EU in Europe and/or the roles of the IMF and the World Bank in promoting VATs to transitional and developing economies. Underlying these accounts, however, is the attribution of the organisational promotion of VAT to the merits of the good VAT.

Bird and Gendron are particularly attuned to the role of intergovernmental organisations in facilitating the rise of VAT in transitional and developing economies:[78]

> The principal reasons for the rapid spread and success of VAT are twofold. The first reason is undoubtedly the early adoption of VAT in the EU and the perceived success of both the EU and its VAT. The second is the key role played by the IMF in spreading the word to developing countries. The *demonstrated success* of VAT in the EU showed that VAT worked. The consistent support and advocacy of this form of taxation by the IMF in emerging countries, first in Latin America and then around the world, introduced the idea of VAT and facilitated its adoption even by countries with much less developed economic and administrative structures.

Bird and Gendron's acknowledgement of the role played by the IMF is limited by the implicit attribution of the motives for the VAT's promotion to the merits (or demonstrated success) of the VAT itself. The authors say little about the broader context and reasons behind the VAT's appeal to the IMF and little about the

75 Richard Goode, 'Tax Advice to Developing Countries: An Historical Survey', *World Development* 21(1) (1993), 37, 38; Miranda Stewart and Sunita Jogarajan, 'The International Monetary Fund and Tax Reform', *British Tax Review* (2) (2004), 146, 147.

76 Richard Goode, 'Tax Advice to Developing Countries: An Historical Survey', *World Development* 21(1) (1993), 37, 40.

77 For an example of such a consideration, see, e.g., Miranda Stewart and Sunita Jogarajan, 'The International Monetary Fund and Tax Reform', *British Tax Review* (2) (2004), 146, 147.

78 Richard Bird and Pierre-Pascal Gendron, *The VAT in Developing and Transitional Countries* (Cambridge University Press, New York, 2007), 19–20 (emphasis added).

manner in which the IMF has exerted its influence. This is a surprising omission, given the shock these authors express elsewhere at the limited capacity of officials in developing and transitional countries to understand, let alone implement, VATs. This is discussed in the following section.

4.2.1 Capacity imbalances

Organisations such as the IMF can exert considerable influence over the recipients of their advice or funding, courtesy of capacity and information imbalances. In a review of IMF activity in Ghana, Pakistan, Uganda and Zimbabwe, the UK's Department of International Development notes that negotiations 'between the IMF and the ministry of finance usually determine the framework of tax policy, although all four governments lacked the ability to analyse it'.[79] Bird and Gendron acknowledge that efforts to facilitate dialogue between developing and developed countries are 'not completely successful' because representatives from these countries 'are in such different worlds that it was not always easy to communicate with each other'.[80] Reflecting on the outcomes of the ITD's First Global Conference on VAT in 2005, the authors conclude that:[81]

> Those concerned with improving how financial sector activities are taxed in a complex developed economy…or with extending the scope and reach of electronic invoicing…are not operating in the same reality as those coping with the initial task of introducing a VAT in an environment in which tax payments are still generally made in person at tax offices and the idea that tax administrations should first collect a tax and then pay (much of) it back is completely novel…They [representatives from developed countries] did not appear to understand the reality of scarce resources (and often equally scarce political support) within which tax administrators in many developing countries must often operate on a daily basis.

If the officials who play a key role in implementing VAT reform lack the capacity to understand the merits of the VAT, let alone realise these merits, this indicates that, as a minimum, merits are mediated and that more is needed than mere appeals to the merits to explain the real VATs that get adopted.

However, even in a situation where the government in a jurisdiction and an intergovernmental organisation have equivalent capacities, good VAT outcomes are equally uncertain. For example, most would agree that the pull to the VAT has been strongest in the EU. Despite this, moves toward greater harmonisation and reform of VATs so as to better reflect the good VAT have been consistently

79 UK Department for International Development, *DFID Evaluation of Revenue Projects (Evaluation Summary)* (DFID, 2001), [14].

80 Richard Bird and Pierre-Pascal Gendron, *The VAT in Developing and Transitional Countries* (Cambridge University Press, New York, 2007), 22.

81 Ibid., 22–23.

hampered by domestic political resistance and by the resistance of member states at the community level.[82]

4.2.2 Increasing reliance on lending conditionality to promote VAT

Richard Goode, the inaugural director of FAD, traces a shift in approach by the IMF from the provision of assistance throughout the 1960s to the linking of assistance to various adjustment and lending programs in the 1980s and 1990s.[83] Keen and Lockwood confirm the 'widespread perception' that the IMF has played a 'significant role in the spread of the VAT', with countries participating in a non-crisis program 25 per cent more likely to introduce a VAT one year later.[84]

Stewart and Jogarajan stress that tax conditionality attached to IMF funding has focused on consumption tax reform and specifically the introduction of VATs, which featured in 20 per cent of 490 Letters of Intent, the primary document outlining loan conditionality, from 1997 to 17 February 2004. The authors conclude that the 'data reveals the pre-eminent role of the IMF in the continued spread of the VAT around the globe'.[85]

At the same time as the IMF increased its emphasis on loan conditionality, the World Bank focused more heavily on the revenue side of fiscal policy and increased its involvement in taxation advice and linked funding to tax reform.[86] A World Bank publication outlines the different approaches taken by the bank in VAT promotion: sometimes recommending VAT as a condition of lending (such as Cameroon in 1989, Hungary in 1986 and Tanzania in 1988); sometimes providing technical assistance; and sometimes where 'the Bank and the borrower disagree strongly' on VAT, in recommending feasibility studies to foster acceptance of the VAT among government officials (as occurred in Ghana, the Philippines, Thailand and Venezuela).[87]

Stewart and Jogarajan further highlight that the activities of the IMF and World Bank should not be considered in isolation. For example, in order to be eligible for

82 See Chapter 5, §4.1.

83 Richard Goode, 'Tax Advice to Developing Countries: An Historical Survey', *World Development* 21(1) (1993), 37, 40.

84 Michael Keen and Ben Lockwood, 'The Value Added Tax: Its Causes and Consequences', *Journal of Development Economics* 92(2) (2010), 138, 144.

85 Miranda Stewart and Sunita Jogarajan, 'The International Monetary Fund and Tax Reform', *British Tax Review* (2) (2004), 146, 155. These findings are supported by Lauren Damme, Tiffany Misrahi and Stephanie Orel, 'Taxation Policy in Developing Countries: What Is the IMF's Involvement?' (Consultancy Project No. DV406 for the Bretton Woods Project, 2008), 12.

86 Richard Goode, 'Tax Advice to Developing Countries: An Historical Survey', *World Development* 21(1) (1993), 37, 40.

87 Z. Shalizi and World Bank Group, *Lessons of Tax Reform* (World Bank, Washington, DC, 1991), 67.

World Bank lending, countries must be members of the IMF and comply with IMF conditionality. Indeed, the influence extends even further, with commercial lenders heavily reliant on IMF approval of a country's macroeconomic program in assessing creditworthiness.[88]

4.2.3 A shift in the content of advice and assistance

In addition to intergovernmental organisations adopting a more interventionist stance, some within the conventional approach identify a shift in the *content* of advice given by these organisations over the second half of the twentieth century. As Goode explains:[89]

> Until about the mid-1970s many advisers recommended progressive taxation as a means of lessening inequality of income and wealth. This advice reflected prevailing public finance doctrines and values of the advisers, though not necessarily the priorities of political leaders. Progressivity was advocated also for equity and to encourage better tax compliance and to improve the prospects for "peaceful, constitutional evolution of society"...In the 1980s and early 1990s advisers were cool to progressivity and redistribution.
>
> Emphasis is [now] put on negative advice. Governments are counselled to avoid: interference with market-directed allocation of resources, disincentives due to high and progressive tax rates, provoking capital flight and discouraging foreign investment by tax rates higher than those of capital-exporting countries, detracting from comparative advantage by high effective protection and export taxes. The value-added tax is often ranked ahead of the income tax.

The shift in the content of advice may go some way to explaining why the developing world came so quickly to embrace the VAT toward the end of the twentieth century. As Chapter 1 noted, of the more than 150 countries with VAT, approximately three-quarters of countries with VAT are low- to middle-income countries[90] and two-thirds of the least developed countries in the world have VATs.[91]

While the conventional approach attributes the growth of the VAT in the developing world to its merits, this proposition has not been universally accepted. Cooper, for example, suggests that part of the answer as to why the new world has found the VAT such a 'captivating creature...has little to do with the tax per se but rather the influence of external factors such as the EU, IMF and World Bank, and

[88] Miranda Stewart and Sunita Jogarajan, 'The International Monetary Fund and Tax Reform', *British Tax Review* (2) (2004), 146, 148.

[89] Richard Goode, 'Tax Advice to Developing Countries: An Historical Survey', *World Development* 21(1) (1993), 37, 41 and 49.

[90] See Chapter 1, n 9 of this book. [91] See Chapter 1, n 10 of this book.

the WTO'.[92] Emran and Stiglitz highlight a trend toward VAT but elsewhere dispute the merits of the VAT:[93]

> Over the last few decades, a general consensus regarding the indirect tax reform in developing countries has emerged that spans academic economists and policy practitioners alike. A reduction in the trade tax with a compensating or revenue-enhancing increase in value-added tax (henceforth VAT) has been the center-piece of such a reform, and it has been implemented in a large number of developing countries under the structural adjustment and stabilization policy conditionalities of the IMF and the World Bank.

The fact that others who note the rising preference for VAT by these organisations dispute the VAT's merits suggests that the merits of the VAT alone do not explain its rise. Even if it is conceded that the shift in advice reflects a reassessment of the merits of best-practice tax policy by the conventional approach, much is left unsaid. For example, factors informing the reassessment of merits are not examined. Norregard and Khan attempt to do so by attributing the shift in the content of advice in favour of VATs to a number of potential factors, such as the 'forces of globalization', negative experience of the income tax or 'a subtle change of views on the equity-efficiency tradeoff'.[94] Each of these factors alone encompasses either complex social processes or contests of ideas. The disparity between the good VAT and real VATs calls for attention to be drawn to these factors to explain the VAT's rise. This should be the beginning of an inquiry, not headed off by simply attributing the VAT's rise to its merits.

4.3 *Failing to account for indirect influence*

The conventional approach rarely, if ever, accounts for the indirect influence of intergovernmental organisations, such as when the organisations influence reform outcomes through dominating data collection and research dissemination, or when countries adopt VATs outside obvious or direct regional or international organisational pressure.[95] This tendency to overlook the more subtle influences of

[92] Graeme Cooper, 'The Discrete Charm of the VAT' (University of Sydney Law School Legal Studies Research Paper No. 07/65, University of Sydney, 2007), 3.

[93] M. Shahe Emran and Joseph E. Stiglitz, 'On Selective Indirect Tax Reform in Developing Countries', *Journal of Public Economics* 89 (2005), 599, 600. See also Stiglitz – '[w]e focus on the VAT because it is the tax structure that has been consistently pushed on developing countries by the IMF and others': Joseph E. Stiglitz, 'Development-Oriented Tax Policy', in R. H. Gordon (ed.), *Taxation in Developing Countries: Six Case Studies and Policy Implications* (Columbia University Press, New York, 2010), 11, 18–19.

[94] John Norregaard and Tehmina S. Khan, 'Tax Policy: Recent Trends and Coming Challenges' (Working Paper No. WP/07/274, IMF, 2007), 5.

[95] The OECD provides a rare acknowledgement when it identifies globalisation as facilitating 'the rapid spread of ideas and techniques, including taxation': OECD, *Consumption Tax*

intergovernmental organisations again appears to be a product of the dominance of the merits-based approach.

Chapter 1 outlined the dominance of intergovernmental organisations in the collection, analysis and dissemination of information on the VAT. However, little mention is made within the conventional approach of the influence exercised by intergovernmental organisations as a result of this dominance. Elsewhere, public policy analysis has acknowledged the influence of *epistemic communities*, defined by Haas as a 'network of professionals with recognized expertise and competence in a particular domain and an authoritative claim to policy-relevant knowledge within that domain or issue-area'.[96] These epistemic communities influence policy trends by, for example, defining problems and issues and canvassing solutions. Accordingly, they exercise a powerful agenda-setting function.[97]

The highly specialised and technical nature of tax policy lends itself to influence by such epistemic communities. The ability of intergovernmental organisations to cover the field of VAT policy affords them great influence, even though the effect of this activity on reform outcomes is less directly measurable than the advice and funding functions. Perhaps part of the failure to highlight the influence of this epistemic community is as a result of proximity, given that the authors of the conventional approach also constitute the epistemic community itself (see §5.1).

Bird and Gendron, for example, are unable to account for why developed countries outside the EU introduced VAT:[98]

> At the same time, *for reasons of their own*, all the non-EU countries of the Organisation for Economic Co-Operation and Development (OECD) – other than the United States – have also, one by one, introduced VATs of their own in recent years – New Zealand in 1986, Japan in 1989, Canada in 1991, and Australia in 2000.

Similarly, Schenk and Oldman identify 'several reasons why the VAT has become such a popular source of revenue',[99] such as the influence of the EU, IMF and GATT/WTO, but then go on to separately list the adoption of VAT in New Zealand, Japan, Canada and Australia without specifically addressing the reasons for the adoption of VAT in these jurisdictions.[100] This vacuum might be implicitly

Trends 2012: VAT/GST and Excise Rates, Trends and Administration Issues (OECD Publishing, Paris, 2012), 58.

96 Peter M. Haas, 'Introduction: Epistemic Communities and International Policy Coordination', *International Organization* 46(1) (1992), 1, 3.

97 See Chapter 5, §4 of this book for a discussion of agenda-setting.

98 Richard Bird and Pierre-Pascal Gendron, *The VAT in Developing and Transitional Countries* (Cambridge University Press, New York, 2007), 20 (emphasis added).

99 Alan Schenk and Oliver Oldman, *Value Added Tax: A Comparative Approach* (rev. edn., Cambridge University Press, Cambridge; New York, 2007), 17.

100 Ibid., 6, 17–19. The authors make some reference to South Africa copying the New Zealand approach: at 18.

filled by references to the merits of the VAT elsewhere in the book, but such accounts leave much unsaid.[101]

The absence of direct influence by intergovernmental organisations does not mean a total absence of influence. For example, Australia's position, prior to the introduction of the GST, of being one of the last OECD countries without a VAT was frequently mobilised in support of VAT reform.[102] Whereas a relatively small nation like Australia might respond to this pressure, larger, more powerful nations such as the US are more able to resist it.[103]

These preliminary points demonstrate that the conventional approach's ready attribution of organisational promotion to the merits of the VAT leaves unexplored a number of important lines of inquiry, which might help elucidate the reasons behind the VAT's rise. These avenues of inquiry, however, deserve serious investigation rather than neglect.

5 ACTORS FREQUENTLY OVERLOOKED BY THE CONVENTIONAL APPROACH

Despite helping facilitate the rise of the VAT, the role of individuals, non-government organisations, and aid and development agencies is virtually absent from the accounts given by the conventional approach of the VAT's rise.

5.1 *Advisers and consultants*

As the previous sections have indicated, the failure to recognise individual actors in the accounts of VAT reform under the strong articulation of the merits rationale and the reluctant or limited recognition of individual agents under the weak versions is notable, given the strong links between the authors whose work constitutes the conventional approach and the organisations that dominate both VAT analysis and promotion. As §4.3 indicated, these contributors themselves may constitute an epistemic community. The absence of agent recognition is even more notable, given the prominent role individual contributors to the conventional approach have played in the promotion and implementation of VATs (often in conjunction with these organisations). As Chapter 1 explained, most contributors to the conventional approach are the very same policy experts who have played a prominent role in analysing and promoting the VAT.

Richard Goode, the first director of the Fiscal Affairs Department, offers a more candid (albeit limited) acknowledgement of the impact of international consultants when he states that the post–World War II attainment of independence by many countries opened a 'large potential number of clients for tax advice'[104] and that '[f]

[101] See, e.g., ibid., 33. [102] See Chapter 6 of this book. [103] See Chapter 7 of this book.

[104] Richard Goode, 'Tax Advice to Developing Countries: An Historical Survey', *World Development* 21(1) (1993), 37, 38.

oreign advisers no doubt contributed to the changes [in the tax systems of developing countries] but their influence can easily be exaggerated'.[105] When it comes to the conventional approach, neglect is the more appropriate charge, rather than exaggeration.

Bodin and Koukpaizin, by contrast, go further than most and identify the key role of policy experts in shaping real VATs:[106]

> As in many developing countries where technical assistance has been provided, the features of the VAT have often been influenced by foreign experts. In several cases, these experts' advice simply replicated practices that had been developed in their own country. This explains, for example, the complex rate and threshold structures, and widespread exemptions in the "first generation" VATs that were introduced in francophone countries until the end of the 1980s, as well as the very low registration thresholds in hispano and lusophone countries (for example Cape Verde and Mozambique), and the uncertainty regarding the most suitable organization for VAT administration in most Anglophone countries (for example in Malawi, where VAT was initially administered by customs and, subsequently, by a VAT directorate that was eventually merged with the income tax administration).

In examining the role of individual actors in promoting VAT reform, the authors already move beyond the standard account in the conventional approach. This enables them to highlight how real VATs were influenced by more than just the merits of the good VAT but often from real VATs already in place in the expert's home country.

Bodin and Koukpaizin buck the general trend, whereby authors closely associated with institutions such as the IMF and World Bank are reluctant to acknowledge their own role in VAT promotion or the role of the organisation they may be affiliated with. Others outside the conventional approach have been more forthcoming.[107] Non-government organisations, such as global accountancy firms, are far more direct in acknowledging the role of intergovernmental organisations. For example, Lejeune, Daou-Azzi and Powell, of PricewaterhouseCoopers, contend that:[108]

[105] Ibid., 47.

[106] Jean-Paul Bodin and Vincent Koukpaizan, 'The Rise of VAT in Africa – Impact and Challenges', *International VAT Monitor* (2009), 178, 180. See also Richard Bird and Pierre-Pascal Gendron, *The VAT in Developing and Transitional Countries* (Cambridge University Press, New York, 2007), 222.

[107] See also Stiglitz, who notes that '[d]eveloping countries are often advised (or instructed) to undertake reforms recommended by "experts" who are called "technocrats" and are often backed by the IMF': Joseph E. Stiglitz, 'Don't Trust Technocrats', *The Guardian* (online), 16 July 2003 (guardian.co.uk/politics/2003/jul/16/globalisation.economy).

[108] Ine Lejeune, Jeanine Daou-Azzi and Mark Powell (of PricewaterhouseCoopers), 'The Balance Has Shifted to Consumption Taxes – Lessons Learned and Best Practices for VAT', in M. Lang, P. Melz and E. Kristoffersson (eds.), *Value Added Tax and Direct Taxation: Similarities and Differences* (IBFD, Amsterdam, 2009), 59, 65.

> Much of the growth of VAT outside the OECD can be attributed to the International Monetary Fund (IMF) and the World Bank, both of whom have been staunch proponents of VAT introduction in the developing world as a major component of sustainable fiscal and trade reform, as well as international consultants more generally acting in concert with the IMF.

In addition, as the next section demonstrates, these private actors and business organisations are also much more candid about their own roles in promoting VAT reform.

5.2 *Business organisations*

Virtually absent from the conventional approach is an acknowledgement of the role of non-government organisations, such as multinational accountancy firms, in assisting with the spread and development of the VAT. In contrast to the modesty of intergovernmental organisations in relation to their role in VAT promotion, the large accountancy firms are more readily forthcoming about their support and promotion of VAT. Indeed, these firms readily avail themselves of opportunities to boast of their involvement in VAT reform as a means to market their services. PricewaterhouseCoopers alone claims it has provided assistance in VAT design and implementation in 37 countries, ranging from developed economies such as EU member states, New Zealand and Australia to developing countries such as Uganda, Singapore, Ethiopia, Pakistan, Tanzania, Rwanda, Jordan, Russia, Montenegro, Bangladesh, Mozambique, Albania, Malta, Mauritius and Romania.[109]

Le Lejuene, Daou-Azzi and Powell, of PricewaterhouseCoopers, openly identify an additional agent in bringing about VAT reform as 'governments *and* businesses [who] have driven and embraced the shift to VAT as the most popular form of taxation'.[110] Another PricewaterhouseCoopers publication encourages business to urge the 'need for convergence', and to make the case for VAT reform in line with the good VAT in order to facilitate business-friendly trading environments.[111] The identification of business (and its representatives) as a driver in VAT reform departs from the treatment given by the conventional approach which, despite repeatedly considering the impact of VAT design on business, does not attribute to business and its representatives any role in facilitating or shaping the VAT's rise.

[109] PricewaterhouseCoopers, *Shifting the Balance: The Evolution of Indirect Taxes* (PricewaterhouseCoopers, 2007), 7. See also KPMG, *Driving Indirect Tax Performance: Managing the Global Reform Challenge* (KPMG, 2010), 7–8.

[110] Ine Lejeune, Jeanine Daou-Azzi and Mark Powell (of PricewaterhouseCoopers), 'The Balance Has Shifted to Consumption Taxes – Lessons Learned and Best Practices for VAT', in M. Lang, P. Melz and E. Kristoffersson (eds.), *Value Added Tax and Direct Taxation: Similarities and Differences* (IBFD, Amsterdam, 2009), 59, 60 (emphasis added).

[111] PricewaterhouseCoopers, *Shifting the Balance: The Evolution of Indirect Taxes* (PricewaterhouseCoopers, 2007), 3.

A KPMG publication largely follows the conventional approach's deferral to the good VAT's merits in identifying three factors behind the VAT's rise: (1) the VAT's facilitation of fiscal stability and growth; (2) the VAT's simplification of tax administration; and (3) 'external influences' such as the IMF, EU and OECD that have promoted VAT in order to eliminate economic distortions.[112] However, the publication also identifies the key role of business in promoting VAT reform when it advises that:[113]

> Understanding this evolving process [of VAT reform] is not just an academic exercise for business – by being involved from the early stages business can achieve the twin objectives of influencing the ultimate VAT system design as well as being well informed, and thus, prepared for its implementation.

The ability to influence VAT reform outcomes is later identified as a key strategy in promoting the interests of the firm's business clientele:[114]

> Traditionally, VAT management has been viewed primarily as a compliance function...However, there is a growing realization that effectively managing the indirect tax function can add to the bottom line of the enterprise. Basic measures, such as enhancing VAT cash flow or reducing the amount of unrecovered VAT, can contribute to the profitability of a business. Similarly, reducing the overall costs of compliance helps deliver a competitive advantage in the marketplace. However, to achieve this, global organizations must be pro-active in responding to global VAT reforms that are relevant to their business.
>
> The following are some of the key actions which organizations should NOW be addressing in order to stay ahead of the game:
>
> Influence change – by playing an active part in the reforms that are occurring, organizations have the power to influence the direction of changes which impact on their business. There are many unresolved issues where input from business is being sought and where there is a genuine opportunity to positively shape how change is introduced. This is not simply about lobbying for special treatment for your business or industry: this is also about working collaboratively with government on issues such as the reduction in unnecessary compliance and drafting legislation which deals clearly and practically with modern business transactions.

The quote is critical in highlighting some key features of the role of business and its representatives in VAT reform. First, it demonstrates an alignment between business and the conventional approach in their perception of the good VAT's merits and willingness to identify those merits as underpinning the VAT's rise. While business is of course not monolithic, it is clear that there exists much support for VAT reform among the multinational accountancy firms that represent business interests. It highlights the shared perception that VAT is a compliance cost but not

[112] KPMG, *Driving Indirect Tax Performance: Managing the Global Reform Challenge* (KPMG, 2010), 6–7.

[113] Ibid., 11. [114] Ibid., 37 (emphasis in original).

a direct impost on business (i.e., that VAT is forward shifted to consumers). Second, it highlights the growing recognition by business of the opportunities that the VAT provides – a realisation that might increase avoidance and minimisation activity as much as it might lead to improving policy outcomes. Third, it demonstrates the strategic importance of influencing fiscal policy outcomes at all stages of the policy process, from the promotion of ideas to implementation. The technical subject matter of tax policy and the general public apathy toward this perceived technical detail means these groups can have a prominent impact on tax policy formation, development and implementation. The failure to identify these agents in accounting for VAT reform is therefore a significant omission in the conventional approach's account of the VAT's rise.

5.3 *Aid and development agencies*

Little mention is made by the conventional approach of the role of aid and development organisations in promoting and facilitating VAT reform. For example, Ebrill et al. attribute the early rise of the VAT in Latin America during the 1960s and 1970s to the lead of Brazil and to the fact that 'the VAT was seen as a more efficient revenue-raising tax that would be consistent with the increasingly outward orientation of economic policies'.[115] No mention is made of the role played by intergovernmental organisations such as the Inter-American Development Bank and other pan-American organisations that, for example, founded the Joint Tax Program in the early 1960s that, among other things, promoted VAT reform.[116] Nor is mention made of the USAID-funded one-man mission to Brazil made by Professor Carl Shoup in 1964 to recommend VAT reform.[117]

More recently, USAID has provided funding and technical assistance on VAT reform to a range of developing and transitional economies. Recent examples of countries that have received assistance from USAID to introduce VATs include Serbia, Egypt, El Salvador, Guatemala and Jamaica.[118] In addition, a number of aid and development agencies have provided assistance with VAT introduction – German aid and development agency German Technical Co-Operation (GTZ) has provided technical assistance to introduce and reform VATs in Serbia, Croatia,

[115] Liam Ebrill et al., *The Modern VAT* (IMF, Washington, DC, 2001), 6.

[116] The organisations included the Organization of American States and the Economic Commission for Latin America. For further details, see Richard Goode, 'Tax Advice to Developing Countries: An Historical Survey', *World Development* 21(1) (1993), 37, 38.

[117] Shoup's recommendations were not introduced, although arguably they had some influence on the VAT reform process: Carl S. Shoup, 'Retrospectives on Tax Missions to Venezuela (1959), Brazil (1964), and Liberia (1970)', in M. Gillis (ed.), *Tax Reform in Developing Countries* (Duke University Press, Durham, NC; London, 1989), ch. 8.

[118] See, e.g., 'Case Studies from Fiscal Reform and Economic Governance', a joint project funded by USAID (United States Agency for International Development): Fiscal Reform and Economic Governance, *Case Studies: USAID Assistance in Fiscal Reform* (2010) (www.fiscalreform.net/index.php?option=com_content&task=section&id=9&Itemid=65).

Macedonia and Pakistan.[119] The UK Department for International Development has similarly provided assistance with VAT reform to countries such as Ghana and Pakistan.[120] The Asian Development Bank (ADB) has been a strong advocate of VAT reform in the Asia Pacific region.[121]

Although highlighting the role of these organisations may not alone explain the rise of VAT, these organisations are one of many factors, outside of merits, that have influenced the uptake of real VATs. Accounts that seek to address the global rise of VAT without at least acknowledging the motives and activities of these organisations provide only a partial account of why the VAT has risen in the manner that it has.

6 THE NEGLECT OF DOMESTIC CONTEXT

The conventional approach tends to present economic factors (such as global competition and mobile capital) as inevitable and formidable drivers of VAT reform and transnational actors as mere messengers of the good VAT. Very little mention is made of the broader agendas of these actors, nor of the mechanisms through which the good VAT gets realised, nor of the domestic social, historical, cultural and political factors that shape real VATs.[122] This is despite widespread acknowledgement outside the conventional approach of the importance of these factors in shaping policy outcomes.[123]

The frequent and often intense resistance to the introduction of VATs throughout both the developed and the developing world underscores the importance of domestic context in influencing real VAT outcomes. The VAT has produced not simply opposition, but fierce resistance, ranging from street protests in Canada[124]

[119] For details, see generally Birger Nerré and Christiane Schuppert, *Combating Tax Evasion and Tax Avoidance: Tax Reform in Croatia* (November 2008), Deutsche Gesellschaft für Technische Zusammenarbeit (GTZ) GmbH (gtz.de/de/dokumente/en-factsheet-combating-tax-evasion-avoidance-tax-reform-croatia.pdf).

[120] John Gray and Emma Chapman, *Evaluation of Revenue Projects Synthesis Report: Volume 1* (United Kingdom Department for International Development 2001), 11–12.

[121] For a list of projects, see, e.g., those listed at Asian Development Bank (2014) (adb.org/)[search "value added tax"].

[122] OECD, *Consumption Tax Trends 2012: VAT/GST and Excise Rates, Trends and Administration Issues* (OECD Publishing, Paris, 2012), 58 cf 66.

[123] See, e.g., Joshua Aizenman and Yothin Jinjarak, 'The Collection Efficiency of the Value Added Tax: Theory and International Evidence' (NBER Working Paper No. 11539, National Bureau of Economic Research, 2005), 13; Scott Riswold, 'VAT in Sub-Saharan Africa – A Critique of IMF VAT Policy', *International VAT Monitor* (March/April 2004), 97, 107; Robin Burgess and Nicholas Stern, 'Taxation and Development', *Journal of Economic Literature* 31(2) (1993), 762, 796. See also Chapter 5 of this book generally.

[124] Neil Brooks, 'An Overview of the Role of the VAT, Fundamental Tax Reform, and a Defence of the Income Tax', in R. Krever and D. White (eds.), *GST in Retrospect and Prospect* (Brookers, Wellington, 2007), 597–99. See generally Neil Brooks, *The Canadian Goods and Services Tax: History, Policy, and Politics* (ATRF, Sydney, 1992).

and Mexico[125] to the electoral defeat of political parties in Australia and Canada.[126] The introduction of VAT in developing nations such as Grenada and Ghana ended in repeal, reenactment and, in the latter case, serious riots.[127] As Chapter 5, §4.1 will later document, even within the VAT's traditional heartland of the EU the story is not as straightforward as the conventional approach might suggest. The political scientist Junko Kato reflects a common perception of VAT reform in the EU that is consistent with many of the accounts offered by the conventional approach:[128]

> The VAT as a technically superior form of taxation may be an obvious choice to facilitate the market integration under its mandatory adoption by the European Union (EU, formerly European Community or EC). In this regard, the implementation of the VAT has been regarded as a purely economic phenomenon independent of the influence of domestic politics in each country.

However, as the conventional approach acknowledges elsewhere, VAT reform and harmonisation in the EU has encountered persistent resistance at the state and community level. This point is not insignificant, given the general acknowledgement within the conventional approach that the move to a common market has provided the greatest pull to reform and harmonise disparate real VATs so as to achieve a single good VAT. This resistance to reform, at a minimum, shows that the good is not self-evident to all actors in the policy process – a point that requires further exploration, not diminution. However, rather than explore these and other issues that bear on the VAT's rise and the consequent resistance the rise engenders, the conventional approach ignores or minimises them. Whereas the histories of the VAT's rise are treated as having little or no bearing on the VAT's design and operation, the design and merits of the VAT (good or real) are presented as having ultimate bearing in explaining the history of the VAT's rise.

Instead, the conventional approach often explains VAT uptake through equating the preferences of national government actors that have introduced VATs with their own. For example, an OECD Policy Brief attributes 'government'[129] interest

[125] Richard Bird and Pierre-Pascal Gendron, *The VAT in Developing and Transitional Countries* (Cambridge University Press, New York, 2007), 24.

[126] See Chapter 6, §1.3 of this book for the Australian case. For an overview of the Canadian history, see Neil Brooks, *The Canadian Goods and Services Tax: History, Policy, and Politics* (ATRF, Sydney, 1992).

[127] Grenada introduced a VAT in 1986, gradually dismantled it and reintroduced the VAT in 2010. Ghana introduced a VAT in March 1995, removed it two months later and then reintroduced the VAT in 1998: Liam Ebrill et al., *The Modern VAT* (IMF, Washington, DC, 2001), 14; Christophe Grandcolas, 'The Occasional Failure in VAT Implementation: Lessons for the Pacific', *Asia-Pacific Tax Bulletin* (2005), 6; Miranda Stewart and Sunita Jogarajan, 'The International Monetary Fund and Tax Reform', *British Tax Review* (2) (2004), 146, 155; Richard Bird and Pierre-Pascal Gendron, *The VAT in Developing and Transitional Countries* (Cambridge University Press, New York, 2007), 20.

[128] Junko Kato, *Regressive Taxation and the Welfare State: Path Dependence and Policy Diffusion* (Cambridge University Press, Cambridge, 2003), 41.

[129] OECD, 'Consumption Taxes: The Way of the Future? (Policy Brief)', *OECD Observer* (2007), 1.

in increasing the share of consumption taxes through instruments like the VAT to 'two main reasons': first, 'international tax competition',[130] which has made it more difficult to collect corporate and personal income taxes; and second, to the general advantage of consumption taxes (over income taxes) whereby taxes on consumption 'improve economic efficiency and increase the rate of growth, or. . .improve competitiveness and protect employment'.[131] Others attribute the VAT's popularity with governments to its specific design features. Erik Jørgensen (IMF) and Jeffrey Owens (OECD), for example, identify 'two main reasons' for the VAT's popularity with governments and therefore its 'widespread adoption' – the crediting of VAT paid at each stage of production up to consumption and the greater difficulty in evading VATs rather than wholesale or retail sales taxes.[132]

These accounts loosely identify 'governments' as the relevant agents to whom the good VAT appeals and rest on a number of unspoken assumptions. For example, they implicitly assume that 'governments' not only recognise and desire the benefits of a good VAT but are also able to act to achieve them (through introducing the good VAT). Of course, the ready admission by the conventional approach of the imperfections of real VATs clearly undermines the implicit assumption in the explanation offered. Indeed, the admissions of the failings of real VATs by the conventional approach are more frequent and frank in the face of the persistence of deviations from the good VAT, such as rate variations and domestic exclusions to the base, and in light of new challenges that arise in relation to frontier issues such as the taxation of financial services and cross-border supplies.[133] Nevertheless, despite the acknowledgement of the imperfections of real VATs, those within the conventional approach continue to express surprise at just why the VAT engenders such resistance to both its introduction and reform. Keen and de Mooij, for example, note that despite the strength of the counter-arguments developed by the conventional approach to defend the VAT against the charge of regressivity,[134] perceptions of regressivity have impeded efforts to expand the VAT base. The authors then muse that '[q]uite why resistance is so deep remains somewhat mysterious'.[135] The mystery, however, remains so deep because of the commitment

[130] Ibid. [131] Ibid.

[132] Erik Jørgensen and Jeffrey Owens, 'The Move to VAT', *OECD Observer* (August/September 1995), 21.

[133] Michael Keen and Ruud de Mooij, '"Fiscal Devaluation" and Fiscal Consolidation: The VAT in Troubled Times', in Alberto Alesina and Francesco Giavazzi (eds.), *Fiscal Policy After the Financial Crisis* (University of Chicago Press, 2013), 443, 466–73; OECD, *Consumption Tax Trends 2012: VAT/GST and Excise Rates, Trends and Administration Issues* (OECD Publishing, Paris, 2012), 66–67.

[134] See Chapter 2, §2.2.6 of this book for a summary.

[135] Michael Keen and Ruud de Mooij, '"Fiscal Devaluation" and Fiscal Consolidation: The VAT in Troubled Times', in Alberto Alesina and Francesco Giavazzi (eds.), *Fiscal Policy After the Financial Crisis* (University of Chicago Press, 2013), 443, 473. In answer to the question he poses of '[w]hy is it. . .that the introduction of the VAT has been so unpopular in so many countries?', Keen notes that in some cases, resistance 'seems largely to have been

within the conventional approach to an account that attributes the VAT's rise to its merits. This is demonstrated by the repeated refrain, detailed later in this section, that if only the merits were more clearly communicated, the resistance would dissipate.

This mystery remains despite the conventional approach elsewhere recognising that domestic context often results in departures from good VAT outcomes.[136] As the OECD has acknowledged:[137]

> there is a wide diversity in the way countries have implemented VAT. Each country has a specific mix of rates, exemptions, thresholds, etc. derived from local historic, economic and political conditions.

In light of their examination of the VAT in developing and transitional economies, Bird and Gendron take the acknowledgement of the power of local context one step further:[138]

> The best (the ideal model – uniform rate, minimal exemption, no domestic zero-rating) may be the enemy of the 'good' (what is politically and administratively feasible).

However, this potentially useful line of inquiry into the local factors that shape real VATs is cut short by the commitment of the conventional approach to explaining the VAT's rise by reference to its merits. Rather than examining the local circumstances that produce real VATs, the conventional approach retreats to a defence of the VAT's merits. One line of defence suggests that the deviations that result from the good VAT are marginal enough to leave some of the promises of the good VAT

resistance to strengthening the income tax by use of information acquired from the VAT'. This useful observation, however, is not explored further by Keen or others elsewhere in the conventional approach, perhaps because it is an instance where the conventional approach's perception of the VAT's merits (i.e., it improves tax administration) is not translated at a domestic political level where the merit is in fact perceived as a liability: Michael Keen, 'What Do (and Don't) We Know about the Value Added Tax? A Review of Richard M. Bird and Pierre-Pascal Gendron's *The VAT in Developing and Transitional Countries*', *Journal of Economic Literature* 47(1) (2009), 159, 167.

136 Alan Schenk and Oliver Oldman, *Value Added Tax: A Comparative Approach* (rev. edn., Cambridge University Press, Cambridge; New York, 2007), ch. 3; OECD, *Consumption Tax Trends 2012: VAT/GST and Excise Rates, Trends and Administration Issues* (OECD Publishing, Paris, 2012), 66; International Tax Dialogue (ITD), 'The Value Added Tax: Experience and Issues' (Background Paper Prepared for the International Tax Dialogue Conference on the VAT, Rome, March 15–16, 2005, ITD), 10, 29; Malcolm Gillis, Carl S. Shoup and Gerardo P. Sicat, 'Lessons for Developing Countries', in M. Gillis, C. S. Shoup and G. P. Sicat (eds.), *Value Added Taxation in Developing Countries (A World Bank Symposium)* (World Bank, Washington, DC, 1990), 219.

137 OECD, *Consumption Tax Trends 2010 – VAT/GST and Excise Rates, Trends and Administration Issues* (OECD, Paris, 2011), 106. See also OECD, *Consumption Tax Trends 2012: VAT/GST and Excise Rates, Trends and Administration Issues* (OECD Publishing, Paris, 2012), 66.

138 Richard Bird and Pierre-Pascal Gendron, *The VAT in Developing and Transitional Countries* (Cambridge University Press, New York, 2007), 25, and at 8.

intact or that real VATs have sufficient merit in a second-best sense to warrant their uptake. Under this line, too strong an acknowledgement of the departures from the merits of the good VAT at the domestic level might call into question the conventional approach's explanatory account. Gillis et al. can reconcile the inconsistency between their merits-based arguments for the VAT's rise and the imperfections of real VATs only by noting that the 'larger is the base of the VAT with only a single rate and a minimum of exemptions – the status of a near perfect VAT – the more important will these superior attributes of the VAT be'.[139] Another line of defence is to lambast those who question the VAT's merits for failing to propose suitable alternatives. Bodin and Koukpaizan, for example, claim that:[140]

> Since the release of *The Modern VAT* in 2001, the literature on VAT and its impact on the tax systems of developing countries has expanded, including articles that raise a number of questions regarding the suitability of VAT for developing countries, but do not suggest credible alternatives.

This defence might be relevant to a debate on what the best tax is for (developing) countries, but it is not an adequate defence to the charge that the explanation that the VAT has risen *because* of its merits is inadequate to account for the variety of real VATs in practice.

An alternative line of defence arising from the commitment to a merits-based explanation urges policy-makers to stay the course and resist (misguided) domestic opposition to the VAT so as to move closer to the good VAT.[141] This might be sage advice; however, it reveals an explanatory account that puts the cart before the horse – if merits underpin the VAT's rise, but further reform is needed to achieve those merits, what then has driven the rise of real VATs as they stand?

In a review of contributions to a conference that explored the broader issue of tax reform in developing countries since World War II, the political scientist Robert Bates commented that:[142]

> Throughout the papers there runs a highly prescriptive tone. The papers strive to develop useful insights for policy makers. But, in key instances, the lessons posited by one expert appear to be contradicted by the lessons prescribed by another. . .The impact of the studies they conducted, the training programs they put in place, or the advice they offered, they indicated, was largely determined by

139 Malcolm Gillis, Carl S. Shoup and Gerardo P. Sicat, 'Lessons for Developing Countries' in M. Gillis, C. S. Shoup and G. P. Sicat (eds.), *Value Added Taxation in Developing Countries (A World Bank Symposium)* (World Bank, Washington, DC, 1990), 219, 230.

140 Jean-Paul Bodin and Vincent Koukpaizan, 'The Rise of VAT in Africa – Impact and Challenges', *International VAT Monitor* (2009), 178.

141 See, e.g., International Tax Dialogue (ITD), 'The Value Added Tax: Experience and Issues' (Background Paper Prepared for the International Tax Dialogue Conference on the VAT, Rome, March 15–16, 2005, ITD), 29–31.

142 Robert Bates, 'A Political Scientist Looks at Tax Reform', in M. Gillis (ed.), *Tax Reform in Developing Countries* (Duke University Press, 1989), 473, 474–75.

> domestic politics. For Harberger, it was the wise leadership of a few distinguished politicians and civil servants that made all the difference; for Gillis, the core group of technocrats who maintained positions of leadership in the making of economic policy. For Jenkins, Shoup, and Bahl, the decisive force was the leadership brought to power by recent changes in government. If there was any consensus. . .it was that domestic politics is decisive in affecting the success of tax reform. But the papers do not provide an empirical basis for distinguishing the specific political forces or conditions that make a difference in implementing tax reforms.

The conventional approach's explanations for the VAT's rise are equally susceptible to this critique. While most would agree that domestic circumstances matter, few offer an adequate account of how domestic circumstances impact on actual VAT reform outcomes. One exception to this trend is in the observation made within the conventional approach that federal states, especially those with strong sub-national taxing powers, might face more difficulty in implementing a VAT because of the coordination issues involved and therefore might be less likely to adopt a VAT. The observation is more likely a product of the fact that the coordination issues involved in VAT implementation are perceived as technical rather than political issues, which can be solved with technical solutions readily proffered by the conventional approach.[143]

The inadequacy of the conventional approach's investigation of domestic influences is compounded rather than alleviated by domestic accounts of VAT reform, whereby authors frequently express frustration that, for reasons all their own, their country has failed to enact the good VAT. Countless domestic accounts of VAT reform bemoan how the real VAT in [insert country name] fails to measure up to the good VAT.[144] While better accounts seek to explore the broader reasons behind

[143] Michael Keen and Ben Lockwood, 'The Value Added Tax: Its Causes and Consequences', *Journal of Development Economics* 92(2) (2010), 138, 141, 143; Liam Ebrill et al., *The Modern VAT* (IMF, Washington, DC, 2001), ch. 17; OECD, *Consumption Tax Trends 2012: VAT/GST and Excise Rates, Trends and Administration Issues* (OECD Publishing, Paris, 2012), ch. 7.

[144] See, e.g., Yan's statement that '[c]ompared with a classical VAT, Chinese VAT can be described as impure': Wu Yan, 'Putting the "Value Added" in China's VAT', *Tax Notes International* (2010), 487, 490. A review of articles in the *International VAT Monitor*, the only journal specifically dedicated to VAT analysis at an international level, is revealing on this point. See, e.g., Reginald Dirks, 'Reform of Swiss VAT – The VAT Act from 2010', *International VAT Monitor* (2009), 481, 487:

> The relatively late introduction of VAT enabled Switzerland to learn lessons and pick the best practices from other VAT systems. However, it has not prevented the legislator and tax administration from suffering the teething troubles that normally accompany the introduction of VAT.

See also Osita Aguolu, 'VAT in Nigeria – Theory and Practice', *International VAT Monitor* (2009), 296, where the byline notes the author's observations of 'quite a difference between the functioning of the VAT system in theory and the actual functioning of VAT in Nigeria', and that 'there is quite a difference between the legal system laid down by the VAT Act and the actual application of the tax in practice': at 296. The author suggests as a response that the

these departures from good VAT design,[145] they often do so in an ad hoc and non-systematic manner. Some describe isolated case studies without reference to a broader analytical framework,[146] while others conflate description with prescription by offering potential policy-makers tips on how to successfully introduce a VAT.[147]

7 CONCLUSIONS ON THE CONVENTIONAL APPROACH TO EXPLAINING THE RISE OF THE VAT

This chapter has demonstrated that the conventional approach posits the normative merits of the VAT as sufficient to answer the empirical question of why the VAT has risen.

Under the strong articulation of the argument, the merits of the VAT are presented as *the* reason behind the VAT's rise. This seems to be little more than an expression of faith – a belief that the VAT's virtue is sufficient in and of itself to explain its adoption in more than 150 countries. The account assumes that the reasons the VAT appeals to the conventional approach are sufficient to explain why the VAT has risen.

Under weak articulations of the merits rationale, other factors behind the rise of the VAT are identified, such as fashionable trends or yardstick competition or the role played by transnational actors. While the weak articulations are not without promise, this promise is frequently undermined by the repeated insistence that these factors are also simply outcomes of the VAT's merits; that is, that the VAT is fashionable because it is good, and that transnational actors are mere messengers of the good VAT. There is little discussion, for example, of what deeper forces, if any, lie behind the fashionable trend toward the VAT; how key intergovernmental actors have shaped VAT reform; and virtually no discussion of the role of other transnational actors, such as consultants, private firms and aid and development agencies, in promoting VAT reform.

Both strong and weak versions tend to rely on the merits of the good VAT in explaining the VAT's rise. However, the argument that the VAT has spread because it is good falters when confronted by the fact that in practice no one has a good VAT. This does not suggest the VAT is flawed (or more flawed than any other tax instrument), as real-world implementation of any tax can compromise normative

government 'should set up an effective and cost-efficient information campaign to make people fully understand and accept VAT for its merits': at 301.

145 See, e.g., Reginald Dirks, 'Reform of Swiss VAT – The VAT Act from 2010', *International VAT Monitor* (2009), 481.

146 See, e.g., Vicki Beyer, 'Japan's Consumption Tax: Settled in to Stay', *Revenue Law Journal* 10 (2000), 98.

147 See, e.g., Richard Bird, Jack Mintz and Thomas Wilson, 'Coordinating Federal and Provincial Sales Taxes: Lessons from the Canadian Experience', *National Tax Journal* (2006), 889. See also Alan Schenk and Members of the IMF Legal Department, *Value Added Tax Act of the Commonwealth of New Vatopia* (IMF, 2006), discussed in Chapter 2 of this book.

ideals. Nor does it necessarily contradict the claim that the VAT is the best form of consumption tax, as the VAT may be the best form of tax from a best and second-best perspective. However, when the causal account for the VAT's rise rests on a claim based primarily on the good VAT, and virtually no one in practice realises this good VAT, then the explanation has failed to sufficiently account for why the VAT has risen in the manner it has. Put simply, if real VATs are not the good VAT, then the good VAT alone cannot explain their existence.

When the conventional approach instead rests on the merits of real VATs to explain the VAT's rise, the explanation is incomplete because the merits of real VATs operate in different and, at times, conflicting ways. So, the VAT is taken up in developed countries because it does not tax exports, but it is taken up in developing countries because it does act as a de facto tax on exports. Under this account of the VAT's rise, the VAT becomes all things to all people.

Whether relying on the merits of the good VAT or real VATs to explain the VAT's rise, the conventional approach fails. There is no one good VAT in practice, just as there is no one meritorious real VAT that appeals to all people in all places at all times. Instead, there are a number of real VATs that appeal for overlapping, different, and sometimes contradictory reasons, often depending on local context.

The attribution of the VAT's rise to its merits stems primarily from the commitment by the conventional approach to promoting the good VAT. The domination of VAT analysis by people so closely involved in its formation and promotion means that analysis of the VAT's rise is compromised by proximity or an agenda that seeks to promote rather than explore complex histories. The conventional approach conflates an imputed perception of rational motivation (policy-makers should implement the good VAT) with an actual causal explanation (motivated by the perception of goodness, policy-makers have introduced good VATs). However, the fact that few, if any, real VATs resemble the good VAT immediately casts this explanation into doubt. The assumption within the conventional approach that rational motivations are sufficient causal explanations is made without an account of the policy process to demonstrate how reasons might (if at all) produce causes. There is no effort, for example, to distinguish the initiation of a policy idea (such as developing the normative prescriptions for the good VAT) from the actual implementation of that policy (realising the prescriptions of the good VAT). This book does not suggest that beliefs about merits are not important, but rather that, in light of the discrepancy between the good VAT and real VATs, beliefs about merits are not alone determinative. As Chapter 3 demonstrated, the *truth* about merits is wholly subsidiary in most existing accounts of the VAT's rise, with attempts to assess the correctness or otherwise of the claims made for the VAT rarely undertaken and not easily verified.

Even if the claims about the VAT's merits are verified, and even if it is accepted that the good VAT is the best tax of all or that real VATs are the best tax instrument in a second-best sense, a number of unspoken assumptions have to hold for the conventional approach's account to be borne out. The account assumes that those to whom the merits of the good VAT appeal also have the ability to introduce the good VAT. The discrepancy between the good VAT and real VATs suggests that at a minimum, this influence is not determinative, and that policy outcomes are similarly influenced by actors who may perceive the merits of the good VAT differently or may instead be motivated by considerations outside the VAT's merit. These actors' preferences and actions are shaped by the institutions and context within which the policy process is located. An examination of the domestic context within which VAT reform occurs should therefore be revealing. However, right at the point where the conventional approach could explore this context and derive some useful understandings of the manner in which real VATs have come about, it circumvents the analysis by simply attributing the VAT's rise back to its merits. As a result, rather than exploring the ways in which domestic context influences real VAT outcomes, the conventional approach too often retreats into a largely irrelevant defence of the VAT's merits to save its flawed causal account.

By contrast, Chapter 5 explores alternative ways to analyse the rise of the VAT that draw on, rather than minimise, the real-world implementation of VATs at the domestic level, and thus improve upon overall understandings of the VAT's rise.

5

Toward an alternative approach to explaining the rise of the VAT

Chapter 4 of this book demonstrated that the merits-based explanations for the VAT's rise put forward by the conventional approach do little to explain the rise of the VAT. This chapter shows that, as well as being unable to account for the empirical reality of real VATs, the merits-based explanations of the conventional approach would also be rejected by public policy analysis. It draws on two leading yet divergent approaches to policy analysis, those of public choice and historical institutionalism, to show that even these very different approaches would reject outright an explanation for the rise of a policy (i.e., the VAT) by reference to its merits.

This chapter also begins the positive component of this book, to address the significant task of explaining the rise of the VAT. The chapter contends that understanding the rise of the VAT requires a refocus of the inquiry to ask what has led to the rise of the *real VATs* that have actually been introduced. To address this question, thereby filling the significant gap left by the conventional approach, §4 outlines an alternative approach to explain the rise of the VAT so as to better account for the rise of real VATs.

1 THE APPLICATION OF PUBLIC POLICY ANALYSIS TO TAXATION

Public policy, as the field of study within the discipline of political science that is centred on the study of 'whatever governments choose to do or not to do',[1] is well placed to offer a means by which to understand the rise of the VAT, given that taxation determines the ability of governments to do things. Lieberman contends that:[2]

[1] Thomas Dye, *Understanding Public Policy* (13th ed., Longman, 2011), 1, 9.

[2] Evan S. Lieberman, 'Taxation Data as Indicators of State-Society Relations: Possibilities and Pitfalls in Cross-National Research', *Studies in Comparative International Development* 36(4) (2002), 89, 92 – the quote is reconfigured from two separate quotes that appear in reverse chronological order and are separated by text.

> Tax collection is ultimately the product of policy making, the monitoring of economic activity, the administration of complex laws, and judicial and punitive enforcement...[and therefore] tax collection provides a lens for understanding more general processes of political life and the relationship between state and society.

While Lieberman's focus is on tax collection, the quote is relevant to all aspects of tax policy, which involves fundamental political decisions relating to how revenue is to be raised, how resources might be redistributed and who is to contribute to the funding of the state and its services. Thus taxation lies at the heart of the relationship between the state and its citizens.

Although analysis of taxation within public policy has received less attention by comparison to the study of state expenditure,[3] a number of studies have sought to examine taxation through a public policy lens.[4] Hettich and Winer remind us of the importance of doing so:[5]

> Taxes...give the government access to private economic resources and make possible the provision of essential public services, such as defense, police protection, and the enforcement of property rights through the courts. Their imposition influences the distribution of personal income and may alter the division of wealth among different groups. How a society employs taxation reveals much about the relation between its citizens and the state, and thus defines an important part of the nation's character.

3 Walter Hettich and Stanley L. Winer, *Democratic Choice and Taxation: A Theoretical and Empirical Analysis* (Cambridge University Press, Cambridge, 1999), 285–86; John L. Campbell, 'The State and Fiscal Sociology', *Annual Review of Sociology* 19 (1993), 163, 164; Margaret Levi, *Of Rule and Revenue* (University of California Press, Berkeley, 1988), 6–7; B. Guy Peters, *The Politics of Taxation: A Comparative Perspective* (Blackwell, Cambridge MA, 1991), 3; Steinmo contends that '[i]n short, the politics of taxation is one of the most important policy concerns in the modern industrial state; yet we know very little about it': Sven Steinmo, *Taxation and Democracy: Swedish, British and American Approaches to Financing the Modern State* (Yale University Press, New Haven, 1993), 3.

4 Public policy analysis of taxation has generally focused on two separate questions. The first shares the concern of development economics and considers the relationship between taxation and state building or taxation as a determinant of the state. The second examines taxation as an object of analysis within the state or society and considers how state or societal institutions might impact taxation. The latter approach is more obviously relevant for the purpose of this book, given that it takes for granted that states exist (albeit with varying abilities to tax): Isaac William Martin, Ajay K. Mehrotra and Monica Prasad (eds.), *The New Fiscal Sociology: Taxation in Comparative and Historical Perspective* (Cambridge University Press, New York, 2009), 2; Evan S. Lieberman, *Race and Regionalism in the Politics of Taxation in Brazil and South Africa* (Cambridge University Press, Cambridge, 2003); Miranda Stewart, 'Introduction: New Research on Tax Law and Political Institutions', *Law in Context* 24(2) (2006), 1.

5 Walter Hettich and Stanley L. Winer, *Democratic Choice and Taxation: A Theoretical and Empirical Analysis* (Cambridge University Press, Cambridge, 1999), 1.

Indeed, the more one moves beyond Hettich and Winer's extremely limited conception of the state, the more taxation assumes an ever greater significance. Murphy and Nagel contend that:[6]

> It is now widely believed that the function of government extends far beyond the provision of internal and external security through the prevention of interpersonal violence, the protection of private property, and defense against foreign attack. The question is how far. Few would deny that certain positive public goods, such as universal literacy and a protected environment, that cannot be guaranteed by private action, require government intervention. There are political differences about the appropriate level of public provision of such goods. But what arouses the most controversy is the use of government power not only to provide what is good for everybody but also to provide extra resources for those who are worse off, on the ground that certain sorts of social and economic inequality are unjust or otherwise bad, and that we have an obligation to our fellow citizens to rectify or alleviate these problems.

These fundamental questions of political and moral significance speak not just to the debate as to the state's appropriate deployment of the resources of its citizens but to the most appropriate method by which to extract the resources of its citizens. Accounting for the rise of the VAT speaks most directly to this latter issue. Simple merits-based explanations for the decision to introduce a VAT seem inadequate to capture the complexity of the decisions suggested by Murphy and Nagel. Alternatively, Peters suggests that 'politics is trumps'[7] in the tax policy-making game, because the other criteria for judging tax policy (e.g., economics, morality) carry little weight 'unless government is willing to accept it and enact it into law through the political process'.[8]

As the purpose of this book is to better explain the rise of the VAT, the following discussion of the approaches of public choice and historical institutionalism is focused first on highlighting the flaws in the conventional approach's explanation of the VAT's rise, and second on suggesting alternative means of explanation. While a number of approaches could have been mobilised for this task, public choice and historical institutionalism were chosen because, in many ways, the approaches sit at opposing ends of the analytical spectrum. Public choice is a strong instance of an actor-centric mode of analysis, whereby policy outcomes are explained by the behaviours and choices of the individual under constraints. By contrast, historical institutionalism is a more societal-based approach, whereby outcomes are explained by reference to the behaviour of actors with an emphasis on the historical and institutional context in which they operate.

6 Liam Murphy and Thomas Nagel, *The Myth of Ownership: Taxes and Justice* (Oxford University Press, New York, 2002), 6.

7 B. Guy Peters, *The Politics of Taxation: A Comparative Perspective* (Blackwell, Cambridge, MA, 1991), 3.

8 Ibid.

2 PUBLIC CHOICE

Public choice is described by one of its proponents 'as the economic study of non-market decision-making, or simply the application of economics to political science'.[9] Public choice theorists argue that, like market decisions, political decisions can be explained largely by examining the rational choices of utility-maximising actors made under certain constraints.[10] Therefore, central to public choice analysis are the choices made by rational actors and the constraints that inform those choices and shape the outcomes of decisions. Before examining what public choice might add to accounts of the VAT's rise, a few common but non-fatal criticisms of the method will be addressed.

Given its considerable influence over the past four decades,[11] it is perhaps not surprising that public choice has attracted no shortage of criticism.[12] However, much of the criticism more accurately attaches to specific, and indeed common, applications of public choice, rather than to the method itself. This is not to suggest that public choice is immune from criticism, but rather that once the method of public choice is separated from a typical ideological agenda, the criticisms of public choice as a method can be seen to be overstated.[13] Two common criticisms

[9] Dennis Mueller, *Public Choice III* (Cambridge University Press, Cambridge 2003), 1. This book specifically refers to public choice but, in an acknowledgement of the fact that public choice is an instantiation of rational choice theories in economics and philosophy, sources relevant to the discussion of both public choice and rational choice are drawn upon.

[10] James M. Buchanan, 'Public Choice: Politics Without Romance', *Policy* 19(3) (2003), 13, 17.

[11] Robert E. Goodin and Hans-Dieter Klingemann, 'Political Science: The Discipline', in R. E. Goodin and H.-D. Klingemann (eds.), *A New Handbook of Political Science* (Oxford University Press, Oxford; New York, 1996), 3, 20; Bernard Grofman, 'Public Choice, Civic Republicanism, and American Politics: Perspectives of a Reasonable Choice Modeler', *Texas Law Review* 71 (1992–1993), 1541, 1544.

[12] See, e.g., Donald P. Green and Ian Shapiro, *Pathologies of Rational Choice Theory: A Critique of Applications in Political Science* (Yale University Press, New Haven, 1994), cf Jeffrey Friedman (ed.), *The Rational Choice Controversy: Economic Models of Politics Reconsidered* (Yale University Press, New Haven, CT, 1996); Jon Elster, *Explaining Social Behavior: More Nuts and Bolts for the Social Sciences* (Cambridge University Press, Cambridge; New York, 2007), 5; Daniel A. Farber and Philip P. Frickey, *Law and Public Choice: A Critical Introduction* (University of Chicago Press, Chicago, 1991); Steffen Ganghof, *The Politics of Income Taxation: A Comparative Analysis* (ECPR Press, Colchester, 2006), 13–17. Peters argues that the 'mode of political behaviour' presented by public choice:

> makes a number of assumptions about the ability of complex political systems to transmit discontent about taxes directly into policy changes. . .[It] also makes the assumption that voters respond only, or perhaps primarily, to aggregate levels of taxing and spending, rather than to the quality of the services being provided, the personal characteristics of political leaders, or any number of possible influences on their behaviour.

B. Guy Peters, *The Politics of Taxation: A Comparative Perspective* (Blackwell, Cambridge, MA, 1991), 8.

[13] See generally Bernard Grofman, 'Public Choice, Civic Republicanism, and American Politics: Perspectives of a Reasonable Choice Modeler', *Texas Law Review* 71 (1992–1993), 1541.

relevant to application rather than method are addressed here, while more fundamental criticisms relating to the method are discussed at §2.4.

James Buchanan, one of the pioneers of public choice, describes the theory as 'politics without romance',[14] but it is not always politics absent ideological commitment. Some criticism of public choice stems from a perception that the method conflates its ostensibly positive agenda (to explain political decisions) with a normative anti-government agenda.[15] The theory's 'profoundly individualist'[16] orientation has meant that it has a natural association with libertarianism, because if choice is an expression of the individual, then curtailing choice undermines freedom. Individual proponents of public choice might also be accurately described as sharing a libertarian commitment.[17] However, the association of public choice with libertarianism is not inevitable. Public choice methodology, for example, has also been employed in individualist Marxist accounts.[18] In relation to the task of this book, to gain a better understanding of the rise of the VAT, public choice as a method is at its most useful when dissociated from this libertarian commitment. That is, the most interesting and effective contribution that public choice can make to analysing policy outcomes is not so much in the Leviathan conceptions of the state (see §2.3), but rather in highlighting the manner in which individual choices and constraints are shaped by collective choices, constraints and actions (see §2.1 and §2.2).

Others criticise public choice for its narrow conception of political motivation, whereby actors are simply driven by the pursuit of self-interest.[19] Under this

[14] James M. Buchanan, 'Public Choice: Politics Without Romance', *Policy* 19(3) (2003), 13.

[15] In response to the anti-government charge, Buchanan contends:

> In a very real sense, public choice became a set of theories of governmental failures, as an offset to the theories of market failures that had previously emerged from theoretical welfare economics. . .The public choice research programme is better seen as a correction of the scientific record than as the introduction of an anti-governmental ideology.

James M. Buchanan, 'Public Choice: Politics Without Romance', *Policy* 19(3) (2003), 13, 16.

[16] James M. Buchanan, *The Limits of Liberty: Between Anarchy and Leviathan* (University of Chicago Press, Chicago, 1975), 1.

[17] See, e.g., James M. Buchanan and Geoffrey Brennan, *The Power to Tax: Analytical Foundations of a Fiscal Constitution* (Cambridge University Press, Cambridge, 1980), which is informed by a strong libertarian impulse: at 15, 23–26.

[18] See, e.g., G. A. Cohen, *Karl Marx's Theory of History: A Defence* (Expanded ed., Princeton University Press, Princeton, NJ, 2000); Jon Elster, *Making Sense of Marx* (Cambridge University Press, Cambridge; New York 1985).

[19] Sven Steinmo, *Taxation and Democracy: Swedish, British and American Approaches to Financing the Modern State* (Yale University Press, New Haven, CT, 1993), 4–5; Michael J. Trebilcock, 'The Choice of Governing Instrument: A Retrospective', in P. Eliadis, M. M. Hill and M. Howlett (eds.), *Designing Government* (McGill-Queens University Press, 2005), 51, 54; Miranda Stewart, 'Introduction: New Research on Tax Law and Political Institutions', *Law in Context* 24 (2) (2006), 1, 5; David Duff, 'The Abolition of Wealth Transfer Taxes: Lessons from Canada, Australia, and New Zealand', *Pittsburgh Tax Review* 3(1) (2005), 1, 7; Richard Simeon, 'Studying Public Policy', *Canadian Journal of Political Science* 9(4) (1976), 548, 554, 577; Mark Kelman, 'On Democracy-Bashing: A Skeptical Look at the Theoretical and "Empirical" Practice of the Public Choice Movement', *Virginia Law Review* 74 (1988), 199, 202–3.

approach, politicians act to secure reelection; bureaucrats act to increase their own prestige or power or that of their department; and voters choose a politician or party that will increase their own utility or voters will not vote at all. Although individual public choice proponents might write as though self-interest is dominant, the method of public choice can account for non-selfish or altruistic motivations.[20] Rationality relates not to the assessment of an agent's ends, but rather to the *means* by which the agent pursues those ends.[21] Public choice can therefore accept that actors can have other-regarding preferences. At a basic level, for example, there may be incentives to act in an other-regarding way (e.g., payment to take care of a child). Even absent the incentive to do so, public choice can accept that people can act in other-regarding ways (e.g., a parent taking a child to the doctor does so for reasons beyond the mere self-interest of avoiding contracting the child's illness). Similarly, public choice as a method applied to political decisions can accept that behaviour can be informed by non-selfish considerations, as is suggested by the fact that people vote in voluntary elections even with the knowledge that their vote is unlikely to influence the final result.[22] Public choice does not, for example, break down by acknowledging that a politician might act motivated by ideals.[23] Nevertheless, whatever the criticism of public choice on this measure, even on a narrow reading of political motivation, it is still able to highlight the failures in the merits-based account of the VAT's rise and offers a far more robust alternative to the explanations provided by the conventional approach (see §2.3).

[20] Mueller contends that the 'basic behavioural postulate of public choice, as for economics, is that man is an egoistic, rational utility-maximiser': Dennis Mueller, *Public Choice III* (Cambridge University Press, Cambridge, 2003), 1–2; *Contra* Karl Widerquist, 'Public Choice and Altruism', *Eastern Economic Journal* 29(3) (2003), 317. Elster states that 'rational choice theory can easily accommodate non-material or non-selfish interests': Jon Elster, 'Rational Choice History: A Case of Excessive Ambition', *American Political Science Review* 94(3) (2000), 685, 692. Levi contends that public choice 'is committed to methodological individualism but does not reduce actors to antisocial or asocial creatures lacking regard for or influence on one another': Margaret Levi, *Of Rule and Revenue* (University of California Press, Berkeley, 1988), 8.

[21] Jon Elster, 'Rational Choice History: A Case of Excessive Ambition', *American Political Science Review* 94(3) (2000), 685, 692. Downs contends that rationality refers to instrumental rationality and efficiency in the pursuit of those goals, either by 'maximizing output for a given input, or minimizing input for a given output': Anthony Downs, *An Economic Theory of Democracy* (Harper and Bros, New York, 1957), 5; Dennis Mueller, *Public Choice III* (Cambridge University Press, Cambridge, 2003), 659; James M. Buchanan, 'Public Choice: Politics Without Romance', *Policy* 19(3) (2003), 13, 17.

[22] Anthony Downs, *An Economic Theory of Democracy* (Harper and Bros, New York, 1957), 299; Gerry Mackie, *Democracy Defended* (Cambridge University Press, Cambridge, 2003), ch. 12–14. See below, n 44.

[23] See also Grofman's discussion of the innovation of elected officials: Bernard Grofman, 'Public Choice, Civic Republicanism, and American Politics: Perspectives of a Reasonable Choice Modeler', *Texas Law Review* 71 (1992–1993), 1541, 1581–82.

2.1 *Choice under constraints*

At a very basic level, when individual choices are made in social settings, the relevant constraints that inform individual choices include the choices of others and access to information relevant to those choices.

As a simple example of how the choices of others impact individual choice, consider two friends wanting to catch up for dinner at a restaurant. Chloe has a strong preference for French cuisine but knows that her friend, Ed, although never having tried French fare, has a strong preference for Japanese. Neither Chloe's preference (to eat at a French restaurant) nor the preference of Ed (to eat at a Japanese restaurant) will conclusively settle the choice as to where the friends will ultimately dine. Chloe, for example, will need to consider the preferences of her friend, Ed, and develop a response. She may select from a number of strategies to further her interest. She might attempt to convince Ed of the merits of French cuisine, or she might try to bluff Ed that the French restaurant she has chosen also serves Japanese fare, or she might decide it is easier to submit to the preferences of Ed. In this example, Chloe's self-regarding preference (to eat at a French restaurant and to dine with Ed) will need to be weighed against her other-regarding preferences (Ed's preference for Japanese), and vice versa.[24] The eventual outcome will be determined by the choices, preferences, information and strategies employed by both friends to resolve this coordination problem.[25]

Resolving the choice of dinner rests on coordination or cooperation in collective decision-making, given each party's preference to share the other's company (over pursuing their own preferred activity) and the ability of both to talk their decisions through.[26] However, as the famous prisoner's dilemma illustrates, a collective action problem can arise when individuals, faced with a choice, may choose to act in an individually rational manner but, in doing so, make the outcome worse for all involved than if the individual had acted in a manner contrary to their self-interest. Or, in other

[24] Chloe would at least need to take Ed's preferences into account. But, if she is a good friend, her other-regarding preferences might be expanded. If she also cares whether Ed is happy, for example, she will have a preference that Ed's preferences are satisfied, and her desire to see Ed happy and her knowledge that Ed likes Japanese food will come into play.

[25] This scenario is a simplified version of the 'battle of the sexes' scenarios developed by Luce and Raiffa, based on what Hampton describes as an 'unfortunately sexist example' of a husband and wife who each prefer different evening activities (he prefers a prizefight, while she prefers the ballet). The scenario employs game theory to analyse the likely outcome when both would prefer to go out with the other to the other's favourite activity rather than attend their preferred activity alone: R. Duncan Luce and Howard Raiffa, *Games and Decisions* (Wiley, New York, 1957), 90–94, ch. 6; Jean Hampton, 'Free-Rider Problems in the Production of Collective Goods', *Economics and Philosophy* 3(2) (1987), 245, 252.

[26] Unlike the prisoner's dilemma, the 'battle of the sexes' game rests on coordination or cooperation in collective decision-making, given each party's preference to share the other's company (over pursuing their own preferred activity): Jean Hampton, 'Free-Rider Problems in the Production of Collective Goods', *Economics and Philosophy* 3(2) (1987), 245, 252; R. Duncan Luce and Howard Raiffa, *Games and Decisions* (Wiley, New York, 1957), 90–94, ch. 6.

words, a 'prisoner's dilemma is one in which noncooperation dominates over cooperation'.[27] Collective action problems therefore give rise to questions of when, and under what constraints, actors will choose cooperation or conflict, and what norms or legal rules are required to produce the best outcomes (i.e., cooperation over conflict).[28]

'Free-rider problems' are a specific type of collective action problem often relating to public goods, which are goods that benefit a collective but which are indivisible and non-excludable.[29] A free-rider is an agent who chooses not to cooperate and contribute to a public good (e.g., a clean environment, national defence, public infrastructure) because they benefit from the good that most people have chosen to cooperate and contribute to.[30] As Rawls explains:[31]

> Where the public is large and includes many individuals, there is a temptation for each person to try to avoid doing his share. This is because whatever one man does his action will not significantly affect the amount produced.

However, if too many people elect to free-ride, the result might be no production or suboptimal production of the collective good; that is, if everyone fails to pay, the entire system may fail.[32] Taxation gives rise to a particularly acute instance of the free-rider

[27] Jean Hampton, 'Free-Rider Problems in the Production of Collective Goods', *Economics and Philosophy* 3(2) (1987), 245, 252. The classic formulation of the prisoner's dilemma has two separately confined accused offered a deal by a shrewd prosecutor who has insufficient evidence to secure a conviction absent a confession. The prosecutor presents the deal to each of the accused separately: confess, and if your accomplice is silent, you go free; confess, and if your accomplice confesses, you will be convicted although with a reduced sentence for the confession; or remain silent, and if you both remain silent, the prosecutor can only secure a conviction on lesser charges. The dilemma in this scenario is that each individual is personally better off confessing than remaining silent if the other confesses (because then s/he will also get the discount) and is better off confessing if the other remains silent (because s/he will then go free). When each reasons in this fashion, both confess, and therefore the outcome is worse than if both had remained silent. The scenario therefore demonstrates conflict between individual and group rationality because a group whose members pursue rational self-interest may collectively end up worse off than a group whose members act contrary to their own self-interest. The prisoner's dilemma can also be viewed as an illustration of a failure of coordination – if the two prisoners could meet to discuss their options, each has an incentive to defect once they leave the discussion, given the payoffs outlined above. Cooperation will not emerge because of a lack of incentives to act cooperatively. Therefore, much discussion of the prisoner's dilemma involves the need for norms and legal rules to incentivise cooperation: Steven Kuhn, "Prisoner's Dilemma", *The Stanford Encyclopedia of Philosophy* (Spring 2009), plato.stanford.edu/archives/spr2009/entries/prisoner-dilemma/; John Rawls, *A Theory of Justice* (original ed., Clarendon Press, Oxford, 1972), 269, who attributes the idea to A. W. Tucker.

[28] Jean Hampton, 'Free-Rider Problems in the Production of Collective Goods', *Economics and Philosophy* 3(2) (1987), 245, 272.

[29] So that making goods 'available to one person in the community makes them available to all': Ibid., 247.

[30] Ibid., 247–48; Anthony Downs, *An Economic Theory of Democracy* (Harper and Bros., New York, 1957), 170.

[31] John Rawls, *A Theory of Justice* (Clarendon Press, Oxford, 1972), 246.

[32] As in the prisoner's dilemma scenario: Jean Hampton, 'Free-Rider Problems in the Production of Collective Goods', *Economics and Philosophy* 3(2) (1987), 245, 246.

problem because everyone benefits from the services of government, which are diffusely shared and may not be readily appreciated, but not everyone is willing to pay for the costs which, in contrast to the benefits, are keenly and directly felt.[33]

2.2 *A focus on how the choices under constraints of political actors might impact the good VAT*

From the outset, the acknowledgement that individual choice is the product of the choices of others immediately challenges an account that seeks to explain political decisions exclusively or predominantly by reference to the merits of a policy idea or instrument. Even if an actor perceives the merits of an idea and this perception motivates them to act toward its realisation, in attempting to achieve this outcome the actor must have regard to more than the mere merits of the idea.

At a minimum, public choice highlights that the actor would need to consider the likely choices and behaviour of others (and perhaps the underlying preferences that might inform those choices), as well as the constraints imposed by the system through which the reform needs to be achieved (for example, constitutional constraints that determine when something becomes a binding law). In a parliamentary democracy, attention is therefore often turned to elected officials and the voters who elect them; bureaucrats who advise the elected officials; and interest groups constituted by individuals who come together to further their shared interest. A highly simplified hypothetical example can be used to highlight some key concepts within public choice that challenge the merits-based explanations of the conventional approach.

Let's suppose a senior Treasury or Ministry of Finance official in an advanced democracy, labelled the 'Treasury official', is familiar with the arguments of the conventional approach and finds the merits of the good VAT compelling for all the reasons outlined in Chapter 2. In addition, let's assume the Treasury official is benevolent; that is, the official is motivated by the belief that introducing the VAT is good for the country rather than in maximising his/her own position or that of his/her department.[34] In rationally calculating how to achieve the implementation

[33] Steinmo states that:

> Because benefits are often diffuse, citizens are insensitive to or unaware of the large share of the benefits they receive. Because taxes are direct, citizens are painfully aware of the costs of government. Because they are rational, they will oppose paying for benefits that they do not perceive.

Sven Steinmo, *Taxation and Democracy: Swedish, British and American Approaches to Financing the Modern State* (Yale University Press, New Haven, CT, 1993), 193. See also Richard Eccleston, *Taxing Reforms* (Edward Elgar, Cheltenham, 2007), 2–3; Anthony Downs, *An Economic Theory of Democracy* (Harper and Bros., New York, 1957), 16; Robert Bates, 'A Political Scientist Looks at Tax Reform', in M. Gillis (ed.), *Tax Reform in Developing Countries* (Duke University Press, Durham, NC, 1989), 473, 478–83.

[34] Many public choice accounts contend that bureaucrats need not be motivated by the good but may be motivated to promote policies that maximise their power, pay and prestige and the

of the good VAT (i.e., the maximisation of the goal at minimal cost), the official must consider other actors and the relevant constraints of the political system through which the VAT will need to pass in order to be introduced. Some of the many considerations the Treasury official would need to take into account are outlined below.

The Treasury official will need to convince any elected officials, with the power to introduce laws, to support the VAT. In convincing the elected officials, the Treasury official could choose from a range of options, from appeals to the merits of the VAT to mere bluffing. To limit the options, let's suppose the Treasury official perceives that the elected officials will be reluctant to enact policies that will compromise their reelection.[35] As the Treasury official has information on the controversial history of VAT reforms in similar jurisdictions elsewhere, which have led to the electoral defeat of other governments, the official might try to downplay or distinguish the experience of other jurisdictions or consider ways to structure the reform package in a way to make it appeal to voters, so as to attempt to avoid the mistakes made elsewhere.

The example is premised upon the assumption that the Treasury official has a privileged position in relation to agenda-setting which, as §4 later explains, is the ability to define problems and offer solutions.[36] The dominance of tax policy by

respective budget, power and prestige of their departments. The argument generally rests on an analogy of bureaucracy with a monopoly provider, and concern stems from the fact that bureaucrats are not restricted by electoral constraints: Michael J. Trebilcock, 'The Choice of Governing Instrument: A Retrospective', in P. Eliadis, M. M. Hill and M. Howlett (eds.), *Designing Government* (McGill-Queens University Press, 2005), 51, 52; William A. Niskanen, *Bureaucracy and Representative Government* (Aldine, Chicago, 1971); Dennis Mueller, *Public Choice III* (Cambridge University Press, Cambridge, 2003), 661; Thomas Romer and Howard Rosenthal, 'Bureaucrats versus Voters: On the Political Economy of Resource Allocation by Direct Democracy', *Quarterly Journal of Economics* 93(4) (1979), 563; James M. Buchanan and Geoffrey Brennan, *The Power to Tax: Analytical Foundations of a Fiscal Constitution* (Cambridge University Press, Cambridge, 1980), 23–24. For criticisms of the claims, see Walter Hettich and Stanley L. Winer, *Democratic Choice and Taxation: A Theoretical and Empirical Analysis* (Cambridge University Press, Cambridge, 1999), 29; Mark Kelman, 'On Democracy-Bashing: A Skeptical Look at the Theoretical and "Empirical" Practice of the Public Choice Movement', *Virginia Law Review* 74 (1988), 199, 214, 218, 268.

[35] Michael J. Trebilcock, 'The Choice of Governing Instrument: A Retrospective', in P. Eliadis, M. M. Hill and M. Howlett (eds.), *Designing Government* (McGill-Queens University Press, 2005), 51, 52. As the start of §2 highlighted, this assumption is not a necessary feature of the public choice account: Bernard Grofman, 'Public Choice, Civic Republicanism, and American Politics: Perspectives of a Reasonable Choice Modeler', *Texas Law Review* 71 (1992–1993), 1541, 1578–82.

[36] In public choice accounts the privileged agenda-setting position of bureaucrats is attributed to the bureaucrats' monopoly supply of public goods and services: Walter Hettich and Stanley L. Winer, *Democratic Choice and Taxation: A Theoretical and Empirical Analysis* (Cambridge University Press, Cambridge, 1999), 29; Thomas Romer and Howard Rosenthal, 'Political Resource Allocation, Controlled Agendas, and the Status Quo', *Public Choice* 33(4) (1978), 27–28; James M. Buchanan and Geoffrey Brennan, *The Power to Tax: Analytical Foundations of a Fiscal Constitution* (Cambridge University Press, Cambridge, 1980), 23–24.

Ministries of Finance and Treasury is suggestive of the importance of their agenda-setting role. However, others can also set agendas. Elected officials, for example, can clearly do so through campaigning and/or persuasion.[37] In addition, other powerful actors and groups can clearly do so. This might therefore require the Treasury official to consider who the likely winners and losers from any reform are and what their relative power is.

Potential losers from the introduction of a VAT might include actors or industries that have benefited from preferential taxation that might be lost with the VAT's introduction, and who might therefore engage in 'rent-seeking' behaviour to preserve the rents (or benefits) accruing from the previous policy.[38] The Treasury official might be mindful of the fact that, although the benefit of any tax concession obtained or retained is offset by the cost of lobbying, often the payoff far outweighs these costs.[39] However, rent seeking need not be the only motivation for acting.

[37] Bernard Grofman, 'Public Choice, Civic Republicanism, and American Politics: Perspectives of a Reasonable Choice Modeler', *Texas Law Review* 71 (1992–1993), 1541, 1577–86.

[38] Public choice theorists label the behaviour of actors who expend resources in order to obtain or retain government benefits as rent seeking, whereby the actors seek a benefit without producing more in return. In taxation, rent seeking generally transfers the cost of a tax concession to another taxpayer: Robin Burgess and Nicholas Stern, 'Taxation and Development', *Journal of Economic Literature* 31(2) (1993), 762, 801. See also Charles Kershaw Rowley, Robert D. Tollison and Gordon Tullock, *The Political Economy of Rent-Seeking* (Kluwer Academic Publishers, Boston, 1988); James M. Buchanan, Robert D. Tollison and Gordon Tullock, *Toward a Theory of the Rent-Seeking Society* (Texas A&M University, College Station, 1980); see especially Gordon Tullock, 'Efficient Rent-Seeking', in J. M. Buchanan, R. D. Tollison and G. Tullock (eds.), *Toward a Theory of the Rent-Seeking Society* (Texas A&M University, College Station, 1980), 97. The term is attributed to Kreuger: Anne O. Krueger, 'The Political Economy of the Rent-Seeking Society', *American Economic Review* 64 (3) (1974), 291. See also David R. Henderson, *Rent Seeking* (2008), Library of Economics and Liberty (econlib.org/library/Enc/RentSeeking.html).

[39] These victories for individual taxpayers and groups often, however, result in pure loss to the economy as a whole because real resources are expended in getting a transfer from others: David R. Henderson, *Rent Seeking* (2008), Library of Economics and Liberty (econlib.org/library/Enc/RentSeeking.html). See the recent efforts of the mining industry to stymie a new mining tax in Australia as an example. For the original proposal, see Commonwealth of Australia Treasury, Australia's Future Tax System Review Panel, *Australia's Future Tax System: Report to the Treasurer* (Australia's Future Tax System Review Panel: The Treasury, Canberra, 2009), 215–47. For what it became after a fierce advertising campaign by the mining industry led the government to renegotiate the tax with three mining companies (Rio Tinto, Xstrata and BHP Billiton), see *Minerals Resource Rent Tax Act 2012* (Cth). A new government came to power on the promise to completely repeal the tax and has successfully done so. For newspaper accounts of the controversy, see David Uren et al., 'Treasury Exposes Mining Tax Flaws: Parkinson Blames Labor's Concessions to Miners for Shortfall in Revenue', *The Australian*, 15 February 2013, 1, 4; Phillip Coorey, 'Taxpayers Lose $60b in Mining Profits Compromise', *Sydney Morning Herald* (online), 16 February 2011 (smh.com.au/national/taxpayers-lose-60b-in-mining-profits-compromise-20110215-1av7f.html); Mark Davis, 'A Snip at $22m to Get Rid of PM', *Sydney Morning Herald* (online), 2 February 2011 (smh.com.au/business/a-snip-at-22m-to-get-rid-of-pm-20110201-1acgj.html); Laurie Oakes, 'Mining New Depths of Political Bastardry', *Daily Telegraph* (online), 29 May 2010 (dailytelegraph.com.au/news/opinion/mining-new-depths-of-political-bastardry/story-e6frezzo-1225872694228).

Small business might oppose the VAT because of concerns over compliance burdens, or social welfare groups might act to oppose the VAT because of concerns about regressivity.

Given that '[p]olitical power is often closely allied to groups which have large asset or wealth holdings',[40] and given that groups with significant resources to tax often perceive they have the most to lose, the Treasury official might compare the relative resources available to groups likely to oppose the tax against the resources of groups likely to support it. The official might try to leverage the likely support of groups, such as export reliant industries (e.g., mining), big business groups and/or their representatives who do not view the VAT as a cost to business other than a compliance cost (see Chapter 4, §5.2). These groups may make their support contingent on the VAT being used to replace taxes that they do perceive as particularly detrimental to their interests, such as the corporate income tax.[41]

The Treasury official (or the elected officials) might be mindful of how to present information so as to best ensure the passage of the VAT. As choices are often made against imperfect information,[42] actors with access to greater information can exploit *asymmetries of information* (the unequal access to information relevant to policy decisions that different actors possess).[43] The general public might choose to remain *rationally ignorant* (i.e., decide not to acquire information because the perceived costs of doing so outweigh the benefits).[44] Public choice contends that small, concentrated sectional interest groups with a strong incentive

[40] Robin Burgess and Nicholas Stern, 'Taxation and Development', *Journal of Economic Literature* 31(2) (1993), 762, 801.

[41] This could give rise to a form of log-rolling, where different coalitions support each other's policies in return for support of their own: Barry R. Weingast, Kenneth A. Shepsle and Christopher Johnsen, 'The Political Economy of Benefits and Costs: A Neoclassical Approach to Distributive Politics', *Journal of Political Economy* 89(4) (1981), 642–43.

[42] Anthony Downs, *An Economic Theory of Democracy* (Harper and Bros., New York, 1957), 207. Some models assume perfect information: Walter Hettich and Stanley L. Winer, *Democratic Choice and Taxation: A Theoretical and Empirical Analysis* (Cambridge University Press, Cambridge, 1999), 26.

[43] The concept is adapted from economics; see generally George A. Akerlof, 'The Market for "Lemons": Quality, Uncertainty and the Market Mechanism', *Quarterly Journal of Economics* 84(3) (1970), 488; M. Spence, 'Job Market Signaling', *Quarterly Journal of Economics* 87 (1973), 355.

[44] Steinmo contends that voters 'are largely uninformed but rationally self-interested': Sven Steinmo, *Taxation and Democracy: Swedish, British and American Approaches to Financing the Modern State* (Yale University Press, New Haven, 1993), 193. Public choice has much to say about the impact of information asymmetries and rational ignorance on other choices. For example, Downs contends that, in relation to voting, the cost of obtaining information is relatively high while the probability of influencing an electoral outcome with one vote is low. As a result, voters can remain rationally ignorant: Anthony Downs, *An Economic Theory of Democracy* (Harper and Bros., New York, 1957), ch. 6, 13, 14, and at 298; Douglas McTaggart, Christopher Findlay and Michael Parkin, *Economics* (2nd ed., Addison-Wesley, Sydney, 1996), 398. Downs and many since have attempted (with limited success) to explain the paradox of voting ('Downs paradox'), which arises when people do vote even though they are unlikely to affect the electoral outcome in representative systems where voting is voluntary:

to mobilise for special treatment are often more likely to gain benefits than the general public, because the general public lacks the equivalent incentive to be informed.[45] As a result of this rational ignorance, voters may therefore lack the incentive to mobilise because benefits are widely spread and their political power is relatively peripheral.[46] Duff contends that the phenomenon of rational ignorance in tax policy 'is likely to be particularly pronounced given the complexity of the issues involved'.[47] Elected officials may exploit *asymmetries of information* between well-informed voters and ill-informed voters and between concentrated and diffuse interest groups with different political mobilisation costs.[48] So, the elected official might bluff the general public while keeping sectional interests informed.

Collective action problems can occur at both the policy development stage and the implementation and collection stages.[49] If the Treasury official is particularly forward thinking, he or she might consider how dynamics might change over time. For example, big business might be allies in supporting the introduction of a VAT, but less helpful later on. So, they might attempt to exert influence to obtain special

Downs at ch. 12–14. The fact that people do bother to vote in the absence of compulsion is explained by identifying other motivations for voting beyond narrow self-interest and a desire to affect the outcome of an election, such as the pleasure in exercising a civic or moral duty or through expressing an opinion: see generally Gerry Mackie, *Democracy Defended* (Cambridge University Press, Cambridge, 2003); Dennis Mueller, *Public Choice III* (Cambridge University Press, Cambridge, 2003), 658; Aaron S. Edlin, Andrew Gelman and Noah Kaplan, 'Vote for Charity's Sake', *Economists' Voice* 5(6) (2008), 1; Aaron Edlin, Andrew Gelman and Noah Kaplan, 'Voting as a Rational Choice', *Rationality and Society* 19(3) (2007), 293. However, rational ignorance need not be viewed negatively. For example, it might be in your own interest to defer to the expertise of your doctor. For an extension of this idea to an account of legal authority, see Joseph Raz, 'Problem of Authority: Revisiting the Service Conception', *Minnesota Law Review* 90 (2005–2006), 1003. Rational ignorance plays out in elections through allegiance to political parties when party allegiance might determine voting choices rather than specific calculation of the issues.

45 Alan Fenna, *Australian Public Policy* (2nd ed., Pearson Education Australia, Frenchs Forest, NSW, 2004), 295; Ira Katznelson and Helen V. Milner, 'American Political Science: The Discipline's State and the State of the Discipline', in I. Katznelson and H. V. Milner (eds.), *Political Science: State of the Discipline* (Norton; American Political Science Association, New York, Washington, DC, 2002), 1, 144.

46 Mancur Olson, *The Logic of Collective Action* (1965); Anthony Downs, *An Economic Theory of Democracy* (Harper and Bros., New York, 1957), ch. 13 and at 299. For a specific application of the approach to the analysis of tax reform, see Robert Bates, 'A Political Scientist Looks at Tax Reform', in M. Gillis (ed.), *Tax Reform in Developing Countries* (Duke University Press, Durham, NC, 1989), 473.

47 David Duff, 'The Abolition of Wealth Transfer Taxes: Lessons from Canada, Australia, and New Zealand', *Pittsburgh Tax Review* 3(1) (2005), 1, 6. See also B. Guy Peters, *The Politics of Taxation: A Comparative Perspective* (Blackwell, Cambridge, MA, 1991), 12.

48 Michael J. Trebilcock, 'The Choice of Governing Instrument:A Retrospective', in P. Eliadis, M. M. Hill and M. Howlett (eds.), *Designing Government* (McGill-Queens University Press, 2005), 51, 52.

49 Evan S. Lieberman, 'Taxation Data as Indicators of State-Society Relations: Possibilities and Pitfalls in Cross-National Research', *Studies in Comparative International Development* 36(4) (2002), 89, 93.

preferences/rents during the drafting and implementation of the VAT, or they may try to minimise VAT liability at the collection stage.[50] The Treasury official will be cognisant of the need to balance stakeholder consultation against the risk of *capture*, whereby policy-makers and regulators become too close with the very people they are charged to regulate at the expense of the public good.[51] The Treasury official may need to consider rules to guard against such capture.

Although the public may perceive their power as peripheral, one exercise of public power is the act of voting.[52] Much of public choice concerns the development of voting models to account for the choices made by voters and by the elected officials appointed by them in a representative democracy.[53] Some of the factors

[50] The recognition by KPMG of the ability of VAT to contribute to a business's bottom line alongside the vulnerability of real VATs to avoidance and evasion highlights this issue: see Chapter 4, §5.2 of this book.

[51] Trebilcock highlights the argument that regulators might become captive to those they seek to regulate so as to, for example, reduce the impact of their own workload or perhaps to enhance future employment prospects: Michael J. Trebilcock, 'The Choice of Governing Instrument: A Retrospective', in P. Eliadis, M. M. Hill and M. Howlett (eds.), *Designing Government* (McGill-Queens University Press, 2005), 51, 52. *Contra* Mark Kelman, 'On Democracy-Bashing: A Skeptical Look at the Theoretical and "Empirical" Practice of the Public Choice Movement', *Virginia Law Review* 74 (1988), 199, 267–68.

[52] *Contra* Brennan and Buchanan, who contend that 'the assumption that electoral processes are sufficient to constrain self-seeking government is extremely vulnerable': James M. Buchanan and Geoffrey Brennan, *The Power to Tax: Analytical Foundations of a Fiscal Constitution* (Cambridge University Press, Cambridge, 1980), 17, and at 15 – 16.

[53] Public choice is not wedded to analysing any particular model. For example, there exist public choice analyses of direct democracies and dictatorships. Downs states that '[o]f course, political rationality need not operate democratically, as it does in our model. As long as uncertainty is diminished and stable order introduced and maintained, rational action is possible, even if tyranny prevails': Anthony Downs, *An Economic Theory of Democracy* (Harper and Bros, New York, 1957), 11. Models vary in their degree of complexity. A voting model commonly applied to the analysis of tax policy outcomes is the median voter model developed by Duncan Black, *The Theory of Committees and Elections* (Cambridge University Press, Cambridge, 1958). In simple terms, the median voter theory provides that, given certain assumptions, the most favoured policy alternative is set at the median point of voters' preference distributions: Walter Hettich and Stanley L. Winer, *Democratic Choice and Taxation: A Theoretical and Empirical Analysis* (Cambridge University Press, Cambridge, 1999), 13, 18; Anthony Downs, *An Economic Theory of Democracy* (Harper and Bros, New York, 1957), 52, ch. 4. Peters explains the implications of the simple median voter model for tax policy:

> The argument of the public choice school is that in a functioning democracy tax and expenditure levels that go above the level desired by the average (median) voter will ultimately produce political retribution against the officials responsible for adopting them.

B. Guy Peters, *The Politics of Taxation: A Comparative Perspective* (Blackwell, Cambridge, MA, 1991), 8. The quote captures but oversimplifies the median voter theory. The application of the simple median voter model to choices in tax policy has commonly focused on the setting of tax rates in a manner that maximises the median voter's fiscal surplus: Walter Hettich and Stanley L. Winer, *Democratic Choice and Taxation: A Theoretical and Empirical Analysis* (Cambridge University Press, Cambridge, 1999), 13; David Duff, 'The Abolition of Wealth Transfer Taxes: Lessons from Canada, Australia, and New Zealand', *Pittsburgh Tax*

the Treasury official might consider include: What is the best way to structure the package in light of the given constraints? What information is necessary to inform voters of the merits of the good VAT so they will support reform? How is the message best communicated, especially in light of the anticipated information campaigns by actors opposing the VAT? What will be the impact of the electoral system? This involves considering the length of the electoral cycle (whereby the longer the cycle, the more likely voters will forget or at least be less inclined to punish the government for the imposition of a new tax, while the shorter the cycle, the greater the incentive for politicians to pursue short-term gains over long-term costs). In addition, the Treasury official will need to consider the method adopted for choosing winners (e.g., first past the post, preferential, proportional voting systems) and how these methods of aggregating preferences will likely impact electoral outcomes.

As a result of these considerations, the Treasury official must decide upon the most appropriate method for achieving the introduction of the good VAT. This will include considering how to best structure compensation for the VAT's introduction, both to appease opponents and to increase the likely support of voters. Cognisant of the conventional approach's edict to avoid doing this through departing from the three design norms necessary to achieve the good VAT, the official will have to consider how best to structure compensation, which might involve targeted expenditure, cutting other taxes such as the income tax or a combination of these and other options no doubt informed by experience with real VATs elsewhere. The official will also need to consider how to present this compensation as preferable to alterations to the good VAT and the likely responses to the compensation package. For example, the official might consider whether the compensation might further intensify opposition to the VAT (for example, if income tax cuts favour the rich too heavily over the poor; or if the compensation is so much that it fuels concerns over the growth of government).

This highly simplified example raises only some of the many constraints that one actor will need to take into account in order to attempt the introduction of the good VAT. Alongside this, of course, sits a host of constraints governing the preferences, choices and actions of the many other actors in the policy process. The Treasury

Review 3(1) (2005), 1, 6; W. Irwin Gillespie, *Tax, Borrow, and Spend: Financing Federal Spending in Canada, 1867–1990* (Carleton University Press, Ottawa, Canada, 1991), 17; Michael J. Trebilcock, 'The Choice of Governing Instrument: A Retrospective', in P. Eliadis, M. M. Hill and M. Howlett (eds.), *Designing Government* (McGill-Queens University Press, 2005), 51, 52. The median voter model is subject to a number of criticisms, not the least of which is its inability to deal with real-world complexity, whereby the model's assumption that policy issues are decided one at a time does not fit with the reality of multidimensional policy issues. See generally Andrew C. Gould and Peter J. Baker, 'Democracy and Taxation', *Annual Review of Political Science* 5 (2002), 87, 98–99; Walter Hettich and Stanley L. Winer, *Democratic Choice and Taxation: A Theoretical and Empirical Analysis* (Cambridge University Press, Cambridge, 1999), 14–15, 37; Rudolf Richter, 'Democratic Choice and Taxation: A Theoretical and Empirical Analysis (Book Review)', *Public Choice* (2000), 194, 195.

official may wish that the introduction of a VAT be determined solely on the basis of the merits of the good VAT, as perceived by the conventional approach. However, even if this were to occur, it would be the result of the choices and behaviour of a number of actors under different constraints, all of which the conventional approach gives us no guide to understanding.

2.3 *The challenge of public choice to the conventional approach*

Public choice points to the problems that arise as a result of the interaction between individual and collective choices. In doing so, it can potentially explain policy decisions that may be judged inefficient from an economic perspective, such as why real VATs get enacted over good VATs.

Some public choice accounts arose from dissatisfaction with public finance economists who, in the words of Buchanan, ignored 'political constraints…in the determination of tax policy'.[54] Brennan and Buchanan's aim in their classic text, *The Power to Tax: Analytical Foundations of a Fiscal Constitution*, is in many ways shared by this book:[55]

> We do not ask the question 'What is a good tax system?'…our major object is not to demonstrate that much of the policy advice proffered by current tax advocates to governments may be wrong, even on its own grounds. Rather, we are seeking to offer a different *understanding* of the nature and process of taxation – a different "window" through which fiscal phenomena can be viewed.

The model proposed by Brennan and Buchanan to contest the standard public finance account deliberately departed from what they perceived as a presumption of benevolent government employed by public finance scholars. Instead, they proposed a predatory model of government as a 'revenue-maximising Leviathan',[56] which could be effectively constrained only by constitutional limitations.[57] It is worth noting in passing the manner in which this Leviathan model has itself

[54] Geoffrey Brennan and James M. Buchanan, *The Power to Tax: Analytical Foundations of a Fiscal Constitution* (online) (Library of Economics and Liberty; Indianapolis, 2000), econlib.org/library/Buchanan/buchCv9co.html, foreword by Brennan (1998), 9.F.2.

[55] James M. Buchanan and Geoffrey Brennan, *The Power to Tax: Analytical Foundations of a Fiscal Constitution* (Cambridge University Press, Cambridge, 1980), 2 (emphasis in original). See also Hettich and Winer, who attempt to address a perceived gap left both by public choice theorists who fail to examine tax policy (at 285–86) and by 'a large part of the economic literature' that treats 'taxation and politics as two distinct fields' (at 2): Walter Hettich and Stanley L. Winer, *Democratic Choice and Taxation: A Theoretical and Empirical Analysis* (Cambridge University Press, Cambridge, 1999). The authors contend that '[m]uch of the literature on public economics is written from a normative point of view and does not attempt to explain observed policy outcomes. Policy recommendations are derived in a framework that is restricted to economic variables and that excludes politics': at 5.

[56] James M. Buchanan and Geoffrey Brennan, *The Power to Tax: Analytical Foundations of a Fiscal Constitution* (Cambridge University Press, Cambridge, 1980), xii, ch. 2.

[57] Ibid., 17, 15–16.

acquired political significance in the VAT debate in the United States (US), whereby strong opposition to VAT reform is motivated by a fear that introducing a VAT will unleash the Leviathan of big government by virtue of the VAT's reputation as a money machine.[58] Brennan and Buchanan's controversial model has been subject to much contestation and debate, which is beyond the scope of this book.[59] However, it is sufficient to note that for the purposes of this book, the whole of government model appears less useful than public choice models focused on individual choice made under constraints,[60] as the following model of tax policy developed by Hettich and Winer demonstrates.[61]

Hettich and Winer conclude that in modern representative democracies, complex tax structures are politically rational.[62] The authors view tax systems as complex combinations of a limited number of parts, which include the tax base; rate structures; and special provisions such as exemptions, credits and deductions.[63]

58 See Chapter 7 of this book.

59 For applications of the model, see Margaret Levi, *Of Rule and Revenue* (University of California Press, Berkeley, 1988); Adam Gifford Jr and Roy W. Kenney, 'Socialism and the Revenue Maximizing Leviathan', *Public Choice* 42 (1984), 101; Robert Higgs, *Crisis and Leviathan: Critical Episodes in the Growth of American Government* (Oxford University Press, New York, 1987), cited in Isaac William Martin, Ajay K. Mehrotra and Monica Prasad, 'The Thunder of History: The Origins and Development of the New Fiscal Sociology', in I. W. Martin, A. K. Mehrotra and M. Prasad (eds.), *The New Fiscal Sociology: Taxation in Comparative and Historical Perspective* (Cambridge University Press, New York, 2009), 1, 10; Walter Hettich and Stanley L, Winer, *Democratic Choice and Taxation: A Theoretical and Empirical Analysis* (Cambridge University Press, Cambridge, 1999), 20–21. For criticisms, see Hettich and Winer at 21–34; Anthony Downs, *An Economic Theory of Democracy* (Harper and Bros., New York, 1957), who contends that whole of government models, such as Leviathan, are 'useless as a guide to practical decisions' (at 15); and that 'the organismic view of government is untrue because it is based upon a mythical entity: a state which is a thing apart from individual men' (at 17).

60 'Rational choice explanations divorced from methodological individualism have a dubious value': Jon Elster, 'Rational Choice History: A Case of Excessive Ambition', *American Political Science Review* 94(3) (2000), 685, 693.

61 Hettich and Winer adopt a probabilistic voting model (under this model, a small change in a party's policy platform might alter the probability of support from a voter): Walter Hettich and Stanley L. Winer, *Democratic Choice and Taxation: A Theoretical and Empirical Analysis* (Cambridge University Press, Cambridge, 1999), 18–20. The authors base the model on a competitive political environment, whereby parties compete on a fiscal platform that maximises the total expected vote. It is generally assumed that parties believe the provision of public services will increase the probability of voter support while an increase in tax will decrease the likelihood of voter support: at 18–19. The authors acknowledge the limitations of their model but contend that their research is a starting point for the exploration of these issues: at 39, conclusion. For criticisms of this model, see Rudolf Richter, 'Democratic Choice and Taxation: A Theoretical and Empirical Analysis (Book Review)', *Public Choice* (2000), 194; Andrew C. Gould and Peter J. Baker, 'Democracy and Taxation', *Annual Review of Political Science* 5 (2002), 87, 98; David Austen-Smith, 'Interest Groups, Campaign Contributions and Probabilistic Voting', *Public Choice* 54 (1991), 123.

62 Walter Hettich and Stanley L. Winer, *Democratic Choice and Taxation: A Theoretical and Empirical Analysis* (Cambridge University Press, Cambridge, 1999), 292.

63 Ibid., 42.

Each part is interdependent, so that decisions affecting one part will affect another. For example, while politicians might get the best electoral outcome in taxing each individual according to his or her own circumstances, administrative efficiency requires that taxpayers are grouped (e.g., according to tax bases and subject to different tax rates). However, this might in turn make it politically desirable to create special provisions for certain groups (depending on the groups' likely economic and political response to inclusion in that base).[64] For Hettich and Winer, tax changes must 'pass a political as well as an economic test, and reforms in one part of the system may lead to unexpected repercussions elsewhere',[65] so in the end complex tax structures are politically (as opposed to economically) efficient:[66]

> . . .tax complexity is a logical outcome of a political process in which politicians attempt to maximise expected votes in order to obtain power or to stay in power. When taxpayers are grouped into *rate bands* and taxable activities are combined into *bases* in response to *administration costs* and *self-selection behaviour*, the resulting tax structure remains complex. Although the theoretical discussion does not rule out equilibrium tax systems that are as simple as those suggested in some recent flat-tax proposals, it suggests such schemes, or any broadly-based tax without special provisions, are not compatible with *vigorous political competition* and do not represent lasting equilibrium outcomes of democratic societies.

The quote is equally applicable to explain the failure to realise the good VAT and why an explanation of the rise of the good VAT based on its perceived normative appeal is wholly insufficient to explain the existence of real VATs with their multiple rates, exemptions and imperfect administration. The real VATs more accurately reflect the complex political outcomes that Hettich and Winer predict.[67] The authors contend that their model 'presents a serious challenge for normative views that are not cognizant of how democracies actually work'.[68] However, Hettich and Winer's critique is applicable to normative views, which fail generally to understand how policy processes work, democratic or otherwise. While the authors themselves acknowledge that there is more to do to develop their model, for example in dealing more effectively with the problem of measuring the political

[64] Ibid., ch. 3. [65] Ibid., 59. [66] Ibid., 292 (emphasis added).

[67] Hettich and Winer thus help explain how the enactment of a real VAT rather than a good VAT might be perfectly efficient from a political economic perspective, such as when a real VAT is the result of a political equilibrium (a situation in which the choices of the relevant political players such as voters, politicians and bureaucrats are compatible and no group can improve its position by making a different choice). This equilibrium reflects the cumulative impact of each actor's self-interested choice within the constraints of collective decision-making in the relevant political system: ibid., 284; Douglas McTaggart, *Microeconomics* (6th ed., Pearson, Frenchs Forest, 2010), 353–54; Michael J. Trebilcock, 'The Choice of Governing Instrument: A Retrospective', in P. Eliadis, M. M. Hill and M. Howlett (eds.), *Designing Government* (McGill-Queens University Press, 2005), 51, 52.

[68] Walter Hettich and Stanley L. Winer, *Democratic Choice and Taxation: A Theoretical and Empirical Analysis* (Cambridge University Press, Cambridge, 1999), 93.

influence of different groups in society, the model suffices to show the deficiencies in the conventional approach's explanation for how real VATs come about.[69]

Even this relatively limited discussion shows that public choice proponents (regardless of their independent support for the VAT) would not simply attribute the VAT's rise to its merits, nor would they attribute the repeated failures to realise the good VAT to marginal or temporary aberrations of the policy process.

2.4 *Limitations of public choice*

As §2 noted, some criticisms of public choice relate more to specific applications of the approach, rather than the method itself. However, there exist a number of criticisms of the method itself that warrant attention. Some contend that public choice has difficulties explaining real-world outcomes because it needs to limit the factors influencing decisions in order to maintain a degree of theoretical rigour.[70] Others criticise public choice for being able to retrospectively explain (or rationalise) any policy outcome.[71] Alternatively, the simple fact that actors may not act in instrumentally rational ways challenges one of the key underlying assumptions of the approach.[72]

Of more interest to this book is the difficulty that public choice has in accounting for the way that history constrains individual choice.[73] Public choice approaches have been criticised for struggling to account for subtle changes in the institutional constraints within which decision-makers act that can have a profound impact on policy outcomes.[74] More fundamental, however, is the fact that the more one admits that the underlying preferences and beliefs that inform individual choice are influenced by external factors, and capable of being changed by the actions of others, the

69 Ibid., 291.

70 Ibid., 41; Donald P. Green and Ian Shapiro, *Pathologies of Rational Choice Theory: A Critique of Applications in Political Science* (Yale University Press, New Haven, CT, 1994), 6–7, ch. 1–5.

71 James M. Buchanan, *The Limits of Liberty: Between Anarchy and Leviathan* (University of Chicago Press, Chicago, 1975), 7.

72 Jon Elster, 'Rational Choice History: A Case of Excessive Ambition', *American Political Science Review* 94(3) (2000), 685, 692; Jon Elster, 'Some Unresolved Problems in the Theory of Rational Behavior', *Acta Sociologica* 36 (1993), 179.

73 For a critical review of an attempt to incorporate history into the public choice approach, see Jon Elster, 'Rational Choice History: A Case of Excessive Ambition', *American Political Science Review* 94(3) (2000), 685. See also Walter Hettich and Stanley L. Winer, *Democratic Choice and Taxation: A Theoretical and Empirical Analysis* (Cambridge University Press, Cambridge, 1999), 291.

74 Michael J. Trebilcock, 'The Choice of Governing Instrument:A Retrospective', in P. Eliadis, M. M. Hill and M. Howlett (eds.), *Designing Government* (McGill-Queens University Press, 2005), 51, 54, 69–70; Hettich and Winer acknowledge the need to better incorporate institutions into public choice models: Walter Hettich and Stanley L. Winer, *Democratic Choice and Taxation: A Theoretical and Empirical Analysis* (Cambridge University Press, Cambridge, 1999), 289.

more complicated it is for public choice to take this into account.[75] That people may make choices on the basis of being tricked (by false information) can be accounted for by public choice because an individual can make a rational choice, albeit on the basis of false information.[76] However, real difficulties arise when one opens up the possibility that the underlying preferences that inform choice are really shaped by background beliefs or values that themselves are shaped by external forces rather than inherent to the individual, such as historical change or influence by other actors with access to greater information. The more public choice admits these influences, the more complex the models become, and the more implausible the claim of the theory to model rational choices seems.[77]

While the difficulty of incorporating history into public choice models is a serious challenge, none of the criticisms operate to save the conventional approach's account of the VAT's rise. If anything, the limitations of public choice bring the inadequacies of the conventional approach into even more sharp relief, given that the conventional approach fails to address these issues at all. It is clear from the above discussion that, even despite its limitations, public choice offers a far more robust account of the policy process than the conventional approach provides. This is especially significant because it demonstrates that the method of policy analysis most likely to appeal to the conventional approach, based on the overlapping preference for market-based solutions that often inform both approaches, would itself reject the merits-based explanations for the VAT's rise put forward by the conventional approach.[78]

3 HISTORICAL INSTITUTIONALISM

Whereas public choice might struggle to account for history, historical institutionalism brings the historical constraints on policy choice to the fore.[79] As Pierson

[75] Bernard Grofman, 'Public Choice, Civic Republicanism, and American Politics: Perspectives of a Reasonable Choice Modeler', *Texas Law Review* 71 (1992–1993), 1541, 1579–80.

[76] Ibid., 1546.

[77] For some of the issues, see Claus Offe, 'Political Economy: Sociological Perspectives', in R. E. Goodin and H. D. Klingermann (eds.), *A New Handbook of Political Science* (Oxford University Press, Oxford, 1998), 675.

[78] See, e.g., Keen and Lockwood's preference for analysis of policy outcomes through a public choice approach: Michael Keen and Ben Lockwood, 'Is the VAT a Money Machine?', *National Tax Journal* 69(4) (2006), 905, 921.

[79] Historical institutionalism forms part of the 'new institutionalism', which seeks to explain policy outcomes through emphasising the importance of institutions in mediating the behaviour of actors and in shaping policy outcomes. Whereas the old institutionalism referred to a body of state-centric atheoretical explanations tinged with a normative concern for good governance, new institutionalism marked a departure from old state-based accounts of politics largely premised on a narrow conception of institutions as the formal, neutral and static structures of the state. New institutionalism sought to 'bring the state back in' to political science discourse after decades of research dominated by behaviouralist, rational choice, structural functional and group conflict approaches, all of which tended to subordinate the

explains, the approach is historical because 'it recognises that political development must be understood as a process that unfolds over time' and institutionalist because 'it stresses that many of the contemporary political implications of these temporal processes are embedded in institutions – whether formal rules, policy structures or norms'.[80]

In some respects, this might seem like nothing more than a restatement of the obvious and unremarkable aphorism that history matters.[81] It seems obvious, for example, that one factor that explains why Australian states no longer levy sales taxes and US states do is the different constitutional structures that determine the limits of state and federal taxing powers. However, the contribution of the approach lies in highlighting the way in which the accretions of history manifest in institutions over time and impact the perceptions and behaviour of actors in the policy process. Historical institutionalism explores the manner in which institutions mediate the socio-economic environment and shape the power, ideas and perceptions of participants in the policy process so as to influence policy outcomes.[82] In this way, an idea that might have compelling merit may never be acted upon because of the constraints imposed by past choices. Alternatively, an idea without merit might be picked up because of happenstance. Historical institutionalism stresses, however, that the very assessment of merit is shaped by historical and institutional constraints. As a very simple illustration of the point, while the

impact of institutions on policy outcomes to individual behaviour or broader structural trends. March and Olsen coined the label 'new institutionalism' with a number of publications culminating in a book: J. G. March and J. P. Olsen, 'The New Institutionalism: Organizational Factors in Political Life', *American Political Science Review* 78 (1984), 734; J. G. March and J. P. Olsen, *Rediscovering Institutions: The Organizational Basis of Politics* (Free Press, New York, 1988); B. Guy Peters, *Institutional Theory in Political Science: The New Institutionalism* (Pinter, Washington, DC, 1999), 15. There are at least three dominant approaches within new institutionalism – rational choice, sociological and historical institutionalism: Peter Hall and Rosemary C. Taylor, 'Political Science and the Three New Institutionalisms', *Political Studies* 44 (1996), 936, 938; Peter B. Evans et al., *Bringing the State Back In* (Cambridge University Press, Cambridge; New York, 1985); Peters claims there are at least six versions: at 17.

80 Paul Pierson, 'Increasing Returns, Path Dependence, and the Study of Politics', *American Political Science Review* 94(2) (2000), 251, 264–65. The historical institutionalist label was coined by Theda Skocpol but articulated comprehensively as an approach by Steinmo: Sven Steinmo, Kathleen Thelen and Frank Longstreth (eds.), *Structuring Politics: Historical Institutionalism in Comparative Analysis* (Cambridge University Press, Cambridge, 1992); B. Guy Peters, *Institutional Theory in Political Science: The New Institutionalism* (Pinter, Washington, DC, 1999), 71.

81 Paul Pierson, *Politics in Time: History, Institutions, and Social Analysis* (Princeton University Press, Princeton, NJ, 2004), 20; Robert E. Goodin and Hans-Dieter Klingemann, 'Political Science: The Discipline', in R. E. Goodin and H.-D. Klingemann (eds.), *A New Handbook of Political Science* (Oxford University Press, Oxford; New York, 1996), 3, 17.

82 Steinmo contends that 'domestic political institutions operate within – and must be understood in the context of – the broader social, economic, and political setting in which they are embedded': Sven Steinmo, *Taxation and Democracy: Swedish, British and American Approaches to Financing the Modern State* (Yale University Press, New Haven, CT, 1993), 12.

differing constitutional restrictions in the US and Australian states might explain the federal division of taxing power, they also influence (among other things) perceptions of the VAT's merits in these jurisdictions.[83]

This section explores historical institutionalism through a number of important themes within the approach, those of history (see §3.1), institutions (see §3.1.1), and the role of ideas, power and individual agency in enabling policy change (see §3.1.2 and §3.2). The limitations of the approach are canvassed under each theme. The section concludes by drawing out some key comparisons with public choice (see §3.3) and by considering the renewed interest in fiscal sociology, which shares a similar agenda and approach with historical institutionalism (see §3.4).

3.1 *The important legacy of history*

Time is critical in the historical institutionalist account of policy change. As Tilly contends, '*when* things happen in a sequence affects *how* they happen'.[84] Historical institutionalist scholars emphasise how policy outcomes are influenced by small and incremental changes over time. They borrow the concept of *path dependence* to explain how earlier decisions, even seemingly inconsequential ones, impact the perception of policy issues and the range of options available at a later stage. At its most banal, path dependence can simply mean 'that what happened at an earlier point in time will affect the outcomes of a sequence of events occurring at a later point in time'.[85] However, what are not banal are the insights that can be gained from attention to the mechanisms through which path dependence occurs.

The notions of *increasing returns* or *positive feedback mechanisms* suggest that 'the probability of further steps along the same path increases with each move down that path' because the cumulative costs of change (or the cost of exit) increase.[86] Notions of path dependence and increasing returns tend to emphasise continuity in policy outcomes, given that the 'path may be altered, but it requires a good deal of political pressure to produce that change'.[87]

[83] See Chapters 6 and 7 of this book.

[84] Quoted in Paul Pierson, 'Increasing Returns, Path Dependence, and the Study of Politics', *American Political Science Review* 94(2) (2000), 251, 264 (emphasis in original).

[85] William Sewell, 'Three Temporalities: Toward an Eventful Sociology', in T. J. McDonald (ed.), *The Historic Turn in the Human Sciences* (University of Michigan Press, Ann Arbor, 1996), 245, quoted in Paul Pierson, 'Increasing Returns, Path Dependence, and the Study of Politics', *American Political Science Review* 94(2) (2000), 251, 252.

[86] Paul Pierson, 'Increasing Returns, Path Dependence, and the Study of Politics', *American Political Science Review* 94(2) (2000), 251, 252. Pierson also contends that 'recognizing the possibility of path dependence necessarily draws social scientists to an investigation of history, if only to evaluate the validity of functionalist assertions': at 264. The terms 'increasing returns' and 'positive feedback mechanisms' are used interchangeably in this book.

[87] B. Guy Peters, *Institutional Theory in Political Science: The New Institutionalism* (2nd ed., Pinter, Washington, DC, 2005), 710.

An understanding of the way in which the accretions of history shape choices defies any account that treats the rise of a policy instrument as linear or inevitable. As Orloff contends:[88]

> we need to take a historical approach to understanding policy outcomes, for there is no standard development sequence of policy-making, but rather a variety of paths to qualitatively varying policy regimes. The temporal sequence in which determinative processes take place makes a difference for outcomes. Some causal factors, such as the political "feedback effects" of the policy legacy, can only be observed over time, and other factors, such as popular unrest…have irreversible effects on policy developments…Political choices are never fully determined, and choices made at one point in time influence later options.

A simple example of the way in which the past constrains the present is Lieberman's observation of path dependence in taxation that no 'factor is a better predictor of the functioning of a tax system for a given state, in a given year, than the operations of the previous year'.[89] However, the conventional approach often overlooks or cannot account for the impact of path dependence in their explanation of real VAT outcomes. The following quote from Messere et al. captures the difficulty:[90]

> Most public finance theorists for very valid reasons – neutrality, simplicity, greater protection against evasion – would prefer a single rate, but apart from New Zealand no OECD government *with a previous single rate sales tax* which exempted food and similar products has been able to overcome political resistance to such a change, though some have tried.

The observation could prompt a useful line of inquiry into how exclusions to pre-existing sales tax bases contribute to the base and rate structure of real VATs in a manner that reflects those prior exemptions. However, rather than investigating how the path-dependent effect of pre-existing taxes impact real VATs, the conventional approach leaves these lines of inquiry largely unexplored.

A more developed example of the influence of path dependence on tax policy is provided by the political scientist Junko Kato, who uses the concept to explore the relationship between regressive taxes and the size of the welfare state. She contends that states that were able to institute regressive taxes, such as the VAT, early

88 Ann Shola Orloff, *The Politics of Pensions: A Comparative Analysis of Britain, Canada, and the United States, 1880–1940* (University of Wisconsin Press, Madison, 1993), 26.

89 Evan S. Lieberman, 'Payment for Privilege? Race and Space in the Politics of Taxation in Brazil and South Africa' (PhD thesis, University of California, Berkeley, 2000), 24. This dissertation was later published as a monograph. All references will be to the monograph unless a direct quotation was not replicated from the thesis to the book, as is the case in this instance: Evan S. Lieberman, *Race and Regionalism in the Politics of Taxation in Brazil and South Africa* (Cambridge University Press, Cambridge, 2003).

90 Ken Messere, Flip de Kam and Christopher Heady, *Tax Policy: Theory and Practice in OECD Countries* (Oxford University Press, Oxford, 2003), 22 (emphasis added).

(defined as post–World War II but prior to the economic instability of the 1970s) were able to fund larger welfare states. Lindert reaches a similar conclusion through the lens of economic history and finds that European welfare states have achieved impressive postwar growth through relying on a larger share of regressive but pro-growth taxes (such as the VAT) to fund universalist welfare states. He concludes that the funding of the welfare state has therefore not been at the expense of economic growth.[91]

Although not specifically directed to explaining the VAT's rise, Kato's thesis is still relevant to the question of what contributed to the rise of, and resistance to, the VAT. Her argument rests on *path dependence*, whereby the *early* implementation of strong revenue raising and largely invisible regressive taxes like the VAT in the postwar boom meant that states had greater capacity to fund a universalist welfare state. This in turn led to greater public support for higher levels of taxation and a larger welfare state because the public could readily perceive the benefits provided by the state.[92] Kato contends that the public support for VAT reform stemmed in part from ignorance of both the revenue-raising potential of the VAT and in part from the postwar boom-inspired ignorance of the prospect of large budget deficits – the latter becoming apparent only after the economic instability of the 1970s.[93] However, by the time of the 1970s instability, these publics were tolerant to high taxation levels.[94] She primarily cites Scandinavian states, with the exception of Denmark, in support of the proposition.[95]

By contrast, Kato contends that countries with heavy reliance on direct taxes, such as the income tax, had weaker revenue-raising capacities that led to weaker or smaller more targeted welfare states. With the public less able to perceive the benefits of high taxes and the welfare state, they were in turn less likely to support later attempts to increase revenue-raising capacity. Therefore, countries that later sought to address budget deficits through the introduction of a VAT faced greater public resistance because of greater antipathy toward the targeted welfare state and an associated suspicion that taxes would simply be directed at reducing government debt rather than providing services. She points to a key source of resistance to regressive taxes arising from mistrust in government promises that regressivity would be addressed and attributes this mistrust to the absence of public memory of high spending and its associated benefits.[96] This observation might explain why policy-makers opt for carveouts to the VAT base (to both alleviate public fears of a

[91] Peter H. Lindert, *Growing Public: Social Spending and Economic Growth since the Eighteenth Century* (Cambridge UK; New York, Cambridge University Press, 2004), 235–45.

[92] Junko Kato, *Regressive Taxation and the Welfare State: Path Dependence and Policy Diffusion* (Cambridge University Press, Cambridge, 2003), 196.

[93] Ibid., 206. [94] Ibid.

[95] Denmark maintained strong reliance on income taxation despite being one of the earliest countries to introduce a VAT, and Denmark has experienced severe tax revolts despite maintaining a relatively generous welfare state: ibid., 30.

[96] Ibid., 214.

revenue grab and allay concerns of regressivity) rather than through addressing regressivity through spending or other taxes. In other words, perceptions of the merits of the VAT are path dependent:[97]

> In a low-tax and -welfare country the politicians are deprived of an effective revenue-raising means and face hostile opposition toward a tax increase from the public without a prospect for compensation *assured by the past.*

Kato cites the US, Australia, Japan and Canada in support of this argument, but acknowledges New Zealand as an 'outlier' based on that country's historically heavy reliance on direct taxes and status as a relatively low-tax and targeted welfare state but a country in which there was relatively strong support for the late introduction of a VAT.[98]

Through analysing quantitative data from 18 advanced industrialised democracies from 1960 to 1996[99] and nine case studies,[100] Kato rejects the conventional characterisation of the VAT as a 'purely economic phenomenon independent of the influence of domestic politics in each country'.[101] She casts doubt on the argument that the rise of the VAT can be attributed solely to its technical superiority or simply to the impact of European integration.[102] Although timing or path dependence is critical in Kato's account, she also identifies a number of other factors that have shaped the VAT's rise, such as economic globalisation; partisanship; the intention of policy-makers; and social class.[103] Kato cites regressivity as 'the most legitimate reason for opposition to tax reform', so that the government's ability to persuade the public that welfare spending would alleviate regressivity was crucial to overcoming resistance in later VAT reforms.[104]

Kato makes an important contribution by highlighting the direct link between revenue capacity and the nature of the welfare state, and by challenging the idea that regressive taxes are anathema to a well-functioning welfare state. Her focus on path dependence emphasises the importance of a nation's previous tax history to the policy choices and reform options available to policy-makers. Although Kato's account further reveals the severe limitations of the conventional approach's merits-based explanation for the VAT's rise, §4 details how Kato's deferral to the conventional approach in assessing key technical issues relating to the VAT undermines her own explanatory account. However, that criticism notwithstanding, Kato's account is but one instance of how perceptions of merits are influenced by local history and previous policy choices across a range of areas relating to both

97 Ibid., 214 (emphasis added). 98 Ibid., 196. See also §4.1 of this chapter.

99 Sweden, Denmark, Finland, Belgium, France, Austria, Italy, Netherlands, Norway, Germany, United Kingdom, Canada, New Zealand, Switzerland, Ireland, Australia, United States, Japan: ibid., 12.

100 The case studies are taken from eight industrialised economies: Sweden, France, United Kingdom, US, Canada, Australia, New Zealand, Japan and the newly industrialised economy of South Korea: ibid., vii–viii.

101 Ibid., 41. 102 Ibid. 103 Ibid., 195, 215. 104 Ibid., 213–14.

taxation and spending, so that merits that might seem obvious in one locality may be entirely absent in another.

3.1.1 Constraints on history – Institutions

Historical institutionalism focuses on the mediating role of institutions, whereby institutions shape the behaviour, relative power and interests of actors and are the means by which the past imposes on the present.[105] At their most simple, institutions are just the names given to salient accretions of history that constrain choices into the future.[106] However, historical institutionalists are keen to stress that, although institutions mediate broader social, economic and political structures and impact agents' preferences, choices and actions, they alone are not solely determinative.[107] As Steinmo contends, institutions 'are not everything in politics'.[108] Nevertheless, definitions over what counts as an institution are contested. It is, however, important to preface this brief discussion of definitional disputes with the observation that, irrespective of the differing views as to what counts as an institution, there is a shared appreciation that institutions mediate broader socio-economic structures and shape agent action. Institutions are in turn shaped by these agents and structures. Under this approach, the good is not self-actualising, nor are institutions wholly determinative. An approach that incorporates even a narrow conception of institutions will improve upon the deterministic explanations for the VAT's rise under the conventional approach.

[105] Ira Katznelson and Helen V. Milner, 'American Political Science: The Discipline's State and the State of the Discipline', in I. Katznelson and H. V. Milner (eds.), *Political Science: State of the Discipline* (Norton; American Political Science Association, New York, Washington, DC, 2002), 1, 17.

[106] Hugh Heclo, *Modern Social Politics in Britain and Sweden: From Relief to Income Maintenance* (Yale University Press, New Haven, CT, 1974), 63; Evan S. Lieberman, *Race and Regionalism in the Politics of Taxation in Brazil and South Africa* (Cambridge University Press, Cambridge, 2003), 274–75.

[107] Sven Steinmo, *Taxation and Democracy: Swedish, British and American Approaches to Financing the Modern State* (Yale University Press, New Haven, CT, 1993), 12. Eccleston explains that 'institutions don't explain everything. While they are important mid-level variables which structure the policy environment and both enable and constrain certain types of political actions, they are just one aspect of the political world': Richard Eccleston, *Taxing Reforms* (Edward Elgar, Cheltenham, 2007), 6. Hall and Taylor contend that 'although they draw attention to the role of institutions in political life, historical institutionalists rarely insist that institutions are the only causal force in politics': Peter Hall and Rosemary C. Taylor, 'Political Science and the Three New Institutionalisms', *Political Studies* 54 (1996), 936, 942; Thelen and Steinmo state that 'institutions constrain and refract politics but they are never the sole "cause" of outcomes': Kathleen Thelen and Sven Steinmo, 'Historical Institutionalism in Comparative Politics', in S. Steinmo, K. Thelen and F. Longstreth (eds.), *Structuring Politics: Historical Institutionalism in Comparative Analysis* (Cambridge University Press, Cambridge, 1992), 1, 3.

[108] Sven Steinmo, *Taxation and Democracy: Swedish, British and American Approaches to Financing the Modern State* (Yale University Press, New Haven, CT, 1993), 12.

At their narrowest, institutions are the formal structures that provide the rules of the game in a given society, such as constitutional rules, laws and the formal apparatus of the state such as courts, parliaments and the executive.[109] A narrow conception of institutions enables formal institutions, such as constitutions, to be distinguished from informal influences such as culture.[110] However, a definition of institutions that is too narrow runs the risk of missing or ignoring important informal rules or influences that might structure political behaviour in an institutional sense. For example, Lieberman criticises narrow conceptions of the relevant institutions of the 'tax state' for failing:[111]

> to capture the various ways in which the political environment can be affected by socially constructed factors, such as the mobilization of group identities, or rhetorical appeals to normative concerns. In emphasizing the centrality of the state…[such approaches do] not adequately address the influence of the varied political configurations of society.

At their broadest, definitions of institutions can include informal rules that shape behaviour consisting of routines, habits, customs or even social norms and culture.[112] Kay contends that broad definitions mean that it can make good sense to have public policies counted as institutions, as 'past policy decisions are institutions in terms of current policy decisions: they can act as structures that can limit or shape current policy options'.[113] However, broad definitions of institutions are criticised for running the risk of dilution, so that every possible explanatory factor is included in the definition of institution to such an extent that institutional accounts explain nothing.[114] A broad definition of institutions can have difficult

109 Levi adopts a narrow definition of institutions as the 'formal arrangements for aggregating individuals and regulating their behaviour through the use of explicit rules and decision processes enforced by an actor or set of actors formally recognized as possessing such power': Margaret Levi, 'A Logic of Institutional Change', in M. Levi and K. S. Cook (eds.), *The Limits of Rationality* (University of Chicago Press, Chicago, 1990), 405.

110 Bo Rothstein, 'Political Institutions: An Overview', in R. E. Goodin and H.-D. Klingemann (eds.), *A New Handbook of Political Science* (Oxford University Press Oxford; New York, 1996), 133, 145.

111 Evan S. Lieberman, *Race and Regionalism in the Politics of Taxation in Brazil and South Africa* (Cambridge University Press, Cambridge, 2003), 24–25. For Lieberman's distinctive conception of the tax state, see below, nn 156 and 157 and the text thereto.

112 Bo Rothstein, 'Political Institutions: An Overview', in R. E. Goodin and H.-D. Klingemann (eds.), *A New Handbook of Political Science* (Oxford University Press Oxford; New York, 1996), 133, 145–46.

113 Adrian Kay, *The Dynamics of Public Policy: Theory and Evidence* (Edward Elgar, Cheltenham UK, 2006), 30.

114 Bo Rothstein, 'Political Institutions: An Overview', in R. E. Goodin and H.-D. Klingemann (eds.), *A New Handbook of Political Science* (Oxford University Press Oxford; New York, 1996), 133, 145–46; Kathleen Thelen and Sven Steinmo, 'Historical Institutionalism in Comparative Politics', in S. Steinmo, K. Thelen and F. Longstreth (eds.), *Structuring Politics: Historical Institutionalism in Comparative Analysis* (Cambridge University Press, Cambridge, 1992), 1, 15. Steinmo criticises the breadth of these types of definitions as being 'so vague that

methodological implications, occasioned by the fact that institutions are both the object, and means, of explanation.[115]

Hall provides one much-used definition of institutions as the 'formal rules, compliance procedures, and standard operating practices that structure the relationship between individuals in various units of the polity and economy'.[116] This definition is open to a charge of circularity: what counts as 'formal' or 'standard', for example, might itself be an institutional matter. The characterisation of institutions as 'salient accretions of history that constrain choices' is likewise subject to this criticism, for 'salience' may also be partly institutionally determined. However, this charge of circularity is not fatal when regard is had to the purpose of such definitions. They are not intended to be formally adequate, but rather to describe data that, upon inspection, reveal the salience of certain patterns. For example, in the language used by Hall, determining what factors will be sufficiently 'formal' or 'standard' to satisfy the observer that the observed factors structure the relationships between individuals in the polity – and therefore are genuinely institutional in nature – will require recourse to the data itself. What is clear, however, is that under both a narrow and broad definition, institutions are enduring (but not unchanging) accretions of history that cannot simply be changed at the whim of an agent. Two leading historical institutionalist analyses of tax policy show that

they leave nothing out': Sven Steinmo, *Taxation and Democracy: Swedish, British and American Approaches to Financing the Modern State* (Yale University Press, New Haven, CT, 1993), 12.

115 Richard Eccleston, *Taxing Reforms* (Edward Elgar, Cheltenham, 2007), 23; Peter Mair, 'Comparative Politics: An Overview', in R. E. Goodin and H.-D. Klingemann (eds.), *A New Handbook of Political Science* (Oxford University Press, Oxford; New York, 1998), 309, 321–22.

116 Peter Hall, *Governing the Economy* (Oxford University Press, New York, 1986), 19. See also Bo Rothstein, 'Political Institutions: An Overview', in R. E. Goodin and H.-D. Klingemann (eds.), *A New Handbook of Political Science* (Oxford University Press, Oxford; New York, 1996), 133, 152. Thelen and Steinmo point to the similarity between Hall's definition and that of the rational choice institutionalist scholar Douglas North, who defines institutions to include 'any form of constraint that human beings derive to shape human interaction', which includes both the formal constraints of rules and the informal constraints of conventions and codes of behaviour: Douglas C. North, *Institutions, Institutional Change, and Economic Performance* (Cambridge University Press, Cambridge, 1990), 4, quoted in Kathleen Thelen and Sven Steinmo, 'Historical Institutionalism in Comparative Politics', in S. Steinmo, K. Thelen and F. Longstreth (eds.), *Structuring Politics: Historical Institutionalism in Comparative Analysis* (Cambridge University Press, Cambridge, 1992), 1, 28. See also Hall and Taylor, who define institutions as 'the formal or informal procedures, routines, norms and conventions embedded in the organizational structure of the polity or political economy': Peter Hall and Rosemary C. Taylor, 'Political Science and the Three New Institutionalisms', *Political Studies* 44 (1996), 936, 938. Eccleston defines institutions as 'the embedded practices, formal state structures and institutionalized patterns of state-society relations which shape the preferences and power of political actors and the processes they tend to follow': Richard Eccleston, *Taxing Reforms* (Edward Elgar, Cheltenham, 2007), 6. See also B. Guy Peters, Jon Pierre and Desmond S. King, 'The Politics of Path Dependency: Political Conflict in Historical Institutionalism', *Journal of Politics* 67(4) (2005), 1275, 1286.

under either a broad or narrow definition of institutions, progress can be made on the merits-based accounts of the conventional approach.

In his celebrated account of tax policy in Britain, Sweden and the US in the twentieth century, Steinmo adopts a narrow definition of institutions as 'the political institutions that write tax law',[117] which more specifically are the formal structures of government – such as the parliament, president, electoral system and the bureaucracy.[118] The limited definition corresponds with the belief that 'institutions are not everything in politics' but instead must be understood as operating in the 'context of – the broader social, economic, and political setting in which they are embedded'.[119]

Through employing a comparative historical analysis, Steinmo identifies two trends of common paths and divergent patterns. The common paths result from the fact that similar structural conditions and challenges in the international economy and polity produced similar pressures on industrialised governments, which responded in broadly similar ways in tax policy. For example, the pressures of financing war efforts in the first and second world wars led to the introduction and expansion of income taxes in most industrialised democracies.[120] However, Steinmo contends that important differences in the institutional configurations of each state account for the different *patterns* in the paths taken by each country, and that these institutional factors have a far stronger impact than do other factors commonly cited for producing divergence, such as differences in the power of political interests or varying cultural preferences for different values in taxation.[121] Steinmo claims that while crises offer an opportunity for reform, the choice of reform options is limited by the institutional configuration of the state.

Steinmo also indirectly attributes the rise of the VAT to a general preference among 'political elites'[122] to increase tax rates and the tax base during times of crisis and attempt to 'hide tax hikes via indirect, or hidden, taxes'.[123] He claims that this preference is partly in response to a desire not to impede economic growth in a capitalist economy and partly a response to a public that is loathsome of taxes but simultaneously demanding of fairer taxes and greater spending.[124] Steinmo contends that citizen resistance to taxation arises more from the type of tax instrument used than the overall tax burden.[125]

Steinmo's analysis enables us to see how the narrowly defined political institutions of the state constrain the path-dependent patterns of taxation through producing positive feedback mechanisms that shape the negotiation of tax policy

[117] Sven Steinmo, *Taxation and Democracy: Swedish, British and American Approaches to Financing the Modern State* (Yale University Press, New Haven, CT, 1993), 12.

[118] For a similar approach see Martin Daunton, *Just Taxes: The Politics of Taxation in Britain, 1914–1979* (Cambridge University Press, Cambridge, 2002), 18–28.

[119] Sven Steinmo, *Taxation and Democracy: Swedish, British and American Approaches to Financing the Modern State* (Yale University Press, New Haven, 1993), 12.

[120] Ibid., ch. 2. [121] Ibid., 4–7. [122] Ibid., 195. [123] Ibid. [124] Ibid., 19–21, 195.

[125] Ibid., 195.

outcomes. He claims that strong majoritarian governments in Britain led to a dramatic seesawing of politically acceptable policies occasioned by changes in government. In Sweden, the institutionalisation of a neo-corporatist style of extra-parliamentary decision-making between government and strong economic interests such as corporations and trade unions led to a compromised position of a more regressive revenue system funding a much larger welfare state.[126] He cites the disparate nature of political decision-making in the US, with its strict division between legislative and executive power and a strong legislative committee system as contributing to fragmented tax changes often in favour of constituent interests. He identifies this as a reason why the US has no VAT:[127]

> These proposals [for consumption tax reform] were defeated because the fragmentation of the American decision-making structure provides numerous veto-points for those who oppose new legislation to defeat it – even when a popular president offers the proposal.

Steinmo prefers this account to one that suggests that the US public is more resistant to major consumption tax reform than those of Britain or Sweden.[128]

In an erudite analysis of the impact of institutions on tax reform outcomes in Brazil and South Africa, Lieberman avoids committing to a universal definition of institutions but rather chooses to focus on one particular institution that he labels the 'national political community', which he defines as a set of rules officially entitling a group of people 'to the rights and responsibilities of citizenship'.[129] Lieberman implicitly adopts a broad definition of institutions when he includes in the definition of national political community the rules in constitutions, codified in laws, policy and practice *and* reinforced by important documents and symbols – including the media, census and maps.[130] Lieberman emphasises the importance of institutions (specifically the institution of the national political community) in mediating the impact of economic structure and the international environment on producing or constraining transformation in taxation:[131]

> While changes in the mode of production; variations in the timing of development; and international ideas, conflicts, and structures all affect taxation outcomes, historically-rooted institutions, which give political salience to certain group identities and not others, mediate those pressures into specific sets of class configurations and coalitions that lead to distinctive types of tax states.

In a comparison of the relative development of the South African and Brazilian tax states, Lieberman concludes that the relative cohesion of economic elites along racial lines in South Africa provided a 'political glue' among the predominantly

[126] Ibid., 202–7. [127] Ibid., 197. [128] Ibid., 5.

[129] Evan S. Lieberman, *Race and Regionalism in the Politics of Taxation in Brazil and South Africa* (Cambridge University Press, Cambridge, 2003), 3.

[130] Ibid., 14. [131] Ibid., 9–10.

white upper classes to overcome the usual collective action problems that lie in collecting tax from this powerful group.[132] By contrast, the political fragmentation of Brazilian elites along regional (as opposed to racial) lines exacerbated the collective action and coordination problems associated with taxation, leading to a much weaker tax state.[133] Lieberman provides an explanation of the way in which history constrains and enables outcomes through highlighting the mediating impact of just one institution on tax policy. Lieberman is able to highlight the manner in which historical actions in one area (e.g., race and citizenship) shape other choices (e.g., tax policy), leading sometimes to unintended consequences. For example, Lieberman contends that, as a result of these divergent paths, South Africa now has a far stronger tax system to redistribute resources to poorer blacks than Brazil, thus suggesting that 'the forces of domestic politics can be more influential than the logic of global capitalism' in shaping tax systems.[134] These historically produced, institutionally mediated and unintended consequences cannot be accounted for in the simplistic merits-based explanations of the conventional approach.

This is not a book on social science methodology, but rather a book that seeks to better explain the rise of the VAT through applying some insights from public policy. The above discussion shows that it is not necessary to engage in the definitional disputes over what counts as an institution in order to improve understandings of the VAT's rise because most definitions of institutions can provide a useful account of the manner in which history constrains policy outcomes. While different authors have found different accretions of history salient, the common theme across all accounts is the way that history influences reform.

3.1.2 Constrainers or enablers of change – The role of ideas

As Hall and Taylor highlight, 'historical institutionalists have been especially attentive to the relationship between institutions and ideas or beliefs'.[135] A renewed interest in the role of ideas emerged, in part, as a response to the application of public choice in a manner that narrowly focused on the self-interest of individuals in policy-making. Whereas these public choice accounts tended to reduce ideas to the 'individual utility calculi' of the rational actor,[136] historical

[132] Ibid., 4. For more on this argument, including Lieberman's notion of the tax state, see below, nn 156 and 157 and the text thereto.
[133] Ibid.
[134] Evan S. Lieberman, 'Payment for Privilege? Race and Space in the Politics of Taxation in Brazil and South Africa' (PhD thesis, University of California, Berkeley, 2000), 363.
[135] Peter Hall and Rosemary Taylor, 'Political Science and the Three New Institutionalisms', *Political Studies* 44 (1996), 936, 942.
[136] Mark M. Blyth, '"Any More Bright Ideas?" The Ideational Turn of Comparative Political Economy', *Comparative Politics* 29(2) (1997), 229, 230. See also Judith Goldstein and Robert O. Keohane, *Ideas and Foreign Policy: Beliefs, Institutions, and Political Change* (Cornell

institutionalists responded by focusing instead on how institutions privilege some ideas over others at certain times.[137]

Steinmo, for example, attributes a shift in preferences for consumption taxes to a broader shift in ideas toward the latter stages of the twentieth century. According to Steinmo, the economic upheaval in the 1970s and widespread dissatisfaction with the tax system called into question the previous logic that taxes could be used as a means by which to actively affect social and political outcomes. The apparent answers provided by neo-liberal economics, the associated resurgence of free-market ideals and consequent abandoning of support for notions such as ability to pay, led to a preference for consumption taxes by policy-makers who favoured the VAT for its perceived neutrality and capacity to generate economic growth.[138]

Although a comprehensive account of the manner in which ideas impact policy outcomes under historical institutionalism has yet to be sufficiently articulated,[139] an analysis that separately focuses on the role of ideas in taxation is useful for challenging many uncontested notions in the conventional approach. For example, Lieberman contends that:[140]

> Typically equity issues are evaluated from one of two angles – either from the perspective of 'vertical', or 'horizontal' equity. Again, within the economics literature, and in policy studies more generally, such concepts are often treated as

University Press, Ithaca, 1993); Peter Hall and Rosemary C. Taylor, 'Political Science and the Three New Institutionalisms', *Political Studies* 44 (1996), 936, 939; Bo Rothstein, 'Political Institutions: An Overview', in R. E. Goodin and H.-D. Klingemann (eds.), *A New Handbook of Political Science* (Oxford University Press, Oxford; New York, 1996), 133, 147.

137 Margaret Weir, 'Ideas and Politics: The Acceptance of Keynesiansim in Britain and the United States', in P. Hall (ed.), *The Political Power of Economic Ideas* (Princeton University Press, Princeton, NJ, 1989), 53. For criticisms of the treatment of ideas in historical institutionalism, see Blyth, who contends that ideas 'become desiderata, catch-all concepts to explain variance' where no 'progressive attempt is made to analyse ideas themselves', and question '"what are ideas" and "what do they do."' Mark M. Blyth, '"Any More Bright Ideas?" The Ideational Turn of Comparative Political Economy', *Comparative Politics* 29(2) (1997), 229, 231.

138 Sven Steinmo, 'The Evolution of Policy Ideas: Tax Policy in the 20th Century', *British Journal of Politics and International Relations* 5(2) (2003), 206, 219, 225, 229.

139 Perhaps the most comprehensive account so far is provided by Hall: Peter A. Hall (ed.), *The Political Power of Economic Ideas: Keynesianism across Nations* (Princeton University Press, Princeton, NJ, 1989). For an earlier treatment of the issue, see Anthony King, 'Ideas, Institutions and the Policies of Governments: A Comparative Analysis: Parts I and II', *British Journal of Political Science* 3(3) (1973), 291; Anthony King, 'Ideas, Institutions and the Policies of Governments: A Comparative Analysis: Part III', *British Journal of Political Science* 3(4) (1973), 409. *Contra* Mark M. Blyth, '"Any More Bright Ideas?" The Ideational Turn of Comparative Political Economy', *Comparative Politics* 29(2) (1997), 229. For Blyth's own effort, see Mark M. Blyth, *Great Transformations: Economic Ideas and Institutional Change in the Twentieth Century* (Cambridge University Press, Cambridge, 2002).

140 Evan S. Lieberman, 'Taxation Data as Indicators of State-Society Relations: Possibilities and Pitfalls in Cross-National Research', *Studies in Comparative International Development* 36(4) (2002), 89, 94.

unproblematic, while in practice, definitions are highly contested among analysts as well as stakeholders within tax systems.

This point is especially relevant to an understanding of the VAT's rise. Chapter 4 identified the significance of epistemic communities in tax policy and suggested that it might be possible to see the conventional approach as constituting an epistemic community. The basis for such a community lies in the shared organisational affiliations of the authors whose work constitutes the approach (see Chapter 1, §1), as well as these authors' concentrated technical expertise in VAT and shared normative appreciation of the merits of the good VAT. Chapter 4, §5.2 also highlighted how business groups and their representatives have a shared appreciation of the good VAT's merits that they also perceive to be in their self-interest. As Lieberman contends:[141]

> Because political discourse around the allocation of the tax burden is so often couched in terms of fairness and justice, as opposed to naked self-interest, the repertoire of political idioms available for such political discussion is critical to how outcomes emerge. To be effective, political claims must be received with a shared understanding of which groups are politically salient and how resources *ought* to be distributed.

It is more likely to be an effective strategy to advocate for tax reform on the basis of economic efficiency or growth, for example, than to do so by simply declaring dissatisfaction with your own tax burden.

However, when framing ideas in the pursuit of, or opposition to, tax reform, whether motivated by the pursuit of naked self-interest or the greater good, actors must be mindful of the institutional context that might make some ideas salient to other actors while other ideas jar. The merits of VAT that seem so self-evident within the epistemic community that might be constituted by the conventional approach are contested when attempts are made to introduce VATs at the domestic level (see Chapter 3 of this book). Given the fierce contests over what the introduction of the VAT means in national political debates, examining the role of ideas can therefore provide a useful lens by which to examine the rise of real VATs.

3.2 *Institutions and the dynamics of agency, ideas, power and change*

Historical institutionalists have typically viewed institutions as 'constraining rather than enabling political action'.[142] Notions of path dependence are useful to explain

[141] Evan S. Lieberman, 'Payment for Privilege? Race and Space in the Politics of Taxation in Brazil and South Africa' (PhD thesis, University of California, Berkeley, 2000), 17 (emphasis in original).

[142] Richard Eccleston, *The Thirty Year Problem: The Politics of Australian Tax Reform* (ATRF, Sydney, 2004), 175; Mark M. Blyth, '"Any More Bright Ideas?" The Ideational Turn of Comparative Political Economy', *Comparative Politics* 29(2) (1997), 229, 230.

policy inertia; that is, how policy change is incremental rather than sudden. But notions of path dependence and incrementalism are less suited to accounting for significant and rapid change or *path-breaking* reforms such as, perhaps, the introduction of VAT. For this reason, historical institutionalism has been criticised for being able to account for policy continuity but not change.[143]

In many historical institutionalist accounts, rapid or major policy change is explained through concepts such as *critical junctures*, defined as 'a period of significant change, which occurs in distinct ways in different countries' and which 'produce distinct legacies'.[144] Critical junctures are often attributed to exogenous change; that is, those changes produced by broader shifts in the structural context within which institutions operate,[145] such as war or economic depression. The critical junctures create the conditions necessary for new ideas to take hold and for actors to undertake significant change.[146] The choices made during these periods in turn have a lasting impact because these 'choices close off alternative options and lead to the establishment of institutions that generate self-reinforcing path-dependent processes'.[147] In other words, 'critical junctures constitute the starting points for many path dependent processes'.[148] Exogenous change might

143 Rothstein describes this as 'the weakest and most difficult point in political institutionalist analysis': Bo Rothstein, 'Political Institutions: An Overview', in R. E. Goodin and H.-D. Klingemann (eds.), *A New Handbook of Political Science* (Oxford University Press Oxford; New York, 1996), 133, 153, and at 154; Peters claims that 'the approach appears much better suited to explain the persistence of patterns than to explain how those patterns might change': B. G. Peters, *Institutional Theory in Political Science: The 'New Institutionalism'* (Continuum, London, 2005), 76–77; Sven Steinmo, *Taxation and Democracy: Swedish, British and American Approaches to Financing the Modern State* (Yale University Press, New Haven, CT, 1993) 12; Richard Eccleston, *Taxing Reforms* (Edward Elgar, Cheltenham, 2007), 180; Kathleen Thelen and Sven Steinmo, 'Historical Institutionalism in Comparative Politics', in S. Steinmo, K. Thelen and F. Longstreth (eds.), *Structuring Politics: Historical Institutionalism in Comparative Analysis* (Cambridge University Press, Cambridge, 1992), 1, 16; B. Guy Peters, Jon Pierre and Desmond S. King, 'The Politics of Path Dependency: Political Conflict in Historical Institutionalism', *Journal of Politics* 67(4) (2005), 1275, 1276–77, 1286–88.

144 Ruth Berins Collier and David Collier, *Shaping the Political Arena* (Princeton University Press, Princeton, 1991), 29. See also Giovanni Capoccia and R. Daniel Kelemen, 'The Study of Critical Junctures: Theory, Narrative, and Counterfactuals in Historical Institutionalism', *World Politics* 59 (2007), 341, 347.

145 Richard Eccleston, *Taxing Reforms* (Edward Elgar, Cheltenham, 2007), 19.

146 Ibid.; Andrew C. Gould and Peter J. Baker, 'Democracy and Taxation', *Annual Review of Political Science* 5 (2002), 87, 89. Punctuated equilibria is a term that is alternatively used to describe these moments. This entails the notion that generally institutions endure in an equilibrium state, but there may be multiple equilibria that achieve stability, and the choice of alternative equilibria is often triggered by exogenous change – leading to punctuated equilibria: B. G. Peters, *Institutional Theory in Political Science: The 'New Institutionalism'* (Continuum, London, 2005), 68, 77, quoting Stephen D. Krasner, 'Approaches to the State: Alternative Conceptions and Historical Dynamics', *Comparative Politics* 16(2) (1984), 223. This book prefers the term 'critical junctures'.

147 Giovanni Capoccia and R. Daniel Kelemen, 'The Study of Critical Junctures: Theory, Narrative, and Counterfactuals in Historical Institutionalism' (2007), *World Politics* 59, 341.

148 Ibid., 342.

be contrasted to *endogenous change*, which is generally conceived of as the incremental changes brought about via a process internal to institutional regimes, such as positive feedback mechanisms.[149]

On an historical institutionalist account, major change in tax policy will be hampered by the coercive nature of taxation and by the distributional consequences of change, because powerful groups and privileged interests that might benefit from the status quo can mobilise to oppose unfavourable change. Their lobbying can create a *positive feedback mechanism* to reinforce the maintenance of this status quo. This exacerbates the collective action problems identified in public choice accounts, whereupon a minority have greater incentive and resources to mobilise to oppose change that may be favourable to a majority.[150] As a result, policy inertia is seen to be a particular feature of taxation, because the political costs of change are perceived to be high, given the likely unpopularity of any reforms to increase taxation.[151] The result is that incremental change is more likely than major change or, alternatively, that for major change to be realised, timing is everything. For that reason, many have held the view that, consistent with the historical institutionalist approach, major tax reform has often required some form of crisis (or at least the appearance of a crisis) to precipitate it, such as war or economic depression.[152]

Notions such as critical junctures assist but do not necessarily remedy the problems of explaining major change under historical institutionalism.[153] Peters, for example, criticises these explanations as bordering on tautologous because 'when a major institutional. . .change does occur. . .after the fact it can be argued that there was a sufficient force available to produce a movement away from the equilibrium and inertia affecting an institution'.[154] Alternatively, others have argued that a renewed emphasis on *incremental change*, *agency* and *group conflict* can provide a more complete account of policy change. Each area for improvement likewise reflects on areas that would improve upon the accounts of the conventional approach, and each is briefly discussed here and then taken up further in §4 of this chapter and the remainder of the book.

As §4 further explains, a focus on *incremental change* might not just help explain how broader patterns of change in public policy occur, but a focus on the detail of

149 Richard Eccleston, *Taxing Reforms* (Edward Elgar, Cheltenham, 2007), 19.

150 Ibid., 3–4.

151 Neil Brooks, *The Canadian Goods and Services Tax: History, Policy, and Politics* (ATRF, Sydney, 1992), 163.

152 See, e.g., Fred Block, 'The Ruling Class Does Not Rule', in Fred Block, *Revising State Theory: Essays in Politics and Postindustrialism* (Temple University Press, Philadelphia, 1987), 51, 65–68. See also the discussion in Chapters 6 and 7 of this book.

153 See, e.g., B. Guy Peters, *Institutional Theory in Political Science: The 'New Institutionalism'* (Continuum, London, 2005), 76–80; Richard Eccleston, *Taxing Reforms* (Edward Elgar, Cheltenham, 2007), 23.

154 B. Guy Peters, *Institutional Theory in Political Science: The 'New Institutionalism'* (Continuum, London, 2005), 78.

VAT design and implementation will also enable insights into how real VATs arise, if they do at all, and why they endure.

Peters et al. contend that a broader focus on *agents* would better account for the dynamics of policy change. They criticise historical institutionalism for being too focused on bureaucrats and overlooking, for example, the creative role of other political actors to help account for change.[155] This book responds to the call for a broad focus on agents in the context of VAT reform, to include those who, as Chapter 4, §5.2 explained, have acknowledged their own role in VAT promotion, such as business and its representatives (see §4 of this chapter). The role of business is especially important in light of its economic power and in light of the fact that business is responsible for VAT collection, which means that business support in VAT reform is particularly crucial. The advantage of extending the focus to a broader range of actors is demonstrated by Lieberman's analysis of the comparative development of the tax states in South Africa and Brazil. Lieberman's model of the 'tax state' focuses on 'upper group' actors (capitalists [investors and company heads], professionals and other high-income groups) as well as the usual inclusion of the executive government and bureaucracy.[156] He bases this inclusion on the contention that:[157]

> Upper groups – comprised of high-income individuals, firms, and organizations – are critical to the development of the tax state because they control the lion's share of taxable resources, particularly in highly unequal societies such as Brazil and South Africa. [Indeed, the financial solvency of the state is in the interest of such upper groups, as they require a political authority that can maintain law and order, protect property rights, and provide needed infrastructure. Nevertheless, the collective action and coordination problems of allocating the tax burden *among* upper groups can impede the realization of such objectives.] The incentives for all individuals and groups to free ride on the tax payments of others are high, and wealthier actors within society generally possess extensive capabilities to influence the development of tax policy, and to avoid and/or evade the tax burden when they are so inclined.

The quote also indicates an appreciation of the manner in which powerful actors or groups can influence tax policy. The reference to free-riding acknowledges the role of powerful and privileged groups with much to gain from either preserving the status quo or pushing for change. Historical institutionalists accept the contention that politics is marked by *conflict* between rival groups for scarce resources or

155 B. Guy Peters, Jon Pierre and Desmond S. King, 'The Politics of Path Dependency: Political Conflict in Historical Institutionalism', *Journal of Politics* 67(4) (2005), 1275, 1283.

156 Evan S. Lieberman, *Race and Regionalism in the Politics of Taxation in Brazil and South Africa* (Cambridge University Press, Cambridge, 2003), 42.

157 Ibid., 16. Portion of quote in parentheses from Evan S. Lieberman, 'Payment for Privilege? Race and Space in the Politics of Taxation in Brazil and South Africa' (PhD thesis, University of California, Berkeley, 2000), 19 (emphasis in original).

struggles for power. However, unlike the group-conflict theories of the 1960s and 1970s,[158] historical institutionalists seek to elevate institutions to more than merely the arena for these battles, but as factors shaping the outcome of these battles, for example by mobilising resources in favour of one group over another.[159] Rothstein, for example, ties the notion of power differentials to institutions and observes that powerful agents can attempt to influence the institutional rules of the game to serve their own perceived self-interest, thereby increasing their power (coming now from both the control of resources and favourably designed institutions).[160]

By contrast, the conventional approach gives only limited recognition to the role of agents in the VAT's rise, and lacks a coherent account of exactly how domestic institutions shape perceptions of the good VAT and the translation of the good VAT into real VATs. Eccleston, by contrast, adopts an historical institutionalist approach to emphasise that, even when the conditions for VAT reform were ripe (such as when there was strong promotion by the IMF, World Bank or EU and favourable economic conditions), the implementation of VAT was profoundly shaped by domestic political institutions.[161] A greater focus on how institutions privilege certain groups over others should be instructive in explaining who has played a part in driving (and resisting) the rise of the VAT. This opens an opportunity to test the logic of the conventional approach that policy-makers' hands were in effect forced by the VAT's merits.

However, it should be remembered that institutions are not the totality of politics under historical institutionalism. They mediate from the outside in and from the inside out; that is, institutions shape individual preferences and actions and also mediate the impact of external factors. Historical institutionalism need not deny that change brought about by new ideas or innovation is possible.[162]

[158] The community power debate involved a contest over how to perceive of the power and influence of different groups over the political process: see generally Barry Hindess, *Discourses of Power: From Hobbes to Foucault* (Blackwell Publishers, Oxford, UK; Cambridge, MA, USA, 1996), 5; Alan Fenna, *Australian Public Policy* (2nd ed., Pearson Education Australia, Frenchs Forest, NSW, 2004), 127–32.

[159] Peter Hall and Rosemary C. Taylor, 'Political Science and the Three New Institutionalisms', *Political Studies* 44 (1996), 936, 937; Bo Rothstein, 'Political Institutions: An Overview', in R. E. Goodin and H.-D. Klingemann (eds.), *A New Handbook of Political Science* (Oxford University Press Oxford; New York, 1996), 133, 139; Kathleen Thelen and Sven Steinmo, 'Historical Institutionalism in Comparative Politics', in S. Steinmo, K. Thelen and F. Longstreth (eds.), *Structuring Politics: Historical Institutionalism in Comparative Analysis* (Cambridge University Press, Cambridge, 1992), 1, 5; Paul Pierson, 'Increasing Returns, Path Dependence, and the Study of Politics', *American Political Science Review* 94(2) (2000), 251, 259.

[160] Bo Rothstein, 'Political Institutions: An Overview', in R. E. Goodin and H.-D. Klingemann (eds.), *A New Handbook of Political Science* (Oxford University Press Oxford; New York, 1996), 133, 145, 153.

[161] Richard Eccleston, *Taxing Reforms* (Edward Elgar, Cheltenham, 2007), 9.

[162] For well-known accounts of innovation that set this innovation in an historical framework, see, e.g., Joseph Schumpeter, *Capitalism, Socialism and Democracy* (Harper, New York, 1943); Max Weber, *Economy and Society: An Outline of Interpretive Sociology* (University of California Press, Berkeley, 1978).

The contribution of historical institutionalism, however, lies in showing how the taking up of ideas is influenced by what has gone before.

Even in the face of its limitations, historical institutionalism offers a significant advance on the simple yet misleading determinism of the explanations for the VAT's rise put forward by the conventional approach whereby change in complex systems is reduced to a simple appeal to policy merits. The work of Kato, Lieberman and Steinmo illustrates that one need not resolve all the methodological tensions within historical institutionalism to improve upon the existing accounts of VAT reform by the conventional approach.

3.3 *Further comparisons with public choice*

Both historical institutionalism and public choice seek to explain real-world policy outcomes. Both admit of the importance of agents in the policy process, and both can admit of the importance of institutions in influencing policy outcomes.[163] Although there are differences in the approaches, some of which are explored further below, this book has shown that both methods would be united in rejecting an account that attributes the VAT's rise to its putative merits.

Historical institutionalism acknowledges the need for choices in policy-making, however, the approach is less individualist in orientation and proceeds from the assumption that the choices of actors in the policy-making process are shaped by a far greater range of constraints. These constraints include not just the choices of others or the rules of the game but all manner of factors, including traditions, beliefs (rational or otherwise), ideas, practice, language, history and so on. Katznelson and Milner contend that the differences in approach between methods like public choice and historical institutionalism represent the positioning of political science as a discipline between economics and the social sciences, whereby:[164]

> Some colleagues emphasize the structural restrictions under which any choice occurs. . .for. . .historical institutionalists. . .these circumstances are paramount and derive from history. Mechanisms by which the past imposes itself on the present

[163] Peter Hall and Rosemary C. Taylor, 'Political Science and the Three New Institutionalisms', *Political Studies* 44 (1996), 936, 937–46; Kathleen Thelen and Sven Steinmo, 'Historical Institutionalism in Comparative Politics', in S. Steinmo, K. Thelen and F. Longstreth (eds.), *Structuring Politics: Historical Institutionalism in Comparative Analysis* (Cambridge University Press, Cambridge, 1992), 1, 7–10, 29. See, e.g., Douglas C. North, *Institutions, Institutional Change, and Economic Performance* (Cambridge University Press, Cambridge, 1990).

[164] Ira Katznelson and Helen V. Milner, 'American Political Science: The Discipline's State and the State of the Discipline', in I. Katznelson and H. V. Milner (eds.), *Political Science: State of the Discipline* (Norton; American Political Science Association, New York, Washington, DC, 2002), 1, 17 (citations omitted); see also Mark M. Blyth, '"Any More Bright Ideas?" The Ideational Turn of Comparative Political Economy', *Comparative Politics* 29(2) (1997), 229, 244–45.

> including path dependence, and the weight of culture and language shape and narrow choices open for individuals. Sharing much with sociologists, historians, and anthropologists, these political scientists emphasize the constraints on behaviour that institutions, among other structures, impose. . .Another part of the discipline [public choice] places these confining structures in the background and emphasizes the acts of choice.

Perhaps it is more accurate to say that public choice emphasises different constraints, such as the mechanisms by which choices are constrained by others or the availability of information or the rules that structure certain choices. However, for historical institutionalism, the key focus is on the mechanisms by which the past imposes itself on the present. In keeping with its broader conception of the constraints that shape the preferences and choices of actors in the policy process, historical institutionalism broadens the field of options within which actors operate and more readily encompasses discussions of the role of ideas and the influence of power in shaping actors' behaviour and policy outcomes. The difference between the approaches is also evident in the method. Public choice relies on models of individual choice informed by game theory, whereas historical institutionalism tends to rely on historical case studies sometimes supported by broader quantitative data analysis.[165]

A key point of distinction between public choice and historical institutionalism lies in the manner in which the different approaches perceive of the relationship between institutions and individual behaviour. Public choice accounts that incorporate institutions adopt more of a 'calculus' approach, whereupon actors' preferences are formed exogenous to institutions but these institutions figure in their strategic calculations of how to further these preferences.[166] By contrast, many historical institutionalists deny that preferences are formed exogenous to institutions and contend that institutions do more than simply mediate the strategies

[165] The following analyses rely on a case-study approach: Sven Steinmo, *Taxation and Democracy: Swedish, British and American Approaches to Financing the Modern State* (Yale University Press, New Haven, CT, 1993); Ann Shola Orloff, *The Politics of Pensions: A Comparative Analysis of Britain, Canada, and the United States, 1880–1940* (University of Wisconsin Press, Madison, 1993); Richard Eccleston, *Taxing Reforms* (Edward Elgar, Cheltenham, 2007). The following studies support case-study analysis with quantitative data: Evan S. Lieberman, *Race and Regionalism in the Politics of Taxation in Brazil and South Africa* (Cambridge University Press, Cambridge, 2003); Junko Kato, *Regressive Taxation and the Welfare State: Path Dependence and Policy Diffusion* (Cambridge University Press, Cambridge, 2003); Steffen Ganghof, *The Politics of Income Taxation: A Comparative Analysis* (ECPR Press, Colchester, 2006).

[166] Peter Hall and Rosemary C. Taylor, 'Political Science and the Three New Institutionalisms', *Political Studies* 44 (1996), 936, 939; Bo Rothstein, 'Political Institutions: An Overview', in R. E. Goodin and H.-D. Klingemann (eds.), *A New Handbook of Political Science* (Oxford University Press Oxford; New York, 1996), 133, 147; Walter Hettich and Stanley L. Winer, *Democratic Choice and Taxation: A Theoretical and Empirical Analysis* (Cambridge University Press, Cambridge, 1999), 289; Mark M. Blyth, '"Any More Bright Ideas?" The Ideational Turn of Comparative Political Economy', *Comparative Politics* 29(2) (1997), 229, 230.

adopted by actors but contribute to the shaping of their very preferences.[167] Hall, for example, claims that:[168]

> Institutional factors play two fundamental roles. . .On the one hand, the organization of policy-making affects the degree of power that any one set of actors has over the policy outcomes. . .On the other hand, organizational position also influences an actor's definition of his own interests, by establishing his institutional responsibilities and relationships to other actors. In this way, organizational factors affect both the degree of pressure an actor can bring to bear on policy and the likely direction of that pressure.

Public choice struggles to account for externally derived and historically constituted influences, which might mean that the formation of an individual's preferences and beliefs is not wholly his or her own. By contrast, historical institutionalism acknowledges a broad range of factors that contribute to preference formation and can therefore more readily examine the influence of ideas and rhetoric on preference formation. Being less individualist in focus, historical institutionalism need not commit to an account of individual and revealed preferences. However, being more individualist in focus means that public choice resists the charge of being unable to account for change because the mechanism by which to produce change is the choice of individual rational agents. These issues need not be explored further for the purposes of this book, because to admit that institutions have a role in shaping the preferences and actions of individual agents in the tax policy process does not require a contention that *all* preference formation is shaped by institutions.

3.4 *Fiscal sociology*

In recent years, there has been a renewed interest in 'fiscal sociology'.[169] Fiscal sociology is generally defined as 'the study of the social processes behind taxation and public finances', where the focus of inquiry is on 'how taxes and expenditures are determined [by] and affect society'.[170] The 'new fiscal sociology' has focused on

[167] Peter Hall and Rosemary C. Taylor, 'Political Science and the Three New Institutionalisms', *Political Studies* 44 (1996), 936, 939; Bo Rothstein, 'Political Institutions: An Overview', in R. E. Goodin and H.-D. Klingemann (eds.), *A New Handbook of Political Science* (Oxford University Press Oxford; New York, 1996), 133, 147.

[168] Peter Hall, *Governing the Economy* (Oxford University Press, New York, 1986), 19.

[169] Schumpeter is credited with popularising fiscal sociology, although the term was borrowed from Rudolf Goldschield: Isaac William Martin, Ajay K. Mehrotra and Monica Prasad, 'The Thunder of History: The Origins and Development of the New Fiscal Sociology', in I. W. Martin, A. K. Mehrotra and M. Prasad (eds.), *The New Fiscal Sociology: Taxation in Comparative and Historical Perspective* (Cambridge University Press, New York, 2009), 1, 2; Joseph Schumpeter, 'The Crisis of the Tax State', in R. Swedberg (ed.), *The Economics and Sociology of Capitalism* (Princeton University Press, Princeton, NJ, [1918] 1991), 99–140.

[170] John L. Campbell, 'The State and Fiscal Sociology', *Annual Review of Sociology* 19 (1993), 163.

the two-way relationship between taxation and the state – focusing on how taxation both shapes social, political and economic relations and is in turn shaped by these forces.[171] Rather than constituting a specific methodological approach, the term includes a range of approaches spanning a number of disciplines that all share a concern to explore taxation and its relationship with society, the economy and the polity.[172]

Although spanning many disciplines (history, sociology and political science), much of the method and sympathies of the new fiscal sociology closely aligns with historical institutionalism and therefore is included within the discussion of historical institutionalism. For example, Martin et al. identify three key characteristics of the new fiscal sociology – all of which will be familiar from the discussion of historical institutionalism. First, the approach emphasises the importance of institutions (defined in the broad sense) in shaping fiscal policy outcomes with particular focus on *informal social institutions*. This broad approach to conceptualising institutions reflects a 'discovery that taxation is deeply enmeshed in social relationships that are no less institutionalized for not being written down'.[173] Second, the new fiscal sociology treats historical sequence and context seriously and rejects linear accounts of policy change. Concepts such as *path dependence*, *positive feedback mechanisms* and *critical junctures* feature prominently in the new fiscal sociology.[174] Third, and as a riposte to the public choice approach, the new fiscal sociology focuses on the role of taxation at a societal rather than individual level.[175] Many of the key contributions to the new fiscal sociology rely on methods similar to those employed by historical institutionalism – using a mix of historical case-study analysis as well as larger quantitative analysis and longitudinal studies.[176] Martin et al. contend that the studies under the new fiscal sociology show that:[177]

[171] For a recent concise summary of the new fiscal sociology, see the contributions to Isaac William Martin, Ajay K. Mehrotra and Monica Prasad (eds.), *The New Fiscal Sociology: Taxation in Comparative and Historical Perspective* (Cambridge University Press, New York, 2009); see also Miranda Stewart, 'Introduction: New Research on Tax Law and Political Institutions', *Law in Context* 24(2) (2006), 1; John L. Campbell, 'The State and Fiscal Sociology', *Annual Review of Sociology* 19 (1993), 163; Richard E. Wagner, *Fiscal Sociology and the Theory of Public Finance: An Exploratory Essay* (Edward Elgar, Cheltenham, UK; Northampton, MA, 2007).

[172] Isaac William Martin, Ajay K. Mehrotra and Monica Prasad, 'The Thunder of History: The Origins and Development of the New Fiscal Sociology', in I. W. Martin, A. K. Mehrotra and M. Prasad (eds.), *The New Fiscal Sociology: Taxation in Comparative and Historical Perspective* (Cambridge University Press, New York, 2009), 1, 2, 12.

[173] Ibid., 13.

[174] 'The new studies treat history instead as a garden of forking paths, with critical junctures – usually war and economic crises – marking moments of choice': ibid., 14, and at 13.

[175] 'The observation of an economic or political equilibrium at any single point in time is not sufficient to explain observed outcomes in a world where multiple equilibria are possible': ibid., 14.

[176] See above, n 165.

[177] Isaac William Martin, Ajay K. Mehrotra and Monica Prasad, 'The Thunder of History: The Origins and Development of the New Fiscal Sociology', in I. W. Martin, A. K. Mehrotra and

economic development does not inevitably lead to a particular form of taxation, but rather that institutional contexts, political conflicts, and contingent events lead to a diversity of tax states in the modern world.

The quote indicates that along with public choice and historical institutionalism, fiscal sociology rejects linear causal accounts that attribute policy outcomes to the putative merits of a policy idea. Given that fiscal sociology shares much with the historical institutionalist method, this book also contributes to the new fiscal sociology agenda by furthering understanding of the VAT's rise.

4 A NEW APPROACH TO EXPLAINING THE RISE OF THE VAT

This book has so far demonstrated that the merits-based explanation for the VAT's rise provided by the conventional approach is insufficient in two main ways. First, given the empirical reality that it is real VATs that have actually risen, a merits-based explanation primarily premised on the merits of the good VAT cannot explain this rise. Second, the explanation does not withstand theoretical scrutiny, as the analysis of two dominant yet markedly different approaches to analysing policy outcomes, those of public choice and historical institutionalism, reveals that both approaches provide insight into why the good is not self-realising and both would therefore comprehensively reject an account of the rise of a policy instrument based on its merits.

This therefore leaves the question of how to improve upon this inadequate account of the VAT's rise provided by the conventional approach. This book contends that in light of the fact that it is real VATs that have actually arisen, a crucial first step is to refocus the inquiry from a general investigation into how the VAT has risen to one that examines how *real VATs* have risen.

The need to introduce the distinction between the good VAT and real VATs as an object of inquiry is further warranted by the state of existing policy-based accounts of the rise of the VAT. The public choice approach suggests that choices and behaviour of key individuals and groups in the policy process can lead to politically optimal outcomes that might be viewed as suboptimal from a public finance perspective. As a result, public choice offers a method by which to understand how the good VAT favoured by the conventional approach is rarely, if ever, realised. Historical institutionalism also provides a means by which to analyse how real VATs are shaped by various actors and the historical and institutional context in which they operate, to produce outcomes that might frequently depart from the good VAT. However, an examination of the existing public policy accounts of VAT reform reveals a peculiar result: despite offering the means by which to highlight the flaws in the conventional approach, existing policy analyses

M. Prasad (eds.), *The New Fiscal Sociology: Taxation in Comparative and Historical Perspective* (Cambridge University Press, New York, 2009), 1, 14.

have instead tended to *reinforce* rather than challenge or improve upon the accounts of the rise of the VAT provided by the conventional approach. This is because existing public policy accounts of the VAT's rise tend to defer to the technical expertise of the conventional approach, especially on questions of the VAT's merits, in a manner that undermines the explanatory power of their approach. In short, because analyses of VAT reform outside the conventional approach do not take account of the difference between the good VAT and real VATs, these accounts fall victim to the same flawed assumptions of the conventional approach. Some examples will suffice to demonstrate the point.

Kato's account of the VAT might just as easily be located within the conventional approach.[178] Despite rejecting a merits-based explanation that attributes the VAT's rise to its technical superiority,[179] Kato largely adopts at face value the claims of the conventional approach. She variously repeats without questioning the merits claims made of the good VAT in relation to real VATs: the VAT is simple and neutral, is passed on to consumers, and has stronger revenue raising power than other taxes. The following quote illustrates the point:[180]

> As a flat-rate regressive tax on a broad-base, the VAT, when implemented, has a strong revenue-raising power that the income tax lacks. The broad tax base on consumption, which does not fluctuate as much as income during economic ups and downs, guarantees large amounts of revenue even with a slight increase in a flat tax rate. The tax base has not been narrowed as much as the income tax by political pressure: taxing the added value at each transaction stage makes tax exemptions technically more difficult than otherwise. Moreover, the VAT is likely to increase tax compliance in general because, in all transaction activities, tax-filing units (i.e., firms) must report their transactions to the tax authority.

Kato further contends that the strength of the VAT rests on its regressivity:[181]

> Regressive taxes more effectively increase the state funding capacity that results from flat rates and a tax base resistant to erosion. Politics preclude an efficient direct transfer from rich to the poor and needy who lack a majority support, and prevent progressive taxation from raising large revenues by increasing loopholes and special tax measures.

Kato's account therefore largely defers to the merits of the good VAT, despite the evidence to suggest that it is real VATs, which fail to realise these merits, that have actually arisen. This oversight is significant. As Chapter 3 outlined, in practice the VAT has not been immune from erosion arising from the granting of exemptions, multiple rates or through fraud and evasion activity. VAT revenues have proven to be susceptible to fluctuation during the fiscal crises experienced

[178] Junko Kato, *Regressive Taxation and the Welfare State: Path Dependence and Policy Diffusion* (Cambridge University Press, Cambridge, 2003), 27. See above §3.1.

[179] Ibid., 41. [180] Ibid., 27, and at 41–42. [181] Ibid., 215.

in some form or another by most economies since 2007. While it is generally agreed that a broad base amounts to less evasion and therefore greater funding capacity, there is no necessary reason why a broad base is better achieved with a *regressive* tax than a progressive or proportionate one. Moreover, there is nothing intrinsic to a regressive tax that necessarily makes it harder to avoid or evade (other than reducing the incentive for higher-income taxpayers to do so). One can have a highly regressive tax, such as a poll tax, that is highly visible, violently protested and easily avoided or evaded.[182] Although most VATs in practice are regressive, there is nothing that necessarily makes them so, given appropriate compensation or adjustments.[183] While alleviating regressivity through multiple rates and exemptions can reduce the VAT's putative virtues of simplicity and neutrality, many of the VAT's virtues do not rest solely on regressivity. For example, both the retail sales tax (RST) and the VAT achieve the same effect economically, and both can be regressive taxes, but it is the VAT's collection mechanism that makes the VAT the preferred consumption tax instrument. Crucially, Kato seems to conflate regressivity with *invisibility*, as indicated by her comment that countries with 'invisible taxes' (excluding Denmark and Finland) have had higher tax levels and more universal welfare provisions than countries with visible taxes.[184] Invisibility is not a virtue unique to the VAT – an RST can be even less visible. By adopting without questioning many of the claims under the conventional approach, Kato falls victim to the same approach she implicitly criticises.[185]

Lindert's account of the link between regressive taxes (such as the VAT) and the size of postwar welfare states similarly relies on the good VAT. The following quote from Lindert's text echoes the evolutionary march of Tait's account of the VAT in Chapter 4, §3:[186]

[182] The high visibility and unpopularity of poll taxes was evidenced by the Thatcher government's introduction of the community charge from 1989 to 1990 – a type of poll tax to pay for local government services. The charge was levied on the number of occupants in a household rather than the property's worth, and was thus said to disproportionately transfer the burden from the rich to middle- and lower-income households. The poll tax led to a number of protests and was repealed by Thatcher's successor, John Major, in 1990: Sven Steinmo, *Taxation and Democracy: Swedish, British and American Approaches to Financing the Modern State* (Yale University Press, New Haven, CT, 1993), 177–78.

[183] Kato acknowledges this but strangely cites the Hall Rabushka flat tax as an example of a progressive tax that exists with a flat rate: Junko Kato, *Regressive Taxation and the Welfare State: Path Dependence and Policy Diffusion* (Cambridge University Press, Cambridge, 2003), 199.

[184] Ibid., 8.

[185] For further criticisms of Kato, see Steffen Ganghof, 'Tax Mixes and the Size of the Welfare State: Causal Mechanisms and Policy Implications', *European Journal of Social Policy* 16(4) (2006), 360.

[186] Peter H. Lindert, *Growing Public: Social Spending and Economic Growth since the Eighteenth Century* (Cambridge UK; New York, Cambridge University Press, 2004), 302, ch. 2.

> The rise of rich democracies has brought a gradual march from narrow and expensive taxes toward broader, more efficient taxes like the general consumption tax. We have already caught glimpses of the later part of that march from more complex income taxes toward the simpler, broader VAT in postwar welfare states.

As Chapter 3, §2.6 demonstrated, simplicity is not generally regarded as a virtue of the good VAT, let alone real VATs. Nor has the VAT necessarily offered as broad a base in these postwar welfare states as its supporters might have hoped for or as the quote implies. Income taxes still constitute the largest share of overall taxation revenues even in the more heavily VAT dependent social-democratic states to which Lindert refers.[187] Lindert's account of the VAT's merits therefore appears at least underdeveloped or overstated because it is based on the good rather than real VATs.

In their concise overview of the state of the new fiscal sociology, Martin et al. rely on a similar good VAT assumption when they claim that the social democratic welfare states of Scandinavia have survived the internationalisation of capital markets 'because they rely on consumption taxes, which are not vulnerable to the globalization of finance or trade'.[188] As Chapter 3 demonstrated, contrary to the authors' contention, the VAT is vulnerable on both these fronts. The taxation of financial supplies under even the good VAT is a difficult frontier issue,[189] as is the application of the VAT to goods and services that are traded in a manner that no longer respects traditional state border-adjustment facilities.[190] Once again, the failure to employ the good VAT/real VATs distinction undermines the authors' explanatory account.

Steinmo alternatively contends that 'if the United States had such a tax [as the VAT], we probably would not consider America a social welfare state laggard'.[191] However, the explanation assumes a causal relationship that is not necessarily there. Ganghof's criticism of Kato is equally apposite here:[192]

> The explanation offered here highlights a kind of asymmetry not sufficiently acknowledged by the tax mix argument: while policy makers with strong spending commitments have no choice but to strongly rely on regressive taxes, those with

[187] This is true to the greatest extent of Denmark and also of Finland, Norway and Sweden: OECD, *Revenue Statistics: 1965–2012* (OECD Publishing, Paris, 2013), 147.

[188] Isaac William Martin, Ajay K. Mehrotra and Monica Prasad, 'The Thunder of History: The Origins and Development of the New Fiscal Sociology', in I. W. Martin, A. K. Mehrotra and M. Prasad (eds.), *The New Fiscal Sociology: Taxation in Comparative and Historical Perspective* (Cambridge University Press, New York, 2009), 1, 15.

[189] See Chapter 2, §4.2.5.1 of this book. [190] See Chapter 3, §6 of this book.

[191] Sven Steinmo, *Taxation and Democracy: Swedish, British and American Approaches to Financing the Modern State* (Yale University Press, New Haven, CT, 1993), 196.

[192] Steffen Ganghof, 'Tax Mixes and the Size of the Welfare State: Causal Mechanisms and Policy Implications', *European Journal of Social Policy* 16(4) (2006), 360, 371. Sullivan makes a similar point in relation to the US: Martin A. Sullivan, 'Was the VAT a Money Machine for Europe?', *Tax Notes* (2012), 143, 145.

weak spending commitments do have a choice but may choose regressive taxation nevertheless – for the same reason that they choose lower spending.

These gaps in policy-based accounts of the rise of the VAT result from a failure to incorporate a key distinction developed by this book – the difference between the good VAT and real VATs. Through inadvertence or mistake, policy analysts confuse the object of analysis as the good VAT when it should in fact be real VATs. This is due, in part, to the deference to the conventional approach on technical matters, which also has the dual effect of undermining the explanatory value of these policy accounts and inadvertently reinforcing the insufficient merits-based explanations put forward by the conventional approach. The deployment of the good VAT/real VATs distinction in this book will ensure that the mistakes of these policy accounts are not repeated and will enable insights into real VATs that are currently ignored by policy analyses or downplayed by the conventional approach.

Having established the importance of refocusing the object of inquiry to one of investigating the rise of real VATs, the next question is what method offers an improved means by which to explore this line of inquiry. While either public choice or historical institutionalism lends itself to the study of the rise of real VATs, the remaining empirical and analytical parts of this book draw upon the historical institutionalist method. The choice of this method does not imply a rejection of the public choice approach because, as §2 of this chapter indicated, public choice offers much by which to improve upon the conventional approach's account of the VAT's rise. Rather, historical institutionalism is merely one means by which to demonstrate the benefits of an alternative approach. Further research using the method of public choice to explain the VAT's rise would most likely yield equally interesting (but not necessarily the same) insights.

The choice of historical institutionalism is motivated by a desire to address the inattention to history by the conventional approach, which, as §2.4 explained, the public choice approach is less well suited to addressing. The historical institutionalist method aligns with the aim of this book, which is positioned between public policy and legal analysis. The aim is to improve understanding of the rise of real VATs by examining how context and the policy-making process impact policy outcomes, and to do this by employing some of the tools of historical institutionalism.

As Chapter 4 highlighted, the conventional approach neglects the domestic context of VAT reform to the detriment of its overall explanation. Given the inattention to history and the neglect of domestic context by the conventional approach, the book adopts an historical case-study approach with carefully selected case studies designed to generate new insights into the local histories that give rise to real VATs.[193] The adoption of an historical case-study approach focuses squarely

[193] For use of this method in historical institutionalism, see above, n 165. The use of historical case studies has a distinguished legacy of providing lasting insights, as might be evidenced by the ongoing contribution of Tocqueville's classic *Democracy in America* to analysis of the

on domestic context and seeks to explain how the response of actors to similar pressures and policy options varies according to local conditions in ways that matter to the shape of real VATs. The focus on case studies over *time* offers a method from which to explore how historical events and localised conditions affect the reception and implementation of global policy ideas like the good VAT. This focus will also assist in demonstrating how policy merits are insufficient to account for the rise of real VATs.

However, the book departs from most historical institutionalist accounts of VAT reform by continuing to a level of detailed legal analysis generally not offered by these accounts. Most historical institutionalist accounts of VAT reform stop at the point of the VAT's introduction. Kato focuses on how regressive consumption taxes such as the VAT impact the size of the modern welfare state, as does Lindert (although through the discipline of economic history).[194] Eccleston focuses on what factors were necessary and/or sufficient for VAT adoption in Australia, Canada, Japan and the US.[195] Steinmo examines the VAT only as part of a late-twentieth-century move to consumption taxes in modern developed economies.[196]

Public policy analysis provides a number of heuristic and stylised models of the policy-making process. No model is said to accurately reflect the reality (being

evolution of the modern American state: Jon Elster, *Explaining Social Behavior: More Nuts and Bolts for the Social Sciences* (Cambridge University Press, Cambridge; New York, 2007), 447; Alexis de Tocqueville and Henry Reeve, *Democracy in America* (rev. edn., Collier, New York, 1900). Flyvbjerg highlights how carefully selected case studies have been critical to the development of knowledge across many disciplines: Bent Flyvbjerg, 'Five Misunderstandings About Case-Study Research', *Qualitative Inquiry* 12(2) (2006), 219, 226. Mair contends that case-study analysis emphasises the full context in which decisions are made and offers a basis from which to derive new insights in both public choice and historical institutionalism: Peter Mair, 'Comparative Politics: An Overview', in R. E. Goodin and H.-D. Klingemann (eds.), *A New Handbook of Political Science* (Oxford University Press, Oxford; New York, 1998), 309, 319. Nørgaard argues that an approach that focuses on carefully selected case studies is often more useful where the concepts behind, and causal theories about, certain phenomena are weak. The weaknesses of the conventional approach outlined in Chapter 4 and the gaps in existing public policy accounts of the VAT's rise therefore call for such an approach: Asbjørn S. Nørgaard, 'Political Science: Witchcraft or Craftsmanship? Standards for Good Research', *World Political Science Review* 4(1) (2008), art. 5, 1, 22.

[194] Junko Kato, *Regressive Taxation and the Welfare State: Path Dependence and Policy Diffusion* (Cambridge University Press, Cambridge, 2003); Peter H. Lindert, *Growing Public: Social Spending and Economic Growth since the Eighteenth Century* (Cambridge UK; New York, Cambridge University Press, 2004).

[195] Richard Eccleston, *Taxing Reforms* (Edward Elgar, Cheltenham, 2007). For a critique, see Martin, who contends that Eccleston's account 'verges on the claim that policymakers enacted a VAT because they had the idea to pass a VAT – or the similarly trivial claim that interest groups changed their position on VAT because they changed their ideas about VAT': Isaac W. Martin, 'Taxing Reforms: The Politics of Consumption Tax in Japan, the United States, Canada and Australia (Book Review)', *Journal of Economic Literature* 47(1) (2009), 192, 193.

[196] Sven Steinmo, 'The Evolution of Policy Ideas: Tax Policy in the 20th Century', *British Journal of Politics and International Relations* 5(2) (2003), 206, 225; Sven Steinmo, *Taxation and Democracy: Swedish, British and American Approaches to Financing the Modern State* (Yale University Press, New Haven, CT, 1993), 197.

too neat and linear for the real world), but most encapsulate the essence of the policy-making process. Generally, the models identify a number of stages in the policy-making process:[197]

(a) Agenda-setting (whereby problems and issues are recognised, defined and prioritised and potential solutions canvassed);
(b) Policy formation/lawmaking (whereby solutions are considered, consultation [ideally] occurs and one might ask which interests are given access to the policy process and which institutional factors are of influence); and
(c) Implementation (whereby policies are coordinated, resourced, evaluated and amended).

This book focuses on all three aspects of the policy-making process but with specific emphasis on lawmaking and implementation. In addition, because taxation and law are inherently linked to institutions,[198] the focus is on key formal institutions involved in lawmaking and the implementation of tax law.[199] The narrow focus on formal institutions helps avoid a simple broad-ranging narrative account and instead enables a focus on small incremental aspects of the policy process to reveal issues often overlooked in more sweeping public policy accounts. For example, the book moves beyond the obvious examples of standard exemptions to the VAT base, such as food, and examines the operation of specific carveouts, in particular the treatment of financial supplies – a frontier issue in VAT design and application. The detailed focus also lends itself to examining the roles of a broader range of actors in the tax policy process to move beyond the conventional approach's generic portrayal of the only relevant agent being the 'whole of government', and so as to focus on the involvement of key actors and groups in shaping or opposing real VATs.

This book contends that, in order to understand the rise of real VATs, one cannot stop at the point of introduction because it is up to, at, and *after* the introduction of VATs that real VATs come about. This book also argues for a focus on technical

[197] Alan Fenna, *Australian Public Policy* (2nd ed., Pearson Education Australia, Frenchs Forest, NSW, 2004), 17–19. See also Andrew C. Gould and Peter J. Baker, 'Democracy and Taxation', *Annual Review of Political Science* 5 (2002), 87, 88–91; Cedric Sandford, *Why Tax Systems Differ: A Comparative Study of the Political Economy of Taxation* (Fiscal Publications, Bath, 2000), 162; Gregory J. Inwood, *Understanding Canadian Public Administration* (3rd ed., Pearson, Prentice Hall, Toronto, 2009), 210.

[198] Evan S. Lieberman, 'Taxation Data as Indicators of State-Society Relations: Possibilities and Pitfalls in Cross-National Research', *Studies in Comparative International Development* 36(4) (2002), 89, 94; Eccleston contends that institutional theory 'yields the most promising approach to furthering our understanding of the politics of taxation': Richard Eccleston, *Taxing Reforms* (Edward Elgar, Cheltenham, 2007), 5.

[199] Sven Steinmo, *Taxation and Democracy: Swedish, British and American Approaches to Financing the Modern State* (Yale University Press, New Haven, CT, 1993), 12.

detail because considerations relating to detail, or in the case of this book considerations of legal detail, influence decisions relating to the introduction, design and *continued implementation* of real VATs. In so doing, the book addresses a long-acknowledged gap in many policy accounts by giving due focus on the interdependent relationship between decisions relating to whether to introduce a policy and how to effectively realise a policy through implementation.[200] Moreover, the focus on detail allows for an account of *incremental change* and the key *agents* that drive and oppose such change – factors identified in §3.2 as being necessary inclusions to improve accounts of change from within the historical institutionalist approach.

In moving beyond superficial conceptions of the VAT and engaging with the technical detail of the VAT, the analysis fills a gap left by the merits-based explanations of the conventional approach and by public policy accounts that, for reasons of specialisation and expertise, tend to defer to the conventional approach on technical matters at the expense of their own explanatory accounts. The distinction drawn in Chapters 2 and 3 of this book will mean that the analysis does not repeat the errors of the conventional approach and public policy analysis; that is, it will not conflate real VATs with the good VAT.

4.1 *Selecting the case studies of reform*

As the case-study method employed by this book is designed to advance understanding of the rise of real VATs, the selection of cases is deliberate rather than

[200] Reuschemeyer and Mahoney, for example, identify a gap in the investigation of some macro-topics, such as law in the social sciences: Dietrich Rueschemeyer and James Mahoney, 'Comparative Historical Analysis: Achievements and Agendas', in D. Rueschemeyer and J. Mahoney (eds.), *Comparative Historical Analysis in the Social Sciences* (Cambridge University Press, New York, 2002), 3, 7. The observation is even more apt to the application of the social sciences to taxation law. The book employs a focus on lawmaking and legal implementation as one way to address this gap, so as to better understand how issues relating to legal design and implementation shape policy choice. See further Evan S. Lieberman, 'Taxation Data as Indicators of State-Society Relations: Possibilities and Pitfalls in Cross-National Research', *Studies in Comparative International Development* 36(4) (2002), 89, 93. Gould and Baker claim that there 'is little analysis of how the politics of implementation explains observed policy choices': Andrew C. Gould and Peter J. Baker, 'Democracy and Taxation', *Annual Review of Political Science* 5 (2002), 87, 90; B. Guy Peters, *The Politics of Taxation: A Comparative Perspective* (Blackwell, Cambridge, MA, 1991), 3; Gregory J. Inwood, *Understanding Canadian Public Administration* (3rd ed., Pearson, Prentice Hall, Toronto, 2009), 224–32; Robert E. Goodin and Hans-Dieter Klingemann, 'Political Science: The Discipline', in R. E. Goodin and H.-D. Klingemann (eds.), *A New Handbook of Political Science* (Oxford University Press, Oxford; New York, 1996), 3, 21; Brian J. Arnold, 'The Process of Tax Policy Formulation in Australia, Canada and New Zealand', *Australian Tax Forum* 7(4) (1990), 379, 383. For one of the pioneering studies identifying the need to address implementation as a key part of the policy process, see L. Presman and Aaron Wildavsky, *Implementation* (2nd ed., University of California Press, Berkeley, 1979).

random and driven by the need to further this aim.[201] Given that the book focuses on how real VATs come to be and given that real VATs are frequently the outcome of domestic political contests, the remaining empirical analysis of this book focuses on two case studies where VAT reform has been particularly contested. The history of VAT reform in Australia and the US from 1960 to 2010 will therefore be examined. Over this half-century period, global VAT uptake peaked but VAT reform in both jurisdictions remained controversial.

Australia and the US are typically viewed as sharing similar political and fiscal histories: both are English-speaking liberal democracies; both are federal states with written constitutions that arose from a number of sovereign states or colonies surrendering some of their power to a central government; both can be broadly located in the Anglo-American legal tradition; and both are relatively open economies. By OECD standards, Australia and the US are low-tax states.[202] Both jurisdictions rely on a small number of taxes to generate revenue, with most revenue derived from income taxation and an increasingly greater share from consumption taxation.[203] The history of taxation in both countries is broadly similar: over the course of the twentieth century, the World Wars and the postwar welfare state triggered the introduction and/or rapid expansion of direct progressive income taxation.[204] Both Australia and the US sit low in the levels of public social spending against comparable OECD economies.[205]

[201] Steinmo illustrates the value of carefully selected case studies to improve analysis of tax policy outcomes: see §3.1.1. See also the above analysis of Kato (at §3.1) and Eccleston (§3.2).

[202] Tax revenue has hovered around 25–30 per cent of GDP in the US from 1965 to 2010 and from 1975 to 2010 in Australia (revenue was approximately 20 per cent of GDP in the period prior to 1965). This was consistently about 5 per cent below the OECD average: OECD, *Revenue Statistics: 1965–2012* (OECD Publishing, Paris, 2013), 24, 91–95.

[203] Ibid., 99–123.

[204] Australia's involvement in World War I was the catalyst for the introduction of the personal income tax and the corporate tax. The economic depression was the catalyst for the introduction of the Wholesale Sales Tax in 1930, and World War II was the catalyst for the expansion of mass income taxation at the federal level: Richard Eccleston, *The Thirty Year Problem: The Politics of Australian Tax Reform* (ATRF, Sydney, 2004), 32–39. In the US, the passage of the Sixteenth Amendment, which took effect on 25 February 1913, paved the way for the enactment of net income taxes on individuals and corporations in 1916. The Depression contributed to the introduction of social security taxes in 1935. The need to fund the US commitment in World War II transformed the income tax into a mass tax: Michael J. Graetz and Deborah H. Schenk, *Federal Income Taxation: Principles and Policies* (6th ed., Foundation Press, New York, 2009), 4–23. See generally Carolyn Webber and Aaron Wildavsky, *A History of Taxation and Expenditure in the Western World* (Simon and Schuster, New York, 1986), ch. 8–9; Sven Steinmo, 'The Evolution of Policy Ideas: Tax Policy in the 20th Century', *British Journal of Politics and International Relations* 5(2) (2003), 206.

[205] Willem Adema, and Maxime Ladaique, 'Net Social Expenditure (2005 edition) – More Comprehensive Measures of Social Support' (Social, Employment and Migration Working Paper No. 29 – Net Social Expenditure, OECD, 2005), 12; Brooks and Hwong classify Australia and the US as low-tax countries based on annual average tax revenue as a percentage of GDP: Neil Brooks and Thaddeus Hwong, *The Social Benefits and Economic Costs of*

Nevertheless, despite their similarities, the outcome of each case study is very different. Australia offers an example of a country that introduced a 'modern VAT' which, as Chapter 3 explained, is a VAT viewed by the conventional approach as more closely resembling the good VAT.[206] Indeed, Australia has been cited as a model from which the US could learn if it were to adopt a VAT.[207] The US, as the only OECD country without a federal VAT, offers a particularly useful case because, as Chapter 1 explained, the high-profile absence of a VAT in the US might be characterised as a frontier issue in relation to the spread of the VAT a cross the globe. As the only developed country without a national VAT, despite having long pioneered the VAT and long considered VAT reform, it is the one developed jurisdiction where the debate on merits as a basis for the introduction of the tax is still a live issue.[208] As the world's most powerful trading nation, it is an especially useful subject of investigation, because, to unlike many developing nations, the economic and political power of the US means that external pressure to reform, by intergovernmental organisations or by mimicking others, is greatly reduced. So, the merits arguments should in many ways stand alone. The aim, however, is not comparison per se between the two cases but rather to identify the internal dynamics of each case. The fact that the two case studies exhibit many similarities will facilitate the identification of distinctive local determining factors.[209]

Given that Australia has a VAT, the focus on the manner in which law influences questions of VAT design and implementation means that, for the Australian case study, close attention will be paid to legislative and case analysis in historical and political context. The Australian case study draws on original policy documents, media reports, commentary, and legal sources such as case law, legislation and the extrinsic materials in support of the relevant legislation. Given that the US does not have a VAT, attention will instead focus on how considerations of legislative process and legal implementation have influenced support for the VAT. The absence of a VAT in the US means legislation and case law are not as relevant, but proposed legislation (bills) is drawn upon, as are original policy documents, media reports and commentary. In addition, reference is made to

Taxation: A Comparison of High and Low Tax Countries (Canadian Centre for Policy Alternatives, Ottawa, 2006), 12.

[206] See Chapter 3, §4.2 of this book.

[207] In testimony to the Committee on Ways and Means on VAT reform, Graetz remarked that 'the VATs to use as your models are Singapore, South Africa, New Zealand, Australia and Canada': US House of Representatives, Committee on Ways and Means, (112th Cong., 1st session), Hearing on Tax Reform and Consumption-Based Tax Systems (26 July 2011, serial 112–15). See also the remarks of Schenk suggesting the US adopt the Australian approach of applying a reduced input tax credit to exempt financial supplies, discussed at Chapter 7, §3.2.

[208] Orloff contends that examining 'failures' as well as 'successes' is a useful approach to highlight key issues: Ann Shola Orloff, *The Politics of Pensions: A Comparative Analysis of Britain, Canada, and the United States, 1880–1940* (University of Wisconsin Press, Madison, 1993), 36.

[209] Ibid., 33; David Nelken, *Comparing Legal Cultures* (Dartmouth, Aldershot, Hants, UK; Brookfield, VT, 1997), 6.

relevant archival material evidencing consideration of VAT reform by the US federal government during the 1970s. This closer focus will reveal issues that have shaped real VATs but that often escape the notice of the political scientist. The focus on legal design and implementation explores the ways in which the good VAT is rarely realised, and the often overlooked political processes that lead to these departures in real VATs. In particular, analysis of approaches in both jurisdictions to the difficult frontier issue of the taxation of financial supplies will reveal the value of this close and extended legal analysis.

The cases provide sites for not simply developing a greater understanding of the histories of VAT reform in Australia and the US, but developing broader understandings of how local histories might impact the realisation of real VATs. However, the cases are not posited as a representative sample of what produces real VATs in all cases. Indeed, the very contention of this book, that local histories matter, guards against this claim, and the selection of Australia and the US is simply one way of demonstrating this. The focus on these nations does not deny that an analysis of other cases could be equally instructive. Three are mentioned to demonstrate the point.

One could focus on the interesting case of New Zealand, which is frequently cited with approval by the conventional approach as coming closer to approximating the good VAT than any other jurisdiction. Instead of simply imploring others to follow the New Zealand lead, a more interesting line of inquiry might be to ask what institutionalised features might have produced this outcome. New Zealand's unitary system of government, unicameral parliament, broader embrace of neoliberal reforms at the time of the VAT's introduction and the associated desire to be validated as a leading reformer in light of its relatively limited economic power would all be useful places to begin (but not end) the inquiry.[210]

One could also focus on countries in the developing world, where an examination of local histories of VAT reform might bring to light the extent of the influence of intergovernmental organisations as well as aid and development agencies. It might also help explain why the introduction of the VAT has been resisted and why the operation of the VAT has been undermined by poor implementation as well as avoidance and evasion activity, despite the view of the conventional approach (and articulated here by one of the leading contributions to development tax theory) that '[i]ndirect taxes, being less visible, tend to encounter less resistance than direct taxes'.[211]

[210] See generally the contributions to Richard Krever et al., *GST in Retrospect and Prospect* (Thomson Brookers, Wellington, NZ, 2007), especially Part I. See also Shaun Goldfinch, *Remaking New Zealand and Australian Economic Policy: Ideas, Institutions, and Policy Communities* (Georgetown University Press, Washington, DC, 2000).

[211] Robin Burgess and Nicholas Stern, 'Taxation and Development', *Journal of Economic Literature* 31(2) (1993), 762, 802.

One could focus on the interesting case of real VATs in jurisdictions within the European Union (EU).[212] The EU is regarded as being at the forefront of VAT reform.[213] As Chapter 4, §2 and §4 highlighted, accounts of the rise of the VAT within the EU are strongly influenced by merits and generally attribute the VAT's rise to the fact that it offered a technical improvement on existing taxes in member states such as turnover taxes and a means by which to harmonise taxes to facilitate the formation of a common market. However, these explanations overlook a number of factors that challenge this straightforward account. The imposition of VAT through Directives, which bind member states to a shared result but allow each state the flexibility to choose the means to this end, has resulted in the enactment of a variety of VAT laws across the EU.[214] The passage of later Directives, including the *Recast VAT Directive*,[215] has attempted to narrow this early flexibility and diversity through defining key terms and limiting exemptions, but moves toward a truly harmonised European VAT have met intractable domestic resistance.[216] The end result is far from harmonious, with 28 different regimes with more than 10 different standard rates, 28 different registration thresholds, 28 unique sets of exemptions and 28 different administrative regimes. As Chapter 3 highlighted, in light of the pressing need for revenue and the massive revenue loss produced by VAT fraud that seeks to exploit the removal of trading barriers and the difference in EU VAT regimes, the calls for greater reform are numerous.[217] Terra and Kajus conclude that:[218]

[212] There exists an extensive literature on the history of the European VAT and a mass of writing on the design and implementation of the VAT within the EU, but none from the perspective proposed by this book. For overviews, see generally Ben Terra and Julie Kajus, IBFD, *A Guide to the European VAT Directives* [online] (15 April 2011); Rita de la Feria, *The EU VAT System and the Internal Market* (IBFD, Amsterdam, 2009); Walter van der Corput and Fabiola Annacondia (eds.), *EU VAT Compass* (IBFD Publications, Amsterdam, 2007).

[213] OECD, *Consumption Tax Trends 2012 – VAT/GST and Excise Rates, Trends and Administration Issues* (OECD, Paris, 2012), 31.

[214] This was especially so as the early Directives provided great flexibility to member states for the manner in which each state could introduce a VAT. The First Council Directive outlined the definition and aims of the proposed VAT: *First Council Directive 67/227/EEC of 11 April 1967 On the Harmonisation of Legislation of Member States Concerning Turnover Taxes* [1967] OJ L 1/14; [1967] OJ Spec Ed 14. The Second Council Directive 67/228/EEC of 11 April 1967 provided the details for the new system (by, for example, outlining key terms such as taxable transactions and place of supply) but gave member states considerable scope to determine the content of their domestic VATs with freedom to determine their own VAT rate structure and exemptions: *Second Council Directive 67/228/EEC of 11 April 1967 on the Harmonisation of Legislation of Member States Concerning Turnover Taxes – Structure and Procedures for Application of the Common System of Value Added Tax* [1967] OJ 1/14; [1967] OJ Spec Ed 16. See also Rita de la Feria, *The EU VAT System and the Internal Market* (IBFD, Amsterdam, 2009), 2.2.2.

[215] *Council Directive 2006/112/EC of 28 November 2006 on the Common System of Value Added Tax* [2006] OJ L 347/1 (referred to hereafter as '*Recast VAT Directive 2006/112/EC*').

[216] See, e.g., European Commission, *VAT Rates Applied in Member States of the European Union (situation as at 14th January 2013)* (Brussels, 2013).

[217] See Chapter 3, §4.3, §5.2 and §6.

[218] Ben Terra and Julie Kajus, IBFD, *A Guide to the European VAT Directives* [online] (15 April 2011), Preface.

> It is an indictment of the Member States that a concept which was accepted in principle 40 years ago still seems as far from realization as it was then. The history of VAT legislation in Europe is a catalogue of failure, not on the part of the Commission, which has acted with commendable consistency and unrelenting effort in attempting to move the situation forward, but on the part of the Member States, who have continually frustrated these efforts.

If merit was all that mattered, then one might expect the further harmonisation of European VATs. The inability to progress toward a truly harmonised European VAT, despite the pressing need to do so, provides strong evidence that much more than merits is required to explain these real VAT outcomes.

That this book chooses to focus on the US and Australia is not to deny that these other cases might offer valuable lines of inquiry, but rather serves to demonstrate that such a line of inquiry is possible, useful and long overdue. The development of a new approach to explaining the rise of the VAT is therefore the beginning of what will hopefully be a much longer-term endeavour.

PART III

Case studies on the real-world challenges of VAT reform

6

Australia

Australia legislated to introduce a value-added tax, known as the Goods and Services Tax ('GST'), on 8 July 1999.[1] Australia is the latest member of the Organisation for Economic Co-operation and Development (OECD) to adopt a VAT. Although the Australian GST is considered a 'modern VAT' due to features such as its single rate, upon closer inspection it becomes apparent that the GST is a real VAT. The focus of this chapter is not on documenting all the areas in which the Australian VAT is real rather than good, but rather in showing how Australia came to get a real VAT. To do this, §1 details the history leading to the introduction of the GST, while §2 draws upon historical institutional theory to show how institutionalised features of the Australian political landscape have shaped and continue to shape the GST. Unlike most public policy accounts of the VAT, which end at the point of the VAT's introduction, this history provides the basis for a closer examination of some key features of the Australian GST.

The GST is assessed against the three norms for good VAT design (see §3 and §4), with a particular focus on the first design norm (see §4) due to the fact that the GST only manages to tax half of total domestic consumption. The impact of law on the ability of the GST to tax consumption is discussed at §4.3. The discussion includes specific issues relating to the drafting and interpretation of the laws governing concepts such as taxable supply and entitlement to input tax credits, and further includes a detailed consideration of the frontier issue of the taxation of financial supplies. The extension of the analysis to such a high degree of legal detail highlights key political contests that shape the operation of the GST, which are absent from most public policy accounts of the VAT's rise.

In showing how Australia came to introduce its own real VAT, the limits of the merits-based account of the VAT's rise by the conventional approach become

[1] The relevant legislation commenced on 1 July 2000: A *New Tax System (Goods and Services Tax) Act 1999* (Cth).

apparent. The GST is the product of the actions of real political actors whose preferences and actions have been shaped by their historical and institutional context, which the historical case-study method outlined in Chapter 5 (§4) is well suited to capturing.

1 WE OF THE 'NEVER EVER' – THE HISTORY OF THE INTRODUCTION OF A GOODS AND SERVICES TAX IN AUSTRALIA[2]

The introduction of the GST in Australia came after more than 25 years of reform efforts. This section provides a brief chronological history of the four major phases of reform. Later sections draw upon specific aspects relating to the history of GST reform to demonstrate how this history matters in explaining the shape of the Australian GST.

1.1 *The 1970s and the Asprey Committee*

A VAT was first officially endorsed in the mid-1970s by the Asprey Committee, as part of a wide-ranging review of the Australian tax system conducted amidst growing criticism of the system's inefficiency and inadequacy.[3] The Asprey Committee recommended the introduction of a broad-based VAT[4] and the abolition of the existing wholesale sales tax (WST) – a schedular tax levied on a narrow base of goods at the wholesale level.[5] The central recommendation of the Asprey Reports was that 'the weight of taxation should be shifted towards the taxation of goods and services and away from the taxation of income'.[6] The Asprey Reports sought to address equity concerns through recommending proposals to broaden the income tax base to include capital gains, strengthen estate taxes and alleviate the regressivity of the VAT through appropriate transfer provisions and adjustments to the income tax.[7]

2 A more detailed version of this history can be found in Kathryn James, 'We of the "Never Ever": The History of the Introduction of a Goods and Services Tax in Australia', *British Tax Review* (2007), 320.

3 Taxation Review Committee (Asprey), Parliament of Australia, *Full Report* (Australian Government Publishing Service, Canberra, 1975); Taxation Review Committee (Asprey), Parliament of Australia, *Preliminary Report* (1974). The recent '*Henry Review*' is the most recent broad-based review of the tax system since Asprey but was undertaken from within the Treasury rather than by an external independent committee: Commonwealth of Australia Treasury, Australia's Future Tax System Review Panel, *Australia's Future Tax System: Report to the Treasurer* (Australia's Future Tax System Review Panel: The Treasury, Canberra, 2009).

4 The Committee proposed including food and clothing in the VAT base, but excluding financial services and rent on pragmatic grounds: Taxation Review Committee (Asprey), Parliament of Australia, *Full Report* (Australian Government Publishing Service, Canberra, 1975) ch. 27, 27.23, 27.42.

5 Ibid., 27.39, 27.48. 6 Ibid., 28.9.

7 This included taking into account the regressive effect of the VAT in the setting of minimum wages: ibid., 27.23, 27.44, 27.49.

The recommendation failed to attract government support for the remainder of the decade,[8] despite the later promotion of consumption tax reform by the then Treasurer of the conservative government, John Howard.[9]

1.2 *The 1980s Draft White Paper and National Taxation Summit*

It was not long before tax reform returned to the agenda in the early 1980s. Calls for reform[10] were made in response to an economic recession; a perceived overreliance on the income tax; and concerns over rampant tax avoidance and evasion.[11]

Six months after the reelection of the Hawke Labor government, Treasury released a Draft White Paper, which canvassed three alternatives for reform[12] but

[8] While the Asprey Reports were widely criticized by the tax community, it was political delay and indifference to the Reports that ensured the recommendations were never realized. Any chance of reform was completely extinguished with the Whitlam Labor government's extraordinary demise in November 1975. The 1975 crisis arose from the Australian Senate (the upper house of the Commonwealth parliament) blocking the government's supply bills, which led to the sacking of the Whitlam government by then Governor-General Sir John Kerr on 11 November 1975 and the calling of a double dissolution election: Jack Richardson, *Resolving Deadlocks in the Australian Parliament: Research Paper 9 (2000–01)* (Department of the Parliamentary Library, Canberra, 2000); Robert Haupt, 'Asprey Tax Flop', *Australian Financial Review*, 6 June 1974, 1; Editorial, 'The Persuasive Mathews Report', *Australian Financial Review*, 30 May 1975, 2; AR Prest, 'The Australian Tax System Reviewed' *Economic Record* 51(136) (1975), 576; R. H. Wallace, 'Taxation Reform: But What Is the Agenda?', *Economic Record* 51(136) (1975), 564; P. D. Groenewegen, *Everyone's Guide to Taxation in Australia* (George Allen & Unwin, Sydney, 1985), 137–38.

[9] The main conservative political parties in Australia are the Liberal and National parties. Both parties have maintained a power-sharing coalition during the reform period. The term 'conservatives' is used in this book to refer to these parties. Howard made three unsuccessful attempts at consumption tax reform in the late 1970s: an attempt to introduce a retail sales tax (RST) in 1978 sparked a fierce scare campaign by the Retail Traders Association that attracted substantial media coverage and resulted in over 45,000 letters sent to federal members of Parliament; the discussion of consumption tax alternatives including a VAT in 1980; and efforts to expand the WST base in 1981: Commonwealth of Australia, *Parliamentary Debates*, House of Representatives, 25 February 1981, 133 (John Howard, Treasurer); P. D. Groenewegen, *Everyone's Guide to Taxation in Australia* (George Allen & Unwin, Sydney, 1985), 46–47, 242–45.

[10] By the early 1980s, politicians and commentators alike viewed the decline in tax morality as destroying the Australian tax system: John Howard, 'Taxation Reform', *Australian Tax Forum* 1 (1) (1984), 8; P. D. Groenewegen, *Everyone's Guide to Taxation in Australia* (George Allen & Unwin, Sydney, 1985), 72; John G. Head, Monash University Centre of Policy Studies and Australian Tax Research Foundation, *Taxation Issues of the 1980s: Papers presented at a Conference* (Australian Tax Research Foundation, Sydney, 1983), 15.

[11] This tax evasion was exposed by the Costigan Royal Commission into the Activities of the Federated Ship Painters and Dockers Union: Government of the Commonwealth of Australia and Government of the State of Victoria, Royal Commission on the Activities of the Federated Ship Painters and Dockers Union, *Interim Report No. 4* (Australian Government Publishing Service, Canberra, 1982); Royal Commission on the Activities of the Federated Ship Painters and Dockers Union, *Final Report* (Australian Government Printer, Canberra, 1984); Commonwealth of Australia Treasury, *Reform of the Australian Tax System: Draft White Paper* (Australian Govt Pub Service, Canberra, 1985), 1.

[12] Commonwealth of Australia Treasury, *Reform of the Australian Tax System: Draft White Paper* (Australian Govt Pub Service, Canberra, 1985), ch. 22.

promoted 'Option C'. This reform option entailed broadening the direct tax base through introducing capital gains and fringe benefits taxation (previously untaxed under the Australian income tax), plus a shift in the tax mix from income to consumption with the introduction of a retail sales tax (RST) of 12.5 per cent to replace the WST.[13]

The options for reform were debated one month later by community groups at the National Tax Summit so as to agree upon a reform agenda.[14] Agreement, however, was elusive. Business, represented by lobby groups such as the Australian Chamber of Commerce and Industry and the newly formed Business Council of Australia (BCA),[15] declared their support for a consumption tax but firmly opposed the expansion of the direct tax base.[16] Welfare and union groups were generally supportive of the expansion of the direct tax base, but opposed a consumption tax on equity grounds. A newspaper editorial at the time summarised the state of affairs: '[e]veryone complains about Option C, but no one comes up with anything better'.[17]

In the end, Treasurer Paul Keating, who had been a vocal supporter of tax reform, including the introduction of a consumption tax, was left to negotiate and announce significant albeit less ambitious reforms consisting of a watered-down capital gains tax, a fringe benefits tax and some base broadening of the WST.[18]

[13] Ibid., 242–55.

[14] Robert Hawke, 'Australian Labor Party Policy Speech' (speech delivered at the Australian Labor Party Policy Launch, Opera House, Sydney, 13 November 1984); Commonwealth of Australia Treasury, *Reform of the Australian Tax System: Draft White Paper* (Australian Govt Pub Service, Canberra, 1985), 2.

[15] The BCA is an association of chief executives from Australia's largest corporations: Business Council of Australia (2012) (bca.com.au). The Business Council of Australia (BCA) was formed in September 1983 with a view to representing the interests of Australia's 100 largest companies. The BCA was a departure from state-based, sectoral business groups. The BCA was formed in part as a response to business being left out of negotiation between the Labor government and unions over the Prices and Income Accord. The Accord involved unions agreeing to exercise wage restraint in exchange for government assurances for the maintenance of real wages through wage indexation, tax relief and the provision of universal public health services such as Medicare: Richard Eccleston, 'The Significance of Business Interest Association in Economic Policy Reform: The Case of Australian Taxation Policy', *Business and Politics* 2(3) (2000), 309, 315, 322.

[16] Commonwealth of Australia, *National Taxation Summit: Record of Proceedings* (summit held from Monday July 1 to Thursday July 4, 1985, Parliament House, Canberra, Australian Government Publishing Service), 55, 118–19, 166.

[17] 'The Curious Case of Option C', *Australian Financial Review*, 2 July 1985, 1.

[18] Reforms occurred in two stages. Stage 1 reforms also included imputation for corporate and shareholder tax, reforms to tax administration, a reduction in the number of income tax brackets, and a reduction in the top marginal rate from 60 to 49 per cent (in alignment with the company tax rate). Stage 2 occurred in May 1988 and consisted mostly of company tax reform measures, including a reduction of the company tax rate from 49 to 39 per cent (thereby undermining the tax symmetry established during the first stage): Paul Keating, *Reform of the Australian Taxation System: Statement by the Treasurer (Press Release)* (AGPS, Canberra, 19 September 1985); Cedric Sandford, *Successful Tax Reform: Lessons from an Analysis of Tax Reform in Six Countries* (Fiscal, Bath, 1993), 78–81.

1.3 *Fightback!* and the 1993 federal election

After almost a decade in office, the Labor government was plagued by leadership tensions between Prime Minister Hawke and Treasurer Keating, and was presiding over an economy in deep recession since 1991.[19]

The conservatives looked poised for election victory after reinventing themselves in April 1990 with a new and popular leader, John Hewson, a professional market economist and relative political novice. However, rather than watch a government unravel, in October 1990, Hewson embarked on a clandestine process of policy development and relied on a private economics firm, Access Economics,[20] rather than his own shadow cabinet to do so.[21] In November 1991, Hewson released *Fightback!* – a comprehensive 650-page neo-liberal economic manifesto. Its central component was a 15 per cent GST, levied on a broad base, including food, with minimal exclusions.[22]

Despite an initially favourable reception, the release of 650 pages of major tax reform halfway through an election term enabled opposition to mobilize.[23] Paul Keating succeeded Bob Hawke as prime minister on 19 December 1991, and harnessed all the political lessons of the failure to achieve broad-based consumption tax reform in 1985 to launch a 'masterful'[24] scare campaign against the GST. This was epitomised by his declaration that 'if you don't understand the GST, don't

[19] Interest rates were up to 17 percent, unemployment was at 11 percent, and there was an $11.6 billion budget deficit and record levels of foreign debt: Alan Fenna, *Australian Public Policy* (2nd ed., Pearson Education Australia, Frenchs Forest, NSW, 2004), 207–8.

[20] Access Economics was established in 1988 by two senior ex-Commonwealth Treasury officials, Geoff Carmody and David Chessell, who marketed the firm as offering the private sector access to the expert advice given to government. After merging with the local member firm of Deloitte, the firm is now known as Deloitte Access Economics and provides advice to a range of private and government clients: Deloitte Access Economics (2014) (deloitteaccesseconomics.com.au). Hewson was therefore able to gain indirect knowledge of the Treasury approach to policy-making, thus demonstrating the continuing impact of Treasury support for a consumption tax on the development of tax policy.

[21] The shadow cabinet reportedly was shown only a 10-page proposal with an 8 per cent GST before its public release: Richard Eccleston, *The Thirty Year Problem: The Politics of Australian Tax Reform* (ATRF, Sydney, 2004), 105.

[22] The resulting revenue would facilitate the abolition of a number of indirect taxes (including the WST) and provide for a 30 per cent reduction in income taxation: Liberal and National Parties of Australia, *Fightback!: The Liberal and National Parties' Plan to Rebuild and Reward Australia, 21 November 1991* (Liberal and National Parties, Canberra, 1991) 2 (hereinafter referred to as '*Fightback!*').

[23] Phillip McIntosh, 'Coalition Support Surges After Package', *Sydney Morning Herald*, 27 November 1991, 4; Robert Gottliebsen, 'Finding a Way Out of the Mess', *Business Review Weekly*, 29 November 1991, 6; Michelle Grattan, 'GST Numbers Game – A Matter of Leadership', *The Age*, 23 November 1991, 2.

[24] Neil Brooks, 'Lessons for Australia from the Canadian Experience with the GST: Don't Do It!', in B. Tran-Nam (ed.), *Tax Reform and the GST: An International Perspective* (Prospect Media, St Leonards, 1998) 109, 112.

vote for it. And if you do understand it, I know you will never vote for it'.[25] Keating promised to match *Fightback!*'s proposed personal income tax cuts without a GST.[26] He was also able to capitalize on growing opposition to *Fightback!* from unions,[27] church and welfare groups, and the occasional business sector that stood to lose from a GST, such as the tourism industry.[28] If any one individual demonstrates the limitations of the merits-based argument of the conventional approach, it is Paul Keating who, despite being convinced of the merits of broad-based consumption tax reform and the lead advocate for such reform during the 1980s, turned into its most powerful opponent in the 1990s. His reversal shows how political opportunism can easily trump merits as a motive for action.

Hewson responded to growing public opposition to reform with the release of *Fightback! II* on 18 December 1992,[29] which exempted food and childcare from the GST.[30] However, unlike Keating, Hewson's campaign performance was clumsy and awkward, as epitomised by an infamous television interview where he appeared at a loss to explain how the GST would apply to a birthday cake.[31] McAllister and Bean conclude that 'it was the GST that proved to be the most electorally damaging' issue for the conservatives during the 1993 election.[32] Labor was returned to office, and Keating relished 'the sweetest victory of all'.[33] In contrast, Hewson was left to lament the loss of the seemingly 'unlosable' election, a loss specifically attributed to the GST.[34]

25 Ibid.

26 Paul Keating, 'One Nation' (Statement by the Prime Minister, 26 February 1992).

27 The Labor campaign was supplemented by an estimated $2 million union push against the GST. Jerome Brown, 'The Tax Debate, Pressure Groups and the 1998 Federal Election', *Policy, Organisation and Society* 18 (1999), 75, 80; John Harrison and Marilyn Stretton, *The GST Debate* (originally published as *The GST Debate – A Chronology: Background Paper No. 1 1997–1998*; Updated by Marilyn Stretton to February 1999) (AGPS, Canberra, 1999).

28 Jerome Brown, 'The Tax Debate, Pressure Groups and the 1998 Federal Election', *Policy, Organisation and Society* 18 (1999), 75, 89; David Uren, 'Editor's Note', *Business Review Weekly*, 11 December 1992, 10.

29 Peter Hartcher, 'Opposition Fears GST Cost Votes', *Sydney Morning Herald*, 14 April 1992, 3; Tim Dodd, 'Coalition Will Turn to Crime in Bid to Sell Fightback! Package', *Australian Financial Review*, 29 May 1992, 7; Michael Gordon, 'Libs' GST: On Sale Again', *Sunday Age*, 19 April 1992, 1.

30 Liberal and National Parties of Australia, *Fightback! Fairness And Jobs* (Liberal and National Parties, Canberra, 1992) (referred to hereafter as '*Fightback! II*').

31 Mike Willesee, interview with John Hewson (3 March 1993). See also 'GST? It's a Piece of Cake', *Sydney Morning Herald*, 4 March 1993, 1.

32 Ian McAllister and Clive Bean, 'Electoral Politics of Economic Reform in Australia: The 1998 Election', *Australian Journal of Political Science* 35(3) (2000), 383, 388.

33 The victory was narrow, with the outcome being determined by 1500 votes across eight marginal seats: Neil Brooks, 'Lessons for Australia from the Canadian Experience with the GST: Don't Do It!', in B. Tran-Nam (ed.), *Tax Reform and the GST: An International Perspective* (Prospect Media, St Leonards, 1998), 109, 113.

34 Ian McAllister and Clive Bean, 'Electoral Politics of Economic Reform in Australia: The 1998 Election', *Australian Journal of Political Science* 35(3) (2000), 383, 388.

1.4 'A *new tax system*'

The fallout from the electoral disaster of *Fightback!* prompted the then leader of the conservatives, John Howard, to publicly abandon his career-long commitment to consumption tax reform when, in order to quell electorally damaging speculation as to the resurrection of the GST, he declared, '[t]here's no way the GST will be part of our policy. It's dead. Never ever. It's dead'.[35] Howard's 'small target' strategy secured the election of the conservatives in 1996.[36] However, the conservatives' first term in office was marred by political instability following the abandonment of election commitments upon 'discovering' a $5 billion revenue shortfall.[37] Howard hoped to use his career-long commitment to consumption tax reform to salvage his declining credibility on a range of issues and therefore, like Lazarus rising from the dead, less than three years after the 'never ever' declaration, proposed a 10 per cent GST.[38]

The resurrection was facilitated by an 'unholy'[39] alliance between the peak business association, the Australian Chamber of Commerce and Industry (ACCI), and peak welfare body, the Australian Council of Social Service (ACOSS), which both campaigned for consumption tax reform (see §2.5).[40] The government's tax reform agenda was aided by a High Court decision on 5 August 1997 that effectively prevented the states from levying indirect consumption taxes, at a loss of approximately $5 billion or 17 per cent of their revenue.[41] The government was quick to seize on the 'opportunity of the decade' to get state governments on the side of reforming the tax system by tying the GST into federal-state fiscal reform.[42]

35 Ibid.; Michelle Grattan, 'Howard Bans GST "Forever"', *The Age*, 3 May 1995, 5.

36 Australian Electoral Commission (AEC), *Members of the 38th Parliament (1996)* (27 January 2011) (aec.gov.au/Elections/federal_elections/1996/members.htm); Australian Electoral Commission, *Senators of the 38th Parliament* (27 January 2011) (aec.gov.au/Elections/federal_elections/1996/senators.htm).

37 Laura Tingle, 'Pledges Kept, Says Howard', *The Age*, 22 August 1996, 7.

38 Commonwealth of Australia, Treasury, *Tax Reform: Not a New Tax, a New Tax System: The Howard Government's Plan for a New Tax System* (AGPS, Canberra, 1998).

39 Rick Krever, 'The Political Economy of the GST: A Comment on Professor Brooks' Paper', in B. Tran-Nam (ed.), *Tax Reform and the GST: An International Perspective* (Prospect Media, St Leonards, NSW, 1998), 141, 144.

40 Whether directly or indirectly resulting from the ACOSS/ACCI campaign, public support for the GST peaked in 1997, with supporters almost doubling the number of opponents. In 1996, some polls showed supporters at 56 per cent to opponents at 37 per cent, and in 1997, 59 per cent to 31 percent: Simon Blount, 'Public Opinion and Tax Aversion in Australia', *Journal of Sociology* 36(3) (2000), 275, 279.

41 *Ha v. New South Wales* (1997), 189 CLR 465: the High Court ruled that franchise fees levied by states on licences for the sale of tobacco (and by implication petrol and alcohol) were excise duties, which could therefore be levied only by the Commonwealth under section 90 of the *Australian Constitution*.

42 Treasurer Peter Costello, quoted in Jerome Brown, 'The Tax Debate, Pressure Groups and the 1998 Federal Election', *Policy, Organisation and Society* 18 (1999), 75, 86.

The statement ('*ANTS Statement*') announcing the *A New Tax System* package ('*ANTS package*') was released on 16 August 1998 and proposed a GST levied at 10 per cent on a broad range of goods and services, including food. Forecast revenue and budget surpluses allowed for the abolition of a range of indirect taxes and for personal income tax cuts squarely targeted at middle-income earners totalling $13 billion per annum. Crucially, the public was given much less detail than *Fightback!* (the 208-page package was one-third of *Fightback!*'s size) and much less time to respond, with an election called within two weeks of the release on 30 August 1998 for 3 October 1998.[43]

The election campaign was closely contested and dominated by the issue of the GST.[44] The main feature of the Labor party's tax package was the absence of a GST.[45] Although the conservatives won office on 3 October 1998 with a 13-seat majority in the lower house, the House of Representatives,[46] they lost the two-party preferred vote 49 to 51 per cent and would still require the support of at least two non-government senators in order to pass the reforms through the Australian upper house, the Senate.[47] After a protracted and controversial period of negotiation and the failure to secure the support of one key independent Senator, Brian Harradine from Tasmania, a compromise was announced on 28 May 1999 with the Australian Democrats, a centre-left political party, which held the balance of power in the Senate. Chief among the concessions was the zero-rating of basic food and increased compensation for low-income earners.[48]

The Howard government was largely spared the electoral consequences of introducing the GST subsequent to the introduction of the tax. In its place, the electoral sword fell squarely on the Democrats who, despite deposing party leader

43 Commonwealth of Australia, Treasury, *Tax Reform: Not a New Tax, a New Tax System: The Howard Government's Plan for a New Tax System* (AGPS, Canberra, 1998) (hereafter referred to as '*ANTS Statement*'), 3–33.

44 Ian McAllister and Clive Bean, 'Electoral Politics of Economic Reform in Australia: The 1998 Election', *Australian Journal of Political Science* 35(3) (2000), 383, 390–91; Marian Simms and John Warhurst (eds.), *Howard's Agenda: The 1998 Australian Election* (UQP, St Lucia, 2000), 3.

45 Richard Eccleston, *The Thirty-Year Problem: The Politics of Australian Tax Reform* (ATRF, Sydney, 2004), 141.

46 Unlike in 1993, the GST brought the Howard government a slight electoral advantage: Ian McAllister and Clive Bean, 'Electoral Politics of Economic Reform in Australia: The 1998 Election', *Australian Journal of Political Science* 35(3) (2000), 383, 398; Marian Simms and John Warhurst, 'Editors' Introduction: The Nature and Scope of Howard's Victory', in Marian Simms and John Warhurst (eds.), *Howard's Agenda: The 1998 Australian Election* (UQP, St Lucia, 2000) 1, 8.

47 Australian Electoral Commission, *Electoral Newsfile 79: Federal Election 1998 Results Guide* (7 December 2007) (aec.gov.au/About_AEC/Publications/Newsfiles/1998/No_79.htm).

48 The compromise also included a number of other proposals, such as a significant cut in diesel fuel excise and a change in the taxation of financial supplies (see §4.3.3.4). Paul Kelly, 'Over the Line', *The Australian*, 29 May 1999, 21; Alan Mitchell, 'Inefficiencies Won't Be the End of the World', *Australian Financial Review*, 29–30 May 1999, 5 - where the author describes the excise cut as an irresponsible concession that was a 'sop to the bush'.

Meg Lees for her role in passing the *ANTS package*, have been decimated in subsequent federal elections.[49]

The introduction of the GST into Australia is undoubtedly one of Australia's most significant tax reforms in the twentieth century. However, the *ANTS package* that introduced the GST has not lived up to the grand ambitions its name implies. In response to the perennial charge of crises in the tax system, in 2009 Labor Treasurer Wayne Swan announced the establishment of a comprehensive review of the Australian tax system undertaken by the Commonwealth Treasury and led by then Treasury Secretary Ken Henry (referred to as the '*Henry Review*').[50] Despite the claims to be a 'root and branch'[51] review of the Australian tax system, in a sign of the continued political potency of the GST in Australia, the GST was excluded from the review panel's terms of reference.[52] Nevertheless, the *Henry Review* did examine the GST, and this chapter will refer to several of its findings throughout.

2 PATHWAYS TO REFORM

The introduction of the GST reveals that even when a government, convinced of the merits of the good VAT, attempts to introduce a good VAT, local conditions shape the real VAT that is ultimately realised. This section highlights the ways in which history mattered in shaping the Australian GST.

2.1 *Path-dependent framing of the merits of the GST*

Various claims were made by the conservatives in support of the introduction of the GST. The communication of these claims during the election was facilitated through the use of $15 million of public funding toward advertising the need for tax reform.[53]

In keeping with the nature of political campaigning, some of the claims were hyperbolic versions of the merits arguments given by the conventional approach but framed in a path-dependent and parochial manner. Much of the GST's virtue was presented by comparison to what it was not – namely, the WST and, to a lesser

[49] Although not solely attributable to the GST, the Democrats' demise followed, and was in some part a result of, the party's involvement in the passage of the ANTS legislation.

[50] Commonwealth of Australia Treasury, Australia's Future Tax System Review Panel, *Australia's Future Tax System: Report to the Treasurer* (Australia's Future Tax System Review Panel: The Treasury, Canberra, 2009).

[51] Commonwealth of Australia Treasury, *Australia's Future Tax System* (2011) (taxreview.treasury.gov.au/Content/Content.aspx?doc=html/home.htm).

[52] Wayne Swan, 'Australia's Future Tax System' (Media release No. 036, 13 May 2008). The Labor government also attempted to exclude consideration of the GST at a national tax forum: Colin Brinsden, 'Tax Forum – A GST-Free Zone', *The Australian* (online), 16 September 2011 (www.theaustralian.com.au/business/breaking-news/tax-forum-a-gst-free-zone/story-e6frg90f-1226138927909).

[53] Jerome Brown, 'The Tax Debate, Pressure Groups and the 1998 Federal Election', *Policy, Organisation and Society* 18 (2000), 75, 94.

extent, the income tax. The WST was labelled inefficient, complex, a cost to business and subject to multiple rates and exemptions.[54]

However, as a largely invisible tax to the consumer, these claims were not necessarily a vote winner. So, in addition, the GST was presented as a cure for all national ills. That is, the rhetoric drew on many of the more spectacular yet unsupported claims of the good VAT, and many of these more extreme claims went largely unchecked in a relatively superficial political debate.[55] The *ANTS Statement* predicted that the GST would help encourage savings, investment and work effort;[56] deliver higher economic growth and more jobs; reduce compliance costs; secure more revenue; remove the need for ad hoc tax redesign; lift the 'tax burden on our exports';[57] improve living standards;[58] make the tax system fairer and promote 'a more prosperous, more egalitarian and fairer Australian society';[59] and even 'liberate the potential of Australia's unique human and natural assets through removing the dead hand of centralised control'.[60] It was also promised that the ANTS reforms would 'reduce tax avoidance and the cash economy'[61] and simplify the tax system:[62]

> The current tax system is unnecessarily complex. Income tax legislation has grown from about 120 pages to more than 7,000 as a result of 60 years of patching and filling. Over the past fifteen years there have been over 650 different tax policy changes announced...The complexity of the tax system has resulted in over 70 percent of tax returns being handled by tax agents.

In addition to parochial appeals, the *ANTS Statement* drew on international comparisons to present Australia as an outlier in maintaining reliance on the WST:[63]

[54] ANTS Statement, 71–72.

[55] *Contra* Quiggin, who argued that the benefits of a GST 'are not as great as was once supposed. In the course of successive debates, claims that a GST would greatly enhance exports, save jobs and eliminate tax evasion have been shown to be unfounded': John Quiggin, 'Forget the GST and Focus on Real Issues', *Australian Financial Review*, 20 May 1999, 19; Neil Brooks, 'Lessons for Australia from the Canadian Experience with the GST: Don't Do It!', in B. Tran-Nam (ed.), *Tax Reform and the GST: An International Perspective* (Prospect Media, St Leonards, 1998), 109; Graeme Cooper and Richard Vann, 'Implementing the Goods and Services Tax', *Sydney Law Review* 23 (1999), 337. See also the comment of Dr Neil Warren, ATAX Studies Group, University of New South Wales:

> I mean look, people are saying that GST will solve all our ills. I mean a GST will not and I think it's a mistake to say that it's going to cure our foreign debt and create thousands of jobs. It's just not going to do that but what it is going to do is to result in a tax system which improves economic efficiency. These'll be things that are not dramatic or profound, they'll just be the small things, the things that you have to do.

Australian Broadcasting Corporation, 'Never say Never', 18 May 1998 (abc.net.au/4corners/stories/s12274.htm).

[56] ANTS Statement, 6. [57] Ibid., 3, 9, 10, 155–56.

[58] Commonwealth of Australia, *Parliamentary Debates*, House of Representatives, 2 December 1998, 1091 (Peter Costello, Treasurer).

[59] ANTS Statement, 9. [60] Ibid., 11. [61] Ibid., 150. [62] Ibid., 8, 15.

[63] Ibid., 7, 71–72.

> Australia is virtually alone in the world operating a wholesale sales tax system. Only Botswana, Ghana, Swaziland and the Solomon Islands share with Australia a persistence with this form of tax.

The importance of external validation was also reinforced through reference to the fact that Australia was one of the last OECD countries, besides the US, yet to adopt a GST.[64]

Despite the promised merits, the conservatives proposed a number of safeguards to alleviate opposition to the tax. In many ways, these safeguards were in response to perceived scepticism or rejection of the claimed merits. Public fears about the potential future growth of the GST were addressed through a promise that variations to the rate and base of the GST could be made only with the agreement of the states.[65] Although the promise is essentially meaningless from a legal perspective, because adherence to the doctrine of parliamentary sovereignty in Australia means that no parliament can bind its successors, it is not politically meaningless, as subsequent federal governments have invoked the promise as a guaranteed protection against public fears over the extension of the GST.[66] There has been no increase in the rate or significant alteration to the base of the GST since its introduction.

In order to keep the states on side, the *ANTS Statement* promised reform of the 'antiquated Commonwealth-State financial relations' by giving all revenues collected from the GST to the states.[67] The support of the states for the GST was itself the product of history, whereby a series of wartime federal government actions and constitutional decisions by the High Court effectively gave the Commonwealth exclusive de facto power to levy income taxes and exclusive de jure power to levy sales taxes to the exclusion of the states.[68] However, despite providing the

64 Ibid., 80.

65 Ibid., 16, 25, 85; Council of Australian Governments (COAG), Intergovernmental Agreement on the Reform of Commonwealth-State Financial Relations (25 June 1999).

66 Commonwealth of Australia Treasury, Australia's Future Tax System Review Panel, *Australia's Future Tax System: Report to the Treasurer* (Australia's Future Tax System Review Panel: The Treasury, Canberra, 2009), 284:

> The current GST system achieves stability of the tax base by requiring unanimous agreement between the Australian government and the States before any changes can be made to the base or rate of GST. However, while this administrative arrangement has been effective in protecting the GST tax base, it makes it difficult to make improvements to the GST, as any government has an effective veto.

67 *ANTS Statement* 5; Commonwealth of Australia, *Parliamentary Debates*, House of Representatives, 2 December 1998, 1089 (Peter Costello, Treasurer).

68 The concurrent taxing power between the Commonwealth and states under section 51(ii) of the *Australian Constitution* has been severely circumscribed by two key lines of High Court decisions. First, in 1942 the Commonwealth, in order to meet its wartime revenue needs, successfully made grants of financial assistance to the states under section 96 of the *Australian Constitution* conditional on the states abandoning their income taxes. This resulted in the Commonwealth's monopolization of income taxation: *State of South Australia v. Commonwealth (Uniform Tax Case (No. 1))* (1942) 65 CLR 373; *Victoria & New South Wales v.*

'opportunity of the decade'[69] to reform federal fiscal relations, the GST has failed to do so.[70] Although the Howard government initially labelled the GST a state tax, in 2008 the newly elected Labor government departed from this practice, so as to reflect the fact that the Commonwealth administers and collects the GST and controls the distribution of GST revenue to the states.[71] However, although labelling the GST a Commonwealth rather than state tax better reflects reality, distribution of GST revenues to the states and territories continues to be contested, particularly in light of lower and more volatile GST revenues since 2007–2008 (see §4.2). Despite a recent review of the issue, in 2013 the Labor government ruled out major reforms in the area.[72]

Commonwealth (Uniform Tax Case (No. 2)) (1957), 99 CLR 575. Second, the High Court's expansive interpretation of the Commonwealth's exclusive power to impose customs and excise duties under section 90 of the *Australian Constitution* has effectively excluded the states' levying sales taxes: see, e.g., *Ha & Lim v. New South Wales* (1997), 189 CLR 465; *Capital Duplicators Pty Ltd. v. Australian Capital Territory (No. 2)* (1993), 178 CLR 561.

69 Treasurer Peter Costello, quoted in Jerome Brown, 'The Tax Debate, Pressure Groups and the 1998 Federal Election' *Policy, Organisation and Society* 18 (1999), 75, 86.

70 Australian Associated Press, 'GST Failures the Fault of States: Costello', *CCH Tax and Accounting News Headlines*, 27 June 2006 – documenting an interview on Southern Cross Broadcasting where Treasurer Costello was reported as conceding 'that aspects of the GST had not gone according to plan, particularly when it came to the way the states and territories spent their funds'. He stated that:

> The GST was a success, what was a failure was that giving the revenue to the states was designed to give the states a growth revenue. . .My great hope in doing that was that with this increasing revenue, (the states) could plan long term. . .They would be more able to operate like independent governments and take responsibilities in particular areas and you wouldn't have this overlap and I don't think that has been a success.

71 Council of Australian Governments (COAG), *Intergovernmental Agreement on the Reform of Commonwealth-State Financial Relations* (25 June 1999). Commonwealth of Australia Treasury, *Budget Paper No. 1: Budget Strategy and Outlook 2008–09, Statement 5: Revenue* (Commonwealth of Australia Treasury, Canberra, 2009), 5–26–5–27, 'Box 5: Reporting the GST as an Australian Government Tax'. The Commonwealth collects the GST and distributes GST revenues to the states (less the administrative cost of collection). The Commonwealth Grants Commission makes recommendations in relation to the distribution of funding according to a specified funding formula: *Federal Financial Relations Act 2009* (Cth); Julie P. Smith, *Taxing Popularity: The Story of Taxation in Australia* (rev. edn., ATRF, Canberra, 2004). The GST Administration subcommittee coordinates GST policy-making among the relevant Commonwealth and state bodies: Commonwealth of Australia Treasury, *Australia's Future Tax System Review Panel, Architecture of Australia's Tax and Transfer System* (Commonwealth of Australia Treasury, Canberra, 2008), 54. A state and territory representative is present on every key Australian Taxation Office committee associated with the administration of the GST: Michael D'Ascenzo, 'The Australian Approach to GST Administration', in R. Krever and D. White (eds.), *GST in Retrospect and Prospect* (Thomson Brookers, Wellington, 2007), 389, 398.

72 Jonathan Barrett and Mathew Dunckley, 'Treasury Boss Slams Door on GST Reform', *Australian Financial Review*, 29 January 2013, 1; Commonwealth of Australia Government, *GST Distribution Review Final Report* (Australian Govt Pub Service, Canberra, October 2012). This followed from an abandoned attempt by the Commonwealth government to retain one-third of GST revenue to fund healthcare reforms. See Council of Australian Governments,

2.2 *Drafting the GST*

Mindful of the mistakes of *Fightback!*, the government carefully stage-managed the ANTS reform process.[73] A parallel process of policy development was adopted. The first established a Tax Consultative Task Force,[74] which consisted of government backbenchers and consulted the public through largely private hearings 'apart from the odd photo opportunity to showcase its role'.[75] Despite receiving 600 submissions, it made no policy recommendations, as its role was to simply summarise public opinion on the GST. Its report was handed to the Treasurer in February 1998, but never publicly released.

The real locus of policy development fell to the Tax Reform Task Force (the '*Task Force*'), established in 1997, consisting mostly of a select group of elite bureaucrats from the Treasury, Australian Taxation Office (ATO) and Department of Prime Minister and Cabinet.[76]

There is little doubt that those who played a key role in the design of the GST were influenced by the merits of the good VAT, as outlined by the conventional approach. First, the *Task Force* was charged with implementing the *ANTS package* that the conservatives had taken to the election. The package itself was very much the path-dependent product of the previous *Fightback!* package developed by the 'GST Planning and Coordination Office' of the Liberal party (known as the Cole Committee), which had studied a number of real VATs[77] and developed a best-practice approach to VAT design.[78] Second, the head of the *Task Force*, Ken

National Health and Hospitals Network Agreement (April 2010) (federalfinancialrelations.gov.au/content/other_related_agreements/NHHN_Agreement.pdf).

73 Australian Broadcasting Corporation, 'Never say Never', 18 May 1998 www.abc.net.au/4corners/stories/s12274.htm).

74 The Tax Consultative Task Force was headed by Senator Brian Gibson: Richard Eccleston, *The Thirty-Year Problem: The Politics of Australian Tax Reform* (ATRF, Sydney, 2004), 134.

75 Australian Broadcasting Corporation, 'Never say Never', 18 May 1998 www.abc.net.au/4corners/stories/s12274.htm).

76 Paul Cleary, 'Treasury's Role in the GST 'Nightmare on Main Street'', *Australian Financial Review*, 12 July 1999, 1, 19. The *Task Force* was based in the Treasury and consisted of two advisers to Treasurer Peter Costello, two Department of Prime Minister and Cabinet advisers, an ATO adviser and David Tune – the only line department representative seconded from the Department of Community Services. The *Task Force* also utilised the skills of a number of consultants.

77 Notably, Canada, New Zealand, South Africa and the United Kingdom: Graeme Cooper and Richard Vann, 'Implementing the Goods and Services Tax', *Sydney Law Review* 23 (1999), 337, 340.

78 The Cole Committee consisted of a Board and Technical Subcommittee and was staffed by a number of tax experts: ibid. Although the report of the committee was never publicly released, McCarthy observes that many of the Cole Committee's recommendations can be seen in our GST law today: Denis McCarthy, 'The Australian GST – Why It Is the Way It Is and Where To from Here?' in C. Peacock (ed.), *GST in Australia: Looking Forward from the First Decade* (Thomson Reuters, Sydney, 2011), 61, 62.

Henry, was a former Treasury representative to the OECD and was described at the time of the introduction of the *ANTS package* as a 'hard-line economic purist'.[79] Third, input into the development of the package was strictly limited. The *Task Force* retained an exclusive hold on the development of the *ANTS package*, even bypassing the ordinary Cabinet procedures of generating a Cabinet submission for other departments to respond to.[80] The *Task Force* consulted only with senior Government Ministers[81] and occasionally with business. Finally, the commitment by the *Task Force* to the good VAT was reflected in the attempts to start with a very broad base in the original *ANTS package* and the original ANTS legislation. The *Task Force* was intent on implementing the GST through adopting a plain-English 'principles-based' drafting style, so as to give effect to the policy intent of the GST.[82]

Business had urged policy-makers to adopt 'off-the-shelf' models for the GST. These off-the-shelf models were of real VATs from other jurisdictions, namely New Zealand and Canada. In a statement of how local institutions and history affect the reception of any policy instrument, regardless of merits, the ATO's deputy commissioner for the GST, Rick Matthews, stated during the policy development of the GST that it 'was not possible to take legislation "off the shelf" from New Zealand or Canada because their design, tax policies and business environments were different'.[83]

Nevertheless, §2.3 and §2.4 will show how the strong commitment of policy-makers to introduce the good VAT resulted in unintended real VAT outcomes.

2.3 *Constitutional constraints and the exclusion of food*

Australian policy-makers endorsed the good VAT and therefore included food in the original *ANTS package*.[84] Given that Australia does not have a good VAT (despite the desire of policy-makers to introduce one), and given that the exclusion

79 Paul Cleary, 'Treasury's Role in the GST "Nightmare on Main Street"', *Australian Financial Review*, 12 July 1999, 1, 19.

80 Ibid.

81 Richard Eccleston, *The Thirty-Year Problem: The Politics of Australian Tax Reform* (ATRF, Sydney, 2004), 134.

82 The Tax Law Improvement Project (TLIP) was underway at the time of the reforms and undertook to rewrite tax legislation from a plain-English principles-based perspective: Commonwealth Office of Parliamentary Counsel, *Tax Law Improvement Project Building the New Tax Law (Information Paper* No. *2)* (April 1995).

83 Paul Cleary and Fiona Buffini, 'GST: Business Hits Delays', *Australian Financial Review*, 25 October 1999, 1, 4, 4.

84 *ANTS Statement* 92–95. The dissatisfaction with the exclusion of food was recently expressed by the *Henry Review*:

> [W]hile the proportion of income spent on GST-free food does fall with income, absolute actual expenditure on GST-free food is almost six times greater for the highest than the lowest income groups. Among food categories, expenditure only on powdered milk, canned meat and offal actually falls with income. As a result, more than one-third of the $5 billion exemption for GST-free food benefits households in the highest

of food is one of the most high-profile departures from the good VAT, it is useful to consider how this real VAT outcome came about.

The standard account of how Australia came to exclude basic food from the base of the GST is that it arose from the need to compromise with the Australian Democrats to pass the reforms through the Senate. While it might be tempting to view this as the product of a unique series of events, closer examination of the political institutions of the Australian federal state reveal that, although the exact outcome might not have been predicted, the outcome was the result of a relatively stable pattern of institutional trends.

The preferential voting system and distribution of electoral seats in the lower house, the House of Representatives, meant that, although losing the popular vote, the conservatives won enough votes in enough seats to win office in the 1998 federal election.[85] However, this was not the case for the upper house, the Senate, where members serve six-year terms with only half due for reelection during each three-year electoral cycle.[86] Since the introduction of proportional representation to the Senate in 1949,[87] the government has rarely controlled the Senate.[88] This lack of government control has meant that the Senate has, to some extent, evolved to become a chamber of review. In addition, the constitutional requirement that each state have an equal number of representatives in the Senate[89] has meant that representatives from smaller states have tended to exercise disproportionate influence. Perhaps none has done more so in recent times than Senator Brian Harradine from Tasmania – one of the key independent Senators whose support the conservatives needed in order to pass the ANTS reforms.

Given Australia's adversarial two-party political system and Labor's continued opposition to the GST after the election, it was not surprising that the government would need to negotiate the ANTS *package* through the Senate. The fact that the Democrats had held the balance of power in the Senate at various stages since the party's formation in 1977 suggests that it was not even particularly surprising

20 percent of the income distribution. These sorts of exemptions add significantly to the complexity of the GST.

Commonwealth of Australia Treasury, Australia's Future Tax System Review Panel, *Australia's Future Tax System: Report to the Treasurer* (Australia's Future Tax System Review Panel: The Treasury, Canberra, 2009), 286 (citations omitted).

85 Australian Electoral Commission, *Electoral Newsfile 79: Federal Election 1998 Results Guide* (7 December 2007) (aec.gov.au/About_AEC/Publications/Newsfiles/1998/No_79.htm). The Commonwealth Parliament is bicameral. The lower house, the House of Representatives, consists of members of parliament drawn from single-member electorates elected every three years by a preferential voting system. The House is strongly majoritarian and adversarial and has been overwhelmingly dominated by two major political groupings – the conservatives (the current incarnation being the Liberal and National Coalition) and the Australian Labor Party (ALP).

86 Australian Constitution, s 7.

87 *Commonwealth Electoral Act 1918* (Cth).

88 Parliament of Australia, *About the Senate* (www.aph.gov.au/About_Parliament/Senate/About_the_Senate).

89 Australian Constitution, s 7.

that, after failing to obtain the support of independent Senators, a deal would need to be made with the Democrats.

The tight grip needed to develop the good VAT in the original *ANTS package* began to unravel as the reforms passed through the Senate. The government was forced to compromise and a number of Senate committees were established to investigate various aspects of the reforms.[90] The scrutiny that the government had tried to avoid during the election campaign came during the hearings of these Senate committees. As one reporter saw it at the time:[91]

> the Howard Government is now paying the price for running a slick advertising campaign and not providing sufficient time for community consultation on its goods and services tax reform package when it was released last year. It was smart tactics in the run-up to the federal election, but it gave weight to Labor and the minor parties' demands for more scrutiny of the package in the Senate. The Senate Committee received 1544 submissions in just four months, demonstrating just how much community and business interest and concern there is.

The Senate Select Committee on the GST revealed the negative distributional consequences of the government's package and highlighted dubious Treasury modelling that had been suppressed during the election campaign.[92] It was shown, for example, that even under generous assumptions, social security recipients would be only 1.5 per cent better off after compensation, and that the benefits offered by compensation for pensioners would phase out after three to four years.[93] This fed into a key concern of many within the welfare sector that compensation was not just insufficient, but that compensation would not last.[94] In his famous 'I cannot' speech, declaring his decision not to support the introduction of a GST, the independent Tasmanian Senator Brian Harradine stated that:[95]

> The government's genuine attempt to compensate and to lock in that compensation is something to be commended, but it cannot be guaranteed. But one thing can be guaranteed, and that is that the goods and services tax, once enshrined in

90 Four Senate committees examined the reforms, the most high profile being the Senate Select Committee on a New Tax System, which considered the recommendations of all other committees: Commonwealth of Australia, Senate Select Committee on a New Tax System, *Main Report* (Parliament of the Commonwealth of Australia, Canberra, 1999); Thomson Reuters 'Senate Tax Reform/GST Inquiries' (8 February 1999) *Weekly Tax Bulletin* (5).

91 Louise Dodson, 'Focus on Scoring Points', *Australian Financial Review*, 20 April 1999, 9.

92 The committee received 1544 submissions and conducted 23 public hearings. The resulting report was more than 500 pages: Commonwealth of Australia, Senate Select Committee on a New Tax System, *Main Report* (Parliament of the Commonwealth of Australia, Canberra, 1999), ch. 2, ch. 4.

93 This caused Professor Ann Harding, a key welfare advocate who supported the GST on food, to abandon her support for the *ANTS package*: Paul Cleary, 'Treasury's Role in the GST "Nightmare on Main Street"', *The Australian Financial Review*, 12 July 1999, 1, 19.

94 Sean Alymer, 'Compensation Too Low', *Australian Financial Review*, 20 April 1999, 8–9.

95 Commonwealth of Australia, *Parliamentary Debates*, Senate, 14 May 1999, 5516 (Brian Harradine).

> legislation, will never be removed. Decisions we make now on this issue are not for the next three years; we are making decisions here that will affect generations. The question that I have to ask myself is whether I am going to be a party to imposing an impersonal, indiscriminate tax on my children, my grandchildren and their children for generations to come. I cannot.

The Democrats had borrowed the idea to exclude basic food from Ireland and supported the exclusion as 'the best and permanent way to compensate families for the adverse effects of a GST'.[96] Indeed, those who lobbied for and won the GST-free treatment of basic food did correctly predict that the compensation package designed to ensure no one would be worse off would in fact be changed by future governments.[97] Whereas changes to the base and rate of the GST are politically difficult although legally insignificant (requiring the consent of all state and territory governments),[98] compensation arrangements are easily changed.

That the conservatives were forced to retreat from their idea of the good VAT and remove basic food despite Prime Minister Howard declaring that such a move would 'represent a gutting of the package'[99] might, as Smith contends, reflect a 'deep historical antipathy in Australia towards taxing the "necessities of life"'.[100] Alternatively, it might simply be an instance of path dependence. The conservatives' reincarnated *Fightback! II* had excluded basic food after much public opposition.[101] The WST itself had only ever taxed luxury (not basic) food.[102] Indeed, the ANTS legislation was 'loosely based on some of the food categories used under the...[pre-existing] wholesale sales tax system'.[103]

[96] Meg Lees, 'Democrats' Recipe', *Australian Financial Review*, 30 April 1999, 41, in which Meg Lees defends the Irish model of zero-rating basic food because 17 out of 23 OECD countries do so and quotes Cedric Sandford as stating that, in relation to the British VAT, the compliance cost of dealing with GST-free food causes relatively few problems. Press reports at the time suggest that the food compromise was suggested by Senator Andrew Murray. This was initially opposed by Meg Lees, who wanted a broader exclusion: Paul Cleary 'Hard-Nosed Democrat Who Saved the GST', *Australian Financial Review* (20 May 1999), 27; Thomson Reuters, 'Democrats Favour "Irish" Model – Zero-Rate Basic Food' (21 April 1999) *GST News Alert* (2).

[97] Michael Evans, 'The Value Added Tax Treatment of Real Property – An Antipodean Context', in R. Krever and D. White (ed.), *GST in Retrospect and Prospect* (Brookers, Wellington, NZ, 2007), 243.

[98] Council of Australian Governments (COAG), Intergovernmental Agreement on the Reform of Commonwealth-State Financial Relations (25 June 1999).

[99] Louise Dodson, 'Catholic Doctrine Bone of GST Dissent', *Australian Financial Review* (7 May 1999), 41.

[100] Alan Kohler quoting Julie Smith: Alan Kohler, 'Tax That Goes against the Tide of History', *Australian Financial Review* (5–6 June 1999), 27.

[101] See §1.3 of this chapter.

[102] *Sales Tax (Exemptions and Classifications) Act 1992* (Cth), sch 1.

[103] Louise Dodson, 'Push to Reduce GST Avoidance', *Australian Financial Review* (18 June 1999), 5.

2.4 *Legislation by regulation*

In avoiding the political mistakes of *Fightback!*, the strategy employed by the conservatives in order to win the 1998 federal election was to release only broad-brush detail of the ANTS *package*, with very little time before the election. This meant that there was much detail to fill in after the election. In a short three-year electoral cycle, changes had to be bedded down quickly, so as to avoid the conservatives losing power at the following election.

Consistent with the implementation of major legislative reform, the ANTS *package* experienced various transitional problems and was subject to numerous amendments – many occurring between the date of enactment on 8 July 1999 and the date of operation on 1 July 2000.[104] However, because this process of implementation was set alongside fierce negotiations to obtain political support for the package to pass through the parliament, there were many opportunities for change. While some of these changes were costly and high profile, such as the exclusion of basic food from the tax base (see §2.3), others were costly but barely rated on the public radar, such as the introduction of the reduced input tax credit in relation to financial supplies (see §4.3.3.4).

One notable feature of the ANTS legislation is the extent to which key provisions are contained in regulations. The move to legislate through regulations was partly in response to the rapid implementation of the tax[105] as well as the intense political deal-making and lobbying that accompanied the introduction of the tax. A press report at the time suggests that the move to legislate by regulation was motivated by a desire on the part of the government not only to amend legislation more easily but also to retain the appearance of simplicity: 'the Treasurer, Peter Costello, confirmed this week that he wanted to keep the detail out of legislation and only put in "broad objectives".'[106]

[104] Those changes intended to clarify core issues or deal with unintended consequences were retrospective in operation and dated back to 1 July 2000. Those changes not designed to deal with unintended consequences were prospective in operation: Ken Fehily, 'Residential Premises', in C. Peacock (ed.), *GST in Australia: Looking Forward from the First Decade* (Thomson Reuters, Sydney, 2011), 201, 203; Richard Krever, *GST Legislation Plus* (Thomson Reuters, Pyrmont, 2014), iii; Fiona Buffini, 'Brace for GST Amendments Galore', *Australian Financial Review* (17–18 July 1999), 4. On 25 October 1999, the Australian Financial Review reported that '[u]p to 1,000 new amendments are expected on top of the 454 tabled last week…' Paul Cleary and Fiona Buffini, 'GST: Business Hits Delays', *Australian Financial Review*, 25 October 1999, 1, 4.

[105] Initially, 16 bills were introduced on 2 December 1998 to introduce the ANTS reforms. These bills underwent significant amendment to secure the passage of the bills through parliament and to address a range of issues not foreseen in the original drafting. The main Acts and Regulations relating to the GST include *A New Tax System (Goods and Services Tax) Act 1999* (Cth) (hereafter referred to as '*ANTS Act 1999*') and *A New Tax System (Goods and Services Tax Administration) Act 1999* (Cth). The main regulations are contained in *A New Tax System (Goods and Services Tax) Regulations 1999* (Cth) (hereafter referred to as '*ANTS Regulations 1999*'). The more than 50 hours spent debating the reforms in the Senate set a record at the time: Thomson Reuters, 'GST Debate Sets Records', *GST News Alert* (49) (29 June 1999).

[106] Paul Cleary, 'The McDonald's Amendment', *Australian Financial Review* (4 June 1999), 41.

As a result, key provisions dealing with controversial issues and the subject of fierce lobbying were buried in regulations where they would attract far less parliamentary and public scrutiny. Although either house of parliament can disallow regulations, the complexity and length of the provisions in question meant that in practice the capacity for scrutiny was not the same as it would have been for legislation requiring passage through both houses.

The substantive provisions relating to food and financial supplies were moved into either the schedules to the primary Act (*ANTS Act 1999*) or the regulations (*ANTS Regulations 1999*) and very quickly abandoned the pretence of principles-based drafting. Instead, the provisions bore greater resemblance to the narrow and schedular drafting of the WST.[107] It was clear that, despite the *Task Force*'s commitment to the good VAT, the merits of the good VAT would not win the day.[108]

2.5 *Lobbying and the divergent fates of the 'unholy alliance'*

As has frequently been highlighted, the alliance between the peak welfare group, ACOSS, and the peak business group, ACCI, was a key factor in returning the GST to the policy agenda. Commentators have pointed to individuals such as Graeme Samuel, the then head of ACCI, and Robert Fitzgerald, the then head of ACOSS, as playing a 'catalytic role'[109] in bringing about GST reform. The general contention is that these key individuals and interest groups learned from previous failed instances of reform and, through a process of self-reflexive policy learning, reassessed their approach to consumption tax reform.[110] Samuel, for example, believed that it was the failure of *Fightback!* to secure support from the welfare sector that led to the demise of the reforms.[111] However, few have sought to either

107 'There is now substantial reliance on non-legislative mechanisms, which is a change and more along the line of what happens in the UK than in New Zealand': Michael Evans, KPMG partner, quoted in Fiona Buffini, 'Brace for GST Amendments Galore', *Australian Financial Review* (17–18 July 1999), 4.

108 'It is also notable that the purity of the. . .GST model was relatively quickly tarnished with a series of significant changes to the original draft of the GST law. In particular, the decision to move the financial supply provisions from the GST Act to the GST Regulations. . .': Denis McCarthy, 'The Australian GST – Why It Is the Way It Is and Where To from Here?' in C. Peacock (ed.), *GST in Australia: Looking Forward from the First Decade* (Thomson Reuters, Sydney, 2011), 61, 64.

109 Richard Eccleston, *Taxing Reforms* (Edward Elgar, Cheltenham, 2007), 182.

110 Ibid., 130, 181; Simon Blount, 'The Politics of Taxation: The Introduction of the GST into New Zealand, Canada, Japan and Australia', *Australian Tax Forum* 16(4) (2001), 439, 441.

111 Graeme Samuel, who was also the treasurer of the Victorian Liberal Party from 1989 to 1992, stated that:

> There's a sort of an accepted wisdom around that Fightback was sold poorly. In fact I think that the Opposition as it was then did an extraordinarily good job of selling a very, very complex package. But it was a package that had some flaws in it. It was a package that had particular flaws when one focussed upon certain sectors of the

explain the historical impetus for the alliance or examine the fate of each sector since the introduction of the GST.[112]

Given the perception of the GST as a regressive tax, the support of welfare groups might be seen as surprising. By OECD standards, Australia is a low-tax state.[113] Tax revenue has hovered around 25 per cent of GDP from 1965 to 2010, placing it consistently about 5 per cent below the OECD average.[114] Welfare spending in Australia is highly targeted. Starved of funding from a revenue shortfall and a corresponding decline in government spending following the 1991 recession, welfare groups needed to focus on ways to *locate* as opposed to *distribute* revenue.[115] Placed in this invidious position, ACOSS opted to support the push by business for a GST on the promise of its revenue-raising potential.

Critically, ACOSS had made its support for the GST contingent on there being no shift in the tax mix (from income to consumption), no undermining of progressivity and there being adequate revenue to support the poor.[116] By contrast, the preference of the conservative government was to facilitate a shift in the tax mix from an income to a consumption tax base.[117] Following its introduction, the GST

> community that vigorously opposed it and of course the welfare sector vigorously opposed it as did the union movement.

Australian Broadcasting Corporation, 'Never say Never', 18 May 1998 (www.abc.net.au/4corners/stories/s12274.htm). See also Sally Neighbour, the reporter from the same program, who stated that:

> The Welfare Lobby's agenda is to shore up the tax base to protect health, social security and other services. Welfare's support is crucial to avoid a damaging campaign against the Government's package. But the strains of reconciling their conflicting interests are showing.

112 Jerome Brown, 'The Tax Debate, Pressure Groups and the 1998 Federal Election', *Policy, Organisation and Society* 18 (1999), 75. Eccleston contends that the formation of a 'cross-class coalition for tax reform' as was represented by the ACCI/ACOSS alliance was essential to the achievement of GST reform in Australia. However, Eccleston's public policy analysis stops at the point of introduction of the GST and, as a result, misses some key underlying and ongoing trends: Richard Eccleston, *Taxing Reforms* (Edward Elgar, Cheltenham, 2007), ch. 3 and at 182.

113 Dick Warburton and Peter Hendy, *International Comparisons of Australia's Taxes*, Commonwealth of Australia Treasury (2006), xv.

114 In 2011, tax revenue to GDP was 26.5 per cent in Australia, compared to an OECD average of 34.1. The lowest tax-to-GDP ratio in Australia over the period 1965–2010 was 20.6 in 1965, and the highest tax-to-GDP ratio was 30.4 in 2000: OECD, *Revenue Statistics: 1965–2012* (OECD Publishing, Paris, 2013) 24. See Chapter 5, §4.1 of this book.

115 Rick Krever, 'The Political Economy of the GST: A Comment on Professor Brooks' Paper', in B. Tran-Nam (ed.), *Tax Reform and the GST: An International Perspective* (Prospect Media, St Leonards, NSW, 1998), 141, 144; Australian Broadcasting Corporation, 'Never say Never', 18 May 1998 (www.abc.net.au/4corners/stories/s12274.htm); Richard Eccleston, *Taxing Reforms* (Edward Elgar, Cheltenham, 2007), 181.

116 ACOSS, *Tax Reform Pack* (ACOSS, Strawberry Hills NSW, 1997).

117 Peter Costello – 'as a general principle I think that the Australian tax system would be better if it taxed consumption more than earnings': Australian Broadcasting Corporation, 'Never say Never', 18 May 1998 (www.abc.net.au/4corners/stories/s12274.htm).

facilitated a partial change in the tax mix.[118] Once the valuable political commodity of their support for a GST had been obtained, ACOSS was effectively frozen out of the policy development process. During the drafting of the package, Robert Fitzgerald of ACOSS complained that 'if we're having a tax reform debate, why is everything happening behind closed doors?'[119] Whereas substantial revenue gains enabled the Howard government to enact a number of provisions mostly in favour of high-income taxpayers,[120] other proposals to broaden the tax base that would target this taxpaying group, such as taxing trusts as companies, were abandoned.[121] By contrast, ACOSS complained that the interaction of the tax system and restrictive welfare provisions left unemployed and low-income earners facing effective marginal tax rates of up to 78 percent.[122]

ACOSS repeatedly called upon business representatives following the release of the *ANTS package* to push for a fairer package. However, in stark contrast to the inclusive approach used to obtain welfare support for a GST, these calls went largely unheeded.[123] Former Democrat Senator Andrew Bartlett bluntly sums up the

[118] John Freebairn, 'Changing the Tax Mix', *Australian Economic Review* 40(2) (2007), 194, 198–99. The relative share of income tax revenue as a percentage of the total Commonwealth taxation revenue fell from 77 per cent to 71 per cent from 1999–2000 to 2004–2005, matched by a corresponding rise in consumption tax revenue from 22 to 28 per cent over the same period: Australian Bureau of Statistics, 5506.0 – *Taxation Revenue, Australia*, 2004–05 (ABS, Canberra, 2006), 9. However, the flattening of GST revenues with the 2008 economic downturn has, in part, arrested this shift, rather than any deliberate policy effort. The Commonwealth Treasury notes that 'tax receipts as a proportion of GDP have moved in a relatively small range over the last two decades. Sales taxes have expanded with the introduction of GST in 2000, while total individuals' income taxes fell': Commonwealth of Australia Treasury, *Pocket Guide to the Australian Tax System* (Treasury, Canberra, 2013), 6.

[119] Australian Broadcasting Corporation, 'Never say Never', 18 May 1998 (www.abc.net.au/4corners/stories/s12274.htm).

[120] For example, the top marginal personal income tax rate was reduced from 47 per cent in 1999 to 45 per cent in 2006, while the threshold at which this top marginal rates commenced was increased from $50,000 to $180,000 in 2008. Other reforms included the introduction of concessional taxation of capital gains: Commonwealth of Australia Treasury, *Pocket Guide to the Australian Tax System* (Treasury, 2006), Table 1; Commonwealth of Australia Treasury, *Budget Overview* (Treasury, Canberra, 2007).

[121] *ANTS Statement*, 113–21; Commonwealth of Australia Treasury, *Historical Material: Entity Taxation – Taxing Trusts Like Companies Overview* (4 April 2001) (archive.treasury.gov.au/contentitem.asp?ContentID=454). The *Australian Financial Review* reported that '[f]ollowing a public outcry, the government has changed its plan to tax cash management trusts as companies and indicated that these investments will be subject to flow-through treatment. . .income will be taxed in hands of investors': 'The GST Guide for Business', *Australian Financial Review* (28 June 1999), 7.

[122] ACOSS, Taxation in Australia: Home Truths and International Comparison (Information Paper 347) (ACOSS, Strawberry Hills NSW, 2003). More recent studies show that Australia maintains a high effective marginal tax rate for various types of low-income earners: see, e.g., Commonwealth of Australia Treasury, Australia's Future Tax System Review Panel, *Consultation Paper* (Commonwealth of Australia Treasury, Canberra, 2008), §4.5.

[123] Louise Dodson, 'ACOSS Appeals to Business', *Australian Financial Review* (30 April 1999), 9. Business groups were largely and overwhelmingly supportive of the *ANTS package*:

sentiment of the welfare sector: 'business got in the cart with the welfare lobby so they could get the cart started, and once they got enough speed up, they said, 'Thanks for the ride.'[124] ACOSS later withdrew its support for reform when it judged that its criteria for supporting reform were not adequately met by the ANTS *package*.[125] However, by this time, the political value of their support had all but expired.

After the GST was introduced, recriminations abounded as to who was responsible for bringing about the unhappy result of a GST excluding basic food. Both business and the government blamed each other for taking too hard line a stance on the GST. Business blamed the government, in particular Prime Minister Howard,, Treasurer Costello and the Treasury, for alienating the welfare lobby,[126] taking a 'miserly'[127]

Helen Trinca and AAP, 'Delivers the Goods, Serves Business Well', *The Sydney Morning Herald* (14 August 1998), 12.

[124] Senator Andrew Murray, who was a key Democrat negotiator, claimed that the big business lobby was 'captured by ideologues who are utterly inflexible in their approach': Lenore Taylor, 'No Business of the Democrats', *Australian Financial Review*, 18. Commenting on the business lobby's approach to the GST, Murray claimed that (at 18):

> If you look at it like a sports match, the first half they played magnificently, they tried for a broad consensus to get the issue on the agenda, but then the Government came to its position, they just fell in behind and showed absolutely no flexibility. . .If they just fall in behind the government of the day, they begin to look like just an extension of the Liberal Party.

[125] Jerome Brown, 'The Tax Debate, Pressure Groups and the 1998 Federal Election', *Policy, Organisation and Society* 18 (1999), 75, 89; ACOSS, *Tax Reform Pack* (ACOSS, Strawberry Hills NSW, 1997); John Warhurst, Jerome Brown and Rohan Higgins, 'Tax Groupings: The Group Politics of Taxation Reform', in Marian Simms and John Warhurst (eds.), *Howard's Agenda: The 1998 Australian Election* (UQP, St Lucia, 2000), 170; John Harrison and Marilyn Stretton, *The GST Debate* (originally published as *The GST Debate – A Chronology: Background Paper* No. 1 1997–1998; updated by Marilyn Stretton to February 1999) (AGPS, Canberra, 1999). For studies on incidence and inequality during the period of the ANTS reforms, see Neil Warren, 'A Review of Studies on the Distributional Impact of Consumption Taxes in OECD Countries' (Social, Employment and Migration Working Paper No. 64, OECD, 2008), 36, 57, 58; Ann Harding, Rachel Lloyd and Neil Warren, 'GST and the Changing Incidence of Australian Taxes: 1994–95 to 2001–2002', *eJournal of Tax Research* 3 (1) (2005), 114; Australian Bureau of Statistics, 6537.0 – *Government Benefits, Taxes and Household Income 2003–2004* (ABS, Canberra, 2006), Table 5; John Creedy, 'The GST and Vertical, Horizontal and Reranking Effects of Indirect Taxation in Australia', *Australian Economic Review* 35(4) (2002), 380: this early study found, on most measures, that the GST led to a slight increase in inequality; Joan R. Rodgers, Peter Siminski and James Bishop, 'Changes in Poverty Rates during the Howard Era', *Australian Economic Review* 42(3) (2009), 300, 314; ACOSS, *Indicators of Inequality Fact Sheet* (ACOSS, 27 March 2011), 1–7.

[126] Paul Cleary and Steve Lewis, 'Hail the New Powerbrokers', *Australian Financial Review* (29–30 May 1999), 4, noting that the Democrats were 'scarred by their treatment at the hands of the Government during the Senate inquiry' and that the Labor party, Greens and 'left' groups were urging the Democrats not to pass the GST.

[127] Paul Cleary, 'Treasury's Role in the GST "Nightmare on Main Street"', *Australian Financial Review* (12 July 1999), 1, 19.

approach to compensation,[128] and not adequately addressing concerns over the GST's perceived regressivity. Criticisms were made of the generous tax cuts (especially to high-income earners), which both fuelled concern over a tax mix switch and contributed to the perceived inadequacy of the compensation by reducing the pool of available funds.[129]

Although unhappy with the exclusion of food, in contrast to welfare groups, business otherwise went from strength to strength during and after the GST reforms. Over the reform period, business lobbyists went from division, fragmentation and parochialism to adopt a largely united front to advocate for GST reform and employed a range of sophisticated lobbying strategies to support their reform agenda.[130] Key to business support for the GST was a perception by business that the GST was not a cost borne by business.[131] However, the business community encompasses many different actors with different and sometimes conflicting preferences. What the introduction of the Australian GST shows is that while business support for reform need not necessarily be uniform, it helps if the most powerful sectors get behind reform.[132] Australia has a small domestic economy and is therefore heavily export dependent. As one of the least industrialized countries in

[128] Louise Dodson, Steve Lewis and Kath Cummins, 'Business Takes Hard Line on GST', *Australian Financial Review* (25 May 1999), 1; Thomson Reuters, 'Small Business Ups Ante over GST without Food', *GST News Alert* (25) (25 May 1999); Steve Lewis and Mark Davis, 'Business Groups at Odds over Scope of Tax', *Australian Financial Review* (20 May 1999), 5; Thomson Reuters, 'Business Eats Its Words on GST', *GST News Alert* (22) (20 May 1999).

[129] Alan Kohler, 'Tax That Goes against the Tide of History', *Australian Financial Review* (5–6 June 1999), 27; Thomson Reuters, 'Business to Urge Income Tax', *GST News Alert* (24) (24 May 1999); Paul Cleary, 'Tax Avoidance Rules Loosen Up', *Sydney Morning Herald*, 23 April 1999, 2.

[130] Helen Trinca and AAP, 'Delivers the Goods, Serves Business Well', *Sydney Morning Herald*, 14 August 1998, 12.

[131] For example, tax adviser Alan Smolak was reported as stating that the 'GST is a flow through expense rather than a cost which sticks. "While it might cause some companies a bit of administrative angst over the short term, I doubt whether it will create any long-term structural or ongoing problems"': John Wasiliev, 'The Full Bite of the GST', *Australian Financial Review* (5–6 June 1999), 29, 30; The *ANTS Statement* provided that 'tax will be collected only on the value added by each business in the production and distribution chain, with the tax being ultimately paid by the final consumer': *ANTS Statement* 80; the Explanatory Memorandum noted that the 'GST is effectively a tax on final private consumption in Australia': Explanatory Memorandum, a New Tax System (Goods and Services Tax) Bill 1998 (Cth) (referred to hereinafter as 'EM ANTS Bill 1998'), 6. The EM further noted that 'GST is effectively borne by consumers when they acquire anything to consume. . .GST is remitted by suppliers who make supplies in carrying on their enterprise. Suppliers do not bear the GST because the tax is included in the price of what they supply': at 6. *Contra* Graeme Cooper and Richard Vann, 'Implementing the Goods and Services Tax', *Sydney Law Review* 23 (1999), 337, 358. Queries over whether the VAT was in fact forward shifted to consumers date back to the Asprey Review: Taxation Review Committee (Asprey), Parliament of Australia, *Full Report* (Australian Government Publishing Service, Canberra, 1975), 27.46.

[132] Australia's major sectors when measured by share of industry output (by gross value-add) from 1990 to 2010 in order of importance as at the time of the introduction of the GST were manufacturing; property and business services; retail and wholesale trade; construction;

the OECD, a large amount of Australia's export revenue comes from mining and agriculture.[133] The mining sector was a major supporter and beneficiary of the GST reforms, including from measures such as GST-free exports, the removal of WST on a range of inputs and significant reductions in diesel fuel excise. The agricultural sector also benefited from these measures, alongside a range of special provisions designed to shield the sector from the full impact of the tax.[134] Although banks and financial institutions benefited from the abolition of WST on a range of inputs and the abolition of some taxes on financial transactions,[135] the input taxation[136] of financial supplies remains a major issue for the sector: see §4.3.3. The property and construction sector similarly perceived benefits from the abolition of the WST on a range of inputs and the (later unrealised) promise to remove state stamp duties, although the application of the GST to real property subsequently caused much consternation.[137] Manufacturers and retailers faced a major new compliance burden, with the GST greatly increasing the number of businesses responsible for collecting the tax. However, this was offset by the removal of the WST, reforms to business taxation and cuts to the corporate tax rate.[138]

Strategies employed by business in bringing about GST reform included consensus building (through the ACCI/ACOSS alliance) and the facilitation of dialogue with potential opponents to reform;[139] the establishment of dedicated lobbying apparatus,

mining; and agriculture: Reserve Bank of Australia, *Chart Pack – Regions and Industry: Industry Share of Output* (7 December 2011) (rba.gov.au/chart-pack/regions-industry.html).

133 Alan Fenna, *Australian Public Policy* (2nd ed., Pearson Education Australia, Frenchs Forest, NSW, 2004), 26; Australian Bureau of Statistics, *1301.0 – 2012 Year Book Australia* (ABS, Canberra, 2012), ch. 15 and 31; Australian Bureau of Statistics, *1301.0 – 2005 Year Book Australia* (ABS, Canberra, 2005), 427–35.

134 Damon Kitney, 'Mining Sector's Good News: "The GST Guide for Business"', *Australian Financial Review* (28 June 1999), 14; Paul Cleary 'Diesel Users Face Tough Penalties, Compliance', *Australian Financial Review* (24 June 1999), 4. Subdiv. 38-O, *ANTS Act 1999* also provides that supplies of farm land are GST free.

135 For example, the financial institutions duty (FID) and bank account debits (BAD) were levied by states on a limited range of financial transactions. Both were abolished with the introduction of the GST: *ANTS Statement*, 74.

136 As Chapter 2 explained, this is the Australian term for exemption.

137 See §4.1.2.

138 Australian policy-makers used the introduction of the GST to reform aspects of business taxation, including by introducing a new form for business tax returns, the Business Activity Statements (BAS), designed to capture information in relation to the GST and a range of other business taxes. The reforms allowed for the rationalisation of the collection of a number of previously separately administered taxes under the PAYG system: *A New Tax System (Pay As You Go) Act 1999* (Cth.): US Government Accountability Office, *Value-Added Taxes: Lessons Learned from Other Countries on Compliance Risks, Administrative Costs, Compliance Burden, and Transition (GAO-08–566)* (Washington, DC, 2008), 40.

139 The 'alliance' convened a National Tax Summit attended by over 200 representatives (excluding politicians), where support was articulated for consumption tax reform. The Australian Council of Trade Unions (ACTU) and BCA were invited but did not participate in the Summit (however, the BCA later joined the Tax Reform Forum). The Summit gave rise to a Tax Reform Forum to maintain ongoing reform dialogue. The forum maintained dialogue through a monthly roundtable discussion between business and welfare groups (namely,

such as the Business Coalition for Tax Reform (BCTR), headed by company director Richard Warburton and staffed by over 10 tax specialists, which worked closely in conjunction with the conservative government in the development of the *ANTS package*;[140] the funding and development of expensive and high-profile public relations and advertising campaigns in support of the GST such as the BCTR's $5 million 'Australians for a fairer tax system' campaign;[141] contributing to the policy debate either through the funding of research in support of industry positions or through business representatives, drawn mostly from the large law and accountancy firms, undertaking research directly; plus the adoption of some old-fashioned lobbying. In a sign of the approach adopted by business lobbyists, the leader of the Democrats at the time of the passage of the *ANTS package*, Meg Lees, commented that:[142]

> Business seemed to think that the more they lobbied us, the greater the chance that we would throw our principles aside and simply back down. It was as if volume and number of phone calls and meetings would make us change our mind and abandon what we believe in.

While there have always been practitioners who have been keen to assist well-heeled taxpayers in minimising their dues, momentum behind taxation becoming a profession in its own right gathered pace in Australia during the 1980s.[143] Tax policy-making is increasingly the preserve of these skilled professionals keen to advocate for their client base. Krever presciently identified how the influence of the profession on the academy would impact the impartiality and quality of academic debate in relation to the introduction of the GST:[144]

> The Australian contingent of quality tax academics who have no constraining ties to the profession is insufficient to establish a quorum for almost any purpose. Serious criticism from the academic community is thus unlikely to be a factor in the tax debate.

This capture of the technical tax policy debate explains in part the superficiality of much of the public discussion of GST reform, wherein some of the wilder claims of the GST's virtues remained largely unchecked.[145]

ACCI, BCA and ACOSS) and continued until 1998: Jerome Brown, 'The Tax Debate, Pressure Groups and the 1998 Federal Election', *Policy, Organisation and Society* 18 (1999), 75, 82–83.

140 John Warhurst, Jerome Brown and Rohan Higgins, 'Tax Groupings: The Group Politics of Taxation Reform', in Marian Simms and John Warhurst (eds.), *Howard's Agenda: The 1998 Australian Election* (UQP, St Lucia, 2000), 169.

141 Ibid., 170.

142 Lenore Taylor, 'No Business of the Democrats', *Australian Financial Review*, 18.

143 Fiona Buffini, 'Tax Professionals Scaling the Heights', *Australian Financial Review* (20 May 1999), 31.

144 Rick Krever, 'The Political Economy of the GST: A Comment on Professor Brooks' Paper', in B. Tran-Nam (ed.), *Tax Reform and the GST: An International Perspective* (Prospect Media, St Leonards, NSW, 1998), 141, 144.

145 See §2.1 of this chapter.

The effectiveness of the strategies employed by business in support of the GST has led many to conclude that without this support, the GST would never have been introduced.[146] In contrast to the treatment of welfare lobbyists, business representatives were consulted during the design and implementation of the GST[147] and many of these same lobbyists now occupy key institutional positions in relation to the ongoing review and operation of the tax. The big end of town and its representatives are no longer merely stakeholders,[148] but their lobbying success has itself been institutionalised in rewarding business lobbyists with roles in tax policy-making and administration. There are numerous examples of this;[149] an

[146] Eccleston contends that '[w]hile inherently difficult to quantify, this organized support from business of a GST (the BCTR strongly promoted the package as in the longer term national interest) was a contributing factor both to the government's decision to promote the agenda in 1997 and its election victory in 1998': Richard Eccleston, 'The Significance of Business Interest Association in Economic Policy Reform: The Case of Australian Taxation Policy', *Business and Politics* 2(3) (2000), 309, 318. A news report at the time of the ANTS reforms claimed that 'the pressure on the Government to prove its reform mettle by taking on tax reform came from the big end of town': Australian Broadcasting Corporation, 'Never say Never', 18 May 1998 (www.abc.net.au/4corners/stories/s12274.htm).

[147] Brown claims that '[b]usiness received a highly privileged position in the preparation of the Government's package...': Jerome Brown, 'The Tax Debate, Pressure Groups and the 1998 Federal Election', *Policy, Organisation and Society* 18 (1999), 75, 97. A former Federal Commissioner of Taxation is somewhat understated when he states that there 'were also a number of amendments made as a result of consultation with business, industry groups and other stakeholders': Michael D'Ascenzo, 'The Australian Approach to GST Administration', in R. Krever and D. White (eds.), *GST in Retrospect and Prospect* (Thomson Brookers, Wellington, 2007), 389, 391.

[148] The ATO consults with a range of groups on various aspects of taxation law. The former Commissioner estimated over 75 consultative forums, including taxpayer, industry and professional representatives, and described these forums as expressing the ATO's 'commitment to consultation, collaboration and co-design': Michael D'Ascenzo, 'The Australian Approach to GST Administration', in R. Krever and D. White (eds.), *GST in Retrospect and Prospect* (Thomson Brookers, Wellington, 2007), 389, 394. Some forums are specifically focused on indirect taxes and the GST, such as the Indirect Taxes Advisory Group and GST Subcommittee of the National Tax Liaison Group (NTLG) – the key forum for recognised professional associations, the law council, and peak industry bodies. Others focus on specific industry sectors, such as the building and construction industry, financial services and business advisory groups (from micro through to large businesses): ATO, *ATO Consultation Framework* (27 October 2014) (ato.gov.au/General/About-consultation/ATO-consultation-framework/#TechAndSpPurposeWorkingGps).

[149] Some further examples include Assistant Treasurer Nick Sherry's announcement in 2009 of the appointment of an Expert Tax System Advisory Panel, established to deliver on the Labor government's 'commitment to enhanced consultation with the business community in the development and design of new tax laws'. The panel consisted of 13 members to consult on policy issues with Treasury and the ATO on a case-by-case basis. According to the media release announcing its establishment, the panel formalised the ad hoc practice of private sector consultation in the past and provided access to 'some of the best private sector brains in the field'. Members of the

examination of the composition of the Board of Taxation (BoT) in the next section is illustrative of how far business has come in its capacity to shape Australian tax policy.

2.6 *Administering the GST*

The institutionalisation of past administrative practices very much shapes the administration of the GST.[150] The Commonwealth Treasury, as the primary source of fiscal policy, undertakes ongoing reviews of, and consults on, the operation of the GST. Despite recent attempts to move away from a traditional approach of private consultation toward public consultation on tax policy issues,[151] much consultation still occurs in private.[152]

panel were selected by public tender and included representatives from five major law firms, five large accountancy firms, two economic organisations and one university: Senator Nick Sherry, Assistant Treasurer, *Rudd Government Appoints Expert Tax Design Advisory Panel (Media Release No. 072)* (2009). David Vos, a partner of PricewaterhouseCoopers and member of the GST Planning and Coordination Office for the Liberal Party in developing *Fightback!*, was later appointed to head the Tax Consultative Committee (the Vos Committee) to review the GST and was later appointed as the inaugural Inspector General of Taxation. The media release announcing his appointment provided that '[i]t is important that the inaugural Inspector-General is an experienced tax professional who can foster the confidence of the business community and has a direct appreciation of business practice and government processes': Senator Helen Coonan (Minister for Revenue and Assistant Treasurer, *Minister Welcomes David Vos as Inaugural Inspector-General of Taxation*, Press Release C075/03 4 August 2003; see biography under 'Members of the Committee'; Tax Consultative Committee (Vos Committee), *The Report of the Tax Consultative Committee* (Commonwealth of Australia Treasury, 1998). Chris Jordan (former KPMG partner and now Federal Commissioner of Taxation) was appointed chair of the government's GST advisory board (introduced to oversee the transition to GST) and was the acting head of the BoT following the resignation of Dick Warburton: Paul Cleary and Fiona Buffini, 'GST: Business Hits Delays', *Australian Financial Review* (25 October 1999), 1, 4.

150 Commonwealth of Australia Treasury, Australia's Future Tax System Review Panel, *Architecture of Australia's Tax and Transfer System* (Commonwealth of Australia Treasury, Canberra, 2008), 51; US Government Accountability Office, *Value-Added Taxes: Lessons Learned from Other Countries on Compliance Risks, Administrative Costs, Compliance Burden, and Transition (GAO-08–566)* (Washington, DC, 2008), 40.

151 Brenda Berkeley, 'GST – The View from Treasury' (speech delivered at GST in Australia: Looking Forward from the First Decade Conference, Melbourne, 17 November 2010).

152 For example, prior to the release of the proposed Minerals Resource Rent Tax for public comment, there was already an extensive confidential consultation process undertaken with key stakeholders from the mining industry, through forums such as the Treasury's Resource Tax Implementation Group and, prior to that, the Policy Transition Group (led by Resources Minister Martin Ferguson and Mr Don Argus AC – former long-standing chairman of mining giant BHP Billiton). The recommendations from this group formed the basis of the draft Minerals Resource Rent Tax legislation: Treasury, Commonwealth Government, *Consultation Paper – Minerals Resource Rent Tax Bill 2011* (10 June 2011) (archive.treasury.gov.au/contentitem.asp?ContentID=2070).

The Australian Taxation Office (ATO) headed by the Federal Commissioner of Taxation is responsible for administering and collecting GST revenues on goods and services produced in Australia but also contributes to policy development.[153] The Australian Customs authority administers the collection of GST on imported goods.[154]

A new addition to tax policy-making and review is the establishment of the Board of Taxation (BoT) in August 2000.[155] The BoT is a 'non-statutory advisory body charged with contributing a business and *broader community perspective* to improving the design of taxation laws and their operation'.[156]

In a sign of the success of business lobbying efforts for the GST, the BoT's inaugural chair, Dick Warburton, had to resign as head of the BCTR (the key business lobbying group formed to support the introduction of the GST) to accept the position.[157] In addition to the ex-officio representatives from government,[158] the board members have been drawn primarily from the business community and the legal and

[153] See §3.1.2 for details on the means by which the ATO administers the GST. A Tax Policy and Legislation Protocol sets out the respective roles of Treasury and the ATO: Commonwealth of Australia Treasury, *Australian Taxation Office/Treasury Protocol – Tax Policy and Legislation* (6 March 2008) (archive.treasury.gov.au/documents/1362/PDF/ATO_Treasury_Protocol.pdf). The operations of the ATO are subject to external scrutiny, including by Parliament, the Inspector-General of Taxation (IGT), the Commonwealth Ombudsman and the Australian National Audit Office (ANAO): Commonwealth of Australia Treasury, Australia's Future Tax System Review Panel, *Architecture of Australia's Tax and Transfer System* (Commonwealth of Australia Treasury, Canberra, 2008) 52–53. The IGT was established in 2003 by the *Inspector-General of Taxation Act 2003* (Cth) following consultation and recommendations undertaken by the BoT. The IGT is an independent statutory office charged with reviewing systemic tax administration issues. The IGT reports to the government and can make recommendations for improving tax administration generally: Inspector-General of Taxation, *Role and Responsibilities of the Inspector-General of Taxation – Summary* (2009) (igt.gov.au/content/role.asp?NavID=4). The Commonwealth Ombudsman and the ANAO have broad powers to review the operations of the public sector. The Ombudsman has a specialist team dealing with tax administration and can address complaints made and conduct 'own motion' investigations, including into systemic issues concerning tax administration. The ANAO supports the Auditor-General, who is an independent officer to the parliament. The ANAO can undertake performance audits in relation to the ATO's administration of the tax system. Both the Ombudsman and ANAO report to parliament: *Ombudsman Act 1976* (Cth); *Auditor-General Act 1997* (Cth).

[154] The Australian Customs Authority is currently named the Australian Customs and Border Protection Service. GST is collected by Customs on the importation of tangible goods and is generally payable when customs duty is payable: *ANTS Act 1999*, s 33–15.

[155] The BoT was established as a response to a major review of business taxation: Review of Business Taxation and John Theodore Ralph (chairman), *A Tax System Redesigned: More Certain, Equitable and Durable* (Review of Business Taxation Canberra, 1999), recommendations 1.4 to 1.7.

[156] The Board of Taxation, *The Charter of the Board of Taxation* (2012) (taxboard.gov.au/content/Content.aspx?doc=about/default.htm) (emphasis added).

[157] Thomson Reuters, 'Tax Advisory Board: Powers and Target Market', *Weekly Tax Bulletin* (53) (13 December 1999).

[158] Ex-officio members include representatives from the Treasury, the ATO and the Office of Parliamentary Counsel.

accounting firms that represent them.[159] Although the original BoT had one representative from the community and welfare sector, this is no longer the case.[160] The absence of a community member on the BoT calls into question the capacity of the BoT to represent a broader community perspective because although business and community perspectives might sometimes align, this is not always the case.

Although the Labor party in opposition initially raised concerns about the extent of business influence in taxation,[161] both major parties in government have relied on the BoT in the development and review of tax policy. In part, this is because of the manner in which the BoT has discharged its functions; it has provided comprehensive advice on a range of issues in accordance with its terms of reference.[162] As an article profiling its inaugural chair, Dick Warburton, observed:[163]

> In his role as chairman of the Board of Taxation he was also under pressure to show a sceptical business community that the board was far more than a rubber stamp for government taxation policies and, in reverse, prove to Treasury that the board was not an industry lobby group.

The success of the BoT in discharging its functions and managing these perceptions has been rewarded not just with the continued existence of the BoT but with an expansion of its duties. As Dick Warburton explains:[164]

> What people have to realise is that the BoT's function in this instance has changed from monitoring of existing legislation and policies to drafting policy recommendations from scratch...

Consultation with stakeholders in the ongoing review and development of any revenue instrument, especially one that relies so heavily on business compliance, is

159 Board of Taxation, *Board Members* (2014) (taxboard.gov.au/content/Content.aspx?doc=about/board_members.htm).

160 Ibid.; Thomson Reuters, 'Tax Advisory Board: Powers and Target Market', *Weekly Tax Bulletin* (53) (13 December 1999).

161 This is captured by the following question on notice from Senator Cook in relation to a separate business advisory body, the GST Advisory Board: 'Is the GST advisory board the first step by business towards gaining greater influence over the operations of the ATO so that the ATO serves the interests of business as opposed to those of the community as a whole?': 'Goods and Services Tax: Advisory Board (Question No. 1576)' Commonwealth, *Parliamentary Debates*, Senate, 6 December 1999, 11272 (Peter Cook, Deputy Leader of the Opposition in the Senate).

162 See, e.g., Board of Taxation, *Review of the Legal Framework for the Administration of the Goods and Services Tax: A Report to the Assistant Treasurer and Minister for Competition Policy and Consumer Affairs* (Australian Government, Canberra, 2008), Part C, and at 189–91 listing those issues 'out of scope' of the BoT's terms of reference. However, in identifying issues beyond scope, the BoT is still able to exercise a powerful agenda-setting role. Three issues in this Review (at ix and x) led to subsequent reviews; see, e.g., the margin scheme (see §4.1.2 of this chapter); the rules relating to cross-border supplies (see §3.2 of this chapter); and the financial supply provisions (see 4.3.3 of this chapter).

163 John Arbouw, 'Dick Warburton: Boardroom Warrior', *Company Director Magazine* 19(1) (1 February 2003), 10, 12.

164 Ibid.

standard and indeed best practice. Business interests lobbying for favourable reform outcomes is also nothing new, nor is regulatory capture whereby tax administrators might become captive to the interests of those they seek to regulate. Peters, for example, contends that we see the influence of interest groups particularly strongly in tax policy, because the complex and technical nature of taxation 'makes it easier to disguise their real influence in legal and economic jargon'.[165] What is notable, however, is the manner in which the past gains from lobbying are institutionalised in such a way as to give the winners from past reforms a continuing and powerful role in agenda-setting, so as to further gains into the future.[166] This privileged role is not shared by the welfare sector.

Historical institutionalism reminds us that power is not simply measured in what gets done (the decision), but also in what does not get done (the non-decision);[167] that is, in the ability to set agendas and define issues in a way that favours some interests over others.[168] One account of this phenomenon is David Good's 'anticipatory model of tax policymaking', whereby governments deliberately mould policy to powerful interests in order to prevent conflict with these powerful groups.[169] However, the developments in Australian tax policy-making just described go beyond this – in a sense, they anticipate anticipation by locating members of powerful groups

[165] B. Guy Peters, *The Politics of Taxation: A Comparative Perspective* (Blackwell, Cambridge, MA, 1991), 12.

[166] See Chapter 5, §2.2, §3.2 of this book. See above n 162.

[167] Peter Bachrach and Morton S. Baratz, 'Two Faces of Power', *American Political Science Review* 56(4) (1962), 947; Peter Bachrach and Morton S. Baratz, 'Decisions and Nondecisions: An Analytical Framework', *American Political Science Review* 57(3) (1963), 632; Peter Bachrach and Morton S. Baratz, *Power and Poverty: Theory and Practice* (Oxford University Press, 1970).

[168] Sven Steinmo, *Taxation and Democracy: Swedish, British and American Approaches to Financing the Modern State* (Yale University Press, New Haven, CT, 1993), 7; John A. Hall and Ralph Schroeder, *An Anatomy of Power: The Social Theory of Michael Mann* (Cambridge University Press, Cambridge, UK; New York, 2006), 135.

[169] David A. Good, *The Politics of Anticipation: Making Canadian Federal Tax Policy* (School of Public Administration, Carleton University, Ottowa, 1980), quoted in B. Guy Peters, *The Politics of Taxation: A Comparative Perspective* (Blackwell, Cambridge, MA, 1991), 12. In the following account by Pierson, this anticipation Good describes would be an instance of the second face of power:

> Increasing returns processes can transform a situation of relatively balanced conflict, in which one set of actors must openly impose its preferences on another set ('the first face of power'), into one in which power relations become so uneven that anticipated reactions ('the second face of power') and ideological manipulation ('the third face') make open political conflict unnecessary. Thus, positive feedback over time simultaneously increases power asymmetries and renders power relations less visible.

Paul Pierson, 'Increasing Returns, Path Dependence, and the Study of Politics', *American Political Science Review* 94(2) (2000), 251, 259. The 'third face' of power exists in the construction of meaning in society, and this construction can occur through manipulating dominant community values, myths, political institutions and procedures. See further Steven Lukes, *Power: A Radical View* (2nd ed., Palgrave Macmillan, New York, 2005); Raymond Geuss, *Philosophy and Real Politics* (Princeton University Press, Princeton, NJ, 2008), 50–54.

within key decision-making bodies. That is, those who once were anticipated have come to occupy positions of agenda control. One can see evidence of the influence of business over the reform agenda by examining reform priorities since the introduction of the GST. There are, for example, repeated calls by business to reform the GST to improve areas that impose a cost to business, such as the reform of financial supplies, but very little effort either to evaluate the incidence of the GST or to introduce measures to reduce its potentially regressive impact.[170]

This section has shown that the shape of the Australian GST has not simply been determined by the merits of the good VAT, even when a government persuaded by those merits tried to introduce a good VAT. The divergent fates of the business and welfare sectors in the implementation of the GST show that the role played by each sector was much more than a cross-class coalition between business and welfare to return consumption tax reform to the agenda. Since the introduction of the GST, business lobbyists have been rewarded with ongoing institutional power, whereas welfare lobbyists have not. This has not necessarily resulted in good VAT outcomes – as the exclusion of food due to the tightfisted approach to compensation demonstrates or as the treatment of financial supplies later indicates (see §4.3.3). This section has shown that particular agents located at the heart of key institutions of tax policy-making have driven real VAT outcomes through actions that are the product of history, institutional constraints and perceived self-interest. These factors have had far greater influence on real VAT outcomes than some remotely defined perception of the merits of the good VAT. The next section considers how the outcome of these actions impacts the extent to which the Australian GST measures up against the three norms of good VAT design.

3 ASSESSING THE AUSTRALIAN GST AGAINST THE THREE DESIGN NORMS FOR A GOOD VAT

An examination of the GST against the good VAT reveals that there are issues in relation to the realisation of all three design norms. This section highlights some issues in relation to the second design norm (invoice-credit method) and the

[170] For example, the Asprey Committee Report recommended that the Commonwealth should maintain national estate and gift duties: Taxation Review Committee (Asprey), Parliament of Australia, *Full Report* (Australian Government Publishing Service, Canberra, 1975), ch. 24. The Commonwealth later abandoned the taxes following the abandonment of these taxes by the states in a classic race to the bottom. The (Ralph) Review of Business Taxation recommended reduction in corporate and capital gains rates in conjunction with other 'tax integrity' measures designed to counter tax avoidance, including unified entity taxation that would tax trusts in the same way as companies: Review of Business Taxation and John Theodore Ralph (chairman), *A Tax System Redesigned: More Certain, Equitable and Durable* (Review of Business Taxation Canberra, 1999). The first two measures were immediately acted upon, but the latter was abandoned: Julie P. Smith, *Taxing Popularity: The Story of Taxation in Australia* (rev. edn., ATRF, Canberra, 2004), 160–161; see above, n 121.

third design norm (destination basis). As the bulk of the issues relate to the first design norm (a broad consumption base), §4 is separately devoted to highlighting these issues.

3.1 *Norm 2 – Calculation of VAT liability using the invoice-credit mechanism*

Like most VATs, the Australian GST is levied using the invoice-credit mechanism.[171] A tax invoice[172] is the key piece of evidence that both documents liability to pay GST[173] and enables eligible entities to claim credit for the GST paid on goods and services used in the course of their enterprise.[174]

Chapter 2, §5.2 outlined the advantages claimed by the conventional approach for the levying of the VAT through the invoice-credit method.[175] However, as was discussed in Chapter 3, §5 and recently confirmed by the *Henry Review*, the compliance benefits of the invoice-credit method can be overstated.[176] The remainder of this section focuses on four key issues in relation to the application of the invoice-credit method under the Australian GST: payment of refunds; avoidance and fraud; administrative costs; and compliance costs.

[171] As Chapter 3, §5 of this book explained, Japan is the only developed country that employs an accounts-based subtraction method for calculating VAT liability.

[172] 'Tax invoice' is generally defined in *ANTS Act 1999*, s 195–1 and s 29–70. For the ATO's position on characterising invoices, which aims to adopt a substantive rather than formal approach to the issue, see ATO, *Goods and Services Tax: Tax Invoices*, GSTR 2013/1, 27 March 2013.

[173] Liability to pay GST is outlined at §4.3.1 of this chapter.

[174] *ANTS Act 1999*: Although a tax invoice is not necessary to satisfy the criteria for a creditable acquisition (s 11–5), nor is an invoice necessary to calculate the amount of an input tax credit (s 11–25), a tax invoice is required in order for a taxpayer to claim an input tax credit in a reporting period: s 29–10(3). Generally, the supplier issues the invoice (s 29–70(2)) unless the circumstances fit into the criteria for a recipient-created tax invoice (s 29–70(3)) or if the Commissioner uses his discretion to treat a document as a tax invoice that would not otherwise be an invoice (s 29–70(1B)). No tax invoice is required to be provided for low-value transactions below a specified threshold ($75, as of June 2011). Similarly, an invoice is not necessary for an input tax credit for these low-value acquisitions: s 29–80 and *ANTS Regulations 1999 reg.* 29–80.01.

[175] Commonwealth of Australia Treasury, Australia's Future Tax System Review Panel, *Australia's Future Tax System: Report to the Treasurer* (Australia's Future Tax System Review Panel: The Treasury, Canberra, 2009), 287.

[176] The *Henry Review* states that:

> While business consumers have an incentive to ask for a tax invoice, consumers have no need for a tax invoice, as they cannot claim a tax credit. As such, tax collected at the final retail stage is not self-enforcing. Moreover, the existence of a tax invoice may assist but does not in itself ensure compliance. A false tax invoice might be used to make a claim for a credit. A missing or absent tax invoice may be used to understate sales.

Ibid.

3.1.1 Payment of refunds

Although GST refunds have been steadily rising[177] and are generally delivered promptly,[178] authorities have at times struggled to balance the need to provide timely refunds against the need to guard against fraud. This balance is not always in the administrators' hands, as was shown by the 2011 case of *Commissioner of Taxation v. Multiflex*.[179] In this case, the full Federal Court dismissed an appeal by the Commissioner of Taxation against an order requiring it to refund VAT to a taxpayer the Commissioner suspected of engaging in missing-trader fraud.[180] The Court based its decision on a construction of the *ANTS Act 1999* alongside relevant provisions of the *Tax Administration Act 1953* (which predate the introduction of ANTS but govern the administration of refunds).[181] In rejecting the Commissioner's argument that the ANTS legislation implied a reasonable time by which to assess the validity of the taxpayer's claim in processing a refund,[182] the Federal Court held that:[183]

> It may readily be accepted that the imperative language of s 35–5 of the GST Act as to the making of a refund is at least attended with the implication that the refund must be made within a time which is reasonable in the circumstances. However, those circumstances must attend what is necessary to discharge the duty concerned, which is to make the refund, not to undertake an investigation which may or may not result in the raising of a GST assessment by the Commissioner.

The *Multiflex* decision involves two conflicting goals (or merits of the VAT): first, to preserve revenue integrity; and second, to prevent the GST from being a cost to business. The decision of the Federal Court in this instance favoured the latter over the former. Although acknowledging that a requirement to refund promptly would

[177] Activity Statement refunds (of which the GST constitutes the majority share) rose from $22,921 million in 2002–2003 to $56,695 million in 2012–2013. GST refunds constitute the largest share of refunds by tax type, constituting well over half of the $97,372 million refunded in 2012–2013: Federal Commissioner of Taxation, *Australian Taxation Office – Annual Report 2012–2013* (ATO, Canberra, 2013), 38; Federal Commissioner of Taxation, *Australian Taxation Office – Annual Report 2011–2012* (ATO, Canberra, 2012), 56.

[178] The ATO aims to process GST returns and refunds within 14 days. The ATO has improved performance on this measure since the introduction of the GST. In 2012–2013, of 1,960,300 original BAS refunds processed, 99.2% of refunds were processed within 14 days: Australian Taxation Office (ATO), *GST Administration Annual Performance Report 2012–13* (ATO, Canberra, 2013), 23.

[179] *Commissioner of Taxation v. Multiflex Pty Ltd.* (2011) 197 FCR 580 (hereafter referred to as '*Multiflex*').

[180] *Commissioner of Taxation v. Multiflex Pty Ltd.* (2011), 197 FCR 580, 583–84, [11]. For a description of missing-trader fraud, see Chapter 3, 5.2 of this book.

[181] Primarily *ANTS Act 1999*, s 35–5; pts 3–10, 4–15 and 5–5 in sch 1 to the *Taxation Administration Act 1953* (Cth).

[182] *Commissioner of Taxation v. Multiflex Pty Ltd.* (2011), 197 FCR 580, 589–90, [28].

[183] Ibid., 592–93, [40].

give rise to the potential for abuse, the Federal Court called for parliament to remedy this defect, which it subsequently has addressed through legislative amendment.[184] The *Multiflex* decision shows that in order to understand how the merits of real VATs will be assessed and realised, it is necessary to understand the institutional context in which decisions relating to real VATs occur. In this instance, this context includes the relevant Acts as made and amended by parliament and the approach of administrators, taxpayers, policy-makers and ultimately the Courts in interpreting and applying the relevant legislative provisions.

3.1.2 Avoidance and fraud

Schemes for avoiding and evading the GST have been undertaken with varying degrees of sophistication and success. Most schemes entail variations on the following themes:[185]

1. Wrongly claiming input tax credits. Schemes can entail the falsification of invoices or business activity statements (a type of GST return); or wrongly registering in the GST system through, for example, entity fraud or identity theft;[186]

[184] Ibid., 581–82, [1], 592, [37]–[38]. The new s8AAZLGA of the *Taxation Administration Act 1953* (Cth) provides that in certain circumstances the Commissioner has authority to retain a refund otherwise due, provided that it is reasonable to require verification of the information provided by the taxpayer. One factor the Commissioner must have regard to in deciding whether to retain the amount is the likelihood of fraud or evasion: s8AAZLGA (2).

[185] For the financial year 2011–2012, the ATO reports that 17 of 39 successful prosecutions for serious tax fraud were related to the GST: Federal Commissioner of Taxation, *Australian Taxation Office – Annual Report 2011–2012* (ATO, Canberra, 2012), 76–79, 83; ATO, "ATO Continues Clamp-Down on GST Fraud and Those Not Reporting Cash Income" (Media release 2011/39). In 2012–2013, the ATO completed 72 GST fraud investigations, referred 31 new matters for prosecution and had 14 fraud cases dealt with by the courts – 13 resulted in convictions and reparation orders of $1.8M: Australian Taxation Office (ATO), *GST Administration Annual Performance Report 2012–13* (ATO, Canberra, 2013), 40. See also Michael D'Ascenzo, 'The Australian Approach to GST Administration', in R. Krever and D. White (eds.), *GST in Retrospect and Prospect* (Thomson Brookers, Wellington, 2007), 389, 402; OECD, *Forum on Tax Administration: Compliance Sub-Group, Information Note, Developments in VAT Compliance Management in Selected Countries* (OECD, Centre for Tax Policy and Administration, Paris, 2009), 18; Robin Woellner et al., *Australian Taxation Law* (20th ed., CCH Australia, Sydney, 2010), 1823 [27–199].

[186] Taxpayers need to register and receive a unique identification number, an Australian Business Number (ABN), in order to obtain input tax credits: *ANTS Act 1999*, s11–5(d). BAS statements require information in relation to the GST and a range of other business taxes: see above, n 138. Twenty-nine people were prosecuted for business activity statement fraud in 2009–2010: Commissioner of Taxation, *Australian Taxation Office – Annual Report 2009–2010* (ATO, Canberra, 2011), 87. In the 2012–2013 tax year, the ATO conducted around 20,000 checks for incorrect or fraudulent registrations and removed over 4,500 GST registrations from the system: Federal Commissioner of Taxation, *Australian Taxation Office – Annual Report 2012–2013* (ATO, Canberra, 2013), 50.

2. Systematic avoidance or minimisation of GST liabilities. Schemes can entail missing-trader fraud; avoiding operating through an 'enterprise' (see §4.3.1) to avoid GST liabilities or not registering in the system at all; under-reporting of GST liabilities; non-lodgement of GST returns; structuring fictitious transactions to avoid GST liability; or the increasing problem of non-payment of GST debts.[187]

The exploitation of complex special rules (such as those relating to zero-rated supplies [see §4.1.1], financial supply transactions [see §4.3.3], and real property transactions [see §4.1.2]) allow for further variations in attempting to maximise input credits or minimise GST liabilities.[188]

The ATO estimated the GST gap at 6.4 per cent (including GST debts) in 2005–2006, and at 5.4 per cent in 2010–2011.[189] The ATO claims that a focus on compliance has reduced the GST gap from an estimated 8.9 per cent in 2001–2002, and further claims that the gap would be more than double the size (12 per cent) without compliance activities.[190]

While a number of reforms have attempted to bolster the self-enforcing mechanism of business-to-business transactions,[191] the absence of a self-enforcement

[187] The ATO has signalled a concern over GST debts, given that outstanding business activity statement debts are higher than income tax debts: Commissioner of Taxation, *Australian Taxation Office – Annual Report 2009–2010* (ATO, Canberra, 2011), 50. Gross GST debts rose to a staggering $4.82B by 30 June 2013, which the ATO states 'reflects the difficulties of collecting debt in the current economic environment'. The ATO is focusing on the use of insolvency to avoid payment of GST liabilities, which is an endemic problem in the property development sector, where phoenix companies later appear for a new development: Australian Taxation Office (ATO), *GST Administration Annual Performance Report 2012–13* (ATO, Canberra, 2013), 18, 21, 34.

[188] The ATO reports that compliance activity in relation to real property transactions from 2012 to 2013 generated $202.2 million in GST liabilities: Federal Commissioner of Taxation, *Australian Taxation Office – Annual Report 2012–2013* (ATO, Canberra, 2013), 49. Approximately 24 per cent of GST litigation involved disputes in relation to property matters: ATO, *GST Administration Annual Performance Report 2012–13* (ATO, Canberra, 2013), 45, and at 31–40 for an overview of compliance areas.

[189] The GST gap is the equivalent of the VAT gap discussed in Chapter 3, §5.2. The Australian results appear to compare favourably to the EU average VAT gap for the same period of 12 percent. Whereas the Reckon Report included VAT debts in its measurement of the VAT gap, the ATO generally excludes GST debt but included it in this instance to enable comparison: Reckon Report, *Study to Quantify and Analyse the VAT Gap in the EU-25 Member States* (Reckon LLP, London, 2009), 5, 9; Federal Commissioner of Taxation, *Australian Taxation Office – Annual Report 2011–2012* (ATO, Canberra, 2012), 76–77.

[190] Australian Taxation Office (ATO), *GST Administration Annual Performance Report 2012–13* (ATO, Canberra, 2013), 16–17. Compliance activities focus on ensuring correct registration, lodgement, reporting and payment by taxpayers: at 18.

[191] For example, legislation provides that businesses that make a payment to an unregistered business that supplies goods and services must withhold the maximum PAYG tax rate of 46.5 per cent from the payment if the supplier does not provide their ABN. Amounts are remitted to the ATO, which presents the supplying business with a payment summary: *A New Tax System (Pay As You Go) Act 1999* (Cth.), s 12–190.

mechanism for business-to-consumer transactions means that the ATO has an increasingly strong compliance focus on the cash economy.[192] Despite the promises in the *ANTS Statement*, the introduction of the GST has led to an increase rather than a diminution in the cash economy.[193]

The administration of the GST by the ATO has shifted from a focus on education and assistance in the first few years of implementation toward one of compliance and enforcement. The ATO uses a variety of arrangements to administer the tax system.[194] These range from determinations having the force of law,[195] to rulings (which may or may not bind the Commissioner),[196] and various interpretive aids and precedential guides indicating how the ATO administers or intends to administer the

[192] Michael D'Ascenzo, 'The Australian Approach to GST Administration', in R. Krever and D. White (eds.), *GST in Retrospect and Prospect* (Thomson Brookers, Wellington, 2007), 389, 404–5.

[193] Martin contends that '[o]ur love affair with cash moved into high gear with the introduction of the goods and services tax a decade ago – defying predictions at the time that it would crack down on the cash economy': Peter Martin, 'Australia Awash in Cold, Hard Cash', *The Age* (online), 26 September 2011 (www.theage.com.au/business/australia-awash-in-cold-hard-cash-20110925-1krty.html). See further *Australian Bureau of Statistics*, 5204.0.55.008 – *Information Paper: The Non-Observed Economy and Australia's GDP* (ABS, Canberra, 2012). Estimates vary depending on the methodology adopted; a World Bank Report estimated the shadow economy in Australia from 1999 to 2007 at 14 per cent of GDP. The ABS disputes this and provides its own estimate of the non-observed economy (of which the cash economy is but one part: at Table 1) at 1.5 per cent of GDP: at 9.2–9.6. In any event, targeting the cash economy is a major component of the ATO's GST compliance and enforcement work. This resulted in recovering an additional $61.4 million in GST liabilities from more than 84,000 activities in 2012–2013: Australian Taxation Office (ATO), *GST Administration Annual Performance Report 2012–13* (ATO, Canberra, 2013), 37.

[194] For a summary, see Commonwealth of Australia Treasury, Australia's Future Tax System Review Panel, *Architecture of Australia's Tax and Transfer System* (Commonwealth of Australia Treasury, Canberra, 2008), 52.

[195] See, e.g., *ANTS Act* 1999, s29–25. The GST Act delegates power to the Commissioner to issue Legislative Determinations, which have the effect of law as delegated legislation. For a list of these determinations, see Australian Taxation Office (ATO), *Legal Database* (2014) (law.ato.gov.au/atolaw/Browse.htm?Node=0&Ima=CollapseAll).

[196] Rulings are a key component of the self-assessment system. They are designed to provide taxpayers some certainty in arranging their tax affairs by outlining the Commissioner's approach to the interpretation and administration of the relevant laws. Rulings can be public (an expression of the Commissioner's opinion of the way in which a relevant provision applies or would apply to entities generally or a class of entities) or private (an expression of the Commissioner's opinion of the way in which a relevant provision applies or would apply to specific taxpayers who apply for the ruling). Rulings bind the Commissioner in certain circumstances. As the previous Commissioner explains, these binding rulings, although 'not the law', are the 'Commissioner's interpretation of the law' and 'do provide protection to taxpayers': Michael D'Ascenzo, 'The Australian Approach to GST Administration', in R. Krever and D. White (eds.), *GST in Retrospect and Prospect* (Thomson Brookers, Wellington, 2007), 389, 392; *Taxation Administration Act 1953* (Cth), pt 5–5 of sch 1, comprises div. 357 (Object and common rules), div. 358 (Public rulings) and div. 360 (Oral rulings). See also GST Bulletins (a form of ruling), GST Determinations (a form of ruling on a particular point), GST Draft Rulings and GST Draft Determinations: Australian Taxation Office, *Legal Database* (2014) (law.ato.gov.au/atolaw/browse.htm?ImA=MainMenu).

relevant laws.[197] At the time of the commencement of the GST legislation on 1 July 2000, there were already 38 GST related rulings and determinations.[198] The ATO also has extensive powers to collect and recover outstanding amounts of revenue, including the ability to issue monetary penalties and interest.[199]

As businesses and their advisers have become familiar with the ANTS legislation, tax planning is growing in sophistication.[200] In response, GST audits[201] have steadily increased since the introduction of the tax, along with taxpayer objections.[202] Taxpayers who object to assessments or rulings by the Commissioner can seek administrative review of these determinations at the Administrative Appeals Tribunal or review by the relevant courts – generally, the Federal Court with final appeals to the High Court by special leave.[203] Litigation has increased from nine cases in 2001–2002 to 15 in 2012–2013.[204]

[197] These include ATO Interpretive Decisions (ATO IDs) – public versions of private rulings which, although binding only on the parties to the private ruling, outline the Commissioner's approach on certain issues; Commissioner's Law Administration Practice Statements, which are directions to ATO staff as to how to administer certain aspects of the law; Decision Impact Statements, which indicate how the Commissioner will respond to key court decisions on the GST: *GST Legislation* Plus, annotated by Richard Krever (Thomson Reuters, Pyrmont, 2014) Preface; Australian Taxation Office, *Legal Database* (2014) (law.ato.gov.au/atolaw/browse.htm?ImA=MainMenu).

[198] Michael D'Ascenzo, 'The Australian Approach to GST Administration', in R. Krever and D. White (eds.), *GST in Retrospect and Prospect* (Thomson Brookers, Wellington, 2007), 389, 392. In 2009–2010, the ATO provided binding advice through 10,647 private rulings (2,002 related to the GST) and 181 public rulings, and further guidance through 18,070 other products: Commissioner of Taxation, *Australian Taxation Office – Annual Report 2009–2010* (ATO, Canberra, 2011), 73–74.

[199] Commonwealth of Australia Treasury, Australia's Future Tax System Review Panel, *Architecture of Australia's Tax and Transfer System* (Commonwealth of Australia Treasury, Canberra, 2008), 49–53. See, for example, the provisions in *Taxation Administration Act 1953* (Cth), Div. 2.

[200] Michael D'Ascenzo, 'The Australian Approach to GST Administration', in R. Krever and D. White (eds.), *GST in Retrospect and Prospect* (Thomson Brookers, Wellington, 2007), 389, 410.

[201] GST audit liabilities have increased from $189 million in 2000–2001 to net audit liabilities of $209 million in 2012–2013 (plus $67 million in penalties from these audit activities): ibid., 404; Australian Taxation Office (ATO), *GST Administration Annual Performance Report 2012–13* (ATO, Canberra, 2013), 50.

[202] GST taxpayer objections tripled from 2003–2004 to 2005–2006: ibid., 410. 2,094 GST objections were lodged in 2012–2013: ATO, *GST Administration Annual Performance Report 2012–13* (ATO, Canberra, 2013), 53.

[203] Australia has a unique system of funding the costs of a taxpayer's litigation in select cases that raise matters of public interest in the administration of revenue laws and where it is therefore desirable to obtain a legal precedent: ATO, *Test Case Litigation Program* (10 May 2013) (ato.gov.au/Tax-professionals/Legal-practitioners/In-detail/Litigation-and-case-law/Test-case-litigation-program/). See also the ATO Annual Report 2009–2010 for a list of test cases funded in the 2009–2010 financial year – six of 16 were GST-related: Commissioner of Taxation, *Australian Taxation Office – Annual Report 2009–2010* (ATO, Canberra, 2011), Appendix 5, 205–8; two matters of 19 were GST related in 2011–2012: Commissioner of Taxation, *Australian Taxation Office – Annual Report 2009–2010* (ATO, Canberra, 2012), Appendix 4, Table 4.6.

[204] Australian Taxation Office (ATO), *GST Administration Annual Performance Report 2012–13* (ATO, Canberra, 2013), 44.

Much of the focus of compliance and enforcement activity is on addressing the 'Achilles heel' of the refund mechanism as well as responding to vulnerable areas such as financial supplies and real property transactions.[205] The ATO uses computerised systems to identify high-risk refund claims.[206] Risk profiling is based on a range of factors that include the size of the refund claimed, the nature of the business and the duration of its registration, as well as its previous compliance history and the existence of other tax debts.[207] In 2012–2013, the ATO reviewed 48,000 GST refund cases and escalated nearly 36,000 to audit, which resulted in one in three claims being adjusted to prevent the incorrect or fraudulent claiming of $401.2 million worth of GST refunds.[208]

Despite the promise that the GST would be more difficult to avoid, policymakers were clearly alive to the potential compliance issues, as indicated by the inclusion of a general anti-avoidance provision in the ANTS legislation.[209] The provision was drafted largely on the basis of the equivalent provisions in the income tax legislation, as was the general anti-avoidance provision in the WST.[210] As is frequently the case with general anti-avoidance provisions, the provision was fiercely unpopular with tax lobbyists and was subject to intense lobbying and subsequent reform.[211] The first judicial consideration of the anti-avoidance provisions by the High Court of Australia has clarified the scope of the provisions, but many questions remain as to the interaction between the general anti-avoidance provisions and the remaining provisions of the GST legislation.[212]

[205] ATO, *GST Administration Annual Performance Report 2012–13* (ATO, Canberra, 2013), 31–40; Federal Commissioner of Taxation, *Australian Taxation Office – Annual Report 2011–2012* (ATO, Canberra, 2012), 79; OECD, *Forum on Tax Administration: Compliance Sub-Group, Information Note, Developments in VAT Compliance Management in Selected Countries* (OECD, Centre for Tax Policy and Administration, Paris, 2009), 18.

[206] OECD, *Forum on Tax Administration: Compliance Sub-Group, Information Note, Developments in VAT Compliance Management in Selected Countries* (OECD, Centre for Tax Policy and Administration, Paris, 2009), 17–18, 30, annex 2, 3, 4.

[207] Ibid., 30; ATO – National Tax Liaison Group, GST Sub-Committee, *Minutes 14 September 2011 – Risk Differentiation Framework (RDF) for Taxpayers* (ATO, Canberra, 2011).

[208] Federal Commissioner of Taxation, *Australian Taxation Office – Annual Report 2012–2013* (ATO, Canberra, 2013), 49.

[209] *ANTS Act* 1999, Div. 165.

[210] *Income Tax Assessment Act* 1936 (Cth), pt. IVA; *Sales Tax Assessment Act* 1992 (Cth), pt. 8.

[211] Andrew Hutchinson, 'GST Anti-Avoidance: Sharper Teeth! – Bigger Bite?' *Weekly Tax Bulletin* (10) (1999), quoting press reports at the time describing the provision as 'fatally flawed' and 'draconian'; Paul Cleary, 'Tax Avoidance Rules Loosen Up', *Sydney Morning Herald*, 23 April 1999, 2.

[212] The general anti-avoidance rule (GAAR) is on its face very broad and captures, among other things, any scheme designed to minimise a taxpayer's GST liability: *ANTS Act* 1999, Div. 165. The breadth is offset by a provision that seeks to exclude from the operation of the GAAR tax benefits that are attributable to a statutory choice in the legislation (or, more accurately in the language of the provision, to catch schemes that provide benefits that 'are not attributable to' the legislation): *ANTS Act* 1999, s165–5(b). The taxpayer engaged in a series of intra-group transfers to obtain the benefit of various concessional provisions in the GST legislation in relation to a property development. In essence, the transactions involved the GST-free sale of

3.1.3 Administrative costs

The cost of administration for any tax instrument is influenced by factors such as the number of taxpayers, the regularity of returns filed and the number of audits conducted.[213] Although Australia has a comparatively high registration threshold, many businesses voluntarily register for the GST.[214] There were more than 2.6 million businesses registered for GST as of February 2014.[215] These businesses may be required to report on a quarterly, monthly or annual basis.[216] The ATO processed 10 million business activity statements in 2012–2013.[217]

Given the large number of registered taxpayers, the regularity of reporting requirements and the need for systematic cross-checking of tax invoices, the costs of administering the GST are significant. The cost was $1.47 for each $100 of revenue in 2012–2013.[218] This compares unfavourably to the $0.80 it costs to collect

two almost complete towers in a residential property development as a GST-free going concern from one GST group member to another and then the application of the margin scheme (see §4.1.2 of this chapter) by the purchaser to minimise the GST payable on the final sale of apartments in the development to end consumers. Despite the transaction being enabled by the relevant legislative provisions, the High Court ruled that a GST benefit (an uplift in the cost base and corresponding reduction in the margin to which the GST applied) had been obtained from a scheme as a result of a choice that was 'not attributable to' the GST law but rather a commercial choice as to the sale price for the intra-group transfers. As this commercial choice was the source of the benefit, and as this was not attributable to the GST law, the scheme was not immune from the operation of Div. 165: at [58]. The specific wording of s165–1(a)&(b) was crucial to the Court's decision: *Commissioner of Taxation v. Unit Trend Services Pty Ltd.* (2013), 297 ALR 190, 200–205. This type of arrangement was later prevented by statutory amendment: Australian Taxation Office (ATO), *GST Administration Annual Performance Report 2012–13* (ATO, Canberra, 2013), 30.

213 US Government Accountability Office, *Value-Added Taxes: Lessons Learned from Other Countries on Compliance Risks, Administrative Costs, Compliance Burden, and Transition (GAO-08–566)* (Washington, DC, 2008), 15.

214 The OECD estimated the Australian threshold to be the equivalent of $48 123USD at 1 January 2012, placing it about the ninth highest in the OECD: OECD, *Consumption Tax Trends 2012: VAT/GST and Excise Rates, Trends and Administration Issues* (OECD Publishing, Paris, 2012), 84.

215 2,655,990 entities were registered for GST purposes as of 19 February 2014: Commonwealth Government, 'ABN Statistics' (2014) (abr.business.gov.au/StatisticalSearchResult.aspx?Postcode=ALL&Year=2011&StateOptions=1,0,0,0,0,0,0,0,0&Options=0,0,1,0).

216 Business with turnovers of less than $20 million can remit on a quarterly basis: *ANTS Act 1999*, s 27–5. This is subject to exceptions: at s 27–15. The quarterly tax periods can provide significant cash-flow benefits to enterprises. Large businesses (with turnovers above $20 million) must remit on a monthly basis: ss 27–5 and s 27–10; 17–5, s33–3, 33–5. There is also an option for eligible entities to file returns on an annual basis: div. 157. See also Mathew Carr, 'Quarterly Payout to Help Small Retailers in "The GST Guide for Business (Liftout)"', *Australian Financial Review*, 9.

217 Australian Taxation Office (ATO), *GST Administration Annual Performance Report 2012–13* (ATO, Canberra, 2013), 33.

218 Australian Taxation Office (ATO), *GST Administration Annual Performance Report 2012–13* (ATO, Canberra, 2013), 9

other Commonwealth taxes.[219] More troublesome is that the cost of collection has not trended down in recent years.[220] If staff costs are an indication, the GST is costly to administer. At the time of the introduction of the GST, the ATO recruited 3,600 new officers to administer the ANTS legislation[221] – staff levels increased from 14,167 prior to the introduction of ANTS to approximately 19,000 after the introduction of ANTS.[222] As the *Henry Review* notes, 'the widespread use of tax invoices as a basis of systematic cross-checking between tax paid and tax claimed, while simple in concept, is costly in practice'.[223]

For 2008–2010, the costs of administering the GST constituted approximately 20 per cent of the ATO's administration costs, while the GST accounted for approximately 15.6–17.4 per cent of revenue during the same period.[224] In 2012–2013, the cost to administer the GST was $705.3 million.[225] The ATO estimates the major components of these costs to be administration costs of $62.2 million for processing and accounts, $99.7 million for debt collection and $255.6 million for 'active compliance' – a significant proportion of which is focused on preventing fraudulent refunds, investigating systematic under-reporting of GST liabilities, following up non-lodgement of reports and debt collection.[226]

3.1.4 Compliance costs

The *Henry Review* notes that 'complying with the GST is costly for many businesses':[227]

[219] Federal Commissioner of Taxation, *Australian Taxation Office – Annual Report 2012–2013* (ATO, Canberra, 2013), 39.

[220] Australian Taxation Office (ATO), *GST Administration Annual Performance Report 2012–13* (ATO, Canberra, 2013), 9 *cf* ATO, *GST Administration Annual Performance Report 2009–2010* (ATO, Canberra, 2010), 51.

[221] Commissioner of Taxation, *Australian Taxation Office – Annual Report 1999–2000* (ATO, Canberra, 2000), ch. 4; Michael D'Ascenzo, 'The Australian Approach to GST Administration', in R. Krever and D. White (eds.), *GST in Retrospect and Prospect* (Thomson Brookers, Wellington, 2007), 389, 392.

[222] In the 2012–2013 financial year, the ATO employed just over 25,000 employees: Commissioner of Taxation, *Australian Taxation Office – Annual Report 2012–2013* (ATO, Canberra, 2013), 81; Federal Commissioner of Taxation, *Australian Taxation Office – Annual Report 1998–1999* (ATO Canberra, 1999), appendix 2.

[223] Commonwealth of Australia Treasury, Australia's Future Tax System Review Panel, *Australia's Future Tax System: Report to the Treasurer* (Australia's Future Tax System Review Panel: The Treasury, Canberra, 2009), 287.

[224] Commissioner of Taxation, *Australian Taxation Office – Annual Report 2009–2010* (ATO, Canberra, 2011), 39, 175.

[225] Commissioner of Taxation, *Australian Taxation Office – Annual Report 2012–2013* (ATO, Canberra, 2013), 90.

[226] Australian Taxation Office (ATO), *GST Administration Annual Performance Report 2012–13* (ATO, Canberra, 2013), 19 41.

[227] Commonwealth of Australia Treasury, Australia's Future Tax System Review Panel, *Australia's Future Tax System: Report to the Treasurer* (Australia's Future Tax System Review Panel: The Treasury, Canberra, 2009), 289, 288.

> The costs incurred by business in complying with the GST arise from registration requirements, issuing tax invoices, distinguishing between different types of supplies, reporting and remitting GST to the ATO, computing and software requirements, record keeping and auditing, understanding the GST law, and impacts on cash flow.

Although there has been no systematic empirical verification of the compliance costs of the GST on Australian business, most agree that the costs of GST compliance are greater, the smaller the business (see Chapter 3, §5.3).[228] For the *Henry Review*, much of this cost arises from departures in relation to the first design norm 'and flows from differential tax treatment of different goods and services. The smallest businesses can [therefore] be under pressure to be in the GST system'.[229] The findings directly contradict the claims made prior to the reforms that the GST would be simple to administer. Whereas approximately 70,000 businesses dealt with this complexity under the WST, more than 2.6 million engage with it now.[230]

There are measures to offset the compliance burden, such as simplified accounting rules for eligible businesses; cash-flow benefits from the time lag between when GST revenue is collected and remitted to government (although these benefits can be overstated); and efficiency benefits in matching the administration of the GST with the Pay As You Go (PAYG) system.[231] However, there are suggestions that reforms should go further.[232] The *Henry Review*, for example, suggested considering the zero-rating of more business-to-business transactions and utilising the reverse-charge mechanism (provided the administrative costs and revenue risk do not outweigh the compliance benefits).[233] As Chapter 3, §4.2.4 and §5.2 explained, both these measures convert the operation of the GST into more of an RST.

228 Ibid., 288–91; US Government Accountability Office, *Value-Added Taxes: Lessons Learned from Other Countries on Compliance Risks, Administrative Costs, Compliance Burden, and Transition (GAO-08–566)* (Washington, DC, 2008), 16–17. See generally Board of Taxation, *Scoping Study of Small business Tax Compliance Costs* (Australian Government, Canberra, 2007).

229 Commonwealth of Australia Treasury, Australia's Future Tax System Review Panel, *Australia's Future Tax System: Report to the Treasurer* (Australia's Future Tax System Review Panel: The Treasury, Canberra, 2009), 289.

230 Michael Dirkis, quoted in Paul Cleary, 'The McDonald's Amendment', *Australian Financial Review*, 4 June 1999, 41. See above, n 215.

231 Australian Taxation Office (ATO), *GST Administration Annual Performance Report 2012–13* (ATO, Canberra, 2013), 23; Robin Woellner et al., Australian Taxation Law (20th ed., CCH Australia, Sydney, 2010), 1815–1816 [27–185]; A *New Tax System (Pay As You Go) Act 1999* (Cth.).

232 US Government Accountability Office, *Value-Added Taxes: Lessons Learned from Other Countries on Compliance Risks, Administrative Costs, Compliance Burden, and Transition (GAO-08–566)* (Washington, DC, 2008), 17, 31. Robin Woellner et al., Australian Taxation Law (20th ed., CCH Australia, Sydney, 2010), 1815–1816 [27–185].

233 Commonwealth of Australia Treasury, Australia's Future Tax System Review Panel, *Australia's Future Tax System: Report to the Treasurer* (Australia's Future Tax System Review Panel: The Treasury, Canberra, 2009), 291. For an explanation of the reverse-charge mechanism, see Chapter 3, §5.2 of this book.

The issues highlighted in this section do not mean that the Australian GST is levied through any mechanism other than the invoice-credit method. However, the discussion demonstrates that, even though formal compliance with this norm of good VAT design might be achieved, practical administrative difficulties can result in departures in real VATs from the intended operation of the good VAT.

3.2 *Norm 3 – Levying VAT on a destination basis*

The GST is levied on a destination basis, meaning that the tax is designed to fall on the domestic consumption of goods and services. In practice, this means that exports generally remain untaxed,[234] while imports are taxed along with domestically produced goods and services for consumption. The ATO reports that in 2012–2013, GST on imports constituted $3 billion (of a total of $48.1 billion).[235]

The application of the GST on a destination basis is not without problems.[236] Many reflect the general difficulty of levying real VATs in the face of the changing nature of commerce and in light of the advances in technology summarised in Chapter 3.[237] As a sign of the nature of the changes, at the time of the ANTS reforms in 1999 only 1.1 million Australians had access to the Internet; by contrast, some 10.4 million Australians had an active Internet subscription in December 2010.[238] One consequence of this is that Australians are purchasing goods from overseas at an increasing rate but not paying GST on the importation of goods with a value of less than $1000.[239] In Australia, as is the case in many other developed economies, the exclusion of GST on low value goods is motivated largely by the belief that the administrative costs of collecting GST would outweigh the revenue

[234] *ANTS Act* 1999, subdiv. 38-E.

[235] Australian Taxation Office (ATO), *GST Administration Annual Performance Report 2012–13* (ATO, Canberra, 2013), 6.

[236] See, for example, the *Travelex* case, where the High Court decided that the supply of foreign currency to an outbound traveller was a GST-free supply, as it was a supply in relation to rights for use outside Australia, under item 4(a) of the table in s 38–190(1) of the *ANTS Act* 1999: *Travelex Ltd. v. Commissioner of Taxation* (2010), 241 CLR 510. See also issues around the treatment of supplies made by inbound tour operators to non-resident travel agents: *ATS Pacific Pty Ltd. v. Commissioner of Taxation*(2014) 219 FCR 302. The High Court of Australia refused special leave to appeal the decision: *ATS Pacific Pty Ltd v. Commissioner of Taxation; Stella Travel Services (Australia) Pty Ltd v. Deputy Commissioner of Taxation* [2014] HCATrans 237 (17 October 2014).

[237] Denis McCarthy, 'The Australian GST – Why It Is the Way It Is and Where To from Here?' in C. Peacock (ed.), *GST in Australia: Looking Forward from the First Decade* (Thomson Reuters, Sydney, 2011), 61, 74. See Chapter 3, §6 of this book.

[238] Australian Bureau of Statistics, 8153.0 – *Internet Activity, Australia* (ABS, 2010), 'Introduction'; Annabel Hepworth, 'Games Lose, PC buyers Win, and the Net Will Be Widened', *Australian Financial Review*, 28 June 1999, 4 (of the Special GST guide for business liftout).

[239] Goods listed under items 32A and 32B, Schedule 4 of the *Customs Tariff Act* 1995 (Cth), namely 'low-value goods' (or goods on which customs duty and taxes is $50 or less and which have a customs value of less than $1,000), are not subject to GST.

benefits.[240] However, recent campaigns by Australian retailers have sought to challenge the exclusion on the basis that it disadvantages Australian retailers and will reduce revenue in the long run if Australian retailers are forced to shut down.[241] Despite a recent review recommending halving the threshold for low-value goods to $500,[242] the government to date has not changed the rules.[243] Further complications to taxing cross-border supplies arise from Australia's unique place-of-supply rules.[244]

[240] OECD, *Consumption Tax Trends 2012: VAT/GST and Excise Rates, Trends and Administration Issues* (OECD Publishing, Paris, 2012), 79; Katharine Murphy and Ben Preiss, 'Retailers Told the Enemy is Within', *The Age*, 1–2.

[241] See, e.g., Clancy Yeates, 'Retail Union Calls for GST on All Imports', *The Age* (online), 9 May 2011 (theage.com.au/business/retail-union-calls-for-gst-on-all-imports-20110508-1ee7c.html#ixzz1Qcv7cDG2).

[242] Productivity Commission, *Economic Structure and Performance of the Australian Retail Industry* (Productivity Commission, Canberra, 2011), 151. In 2012, the OECD assessed that Australia had the highest low-value-import threshold in the OECD (of $642 USD when measured at purchase parity rates). Halving this amount would still leave Australia with the highest threshold, although by a reduced margin: OECD, *Consumption Tax Trends 2012: VAT/GST and Excise Rates, Trends and Administration Issues* (OECD Publishing, Paris, 2012), 100.

[243] Commonwealth of Australia Government, *GST Distribution Review Final Report* (Australian Govt Pub Service, Canberra, October 2012), recommendation 11.2, 160; *Contra* the Commonwealth of Australia Treasury, *The Low Value Parcel Processing Taskforce Final Report* (Commonwealth of Australia Treasury, Canberra, 2012), which identified that little benefit would result from changing the threshold without reforms to improve the administration and collection of GST on low-value imported goods: at 2.

[244] These rules are contained in s 9–25 of the *ANTS Act* 1999, which sets out five circumstances where a supply will be 'connected with Australia'. Three relate to when goods will be connected with Australia, which will occur: (1) If the goods are delivered, made available in, or (2) removed from Australia: s 9–25(1) – (3); or (3) If the goods are imported (or assembled) in Australia: s 9–25(3). One relates to real property whereby a supply is connected with Australia if the real property (or the land to which it relates) is in Australia: s 9–25(4). The final rule relates to 'supplies of anything else' other than 'goods or real property'; e.g., services. A supply of a service is connected with Australia if it is (a) done in Australia; or is (b) supplied by an Australian-based supplier or, in the absence of (a) and (b), the supply is of a right or option to acquire a service connected with Australia, such as the supply to an overseas resident of an Australian holiday package. The place-of-supply rules for services are very broadly framed and, on their face, can potentially include the consumption of services outside Australia or can inadvertently lead to requiring non-residents to remit GST for services provided to businesses located in Australia. As the OECD explains:

> supplies of services performed in Australia, provided through an Australian enterprise, or consisting of rights to receive supplies in Australia are considered to be potentially taxable in Australia. To prevent GST applying to services not consumed in Australia, the Australian GST law includes broad, proxy-based zero-ratings ('GST-free') similar to those used in New Zealand. Australia's most significant variation from the New Zealand GST is its extensive application to non-residents, who may be required to remit GST for services performed in Australia, irrespective of whether their customer is a registered business or a final consumer. Similarly, services supplied from Australia to a non-resident cannot be zero-rated if the services are delivered to another person (whether a business or a consumer) in Australia.

Although beyond the scope of this book,[245] these rules have been added to the calls for further reform of the manner in which the Australian GST applies to cross-border supplies.[246]

4 NORM 1 – A BROAD CONSUMPTION BASE AT A SINGLE RATE WITH MINIMAL EXCLUSIONS

Chapter 2 outlined the consensus within the conventional approach to levy the VAT on a broad-consumption base at a single rate. This section first examines an area of apparent compliance with the requirement to levy the VAT at a single rate but highlights how this leads to unintended and costly consequences. The section then explores an area of clear non-compliance by discussing how the GST fails to tax a broad consumption base. It examines how domestic laws contribute to this outcome. In both cases, the conventional approach offers little by which to understand these real VAT outcomes.

4.1 *Unintended consequences of a single rate*

Unlike many other developed countries, the Australian GST is levied at a single rate (albeit a comparatively low rate of 10 per cent, as well as the zero-rating of certain domestic supplies).[247] The levying of the GST at a single rate was driven by

OECD, Consumption *Tax Trends 2012: VAT/GST and Excise Rates, Trends and Administration Issues* (OECD Publishing, Paris, 2012), 37. The breadth of the Australian laws to non-residents led the BoT to recommend that the Government 'consider reviewing the application of the GST to cross-border transactions with a view to simplifying and reducing the number of non-residents in the system', despite this being outside the Board's terms of reference: *Review of the Legal Framework for the Administration of the Goods and Services Tax: A Report to the Assistant Treasurer and Minister for Competition Policy and Consumer Affairs* (Australian Government, Canberra, 2008), 112. The Australian government responded by announcing only minor changes to the rules for cross-border supplies: Commonwealth of Australia Treasury, *Budget 2012–2013 – Budget Paper No. 2* (AGPS, Canberra, 2012), 26.

[245] For further discussion, see Rebecca Millar, 'The Destination Principle: Past Developments and Future Challenges', in C. Peacock (ed.), *GST in Australia: Looking Forward from the First Decade* (Thomson Reuters, Pyrmont, 2011), 313; OECD, *Consumption Tax Trends 2012: VAT/GST and Excise Rates, Trends and Administration Issues* (OECD Publishing, Paris, 2012), 37–38; Board of Taxation, *Review of the Application of GST to Cross-Border Transactions: A Report to the Assistant Treasurer* (Canberra, 2010), 13–14 (for criticism of the existing rules), and the whole report for other issues and suggested reforms.

[246] Board of Taxation, *Review of the Application of GST to Cross-Border Transactions: A Report to the Assistant Treasurer* (Australian Government, Canberra, 2010).

[247] Of OECD countries, only Japan levies its unique VAT at a single rate with no zero-rating. The OECD identifies four other member countries (including Australia, Canada [this is true of the federal tax, but there are variations of the rate across the provinces], Israel and South Korea) that levy VAT at a single rate but also zero-rate some domestic supplies: OECD, *Consumption Tax Trends 2012: VAT/GST and Excise Rates, Trends and Administration Issues* (OECD Publishing, Paris, 2012), 80–83.

the same concerns shared by the conventional approach that were detailed in Chapter 2, §4.3. As the *Henry Review* explains:[248]

> A single rate of tax that does not require taxpayers to discriminate between different forms of consumption is likely to be the simplest approach, as well as being highly efficient.

Simplicity was undoubtedly a priority after the failure of *Fightback!* to explain the application of even a single-rate GST (see §1.3).

Others have highlighted that the desire to levy the VAT at a single rate was motivated by what the VAT replaced. As Fehily contends:[249]

> there was a very significant desire to not use multiple rates in the (then) new GST, partly because of the assertion of the undesirability of continuing with the old Sales Tax that was in place...[which] was only on goods...[and] subject to a multitude of different rates.

The WST that existed prior to the introduction of the GST had six separate rates ranging from 12 to 45 percent.[250] The WST had started at a single low rate (of 2.5 per cent in 1930) but was then subject to many subsequent rate and base variations.[251]

The decision to set a single-rate GST could be seen as influenced by the merits of the good VAT or as an instance of path-dependent policy learning, produced by a desire to avoid previous complications arising from the multi-rated WST. However, the desire to avoid a multiple-rate VAT has led policy-makers to devise innovative means which, although not registering as rate variations, have a similar effect of providing either a concessionary or additional effective rate of tax. Three are examined below: first, the extensive use of domestic zero-rating; second, the application of the margin scheme on real property transactions; and third, the luxury car tax and wine equalisation tax.

4.1.1 Extensive use of domestic zero-rating

Australia is not alone in applying differential tax treatment to different supplies. However, Table 6.1 shows that Australia leads the OECD in the extent to which it

[248] Commonwealth of Australia Treasury, Australia's Future Tax System Review Panel, *Australia's Future Tax System: Report to the Treasurer* (Australia's Future Tax System Review Panel: The Treasury, Canberra, 2009), 276.

[249] Ken Fehily, 'Comment: Real Property Issues in the GST', in R. Krever and D. White (eds.), *GST in Retrospect and Prospect* (Thomson Brookers, Auckland, 2007), 309, 310.

[250] See schedules 1 to 7 of the *Sales Tax (Exemptions and Classifications) Act 1992 (Cth)*; *Sales Tax Assessment Act 1992* (Cth); Sam Reinhardt and Lee Steel, 'A Brief History of Australia's Tax System', *Economic Roundup* (2006), 1, 20.

[251] Sam Reinhardt and Lee Steel, 'A Brief History of Australia's Tax System', *Economic Roundup* (2006), 1, 20.

TABLE 6.1 – *Comparison of zero-rating of certain domestic supplies in Australia against other OECD country approaches – 2008*[a]

Australian categories of domestic zero-rated supplies	Relevant subdivision of Division 38 ANTS Act	OECD – Zero-rate (excluding Australia)	OECD – Reduced rate	OECD Exempt
Food	38 A	4	17	0
Health	38 B	6	12	26
Education	38 C	0	1	25
Childcare	38 D	0	0	0
Religious services	38 F	0	0	0[b]
Activities of charitable institutions, etc.	38 G	1[c]	0	28
Water and sewerage	38 I	2	10	4
Transport and related matters	38K	4	15	5
Precious metals	38L	3	0	0

[a] Data based on 29 OECD countries with VAT as of 2008. These figures are estimates based on general approaches given that, for example, many countries might exempt some but not all medical supplies and apply reduced or zero-rates to other medical supplies: OECD, *Consumption Tax Trends 2008 – VAT/GST and Excise Rates, Trends and Administration Issues* (OECD, Paris, 2008), 51–56; Dick Warburton and Peter Hendy, *International Comparisons of Australia's Taxes* (Commonwealth of Australia Treasury, Canberra, 2006), 248.
[b] Some countries exempt or have reduced rates for burial and funeral services: OECD, *Consumption Tax Trends 2012 – VAT/GST and Excise Rates, Trends and Administration Issues* (OECD Publishing, Paris, 2012), Tables 3.9 (80–83) and 3.11 (86–88).
[c] The UK zero-rates certain supplies made to charitable organisations: ibid., 56.

zero-rates domestic supplies. Australia zero-rates at least 16 categories of domestic supply where most other OECD jurisdictions might apply a reduced rate or exemption.[252] As zero-rating involves collecting no GST on outputs and refunding GST on inputs, this method of exclusion to the GST base is more costly from a revenue perspective than reduced rates and exemptions. Treasury estimates the cost of the zero-rating of basic food alone to be on the order of $6 billion.[253]

[252] *ANTS Act* 1999, div. 38. At the time of writing, there were 17 categories of GST-free supplies with the final category including certain supplies of eligible emissions units under the Australian emissions trading scheme (subdiv. 38S). The repeal of Australia's emissions trading scheme is likely to reduce this list to 16.

[253] For 2013–2014, the zero-rating of food cost $6.2 billion: Commonwealth of Australia Treasury, *Tax Expenditures Statement 2013* (Australian Government, Canberra, 2013), 12; Commonwealth of Australia Treasury, Australia's Future Tax System Review Panel, *Australia's Future Tax System: Report to the Treasurer* (Australia's Future Tax System Review Panel: The Treasury, Canberra, 2009), 286. As has already been noted, a GST-free supply in Australia is the equivalent of a zero-rated supply: see Chapter 2, §4.2.2 of this book.

The list of exclusions to the Australian GST is the usual grab bag of standard exclusions mixed with deals cut by specific industries and groups. The original *ANTS package* had a much smaller list of only five zero-rated supplies.[254] As two practitioners from PricewaterhouseCoopers advised at the time of the release of the original package, 'given that the final policy for zero-rating is yet to be settled, there may still be room for negotiation'.[255] The fact that the list more than tripled indicates that there certainly was. Some lobbying failed. For example, unlike many OECD countries, Australia does not zero-rate or apply concessional treatment to books and newspapers despite a fierce industry campaign to do so.[256] The GST applies to supplies of clothing in Australia which, unlike other ostensibly equity-based exclusions, did not garner the same intensity of opposition.[257] Other lobbying efforts were clearly more fruitful; Australia is the only OECD country to zero-rate religious services and one of only four countries that zero-rate certain supplies of precious metals.[258] The preferential taxation of supplies of precious metals is an extension of the preferential treatment under the WST. It was lobbied for by the mining industry and was justified on the basis that because the price of precious metals is fixed internationally, to levy GST on supplies would constitute a tax on mining businesses because the GST could not be passed forward in the price to the consumer.[259] This produces an odd situation where gold, the quintessential commodity or luxury good, is not taxed but inputs used in its production can be credited.

[254] The original list consisted of health and medical supplies, educational supplies, childcare, religious services and charitable activities: *ANTS Statement*, 93–95.

[255] Margherita Antonelli and David Oliver (of PricewaterhouseCoopers), 'Practical Thoughts on the GST', *Weekly Tax Bulletin* (37) (1998), 1069. The authors also noted, somewhat prophetically, that:

> [T]he most controversial issue will be, whether to zero-rate food. Unlike Dr Hewson's Fightback package which proposed to zero-rate food, the Government is determined to include all food in the GST base. This is probably the biggest difference between the 1993 GST proposal and the 1998 proposal. Ironically, it may become 'the straw that breaks the camel's back'.

[256] Murray Waldren, Terry Plane and Richard McGregor, 'Words of War on Publishing Tax', *The Australian*, 1 June 1999, 4. The campaign extracted some compromises, including a compensation package (the 'book industry assistance plan') which, among other things, provided a subsidy of 8 per cent for educational textbooks to offset the imposition of the GST: *Appropriation (Supplementary Measures) Act (No. 1) 1999* (Cth). This subsidy expired (and was not renewed, despite calls to do so) in 2005.

[257] Graeme Cooper and Richard Vann, 'Implementing the Goods and Services Tax', *Sydney Law Review* 23 (1999), 337, 386.

[258] The first supply of precious metal after refinement is GST free, while subsequent supplies are input taxed: *ANTS Act 1999*, s 38–385.

[259] *Sales Tax (Exemptions and Classifications) Act* 1992 (Cth), sch 1, ch. 1; Michael Jeffrey and Russell Maynard, 'Australia's GST: What It Means for the Mining Industry', *Australian Mining and Petroleum Law Journal* 18(1) (1999), 54.

The heavy reliance on domestic zero-rating is perhaps the most visible outcome of the desire to adhere to a single rate. The plausibility of this link is supported by the Howard government's admission that the Democrats rejected an offer by the conservatives to tax food at 5 percent. Ultimately, food was zero-rated.[260] Treasurer Costello defended claims that the GST's treatment of food would be more complex than under the WST by claiming that 'the new system has only "one-fifth" the amount of complexity because five rates under the existing sales tax come down to one'.[261]

Not only is zero-rating expensive, but it is dominated by definitional disputes. As was noted in §2.4, the exclusion of basic food from the GST base was, to a significant extent, introduced through regulations and schedules containing key definitions. This approach to legislating for food also closely resembles the previous approach under the WST:[262]

> For the Government is planning that most of the rules governing the GST will not be set in legislation. Instead, just like the old wholesale tax system, the rules will be contained in regulations determined by the Australian Tax Office. In theory, the Tax Office could end up producing lists of goods – identified by brand name – which are taxable. Just as they do under the wholesale tax…This means the Treasurer and Tax Office would have discretion to decide which goods were in or out of the tax-free boundary. And business can be expected to contest this boundary in private, or through the courts.

As §2.4 indicated, the move to place key definitions in schedules and regulations was in response to intense lobbying from industry, including the food industry.[263] The move enables tax policy-makers and administrators to have a greater degree of latitude to settle definitions through amending regulations rather than the primary Act.[264] However, disputes between taxpayers and administrators over the definition of basic food have resulted in much compliance activity. For example, as of

[260] It was reported around the time of the compromise with the Democrats that John Howard revealed that this 5 per cent option had been put to the Democrats but was rejected: Steve Lewis and Paul Cleary, 'Business Tastes a Bitter Defeat', *Australian Financial Review* (29–30 May 1999), 6. It was further reported that Treasurer Peter Costello confirmed that the 5 per cent rate for food was first put to the Democrats but rejected: Paul Cleary, 'The McDonald's Amendment', *Australian Financial Review* (4 June 1999), 41. Business lobbyists also strongly opposed taxing food at different rates but proposed a 5 per cent rate for all food if a compromise was required: Thomson Reuters, 'Business Coalition for Tax Reform – Tax All Food at a Single Rate', *GST News Alert* (26) (1999).

[261] Costello, quoted in Paul Cleary, 'The McDonald's Amendment', *Australian Financial Review* (4 June 1999), 41. Given that the GST is applied at both the standard rate and a zero-rate, it would be more correct to identify two rates rather than one.

[262] Paul Cleary, 'The McDonald's Amendment', *Australian Financial Review* (4 June 1999), 41.

[263] For example, lobbying by McDonald's to have pre-prepared meals supplied by retail outlets taxed the same as meals sold at takeaway restaurants led to an amendment labelled the McDonald's amendment: ibid.

[264] Ibid.

February 2014 there were approximately 95 ATO Interpretive Decisions[265] on the GST-free status of food and food-like products ranging from bovine colostrum powder (GST free when sold for human consumption) to edible chocolate body paint (taxable).[266]

4.1.2 The margin scheme on select real property transactions

The application of the GST to real property transactions is problematic in Australia, as it is under both the good VAT and real VATs, and is yet another instance of a frontier issue. In general terms, the Australian approach is that all supplies of commercial real property are taxable, but only initial supplies of residential real property are taxable, with subsequent supplies of residential property, such as sales and leases, input taxed.[267] It is not the intention of this book to detail the complex treatment of real property under the GST, as the discussion of financial supplies in §4.3.3 is intended to highlight the nature of the difficulties that arise in real VATs when frontier issues that test the limits of the good VAT are reached. This section simply highlights a single unique[268] aspect in the GST's application to certain supplies of real property, the margin scheme, and highlights how one feature of the scheme relates to the levying of the GST at a single rate.

The margin scheme is designed to 'ensure that the GST is only payable on the value added [including capital appreciation] after the commencement of the

[265] Search undertaken through - ATO, *Legal Database* (2014) (http://law.ato.gov.au/atolaw/search.htm); see above, n 197 for a definition of ATO Interpretative Decisions.

[266] ATO, *Goods and Services Tax: GST and Bovine Colostrum Powder*, ATO ID 2004/622, 30 July 2004; ATO, *Goods and Services Tax: GST and Edible Chocolate Body Paint*, ATO ID 2004/38, 27 September 2002.

[267] The treatment of real property transactions varies according to the nature of the property supplied: *ANTS Act* 1999. Taxable supplies include supplies of commercial property, including commercial residential premises (s 40–65); short-term accommodation (s 40–35(1)(b)); the initial supply of residential premises (including newly constructed and substantially renovated premises) (s 40–75 ANTS); or the initial supply of a long-term lease of residential property (of more than 50 years) (s 40–70(1)(b) and s 195–1). Certain supplies are taxed concessionally: for example, supplies of long-term residential commercial accommodation are generally taxed at half the value of the available base (another concession that achieves a similar outcome to a reduced rate) (div. 87). Input-taxed supplies include subsequent supplies of residential property (s 40–65, subdiv. 40-C) and residential leases (s 40–70, subdiv. 40-B). Supplies of certain real property are GST free, including certain grants or leases by government (subdiv. 38N); certain supplies of farm land (div. subdiv. 38O) and land sold as part of a going concern (div. subdiv. 38J).

[268] The Australian GST is unique in applying a margin scheme to supplies of real property. Most OECD jurisdictions employ a margin scheme for the taxation of secondhand goods, travel agencies, works of arts and collectibles. Israel applies a limited margin scheme to the 'sale of dwellings by a real estate dealer, who acquired it from a person who is not a non-profit organisation, a financial institution or a dealer': Organisation for Economic Cooperation and Development (OECD), *Consumption Tax Trends 2012: VAT/GST and Excise Rates, Trends and Administration Issues* (OECD Publishing, Paris, 2012), 91–93, Table 3.13.

GST system'.[269] As a result, if vendors and purchasers elect to apply the margin scheme, GST is payable only on the value added or margin on taxable supplies of certain real property (namely, freehold interests in land, stratum units and long-term leases) calculated after 1 July 2000.[270]

Vendors and purchasers can either agree to choose to apply the basic rules (so that GST is payable on 1/11 of the purchase price and the buyer can claim input tax credits on inputs), or they can elect in writing to apply the margin scheme.[271] If the parties elect to apply the margin scheme, GST is payable at 1/11 of the margin[272] of the property (as opposed to the entire purchase price).[273] However, the quid pro quo is that input tax credits cannot be claimed by the purchaser for the supply of the real property.[274] Given that the choice of the margin scheme entails the denial of input tax credits, the scheme will generally be used only where the purchaser is unregistered for GST purchases (for example, an owner-occupier acquiring the property for personal use) or if the purchaser would ordinarily be denied input tax credits (as might be the case if the purchaser was a financial institution). By contrast, commercial operators acquiring the property in the course of their enterprise would most likely prefer for GST to apply, so as to claim input tax credits for the supply of the property.[275]

There are many issues in relation to the operation of the margin scheme.[276] This discussion is intended to highlight one consequence of the scheme, which is that the margin scheme can operate as a backdoor method of imposing a lower rate of VAT. As Fehily contends:[277]

> [T]axing something at 10% but on an amount lower than the full selling price (e.g., as occurs in Australia under the margin scheme for residential premises), or

[269] Commonwealth of Australia Treasury, *Consultation Paper on the Review of the Margin Scheme* (Australian Government, Canberra, 12 May 2009); EM ANTS Bill 1998; Explanatory Memorandum, Tax Laws Amendment (2008 Measures No. 5), Bill 2008 (Cth).

[270] *ANTS Act* 1999 div. 75, s 75–5(1).

[271] Ibid., s 75–5(1) and (1A). This election is subject to a growing list of restrictions: see s75–5(2)-(4). The election must be exercised on or before the date of supply: *Cyonara Snowfox Pty Ltd. v. Commissioner of Taxation* 208 FCR 471, 490–492; s75(1A).

[272] The margin upon which the GST is payable is calculated either under the 'consideration method' or in specific circumstances the 'valuation method'. The consideration method calculates the margin as the amount by which the consideration for supply exceeds the consideration for the acquisition of the respective interest: *ANTS Act* 1999, s 75–10(2). The valuation method calculates the margin as the amount by which the consideration for supply of the property exceeds the value of the property as of 1 July 2000 or the date the supplier registered or was required to register for the GST: at s 75–10(3), s75–11. See also Commonwealth of Australia Treasury, *Consultation Paper on the Review of the Margin Scheme* (Australian Government, Canberra, 12 May 2009), 3.

[273] *ANTS Act* 1999, s 75–10(1).

[274] Ibid., s 75–20.

[275] Christine Peacock, 'Changes to the Australian GST Immovable Property "Margin Scheme"', *International VAT Monitor* (September/October 2006), 327, 328.

[276] For a fuller discussion of the issues, see, e.g., ibid.

[277] Ken Fehily, 'Comment: Real Property Issues in the GST', in R. Krever and D. White (eds.), *GST in Retrospect and Prospect* (Thomson Brookers, Auckland, 2007), 309, 310.

taxing the full selling price at a rate less than 10%, to my mind, is the same thing. In a sense, it is a mischievous means of enabling the government to argue that there is only one rate of GST, when really there is not.

This circuitous method of achieving a de facto concessional rate has come at great expense. The margin scheme is costly to revenue;[278] complex to administer;[279] subject to significant and largely unanticipated abuse – with taxpayers structuring transactions to take advantage of the margin scheme and other concessional provisions in the ANTS legislation;[280] results in a disproportionate share of adverse audit findings, taxpayer objections and litigation (around one-third of the 30 per cent of GST litigation that concerns real property relates to the margin scheme);[281] and has been subject to numerous ad hoc legislative amendments – mostly in response to avoidance activity.[282]

Despite complaining vociferously about the operation of the margin scheme,[283] a recent proposal to simplify and redraft the margin scheme provisions met with equally vocal opposition from the property and construction industry and its advisers.[284]

278 Christine Peacock, 'Changes to the Australian GST Immovable Property "Margin Scheme"', *International VAT Monitor* (September/October 2006), 327.

279 There are over 200 pages of ATO publications on the margin scheme, many of which have conflicted with the approach of the courts to the scheme. In 2009, the Treasury estimated that ATO official compliance activity in relation to the scheme was at six Goods and Services Tax Rulings (GSTR), one draft GSTR, a Goods and Services Tax Determination (GSTD), four Law Administrative Practice Statements (PSLA), five Margin Scheme Legislative Determinations (MSV), six fact sheets and numerous entries on the ATO Issues Register: Commonwealth of Australia Treasury, *Consultation Paper on the Review of the Margin Scheme* (Australian Government, Canberra, 12 May 2009), 6–7; ATO, *Legal Database* (2014) (law.ato.gov.au/atolaw/execute_search.htm).

280 It is of little surprise that the first High Court case on the application of the general anti-avoidance rule arose as a result of a dispute over the application of the margin scheme: *Commissioner of Taxation v. Unit Trend Services Pty Ltd.* (2013), 297 ALR 190; see above, n 212. Christine Peacock, 'Changes to the Australian GST Immovable Property "Margin Scheme", *International VAT Monitor* (September/October 2006), 327.

281 The Treasury estimated that based on cases as at 27 February 2009, of 155 cases before the courts, 48 related to property and 16 involved the margin scheme: Commonwealth of Australia Treasury, *Consultation Paper on the Review of the Margin Scheme* (Australian Government, Canberra, 12 May 2009), 6. More recent data confirm that these trends continue: Australian Taxation Office (ATO), *GST Administration Annual Performance Report 2012–13* (ATO, Canberra, 2013), 45, 51.

282 The original *ANTS Act* 1999, div. 75 contained five operative provisions and spanned approximately one page. Numerous amendments have been made – largely as ad hoc responses to address unanticipated abuse of the scheme – so that 15 provisions span about 17 pages: *ANTS Act* 1999 Div. 75; Commonwealth of Australia Treasury, *Consultation Paper on the Review of the Margin Scheme* (Australian Government, Canberra, 12 May 2009), 5; see, e.g., *Tax Laws Amendments (2005 Measures No. 2) Act 2005* (Cth), sch 6.

283 Board of Taxation, *Review of the Legal Framework for the Administration of the Goods and Services Tax: A Report to the Assistant Treasurer and Minister for Competition Policy and Consumer Affairs* (Australian Government, Canberra, 2008), ch. 4.

284 Commonwealth of Australia Treasury, *Implementation of the Recommendations of Treasury's Review of the GST Margin Scheme – Discussion Paper* (Australian Government, Canberra, 2010), 2.

As a result, the task of restructuring the provisions has been abandoned.[285] This shows how the sunk costs of business complying with, and finding opportunities not to comply with, the complexities of real VATs can prompt resistance to reform. It also highlights how, beneath the simple overall veneer of the single rate, lies much complexity that cannot be explained by merits but only by localised responses by policy-makers and taxpayers.

4.1.3 Luxury car tax and wine equalisation tax

Some jurisdictions apply an increased VAT rate to luxury goods. In Australia, the GST applies at a single rate across a range of goods.[286] However, because the WST applied an increased rate on a range of luxury goods,[287] the application of a single-rate GST would have led to a dramatic reduction in the cost of some luxury items, such as wine and luxury cars.[288] Rather than introduce increased rates, which would be seen to depart from the good VAT, policy-makers chose to introduce two separate specific sales taxes to apply to the sale of wine (the Wine Equalisation Tax [WET])[289] and luxury cars (Luxury Car Tax [LCT]).[290] The WET and LCT are single-stage sales taxes based on the WST. Therefore, a multi-rated GST is avoided only through the imposition of a tax modelled on the much-derided WST that the ANTS reforms sought to replace.

The WET in particular was fiercely unpopular with the wine industry.[291] It was suggested by the Labor opposition at the time of the bill's introduction that a large part of the motivation behind both taxes was to avoid a multi-rated GST:[292]

[285] Terry Hayes, 'GST Margin Scheme Restructure Will Not Proceed', *Weekly Tax Bulletin* (28) (29 June 2012), 1059.

[286] Other than those that are not otherwise GST free or input taxed.

[287] See schedules 6 and 7 to the *Sales Tax (Exemptions and Classifications) Act 1992* (Cth). There is an obvious vertical equity imperative for this.

[288] As the previous WST rates were approximately 40 percent, the price of wine and luxury cars would have been substantially reduced: ibid.

[289] WET is a single-stage tax applied at the wholesale level to qualifying wine and related products for domestic consumption (generally with a minimum alcohol content of 1.15%) and is applied at a rate of 29%. GST is then generally levied on the WET-inclusive price. Revenue from WET was $729 million in 2011–2012: ATO, *Guide to Wine Equalisation Tax* (13 December 2012) (ato.gov.au/Business/Wine-equalisation-tax/); ATO, *Taxation Statistics: 2011–2012* (ATO, Canberra, 2013), 109; *A New Tax System (Wine Equalisation Tax) Act 1999* (Cth), s2–1.

[290] The Luxury Car Tax is a single-stage sales tax that is levied on taxable supplies and importations of luxury cars at a rate of 33 per cent (on the value above a specified threshold – $ 60,316 as of 14 February 2014). The LCT is applied in addition to, but not inclusive of, the GST. Revenue from LCT was $441 million in 2011–2012: *A New Tax System (Luxury Car Tax) Act 1999* (Cth), s2–1. ATO, *Guide to Luxury Car Tax* (14 February 2014) (ato.gov.au/Business/Luxury-car-tax/); ATO, *Taxation Statistics: 2011–12* (ATO, Canberra, 2013), 109.

[291] Steve Lewis, 'Wine Makers Say New Tax Will Damage a Cellars Market', *Australian Financial Review*, 24 June 1999, 4.

[292] Commonwealth of Australia, *Parliamentary Debates*, House of Representatives, 31 March 1999, 4835 (Simon Crean [Deputy Leader of the Opposition]).

> It arises for one reason and one reason only—that is, the arrogance of the Treasurer. The Treasurer would not embrace the idea of a multirate direct tax. He wanted a single rate GST, and he does not care about the consequences.

The efficiency gains from this approach over levying the GST at multiple rates are unclear and were questioned by the Labor opposition at the time of the bill's introduction:[293]

> Whilst we are totally opposed to the GST, it would have been far more efficient to have a multirate GST to achieve the government's aims, rather than a forcing of the industry to deal with a whole new tax on top of the GST.

Of course, there are valid reasons to avoid introducing multiple rates, as this might lead to pressure to introduce further rate variations (lower or higher). Irrespective of the relative merits of multiple- or single-rate VATs, this discussion demonstrates that, even when policy-makers are motivated by the desire to realise the merits of the good VAT (i.e., a single rate), factors beyond merits, such as the tax position left by the previous WST, perceptions of fairness and pressure from industry groups, shape real VAT outcomes.

4.2 *Failure to reach a broad consumption base*

Although the revenue yield of the GST was initially in accordance with expectations,[294] Table 6.2 shows that, contrary to predictions, GST revenues have proved susceptible to economic fluctuations with 'weaker than anticipated'[295] and 'highly volatile'[296] revenues following the 2008 economic downturn.

The GST has not lived up to expectations in relation to its ability to tax a broad consumption base. The Australian GST taxes approximately only half of the

[293] Ibid.

[294] Before the compromise with the Democrats, the *ANTS Statement* predicted that the GST would raise $27.20 billion (2000–2001), $31.96 billion (2001–2002) and $32.81 billion (2002–2003): *ANTS Statement*, 100. As estimated, annual growth in GST revenues has averaged approximately 6 per cent per year since its introduction, but this masks a significant disparity between pre-global financial crisis revenues, which grew at an average of 8.3 per cent per year up until 2007–2008, and post-global financial crisis revenues, which increased only 2.2 per cent per year from 2008 to 2012: Commonwealth of Australia Government, *GST Distribution Review Final Report* (Australian Govt Pub Service, Canberra, October 2012), 153.

[295] 'GST collections continue to be weaker than anticipated': Commonwealth of Australia Treasury, *Mid-Year Economic and Fiscal Outlook* (Australian Government, Canberra, 2010), Pt. 3, 32.

[296] Commonwealth of Australia Government, *GST Distribution Review Final Report* (Australian Govt Pub Service, Canberra, October 2012), 157.

TABLE 6.2 – *GST revenue and as a proportion of federal government taxation revenue*[297]

	2000–2001	2001–2002	2002–2003	2003–2004	2004–2005	2005–2006	2006–2007	2007–2008	2008–2009	2009–2010	2010–2011	2011–2012
Total Tax Revenue (TTR) ($m)	175,591	177,838	194,881	209,643	229,232	245,313	262,101	285,954	278,363	267,556	289,124	317,888
GST ($m)	23,854	27,389	31,257	34,121	35,655	39,118	41,208	44,381	42,626	46,553	48,093	48,849
GST as a % of TTR	13.6	15.4	16	16.3	15.5	15.9	15.7	15.5	15.3	17.4	16.6	15.3

[297] Based on data from Australian Bureau of Statistics, 5506.0 – *Taxation Revenue, Australia*, 2009–10 (ABS, Canberra, 2011); Australian Bureau of Statistics, 5506.0 – *Taxation Revenue, Australia*, 2011–12 (ABS, Canberra, 2013).

available consumption base.[298] For 2009, the OECD estimates a VAT revenue ratio (VRR) of 0.52 for the GST against an unweighted OECD average of 0.58.[299] Moreover, the VRR has fallen in recent years.[300] This is of concern to authorities because, as the *Henry Review* recently noted, 'few, if any, countries have significantly broadened their main consumption tax base after introduction', which might further be reinforced, at least politically if not legally, through the requirement that changes to the rate and base secure the agreement of all Commonwealth and state governments.[301] The decline in GST revenues and the VRR has led to a number of calls to reform the GST, so as to expand its base.[302] To date, successive governments have resisted any suggestion of reform in this direction.

Figure 6.1 gives an indication of the failure to tax some of the main consumption bases that contribute to this gap. Although the data refer to the impact of all consumption taxes (including excise), the revenue gaps are consistent with the exclusions to the GST base. Figure 6.1 shows that most prominent among these gaps are housing (see §4.1.2), food (see §2.3 and §4.1.1), insurance and financial supplies (see §4.3.3), health and education (see generally §4.1.1).

Justice Edmunds, of the Federal Court of Australia, was recently reported as criticising the GST for being 'expensive to collect, leaking revenue and tying up the courts'.[303] He concluded that the GST had '"failed to meet the generally accepted hallmarks of tax reform" and had in many ways made things worse'.[304] Given that the Federal Court is the forum for most litigation on the GST, it is significant that a judge of the Federal Court presents such a damning assessment of the GST.

The GST, like the good VAT, is intended to reach a broad base of final consumption. However, this economic end needs to be achieved through laws.

[298] Commonwealth of Australia Treasury, Australia's Future Tax System Review Panel, *Australia's Future Tax System: Report to the Treasurer* (Australia's Future Tax System Review Panel: The Treasury, Canberra, 2009), 286.

[299] Since introducing the GST, Australia has generally taxed around half of the available consumption base at around or just below the OECD average: OECD, *Consumption Tax Trends 2012: VAT/GST and Excise Rates, Trends and Administration Issues* (OECD Publishing, Paris, 2012), 113. See Chapter 3, §4.1 of this book.

[300] The VRR fell from 0.54 in 2007 to 0.50 in 2008. This drop should not be a product of the economic downturn and decreased consumer spending because the VRR measures the VAT collected against actual expenditure levels: OECD, *Consumption Tax Trends 2012: VAT/GST and Excise Rates, Trends and Administration Issues* (OECD Publishing, Paris, 2012), 113.

[301] Commonwealth of Australia Treasury, Australia's Future Tax System Review Panel, *Australia's Future Tax System: Report to the Treasurer* (Australia's Future Tax System Review Panel: The Treasury, Canberra, 2009), 273, and at 284. As §2.1 highlighted, this is more of a political barrier than an enforceable legal barrier.

[302] See, e.g., Commonwealth of Australia Government, *GST Distribution Review Final Report* (Australian Govt Pub Service, Canberra, October 2012), ch. 11; the OECD suggests expanding the base and increasing rates: OECD, *Economic Surveys – Australia* (OECD, Paris, 2012), 10; John Daley, Cassie McGannon and Leah Ginnivan, *Game-Changers: Economic Reform Priorities for Australia* (Grattan Institute, Melbourne, 2012), 29.

[303] Peter Martin, 'Judge Hits Out at Leaky, Expensive GST', *The Age*, 15 September 2011, 3.

[304] Peter Martin, 'Judge Hits Out at Leaky, Expensive GST', *The Age*, 15 September 2011, 3.

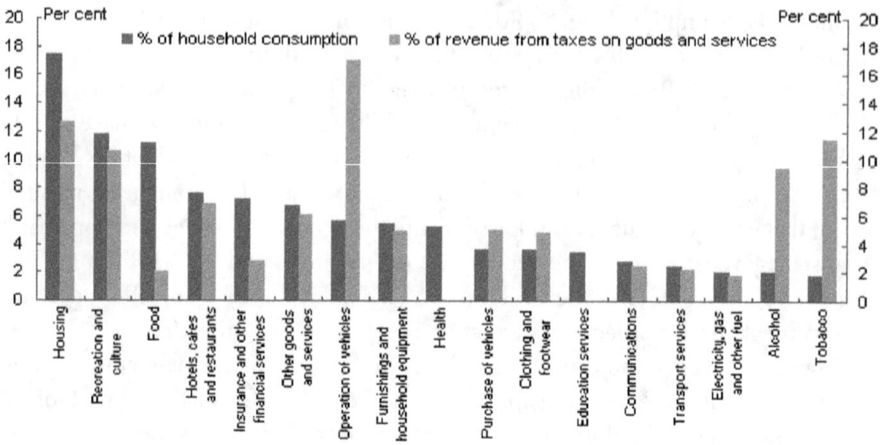

FIGURE 6.1 Household consumption and estimated revenue from Australian government taxes on goods and services in 2006–2007[305]

These laws, in turn, bring to bear local influences that shape drafting styles, as well as the approach of administrators and the interpretation of those laws by the judiciary. Chapter 2, §4 and §5 indicated that laws are needed to identify when a taxable supply occurs (so as to trigger liability to pay VAT) and when a business will be entitled to receive input credits (so as to ensure that the VAT falls on the base of end consumption rather than production).

The remainder of this section explores how the design and implementation of laws designed to tax consumption through the GST contribute to the failure of the GST to tax a broad consumption base. After introducing the basic legislative framework of the GST (see §4.3), this section explores how institutionalised legal practices impact both (1) the liability to pay GST (see §4.3.1) and (2) entitlement to input tax credits (see §4.3.2). The entitlement to credits is further explored through (3) examining the complex treatment of financial supplies (see §4.3.3). There are a number of problems that arise under all three areas, but the discussion focuses on some key issues to illustrate the difficulties and to show how institutions rather than merits explain much more of the real VAT outcomes that have arisen.

4.3 *Legislating for a consumption base*

The ANTS legislation is drafted so as to provide the basic rules (contained in Chapter 2 of the Act), the exemptions (contained in Chapter 3 of the Act) and the

[305] Commonwealth of Australia Treasury, Australia's Future Tax System Review Panel, *Architecture of Australia's Tax and Transfer System* (Commonwealth of Australia Treasury, Canberra, 2008), 278 (reproduced with permission). The high revenues relative to household consumption from the operation of vehicles, alcohol and tobacco are a result of excise taxation.

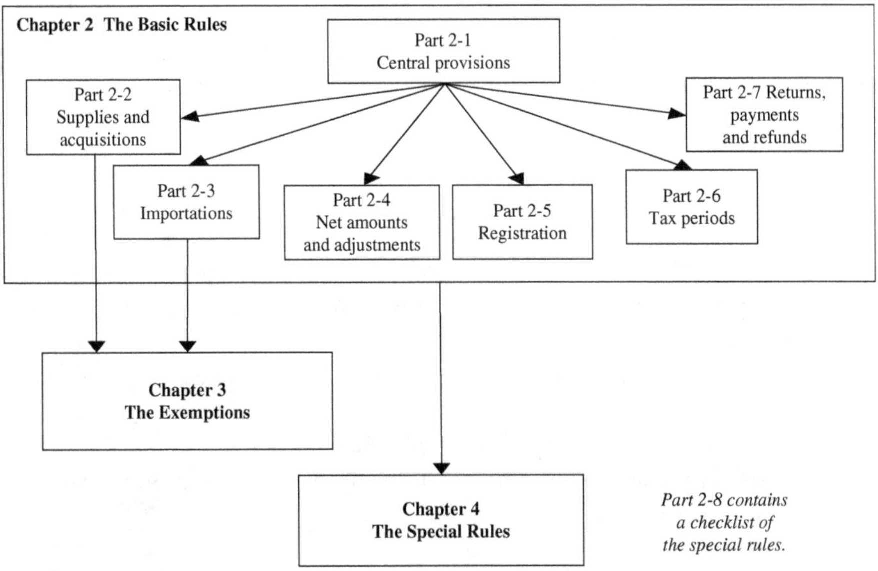

FIGURE 6.2 Overview of legislative structure of Australian GST[306]

special rules (contained in Chapter 4 of the Act).[307] Figure 6.2 is a diagram from the ANTS legislation representing the legislative structure.

The basic rules include the legal rules that determine liability to pay GST (when, how and who is liable to pay, so that registered entities remit the GST but final consumers pay the tax) and entitlement to credit or a refund for GST paid (when, how and who is entitled to credits, so that registered entities, including businesses, do not incur the GST).[308]

The exemptions to the basic rules define when supplies will be GST free (such as food) or exempt, i.e., input taxed (such as financial supplies).

Chapter 4 of the legislation contains the special rules, which modify the operation of the basic rules. These rules constitute over half the legislation and contain special rules relating to religious groups; joint ventures; the supply of secondhand goods; insurance; the application of GST to taxes, fees and charges; gambling; reverse-charge mechanisms for certain offshore supplies; the margin scheme for real property (see §4.1.2); and the anti-avoidance provisions (see §3.1.2). These special rules contain much of the deviation from the design norms of the good

[306] *ANTS Act 1999*, s 2–5. Sourced from ComLaw at 21 March 2014. For the latest information on Australian Government law, please go to comlaw.gov.au/Content/Copyright#attributed. This material is licensed for reuse under a Creative Commons CC BY-NC-SA 3.0 licence.

[307] Chapter 5 of the Act contains miscellaneous provisions, chapter 6 contains provisions relating to the interpretation of the legislation, chapter 1 contains the introduction: *ANTS Act 1999*.

[308] *ANTS Act 1999*, s 2–5.

VAT and are often a product of the political compromises that attended the introduction of the GST. One special rule, the reduced input tax credit for financial supplies, is discussed in depth at §4.3.3.4 to illustrate some of the issues that arise in relation to these rules.

4.3.1 Liability for GST

In Australia, the GST is payable on taxable supplies[309] and taxable importations.[310] Liability to pay the GST generally falls on the supplier.[311] This section will focus on domestic supplies.

An entity makes a taxable supply if the following positive elements are satisfied:[312]

- The entity makes a 'supply'[313] for 'consideration';[314]
- The supply is made in the course or furtherance of an 'enterprise'[315] that the entity carries on;
- The supply is 'connected with Australia';[316] and
- The entity is registered or required to be registered.[317]

A supply is not a taxable supply to the extent that it is (negative elements):[318]

[309] Ibid., s 9–5, 9–40. [310] Ibid., s 13–40.

[311] For exceptions, see Div. 83 and 84 outlining compulsory and voluntary reverse-charge mechanisms: ibid.

[312] Ibid., s 9–40.

[313] Ibid., s9–10. Supply is broadly (if somewhat circularly) defined in the legislation as 'any form of supply whatsoever'. This includes voluntary and involuntary supplies, legal and illegal supplies, and positive supplies and negative supplies (where the supplier refrains from doing an act): at s 9–10(1). The courts have generally interpreted the term supply broadly: *Saga Holidays Ltd. v. Commissioner of Taxation (Cth) and Others* (2006), 156 FCR 256, 265 [35].

[314] *ANTS Act* 1999, s 9–15.

[315] *ANTS Act* 1999, s 9–20 defines enterprise broadly to include business, charities and religious institutions. The enterprise requirement is the Australian legislature's attempt to exclude supplies made in a private or domestic capacity. This is also achieved through the registration requirement and the requirement that suppliers have an Australian Business Number (ABN) in order for the recipient of a supply to obtain an input credit: see further below, n 317; *A New Tax System (Pay As You Go) Act* 1999 (Cth.); *GST Legislation Plus*, annotated by Richard Krever (Thomson Reuters, 2014), see 75–81 for a discussion of alternative approaches used in other comparable jurisdictions to achieve a similar outcome (of not taxing private/personal/non-business supplies).

[316] *ANTS Act* 1999, s 9–25. This concerns the application of norm 3, the destination principle: see §3.2.

[317] Only registered entities are capable of making a taxable supply, and only in so far as the supply relates to carrying on an enterprise. This excludes from taxation supplies made by a registered person in a personal capacity. Registration is compulsory for entities with annual (current and/or projected) turnover exceeding $75,000 for entities other than non-profit entities and $150,000 for non-profit entities: *ANTS Act* 1999, s 23–5; *ANTS Regulations* 1999, reg. 23–15.01, 23–15.02. Registration is voluntary for entities below this threshold: *ANTS Act* 1999, s 23–10.

[318] *ANTS Act* 1999, s 9–5, 9–30, div. 38, div. 40. A supply that could be classified as both input taxed and GST free will generally be treated as a GST-free supply: s 9–30(3).

- 'GST-free';[319] or
- 'Input taxed'.[320]

There are, therefore, three main potential tax outcomes for domestic supplies within the scope of the Act:[321]

- Taxable and therefore subject to GST: as the GST is levied on a GST-inclusive basis, the tax is payable on 1/11 of the GST inclusive price for eligible supplies of goods and services;[322]
- Input taxed: no GST is paid on the supply, but the supplier is not entitled to a credit for GST incurred on inputs used in making the supply (the Australian equivalent of exemption) – see as an example §4.3.3, financial supplies;[323] or
- GST-free: the final consumer pays no GST, but the supplier can obtain input tax credits (the Australian equivalent of zero-rating): see §4.1.1.[324]

Entities are required to file GST returns and remit GST in relation to monthly, quarterly or, in certain circumstances, annual 'tax periods'.[325] GST is attributable to the tax period during which the earlier of two events occurs – either the receipt of consideration for a supply or, if an invoice is issued relating to a supply before any consideration is received, the date the invoice is issued.[326] When the GST charged on supplies exceeds the total input tax credits the taxpayer is entitled to claim over a 'tax period', the taxpayer remits a net amount to the ATO.[327] When the input tax credits exceed the tax charged on supplies over a 'tax period', the taxpayer is entitled to a refund or to offset the amount against other outstanding tax liabilities.[328]

4.3.1.1 INTERPRETING A 'TAXABLE SUPPLY' One might think from surveying the conventional approach that the status of the GST as a consumption tax is irrefutable. However, this is not necessarily the view of Australian courts charged with

[319] Ibid., div. 38. [320] Ibid., div. 40.

[321] These are all supplies that are within the scope of the legislation. As with all jurisdictions, there exist supplies, including those made by registered entities, which are beyond the legislative scope of the Act. This might be, for example, because the supply does not meet the definition of supply within the Act. See further Richard Krever and Rita de la Feria, 'Ending VAT Exemptions: Towards a Post-Modern VAT', in R. de la Feria (ed.), *VAT Exemptions: Consequences and Design Alternatives* (vol. 37, EUCOTAX Series on European Taxation, Kluwer Law International, Alphen aan den Rijn, 2013), 3, 12–22.

[322] 1/11 of the gross amount equals 10 per cent of the net amount: *ANTS Act 1999*, s 9–70.

[323] Other input-taxed supplies include supplies relating to residential rent, residential premises, precious metals (other than the first zero-rated supply), school tuckshops and canteens and charitable fund-raising events: ibid., div. 40.

[324] Ibid., div. 38. [325] Ibid., div. 27 and 151.

[326] Ibid., s29–5(1), qualified by s29–5(2). [327] *ANTS Act 1999*, s 17–5, ss 33–3, 33–5.

[328] Ibid., s35–5; *Taxation Administration Act 1958*, ss 8AAZL-8AAZLB, 8AAZLE.

interpreting the legislation implementing the GST. One example will suffice to demonstrate the point.[329]

In 2008, the High Court of Australia handed down one of its earliest decisions on the GST, the *Reliance Carpet* case.[330] It is interesting to note in passing the eight-year time lag between the introduction of the ANTS legislation and the first substantive consideration of it by the High Court. This delay suggests that outcomes are as much a product of the bodies and institutions that shape tax litigation and the administration and interpretation of tax laws as they are of the merits of the good VAT as perceived by a government whose term in office had ended before the first ultimate appellate decision was handed down.

The High Court ruled in favour of the Commissioner of Taxation, holding that the respondent (the vendor) was liable to pay GST on a deposit that had been forfeited in a contract for the sale of land that had been terminated due to default by the purchaser. The Court ruled that a supply[331] was made upon entry into the contract of sale and that, by virtue of special provisions in the *ANTS Act 1999*, the deposit paid to secure the supply constituted consideration for the supply upon forfeiture of that deposit, thereby transforming the supply into a taxable supply.[332] In its reasons for decision, the High Court commented that:[333]

> An important point respecting the nature of the GST was made as follows by the Full Court of the Federal Court in *Sterling Guardian Pty Ltd. v. Commissioner of Taxation*:
>
> 'In economic terms it may be correct to call the GST a consumption tax, because the effective burden falls on the ultimate consumer. But as a matter of legal analysis what is taxed, that is to say what generates the tax liability (and the obligations of recording and reporting), is not consumption but a particular form of transaction, namely supply...'
>
> *By way of contrast to the Australian system*, counsel for the Commissioner referred to Art 2(1) of the first Council directive on the harmonisation of legislation of

[329] Robert Olding, 'Interpretation of the GST Act – Towards a Principled Basis?' in C. Peacock (ed.), *GST in Australia: Looking Forward from the First Decade* (Thomson Reuters, Pyrmont, 2011), 77, 90. See, e.g., *Gloxinia Investments Pty. Ltd. as trustee for the Gloxinia Unit Trust v. Commissioner of Taxation* (2009), 183 FCR 420 426, [23], where the Court gave little credence to the Commissioner's arguments that the taxpayer's construction failed to represent the policy of the GST to capture the value added to new residential premises. Similarly, the attempt by the parties to argue that their position was more consistent with the policy intent of the GST to tax domestic consumption did not significantly influence the decision in *Travelex Ltd. v. Commissioner of Taxation* (2010), 241 CLR 510.

[330] *Commissioner of Taxation v. Reliance Carpet Co Pty Ltd.* (2008), 236 CLR 342 ('*Reliance Carpet*').

[331] *ANTS Act 1999*, s 9–10.

[332] *ANTS Act 1999*, div. 99 – s99–5 provides that a deposit given as security for the performance of an obligation is not treated as consideration for a supply unless the deposit is either forfeited or applied as all or part of the consideration for supply; *Reliance Carpet*, 355–56, [39]–[42].

[333] *Reliance Carpet*, 345–46, [3], quoting *Sterling Guardian v. Federal Commissioner of Taxation* (2006), 228 ALR 712, 258, [15] (emphasis added). See also EM ANTS Bill 1998.

> member states of the European Community concerning turnover taxes; this indicates that VAT is a general tax on the consumption of goods and services.

The apparent attempt to contrast the European VAT as a tax on general consumption with the Australian GST as a tax on transactions seems perplexing, given that both taxes ultimately seek to tax final consumption through the use of legal rules which, although differing in many respects, do not differ in such a way as to indicate that Australian drafters intended the tax base to be something other than consumption. The *Recast VAT Directive*, for example, refers to the VAT as a consumption tax levied through the taxation of transactions.[334] The ATO's then Deputy Chief Tax Counsel, Robert Olding, characterises the *Reliance Carpet* decision as follows:[335]

> The feature that the GST seeks to tax consumption was quickly dispensed with by the High Court in the *Reliance Carpet* case. The Court noted that that may be its policy but the legal means to achieve that policy is the taxing of supplies.

The *Reliance Carpet* case does not suggest that Australian judges are particularly obstructionist, as some practitioners and business representatives claim,[336] or that Australian legislative drafters were undertaking some bold new legislative attempt to redefine the GST base. Rather, the case demonstrates that the legal terms used to implement the GST differ from the economic concepts used. The case further shows what can occur when the legal terms are interpreted by judges who are bound to apply their own rules and principles, such as local rules of statutory interpretation, which in Australia require the construction of statutes by reference to their language, purpose and context.[337]

The approach to interpreting the GST in the *Reliance Carpet* case demonstrates the inadequacy of the conventional approach's account of the VAT's rise. In this case, we can see that one of the key merits said to underpin the VAT (its

[334] *Council Directive 2006/112/EC of 28 November 2008 on the Common System of Value Added Tax* [2006] OJ L 347/1 (referred to hereafter as '*Recast VAT Directive 2006/112/EC*'), art. 1(2) and 2.

[335] Robert Olding, 'Interpretation of the GST Act – Towards a Principled Basis?' in C. Peacock (ed.), *GST in Australia: Looking Forward from the First Decade* (Thomson Reuters, Pyrmont, 2011), 77, 90.

[336] See discussion of these criticisms: ibid., 78; Michael Wigney SC, 'Text, Context and the Interpretation of a "Practical Business Tax"', *Australian Tax Review* 40 (2011), 94. Cnossen identifies the perception of the VAT as a transaction tax as being a common view among lawyers: Sijbren Cnossen, 'A VAT Primer for Lawyers, Economists, and Accountants', *Tax Notes International* 55(4) (2009), 319, 326. One cannot claim that all decisions go in a certain direction – see the discussion of practical business tax below and the broad interpretation of supply in *Saga Holidays Ltd. v. Commissioner of Taxation (Cth) and others* (2006), 156 FCR 256 265, [35].

[337] For statements of the modern approach to statutory interpretation in Australia, see, e.g., *CIC Insurance Ltd. v. Bankstown Football Club Ltd.* (1997), 187 CLR 384, 408; *Project Blue Sky Inc. v. Australian Broadcasting Authority* (1998), 194 CLR 355, 384; *Alcan (NT) Alumina Pty Ltd. v. Commissioner of Territory Revenue* (NT) (2009), 239 CLR 27, 46–47, [47].

consumption base) is but one part of the context taken into account in interpreting the laws that implement the GST.[338] Few institutional actors are in a position to unilaterally declare (without empirical evidence) that the GST is not a consumption tax and therefore to deny one of the key bases of the GST's putative appeal. However, Australian judges are in an institutional position to do so, and are in an institutional position to do so immune from the political lobbying of vested interests, as they are open only to persuasion by the parties' pleadings on the relevant law. This basic point demonstrates that not all institutional actors are instructed by the merits highlighted by the conventional approach, as this quote from one frustrated commentator demonstrates:[339]

> it would be a sad day indeed if the blood shed by Governments that had the courage to enact taxes in the value added tax form in pursuit of economic efficiency and neutrality were to have those ambitions frustrated by an interpretation or administration of the law that failed to take the economic aims of the tax system into account. The business community in particular, being key supporters of the tax reform that led to GST in New Zealand and Australia, would have cause to feel betrayed.

However, the High Court's approach does not mean that the Australian GST does not tax end consumption, but rather that the conventional approach cannot account for how these real VAT outcomes occur. For example, the ultimate outcome in the *Reliance Carpet* case was in accordance with economic concepts of the GST as a consumption tax. By paying a deposit, the purchaser consumes a service from the vendor; the vendor agrees not to sell the property to anyone else and the purchaser has the ability to walk away. The High Court arrived at this result, however, not through engaging in considerations of the merits of the good VAT as a consumption tax but through applying rules relating to statutory construction, property law and contract law.[340]

[338] Robert Olding, 'Interpretation of the GST Act – Towards a Principled Basis?' in C. Peacock (ed.), *GST in Australia: Looking Forward from the First Decade* (Thomson Reuters, Pyrmont, 2011), 77, 88–91.

[339] Michael Evans, 'The Value Added Tax Treatment of Real Property – An Antipodean Context', in R. Krever and D. White (ed.), *GST in Retrospect and Prospect* (Brookers, Wellington, NZ, 2007), 243, 245.

[340] The taxpayer attempted to argue that no supply had occurred (because of the failure of the principal supply – the sale of land) and that therefore the deposit received could not be consideration for any supply. The High Court preferred the Commissioner's contention that the deposit operated as security for the supply of obligations under the contract, which included not just the obligation to transfer title to the land on payment of the balance of the purchase price, but obligations to refrain from accepting offers from other prospective purchasers, obligations to maintain the land in its current condition, etc.: *Reliance Carpet*, 355 [37]. By virtue of a special provision in the *ANTS Act 1999*, s99–15, which provided that a deposit was not consideration for a supply unless forfeited or applied as all or part of the consideration for supply, the deposit therefore constituted consideration at the time of its forfeiture: 355–356, [38]–[39]. The High Court found that, in accepting the taxpayer's

Ironically, the High Court appears to have been motivated to distinguish the Australian 'transactional' GST from the European 'consumption' VAT because the taxpayer in the case sought to rely on French authority that the forfeiture of a deposit in similar circumstances was not a 'taxable transaction' under the relevant law.[341] This decision was based, not on a different perception of the nature of the VAT or its merits, but on a different treatment of the nature of the forfeiture of a deposit under French contract law and differences in the legislative requirements of the European Union (EU) Directive and the ANTS legislation.[342]

A later High Court decision revisiting the issue of 'taxable supplies' further illustrates how determination of the issues turns on local approaches to construing statutory and contractual provisions, rather than an appeal to the merits. The issue in this case was whether a payment for a fare made to an airline for a flight that was neither taken nor refunded was a taxable supply in accordance with s 9–5 of the *ANTS Act 1999*. The airline contended that the failure to take the flight meant that there was no supply and therefore no liability to remit GST. In holding in favour of the Commissioner, the Court found that what was supplied was not an unconditional promise to carry the passenger and his or her baggage on a particular flight (and therefore no supply if the passenger failed to take that flight), but 'something less than that'.[343] Based on a construction of the contractual terms, the Court found that the supply was of 'a promise to use best endeavours to carry the passenger and baggage, having regard to the circumstances of the business operations of the airline'.[344] This promise rather than the flight itself constituted the taxable supply, and payment of the fare therefore constituted consideration for the supply, with the airline therefore liable to remit GST. Although the case departs from the European

contention, the full Federal Court adopted a narrow characterisation of a supply of real property as entailing a supply of land rather than a bundle of rights. The Court found that the full Federal Court gave 'insufficient weight both to the definition of "real property" in the Act, and to the identity of the subject matter of the contract, in accordance with ordinary principles of conveyancing, as the title or estate of the vendor in a parcel of land rather than merely the parcel itself in a geographical sense': 348, [13]. For the application of contractual principles, see the remainder of this section and *Reliance Carpet*, 349–52, [22]–[28] discussing whether the deposit constituted consideration.

[341] Ibid., 352–53, [29]–[30]. The taxpayer also sought to rely on other overseas authority, but the Court did not discuss these authorities, as they were not sufficiently analogous to the relevant provisions, specifically the *ANTS Act 1999*, ss 99–5–99–10: at 353, [31].

[342] Specifically, the *Recast VAT Directive 2006/112/EC* required a specific connection between the services provided (in that case, provision of a hotel room) and what was received for them, which was not required by virtue of the *ANTS Act 1999*, s 99–10. This connection was not satisfied because under French contract law the forfeited deposit was treated as compensation existing independently of the contract for service (i.e., the provision of the room): *Reliance Carpet*, 352–53, [29]–[30], considering *Société Thermale d'Eugénie-les-Bains v. Ministère de l'Économie, des Finances et de l'Industrie* [2007], 3 CMLR 1003. Therefore, even in the home of the VAT, institutional constraints produce real VAT outcomes. That is, despite a Directive that aims to tax consumption, local institutionalised legal rules meant that the taxpayer was not liable for VAT.

[343] *Commissioner of Taxation v. Qantas Airways Ltd.* (2012), 291 ALR 653, 661 [33].

[344] Ibid.

approach to the issue of the forfeiture of advance payments, the decision is consistent with economic ideas of consumption – that occurred at the point when the passenger purchased the right to attend or not attend the flight.[345] However, importantly and consistent with the contentions of this book, the decision was not informed by such merits-based considerations but rather on principles of contractual and statutory construction.

Unsurprisingly, there are numerous instances where the interpretations adopted by Australian courts do not necessarily accord with the merits of the good VAT. This can be seen in the constant complaint within practitioner circles that the Courts do not give enough emphasis to interpreting the GST as a 'practical business tax'.[346] The term is meant to reflect that, where possible, the GST should be interpreted in a manner so as to ensure that the economic incidence of the GST is on end consumers (rather than business).[347] Frequently, this occurs in cases where business seeks, but is denied, input credits by the Courts.[348] The frustration

345 Krever contends that this expansive approach to the interpretation of 'taxable supply' has the potential to broaden the GST base: Richard Krever, 'Forfeited Airfare (VAT Case Note – Australia)', *International VAT Monitor* (November–December 2012), 453.

346 J. Stone made reference to the term in *Saga Holidays Ltd. v. Commissioner of Taxation (Cth) and Others* (2006), 156 FCR 256, 264, [29]–[30]:

> Consideration of these aspects of the GST Act has led to the tax being described as a "practical business tax"; *Sterling Guardian Pty Ltd. v. FCT* [2005] FCA 1166; (2005) 220 ALR 550 at [39]. The description is appropriate because it draws attention to two related aspects of the tax. The fact that liability to pay the tax is imposed at various stages of the supply chain means that it is a tax on business, but, importantly, one that is designed, where practicable, to quarantine business from the ultimate burden of the tax. This and other aspects of the tax legitimately form part of the context in which the language of the act is interpreted and explains, at least in part, why the description "practical business tax" seems to be appropriate. This does not mean, however, that there is some special canon of construction that should be applied when interpreting the GST Act. The purposive approach to interpretation, of its nature, takes account of the context of the Act and the phrase, "a practical business tax" is a reference to that context...

The high-water mark of the approach is said to be the case of *Brady King Pty Ltd. v. Commissioner of Taxation* (2008), 69 ATR 271, 279, [49]. Recent support for the concept was expressed in *Commissioner of Taxation v. Multiflex Pty Ltd.* (2011), 197 FCR 580, 592, [37]–[38]. See also Robert Olding, 'Interpretation of the GST Act – Towards a Principled Basis?' in C. Peacock (ed.), *GST in Australia: Looking Forward from the First Decade* (Thomson Reuters, Pyrmont, 2011), 77, 84; Michael Wigney SC, 'Text, Context and the Interpretation of a "Practical Business Tax"', *Australian Tax Review* 40 (2011), 94, 99–102.

347 Michael Wigney SC, 'Text, Context and the Interpretation of a "Practical Business Tax"', *Australian Tax Review* 40 (2011), 94–95 (documenting the common complaints); Robert Olding, 'Interpretation of the GST Act – Towards a Principled Basis?' in C. Peacock (ed.), *GST in Australia: Looking Forward from the First Decade* (Thomson Reuters, Pyrmont, 2011), 77, 78.

348 See, e.g., *Gloxinia Investments Pty. Ltd. as trustee for the Gloxinia Unit Trust v. Commissioner of Taxation* (2009), 183 FCR 420; Denis McCarthy, 'The Australian GST – Why It Is the Way It Is and Where To from Here?' in C. Peacock (ed.), *GST in Australia: Looking Forward from the First Decade* (Thomson Reuters, Sydney, 2011), 61, 63.

leads to calls for the reintroduction of a special interpretive approach to taxation legislation, including the GST.[349] Justice Kirby sums up to the response of the judiciary to such calls from the tax profession:[350]

> It is hubris on the part of specialised lawyers to consider that 'their Act' is special and distinct from general movements in statutory construction which have been such a marked feature of our legal system in recent decades. The Act in question here is not different in this respect. It should be construed, like any other federal statute, to give effect to the ascertained purpose of the Parliament.

Legal rules come up trumps over notions of policy merits in the high-stakes game of interpreting the Australian GST. The merits-based account of the conventional approach is unable to explain these outcomes which, in this instance, arise not from overt political machinations, but from the relatively enduring and stable institutional rules of statutory construction employed by the High Court. One can see the futility of relying on the merits-based account of the VAT's rise when, in achieving an outcome consistent with the merits of the good VAT as a consumption tax, the High Court of Australia denies the very basis for the merit itself (that the GST is a consumption tax). It shows that explanations of outcomes by reference to merits would either fail to explain the outcome at all or do so only by accident.

4.3.2 Eligibility for input tax credits

The rules governing entitlement to input credits are crucial to ensuring that the GST does not fall on business. In order for an entity to claim an input tax credit for the GST incurred on inputs used in the production of goods and/or services, the acquisition of the relevant input must satisfy four statutory conditions necessary to constitute a *creditable acquisition*.[351] The first and most important is discussed at length in what follows, and requires that (1) the acquisition is solely or partly for a *creditable purpose*. The other three requirements are that (2) the supply of the acquisition was a taxable supply;[352] (3) the entity provided or was liable to provide consideration for the acquisition;[353] and (4) the entity is registered or required to be registered under the Act.[354]

349 The previous approach of Australian courts to interpreting revenue statutes was to construe such statutes strictly meaning that if a provision did not explicitly cover a taxpayer's affairs no tax would be payable, and conversely, a person seeking to obtain a tax benefit would need to fall within the plain words of the relevant provision: CCH Australia Limited, *GST & Sales Tax Guide (Online Reporter Services)*, looseleaf, CCH, North Ryde, NSW, 2–520; *Anderson v. Commissioner of Taxation (Vic)* (1937), 57 CLR 233, 243. Ironically, the nature of the GST whereby many disputes between business and the ATO involve entitlement to input tax credits leads the tax profession to call for a purposive and contextual approach over a literal approach.

350 *Commissioner of Taxation v. Ryan* (2000), 201 CLR 109, 146, [84].

351 *ANTS Act 1999*, ss 11–5, 11–10. 352 Ibid., defined in s 9–5.

353 Ibid., defined in s 9–15. 354 Ibid., s 25–5, 23–5.

Creditable purpose is positively defined as meaning that 'you acquire a thing…to the extent that you acquire it in carrying on your enterprise'.[355] This *positive limb* of the test is qualified by two negative limbs that provide that 'you do not acquire a thing for a creditable purpose to the extent that':[356]

- The acquisition *relates to making* supplies that would be input taxed [such as a financial supply – the '*first negative limb*']; or
- The acquisition is of a private or domestic nature [the '*second negative limb*'].

As these requirements suggest, an entity that makes a GST-free supply is entitled to input tax credits for acquisitions used in the making of those supplies, as there is no requirement that the supply made as a result of the inputs be a taxable supply (which a GST-free supply is not) but simply that the supply relates to a creditable purpose (which excludes input-taxed supplies but not GST-free supplies).[357] By contrast, an entity will be denied credit on inputs if the acquisition *relates to making* supplies that would be input taxed (and thus fails the *first negative limb* of the creditable purpose test).

The centrality of the requirement of *creditable purpose* in determining entitlement to an input tax credit is unique to Australia. Other jurisdictions, such as those in the European Union, allow for an input credit provided it relates to the making of an equivalent taxable or GST-free supply.[358] By contrast, rather than requiring a

[355] The use of the terms 'to the extent that' allows for apportionment of input credits for inputs used in making composite supplies (i.e., both input-taxed and taxable/GST-free supplies): ibid., s11–5(1), 11–25, 11–3; *HP Mercantile Pty Ltd. v. Commissioner of Taxation* [2005], FCR 553, 560 [21] (Hill J). For a discussion of apportionment issues, see Denis McCarthy, 'The Australian GST – Why It Is the Way It Is and Where To from Here?' in C. Peacock (ed.), *GST in Australia: Looking Forward from the First Decade* (Thomson Reuters, Sydney, 2011), 61, 65–66.

[356] *ANTS Act* 1999, s 11–15(2).

[357] Confirmed by *ANTS Act* 1999, s 38–1. As a GST-free supply generates no GST liability, the recipient of a supply receives no credit. This is also a specific outcome of the legislative drafting that excludes GST-free supplies from the definition of taxable supply (s 9–5) and provides that input tax credits are payable in an amount equal to the GST payable on the thing acquired (s 11–25) which, for a GST-free supply, is an amount equal to zero.

[358] *Recast VAT Directive 2006/112/EC*, art. 168, provides that a 'taxable person' can deduct VAT 'in so far as the goods and services are used for the purposes of the taxed transactions of a taxable person'. New Zealand defines input tax (which in turn determines what is creditable) as being tax levied on the acquisition/importation of 'goods and services' acquired for the 'principal purpose of making taxable supplies'. The UK, Canada and Singapore provide that a registered entity is entitled to a credit if it acquires/imports taxable goods and services for the purpose of making taxable supplies: Denis McCarthy, 'The Australian GST – Why It Is the Way It Is and Where To from Here?' in C. Peacock (ed.), *GST in Australia: Looking Forward from the First Decade* (Thomson Reuters, Sydney, 2011), 61, 65–66; *HP Mercantile*, 560, [21], J. Hill. A Commonwealth Treasury Consultation Paper notes:

> An additional feature of Australia's approach to financial supplies arises from its adoption of the input tax mechanism which, unlike other jurisdictions, does not provide

nexus to a specific type of supply (taxable or GST free), the *creditable purpose* concept provides a broad starting position that brings all acquisitions made in the carrying on of an enterprise into the net but then excludes those acquisitions that relate to input-taxed supplies or those of a private or domestic nature.[359]

The broad scope of the *creditable purpose* concept is designed to reflect the legislative intent of the GST as not being a cost, and specifically not a cost that cascades to business.[360] However, in order to achieve this goal, Australian legislative drafters did not model the approach based on any best-practice VAT, real or imagined, but rather modelled the legislation on the provisions governing the entitlement to deductions for business income in the Australian income tax legislation.[361] As J. Hill noted in *HP Mercantile*:[362]

> for a credit of input tax on acquisitions based on a link between an acquisition and a taxable (or zero-rated or GST free) supply. Under Australian GST law, input tax relief is available on all acquisitions made in carrying on an enterprise, but is denied to the extent that the acquisition relates to making input taxed supplies.

Commonwealth of Australia Treasury, *Review of the GST Financial Supply Provisions – Consultation Paper* (Australian Government, Canberra, 2009), 6.

359 Ross Stitt, 'Uncertanties Surrounding Input Tax Credit Entitlement in Australia', in C. Peacock (ed.), *GST in Australia: Looking Forward from the First Decade* (Thomson Reuters, Pyrmont, 2011), 115, 117; EM ANTS Bill 1998, 1.1.27, 3.2.6.

360 EM ANTS Bill 1998, 1.1.27; 'If you are going to use a thing in your enterprise, for example by selling it on to someone else, GST will be included in that sale. Therefore, to avoid double taxing that thing, you receive a credit for the GST included in the price you paid for the thing. You therefore have a creditable purpose if you acquire a thing for the purpose of your enterprise': at 3.2.4; Denis McCarthy, 'The Australian GST – Why It Is the Way It Is and Where To from Here?' in C. Peacock (ed.), *GST in Australia: Looking Forward from the First Decade* (Thomson Reuters, Sydney, 2011), 61–75, 65–66.

361 The relevant provisions in the income tax legislation are s 8–1, *Income Tax Assessment Act 1997* (Cth), and s 51(1), *Income Tax Assessment Act 1936* (Cth). The EM ANTS Bill 1998 specifically refers to s 8–1, *Income Tax Assessment Act 1997*, in noting that the creditable purpose test is broader than the deductibility for income test because it includes credit for capital goods: at 1.1.27, 3.25; Denis McCarthy, 'The Australian GST – Why It Is the Way It Is and Where To from Here?' in C. Peacock (ed.), *GST in Australia: Looking Forward from the First Decade* (Thomson Reuters, Sydney, 2011), 61, 65–66.

362 *HP Mercantile Pty Ltd. v. Commissioner of Taxation* [2005], FCR 553, 560, [21]. The difference between the Australian and European approaches might also be seen as a path-dependent product of historically different approaches to taxing income. Australia uses a global concept of income which, in general terms, includes a common definition of income (albeit separated into various sources of income such as employment, business and property). In general, the rules for determining net income (i.e., entitlement to deductions) are the same regardless of the type of income, so that losses incurred in generating income from one source can be offset against income from another. The test for establishing entitlement to deductions also exists separately on its own terms to the test for determining assessable income. By contrast, many European countries, such as the UK, France, Germany, Italy and Spain, tend to have schedular definitions of income, meaning that different types of income are defined and taxed differently and losses from one category cannot be used to offset income in other categories. Although the distinction between global and schedular approaches is not a bright-line one (most countries employ a mix of both), the divergent concepts continue to shape approaches to the taxation of income: Victor Thuronyi, *Comparative Tax Law* (Kluwer Law International, The Hague, 2003), 233–35.

> It is, perhaps, not unremarkable that s 11–15 of the GST Act bears, in its structure, some similarity to the general business deduction provisions of the Australian income tax law...In both...there is a need to pass first through a positive test. In the case of GST, the positive test is the requirement that the acquisition has been in whole or in part acquired in carrying on an enterprise. In the income tax context, there is the need to find that the loss or outgoing be incurred in gaining or producing assessable income, or in carrying on a business...Next, both require consideration of negative tests which exclude the allowance of a credit in the GST context or the allowance of a deduction in the income tax context. In the GST context the negative tests are those set out in s 11–15(2) of acquisitions relating to supplies that would be input taxed or acquisitions of a private and domestic nature. In the income tax context, the negative tests also involve the case where the loss or outgoing is of a private and domestic nature as well as where it is capital or of a capital nature.

This is but one of a number of instances throughout the ANTS legislation where key concepts and provisions have been directly adapted from the income tax legislation, and it is yet another instance of the path-dependent effect of existing taxation arrangements on the shape of new reforms.[363]

Although some have described the goal of the *creditable purpose* test (to shield business from the cost of the GST by adopting as a starting point a broad entitlement to input credits) as 'laudable',[364] others have criticised the complexity that the approach entails.[365]

As the structure of the *creditable purpose* test suggests, entitlement to input credits is a major issue in relation to input-taxed supplies, and perhaps no other area highlights the issue better than financial supplies, which are classified as input-taxed supplies under the *ANTS Act*. As this book has highlighted, the application of the VAT to financial supplies is one of a number of frontier issues that test the limits of the good VAT. The following analysis of the complexities of applying the *creditable purpose* test to the taxation of financial supplies in determining access to input tax credits explores how problematic aspects in the design of the good VAT become amplified in real VATs when these sorts of frontier issues come into play.

363 See, e.g., the discussion of the influence of the general anti-avoidance provisions in the income tax legislation on the general anti-avoidance provisions of the *ANTS Act 1999* (discussed at §3.1.2 of this chapter).

364 Denis McCarthy, 'The Australian GST – Why It Is the Way It Is and Where To from Here?' in C. Peacock (ed.), *GST in Australia: Looking Forward from the First Decade* (Thomson Reuters, Sydney, 2011), 61, 66.

365 Stitt, for example, argues that 'the Australian model is arguably more complex' than the approaches used elsewhere: Ross Stitt, 'Uncertainties Surrounding Input Tax Credit Entitlement in Australia', in C. Peacock (ed.), *GST in Australia: Looking Forward from the First Decade* (Thomson Reuters, Pyrmont, 2011), 115, 118.

4.3.3 Eligibility for input credits and financial supplies

Australia adopted a 'modified version'[366] of the input taxation of financial supplies informed by both the difficulty of applying the good VAT to financial supplies (outlined in Chapter 2, §4.2.5.1)[367] and being heavily influenced by real VATs elsewhere (see Chapter 3, §4.2.4). Discussion of this highly complex and technical area is rarely, if ever, engaged in under existing public policy accounts of VAT reform. The analysis shows that, contrary to the tendency of the conventional approach to treat the taxation of financial supplies as merely technical, the taxation of financial supplies is fiercely political and, while merits might motivate some policy-makers, they do so in ways not at all anticipated by the conventional approach. In an indication of how little the merits-based approach offers to explain these real VAT responses, Treasurer Peter Costello defended the input taxation of financial supplies at the time of the ANTS reforms by stating that in 'no country in the world does GST apply to financial services…[therefore] Australia is following world's best practice in relation to financial services'.[368] As McCarthy sees it:[369]

> Key policy decisions made during 1998 and 1999 were either forced upon the Government (such as the GST-free treatment of food), made after careful consideration of overseas experience (such as the treatment of financial supplies, land, Government, GST grouping and international transactions) or made because of situations unique to Australia (such as the financial supplies and insurance regimes). Some of the policy decisions reflect the sentiment of those drafting the law at the time. Interestingly (and not surprisingly), those now charged with administering the GST seem to have different sentiments, particularly in relation to the recovery of input tax.

[366] A Treasury Consultation Paper refers to the Australian system as a 'modified version' of the European approach: Commonwealth of Australia Treasury, *Review of the GST Financial Supply Provisions – Consultation Paper* (Australian Government, Canberra, 2009), 5.

[367] The Explanatory Memorandum to the ANTS Bill 1998 confirms this as the basis for input-taxing financial supplies: 'Most countries that have a GST system exempt financial services as there is no readily agreed identifiable value for supplies consumed by customers of financial services. The approach adopted in the Bill is consistent with the international model': at 40–5. The Explanatory Statement to the ANTS Regulations provides further confirmation:

> The fundamental reason for input taxing financial services is that it is difficult to value most financial services as they are often charged by way of a margin. Where supplies are input taxed, it is not necessary to value the service.

Explanatory Statement, A New Tax System (Goods and Services Tax) Regulations 1999 (Cth), Attachment E, Regulation Impact Statement (hereinafter referred to as '*ES ANTS Regulations 1999*'); see also *AXA Asia Pacific Holdings Ltd. v. Federal Commissioner of Taxation* [2008] FCA 1834, 511, [51] ('*AXA v. FCOT*').

[368] Phillip Hudson, 'No GST Deal For Financial Sector ', *The Age* (Melbourne), 9 March 1999, 6.

[369] Denis McCarthy, 'The Australian GST – Why It Is the Way It Is and Where To from Here?' in C. Peacock (ed.), *GST in Australia: Looking Forward from the First Decade* (Thomson Reuters, Sydney, 2011), 61, 63.

Despite the apparent opportunity for policy learning that McCarthy identifies, the financial supply provisions have been widely criticised. McCarthy sums up the general sentiment among practitioners to the Australian approach:[370]

> Australia's financial supply provisions are unique. Some may say, uniquely complicated! They have been studied by many, but after 10 years our GST approach to financial services is still unique.

There have been disproportionately high numbers of ATO compliance activities on the financial supply provisions.[371] The classification of financial supplies as input-taxed supplies under the GST affects both liability to pay GST (none is payable because the supply is not a taxable supply)[372] and entitlement to input credits (input credits are denied by virtue of the *first negative limb* of the *creditable purpose* test). Although there are many issues relating to the input taxation of financial supplies, which alone could occupy a book in their own right,[373] it is the entitlement to credits that has generated most disputes between businesses seeking input credits and the ATO seeking to deny credits. The remainder of this section highlights some of the issues that arise in relation to the *creditable purpose* test.

[370] Ibid., 70.

[371] A search of the ATO database reveals over 200 ATOIDs, Legislative Determinations, Rulings, Determination, Bulletins, Taxpayer Alerts and Technical Discussion Papers related to the financial supply provisions: ATO, *Legal Database* (2014) (law.ato.gov.au/atolaw/execute_-search.htm). See, e.g., Australian Taxation Office, *Goods and Services Tax: Determining the Extent of Creditable Purpose for Providers of Financial Supplies*, GSTR2006/3, 12 April 2006; Australian Taxation Office, *Goods and Services Tax: Reduced Credit Acquisitions*, GSTR2004/1, 25 February 2004; Australian Taxation Office, *Goods and Services Tax: GST Treatment of Financial Supplies and Related Supplies and Acquisitions*, GSTR 2002/2, 26 June 2002; Australian Taxation Office, *Goods and Services Tax: Financial Acquisitions Threshold*, GSTR 3003/9, 14 May 2003. The Treasury notes a significant amount of private rulings on financial supplies: Commonwealth of Australia Treasury, *Review of the GST Financial Supply Provisions – Consultation Paper* (Australian Government, Canberra, 2009), 10. Some of this compliance activity has resulted in litigation before the appellate courts; see, e.g., *Commissioner of Taxation v. American Express Wholesale Currency Services Pty Ltd; Commissioner of Taxation v. American Express International Inc.* (2010), 187 FCR 398; *Travelex Ltd. v. Commissioner of Taxation* (2010), 241 CLR 510; *AXA Asia Pacific Holdings Ltd. v. Commissioner of Taxation* (2008), 173 FCR 500. *Contra* de la Feria and Walpole, who contend that the number of private rulings (and litigation) is less than other problematic areas such as the supplies of residential premises and the margin scheme: Rita de la Feria and M. Walpole, 'Options for Taxing Financial Supplies in Value Added Tax: EU VAT and Australian GST Models Compared', *International and Comparative Law Quarterly* 58(4) (2009), 926.

[372] *ANTS Act* 1999, s 9–5: see §4.3.1.

[373] For a comprehensive (albeit dated) treatment of financial supplies under the GST, see Peter McMahon and Everton MacIntyre, *GST and the Financial Markets* (CCH, Sydney, 2001). For current accounts, see CCH Australia Limited, *GST & Sales Tax Guide* (online reporter services), looseleaf, CCH, North Ryde, NSW; Commonwealth of Australia Treasury, *Review of the GST Financial Supply Provisions – Consultation Paper* (Australian Government, Canberra, 2009).

4.3.3.1 INTRODUCTION TO THE FINANCIAL SUPPLY PROVISIONS The *ANTS Act* simply provides that:[374]

1. Financial supplies are input taxed; and
2. The term 'financial supply' has the meaning given in the regulations.

It is useful to remember at this point that the classification of financial supplies as input-taxed supplies brings into play the *first negative limb* of the *creditable purpose* test because a *creditable purpose* is denied to the extent that the acquisition relates to making supplies that would be input taxed (as §4.3.2 explained).

The bulk of the rules governing financial supplies are contained in the *ANTS Regulations*.[375] In general terms, the *ANTS Regulations* provide that a *financial supply* is made when:

1. The supply consists of the provision, *acquisition* or disposal of an *interest* (defined as 'anything that is recognised in law or in equity as property in any form')[376] in or under a matter listed as qualifying to be the subject of a financial supply;[377]
2. The supply is made for consideration, in the course of furthering an enterprise and is connected with Australia;[378]
3. The supply is by a party who is registered (or required to be registered) for GST and who is a *financial supply provider*[379] in relation to the supply of the *interest*.[380]

This list condenses a number of requirements, each with a number of complex issues. Some preliminary points will provide some context.

The scope of the financial supply provisions is limited to transactions between principals engaging in transactions such as the borrowing and lending of money or the buying or selling of shares.[381] This is indicated by the requirement that the financial supply be of a proprietary interest[382] and by the definition of *financial*

374 *ANTS Act* 1999, s 40–5.

375 The Regulations relating to financial supplies state that their purpose is to identify both when a supply is a financial supply and when a supply is not a financial supply: *ANTS Regulations* 1999, reg. 40–5.01.

376 Ibid., regs. 40–5.02, 40–5.09(1),.

377 Ibid., regs. 40–5.02, 40–5.09(3).

378 Ibid,. reg. 40–5.09(1). See the discussion of these issues in ATO, *Goods and Services Tax: GST Treatment of Financial Supplies and Related Supplies and Acquisitions*, GSTR 2002/2, 26 June 2002 (hereinafter referred to as '*GSTR* 2002/2'), 45–77 and 104–6.

379 Defined in *ANTS Regulations* 1999 reg. 40–5.06(1) and (2).

380 Ibid., reg. 40–5.09(1)(b).

381 Commonwealth of Australia Treasury, *Review of the GST Financial Supply Provisions – Consultation Paper* (Australian Government, Canberra, 2009), 4.

382 Although the courts have interpreted the term 'interest' broadly (see, e.g., *Commissioner of Taxation v. American Express Wholesale Currency Services Pty Ltd; Commissioner of Taxation v. American Express International Inc.* (2010), 187 FCR 398, 444, [181]), the focus on

supply provider. An entity is a *financial supply provider* in three circumstances: (1) the entity *supplies* an *interest* that was immediately the property of the entity before the supply; or (2) the entity creates an *interest* in making the supply; or (3) the entity *acquires* that *interest*.[383] The result is that, in contrast to many other real VATs, facilitation services such as agency and brokerage services are excluded from the definition of financial supply and therefore constitute taxable supplies.[384] This is further enforced by the distinction drawn between a *financial supply provider* and a *financial supply facilitator* as an entity 'facilitating the supply of the interest for a financial supply provider'.[385] Although this might be seen to result in widening the Australian GST base, §4.3.3.4 explains how this base broadening is limited by other measures.

The *ANTS Regulations* list the interests that are capable of being the subject of a financial supply and those that are not:[386]

- The *ANTS Regulations* list items that can be the subject matter of a financial supply, such as interests in or under bank accounts; lines of credit; charges or mortgages over real or personal property; life insurance; currency exchanges; securities; guarantees and indemnities; and derivatives.[387] A supply is a financial supply only if it appears on this list (or is listed as an *incidental financial supply*) and otherwise meets the requirements of a financial supply in the regulations;[388]
- The list of financial supplies is qualified by a list of supplies that are *not financial supplies*. If something appears on both lists (of financial supplies and not financial supplies), it will not be a financial supply. The list of things that are not financial supplies includes professional

proprietary interests has been criticised for misconstruing the purpose of the financial supply exemption, which is intended to exclude financial intermediation services (because of the difficulty in identifying and attributing the margin on a transactional basis), not the capital flows, which the intermediation services facilitate and which should form no part of a consumption tax base because these capital flows are neither a supply nor consideration for supply: Michael B. Evans, 'The GST Treatment of Financial Services in Australia', in C. Peacock (ed.), *GST in Australia: Looking Forward from the First Decade* (Thomson Reuters, Pyrmont, 2011), 133, 151–52, 156.

383 Defined in *ANTS Regulations* 1999, regs. 40–5.06(1) and (2).

384 Commonwealth of Australia Treasury, *Review of the GST Financial Supply Provisions – Consultation Paper* (Australian Government, Canberra, 2009), 4; Michael B. Evans, 'The GST Treatment of Financial Services in Australia', in C. Peacock (ed.), *GST in Australia: Looking Forward from the First Decade* (Thomson Reuters, Pyrmont, 2011), 133, 145; *ANTS Regulations* 1999, reg. 40–5.12.

385 *ANTS Regulations* 1999, reg. 40–5.07.

386 *ANTS Regulations* 1999, reg. 40–5.09(3); see also GSTR 2002/2, [20]; ATO, *Goods and Services Tax Ruling: Goods and Services Tax: In the Application of Items 2 and 3 and Paragraph (b) of Item 4 in the Table in Subsection 38–190(1) of the A New Tax System (Goods and Services Tax) Act 1999*, GSTR 2004/7, 1 December 2004.

387 *ANTS Regulations* 1999, regs. 40–5.09(3) and (4).

388 Ibid., reg. 40–5.10.

advice relating to financial supplies, brokerage services, debt collection and trustee services;[389]

- The list of things that are *not financial supplies* is further qualified by the concept of *incidental financial supplies* – meaning that when something both is *not a financial supply* and is an *incidental financial supply*, it will be treated as a financial supply.[390] The regulations give as an example of an incidental financial supply the provision of advice in relation to a housing loan for which a separate charge is not made.[391]

The ostensible 'guiding principle' in drafting these lists was that only financial supplies that are 'normally charged for by way of a margin' ought to be input taxed and therefore classified as financial supplies.[392] This was based on the difficulty in valuing the margin for a financial service on a transactional basis (outlined in Chapter 2, §4.2.5.1).[393] Therefore, certain supplies that are not normally charged by way of a margin are generally listed as *not financial supplies*.[394] However, in one of many illustrations of the difficulty of translating economic rationales into legislative language, nowhere in the legislative provisions is reference made to the underlying principle of a margin. In its place is a series of complicated lists of technical transactions that are necessary to engage with to determine the taxable status of a transaction. As a result, supplies that are actually charged through an explicit fee can be treated as a financial supply provided the supply is on the list of financial supplies (i.e., provided the supply is normally charged by way of a margin).[395] The boundary between *financial supplies, incidental financial supplies* and supplies that are *not financial supplies* is not always clear.[396] For example, whereas arranging services are not a financial supply, the provision of advice can be included as an

[389] Ibid., reg. 40–5.12.

[390] Reg. 40–5.10 provides that in order to be an incidental financial supply, the supply must be incidental to the financial supply; it must be supplied at approximately the same time for the same (i.e., not separate) consideration; and normal practice is to supply both supplies together: ibid.

[391] Ibid., reg. 40–5.10.

[392] Commonwealth of Australia Treasury, *Review of the GST Financial Supply Provisions – Consultation Paper* (Australian Government, Canberra, 2009), 2, 4.

[393] Ibid., 1–2.

[394] The Explanatory Statement to the *ANTS Regulations* 1999 states, at 3:

> All other financial services, including agency services, are generally not capable of being charged for by way of a margin. This is because the facilitator of such financial services does not hold a legal interest in a financial product before it is supplied. All other financial services will therefore be taxable. For example, fees or commissions relating to agency services are easily identified and valued and are taxable.

[395] These include account-keeping fees, life insurance premiums, insurance risk and guarantees: *ANTS Regulations* 1999, reg. 40–5.09(3) and (4).

[396] *Commissioner of Taxation v. American Express Wholesale Currency Services Pty Ltd; Commissioner of Taxation v. American Express International Inc.* (2010), 187 FCR 398, 433, [145] (Kenny and J. J. Middleton).

incidental financial supply in certain circumstances.[397] As a result, the lists are supplemented by non-exhaustive, non-binding examples,[398] which themselves become largely determinative of the ultimate classification of the supply.[399]

A Treasury Discussion Paper notes the absence of principles in the financial supply provisions and that 'this unique structure relies heavily on regulations and results in additional complexity and uncertainties'.[400] It fails to point out, however, that these critiques echo those made of the WST – list-based drafting informed not so much by principle as by the success of political lobbying.[401]

While there are clearly a number of issues in relation to the financial supply provisions, the remainder of this discussion focuses on one remarkable[402] feature of the definition of *financial supply* in that the term includes both the supply *and* acquisition of an interest. The latter is commonly referred to as an *acquisition supply*[403] by the ATO in its rulings or by the Courts so as to distinguish the notion from the ordinary meaning of supply even though the term *acquisition supply* appears nowhere in the *ANTS Act* or *ANTS Regulations*. The notion of an *acquisition supply* has been described by the late Justice Hill as counterintuitive and compounding confusion, even calling into question the very validity of the regulations that contain the concept of an *acquisition supply*.[404] McCarthy

[397] *ANTS Regulations* 1999, reg. 40–5.10. [398] Ibid., schedules 7 and 8.

[399] Evans contends that 'ascertaining the scope of input taxation under the Regulations will be particularly difficult without the aid of the examples contained in the Regulations. In effect, the examples operate to define the operative provisions rather than the opposite': Michael B. Evans, 'The GST Treatment of Financial Services in Australia', in C. Peacock (ed.), *GST in Australia: Looking Forward from the First Decade* (Thomson Reuters, Pyrmont, 2011), 133, 153. See also *Commissioner of Taxation v. American Express Wholesale Currency Services Pty Ltd; Commissioner of Taxation v. American Express International Inc.* (2010), 187 FCR 398, 443, [179] (Kenny and J. J. Middleton); *AXA v. FCOT*, 509, [46] (J. Lindgren).

[400] Commonwealth of Australia Treasury, *Review of the GST Financial Supply Provisions – Consultation Paper* (Australian Government, Canberra, 2009) 9. Treasury also notes that the 'legislative structure can result in complexities and administrative costs' (at 14). The paper also notes that some provisions are not consistent with the underlying policy rationale and that the provisions result in arbitrary distinctions. For further criticisms of the drafting of the financial supplies provisions, see Board of Taxation, *Review of the Legal Framework for the Administration of the Goods and Services Tax: A Report to the Assistant Treasurer and Minister for Competition Policy and Consumer Affairs* (Australian Government, Canberra, 2008), 100, and the submissions received; Peter Edmundson, 'GST and Financial Supplies: A Comparative Analysis of Legislative Structure', *Australian Tax Review* 30 (2001), 132.

[401] ANTS Statement, 71–72.

[402] J. Lindgren in *AXA v. FCOT* notes that: 'Remarkably, under regs. 40–5.06 and 40–5.09 an acquisition of an interest can be a supply of the interest', 509, [44].

[403] *GSTR* 2002/2, 8 [25].

[404] *HP Mercantile*, 559, [19] (J. Hill). Presumably, the questioning of the validity of the relevant regulations is based on the definition of supply in the enabling Act. The *ANTS Act* 1999 provides that a 'supply' is 'any form of supply whatsoever' (s 9–10(1)) and lists a financial supply as an example of a supply (s 9–10(2)(f)). The remainder of the Act does nothing to depart from the ordinary meaning of the term 'supply', which would encompass the provision and/or disposal of an interest but would not normally include the acquisition of an interest. The definition of financial supply in the regulations therefore extends the ordinary meaning

describes the idea of an *acquisition supply* as being 'oxymoronic' and inconsistent with principles-based, plain-English drafting.[405]

4.3.3.2 'ACQUISITION SUPPLIES' AND THE *creditable purpose test* The need to include acquisitions in the definition of financial supply arises, in part, from the expansive definition of *creditable purpose*. An example of a supply of shares under the different approaches to the taxation of financial supplies in Australia and the European Union will demonstrate the issue. Figure 6.3 introduces the Australian approach.

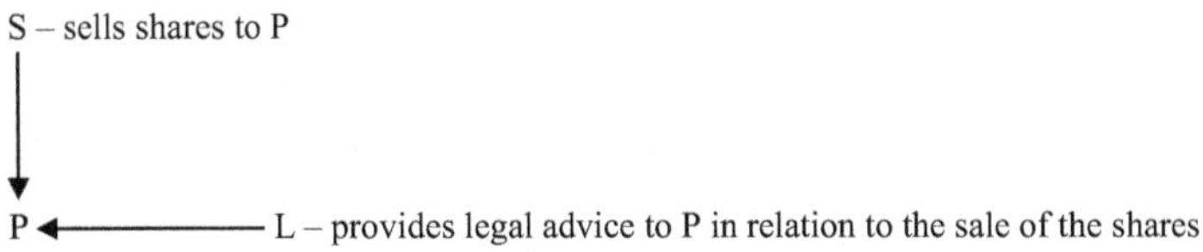

FIGURE 6.3 Australian approach to financial supplies

Can P *obtain credit for the advice of* L? In receiving advice from *L*, *P* paid a fee (1/11 of which includes GST), so the question is whether *P* can obtain an input tax credit for the GST paid in relation to this advice.

Under the expansive definition of financial supply in Australia, not only does S make a financial supply, but so does *P*, by virtue of the notion of *acquisition supply*.[406] S would be denied an input credit for an acquisition made in relation to the sale of the shares, such as legal advice, because although the acquisition is made in carrying on an enterprise (the positive limb of the *creditable purpose* test), the acquisition relates to making a supply that is input taxed (and is therefore excluded under the *first negative limb* of the *creditable purpose* test).[407] By contrast, without the notion of an *acquisition supply*, *P* would be entitled to an input credit for the legal advice received in relation to the purchase of the shares. That is, provided *P* met the *positive limb* of the *creditable purpose* test (that *P* acquired the advice in carrying on its enterprise), the acquisition of the legal advice would not fall afoul of the *first negative limb* of the *creditable purpose* test because the legal advice does not relate to the making of a supply that would be input taxed (as *P* makes no supply but rather acquires the shares). Therefore, provided that

of supply in a manner that might be argued to be inconsistent with the enabling Act (and therefore *ultra vires* or beyond the power provided in the enabling Act): see GSTR 2002/2, 6–7 for the ATO's perspective.

405 Denis McCarthy, 'The Australian GST – Why It Is the Way It Is and Where To from Here?' in C. Peacock (ed.), *GST in Australia: Looking Forward from the First Decade* (Thomson Reuters, Sydney, 2011), 61, 66.

406 ANTS *Regulations* 1999, reg. 40–5.09(3) Item 10 – Securities.

407 ANTS *Act* 1999, s 11–15(2)(a).

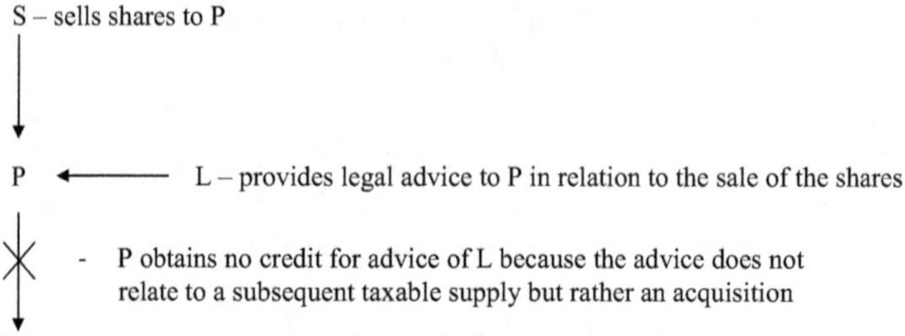

FIGURE 6.4 European approach to financial supplies

the legal advice met the other requirements for a creditable acquisition, which it should, but for the notion of *acquisition supply* P could obtain a credit.[408] To allow P to obtain a credit would be contrary to the policy of input-taxing financial supplies. If *P* were able to obtain a credit for the acquisition and later sold the shares, the effective tax outcome would be akin to zero-rating.

By contrast, as Figure 6.4 shows, under the European approach, *P* would not be entitled to an input tax credit for the legal advice from *L* because, unlike the Australian approach, the European approach requires *P* to make a subsequent taxable supply (or an 'on-supply')[409] in order for *P* to receive credit.[410] Even if *P* were to later sell the shares, because the subsequent supply would be a financial supply and therefore an exempt supply it would not be a taxable transaction.

Some contend that the European approach is more straightforward,[411] as the following comments by Justice Hill in the first major appellate case on the financial supply provisions, *HP Mercantile*, indicate. The issue in the case was whether the

[408] The supply of legal advice would be a taxable supply made for consideration: Ibid., s 11–5. Richard Krever, *GST Legislation Plus* (Thomson Reuters, Pyrmont, 2014), 988–89; Ross Stitt, 'Uncertanties Surrounding Input Tax Credit Entitlement in Australia', in C. Peacock (ed.), *GST in Australia: Looking Forward from the First Decade* (Thomson Reuters, Pyrmont, 2011), 115, 118.

[409] *AXA v. FCOT*, 508, [38] (J. Lindgren).

[410] *Recast VAT Directive 2006/112/EC*, art. 168; the language used in the Directive is a 'taxable transaction', which can include both taxable and zero-rated transactions but not exempt transactions.

[411] Ross Stitt, 'Uncertanties Surrounding Input Tax Credit Entitlement in Australia', in C. Peacock (ed.), *GST in Australia: Looking Forward from the First Decade* (Thomson Reuters, Pyrmont, 2011), 115, 118. Others highlight that the difference is overstated because under the Australian approach the need to apportion input credits between taxable, GST-free and input-taxed supplies in essence requires a degree of tracing or at least a consideration of the use made of the relevant acquisition: at 127; Denis McCarthy, 'The Australian GST – Why It Is the Way It Is and Where To from Here?' in C. Peacock (ed.), *GST in Australia: Looking Forward from the First Decade* (Thomson Reuters, Sydney, 2011), 61, 66; *AXA v. FCOT*, 516, 75 (J. Lindgren). The European approach is similarly beset by complexity and also requires reference to a taxpayer's overall economic activities in addition to a consideration of the link to a taxable supply in order to ascertain entitlement to credits: Ad van Doesum and Gert-Jan van Norden, 'The Right to Deduct under EU VAT', *International VAT Monitor* (September/October 2011), 323, 325–26.

taxpayer, a trustee, who had acquired debts could obtain full input credits for expenses relating to a feasibility study (undertaken *before* the acquisition of the debts for the purpose of deciding whether to acquire the debts) and debt collection services (undertaken *after* the acquisition of the debts for the purpose of recovering the debts).[412] Justice Hill noted that the issue would have been determined relatively simply under the European model because none of the acquisitions made went on to constitute a taxable supply, and therefore no input credits would be forthcoming.[413] By contrast, the Australian provisions required the Court to first assess whether the acquisitions satisfied the positive limb of the *creditable purpose* test (i.e., that they were acquired in carrying on an enterprise) – a matter agreed to by all parties in the case. The Court had to then consider whether the acquisitions fell afoul of the *first negative limb* of the *creditable purpose* test and assess whether the acquisitions related to the making of supplies that *would be* input taxed. The acquisition of the debts was treated as a financial supply and therefore an input-taxed supply due to the notion of an *acquisition supply*.[414] The Court rejected the argument of the taxpayer that the debt collection services did not relate to the making of a supply that *would be* input taxed because the acquisition of the debt collection services was *after* the acquisition of the debt. The Court rejected that the words 'would be input taxed' required futurity and a specific link between the acquisition and an actual supply, but rather the words required a link to the making of input-taxed supplies generally.[415] Although the Federal Court reached a similar conclusion on the facts as would result under the European approach, namely that the taxpayer was not entitled to input tax credits, this conclusion did not turn on the lack of a subsequent on-supply as it would in Europe, but rather on a reading of the *first negative limb* of the *creditable purpose* test.

Irrespective of which approach is better, it is useful to consider at this point how far the analysis has strayed from the merits of the good VAT which, as a tax on final consumption, should not be borne by business at all. This merit is intended to be captured by the broad notion of *creditable purpose*. However, in responding to the good VAT's difficulty in taxing financial supplies by input-taxing financial supplies, highly artificial notions such as *acquisition supplies* are developed to deny business access to input credits. However, all this artificiality and the complexity that flows from that concept is so that business is taxed – precisely the opposite of what the good VAT requires.[416] Whereas the *creditable purpose* test is informed by the

[412] *HP Mercantile Pty Ltd. v. Commissioner of Taxation* [2005], FCR 553, 556, [4] and [6] (J. Hill) (hereafter '*HP Mercantile*').

[413] Ibid., 560. [414] Ibid., 560. [415] Ibid., 562–64, [34]-[53].

[416] This point was acknowledged as much by J. Hill in *HP Mercantile*, 564–66, [45] and [50]; quoted with apparent approval by J. Lindgren in *AXA v. FCOT*, 514, [62]. For this reason, the business community has been a vocal critic of the provisions: Denis McCarthy, 'The Australian GST – Why It Is the Way It Is and Where To from Here?' in C. Peacock (ed.), *GST in Australia: Looking Forward from the First Decade* (Thomson Reuters, Sydney, 2011), 61, 66–67; Commonwealth of Australia Treasury, *Review of the GST Financial Supply Provisions – Consultation Paper*

historic approach to deductions under the Australian income tax, the notion of *acquisition supply* is more akin to the drafting approach under the WST, which relied heavily on deeming provisions.[417] The interaction of *creditable purpose* and acquisition supplies also has a number of unintended consequences, some of which are explored below.

4.3.3.3 MODIFICATIONS TO THE OPERATION OF THE *creditable purpose test* Whereas the notion of an *acquisition supply* is designed to deny business input credits for acquisitions made in relation to financial supplies, a number of other provisions attempt to limit the scope of this denial through modifying the *first negative limb* of the *creditable purpose* test that denies a *creditable purpose* to the extent that it relates to the making of an input-taxed supply.[418] For example, input tax credits may be available for acquisitions that relate to the making of financial supplies if the taxpayer does not exceed a *de minimus* threshold known as the financial acquisitions threshold (FAT).[419] The FAT is designed to limit the broad scope of the financial supply provisions (in part brought about by the notion of an *acquisition supply*).[420] A special borrowing exemption also shields taxpayers from falling afoul of the *first negative limb* of the *creditable purpose* test by also deeming

(Australian Government, Canberra, 2009), 9; Ross Stitt, 'Uncertanties Surrounding Input Tax Credit Entitlement in Australia', in C. Peacock (ed.), *GST in Australia: Looking Forward from the First Decade* (Thomson Reuters, Pyrmont, 2011), 115, 131.

417 Denis McCarthy, 'The Australian GST – Why It Is the Way It Is and Where To from Here?' in C. Peacock (ed.), *GST in Australia: Looking Forward from the First Decade* (Thomson Reuters, Sydney, 2011), 61, 64.

418 *ANTS Act* 1999, s 11–15(2)(a).

419 Ibid., s 11–15(4); Div. 189. The FAT is exceeded if an entity makes (or is likely to make) financial acquisitions (excluding borrowings for non-input taxed supplies) over a 12-month period where the input tax credits related to making those financial acquisitions would exceed the lesser of $150,000 or 10 per cent of the total amount of input tax credits to which the entity would be entitled. Calculation of the threshold includes current acquisitions (made in the 12 months leading up to the month of calculation) or projected acquisitions (over the ensuing 11-month period): ss 189–5, 189–10. Therefore, a small business that acquires a software package in order to manage its accounts relating to a credit facility will be entitled to an input tax credit on the supply, provided this and other financial acquisitions are less than $1,500,000 or that the input tax credits constitute less than 10 per cent of the total input tax credits the business was entitled to over the relevant 12-month period. By contrast, a bank that purchases a software package to manage its accounts will be denied input tax credits on the purchase in the likely event that the bank is over the FAT. See also Australian Taxation Office, *Goods and Services Tax: Financial Acquisitions Threshold*, GSTR 3003/9, 14 May 2003.

420 Because financial acquisitions are included in the definition of financial supply, the financial supply provisions are not simply an issue for financial institutions but any entity that provides, acquires or disposes of a listed financial interest in the course of their enterprise. As noted above at n 404, this is broader than the use of supply elsewhere in the *ANTS Act 1999*: *GSTR2002/2*, 7–8. The Treasury confirms this reading when it contends that 'financial supplies are not exclusively an issue for financial institutions alone, and can affect almost all entities': Commonwealth of Australia Treasury, *Review of the GST Financial Supply Provisions – Consultation Paper* (Australian Government, Canberra, 2009), 2.

that acquisitions made in relation to borrowing to make taxable or GST-free supplies are not treated as relating to input-taxed supplies.[421] Both measures are subject to their own complexities and criticisms;[422] to illustrate some of the issues relating to the modification of the *creditable purpose* test in more detail, another modification, the reduced input tax credit, will be the focus of further discussion.

4.3.3.4 THE REDUCED INPUT TAX CREDIT The reduced input tax credit (RITC) allows for the partial recovery of input credits even for acquisitions (defined as *reduced credit acquisitions*) that relate to the making of financial supplies.[423] In essence, the RITC overrides the *first negative limb* of the *creditable purpose* test[424] by providing that 'the fact that a reduced credit acquisition relates to making

[421] *ANTS Act* 1999, s 11–15(5) and 15–10(5). For the definition of borrowing, see s 195–1, which adopts the meaning given by s 995–1 of the *Income Tax Assessment Act* 1997; *GSTR* 2002/2, 4.

[422] Board of Taxation, *Review of the Legal Framework for the Administration of the Goods and Services Tax: A Report to the Assistant Treasurer and Minister for Competition Policy and Consumer Affairs* (Australian Government, Canberra, 2008), 99–100; Rita de la Feria and M. Walpole, 'Options for Taxing Financial Supplies in Value Added Tax: EU VAT and Australian GST Models Compared', *International and Comparative Law Quarterly* 58(4) (2000), 897, 920; Ross Stitt, 'Uncertanties Surrounding Input Tax Credit Entitlement in Australia', in C. Peacock (ed.), GST in *Australia: Looking Forward from the First Decade* (Thomson Reuters, Pyrmont, 2011), 115, 119. The government recently increased the FAT to $150,000, following advice from Treasury: Commonwealth of Australia Treasury, *Implementation of the Recommendations of Treasury's Review of the GST Financial Supply Provisions* (Australian Government, Canberra, 2010), viii. In relation to the borrowing exemption, if a business seeks to raise capital, there are a number of potential tax treatments that might apply: (a) If capital is raised through borrowing, there is no denial of input credits (because of the borrowing exemption); (b) If the capital is raised through a share issue, then the business is potentially denied full input credits for the GST incurred in relation to the share issue because this relates to the making of a financial supply (i.e., an input taxed supply). This is a particular problem for merger and acquisition activity. For example, if a company acquires shares in another company, a number of different VAT consequences may arise, depending on the structure of the transaction: (1) both may be denied full input credits for the GST incurred in relation to the transaction (as shown in Figure 6.3); (2) if the business acquired the assets of the takeover target, the transaction would be taxable and full input credits would be available; (3) if the business acquired another business as a going concern, the transaction would be GST free. The third potential outcome is a result of the ANTS Act 1999 div. subdiv. 38-J, which provides that the vendor and purchaser may, subject to certain conditions, agree in writing to treat the sale of a going concern (i.e., a business) as GST free (zero-rated) provided that the supply is for consideration, the recipient is registered (or required to be registered) and the supply involves all things necessary for the continued operation of the business, which the supplier must continue to operate until the day of supply: s 38–325. Denis McCarthy, 'The Australian GST – Why It Is the Way It Is and Where To from Here?' in C. Peacock (ed.), *GST in Australia: Looking Forward from the First Decade* (Thomson Reuters, Sydney, 2011), 61, 66–67; Commonwealth of Australia Treasury, *Review of the GST Financial Supply Provisions – Consultation Paper* (Australian Government, Canberra, 2009), 9; Ross Stitt, 'Uncertanties Surrounding Input Tax Credit Entitlement in Australia', in C. Peacock (ed.), *GST in Australia: Looking Forward from the First Decade* (Thomson Reuters, Pyrmont, 2011), 115, 131.

[423] *ANTS Act* 1999, s 70–10, 'Extended Meaning of Creditable Purpose'.

[424] Ibid., s 70–10(3): this section has effect despite s 11–15.

financial supplies does not stop it being for a *creditable purpose* to the extent that it relates to making financial supplies'.[425] The RITC allows for the recovery of 75 or 55 per cent of the total input tax paid on certain financial acquisitions.[426] The extensive list of more than 30 eligible acquisitions includes certain payment and transfer services, debt collection services, fund management services, and insurance services.[427] So, although the taxpayer in *HP Mercantile* was denied full input tax credits for the feasibility study and debt collection services in relation to the acquisition of debts, the Federal Court agreed with the Commissioner of Taxation that the taxpayer was entitled to an RITC for the debt collection services by virtue of their classification as *reduced credit acquisitions*.[428]

The RITC is unique to Australia.[429] The ostensible and indeed widely understood rationale for the RITC is to address the bias to self-supply that arises from the denial of input credits for financial institutions (see Chapter 2, §4.2.1 and §4.2.5.1). As §4.3.3.5 later explains, this is only a partial account of the underlying rationale. It is useful, however, to first provide some explanation for the bias to self-supply rationale. It should be noted from the outset that the RITC was not motivated by a desire to achieve a good VAT, but was rather the product of comparisons to real VATs elsewhere.

Real VATs in many other jurisdictions, such as those in the EU, extend exemption/input taxation of the ancillary services (often referred to as arranging services)

[425] Ibid., s 70–10(1); see also s 70–10(2).

[426] This is for those taxpayers above the FAT: *ANTS Regulations* 1999, reg. 70–5–03.The reduced 55 per cent rate applies to certain supplies acquired by recognised trust schemes: see below, n 443.

[427] Ibid., reg. 70–5.02(2). In addition, services commonly in-sourced, such as human resources, senior executive management and marketing and communications, are listed as reduced-credit acquisitions when supplies are made by an offshore branch of the same entity: regs. 70–5.02A & B.

[428] Ibid., reg. 70–5.02(2) item 17; *HP Mercantile*, 568, [65] (J. Hill).

[429] Singapore also offers a similar credit scheme albeit structured in a different manner and motivated by different policy objectives (although informed by the Australian provisions). Singapore allows financial institutions to claim input tax credits under either the 'special method' (which is the equivalent of zero-rating financial supplies to registrants under certain conditions) or through the 'fixed input recovery method', which allows financial institutions to claim a credit for a fixed percentage of total input taxes. In Singapore, the approach was justified by a concern to prevent the cascading of tax liability. The Singaporean approach uses industrial statistics to calculate the average percentage of recoverable input taxes available to different businesses and provided by different financial service providers (known as 'fixed input tax recovery rates'): *Goods and Services Tax Act* (Singapore, cap 117A, rev. edn. 2005), ss 19, 20(3); *Goods and Services Tax (General) Regulations* (Singapore, cap 117A, rev. edn. 2008), r 30; Lee Burns, 'Consumption Taxation of Supplies of Financial Services in the Asia-Pacific Region', *Asia Pacific Tax Bulletin* 14 (2008), 352, 354–55; Satya Poddar, 'VAT on Financial Services – Searching for a Workable Compromise', in R. Krever and D. White (eds.), *GST in Retrospect and Prospect* (Thomson Brookers, Wellington, 2007), 179, 187; Howell H. Zee, 'VAT Treatment of Financial Services: A Primer on Conceptual Issues and Country Practices', *INTERTAX* 34(1) (2006), 458, 463–64.

commonly acquired by financial institutions so as to prevent the bias to self-supply that arises from the denial of input credits.[430] So, for example, even though the value of debt collection services can be readily ascertained and is generally charged for by a fee, many jurisdictions input-tax rather than tax these services so as to deter the financial institutions that acquire these services from moving these services in-house.[431] This leads to at least two consequences: first, there is much political pressure by various suppliers to the financial services industry to have exemptions applied to their sector; second, there is much tax planning devoted to structuring transactions so as to appear to formally meet the criteria for an exemption.[432] The popular understanding of the RITC is that Australian policy-makers were keen to avoid the legal contests over the classification of services not themselves financial supplies but involving the arranging of financial supplies.[433] Under this view, the RITC was proposed to address the bias to self-supply so as to achieve an equivalent outcome to extending exemptions upstream but without some of these disputes.[434] As the Explanatory Statement to the ANTS Regulations introducing the RITC provides:[435]

> The RITC was designed to reduce the bias to insource and limit any pressure to extend input taxation up the supply chain through litigation. Where a financial institution purchases a service that is taxable and eligible for an RITC, the tax effect is similar to the situation where the purchased service is input taxed. . .Over

[430] The issue in the EU manifests in case law surrounding the interpretation of art. 135, *Recast VAT Directive 2006/112/EC*. For a summary, see Rita de la Feria and M. Walpole, 'Options for Taxing Financial Supplies in Value Added Tax: EU VAT and Australian GST Models Compared', *International and Comparative Law Quarterly* 58(4) (2009), 897, 899–913.

[431] Chapter 2, §4.2.1 of this book explained the effect of extending an exemption upstream.

[432] Further issues arise from the rapidly changing business models adopting new supply structures in the financial services industry: Rita de la Feria and M. Walpole, 'Options for Taxing Financial Supplies in Value Added Tax: EU VAT and Australian GST Models Compared', *International and Comparative Law Quarterly* 58(4) (2009), 897, 900.

[433] *ES ANTS Regulations* 1999, app. E, 2, 3, noting the differences regarding services that are not directly financial supplies but involve 'arranging' financial supplies.

[434] Although the RITC might address the self-supply bias, it does not completely eliminate cascading of tax liability involved with the input-taxing of financial services: Howell H. Zee, 'VAT Treatment of Financial Services: A Primer on Conceptual Issues and Country Practices', *INTERTAX* 34(10) (2006), 458, 465.

[435] *ES ANTS Regulations* 1999, app E, 1. See also *GSTR 2002/2*, 5:

> Other jurisdictions input tax services that are not directly financial supplies but involve arranging financial supplies. This is done partly to address a self-supply bias that arises where a financial service provider uses inputs that would normally be taxable. Reduced input tax credits were introduced in the Australian context to overcome this self-supply bias.

The Treasury noted that the 'reduced input tax credit means that a financial institution will not face a tax incentive to insource a service': Commonwealth of Australia Treasury, *The Application of Goods and Services Tax to Financial Services – Consultation Document* (Australian Government, Canberra, 1999), 19.

the medium to long term, this will substantially reduce the pressure to expand the definition of input taxed financial supplies.

In order to prevent the bias to self-supply, inclusions on the list of reduced-credit acquisitions giving rise to the RITC should be readily substitutable and capable of being in-sourced, and the setting of the rate should be empirically grounded to reflect the value-add of the service provider.[436] However, a Treasury Consultation Paper notes that the 'rationale underpinning the inclusion/exclusion of some items' on lists governing the GST treatment of financial supplies including the RITC is 'not always clear'.[437] For example, although substitutability is supposed to inform inclusions on the RITC list, many of the services identified are not capable of ready substitution. Stitt labels the inclusion of mergers and acquisitions advisory services[438] as 'unduly concessionary',[439] given that self-supply is not a viable option for the acquirers of such services, as the nature of such services requires them to be provided independently. Conversely, Stitt identifies certain services that are readily substitutable as excluded from the list, such as legal services.[440] This is but one of a number of complexities that beset the narrowly prescriptive list-based approach.[441]

[436] Commonwealth of Australia Treasury, *The Application of Goods and Services Tax to Financial Services – Consultation Document* (Australian Government, Canberra, 1999), 21 and at 18:

> the size of the reduced input tax credit should be calculated by reference to the value added by the last supplier of a service into a financial service provider. The reduced input tax credit reimburses the purchaser for the GST effectively applied to the wages and profits of the supplying firm. The reduced input tax credit means that a financial institution will not face a tax incentive to insource a service.

In addition, the self-supply bias is addressed by excluding from the definition of 'enterprise' (one of the requirements for a 'taxable supply', which is, in turn, necessary to give rise to an input credit for that supply) activities done by a person as an employee: *ANTS Act*, s 9–20(2).

[437] Commonwealth of Australia Treasury, *Review of the GST Financial Supply Provisions – Consultation Paper* (Australian Government, Canberra, 2009), 11; see also Rita de la Feria and M. Walpole, 'Options for Taxing Financial Supplies in Value Added Tax: EU VAT and Australian GST Models Compared', *International and Comparative Law Quarterly* 58(4) (2009), 897, 919.

[438] *ANTS Regulations* 1999, reg. 70–5.02(2) item 9(e).

[439] Ross Stitt, 'Financial Supplies and Reduced Input Tax Credits – An Australian Perspective', in R. Krever and D. White (eds.), *GST in Retrospect and Prospect* (Thomson Brookers, Wellington, 2007), 205, 210.

[440] Ibid. Stitt's own position as a partner in a top-tier law firm might motivate the inclusion of the example.

[441] See, e.g., the scope of debt-collecting services: *ANTS Regulations* 1999, reg. 70–5.02(2) item 17; Ross Stitt, 'Financial Supplies and Reduced Input Tax Credits – An Australian Perspective', in R. Krever and D. White (eds.), *GST in Retrospect and Prospect* (Thomson Brookers, Wellington, 2007), 205, 209. While certain data processing services may qualify as a reduced-credit acquisition, information technology services acquired to perform the same data processing functions do not qualify as a reduced-credit acquisition: *ES ANTS Regulations* 1999, app. C, 2. For concerns over the proposed use of list-based drafting in the European Union context, see Rita de la Feria and Ben Lockwood, 'Opting for Opting-In? An Evaluation of the European Commission's Proposals for Reforming VAT on Financial Services', *Fiscal Studies* 31(2) (2010), 171, 178–79.

Empirically grounding the rate of the RITC should result in different rates for different services. For example, where inputs were less significant to the service and labour was more important, the rate should be higher.[442] However, industry preferred, and was granted, a generous average rate (of 75 per cent) for the types of acquisitions identified as being eligible for a reduced input tax credit.[443]

The desire to achieve equivalent outcomes to already imperfect real-world approaches has given rise to its own set of complexities. Treasury notes that the 'RITC goes some way to tackling the problem of [the] self-supply bias but introduces a further layer of complexity'.[444] Rather than, for example, removing the political and legal contests over who should be granted an exemption upstream, these contests are simply transferred to the RITC.[445] The RITC has been subject to much tax planning. The ATO has expressed particular concern about schemes in the context of merger-and-acquisition activity.[446] An example helps illustrate some of the issues.

Figure 6.5 shows a company, the *financial supply provider* (FSP), taking over a target company through the acquisition of shares. This is classified as a financial supply under the *ANTS Regulations* and would therefore be treated as an input-taxed supply.[447] Rather than directly acquiring the services needed to complete the takeover, the FSP interposes an entity, the *financial supply facilitator* (FSF),

[442] For an example of the manner of calculation, see Commonwealth of Australia Treasury, *The Application of Goods and Services Tax to Financial Services – Consultation Document* (Australian Government, Canberra, 1999), 19.

[443] Commonwealth of Australia Treasury, *Review of the GST Financial Supply Provisions – Consultation Paper* (Australian Government, Canberra, 2009), 18–19, 23. A new reduced rate of 55 per cent was recently introduced for supplies acquired by recognised trust schemes. This reduced rate was introduced in part as a response to the use of single-fee trustee arrangements, which enabled trusts to bundle services so as to attract a full RITC of 75 per cent on all services, including those that would otherwise not be eligible for an RITC but for the bundling. This is a variant of the issue discussed at Figure 6.5: *ANTS Regulations* 1999, reg. 70–5.03(a)–(b); Explanatory Statement, A New Tax System (Goods and Services Tax) Amendment Regulation 2012 (no. 1) (Cth), Schedule 1, 'Supplies to Recognised Trust Schemes'.

[444] Commonwealth of Australia Treasury, *Review of the GST Financial Supply Provisions – Consultation Paper* (Australian Government, Canberra, 2009), 9.

[445] Ross Stitt, 'Financial Supplies and Reduced Input Tax Credits – An Australian Perspective', in R. Krever and D. White (eds.), *GST in Retrospect and Prospect* (Thomson Brookers, Wellington, 2007), 205, 210.

[446] This example is one of a number of variations: see generally Commonwealth of Australia Treasury, *Implementation of the Recommendations of Treasury's Review of the GST Margin Scheme – Discussion Paper* (Australian Government, Canberra, 2010), 12–16; John Kehoe, 'Tax Office Chases Dodgy GST Claims', *Australian Financial Review* (19 February 2010), 10; ATO, *Taxpayer Alert 2010/1: GST – Interposing an Associated 'Financial Supply Facilitator' to Enhance Claims for Reduced Input Tax Credits for Expenses Incurred in the Course of a Company Takeover*, TA 2010/1, 19 February 2010; for criticisms of the ATO's approach, see ATO – National Tax Liaison Group, GST Sub-Committee, *GST Minutes 1 March 2010 – Item 11 Taxpayer Alert 2010/1 – Financial Supplies arrangement* (ATO, Canberra, 2010).

[447] *ANTS Act* 1999, s 40–5(1) and *ANTS Regulations* 1999, reg. 40–5.09(1), item 10 of reg. 40–5.09 (3) – i.e., a supply of securities (shares).

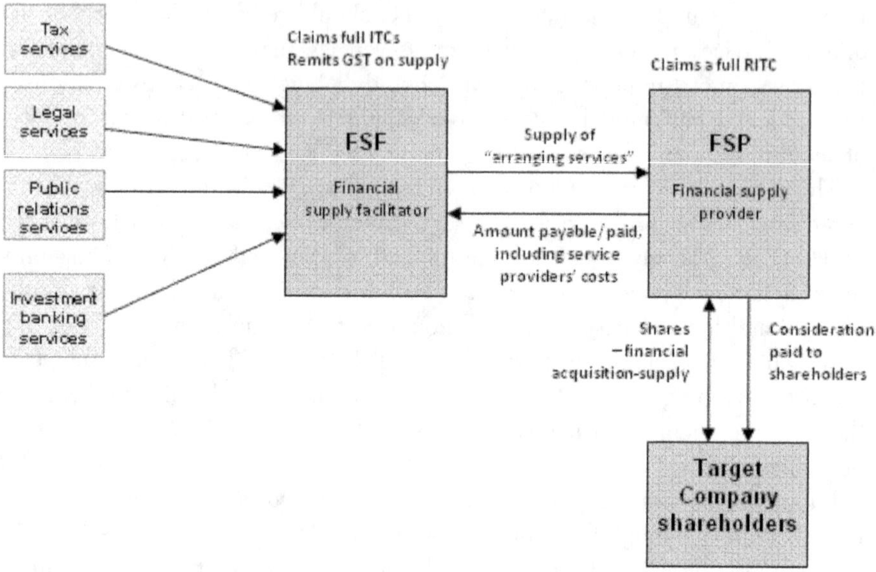

FIGURE 6.5 Exploitation of the RITC[448]

to acquire the requisite services. These services include tax, legal and public relations services as well as investment banking services, such as valuation services. As an FSF, the associate company is able to obtain full input tax credits on all the acquired services. This is because the acquisitions would not fall afoul of the *first negative limb* of the *creditable purpose* test; that is, they do not relate to supplies that would be input taxed, as the associate then passes on the services to the FSP as a taxable supply of an 'arranging service'. The FSP then obtains an RITC for the whole of the arranging services because the 'arrangement' by an FSF of securities transaction services is classified as a reduced-credit acquisition.[449] In this way, the FSP is able to obtain an RITC for the tax, legal and public relations services that it would not have been entitled to had it acquired the services from those entities directly (as these services are not listed as reduced-credit acquisitions).[450] Only the investment banking services would have been eligible for the RITC.[451]

[448] This is taken directly from *GSTD* 2011/3, 5, app. 1.

[449] *ANTS Regulations* 1999, reg. 70–5.02(2), item 9 – securities transactions services.

[450] Ibid., reg. 70–5.02(2).

[451] ATO, *Goods and Services Tax: Do the Acquisitions of the Services Provided under the Arrangement Described in Taxpayer Alert TA 2010/1 Form Part of a Reduced Credit Acquisition Made by the Financial Supply Provider under Item 9 of the Table in Subregulation 70–5.02(2) of the A New Tax System (Goods and Services Tax) Regulations 1999?* GSTD 2011/3, 30 November 2011 (hereinafter referred to as 'GSTD 2011/3'), 4–5, app. 1; see also Ross Stitt, 'Uncertanties Surrounding Input Tax Credit Entitlement in Australia', in C. Peacock (ed.), *GST in Australia: Looking Forward from the First Decade* (Thomson Reuters, Pyrmont, 2011), 115, 121.

The ATO has sought to treat these transactions as giving rise only to a partial RITC – mainly for the investment banking services – and has also raised the prospect that such arrangements may fall afoul of the general anti-avoidance provision.[452] Taxpayers and practitioners are keen to stress that this alleged avoidance and evasion is in keeping with the policy intent of the good VAT as not being a cost to business.[453] Moreover, they contend that the use of an entity to arrange such transactions is a commonplace and legitimate approach justified as much by commercial considerations as it is tax planning.[454] This might all be true, but the RITC was never seeking to achieve the good VAT, but rather to replicate similar outcomes to other real VATs. In doing so, however, policy-makers have encouraged the pursuit of transactions that focus on form over substance and that seek to manipulate the relevant legislative provisions, just as is done in real VATs elsewhere. The difficulties of real VATs in other jurisdictions relating to the classification of 'arranging' services seem to have been transferred rather than avoided. The merits of the good VAT therefore add little to explain this outcome.

As with the financial supply provisions generally, the provisions relating to the RITC are costly to comply with and to administer, constitute a significant share of ATO compliance activity[455] and attract much criticism.[456] As the next section explains, the provisions themselves have undergone significant amendment. Treasury estimates that the current tax treatment of financial supplies results in an over-taxation of business by $760 million and an under-taxation of household consumption of financial services equivalent to $3.9 billion. However, these estimates assume that the cost of input taxation is not forward shifted to final consumers but is borne by businesses that use the products and services of financial supply providers (and are denied input credits otherwise available on their inputs) or are absorbed by the financial supply providers themselves. The figures have not been empirically verified, and it is not clear if they take into account the RITC.[457]

[452] *GSTD 2011/3*, 8–9, app. 1.

[453] John Kehoe, 'Tax Office Chases Dodgy GST Claims', *Australian Financial Review*, 19 February 2010, 10.

[454] As always, the individual factual characterisation of a case will be critical. See the issues raised by respondents to the ATO's draft ruling: ATO, *Ruling Compendium*, GSTD 2011/3EC (2011).

[455] A significant proportion of rulings and ATO compliance activities in relation to financial supplies concern the RITC: see, e.g., ATO, *Goods and Services Tax: Reduced Credit Acquisitions*, GSTR2004/1, 25 February 2004; ATO, *Goods and Services Tax: Determining the Extent of Creditable Purpose for Providers of Financial Supplies*, GSTR2006/3, 12 April 2006.

[456] Board of Taxation, *Review of the Legal Framework for the Administration of the Goods and Services Tax: A Report to the Assistant Treasurer and Minister for Competition Policy and Consumer Affairs* (Australian Government, Canberra, 2008), 98; Commonwealth of Australia Treasury, *Review of the GST Financial Supply Provisions – Consultation Paper* (Australian Government, Canberra, 2009).

[457] Commonwealth of Australia Treasury, Australia's Future Tax System Review Panel, *Australia's Future Tax System: Report to the Treasurer* (Australia's Future Tax System Review Panel: The Treasury, Canberra, 2009), vol. 2, 304. The 2012 Tax Expenditures Statement (TES)

TABLE 6.3 – *Estimate of revenue foregone as a result of the RITC ($m AUD) – 2014*[458]

2009–10	2010–11	2011–12	2012–13	2013–14	2014–15	2015–16	2016–17
680	700	720	780	830	870	920	970

The RITC is costly to revenue. The Australian Treasury treats the RITC as a tax expenditure. Initial estimates predicted the revenue foregone as a result of the RITC would be $50 million in 2000–2001, rising to $70 million in 2003–2004.[459] Press reports at the time suggest that the move to place the financial supply provisions into the regulations was motivated in part by a desire to maintain 'tight control'[460] over the provisions and flexibility to amend the law in light of potential cost blowouts arising from the extension of the RITCs to all financial providers (as the next section highlights). However, as Table 6.3 shows, moving the financial supply provisions into the Regulations has not prevented a cost blowout by a factor of 10, compared to the original estimates.

The input taxation of financial supplies is a cost to business and is not in line with the underlying merits of the good VAT. However, the RITC is a complex and expensive measure to try to lessen the impact on business. The next section explains how this outcome came about.

4.3.3.5 THE HISTORY OF THE RITC The *ANTS Statement*, and *Fightback!* before it, had proposed taxing secondary financial services (or facilitation services) capable

reports that the input taxation of financial supplies constitutes a $3.45 billion tax expenditure (presumably in favour of end consumers). The alleged over-taxation of business is not separately accounted for as a negative tax expenditure: Commonwealth of Australia Treasury, *Tax Expenditures Statement 2012* (Australian Government, Canberra, 2013), 192. However, the TES elsewhere states that removing the input taxation of financial supplies would have negligible revenue gain: at 213; Michael B. Evans, 'The GST Treatment of Financial Services in Australia', in C. Peacock (ed.), *GST in Australia: Looking Forward from the First Decade* (Thomson Reuters, Pyrmont, 2011), 133, 144. See also Chapter 2, §4.2.5.1 of this book.

458 Commonwealth of Australia Treasury, *Tax Expenditures Statement 2013* (Australian Government, Canberra, 2014), 169.

459 The estimates for intervening years were $60 million in 2001–2002 and $70 million in 2002–2003: Commonwealth of Australia Treasury, *The Commonwealth Budget Papers 2000 – 2001*, Appendix A (budget.gov.au /2000–01/papers/bp3/html/appa.htm). Note that owing to the government's presentation of the GST as a state tax, tax expenditure data relating to the GST were not originally included in Tax Expenditure Statements. This practice changed from 2008: Commonwealth of Australia Treasury, *Tax Expenditures Statement 2008* (Australian Government, Canberra, 2009), 1. The 2008 Tax Expenditure Statement had similar figures to those in the 2000–2001 budget papers: 2004–2005 and 2005–2006 were estimated at $60 million, and 2006–2007 $90 million, 2007–2008 $80 million, 2008–2009 $70 million, 2009–2010 $90 million, 2010–2011 and 2011–2012 $100 million: at 197. From the 2009 Tax Expenditure Statement onward, this estimate was revised upward without any obvious change in methodology: Commonwealth of Australia Treasury, *Tax Expenditures Statement 2009* (Australian Government, Canberra, 2010), 183.

460 Paul Cleary, 'Input Credit Details Made Regulations (GST: The Fine Print)', *Australian Financial Review* (24 June 1999), 4.

of being provided for a readily identifiable fee or charge, such as debt collection services.[461] The original intention of policy-makers was to extend the base of the GST (by taxing these ancillary services – in line with the good VAT goal of a broad consumption base) but to deny input credits for financial service providers that acquired these facilitation services (in an extension of most real VATs and contravening the good VAT notion that the tax not be borne by business). Although the ostensible rationale for the RITC is to counteract the self-supply bias, this was not something that originally concerned policy-makers.

Upon closer inspection of the history of the RITC, one can see at least three rationales for the RITC, none of which were raised by policy-makers but were rather raised by lobbyists for the financial services industry, and primarily motivated by real VAT comparisons.[462] A 2010 Treasury Consultation Paper explains that the RITC achieves the same effect that real VATs elsewhere achieve by extending exemptions (here referred to as input taxation) upstream:[463]

> If set at an appropriate rate, a RITC results in the same tax effect as would be the case if the service being provided was input taxed rather than taxed. As smaller financial supply providers outsource more of their activities this provides a greater benefit to them.

The impact of real VATs elsewhere is further evidenced by the Explanatory Statement to the ANTS Regulations introducing the RITC:[464]

> A greater proportion of financial service providers' purchases will be either input taxed, or eligible for an RITC, than would be input taxed in overseas jurisdictions. However, for compliance and simplicity reasons, a broader range of services is taxable than is generally taxed in overseas jurisdictions. Where the scope of taxation has been increased from what is generally input taxed in overseas jurisdictions, an RITC will usually apply.

The banking industry had lobbied strongly for a GST and for financial supplies to be taxable under that GST, and even developed a 'complex, technology-based formula for levying the tax'.[465] This was rejected by the government, in part

[461] *ANTS Statement*, 96; *Fightback!* proposed exempting financial services because the drafters were not satisfied that there was any appropriate way to tax financial supplies under a GST, but the drafters were prepared to receive submissions on the issue: *Fightback!*, 79, *Fightback! II*, 19.

[462] See generally Tim Edgar, 'Exempt Treatment of Financial Intermediation Services Under a Value-Added Tax: An Assessment of Alternatives', *Canadian Tax Journal* 49(5) (2001), 1181.

[463] Commonwealth of Australia Treasury, *Implementation of the Recommendations of Treasury's Review of the GST Financial Supply Provisions* (Australian Government, Canberra, 2010), 8.

[464] *ES ANTS Regulations* 1999, app. E, 2.

[465] Tim Boreham, 'Bankers Charge to Fore in GST Debate', *The Australian*, 20 March 1998, 23. The report also notes that:

> The banks have thrown their collective weight behind a goods and services tax for the first time – especially if $2 billion of government-imposed bank charges disappear as part of the deal. In an unusual stance for an industry body, the Australian Bankers' Association has urged the Federal Government to include financial services in any broad-based consumption tax.

because it was untested elsewhere in the world.[466] When the taxation of financial supplies was not forthcoming, the industry lobbied hard for zero-rating.[467] The banking industry was not happy with input taxation and expressed this dissatisfaction prior to the release of the original *ANTS package*.[468] The dissatisfaction was only partially offset by other reforms in the package that would reduce the banks' tax burden.[469] These benefits were significant enough to prompt David Vos, a PricewaterhouseCoopers partner, to predict that:[470]

> The banks are, in my view, going to provide a cheaper service with an exemption than if they were taxable. . .By the time 22 percent of imbedded costs are removed, I reckon prices will come down or at least marginally so.

Nevertheless, the peak banking organisation, the Australian Bankers' Association, warned even before the release of the *ANTS package* that the input taxation of financial supplies would hurt smaller institutions such as credit unions and building societies (the 'competition rationale').

Australia has a highly concentrated banking and finance sector, with four banks dominating the market share in banking, insurance, wealth management and financial advice. A brief respite to this market dominance occurred during the 1990s when a range of non-bank lenders entered the market facilitated through mortgage securitisation.[471] These smaller institutions were more heavily reliant on the outsourcing of services than larger financial institutions for which it made sense to self-supply due to economies of scale.[472]

Policy-makers have sought for some decades now to position Australia as a global financial services centre[473] and were therefore sensitive to warnings of reduced

[466] Boreham reported that 'Treasury is believed to have expressed strong interest in the proposals. "But they didn't want to do something which hadn't been done anywhere else in the world," one banking source says': Tim Boreham, 'Banks Dealt a Blow on GST Front', *The Australian*, 3 August 1998, 35.

[467] Tim Boreham, 'The Y2K Bug Has a Friend, the GST Slug', *The Australian*, 9 April 1999, 21.

[468] Sean Alymer, 'Banks Fear Backlash over Tax Exemption', *Sydney Morning Herald*, 10 August 1998, 33; Tim Boreham, 'Banks Dealt a Blow on GST Front', *The Australian*, 3 August 1998, 35.

[469] These reforms included reductions from 22 per cent WST to 10 per cent GST on computers and the abolition of a range of indirect taxes on financial transactions: *ANTS Statement*, 76, 79.

[470] Tim Boreham, 'Banks to Be Kept in Line', *The Australian*, 12 August 1998, 2; Miranda McLachlan, 'GST May Hit Bank Fees, Rates', *The Herald-Sun*, 12 August 1998, 27.

[471] The Australian Senate Economics References Committee, *Competition within the Australian Banking Sector* (Canberra, 2011), 10 [2.28].

[472] The managing director of one of the largest non-bank lenders at the time was quoted as saying that the 'resulting increase in the cost of outsourcing would crush mortgage competition and push up interest rates by up to 2 percent': Phillip Hudson, 'No GST Deal For Financial Sector', *The Age* (Melbourne), 9 March 1999, 6; Hans van Leeuwen, 'New Headache for Non-Bank Home Lenders', *Australian Financial Review* (27 April 1999), 4.

[473] John Hewson, 'Facing Global Financial Challenge', *Australian Financial Review* (21 May 1999), 44; Denis McCarthy, 'The Australian GST – Why It Is the Way It Is and Where To

competition in the banking sector. A 1999 Treasury Consultation Document confirms the responsiveness of policy-makers to the competition rationale:[474]

> Larger market participants generally have a greater ability to insource services. For example, smaller financial service providers, such as credit unions or building societies, would have less scope to insource mortgage valuation services than would a large bank. Therefore, input taxing financial supplies has important implications for the relative competitiveness of different segments of the financial sector.

Therefore, buried in the ancillary documentation to the release of the compromised package with the Democrats was an announcement that credit union, building societies and non-bank lenders would obtain a rebate on GST paid on certain commonly outsourced services such as loan processing.[475] The compromise with the financial services sector had been agreed to by the government five weeks prior to the announcement of the compromise with the Democrats on 31 May 1999.[476] The concession was celebrated by smaller institutions and their service providers.[477] Dave Taylor, head of the peak body for credit unions, declared:[478]

> It's absolutely wonderful because the previous GST package, without this amendment, would have been significantly discriminatory to credit unions. Credit unions potentially face a $40 million unrecoverable GST burden. This rebate will claw back nearly all of that.

However, within weeks of the announcement the major banks were campaigning fiercely for the RITC concession to be extended to them in the interests of promoting a 'level playing field' (the 'level playing field rationale') and complained

from Here?' in C. Peacock (ed.), *GST in Australia: Looking Forward from the First Decade* (Thomson Reuters, Sydney, 2011), 61, 71.

474 Commonwealth of Australia Treasury, *The Application of Goods and Services Tax to Financial Services – Consultation Document* (Australian Government, Canberra, 1999), 18.

475 'Financial Services: A partial input tax credit will be provided for the purchase of a specified list of services used to make financial supplies.' Thomson Reuters, 'GST and Tax Reform: It's a Deal!', *GST News Alert* (29) (31 May 1999).

476 O'Riordan reported on 3 June 1999 that '[t]he government agreed to the partial rebate five weeks ago. It chose not to reveal the details until it had concluded negotiations with Independent Senator Brian Harradine and the Democrats on the wider GST package': Bernard O'Riordan, 'Non-Banks' Tax Breakthrough', *Australian Financial Review* (3 June 1999), 4. Some later reports wrongly attribute the measure to the Democrats; however, this was never part of the Democrats' platform: Paul Cleary, 'Input Credit Details Made Regulations', *Australian Financial Review* (24 June 1999), 4.

477 Tim Blue, 'Financial Planners Brace for Shake-Up', *The Australian*, 1 June 1999, 22.

478 Bernard O'Riordan, 'Non-Banks' Tax Breakthrough', *Australian Financial Review*, 3 June 1999, 4. See also a newspaper article that notes that 'the competitive position of the credit union lenders has been enhanced' as a positive aspect of the concession: Robert Harley, 'Buy Now, Wait a While or Give Up?' *Australian Financial Review* (5–6 June 1999), 32.

that 'credit unions are getting a tax credit for outsourcing but we're not getting it when we do it ourselves and we think that's a little bit unfair'.[479] In support of the banks' campaign, consumers were warned of inevitable rises in bank fees that would result from a failure to extend the concession to banks.[480] By 9 June 1999, less than two weeks after the Democrats' announcement, the RITC was extended to all banks.[481]

However, the concession did not appease the threats. Over the ensuing months, banks warned of increased fees that would hit 'mum and dad bank customers'[482] and banks mobilised their own service providers in support of their campaign.[483] One might ask why this was the case, given the boon for the major banks that was the extension of the RITC. The answer seems to be so as to support their bargaining position in relation to the drafting of the financial supply provisions. The government had committed to consult industry on which supplies should be treated as financial supplies and which services should be eligible for input tax credits (by falling outside the definition of financial supplies) or RITCs. Much informal consultation took place before the official release of a Treasury Consultation Document issued in August 1999 that specifically invited participants' feedback on the appropriate rate of the RITC:[484]

> The Government welcomes comments on these proposals. The Government requests that any suggested changes should clearly describe the particular product and preferred treatment.

The government invited specific lobbying and received it. None of the lobbying is headline-generating material, but the difficulties in identifying a consistent policy behind the inclusions on the relevant lists of financial supplies, non-financial supplies and RITCs is at least partly explained by the success of the respective lobbying efforts. This explains why a recent Treasury Report noted that it 'is unlikely that a set of principles could be developed that would mirror the existing

[479] Sean Alymer, 'Big Four to Pass Extra GST Costs to Customers', *Australian Financial Review*, 8 June 1999, 4; Bernard O'Riordan, 'Non-Banks' Tax Breakthrough', *Australian Financial Review*, 3 June 1999, 4, which states that:

> It was unclear whether the same rebates would apply to banks which outsourced portions of their business. The major banks, most of which outsource some parts of their business, were attempting to get some clarification on the guidelines. Commonwealth Bank of Australia's group general manager, financial and risk management, Mr. Michael Ulmer, said, 'I don't see how that would be competitively neutral.'

[480] Sean Alymer, 'Big Four to Pass Extra GST Costs to Customers', *Australian Financial Review*, 8 June 1999, 4.

[481] Annabel Hepworth, 'Banks to Get Input Credits under GST', *Australian Financial Review*, 10 June 1999, 29.

[482] 'Banks' GST Fee Shock', *Sunday Herald Sun* (Melbourne), 25 July 1999, 17.

[483] Andrew McKenzie, ' Industry Fears Impact of GST', *The Australian*, 6 July 1999, 27.

[484] Commonwealth of Australia Treasury, *The Application of Goods and Services Tax to Financial Services – Consultation Document* (Australian Government, Canberra, 1999), 4.

law in full'.[485] Unfortunately for consumers, any concessions obtained in the negotiations over the financial supply provisions did not prevent the banks from lifting fees – ostensibly to recover the cost of the GST – including a 0.02 per cent increase in home lending rates.[486]

The history of the RITC speaks to a tension in real VATs between coverage and neutrality. The merits of the good VAT offer little to help explain how these tensions get resolved in practice. Policy-makers, learning from the experience of real VATs elsewhere, had sought to expand the GST base to include a number of readily taxable supplies to financial institutions (i.e., extend coverage consistent with the broad base of a good VAT). However, the cost of doing so was the RITC, which was driven by actors who defended neutrality in the sense of the VAT not being a cost to business (also consistent with the intent of the good VAT),[487] and who also supported their domestic position by comparison to real VATs elsewhere. However, the history also shows the manner in which concessions multiply, and

[485] Commonwealth of Australia Treasury, *Review of the GST Financial Supply Provisions – Consultation Paper* (Australian Government, Canberra, 2009), 11. See also Denis McCarthy, 'The Australian GST – Why It Is the Way It Is and Where To from Here?' in C. Peacock (ed.), *GST in Australia: Looking Forward from the First Decade* (Thomson Reuters, Sydney, 2011), 61, 70–71.

[486] Bruce Brammall, 'Bank GST Levy', *The Herald-Sun*, 15 August 2000, 1; Steve Burrell, 'Give 'Em All a Good Kicking', *Sydney Morning Herald*, 8 September 2000, 26; Matt Wade, 'Banks Lift Rates to Recoup GST', *Sydney Morning Herald*, 22 July 2000, 3; 'The two biggest banks have braved a customer backlash by raising fees and interest rates and lowering some deposit rates to counter the expected cost of the GST': Tim Boreham, 'Customers Face Hike in Fees', *The Australian*, 22 July 2000, 5; Matt Wade, 'The GST Made Us Do It: Banks Lift Fees', *Sydney Morning Herald*, 17 July 2000, 6; 'Now Heat Is on Bank Fees', *The Herald-Sun*, 28 June 2000, 2; ' "Banks could be around $300 million a year worse off as a result of the GST package," Australian Bankers Association chief Tony Aveling said': Karen Collier, 'Bank Fees Add to Costs', *The Herald-Sun*, 29 May 2000, 44; Morgan Mellish, 'Bank to Raise Fees to Beat GST', *Sydney Morning Herald*, 26 January 2000, 3; Morgan Mellish, 'Banks' GST Bite on Credit Card Users', *Sydney Morning Herald*, 25 January 2000, 1; 'Bank to Raise Fees to cover GST Bill', *The Herald-Sun*, 29 October 1999, 9. *The Herald-Sun* reported that:

> Banks will lift fees and charges as they battle to recoup the millions of dollars the GST will cost them each year. And it will be low-income customers who will be hit hardest, a consumer group warned. The Australian Bankers Association estimates the GST will cost Australia's banks $430 million a year to implement, even though financial services will not attract a GST.

Miranda McLachlan and Peter Gosnell, 'Banks Face $430m Bill', *The Herald-Sun*, 21 January 2000, 4.

[487] These multiple rationales for the RITC were partly reflected in the Explanatory Statement for the ANTS Regulations introducing the RITC:

> The RITC approach – which is unique to the Australian GST – has a number of benefits over the general approach of broader input taxation taken in overseas jurisdictions. These include reduced bias to insource; lower compliance costs for smaller entities; greater legislative certainty; and a better competitive position for domestic service providers.

ES ANTS Regulations 1999, app. E, 3.

the unintended consequences of policy decisions driven by political lobbying. Pressure to extend a concession to one segment of an industry, non-bank financial service providers, on the basis of enhancing competition, set off lobbying by another, big banks, on the basis of competitive neutrality. This has resulted in provisions that lack identifiable and consistent policy rationales, and certainly none of which can be explained by the good VAT. In a sign of the distortion that occurs when policy ideas are considered absent context, the EU recently considered (and rejected) adopting the RITC.[488] Here, rationales for local policy decisions seem to become retrospectively translated, so that the RITC appeals to Europeans as a means to address the bias to self-supply, despite the RITC itself being the unintended consequence of a deliberate decision by Australian policy-makers to depart from European practice and include ancillary financial services in the GST base. Merits offer little from which to understand how these real VAT outcomes arise.

4.3.4 The legacy of the GST treatment of financial supplies

The problems with the RITC mechanism is but one of the many reasons the Australian approach to the taxation of financial supplies is labelled uncertain and 'unnecessarily complex'.[489] In a prescient assessment of the issues, Cooper and Vann in 1999 claimed that:[490]

[488] The rejection was in part informed by dissatisfaction with accurately calculating the RITC to apply to the diverse range of labour costs across the EU: European Commission, *Impact Assessment: Accompanying Document to the Proposal for a Council Directive Amending Directive 2006/112/EC on the Common System of Value Added Tax, as Regards the Treatment of Insurance and Financial Services*, SEC (2007) 1554, 34–35; Rita de la Feria and M. Walpole, 'Options for Taxing Financial Supplies in Value Added Tax: EU VAT and Australian GST Models Compared', *International and Comparative Law Quarterly* 58(4) (2009), 897, 898–99; Alan Schenk, 'Taxation of Financial Services Under a U.S. Value-Added Tax',*Tax Law Review* 63(2) (2010), 409, 429.

[489] The BoT further notes complexity in relation to 'defining what supplies will be financial supplies and what acquisitions may qualify for reduced input tax credits': Board of Taxation, *Review of the Legal Framework for the Administration of the Goods and Services Tax: A Report to the Assistant Treasurer and Minister for Competition Policy and Consumer Affairs* (Australian Government, Canberra, 2008), 100. Edmundson goes so far as to conclude that the 'Australian regime is more complex than overseas regimes' in the UK, EU, Canada and New Zealand: Peter Edmundson, 'GST and Financial Supplies: A Comparative Analysis of Legislative Structure', *Australian Tax Review* 30 (2000), 132. Stitt arrives at a similar conclusion: Ross Stitt, 'Uncertanties Surrounding Input Tax Credit Entitlement in Australia', in C. Peacock (ed.), *GST in Australia: Looking Forward from the First Decade* (Thomson Reuters, Pyrmont, 2011), 115, 118. See also Denis McCarthy, 'The Australian GST – Why It Is the Way It Is and Where To from Here?' in C. Peacock (ed.), *GST in Australia: Looking Forward from the First Decade* (Thomson Reuters, Sydney, 2011), 61, 70–71.

[490] Graeme Cooper and Richard Vann, 'Implementing the Goods and Services Tax', *Sydney Law Review* 23 (1999), 337, 414; *Contra* David F. Bradford, 'The X Tax in the World Economy' (CEPS Working Paper No. 93, Center for Economic Policy Studies [Princeton], 2003), 104.

> Proxy taxes such as Financial Institutions Duty and/or Bank Account Debits Tax, which are to [be] abolished under tax reform, might have been a more effective way of taxing financial services rather than creating the various distortions that the proposed input taxing regime increasingly is causing around the world. . .In this area the GST must be regarded as decidedly inferior to the income tax.

Some express hope that the complexity of the financial supply provisions can be 'solved' through better drafting.[491] However, when Treasury offered to redraft the provisions in a principles-based manner,[492] the offer was comprehensively rejected by stakeholders from the financial services industry who had previously bitterly complained of the complexity of the financial supply provisions.[493] As a result, the Australian government undertook far less ambitious amendments and all but abandoned any efforts toward principles-based reform.[494]

The finance industry's support for the maintenance of the status quo in this instance demonstrates how the sunk costs in complying with a complex tax regime (and the knowledge of the opportunities arising from that complexity) embodies the notion of increasing returns, whereby 'the probability of further steps along the

[491] Edmundson, for example, calls for clearer legislative provisions, as 'any consumption tax on financial services should not stray unduly from the well-explored, orthodox criteria of a good tax': Peter Edmundson, 'GST and Financial Supplies: A Comparative Analysis of Legislative Structure', *Australian Tax Review* 30 (2001), 132, 134. A 2008 BoT report suggested redrafting the financial supply provisions to 'remove unnecessary complexity and ensure clarity and consistency'. The BoT proposed that the 'same policy outcome could be achieved with straightforward provisions': Board of Taxation, *Review of the Legal Framework for the Administration of the Goods and Services Tax: A Report to the Assistant Treasurer and Minister for Competition Policy and Consumer Affairs* (Australian Government, Canberra, 2008), 100. See also Denis McCarthy, 'The Australian GST – Why It Is the Way It Is and Where To from Here?' in C. Peacock (ed.), *GST in Australia: Looking Forward from the First Decade* (Thomson Reuters, Sydney, 2011), 61, 66.

[492] Commonwealth of Australia Treasury, *Review of the GST Financial Supply Provisions – Consultation Paper* (Australian Government, Canberra, 2009), 10–14.

[493] Commonwealth of Australia Treasury, *Submissions to Review of the GST Financial Supply Provisions by the Commonwealth of Australia Treasury* (21 August 2009) (archive.treasury.gov.au/contentitem.asp?ContentID=1603&NavID=).

[494] Relevant reforms included increasing the monetary amount for the FAT from $50,000 to $150,000: see §4.3.3.3; treating hire-purchase agreements as wholly taxable (despite a BOT recommendation that the existing treatment of hire purchase arrangements was appropriate): *ANTS Regulations* 1999, reg. 40–5.09(3), Item 8, reg. 40–5.12, Items 19 and 20; *ANTS Act* 1999, Div. 158; Board of Taxation, *Review of the Legal Framework for the Administration of the Goods and Services Tax: A Report to the Assistant Treasurer and Minister for Competition Policy and Consumer Affairs* (Australian Government, Canberra, 2008), 101; expanding the list of reduced credit acquisitions to include certain supplies of life insurance, lenders' mortgage insurance and transactional fraud monitoring services: reg. 70–5.02 *ANTS Regulations* 1999; introducing the reduced rate of RITC of 55 per cent for certain acquisitions: see above, n 443: Commonwealth of Australia Treasury, *Implementation of the Recommendations of Treasury's review of the GST Financial Supply Provisions* (Australian Government, Canberra, 2010), viii; *A New Tax System (Goods and Services Tax) Amendment Regulation 2012 (No 1)* (Cth); *Tax Laws Amendment Act (2011 Measures No. 9) Act 2012* (Cth).

same path increases with each move down that path' because the cumulative costs of change increase.[495] In turn, the industry's own lobbying in support of the retention of the provisions creates a type of positive feedback mechanism to reinforce the maintenance of the status quo.[496] Increasing returns present a direct challenge to the suggestions within the conventional approach that VATs will move closer toward a good VAT with time.

Others suggest that the problems relating to the GST treatment of financial supplies require the GST to be abandoned altogether in relation to the taxation of financial supplies. Although its terms of reference precluded the *Henry Review* from suggesting reforms to the GST,[497] this did not prevent it from providing a negative assessment of the GST and its application to financial supplies:[498]

> The input taxation of financial services under the GST, and associated provisions to give relief from it, are complex and affect Australia's position as a regional financial services centre.

Such was the dissatisfaction with the GST treatment of financial services, the *Review* proposed, among other things, the replacement of the GST with a 'financial services tax' for the taxation of financial supplies[499] and the introduction of a new consumption tax, the cash-flow tax, effectively an accounts-based subtraction method of taxing consumption, to supplement the GST.[500] While it is not

[495] Paul Pierson, 'Increasing Returns, Path Dependence, and the Study of Politics', *American Political Science Review* 94(2) (2000), 251, 252. A PricewaterhouseCoopers publication to clients states that '[o]verall, the financial services industry will be relieved that there will not be substantial changes to the existing provisions, particularly given the level of investment which has been made to address fundamentally complex provisions': PricewaterhouseCoopers, *Tax-Talk: GST Special Edition* (May 2010) (pwc.com.au/tax/assets/taxtalk/TaxTalkSE_May10.pdf).

[496] Paul Pierson, 'Increasing Returns, Path Dependence, and the Study of Politics', *American Political Science Review* 94(2) (2000), 251, 259.

[497] See §1.4 of this chapter.

[498] Commonwealth of Australia Treasury, Australia's Future Tax System Review Panel, *Australia's Future Tax System: Report to the Treasurer* (Australia's Future Tax System Review Panel: The Treasury, Canberra, 2009), 308.

[499] The Review also recommended considering zero-rating financial services or applying a modified reverse-charge mechanism: Commonwealth of Australia Treasury, Australia's Future Tax System Review Panel, *Australia's Future Tax System: Report to the Treasurer* (Australia's Future Tax System Review Panel: The Treasury, Canberra, 2009), 309–13, see Chapter 2, §4.2.5.1. As Chapter 3 explained, Australia is not alone in pursuing these alternative options to the taxation of financial services: see Chapter 3, §4.2.4. As Chapter 3 further explained these provisions convert the operation of the GST into more of an RST.

[500] The Review acknowledged that taxing financial supplies under the cash-flow tax would not be viable because of significant transitional issues associated with taxing existing businesses with assets already financed by debt:

> From the perspective of a lender, interest payments and repayment of principal would become taxable in the hands of the lender after the introduction of the tax but no deduction would have been provided for the original loan. To avoid this, complex transitional arrangements would be necessary and these would severely undermine the simplicity of a CFT [cash-flow tax].

necessary to discuss these proposals in any detail, it is interesting to note how the reality of GST implementation has caused its main promoter (the Australian Treasury) to almost come full circle in hinting that the GST might not be the best means by which to tax consumption.[501] The Report's discussion of the cash-flow tax is particularly instructive, as it shows that while policy-makers seem to have a better appreciation of the shortcomings of the GST, they lack an appreciation of the institutionalised basis for these shortcomings.

The Report's assessment of the merits of the cash-flow tax hark back to the earlier promises made of the GST – that it would simplify and improve consumption taxes in a more economically efficient manner. The *Henry Review*'s support, in principle, for the cash-flow tax in part turned on a negative assessment of the GST:[502]

> The direct subtraction method is the simplest and likely to be the most consistent with the needs of a modern economy, as it can run off standard business cash flow management practices. For example, where the GST relies on concepts such as 'supplies' and 'creditable acquisitions' that have no business meaning, a cash flow tax would rely on cash flow concepts already familiar to business...

The statement lacks an appreciation of the difficult process of drafting economic concepts into legislative language – as was seen in §4.3.3.1 with the difficulty of translating the economic concept of a 'margin' in the financial supply provisions through a list of technical transactions. In a clear demonstration of the underestimation of the power of these institutional features on the shape of any tax innovation, the *Henry Review* concluded in relation to the cash-flow tax that:[503]

Commonwealth of Australia Treasury, Australia's Future Tax System Review Panel, *Australia's Future Tax System: Report to the Treasurer* (Australia's Future Tax System Review Panel: The Treasury, Canberra, 2009), 281. See also Michael Walpole, 'The Henry Review's Tax on Financial Services: An Alternative Approach for Australia', *International VAT Monitor* 17 (January/February 2013).

[501] Professor Greg Smith, a member of the *Henry Review* panel, claims that the discussion of the cash-flow tax was simply a backdoor way of discussing the GST within the Review's terms of reference. However, this does not take away from the criticisms made by the *Henry Review* of the GST, nor from the sentiments expressed as to ways to overcome the limitations of the GST: 'Professor Greg Smith told a Tax Institute forum the review had sidestepped a ban in its terms of reference on proposing changes to the GST by recommending instead "an alternative to the GST which was the GST without invoices".' Peter Martin, 'GST Rise a Must, Says Tax Expert', *The Age* (online), 1 September 2011 (theage.com.au/national/gst-rise-a-must-says-tax-expert-20110831-1jm09.html#ixzz1ieVi5H9e).

[502] Commonwealth of Australia Treasury, Australia's Future Tax System Review Panel, *Australia's Future Tax System: Report to the Treasurer* (Australia's Future Tax System Review Panel: The Treasury, Canberra, 2009), 279. However, the Report did note the associated compliance risks that this might entail when business, in net refund positions, did not need to support their claims with invoices (but rather accounts): at 280, 282.

[503] Ibid., 283–84.

> By avoiding complex exemptions and special rules, a CFT [cash-flow tax] could be radically simpler than existing consumption taxes, while also improving the efficiency of the tax system...
>
> A direct subtraction method tax would not require the same institutional arrangement as a GST. Because net cash flows, rather than individual goods and services, would be taxed, there would be no need for the GST's system of invoices to enforce different tax treatments for different goods or services. The direct subtraction method would allow specific entities – such as very small businesses – to be removed from the system entirely, without making the system more complicated for those entities that remain (given that the tax makes no distinction between cash flows to or from 'registered' or 'unregistered' entities).

The quote is revealing for the dissatisfaction levelled at key design features that are said to constitute the good VAT, such as the merits of the invoice-credit method.[504] Beyond this, the *Henry Review*'s relatively sober reflection on the merits of the GST confirm that the Australian GST is a real VAT with real flaws, especially in relation to its inability to reach a broad consumption base in line with the first norm of good VAT design. While Treasury appears to have appreciated the design shortcomings of the GST, it does not seem to have arrived at a similar lesson in relation to how history, institutions and politics bring about these shortcomings. It is perhaps ironic that former Treasury Secretary Ken Henry, the chair of the *Henry Review*, offered the following 'compelling' first lesson in tax reform:[505]

> We can't expect citizens to be enthusiastic about tax reform just because it has the word 'reform' in it. Reform may be regarded as self-evidently good in the think tanks and university departments in which many of this audience moves. But for everyday people, reform needs and deserves powerful justification.

A recap of the findings in this chapter should be instructive in revealing explanations for reform beyond the self-evident goodness of a policy.

5 CONCLUSION

This chapter demonstrated the ways in which history mattered to the shape of the GST. Australia provides an example of a country where, consistent with the account of the conventional approach, policy-makers were convinced of the merits of the good VAT. The fact that the GST is a real VAT therefore presents a direct challenge to this account. Unlike the suggestion by the conventional approach that policy learning will eventually lead to good VAT outcomes, this chapter showed various instances of policy learning that did not result in good VAT outcomes.

[504] See Chapter 2, §5 of this book.

[505] Dr Ken Henry, 'Lessons from Tax Reform Past' (speech delivered at the Committee for Economic Development of Australia, Sydney, 15 October 2009) (taxreview.treasury.gov.au/content/Content.aspx?doc=html/speeches/10.htm).

Indeed, the strength of the commitment by policy-makers to introduce a good VAT in many ways contributed to less than meritorious outcomes – the exclusion of basic food from the GST base being the most notable.

The Australian history demonstrates that not all actors who shaped the GST even perceived of the merits of the good VAT, as was seen in the interpretation of the ANTS legislation by judges. Other actors did not agree with the merits or changed their minds on the merits, such as welfare groups. Those actors who did perceive of the merits of the GST, such as Treasury and business, were unable to realise those merits because factors beyond merits quickly took hold. Those factors included high-profile institutionalised influences such as the constitutional and voting rules that contributed to the exclusion of food in order to pass the ANTS legislation through parliament. They also included less obvious institutional influences, which were highlighted by focusing on the impact of law on the (in)ability of the GST to reach a broad consumption base. While the exact outcomes that might be produced by these institutions might not be predictable, the institutions that themselves will influence real VAT outcomes are readily identifiable and, contrary to the apparent desire of the *Henry Review*, by virtue of their institutionalisation cannot be easily bypassed.

The divergent fates of business and welfare in the development of the GST show that the application of the tax to the most powerful industries will determine not just the likelihood of introducing reform but the reform's continued design and operation. However, the influence of these industries will not always produce outcomes in line with the merits of the good VAT. A focus on institutions demonstrates how past gains can become institutionalised in a manner that continues to benefit the victors. The dominance by business of the institutions charged with the ongoing review and administration of the GST contributes to certain issues, such as financial supplies, which impose a cost on business, dominating administrative and compliance activity and discussions of reform. However, ironically, the dominance of these issues, rather than leading to good VAT outcomes, has resulted in the institutionalisation of approaches that depart markedly from anything like the merits promised of the good VAT and has ultimately undermined the support for the GST by Treasury – once its strongest advocate.

While a cash-flow tax might begin, in theory, to be more consistent with economic concepts than the real GST, the need to translate and implement these concepts in a domestic setting requires laws that often produce outcomes that are motivated less by merits than by local drafting practices and the institutionalised rules and practices of administrators and courts. Just as the path-dependent framing of the merits of the cash-flow tax against the GST repeats the path-dependent framing of the merits of the GST vis-à-vis the WST, like the GST before it, any cash-flow tax will bear the imprint of past taxes upon it.

7

The United States

The United States, as the only member country of the Organisation for Economic Cooperation and Development (OECD) without a VAT, presents one of the most potent challenges to the conventional approach's claim that the VAT has risen by virtue of its merits. The US remains the elephant in the room for the conventional approach – if the VAT is so good, why doesn't the US, the world's most dynamic industrial economy, have one? A merits-based explanation does not account for this anomaly. Furthermore, the US is the intellectual and physical home to much of the conventional approach: US experts pioneered the initial development of the VAT; US aid and development organisations have fostered the uptake of the VAT across the developing world, and the US is the home of the Washington consensus. Yet, despite this, the US has not adopted a VAT. This remains the case despite a growing belief among US tax policy experts that the introduction of a VAT is inevitable or, at least a possibility, in light of burgeoning federal government debt and growing spending commitments. Avi-Yonah is one of the few to go on the record and predict that 'by the end of the next decade…the US will then join the rest of the OECD in enacting a federal VAT'.[1] This declaration mirrors the privately held beliefs among many 'informed observers'[2] that a VAT is somehow inevitable in light of the inadequacies of the current system and the burgeoning expenditure demands of the federal government. This belief is shared by adherents to the conventional approach. The International Monetary Fund (IMF) recently recommended that the US consider the adoption of a VAT[3] and restated the merits argument in light of the US situation:[4]

[1] Reuven S. Avi-Yonah, 'Summary and Recommendations', *Tax Law Review* 63(2) (2010), 285, 288.

[2] Ibid., 285.

[3] IMF, *IMF Country Report No. 11/201 – The United States – 2011 Article IV Consultation* (IMF, Washington, DC, 2011), 14, 19, 32.

[4] IMF, *Fiscal Monitor (November 2010) – Fiscal Exit: From Strategy to Implementation* (IMF Publication Services, Washington, DC, 2010), 79.

> VAT is an efficient way of raising revenues, so it is not surprising that introducing VAT in the United States. . .should be considered the focus for fiscal consolidation. . .introducing VAT alongside the income tax – rather than replacing it – would broaden the federal tax base, making it less prone to cyclical fluctuations. Moreover, retaining the progressivity of income tax would allow for a simple and efficient structure of the VAT system.

Even in the event that the US ultimately adopts a VAT, the fact it does not yet have one despite considering it many times suggests that merits will not be sufficient to account for its introduction or ultimate shape.

Given the challenge to the conventional approach posed by US resistance to the VAT, or, in other words, given that the absence of the VAT in the US remains a frontier issue in accounting for the VAT's rise, it is instructive to inquire why the VAT has not become an actuality in the US. This chapter does so in §1 by examining the history of the VAT reform debate in the US over the reform period 1960–2010. This history begins with a brief overview of the US VAT debate *before* the reform period, as these early paths have influenced the later trajectory of the VAT reform debate in the US. Attention is focused primarily on official consideration of VAT reform at the federal government level.

Future paths of VAT reform are explored in §2. The purpose here is not to engage in crystal-ball-gazing to predict whether the US will adopt a VAT, but to draw on the history of the VAT debate in the US to explore what would be the likely blocking factors to the US enacting the type of good VAT that many of its proponents seek. History suggests that, should the US eventually enact a VAT, it will introduce a real VAT, not a good one. A number of institutionalised factors drawn from the history of US VAT reform that will likely shape any real VAT in the US will be considered.

The chapter concludes with an assessment of what a real VAT might look like in the US by assessing a potential US VAT against the three design norms of the good VAT outlined in Chapter 2 and by assessing how the US might deal with the frontier issue of the taxation of financial supplies (see §3). The chapter shows that, should the US enact a VAT, much more than a simple consideration of the merits of VAT will be required to explain its ultimate and undoubtedly real shape.

1 A HISTORY OF THE VAT REFORM DEBATE IN THE UNITED STATES

Although many think of the VAT as being a quintessentially European tax, its intellectual origins lie just as much in the US as in continental Europe, leading Lindholm to declare that the 'VAT is as American as apple pie'.[5]

[5] Richard W. Lindholm, A *New Federal Tax System* (Praeger, New York, 1984), 120. See also Wells and Fisher, who claim that the VAT is a US tax: Steve Wells and Tonya Flesher, 'Lessons for Policy Makers from the History of Consumption Taxes', *Accounting Historians Journal* (1999), 103, 113–14.

1.1 *Early paths*

The status of the US as a modern-day VAT reform laggard is at odds with the early enthusiastic efforts of twentieth-century VAT pioneers.[6] T. S. Adams, for example, has been credited with the development of the invoice-credit method of the VAT almost a century ago,[7] while Professor Carl Shoup has been labelled the 'intellectual father of the value-added tax' and contributed to the development of the VAT in continental Europe, Latin America and the (failed) introduction of what would have been the world's first national VAT in Japan.[8]

A federal sales tax was considered about once every decade throughout the twentieth century before the reform period of 1960–2010.[9] As part of these debates, a VAT was sometimes discussed as a reform option. The sales tax debate is notable in several respects. First, the debate was divisive.[10] Second, the debate did not result

[6] Some have pointed to earlier precursors, such as early gross-receipts taxes and sales taxes, which share some features of the VAT: Robert P. Crum, 'Value-Added Taxation: The Roots Run Deep Into Colonial and Early America', *Accounting Historians Journal* 9(2) (1982), 25. Perhaps the closest approximation to a proposal for a VAT was during the Civil War period in 1863, when Congress rejected a proposal to amend the manufactured articles tax, a select sales tax existing throughout the Civil War period, to tax 'only the increased value of an article when its constituent parts had already been taxed as manufactured articles'. The amendment failed in part because of the loss of revenue such a measure would entail and the 'impossible' administrative burden it would impose on administrators without an effective mechanism to achieve it: Congressional Globe, 37th Cong., 3rd session 1315–17 (1863). See also Harry Edwin Smith, *The United States Federal Internal Tax History from 1861 to 1871* (Houghton Mifflin Company, Boston, New York, 1914), 224–52, esp. 228.

[7] Professor T. S. Adams (1873–1933) was a Professor of Economics, Treasury adviser and one-time president of the National Tax Association. See Chapter 1 of this book.

[8] Carl Shoup was Professor of Economics at Columbia University and one of the earliest proponents of the VAT in the US: Wayne Thirsk, 'Intellectual Foundations of the VAT in North America and Japan', in L. Eden (ed.), *Retrospectives on Public Finance* (Duke University Press, Durham and London, 1991), 133. See also Chapter 4, §5.3.

[9] Junko Kato, *Regressive Taxation and the Welfare State: Path Dependence and Policy Diffusion* (Cambridge University Press, Cambridge, 2003), 125. For a summary of this early history, see Richard W. Lindholm, A *New Federal Tax System* (Praeger, New York, 1984), ch. 7; Steve Wells and Tonya Flesher, 'Lessons for Policy Makers from the History of Consumption Taxes', *Accounting Historians Journal* (1999), 103, 111–18; Charles E. McLure Jr, 'Value Added Tax: Has the Time Come?' in C. E. Walker and M. A. Bloomfield (eds.), *New Directions in Federal Tax Policy for the 1980s* (Ballinger Publishing Company, Cambridge Massachusetts, 1983), 185; Joseph Thorndike, *Early Proposals for an American VAT* (30 June 2009), Tax Analysts (taxhistory.org/thp/readings.nsf/ArtWeb/6F4B8EADA426FDCE852575F600464B81?OpenDocument); Michael Graetz, *100 Million Unnecessary Returns, A Simple, Fair and Competitive Plan for the United States* (Yale University Press, 2008), 70–71.

[10] See, e.g., the observation by Williamson on the general sales tax debate in the early 1920s:

> [T]he country is remarkably divided on this subject. The farmers are represented as against the tax by certain of their alleged spokesman. Labor is opposed to the tax...The business community and others divide. Organizations of business men have been created especially to agitate for the sales tax.

K. M. Williamson, 'The Literature on the Sales Tax', *Quarterly Journal of Economics* 35(4) (1921), 618.

in reform by way of the introduction of a federal sales tax. A number of states, however, introduced variants of the VAT, though none by way of the invoice-credit method.[11] Third, sales tax reform was generally discussed as an option for the reform of existing federal taxes such as the corporate income tax, or as an alternative to wartime excess profits taxes or income surtaxes.[12] Finally, and related to the previous point, the likely incidence or burden of sales taxes was fiercely contested.[13] As the following account of a failed third attempt to introduce an amendment to introduce a general sales tax (including an apparent version of a value-added tax)[14] by Senator Smoot in 1921 indicates:[15]

> The two earlier turnover taxes had been proposed as consumption taxes; it had been argued that they could not become a burden on industry since they would invariably be shifted. The opposition seized upon this feature of the proposals and emphasized the characteristics of such consumption taxes of burdening the poor more heavily than the rich. In defending his third proposal, Senator Smoot argued that it was intended to be a tax on industry and not on the consumer, and that because of its low rate it would not be shifted.

[11] The US state of Michigan introduced an addition-method accounts-based VAT (the Business Activities Tax, later the Single Business Tax, and then later the Michigan Business Tax – a subtraction-type VAT): see generally Robert F. van Brederode, *Systems of General Sales Taxation: Theory, Policy and Practice* (Kluwer Law International Alphen aan den Rijn, 2009), 6 and at §7.4. New Hampshire has also employed an addition-method VAT: see generally Carl S. Shoup, *Public Finance* (Aldine Publishing Company, Chicago, 1969), 258; Alan Schenk and Oliver Oldman, *Value Added Tax: A Comparative Approach* (rev. edn., Cambridge University Press, Cambridge; New York, 2007), 43; Alan A. Tait, *Value Added Tax* (McGraw-Hill, London, New York, 1972), 9–11; Liam Ebrill et al., *The Modern VAT* (IMF, Washington, DC, 2001), 20. More recently Richard Ainsworth has pointed to some state sales tax reforms (in New York and Illinois) that selectively adopt aspects of an invoice-credit method VAT: Richard Ainsworth, 'VAT Experimentation – New York & Illinois ' (Working Paper No. 12–23, Boston University School of Law, 2012).

[12] See, e.g., Joseph Thorndike, *Early Proposals for an American VAT* (30 June 2009) Tax Analysts (taxhistory.org/thp/readings.nsf/ArtWeb/6F4B8EADA426FDCE852575F600464B81?OpenDocument); Gerhard Colm, 'The Basis of Federal Fiscal Policy', *Taxes – the Tax Magazine* 6(17) (1935), 338; Paul Studenski, 'Towards a Theory of Business Taxation', *Journal of Political Economy* 48(5) (1940), 621; K. M. Williamson, 'The Literature on the Sales Tax', *Quarterly Journal of Economics* 35(4) (1921), 618; T. S. Adams, 'The Taxation of Business', *Proceedings of the National Tax Association* (1917), 185; T. S. Adams, 'Fundamental Problems of Federal Income Taxation', *Quarterly Journal of Economics* 35(4) (1921), 527.

[13] Ibid. (all citations).

[14] The amendment was proposed to a House Revenue Bill. The final Smoot proposal included a:

> hastily added amendment allowing credits to merchants and manufacturers for the amount of sales tax included in the prices of commodities purchased by them (which would have completely revolutionized the character of the tax, making it a net value transfer tax, and would have cut its revenue production to less than one-third of the original proposal, although neither the sponsor of the amendment nor the senators voting on it seemed to realize this)...

National Industrial Conference Board Inc., *General Sales or Turnover Taxation* (New York, 1929), 193.

[15] Ibid., 193.

The perception of the VAT as a business tax has at times been prominent in the US VAT debate. This perception, in part, reflects the VAT's origins in the US. Adams had proposed a VAT as an alternative to the business income tax.[16] Adams' focus was federal, and the absence of a federal sales tax therefore meant his concern was not necessarily with the technical modification of an extant sales tax but rather with an alternative to existing federal taxes, particularly as applied to business income and profits.[17] As an addendum to an article on the fundamental flaws of the federal income tax, Adams speculated on long-term proposals that might be available if the income tax were no longer the principal federal tax on business. Adams shifted his focus from a practical discussion of the sales tax as a means to replace existing miscellaneous excise taxes to a theoretical discussion of the sales tax 'of interest here only as a substitute for the tax on net business income'.[18] Adams then envisaged replacing surtaxes with an expenditure tax and replacing the net income tax with a tax on 'modified gross income' which, when applied to business, would operate very much like a VAT:[19]

> In the case of producers and sellers of 'goods, wares and merchandise' further simplicity could be achieved if desired, by giving the tax a form of a sales tax with a credit or refund for taxes paid by the producer or dealer (as purchaser) on goods bought for resale or for necessary use in the production of goods for sale.

This credit mechanism, Adams claimed, would avoid the worst problems of a cascading turnover tax.[20] Although Adams did not directly address the incidence

[16] T. S. Adams, 'Fundamental Problems of Federal Income Taxation', 35(4) (1921), *Quarterly Journal of Economics* 527, 553.

[17] Adams was a supporter of a tax on business justified by the benefits business received from the state where a 'large part of the cost of government is traceable to the necessity of maintaining a suitable business environment': T. S. Adams, 'The Taxation of Business', *Proceedings of the National Tax Association* (1917), 185, 187. Nevertheless, Adams was part of a debate in the US during World War I within the business community as to the virtue of replacing the excess profits tax with a general sales tax. Although eventually a vocal opponent of the excess profits tax, Adams also opposed a general sales tax if it took the form of a cascading turnover tax and if the tax was levied in addition to existing specific sales taxes: T. S. Adams, 'Professor Adams's Views on Tax Revision', *New York Times*, 13 December 1920, 14; K. M. Williamson, 'The Literature on the Sales Tax', *Quarterly Journal of Economics* 35(4) (1921), 618, 625. Following the end of World War I and the repeal of the excess profits tax, Adams focused on the imperfections of the income tax and surtaxes.

[18] T. S. Adams, 'Fundamental Problems of Federal Income Taxation', *Quarterly Journal of Economics* 35(4) (1921), 527, 548.

[19] Ibid., 553. In addition Adams suggested a suite of specific consumption or excise taxes for semi-luxury and harmful goods, such as alcohol and tobacco, and 'of course', estate or inheritance and stamp taxes: at 554. In a sign of the shift in the rhetorical influence of values in the tax debate, Adams acknowledged that his plan had 'little chance of adoption', for the 'historical fact is that modern states prefer equity and complexity to simplicity and equality' (at 554). See further Dennis Ventry, 'Equity versus Efficiency and the US Tax System in Historical Perspective', in D. Ventry Jr and J. Thorndike (eds.), *Tax Justice: The Ongoing Debate* (Urban Institute Press, Washington, DC, 2002), 25.

[20] T. S. Adams, 'Fundamental Problems of Federal Income Taxation', *Quarterly Journal of Economics* 35(4) (1921), 527, 553.

of this nascent VAT, his support for the taxation of business and his labelling of the argument that 'all taxes are shifted' as 'particularly misleading' suggests that Adams envisioned the VAT burden as being borne primarily by business, whom he viewed as benefiting from the state-sponsored market.[21]

In many ways, the fate of the VAT in Western Europe and the US is a product of path dependence. Von Siemens' proposed VAT was viewed as a means to improve what was already there – usually the cascading turnover tax.[22] By contrast, absent a federal sales tax, VAT reformers in the US have been proposing to introduce something new. The VAT is often framed in the domestic setting by reference to what it is not. In the US context, this has meant that framing requires comparison to existing taxes, such as the income tax, which makes VAT reform a far more radical proposition.[23]

1.2 *1960s and 1970s – Task force, blueprints and syndromes*

Interest in the VAT resurfaced in the mid-1960s when a non-profit organisation consisting of business and education leaders, the Research and Policy Committee for Economic Development, studied but then rejected a proposal to introduce a VAT to replace the corporate income tax.[24] Advocates who spoke of the VAT's capacity to improve savings and investment were outweighed by opponents concerned with the distributional implications of replacing the corporate income tax with a VAT. Resolving these concerns over the distribution of the effective burden of reform was complicated by uncertainty over the existing incidence of the corporate income tax. However, McLure claims that at this stage 'there was little

[21] Ibid., 550.

[22] See Chapter 1 of this book. Even despite this, Europe has still resisted various aspects of VAT reform, as Chapter 5, §4.1 explained.

[23] Terra and Kajus highlight as a 'clear example' of the divergent approaches the near-simultaneous enactment of the Michigan Single Business Tax in 1953, an income-type VAT levied on business activity, and the introduction of the 'tax sur la valeur ajoutée' in France in 1954:

> It is remarkable that in Anglo-Saxon countries the VAT system was considered as a system of levying business taxation in conformity with Adams, whereas on the European continent the system was approached consistently as an "ennobled turnover tax".

Ben Terra and Julie Kajus, IBFD, A *Guide to the European VAT Directives* [online] (15 April 2011), 7.1. See also van Brederode, who states that the 'two concepts are different in approach. Adams' design is in essence a business income type VAT, where Siemens' is a consumption type VAT. . .': Robert F. van Brederode, *Systems of General Sales Taxation: Theory, Policy and Practice* (Kluwer Law International Alphen aan den Rijn, 2009), 7.

[24] US Committee for Economic Development, Research and Policy Committee, A *Better Balance in Federal Taxes on Business: A Statement on National Policy* (Committee for Economic Development, New York, 1966).

dispute that a VAT would be borne by consumers of taxed products'.[25] Throughout the early 1970s, business circles continued to discuss VAT as a means to replace the corporate income tax.[26]

Official interest in the VAT was reignited when, in September 1969, President Nixon queried whether a VAT might be able to partially substitute for local property taxes used to fund public schools.[27] This began a decade of intense interest in the VAT by US policy-makers. Throughout the decade, the VAT received constant attention by the US Department of the Treasury ('Treasury') and was the subject of two inquiries (the Task Force on Business Taxation and the Advisory Commission on Intergovernmental Relations) and two (failed) attempts to legislate for a VAT in Congress. A brief chronology of these events follows.

Nixon appointed John H. Alexander, a partner in Nixon's previous law firm, to head a Task Force on Business Taxation (the '1969 *Task Force*'). The 1969 *Task Force* was charged with examining ways to reduce the federal business tax burden, including through the introduction of a comprehensive VAT proposal drafted by the Treasury at Nixon's request. The 1969 *Task Force* considered the VAT as a whole or partial substitute for the corporate income tax,[28] as an alternative for

[25] Charles E. McLure Jr, 'Value Added Tax: Has the Time Come?' in C. E. Walker and M. A. Bloomfield (eds.), *New Directions in Federal Tax Policy for the 1980s* (Ballinger Publishing Company, Cambridge, MA, 1983), 185; Steve Wells and Tonya Flesher, 'Lessons for Policy Makers from the History of Consumption Taxes', *Accounting Historians Journal* (1999), 103, 118; US Committee for Economic Development Research and Policy Committee, *A Better Balance in Federal Taxes on Business: A Statement on National Policy* (Committee for Economic Development, New York, 1966).

[26] Tax Foundation (US), *A Value Added Tax for the United States? Selected Viewpoints* (Tax Foundation, Washington, DC, 1979), 2. Supporters included the United States Chamber of Commerce, the First National City Bank (New York), and academics Dan Throop Smith, C. L. Harris and Richard Lindholm. Opponents included Treasury Assistant Secretary Stanley Surrey and labor groups, as well as opposition expressed in a lead editorial of the *Wall Street Journal* on 17 June 1969: 'Preliminary Draft Paper prepared by US Treasury on "Value Added Tax" September 10, 1969', Attachment 1 to Memorandum from Gerard Brannon (Office of the Treasury Secretary) to Henry C. Wallich, Subject: Materials for the Consultants' Meeting on October 11, 20 September 1969; File WNRC 80–0005; Meeting Files of Henry Wallich, Senior consultant, 1969–1970, Folder 2 October 11, 1969 – Consultants' meeting; Meeting files 1969–1970; Office of the Secretary, General Records of the Department of Treasury, Record Group 56; National Archives at College Park MD (NACP) (hereafter 'Treasury Paper for 1969–1970 Expert Panel 10 Sep 1969').

[27] See, e.g., *The Value-Added Tax: Hearings before the Joint Economics Committee, 92nd Congress, 2nd Session* (Government Printing Office, Washington, DC, 1972); Charles E. McLure Jr, 'Value Added Tax: Has the Time Come?' in C. E. Walker and M. A. Bloomfield (eds.), *New Directions in Federal Tax Policy for the 1980s* (Ballinger Publishing Company, Cambridge MA, 1983), 185–86; Steve Wells and Tonya Flesher, 'Lessons for Policy Makers from the History of Consumption Taxes', *Accounting Historians Journal* (1999), 103, 118.

[28] The 1969 *Task Force* estimated that a complete substitute would exclude a significant portion of Gross National Product (GNP) and require a VAT range of 8–11 per cent, which none bar one member favoured. A partial substitution was estimated to require a rate of 2–5 per cent and a reduction in the corporate income tax of between 8–28 per cent: 'Task Force on Business Taxation, First Report to the President – The Value-Added Tax, 1 December 1969,

payroll taxes,[29] or as a separate additional source of revenue.[30] The 1969 *Task Force* rejected a VAT in the short term, as it feared experimentation with a relatively new tax instrument that had only just been mandated in the European Economic Community (EEC) and feared the inflationary consequences of the tax – the latter was to become a major issue throughout the coming decade.[31] Although the majority recommended considering a VAT, alongside other indirect tax options, to meet future revenue needs, the majority of the 1969 *Task Force* did not believe extra revenue was needed at that time.[32]

Around the time the 1969 *Task Force* was deliberating over these issues, archival documents reveal that the Treasury had privately engaged a panel of experts (the '1969–1970 *Expert Panel*') to consider the VAT. The 1969–1970 *Expert Panel* considered the VAT as 'most saleable' as part of a package where it might substitute for the social security tax, or enable a substantial reduction in the corporate income tax or some rate adjustments in personal income tax.[33]

An assessment of the meetings of the 1969–1970 *Expert Panel*, by Henry C. Wallich, a senior consultant to the Nixon administration and later a member of the Federal Reserve Board, concluded that 'the VAT presents more problems and possibly fewer benefits than I had previously believed'.[34] Wallich noted that the VAT was 'an inefficient tax' beset by administrative and rate problems such that when rates were low the tax was not as good as a Retail Sales Tax (RST), but when rates were high the VAT would inflate prices and revenue. On this last point, Wallich warned that as it was unlikely to be politically palatable to substitute the VAT for the corporate income tax, the introduction of a VAT might lead to more revenue and a 'temptation to enlarge the public sector unduly'.[35] However, Wallich

Attachment 2 to a Memorandum from William L. Horton (White House) to Mr Finch'; File – Value Added Taxes [CFOA 327]; Staff Member and Office Files, Robert H. Finch; White House Central Files; Nixon Presidential Materials Project; NACP (hereafter 'The 1969 Task Force First Report on VAT'), 11–14.

[29] Ibid., 18–19. [30] Ibid., 19–22. [31] Ibid., 12.

[32] Ibid., 19–22. Two members of the 1969 *Task Force*, Dan Throop Smith and Norman Ture, dissented and recommended that the VAT be introduced at once to replace the corporate income tax and believed that the introduction of a low single-rate VAT with minimum exemptions could be developed: 'The 1969 Task Force First Report on VAT' – Minority Report 30 December 1969.

[33] 'Agenda Item III Value-Added Tax' discussion leader Arnold Harberger, Treasury consultants' meeting, October 11 1969'; File WNRC 80–0005; Meeting Files of Henry Wallich, Senior Consultant, 1969–1970, Folder 2 October 11, 1969 – Consultants' meeting; Meeting files 1969–1970; Office of the Secretary, General Records of the Department of Treasury, Record Group 56; NACP.

[34] 'A Note on the Consultants' meeting on Value Added Taxation' from Henry C. Wallich to Secretary Kennedy, August 5, 1970'; File NN3 056–99–002; Meeting Files of Henry Wallich, Senior Consultant, 1969–1970; Folder 4 – August 4, 1970 – Consultants' Meeting; Meeting files 1969–1970, Office of the Secretary; General Records of the Department of Treasury; Record Group 56; NACP (hereafter 'Wallich to Secretary Kennedy Note on the Consultants' Meeting on August 5, 1970').

[35] Ibid.

noted 'on the positive side' that the potential broad appeal of the VAT lay in its *realness*, not its *goodness*, whereby through the use of 'judicious exemptions, rate variations, not just business but a considerable number of other groups could probably be induced to back the VAT'.[36]

On 20 January 1972, President Nixon requested the Advisory Commission on Intergovernmental Relations (the '1972 *Advisory Commission*') to investigate whether a VAT was a viable substitute for the residential school property tax. The Commission concluded against reforming the property tax, but did comprehensively consider the VAT. It too was sceptical of the claims made for the VAT, based on a pragmatic assessment that any VAT enacted in the US was unlikely to be able to realise the claims made in support of it.[37]

Democrats, who opposed introducing the VAT for its regressivity, attempted to obtain a political advantage in the 1973 election year by trying to force President Nixon to reveal a hidden VAT reform agenda. The strategy failed to prevent Nixon's return to office.[38] However, later that year the Nixon administration dismissed VAT reform, fearing it 'would raise too much revenue too fast' and would lead to the rise of federal spending and the growth of government.[39]

A number of factors also conspired against any major tax reforms in the mid-1970s, not least of which was the Watergate scandal that ended Nixon's presidency.[40] During the 1970s, a fiercely partisan tax reform debate occurred in the context of rising energy costs, recessions, high inflation and balance of payment issues.[41] Attempts at base-broadening were offset by tax cuts (including the extension of ostensibly temporary cuts), and '[t]ax preferences and favors to various interest groups were fixtures in those bills'.[42] The tax reform agenda was also shaped

[36] Ibid.

[37] US Advisory Commission on Intergovernmental Relations, *The Value-Added Tax and Alternative Sources of Federal Revenue: An Information Report* (Washington, DC, 1973). See also §1.2.1 of this chapter.

[38] Junko Kato, *Regressive Taxation and the Welfare State: Path Dependence and Policy Diffusion* (Cambridge University Press, Cambridge, 2003), 125–26.

[39] 'Paper Says President Opposes Value-Added Tax as a Danger', *New York Times*, 20 November 1972, 25. For an outside statement of a similar fear, see Dan Throop Smith's statement that '[i]f a VAT leads to excessive government spending which would not otherwise occur, the great revenue potential of VAT may be the best argument against it': Dan Throop Smith, '"VAT" – The Most Neutral Tax', *New York Times*, 28 February 1972, 31.

[40] Scandal also ended the career of the once powerful chair of the Ways and Means Committee, Wilbur Mills, who suffered an ignominious demise at the hands of alcoholism and his association with the exotic dancer 'Fanny Fae'. The disruption to the committee alongside the 1970s oil crises, recession and rampant inflation distracted from major tax reform initiatives: see generally John F. Witte, *The Politics and Development of the Federal Income Tax* (University of Wisconsin Press, Madison, 1985), 188, ch. 9.

[41] Ibid.

[42] C. Eugene Steuerle, *Contemporary US Tax Policy* (2nd ed., Urban Institute Press, Washington, DC, 2008), 73.

by the growing prominence and acceptance of supply-side economic theory[43] and the 1978 passage of Proposition 13, which prompted the 'tax revolt', said to embody dissatisfaction across the US with the tax system.[44]

Alongside the horse trading was the release by the Treasury in 1977 of the *Blueprints for Basic Tax Reform* ('*Blueprints*') which, at the request of the Ford administration, considered comprehensive options for tax reform. *Blueprints* was a largely normative endeavour to recommend systemwide reform so as to 'have a tax system which looks like someone designed it on purpose'.[45] The Treasury proposed two alternative conceptions of the 'ideal' tax system to provide a basis for practical reform plans:[46] the first was based on a comprehensive income tax,[47] and the second was based on a cash-flow consumption tax model.

Although the specific recommendations of *Blueprints* were never realised,[48] analysis of *Blueprints* reveals a number of important insights. First, *Blueprints* showed a clear preference by the Treasury for a consumption tax base.[49] Second, perhaps to support the first preference, the Treasury identified a shift in the existing tax system toward a consumption base:[50]

43 See generally Ronald F. King, 'The Supply-Side Reformation: Business Tax Policies in the Ford Administration', in B. J. Firestone and A. Ugrinsky (eds.), *Gerald R. Ford and the Politics of Post-Watergate America* (Greenwood Press, Westport, CT 1993), 245.

44 Californians voted in a referendum to amend the Californian constitution to limit the property tax rate to 1 per cent of market value and require that new taxes pass a two-thirds majority in each house of the legislature to become law: W. Elliot Brownlee, *Federal Taxation in America: A Short History* (2nd ed., Cambridge University Press, Cambridge, 2004), 140; John F. Witte, *The Politics and Development of the Federal Income Tax* (University of Wisconsin Press, Madison, 1985), 208, 216. See further Isaac W. Martin, *The Permanent Tax Revolt* (Standford University Press, Palo Alto, CA, 2008). This event also partly inspired the writing of James M. Buchanan and Geoffrey Brennan, *The Power to Tax: Analytical Foundations of a Fiscal Constitution* (Cambridge University Press, Cambridge, 1980).

45 US Department of the Treasury, *Blueprints for Basic Tax Reform* (Dept. of the Treasury, Washington, DC, 1977), 1.

46 Ibid.

47 The comprehensive income model was based on the individual or family unit as the relevant filing unit and therefore sought to, among other things, remove the corporate income tax but tax the gains made by shareholders, and to tax other realised capital gains: ibid., ch. 3.

48 Edward R. Kantowicz, 'The Limits of Incrementalism: Carter's Efforts at Tax Reform', *Journal of Policy Analysis and Management* 4(2) (1985), 217, 221. Carter attempted major tax reforms based on the income tax proposals in *Blueprints*. These reforms were geared mostly toward the taxation of capital gains, but despite managing to pass legislation through Congress the end result 'abandon[ed] any pretense of tax reform': John F. Witte, *The Politics and Development of the Federal Income Tax* (University of Wisconsin Press, Madison, 1985), 209. Steuerle has also highlighted the institutional constraints in pursuing such significant reform: '[t]he Blueprints for Basic Tax Reform proposal of the Ford administration had gone nowhere in part because no one knew how to put its changes into place': quoted in Jeffrey H. Birnbaum and Alan S. Murray, *Showdown at Gucci Gulch: Lawmakers, Lobbyists, and the Unlikely Triumph of Tax Reform* (Random House, New York, 1987), 53.

49 US Department of the Treasury, *Blueprints for Basic Tax Reform* (Dept. of the Treasury, Washington, DC, 1977), ch. 2.

50 Ibid., 23.

> In many important ways, a broad-based consumption tax more closely approximates the current tax system than does a broad-based income tax and would constitute less of a change.

Features identified as contributing to this shift were the preferential tax treatment of homeownership and employer and employee contributions to retirement savings;[51] provisions allowing for investment tax credits; accelerated depreciation; and discounted tax rates for capital gains:[52]

> All these techniques have the same practical effect as exempting from tax the income from the investment. To this extent, this is equivalent to converting the base from accretion income to consumption.

Third, despite the clear preference for a consumption base, the consumption tax model outlined in *Blueprints* was not a VAT but a version of an accounts-based cash-flow tax to be levied on individuals or family units, rather than business.[53]

In 1979, as a response to the failure of reform and the perennial fiscal crisis, the new chair of the Ways and Means Committee, Democratic Congressmen Al Ullman, with the support of the Senate Finance Committee chairman, Democratic Senator Russell Long, introduced what at the time was 'probably the most radical approach to tax reform seriously considered by Congress since World War II'.[54] The bill proposing the *Tax Restructuring Act of 1979* outlined an invoice-credit, destination-based VAT levied at all stages of the production chain, including the retail level at a rate of 10 percent.[55] The estimated $130 billion in yearly revenue to be raised by the first proposed VAT was to be directed toward

[51] Ibid., 10–11. [52] Ibid., 23.

[53] The cash-flow consumption tax model was based on the idea that individuals (or family units), rather than businesses, would be designated taxpayers and would be required to file tax returns. Borrowings would be included in the tax base, as would unlimited exemptions for savings: US Department of the Treasury, *Blueprints for Basic Tax Reform* (Dept. of the Treasury, Washington, DC, 1977), 9–13, ch. 1 and 4. The *Blueprint's* primary author, David Bradford, later developed the proposal into the X-tax consumption tax: David F. Bradford, 'The X Tax in the World Economy' (CEPS Working Paper No. 93, Center for Economic Policy Studies (Princeton), 2003). See below, n 281. See generally Alan Schenk and Oliver Oldman, *Value Added Tax: A Comparative Approach* (rev. edn., Cambridge University Press, Cambridge; New York, 2007), 32; Daniel Shaviro, 'Simplifying Assumptions: How Might the Politics of Consumption Tax Reform Affect (Impair) the End Product?' in J. W. Diamond and G. R. Zodrow (eds.), *Fundamental Tax Reform: Issues, Choices, and Implications* (MIT Press, Cambridge, MA; London, 2008), 75, 81.

[54] W. Elliot Brownlee, *Federal Taxation in America: A Short History* (2nd ed., Cambridge University Press, Cambridge, 2004), 139.

[55] The Tax Restructuring Act of 1979, HR 5665, 96th Cong. (1979) (hereafter 'The Tax Restructuring Act of 1979').

reducing income and payroll taxes.[56] Ullman's reforms failed to pass the House of Representatives, despite being later introduced in a revised form in 1980.[57]

The initial proposal included a broad-based VAT with reduced rates of 5 per cent for food, housing (the sale or rental of a principal residence) and medical costs.[58] After the initial reform failed to gain sufficient support, and following 'months of debate – and constructive advice from around the country',[59] Ullman proposed a revised VAT that would zero-rate most supplies of food and non-alcoholic beverages; the sale and lease of residential properties; medical care; tuition from public and private tax-exempt educational institutions; most supplies by charities and non-profits (not charged for by a fee);[60] public transport fares; non-retail farming and fishing sales; interest; and most supplies made to or from government entities.[61] The exclusions revised revenue estimates down to $115 billion per annum – a somewhat optimistic figure given the extent of the zero-rating proposed.[62] Whereas the original proposal prohibited the supplier from showing the VAT separately on the invoice, the revised proposal gave the supplier a choice to do so following criticism that the first approach was an attempt to hide the tax from the consumer who pays it, which in turn could lead to a growth in government.[63]

The Treasury was officially ambivalent about the Ullman reforms, despite simultaneously working on its own design proposal for a possible VAT at the time.[64]

56 This estimate was based on the first VAT proposal: 'Testimony of the Honorable G. William Miller, Secretary of the Treasury, on the 'Tax Restructuring Act of 1979' before the House Ways and Means Committee – released November 8, 1979', p. 2; File: Value Added Tax; Subject Files 1979–1980 of Geoffrey G. Peterson, Deputy Assistant Secretary for Legislative Affairs, 1979–1980, Office of the Secretary, Office of the Deputy Secretary, Office of the Assistant Secretary for Legislative Affairs; General Records, subject files; General Records of the Department of Treasury, Record Group 56; NACP (hereafter 'Secretary Miller Testimony on the Tax Restructuring Act of 1979').

57 The Tax Restructuring Act of 1980, HR 7015, 96th Cong., 2nd session (1980) (hereafter 'Tax Restructuring Act of 1980').

58 The Tax Restructuring Act of 1979.

59 Statement by Congressman Al Ullman (upon Introduction of HR 7015, the "Tax Restructuring Act of 1980", April 2, 1980', p. 1; File: Value Added Tax; Subject Files 1979–1980 of Geoffrey G. Peterson, Deputy Assistant Secretary for Legislative Affairs, 1979–1980, Office of the Secretary, Office of the Deputy Secretary, Office of the Assistant Secretary for Legislative Affairs; General Records, subject files; General Records of the Department of Treasury, Record Group 56; NACP (hereafter 'Statement by Ullman on Tax Restructuring Act of 1980').

60 Although the bill listed these organisations as 'exempt organisations', it allowed credits for all inputs: Tax Restructuring Act of 1980, §4015.

61 Tax Restructuring Act of 1980, §§4012–4015.

62 'Statement by Ullman on Tax Restructuring Act of 1980', above n 59, 1.

63 Tax Restructuring Act of 1980, §4022; PricewaterhouseCoopers, 'Information Guide: Value Added Tax, April 1980 (Supplement to the Information Guide on Value Added Tax'), p. 2; File: Value Added Tax; Subject Files 1979–1980 of Geoffrey G. Peterson, Deputy Assistant Secretary for Legislative Affairs, 1979–1980, Office of the Secretary, Office of the Deputy Secretary, Office of the Assistant Secretary for Legislative Affairs; General Records, subject files; General Records of the Department of Treasury, Record Group 56; NACP.

64 Memorandum from Donald C. Lubick, Assistant Secretary (Tax Policy) to Treasury Secretary Blumenthal, Subject: Value Added Tax, March 15 1979 – Attaching Revised Treasury Staff

Undoubtedly, the Treasury's articulation of its concerns did not enhance the prospect of success for Ullman's reforms. Experts from the business and academic fields were also reluctant to endorse the whole package, despite being in favour of individual elements of the plan.[65] All feared the perceived complexity of the VAT. Liberals decried the perceived regressivity, while conservatives feared that the VAT's revenue generation would lead to a growth in government, despite an express commitment in the 1980 bill to limit federal expenditure to a fixed percentage of Gross National Product (GNP).[66]

Some have suggested that Ullman ultimately paid a heavy and unexpected political price for his championing of VAT reform when he lost his safe seat in the election landslide of 1980.[67] Whether or not this is true, Ullman's fate seemed to impact would-be VAT advocates, as '[n]obody wants to get the Al Ullman syndrome'.[68]

1.2.1 Trends from the VAT policy discussions during the 1960s and 1970s

A number of important trends can be discerned from the consideration of VAT reform during the 1960s and 1970s. First, there was a growing preference for consumption taxation at the official level. However, second, there was scepticism by officials in relation to the capacity of the VAT to realise the promised merits of a consumption tax.[69] Indeed, official consideration of VAT reform during the 1960s

Paper – Value Added Tax: Economic and Political Considerations'; File: Value Added Tax; Subject Files 1979–1980 of Geoffrey G. Peterson, Deputy Assistant Secretary for Legislative Affairs, 1979–1980, Office of the Secretary, Office of the Deputy Secretary, Office of the Assistant Secretary for Legislative Affairs; General Records, subject files; General Records of the Department of Treasury, Record Group 56; NACP.

65 'Value Added Tax', an extract from the American Retail Federation position, p. 8; File: Value Added Tax; Subject Files 1979–1980 of Geoffrey G. Peterson, Deputy Assistant Secretary for Legislative Affairs, 1979–1980, Office of the Secretary, Office of the Deputy Secretary, Office of the Assistant Secretary for Legislative Affairs; General Records, subject files; General Records of the Department of Treasury, Record Group 56; NACP.

66 Ibid., Tax Restructuring Act of 1980, §402. See also Sven Steinmo, *Taxation and Democracy: Swedish, British and American Approaches to Financing the Modern State* (Yale University Press, New Haven, CT, 1993), 143; Junko Kato, *Regressive Taxation and the Welfare State: Path Dependence and Policy Diffusion* (Cambridge University Press, Cambridge, 2003), 126; W. Elliot Brownlee, *Federal Taxation in America: A Short History* (2nd ed., Cambridge University Press, Cambridge, 2004), 139.

67 Cf Alan Schenk, 'Prior US Flirtations with VAT', in C. Phillips (ed.), *The VAT Reader: What a Federal Consumption Tax Would Mean for America* (Tax Analysts, Arlington, VA, 2011), 52, 58; Michael Graetz, *100 Million Unnecessary Returns, A Simple, Fair and Competitive Plan for the United States* (Yale University Press, 2008), 72.

68 Sven Steinmo, *Taxation and Democracy: Swedish, British and American Approaches to Financing the Modern State* (Yale University Press, New Haven, CT, 1993), 144.

69 Even the Europeans were not recommending a VAT: '[t]he Europeans feel that if we are considering a low rate tax it should be an RST and not a VAT. The complexities of a VAT are warranted only when the rate is high, and the compliance advantages of VAT become important': 'Summary of Treasury Consultants' Meeting on Value Added Tax, August 4, 1970 (marked

and 1970s seemed most alive to the disjunct between the good VAT and real VATs. So, for example, while it was generally accepted that consumption taxation was more neutral toward business and savings than other alternatives, such as the income tax,[70] all queried the VAT's claims to neutrality and simplicity, given the likely exclusions to the base and possible rate variations.[71] The 1969 *Task Force*, for example, found that the 'argument that a value-added tax is relatively simple does not appear to be valid',[72] given the record-keeping and filing requirements, which would fall disproportionately on smaller business.[73] It feared that 'if more than a very low rate of tax were used, pressures would shortly develop for different tax rates for different articles'.[74] The 1972 *Advisory Commission* found that:[75]

> The value-added tax enjoys the reputation of being the most neutral form of taxation in theory. The neutrality argument is valid, however, only if the 'ideal' type of value-added tax is enacted, that is if the tax is comprehensive in coverage and applied at a single rate. If either of these conditions is violated, however, the neutrality argument loses its validity.

The 1972 *Advisory Commission* found, in short, that these conditions would likely be violated; the 'preferred form of the value-added tax is a comprehensive, single-rate tax. Enactment of a VAT of this nature, however, does not seem realistic.'[76]

No single VAT proposed during this period, from the Treasury's private deliberations to Ullman's public attempts to legislate a VAT, adopted as its starting point a broad consumption base. The Treasury estimates for the 1969–1970 *Expert Panel* factored in likely exclusions to the VAT base as including health and medical care, private school costs, religious and welfare activities, financial supplies, farms, and the implied rental value of houses and farms.[77] Food and rental payments for housing were included in the tax base, but revenue estimates were provided in the event they could not be included.[78] The 1972 *Advisory Commission* assessed that likely exclusions from the VAT base would include financial supplies, real property[79] and

MSF 8/6/70)', p. 4; File NN3 056–99–002; Meeting Files of Henry Wallich, Senior Consultant, 1969–1970; Folder 4 – August 4, 1970 – Consultants' Meeting; Meeting files 1969–1970, Office of the Secretary; General Records of the Department of Treasury; Record Group 56; NACP (hereafter 'Summary of 1969–1970 Expert Panel meeting of 4 August 1970').

70 US Advisory Commission on Intergovernmental Relations, *The Value-Added Tax and Alternative Sources of Federal Revenue: An Information Report* (Washington, DC, 1973), 7–8; US Department of the Treasury, *Blueprints for Basic Tax Reform* (Dept. of the Treasury, Washington, DC, 1977), 9–10, ch. 2.

71 'The 1969 Task Force First Report on VAT', above n 28, 13–14.

72 Ibid., 13.

73 Ibid., 13.

74 Ibid., 14.

75 US Advisory Commission on Intergovernmental Relations, *The Value-Added Tax and Alternative Sources of Federal Revenue: An Information Report* (Washington, DC, 1973), 9.

76 Ibid., 34.

77 'Treasury Paper for 1969–1970 Expert Panel 10 Sep 1969', above n 26, 4–6.

78 Ibid., 5.

79 The 1972 Advisory Commission noted that: 'Congress never has given serious attention to taxing imputed rents of homeowners under the income tax. It therefore seems far-fetched to believe such consumption expenditures would be incorporated in a value-added tax': US

government services. In addition, it was considered that basic necessities would likely be excluded by virtue of the preferential 'tax treatment for necessities' that is 'a deeply rooted facet of State retail sales taxes, both those adopted long ago and those recently enacted'.[80] The 1972 *Advisory Commission* assessed that after factoring in these likely exclusions, the VAT would reach only about 40 to 50 per cent of the total consumption base.[81] Although none saw state sales taxes as a necessary legal impediment to reform, all viewed the existence of these taxes as a likely political and administrative barrier, given indications made by state governors.[82]

Third, doubt was also expressed as to claims that the VAT was more resistant to fraud and evasion than an RST. For example, Treasury analysis of the VAT found that, because the VAT allows only for cross-checking between registered taxpayers, a 'value-added tax is not necessarily superior to a retail sales tax in controlling fraud at the retail level' because consumers are not registered. An invoice, it was noted, provides "only discouragement and not complete prevention"'.[83]

Fourth, there was scepticism over the broader macro-economic claims made of the VAT, such as the claims that a VAT would lead to an increase in net savings and economic growth.[84] The claim, popular with business at the time, that a VAT would improve the balance of trade was repeatedly rejected by all who considered

Advisory Commission on Intergovernmental Relations, *The Value-Added Tax and Alternative Sources of Federal Revenue: An Information Report* (Washington, DC, 1973), 42.

80 Ibid., 38. 81 Ibid. 82 Ibid., 11–12.

83 Dorothy Johnstone quoted in George N. Carlson, *Value-Added Tax: European Experience and Lessons for the United States* (Office of Tax Analysis, Department of Treasury; US Government Printing Office, Washington, DC, 1980), 74–75.

84 Although accepting that a VAT would lead to an increase in individual savings vis-à-vis an income tax, the 1972 *Advisory Commission* was concerned that increased individual savings would reduce overall national income, therefore leading to a decline in aggregate savings. The 1972 *Advisory Commission* disputed that increased private savings would spur further investment and economic growth because:

> the rate of economic growth is responsive to a number of socio-economic factors but not critically amenable to influence by any one such variable. Furthermore, the investment function is generally considered more dynamic and more sensitive to changes in the rate of interest than the savings function.

US Advisory Commission on Intergovernmental Relations, *The Value-Added Tax and Alternative Sources of Federal Revenue: An Information Report* (Washington, DC, 1973), 13–14. In his testimony to the House Ways and Means Committee on Ullman's 1979 VAT proposal, Treasury Secretary Miller challenged the claims that the VAT would lead to greater investment and capital formation, and increased economic growth, and noted that '[i]t is important to recognize. . .that the responsiveness of saving to more favourable taxation is an unsettled issue' (at 5). Secretary Miller testified that other factors influenced capital formation and observed that 'an increase in savings will increase capital formation only if the higher savings lowers interest rates and therefore the cost of capital' and that 'increased savings in the United States may be invested outside the country' (at 5). Secretary Miller also noted that 'the potential for the value added tax in promoting capital formation 'may be exaggerated by an analysis that compares a pure consumption tax with a pure income tax levied on all returns to capital' (at 6): 'Secretary Miller Testimony on the Tax Restructuring Act of 1979', above n 56.

it at an official level. Internal Treasury documents noted the gulf between the Treasury's view and the perceptions of politicians and business: '[a]lthough the VAT is not expected to significantly improve the trade balance, the contrary perception is widely held in both the business and political communities'.[85] In general terms, the claim of VAT supporters was that a VAT would improve the competitive position of US exports because the rules under the General Agreement on Tariffs and Trade (GATT) allowed for the refund for indirect taxes paid on exports but not direct taxes, such as the corporate income tax.[86] The rejection of the claim arose, in part, from the view that whether a VAT would improve the balance of trade would depend on the tax, if any, it replaced and what the incidence of that tax was.[87] Unlike the situation in Europe, where the VAT was earmarked to replace turnover taxes, which clearly fell on exports, in the US there were a number of candidates that the VAT might replace (such as the corporate income tax or social security taxes) and the effective incidence of these taxes was uncertain. Even if gains could be identified, all considered that these advantages would be offset in the longer term by exchange rate adjustments or border tax adjustments.[88] Indeed, even assuming the validity of the claims made regarding the VAT, many felt the perceived gains might come at too great a cost.[89]

85 'Value Added Tax: Economic and Political Considerations' (Revised Treasury Staff Paper), Attachment to Memorandum from Donald C. Lubick, Assistant Secretary (Tax Policy) to Treasury Secretary Blumenthal, Subject: Value Added Tax, March 15 1979, p. 29; File: Value Added Tax; Subject Files 1979–1980 of Geoffrey G. Peterson, Deputy Assistant Secretary for Legislative Affairs, 1979–1980, Office of the Secretary, Office of the Deputy Secretary, Office of the Assistant Secretary for Legislative Affairs; General Records, subject files; General Records of the Department of Treasury, Record Group 56; NACP (hereafter 'Revised Treasury VAT Staff Paper 1979').

86 See Chapter 2, §6 of this book.

87 See, e.g., George N. Carlson, *Value-Added Tax: European Experience and Lessons for the United States* (Office of Tax Analysis, Department of Treasury; US Government Printing Office, Washington, DC, 1980), 79–80.

88 US Advisory Commission on Intergovernmental Relations, *The Value-Added Tax and Alternative Sources of Federal Revenue: An Information Report* (Washington, DC, 1973), 15; In his testimony on the Ullman 1979 VAT, Secretary Miller stated (at 9) that:

> While these differential rules [allowing for indirect taxes to be refunded on exports and imposed on imports, but prohibiting the same treatment for direct taxes] may seem unfair, it is doubtful that the US trade balance would improve significantly from substituting a value added tax for the corporate income tax.

However, Miller noted that a modest improvement might arise if the VAT replaced social security taxes (but not the corporate income tax): 'Secretary Miller Testimony on the Tax Restructuring Act of 1979', above n 56, 9–10. Robert Gordon, University of Chicago, to Henry Wallich attaching summary of Treasury Consultants' meeting, Oct 17, 1969, p. 12; File WNRC 80–0005; Meeting Files of Henry Wallich, Senior consultant, 1969–1970, Folder 2 October 11, 1969 – Consultants' meeting; Meeting files 1969–1970; Office of the Secretary, General Records of the Department of Treasury, Record Group 56; NACP ('Summary by Gordon of Expert Panel Meeting 17 Oct 1969').

89 See, e.g., US Advisory Commission on Intergovernmental Relations, *The Value-Added Tax and Alternative Sources of Federal Revenue: An Information Report* (Washington, DC, 1973),

The responses to the GATT rules were varied. The 1969 *Task Force* preferred the renegotiation of the GATT rules as a more feasible solution to the VAT.[90] Others thought the introduction of the VAT would be advantageous to relieve pressure to renegotiate the GATT rules.[91] Documents used by the 1969–1970 *Expert Panel* also suggest that the certainty of the European position on the incidence of VAT (i.e., that it is forward shifted to final consumers)[92] appeared to be informed by the advantages gained by the GATT rules and perhaps a determination to protect their own position:[93]

> The Europeans have concluded that indirect taxes are always passed on in price and that direct taxes are not. As a result, they are not likely, under any circumstances, to consider a change in the GATT rules on border tax adjustments.

Actors therefore have good reason to believe in the merits of the VAT as being forward shifted to consumers when this benefits their position under international trade rules.

Finally, concerns were expressed over the downsides of VAT reform, such as the VAT's regressivity[94] or public perceptions of regressivity, which would, for example, make replacing the corporate income tax with the VAT politically impossible.[95] Although mindful of the need to address regressivity through other means, many still favoured doing so through exclusions to the VAT base. The revisions incorporated into Ullman's second VAT proposal, which introduced generous exclusions, suggest the political impetus for such an approach. In addition, the preference for addressing inequity through exclusions to the base was in part attributable to a

15, 17; 'Wallich to Secretary Kennedy Note on the Consultants' Meeting on August 5, 1970', above n 34.

90 'The 1969 Task Force First Report on VAT', above n 28 at 13, 15–16, 17.

91 A Treasury staff paper noted that '[p]oliticians, on the other hand may feel that a VAT would reduce the pressure. . .to rewrite or revise the GATT rules'. 'Revised Treasury VAT Staff Paper 1979', above n 85, 30.

92 See Chapter 2, §4 of this book.

93 Noted by Cohen, 'Summary of 1969–1970 Expert Panel meeting of 4 August 1970', above n 69, 5.

94 US Advisory Commission on Intergovernmental Relations, *The Value-Added Tax and Alternative Sources of Federal Revenue: An Information Report* (Washington, DC, 1973), 9–11; George N. Carlson, *Value-Added Tax: European Experience and Lessons for the United States* (Office of Tax Analysis, Department of Treasury; US Government Printing Office, Washington, DC, 1980), 80. The 1969–1970 *Expert Panel* was split over regressivity; Professor Musgrave opposed a shift to VAT because it lacked progressivity, while Professor Harberger favoured it: 'Summary by Gordon of 1969–1970 Expert Panel Meeting 17 Oct 1969', above n 88, 14. Professor Carey Brown commented that 'on all but equity grounds' the ideal would be a fully general VAT imposed at a single rate. 'This, however, implies regressivity, which can and should be reduced by making exceptions in the coverage for certain necessities' such as food and shelter, but excluding clothing and medical services: 'Summary of 1969–1970 Expert Panel meeting of 4 August 1970', above n 69, 15, 16–18.

95 'Wallich to Secretary Kennedy Note on the Consultants' Meeting on August 5, 1970', above n 34.

belief that to do so through spending might fuel the growth of government and in part because of concern that modifications to the income tax to increase progressivity would do nothing to alleviate the absolute burden on the poor.[96]

1.3 *The 1980s – Reform and Reaganomics*

The *Economic Recovery Tax Act of 1981* ('ERTA1981'),[97] while directed mainly at President Reagan's supply side tax cuts, accelerated the shifting of the tax mix toward a consumption tax base. As a US Treasury document explains:[98]

> The 1981 tax cut actually represented two departures from previous tax policy philosophies, one explicit and intended and the second by implication. The first change was the new focus on marginal tax rates and incentives as the key factors in how the tax system affects economic activity. The second policy departure was the de facto shift away from income taxation and toward taxing consumption. Accelerated cost recovery was one manifestation of this shift on the business side, but the individual side also saw a significant shift in the enactment of various provisions to reduce the multiple taxation of individual saving.

Within months of the enactment of ERTA, subsequent reforms were targeted at redressing the fiscal gap caused by the loss of revenues and the increase in federal government spending, made worse by an economic recession.[99] As part of these reform attempts, Democrat and Republican members of Congress proposed about a dozen bills effectively constituting variations on a theme of the flat tax, in essence proposals to move toward a consumption base by not taxing the returns from savings and investments alongside efforts to flatten tax rates.[100] None resulted in legislative outcomes.

The most significant tax reforms in US postwar history occurred following the release in 1984 of the Treasury report *Tax Reform for Fairness, Simplicity and Economic Growth* (*'Treasury I'*)[101] and the eventual introduction of the *Tax Reform*

[96] 'Summary of Expert Panel meeting of 4 August 1970', above n 69, 9, 12.

[97] *Economic Recovery Tax Act of 1981*, Pub. L No. 97–34, 95 Stat. 172 (1981) (hereafter '*ERTA1981*').

[98] US Treasury, 'History of the US Tax System' (August 2003) Almanac of Policy Issues policyalmanac.org/economic/archive/tax_history.shtml.

[99] To indicate the ongoing impact of the revenue foregone as a result of the *ERTA1981*, Steuerle estimates the cost of the measures at $323 billion or close to 6 per cent GNP for fiscal year 1990 alone: C. Eugene Steuerle, *Contemporary US Tax Policy* (2nd ed., Urban Institute Press, Washington, DC, 2008), 81; *Tax Equity and Fiscal Responsibility Act of 1982* Pub. L No. 97–248, 96 Stat. 324 (1982); *Deficit Reduction Act of 1984* Pub. L No. 98–369, 98 Stat. 494 (1984).

[100] W. Elliot Brownlee, *Federal Taxation in America: A Short History* (2nd ed., Cambridge University Press, Cambridge, 2004), 156.

[101] US Department of the Treasury, *Tax Reform for Fairness, Simplicity, and Economic Growth* (Office of the Secretary, Department of the Treasury, Washington, DC, 1984) (hereafter '*Treasury I*').

Act of 1986 ('*TRA86*').[102] Although these reforms were directed primarily toward the income tax base, *Treasury I* considered a VAT in great detail. This section explores two significant trends arising from this period: first, the Treasury's analysis of a VAT as the 'most appropriate'[103] tax should national sales tax reform be undertaken; and second, the process of income tax reform from the release of *Treasury I* to the enactment of *TRA1986* and what it reveals about the likely trajectory for future federal VAT reform.

1.3.1 The VAT as the 'most appropriate' national sales tax

Although concluding that the VAT was the 'most appropriate'[104] consumption tax for use at the federal level, the Treasury did not recommend embarking on VAT reform because of the 'context' of the review.[105] 'Context' in this sense was revenue neutrality, meaning that because the introduction of a VAT would be only to reduce reliance on the income tax, the cost and complexity of introducing a new tax would not justify the benefits.[106] Nevertheless, the Treasury comprehensively considered the design of a VAT for use at the federal level.[107] *Treasury I* suggests that the Treasury was more convinced of the merits of the VAT than in its more private deliberations in the 1970s, at least in its public commentary. However, despite this, Treasury proposed a path of income tax reform and, even when formulating the design of a theoretical VAT, designed a VAT more in keeping with a real VAT than a good VAT.

The Treasury concluded that the VAT was the most appropriate candidate for federal sales tax reform for the familiar reasons identified by the conventional approach: its neutrality toward production and consumption decisions (vis-à-vis the income tax);[108] the possibility that the VAT might capture revenue missed by the income tax (provided that the income retained through tax fraud was used to purchase taxable goods and services);[109] the VAT's superiority to an RST because of

102 *Tax Reform Act of 1986*, Pub. L No. 99–514, 100 Stat. 2085 (1986) (hereafter '*TRA86*').

103 *Treasury I*, vol. 3, ch. 1, 1. 104 Ibid. 105 Ibid.

106 Ibid. Birnbaum and Murray suggest that the report's conclusion on VAT was something of a *fait accomplit*:

> a VAT would be hugely expensive to administer. Such an extensive new tax system would only be worth doing if it were big – raising $100 billion a year or more. Because the tax bill was not supposed to raise revenue, a large VAT seemed out of the question, and the idea was dropped. The Secretary allowed his tax experts to prepare a book on the pros and cons of a VAT, which they thought might be useful in future budget debates, but he rejected the idea of making a VAT part of tax overhaul.

Jeffrey H. Birnbaum and Alan S. Murray, *Showdown at Gucci Gulch: Lawmakers, Lobbyists, and the Unlikely Triumph of Tax Reform* (Random House, New York, 1987), 52.

107 The consideration went right down to the development, in conjunction with the Internal Revenue Service (IRS), of sample VAT returns: *Treasury I*, vol. 3, App 9-A, 125–27.

108 *Treasury I*, vol. 3, ch. 3, 17–20 and ch. 4, 29–31. 109 Ibid., vol. 3, ch. 2, 16.

the ability to collect revenue incrementally throughout each stage of the production chain (meaning that some revenue could be obtained even if the tax was avoided at the final retail stage);[110] and finally, that the VAT would be better at taxing services (informed largely by the failure of most state sales taxes to tax services on a comprehensive basis).[111]

As Chapter 2 explained, many of the merits cited by the Treasury depend on the enactment of the good VAT.[112] Indeed, the Treasury ostensibly appears to have favoured the good VAT by recommending a VAT broadly in line with the three design norms of the good VAT outlined in Chapter 2:[113]

> If the policy debate in the United States ever focuses on choosing a form of value-added tax, it should concentrate on a value-added tax with the following characteristics:
>
> 1. consumption type [norm 1];[114]
> 2. credit method of determining tax liability [norm 2];[115] and
> 3. destination principle of border tax adjustments [norm 3].[116]
>
> ... the tax should also have a broad base, with only minimal and well justified exclusions, and it should be imposed at a single, uniform rate.[Norm 1]

However, despite expressing a strong preference for a good VAT, this was not what the Treasury in fact proposed.[117] Most departures were from the first design norm of the good VAT – levying the VAT on a broad consumption base.

Treasury I identified problems with the VAT as being its 'regressivity, a onetime increase in prices, federal intrusion into the sales tax area, significant administration and compliance costs, and the possibility of greater public expenditures'.[118]

[110] Ibid., vol. 3, ch. 4, 14. Although not endorsing the claim that a VAT was harder to avoid or evade, *Treasury I* noted (at ch. 3, 26) that:

> To the extent that tax avoidance and evasion are motivated by high income tax rates, a value-added tax would also alleviate these problems and improve the administration and enforcement of the income tax and therefore its image.

[111] Ibid., vol. 3, ch. 6, 47. As Chapter 2 explained, there is no reason in theory why an RST cannot apply to services, but see Chapter 2, §5.2, n 191 for why the VAT is thought superior on this measure.

[112] See Chapter 2, §2 of this book.

[113] *Treasury I*, vol. 3, ch. 2, 16.

[114] The Treasury viewed the consumption-type credit method as the 'only form suitable for the United States': ibid., vol. 3, ch. 2, 2; and at 1, 3, 7.

[115] The preference for the credit method was in part motivated by a pragmatic recognition that the VAT would be levied at multiple rates due to political pressures and the credit method was best equipped to handle this: ibid., ch. 2, 10, 42 and ch. 5.

[116] Ibid., vol. 3, ch. 2, 12 and ch. 5, 245–46.

[117] Ibid., ch. 5–7.

[118] Ibid., vol. 3, ch. 1, 2. Among the estimated costs of introducing a VAT were 18 months implementation time; 20,000 additional personnel; and $700 million in enforcement. It was estimated that the VAT would involve 15–20 million taxpayers: Ibid., vol. 3, ch. 1, 1–2 and ch. 9, 113.

The 'minimal and well justified exclusions'[119] to the VAT base stemmed from many of these perceived disadvantages, but the path-dependent impact of both the income tax and state RSTs is clear from a number of the proposals. Among the Treasury's recommendations were:[120]

- In recognition of the fact that the taxation of housing and construction was a 'major area in which universal application of the value-added tax is simply not feasible',[121] the Treasury proposed taxing non-residential/commercial property transactions but only taxing the first sale of a residential property if not considered 'too harsh' and otherwise exempting sales and rental of residential homes. Alternatively, in line with state sales tax practice, the Treasury proposed taxing the inputs that go into residential real property construction but not the actual supply of the property;[122]
- Exclusion of certain health and medical services – including exempting the services of physicians, dentists and health professionals and zero-rating the services provided by hospitals;[123]
- Zero-rating of education and religious and welfare services;[124] foreign travel; and urban public transport;[125]
- The report proposed a unique approach to a number of difficult sectors whereby, in line with state RST practice, supplies would be exempt but specific inputs into those supplies would be zero-rated. For example, supplies by farmers would be exempt, but common inputs used in making those supplies would be zero-rated such as livestock, feed, seed, fertiliser, farm machines, and probably fuel sold for farm purposes.[126] Similar treatment was proposed for supplies by state and local governments (informed by potential constitutional and political limitations)[127] and by the non-profit sector. The Treasury noted that many of these non-profit organisations are exempt for income tax purposes and although 'exclusion from one form of tax does not necessarily warrant exclusion from another',[128] non-profits that provide services unsuitable to tax, such as hospital, charitable, religious and educational institutions, should be exempt or zero-rated or exempt with zero-rated inputs;[129]

[119] Ibid., vol. 3, ch. 2, 16.

[120] Chapter 6 details the treatment of all problematic areas, including the treatment of fringe benefits and the sale of used durable goods: ibid., vol. 3, ch. 6, 77–83. For the discussion of the treatment of financial supplies, see §3.2 of this chapter.

[121] Ibid., vol. 3, ch. 6, 77. [122] Ibid., vol. 3, ch. 6, 72–77. [123] Ibid., vol. 3, ch. 6, 56–57.

[124] Ibid.

[125] Zero-rating of mass urban transport was recommended partly to encourage further use. Other transport-related proposals were the exemption of taxi fares and the taxation of interstate travel and freight services: ibid., vol. 3, ch. 6, 54–56.

[126] Ibid., 62–67. [127] Ibid., 67–70. [128] Ibid., 70. [129] Ibid., 70–72.

- In direct contrast to the advice of the conventional approach and standard practice, the Treasury advised against setting thresholds for compulsory registration based on annual turnover because 'the case for exemption of small firms is not nearly as strong in the United States' as it is in Southern Europe and developing countries, due to better record-keeping practices. The Treasury preferred the state RST practice of exempting businesses that did not have an established place of business or that traded on a casual non-regular basis and allowing for voluntary registration;[130]
- The Treasury proposed four possible means to address regressivity:[131] the zero-rating of essential goods and services; providing a refundable tax credit reimbursing VAT paid based on average amounts of essential consumption; adjusting transfer payments; and, finally, using a personal exemption type VAT.[132] The Treasury did not favour exclusions to the base,[133] but was relatively ambivalent about all the measures, despite perhaps indicating a preference for the refundable credit option.[134]

Table 7.1 illustrates the revenue effects of the exclusions to the VAT base factored in by the Treasury. The second column shows the cost of exclusions endorsed by the Treasury, and the third column shows exclusions not endorsed by the Treasury but envisaged as political possibilities. Even on the Treasury's recommended exclusions, the VAT base would be reduced to 77 per cent of total consumption expenditure. The exclusion of food and other essential services would have reduced the base to around 55 per cent of total consumption expenditure, which would be roughly in line with the average OECD VAT base.[135]

The Treasury expressed a strong preference for a single-rate VAT, but was mindful that the experience of other countries demonstrated that it may not be possible to avoid multiple-rate VATs.[136] Nevertheless, the Treasury maintained that:[137]

> If a single rate of value-added tax is politically unacceptable, the only other rate should be zero. It should be applied to necessities such as food and medicine, assuming other alternatives for removing the burden of the tax from the poor are not feasible. If zero rates are used, there is little need for, and much complexity created by, the use of reduced "semi-necessity" and increased "luxury" rates of tax.

[130] Ibid., 61. [131] Ibid., vol. 3, ch. 8.
[132] This is a version of a flat tax: see generally ibid., vol. 3, ch. 4, 35–38.
[133] Ibid., vol. 3, ch. 8, 99–100.
[134] However, Treasury expressed concern that this might be regarded as an additional welfare payment and, in the absence of debate on welfare reform, might therefore make the credit susceptible to the charge that the VAT was a means to increase the growth of government: ibid., vol. 3, ch. 8, 100.
[135] See Chapter 3, §4 of this book. [136] *Treasury I*, vol. 3, ch. 2, 11.
[137] Ibid., vol. 3, ch. 5, 45.

TABLE 7.1 – *Estimates from* Treasury I *of a likely US VAT base*[a]

Total consumption expenditure	Less – Recommended exclusions (zero-rated and exempted)		Less – Potential exclusions to remedy regressivity (not endorsed by the Treasury)	
3,127B	Rental value of owner- and tenant/occupied housing (including farms)	–460	Food	–349
	Medical care (including health insurance)	–232	Zero-rating of sales of new housing, prescription drugs, and household energy expenditures for electricity, gas, fuel oil, and water and sanitation services	–346
	Insurance and finance (other than health insurance)	–74		
	Education	–48		
	Religious and welfare	–47		
	Foreign travel	–13		
	Local transportation	–8		
	Other: food produced and consumed on farms, military-issued clothing, domestic services	–7		
		–889B		
PLUS – First sale of new residential housing		+170		
Revised total base		**2,408**		**1,713**

[a] *Treasury I*, vol. 3, ch. 7, 86.

Treasury I shows the impact of path dependency on VAT design with reform options influenced by state sales tax practices (for example, in the taxation of residential housing, the exemption of supplies but zero-rating of certain inputs, and in refusing to recommend business registration thresholds) and the income tax (in extending preferential income tax treatment to education, religious and charitable organisations). *Treasury I* also shows, once again, how the VAT's weaknesses, such as its perceived regressivity and inability to tax difficult sectors, leads to complex policy responses shaped by the institutional context of the policy-making environment. That so many exclusions to the VAT base were factored in at such an early stage of policy development (even before the legislative process is taken into account) suggests that any future US VAT will likely depart in a significant way from the first design norm of a broad consumption base.

1.3.2 The translation of ideals – From *Treasury I* to TRA86

Treasury I ultimately recommended comprehensive reform of the income tax base. In essence, the reforms recommended by the Treasury sought to expand the income tax base through the elimination of a number of preferences in exchange for reduced and compressed marginal tax rates.[138] The substance of these proposals and the reforms that resulted have been extensively canvassed elsewhere.[139] This section reviews the assessment by two experts, McLure and Zodrow, who were closely involved in the development of *Treasury I* and committed to the merits of the proposals it contained. The assessment of reform by these authors is useful in distilling a number of trends from this reform period that are instructive as to the likely fate of any future VAT reform proposals in the US.[140]

First, the Treasury chose fundamental reform of an income tax base. According to McLure and Zodrow, the choice of an income base was the 'most fundamental' and 'for many, the most disappointing'.[141] However, as McLure and Zodrow explain, the decision to stick with an income base was not based just on the path-dependent pull of the familiarity with the income tax, but on complexities in the implementation of a consumption tax, which 'is more problematic than it may seem'.[142] A major sticking point was the appropriate treatment of gifts and bequests under a consumption tax. As was explained in Chapters 2 and 3, the argument that VATs are less inequitable when measured over lifetime incomes (because people

138 Ibid., vol. 1, ch. 4–7.

139 See, e.g., Joel Slemrod (ed.), *Do Taxes Matter? The Impact of the Tax Reform Act of 1986* (MIT Press, Cambridge, MA, 1990); Charles E. McLure Jr and George R. Zodrow, 'Treasury I and the Tax Reform Act of 1986: The Economics and Politics of Tax Reform', *Economic Perspectives* 1(1) (1987), 37; Alan Auerbach and Joel Slemrod, 'The Economic Effects of the Tax Reform Act of 1986', *Journal of Economic Literature* 35 (1997), 589; C. Eugene Steuerle, *Contemporary US Tax Policy* (2nd ed., Urban Institute Press, Washington, DC, 2008), ch. 7; W. Elliot Brownlee, *Federal Taxation in America: A Short History* (2nd ed., Cambridge University Press, Cambridge, 2004), ch. 4–5.

140 Charles E. McLure Jr and George R. Zodrow, 'Treasury I and the Tax Reform Act of 1986: The Economics and Politics of Tax Reform', *Economic Perspectives* 1(1) (1987), 37. McLure was Deputy Assistant Secretary for Tax Analysis, US Treasury Department from 1983 to 1985, see *Curriculum Vitae of Charles E. McLure Jr* (12 September 2003), National Bureau for Economic Research (nber.org/vitae/vita371.htm). McLure has been a leading US proponent of VAT reform; see, e.g., Charles E. McLure, *The Value-Added Tax: Key to Deficit Reduction?* (American Enterprise Institute, Washington, DC, 1987). Zodrow was a visiting economist in the US Treasury Office of Tax Analysis from 1984 to 1985: *Curriculum Vitae – George R. Zodrow* (20 September 2010), Department of Economics, Rice University (economics.rice.edu/~zodrow/).

141 Charles E. McLure Jr and George R. Zodrow, 'Treasury I and the Tax Reform Act of 1986: The Economics and Politics of Tax Reform', *Economic Perspectives* 1(1) (1987), 37, 40.

142 Ibid.

will consume what they earn in a lifetime) can generally be maintained only if something is done to effectively tax intergenerational transfers of wealth.[143] McLure and Zodrow noted that in light of the political moves to eliminate estate and gift taxation[144] and the fact that 'during the formulation of *Treasury I*, it was impossible to gain agreement for even extremely limited taxation of capital gains on assets transferred at death',[145] at least some of those within the Treasury thought that to introduce a VAT in these circumstances would be 'highly inequitable'.[146] The difficulty of selling a consumption tax to the American public and the difficult transitional issues involved also influenced the Treasury's preference to maintain income as the main tax base.[147]

Second, as with the Treasury's proposed VAT, the income tax was not pure, but rather an attempt to restructure the income tax so as to more closely resemble real economic income.[148] Like the Treasury's VAT policy proposals, the proposals for reform of the income tax were influenced by existing taxes (at both the federal and state level) and the likely social and political implications of the recommendations for reform. This shows that, even to policy-makers motivated by the merits of a particular set of reform proposals, considerations beyond merits have a profound impact on the development of recommendations for reform.

Third, from the release of *Treasury I* in November 1984, the reform plan endured two years of political adulteration. The President revised the reform proposal in May 1985,[149] the House Ways and Means Committee then produced its draft in November 1985,[150] and after much to-and-fro in the Senate Finance Committee a compromised report was finally supported by the Senate in September 1986.[151] According to McLure and Zodrow, the process of reform began with the 'conceptually coherent proposals' of *Treasury I* and ended with the 'hodge-podge of proposals' in *TRA86*:[152]

143 See Chapter 2, §2.2.6 and Chapter 3, §2.7 of this book.

144 See generally Michael Graetz, *Death by a Thousand Cuts: The Fight Over Taxing Inherited Wealth* (Princeton University Press, Princeton, NJ, 2005).

145 Charles E. McLure Jr and George R. Zodrow, 'Treasury I and the Tax Reform Act of 1986: The Economics and Politics of Tax Reform', *Economic Perspectives* 1(1) (1987), 37, 40.

146 Ibid., 41. 147 Ibid., 41.

148 McLure and Zodrow state that '[o]f course, Treasury I was not a conceptually pure income tax': Ibid.

149 President of the United States (Ronald Reagan), *The President's Tax Proposals to the Congress for Fairness, Simplicity, and Growth* (US Government Printing Office, Washington, DC, 1985).

150 C. Eugene Steuerle, *Contemporary US Tax Policy* (2nd ed., Urban Institute Press, Washington, DC, 2008), 121.

151 US Joint Committee on Taxation, *Summary of Conference Agreement on HR 3838 (Tax Reform Act of 1986) (JCS-16–86)* (US Government Printing Office, Washington, DC, 1986); C. Eugene Steuerle, *Contemporary US Tax Policy* (2nd ed., Urban Institute Press, Washington, DC, 2008), 121.

152 Charles E. McLure Jr and George R. Zodrow, 'Treasury I and the Tax Reform Act of 1986: The Economics and Politics of Tax Reform', *Economic Perspectives* 1(1) (1987), 37, 57.

> For an economist it is troublesome to see how little influence economic arguments exerted once Treasury I went to the White House and considerations of politics and cosmetics became dominant.

Nevertheless, the enactment of *TRA86* is regarded as one 'of the most far reaching reforms'[153] of the US tax system. Many cite the reforms as a testament to the bipartisan commitment to reform shared by a number of policy entrepreneurs from President Reagan and Treasury Secretaries Don Regan and James Baker to Democrat Congressmen Dan Rostenkowski and Senator Bill Bradley.[154] The reduction and compression of marginal tax rates and expansion of the income tax base through the elimination of many special preferences constituted the most significant postwar reform of the US tax system, and is said to have inspired similar reforms worldwide.[155] The enactment of *TRA86* shows that major reform is possible (even absent major crisis)[156] but that reforms will not resemble initial policy proposals, irrespective of how meritorious the drafters of those proposals might consider them to be.

1.4 *Post-TRA86 – The euphoria is short lived; crisis ensues*

The post-reform euphoria following the enactment of *TRA86* was relatively short lived. In 2005, President Bush's Advisory Panel on Tax Reform estimated that since 1986 there have been over 15,000 changes to the tax code.[157] As Peters argues, 'in almost every revenue bill since the major reform in 1986 some new special tax treatments have appeared, returning the tax system to the same "Christmas tree" it had been prior to reform'.[158]

153 Ibid., 37.

154 B. Guy Peters, *The Politics of Taxation: A Comparative Perspective* (Blackwell, Cambridge, MA, 1991), 287; W. Elliot Brownlee, *Federal Taxation in America: A Short History* (2nd ed., Cambridge University Press, Cambridge, 2004), 175.

155 Sven Steinmo, 'The Evolution of Policy Ideas: Tax Policy in the 20th Century', *British Journal of Politics and International Relations* 5(2) (2006), 206, 219.

156 W. Elliot Brownlee, *Federal Taxation in America: A Short History* (2nd ed., Cambridge University Press, Cambridge, 2004), 247.

157 US President's Advisory Panel on Federal Tax Reform, *Simple, Fair, and Pro-Growth: Proposals to Fix America's Tax System* (2005), 16. Ackerman and Altshuler further contend that such changes followed a pattern of pairing tax benefits with complex rules, such as phase-ins and phase-outs, which have contributed to the tax code's complexity: Jonathan Ackerman and Rosanne Altshuler, 'Constrained Tax Reform: How Political and Economic Constraints Affect the Formation of Tax Policy Proposals', *National Tax Journal* 59(1) (2006), 165, 170. Phase-out provisions are designed to expire with the expectation that they will be extended by subsequent legislation, while, as the name suggests, the commencement of phase-in provisions is delayed so as to reduce the impact of the provisions once they are passed. Auerbach and Slemrod claim that the use of such provisions is 'an unfortunate lesson in obfuscation' learned from the TRA86: Alan Auerbach and Joel Slemrod, 'The Economic Effects of the Tax Reform Act of 1986', *Journal of Economic Literature* 35 (1997), 589, 268. However, Ackerman and Altshuler argue that the practice at least dates back to the 1970s: at 171.

158 B. Guy Peters, *American Public Policy: Promise and Performance* (6th ed., CQ Press, Washington, DC, 2004), 226.

The response of experts, academics, politicians, policy-makers and lobbyists has been to discuss and propose myriad reforms – many proposals are simply different methods of moving toward a consumption base. These include subtraction-based VATs,[159] flat taxes,[160] Unlimited Savings Allowance (USA) tax proposals[161] and proposals for federal retail sales taxes (RSTs) such as the Fair Tax.[162] The VAT has been one of these many consumption tax proposals.[163]

The VAT has periodically been proposed as an option to fund major initiatives, such as healthcare,[164] or in response to concern that the US federal budget deficit

159 See, e.g., the Business Activities Tax endorsed by Senators Danforth and Boren: The Comprehensive Tax Restructuring and Simplification Act of 1994, S 2160, 103rd Cong. (1994); Congressman Gibbons' subtraction-VAT proposals: Revenue Restructuring Act of 1996, HR 4050, 104th Cong. (1996). For further discussion, see Alan Schenk and Oliver Oldman, *Value Added Tax: A Comparative Approach* (rev. edn., Cambridge University Press, Cambridge; New York, 2007), 336, 434, 440.

160 Flat tax proposals vary, but in essence they are variations on origin-based, subtraction-method consumption taxes levied at a single rate. A flat tax formed the centrepiece of billionaire Steve Forbes' bid for the 1996 Republican presidential nomination. Examples of congressional proposals include Congressman Richard Armey's (Rep) The Freedom and Fairness Restoration Act of 1997 HR 1040; Senator Shelby's Tax Simplification Act of 2003, S 1040, 108th Cong., 1st session (2003); Senator Specter's Flat Tax Act of 2003, S 907, 108th Cong., 1st session (2003). See further Alan Schenk and Oliver Oldman, *Value Added Tax: A Comparative Approach* (rev. edn., Cambridge University Press, Cambridge; New York, 2007), 448–51; Robert F. van Brederode, 'Towards a Federal Sales Tax in the United States?' *International VAT Monitor* (March/April 2008), 114; W. Elliot Brownlee, *Federal Taxation in America: A Short History* (2nd ed., Cambridge University Press, Cambridge, 2004), 204–5. For the inspiration for many of these proposals, see Robert E. Hall and Alvin Rabushka, *The Flat Tax* (Hoover Institution Press, Stanford, CA, 1985).

161 The USA tax consists of a subtraction-method VAT and a proposal to replace the income tax with an individual consumption tax (allowing deductions for new net savings): Sen Sam Nunn (Dem) and Pete Dominici (Rep): USA Tax Act of 1995, S 722, 104th Cong., (1995). Variations including a simplified USA tax (proposing a cash-flow tax on business income and a consumed expenditure tax levied on the individual) have been proposed on a number of subsequent occasions: see, e.g., the Simplified USA Tax Act of 2003, HR 269, 108th Cong. (2003). See further Alan Schenk and Oliver Oldman, *Value Added Tax: A Comparative Approach* (rev. edn., Cambridge University Press, Cambridge; New York, 2007), 442.

162 See, e.g., the panel on the fair tax at the 2011 hearing of the House Ways and Means Committee on consumption tax reform proposals: US House of Representatives, Committee on Ways and Means, 112th Cong., 1st session), *Hearing on Tax Reform and Consumption-Based Tax Systems* (26 July 2011, serial 112–15). See also the proposal of Congressman Schaefer (Rep) and Billy Tauzin (Rep) for a National Retail Sales Tax Act of 1996, HR 3039, 104th Cong. (1996); the proposal of Congressman John Linder (Rep) and Senator Chambliss (Rep) for the Fair Tax Act of 2007 HR 25/S 1025, 110th Cong. (2007). See further Robert F. van Brederode, 'Towards a Federal Sales Tax in the United States?' *International VAT Monitor* (March/April 2008), 114; Alan Schenk and Oliver Oldman, *Value Added Tax: A Comparative approach* (rev. edn., Cambridge University Press, Cambridge; New York, 2007), 451–57.

163 See, e.g., Charles E. McLure, *The Value-Added Tax: Key to Deficit Reduction?* (American Enterprise Institute, Washington, DC, 1987).

164 See, e.g., Congressman Dingell's various proposals for a VAT to finance reform of healthcare, e.g., National Health Insurance Act of 2009, HR 15, 111th Cong., 1st session (2005). The VAT was informed by the Ullman VAT: Alan Schenk and Oliver Oldman, *Value Added Tax:*

has reached a crisis point.[165] Although there have been a number of VATs proposed at the congressional level, none have received sufficient support from Congress or the relevant congressional committees to come close to legislative action. Moreover, there have been no serious proposals for VAT reform from the White House. Indeed, the response to even the mere mention of VAT reform has resulted in immediate retractions by Presidents suspected of considering it. For example, when fiscal pressure, resulting from an economic recession and the expenditure demands of the Gulf War, prompted consideration of a VAT by the administration of President George H. W. Bush,[166] consumption tax reform was ruled out as being too administratively costly and too politically costly, owing to the President's infamous 1988 pledge, 'read my lips, no new taxes'.[167] When a VAT was proposed by President Clinton's health policy adviser, Ira Magaziner, in order to raise revenue for healthcare reform, the Clinton administration quickly acted to remove VAT reform from the agenda.[168]

In the absence of any serious legislative action on VAT reform, three trends relevant to VAT reform will be considered: first, the efforts of the American Bar Association to draft a model VAT and Senator Hollings' failed attempts to realise these reforms; second, the acceleration of efforts toward moving the income tax to a consumption base; and finally, the last major official consideration of VAT reform undertaken during the presidency of George W. Bush.

1.4.1 The model VAT

The American Bar Association ('ABA'), although ostensibly not advocating for a VAT, drafted a model VAT statute (the '1989 ABA *Model VAT*'). The 1989 ABA

A *Comparative Approach* (rev. edn., Cambridge University Press, Cambridge; New York, 2007), 433.

[165] See, e.g., the proposal, put forward by Dem Jerry Brown, during his 1992 presidential campaign, for a 13 per cent VAT (to replace social security taxes, the corporate income tax and gasoline taxes) alongside a flat income tax as a 'silver bullet solution' for economic reform: Alan Schenk, 'Recent Activity in the United States Involving the Value Added Tax', *International VAT Monitor* (1992), 2, 10–11.

[166] Brownlee contends that Treasury Secretary Nicholas Brady suggested introducing a VAT, which appeared at one stage to have been suggested by President Bush Sr. However, budget director Richard Darman and Chief of Staff John Sununu preferred energy tax reform for reasons of administrative ease and minimizing political fallout: W. Elliot Brownlee, *Federal Taxation in America: A Short History* (2nd ed., Cambridge University Press, Cambridge, 2004), 188.

[167] Instead, decidedly less ambitious reforms of selectively increasing consumption taxes on petrol and home heating oil were introduced, as well as additional measures such as income tax rate increases: ibid., 183, 189–91.

[168] In the VAT's place were proposals to introduce the politically palatable yet insufficient revenue-raising tools of a cigarette tax and an income tax surcharge on large business: Thomas Friedman, 'New Tax on Goods Is Weighed to Pay for Health Care', *New York Times*, 15 April 1993, A1; Junko Kato, *Regressive taxation and the welfare state: path dependence and policy diffusion* (Cambridge University Press, Cambridge, 2003) 130; W. Elliot Brownlee, *Federal Taxation in America: A Short History* (2nd ed., Cambridge University Press, Cambridge, 2004), 197.

Model VAT mostly conformed with the three norms of good VAT design – proposing a single-rate VAT (with the exact rate to be determined by Congress) on a broad base (with zero-rating only for exports) levied through the invoice-credit method on a destination basis.[169]

The proposed VAT had a few unique approaches informed either by previous VAT proposals, particularly Ullman's VAT, or by an analysis of the issues.[170] The 1989 *ABA Model VAT* preferred to address regressivity through grants or adjustments to the income tax rather than through changes to the VAT base.[171]

Senator Hollings (Dem) proposed a 5 per cent VAT based on the ABA proposals, but modified the base to exclude items such as food and housing. The proposal was motivated by a desire to reduce the deficit. The Hollings proposals were unsuccessful.[172]

1.4.2 Accelerating the shift from income to consumption

President George W. Bush conducted his 2001 election campaign on the promise of tax cuts. He wasted no time acting on the rhetoric when, three months after his inauguration on 20 January 2001, the *Economic Growth and Tax Relief Reconciliation Act of 2001* was passed by the Republican-controlled Congress. The centrepiece of the Act was across-the-board tax cuts.[173] Bush's apparent motive was

[169] Alan Schenk (Reporter), American Bar Association Section of Taxation, *Value Added Tax: A Model Statute and Commentary (A Report of the Committee on Value Added Tax of the American Bar Association Section of Taxation)* (American Bar Association 1989).

[170] For example, as with *Treasury I*, there was no proposal for a minimum compulsory registration threshold. Treasury was also granted discretion to classify certain transactions as non-taxable (i.e., zero-rated) to reduce adverse cash-flow effects, such as in the sale of going concerns or for high-priced capital assets. Similar provisions were in the Ullman proposal and can be found in VATs elsewhere: Alan Schenk, 'A Model Value Added Tax Statute for the United States', *International VAT Monitor* (September 1990), 2, 4–5.

[171] Alan Schenk (Reporter), American Bar Association Section of Taxation, *Value Added Tax: A Model Statute and Commentary (A Report of the Committee on Value Added Tax of the American Bar Association Section of Taxation)* (American Bar Association 1989), 11 and 71.

[172] Deficit and Debt Reduction and Social Security Solvency Act of 1999, S. 1376, 106th Cong., 1st session (1999). See further Alan Schenk and Oliver Oldman, *Value Added Tax: A Comparative Approach* (rev. edn., Cambridge University Press, Cambridge; New York, 2007), 434.

[173] The reforms included a new 10 per cent individual income tax rate bracket; doubling of the child credit and extending its refundability; reducing marriage penalties; eliminating the phase-out of personal exemptions and the limitation on certain itemized deductions for high-income taxpayers; providing tax incentives for education; increasing Individual Retirement Accounts (IRAs) and pension tax incentives (IRAs provide tax deductions for employee contributions to retirement savings, various pension plans where employers contribute to an employee's retirement savings are also taxed preferentially): see generally Michael J. Graetz and Deborah H. Schenk, *Federal Income Taxation: Principles and Policies* (6th ed., Foundation Press, New York, 2009), 654–756; a phased-in reduction of the estate tax and modifications to the gift tax; and relief from the alternative minimum tax (AMT). The AMT was introduced in the *TRA1986* reforms as a means to ensure that high-income taxpayers above a specified income threshold, who take advantage of various tax preferences, still pay a

twofold: to create a supply-side inspired boost to economic activity in response to an economic recession with the intended collateral effect that restricting revenue would control the growth of government. As Brownlee contends:[174]

> Bush. . .followed Reagan's example by promoting tax cuts as an effective way to stimulate the growth of the economy. . .In contrast to Reagan, however, Bush emphasized how tax cuts would force future Congresses to slow the growth of the federal government.

After the events of 9/11, Bush again proposed tax cuts to arrest the increasing fiscal pressure caused by a sluggish economy and increasing defence and security expenditure demands. The 2002 and 2003 reforms were unashamedly beneficial to the affluent, on the ostensible promise of stimulating economic growth.[175] The reforms marked a deliberate turn away from the taxation of investment, accumulated wealth and capital gains, at a cost to revenue of approximately $2.7 trillion.[176]

The Bush reforms pleased conservative tax reformers, who have proposed variants of the 'five easy pieces' approach to tax reform developed by Gary Robbins and Republican lawyer Ernest Christian in 2002.[177] As Stephen Moore from the Club for Growth declares:[178]

> People like me have been advocating a flat tax for decades. . .No one could get it done politically. What Bush has done, in a hidden way, is move us in baby steps towards the flat tax.

The approach is to substitute overt big-bang reform with reform by covert 'baby steps', so as to accelerate the transformation of the income tax base into a

minimum amount of tax. The AMT is levied on a broader base at a lower rate, and taxpayers pay tax if the amount payable under the AMT exceeds the net tax payable under the income tax. A separate AMT applies for both individuals and corporations: Graetz and Schenk at 776–77; *Economic Growth and Tax Relief Reconciliation Act of 2001*, Pub. L No. 107–16, 115 Stat. 38 (2001). See also C. Eugene Steuerle, *Contemporary US Tax Policy* (2nd ed., Urban Institute Press, Washington, DC, 2008), 123, ch. 11.

174 W. Elliot Brownlee, *Federal Taxation in America: A Short History* (2nd ed., Cambridge University Press, Cambridge, 2004), 221.

175 See, e.g., the laws slashing taxes on investment and accumulated wealth and reducing taxes on capital and dividends, expanding the 10 per cent tax bracket, increasing tax breaks for married couples, temporarily increasing the AMT exemption, and expanding depreciation rules: *Job Creation and Worker Assistance Act of 2002*, Pub. L No. 107–47, 116 Stat. 21 (2002); *Jobs and Growth Relief Reconciliation Act of 2003*, Pub. L No. 108–27, 117 Stat. 752 (2003). See also C. Eugene Steuerle, *Contemporary US Tax Policy* (2nd ed., Urban Institute Press, Washington, DC, 2008), 210–11.

176 US Dept. of the Treasury, *General Explanations of the Administration's Fiscal Year 2008 Revenue Proposals* (2007).

177 Ernest Christian and Gary A. Robbins, 'Stealth Approach to Tax Reform', *Washington Times*, 1 November 2002, A21. See also Daniel Shaviro, 'Simplifying Assumptions: How Might the Politics of Consumption Tax Reform Affect (Impair) the End Product?' in J. W. Diamond and G. R. Zodrow (eds.), *Fundamental Tax Reform: Issues, Choices, and Implications* (MIT Press, Cambridge, MA; London, 2008), 75, 83–85.

178 John Cassidy, 'Tax Code' (6 September 2004), *The New Yorker*, 70.

consumption base.[179] There are a number of versions of the five easy pieces approach, but the proposals from the original model include (1) reducing marginal tax rates; (2) eliminating the 'double taxation' of corporate earnings by integrating the taxation of corporate and shareholder income; (3) moving to immediate deductions on all business expenses; (4) expanding the preferential tax treatment of savings; and (5) excluding the export and foreign trade earnings of US companies (i.e., tax on a territorial rather than a worldwide basis).[180] Other variations include proposals for eliminating the estate tax; eliminating the taxation of capital gains; and abolishing the Alternative Minimum Tax (AMT).[181] Under the administration of President George W. Bush, many of these reforms were well underway, as Grover Norquist, president of the conservative anti-tax lobby group Americans for Tax Reform, states:[182]

> Do you think it was an accident that the first three tax cuts moved toward expensing business expenditures, toward universal I.R.A.s, toward getting rid of the capital gains tax, toward getting rid of the double taxation of dividend income, toward getting rid of the death tax? No. It is consistent with a vision.

Many aspects of the temporary 'tax relief' enacted by the Bush administration have remained, despite the ostensible intention that they expire in 2010.[183] While acting consistently with this 'vision' might move the tax base toward consumption, this has been absent the compensating revenue that a new tax might provide, and has therefore increased the calls for tax reform to prevent the exacerbation of a fiscal crisis.

1.4.3 Simple, fair and pro-growth: Proposals to fix America's tax system

In January 2005, President George W. Bush established a bipartisan panel to report on revenue-neutral ways to reform the tax system, with a view to simplicity, fairness

[179] Ibid.

[180] Ernest Christian and Gary A. Robbins, 'Stealth Approach to Tax Reform', *Washington Times*, 1 November 2002, A21.

[181] See above, n 173, for a description of the AMT.

[182] John Cassidy, 'Tax Code' (6 September 2004), *The New Yorker*, 70. Interestingly, the Senate blocked President George W. Bush's second-round attempt to permanently repeal estate taxes because of lobbying by some of the United States' wealthiest citizens – Bill Gates, Warren Buffett, George Soros, and Ed Turner – who formed a group called 'Responsible Wealth': W. Elliot Brownlee, *Federal Taxation in America: A Short History* (2nd ed., Cambridge University Press, Cambridge, 2004), 232.

[183] The *American Taxpayer Relief Act of 2012*, Pub. L 112–240, 126 Stat. 2313 (2013) has permanently extended many of the tax preferences for taxpayers with incomes of less than $400,000 (or $450,000 for joint filers). Originally, the Obama administration's 2010 budget proposed to extend a number of the temporary reforms enacted under the Bush administration. The preservation of benefits largely extended to a broadly defined middle class earning up to $250,000: US Joint Committee on Taxation (111th Cong., 1st session) *Description of Revenue Proposals Contained in the President's Fiscal Year 2010 Budget Proposal; Part One: Individual Income Tax and Estate and Gift Tax Provisions JCS-2–09* (US Government Printing Office, Washington, DC, 2009).

(including progressivity) and the promotion of economic growth (hereafter the '2005 *Tax Advisory Panel*').[184] In a sign of both the size of the task and the need for reform, the Panel's final report released in November 2005 quoted a Treasury estimate that in 2006 over 6600 taxpayers with incomes greater than $200,000 and over 1300 taxpayers with incomes greater than $700,000 would pay no tax at all, through the use of legitimate tax avoidance.[185]

The final report proposed two alternatives for reform. The first, the simplified income tax plan, focused on 'streamlining' elements of the existing income tax.[186] The second option, the growth and investment tax plan, went further and aimed to 'move our tax system closer to a consumption tax'.[187] It proposed to do so by making all business investment immediately deductible,[188] by further extending and reforming tax-preferred savings accounts and by moving to a 15 per cent tax on capital income.[189] In effect, the 2005 *Tax Advisory Panel*'s recommendations brought to light a tax reform plan that had hitherto been conducted under the cover of stealth.

The 2005 *Tax Advisory Panel* also considered, but failed to obtain consensus on, a progressive consumption tax, a VAT and a national RST.[190] The panel was not willing to countenance a complete shift from an income tax to a VAT, preferring a hybrid model combining a 15 per cent VAT (labelled a partial replacement VAT) with a modified income tax (based on the simplified income tax proposal).[191]

[184] US President's Advisory Panel on Federal Tax Reform, *Simple, Fair, and Pro-Growth: Proposals to Fix America's Tax System* (2005), 16 (hereafter '2005 *Tax Advisory Panel*').

[185] Ibid., 10.

[186] Among the recommendations were limiting rate reductions and compressions, removing the AMT, extending the tax-preferred treatment of homeowner and charitable benefits, and expanding and simplifying tax-preferred savings accounts: ibid., ch. 5.

[187] Ibid., 59. Graetz labels this a modified version of Bradford's X-tax: Michael Graetz, *100 Million Unnecessary Returns, A Simple, Fair and Competitive Plan for the United States* (Yale University Press, New Haven, CT, 2008), 73, 166. See below, n 281.

[188] But denying deductions for interest payments: ibid., 189.

[189] Ibid., ch. 5. The proposal included a progressive tax on income from labor and a cash-flow tax on business activity levied at a single rate: at 61–62.

[190] Ibid., xiv.

[191] Ibid. The Panel estimated that the adoption of a VAT would enable the highest tax rates under the simplified income tax to be reduced to from 33 per cent to 15 per cent (for both the top marginal rate of income tax and corporate income tax – reduced from 31.5 per cent for large businesses): at 108–9, 191. This approach was influenced by the reform proposals advocated by Graetz, whose 'Competitive Tax Plan' proposes, among other things, a VAT to replace the individual income tax for taxpayers with incomes below a certain threshold: Michael Graetz, *100 Million Unnecessary Returns, A Simple, Fair and Competitive Plan for the United States* (Yale University Press, New Haven, CT, 2008). Graetz estimates that a VAT imposed on a broad base with minimal exclusions (such as medical care and education, but not food) at a rate between 10 and 14 per cent could enable an exemption from income tax for families with an annual income of less than $100,000 and the substantial reduction of rates for incomes above that amount: at 67. The proposal would exempt from registration businesses with an annual gross turnover of less than $100,000: at 69. Graetz's plan also involves a significant reduction in the corporate income tax rate (to 15–20 per cent) and the repeal of the earned

The 2005 *Tax Advisory Panel* accepted the potential for a VAT to realise the merits of a consumption tax and therefore promote economic growth,[192] stimulate savings and promote the trading competitiveness of the US.[193] This positive assessment was influenced by a belief in the benefits that would flow from reducing reliance on income taxes[194] and was based on a proposed VAT that was closer to the good VAT than any of the earlier Treasury proposals:[195]

> A broad-based VAT applied at a single rate is economically efficient because it generally does not distort consumers' choices among goods and services and does not discourage savings or distort the allocation of capital. Economists agree that a well-designed VAT imposes a lower excess burden than most other taxes for any given amount of revenue raised. Reducing the excess burden of taxation on the economy is an important way that the tax system can encourage economic growth.

The 2005 *Tax Advisory Panel* was optimistic of being able to benefit from 'best practice' experience to achieve the good VAT:[196]

> In implementing the VAT, the United States would be able to take advantage of the wealth of worldwide experience in administering and complying with the tax. The VAT has been adopted by every major developed economy except the United States. Thus, the Treasury Department and IRS could study and apply best practices from around the world.

So confident was the 2005 *Tax Advisory Panel* of the capacity to learn from the experience of other jurisdictions, that the Panel predicted that VAT fraud and evasion would be less of an issue in the US than in countries such as the UK because the VAT proposed by the Panel would be levied on a broader base.[197]

income tax credit to be replaced with measures to compensate for the regressivity of the VAT, such as through the use of one or both of tax offsets (at 170–77) and digital smart cards to provide relief from the VAT on the consumption of eligible citizens (at 178–81). See also Michael Graetz, '100 Million Unnecessary Returns: A Fresh Start for the US Tax System', *Yale Law Journal* 112 (2002–2003), 261, 286–90.

[192] US President's Advisory Panel on Federal Tax Reform, *Simple, Fair, and Pro-Growth: Proposals to Fix America's Tax System* (2005), 200.

[193] Ibid., 201. [194] Ibid., 200. The 2005 *Tax Advisory Panel* noted (at 200) that:

> The Partial Replacement VAT also would make it possible to substantially reduce income tax rates for all individual and corporate taxpayers. Lower marginal income tax rates on individuals and businesses would strengthen incentives to save, invest, work, and innovate while making our tax system more efficient.

[195] Ibid. [196] Ibid., 201.

[197] Ibid., 202. However, the Panel also acknowledged that the compliance benefits of the VAT over an RST should not be overstated (at 205):

> Further, more transactions are subject to a VAT than to a retail sales tax, creating additional opportunities for evasion. Under a VAT, firms could fabricate invoices to claim input credits, even if such purchases were never made. Claiming excess input credits in a VAT also can produce a tax refund for a business. This temptation does not exist under the retail sales tax.

The optimistic sentiment that the US might benefit from the policy learning of the experience with VAT in jurisdictions elsewhere has similarly been expressed by those within the conventional approach (see §3.2 of this chapter). This broad base was listed under the heading 'Design Assumptions', which, consistent with the good VAT, proposed that:[198]

- The VAT should be imposed on the broadest consumption base consistent with:
  - The structure of our federal system of government, and
  - The need to maintain neutrality between public and private sector provision of goods and services.
- The VAT should use the credit-invoice method.
- The VAT should be border adjusted.
- The VAT should be imposed at a single uniform rate.
- The VAT should be set at a rate that is high enough to raise sufficient revenue to accomplish substantial income tax reform, justify the administrative burden of the VAT on businesses and government, and discourage subsequent rate increases.

The VAT base proposed by the *2005 Tax Advisory Panel* included all domestic consumption except non-commercial government services; primary and secondary education (but including tertiary education); existing residential housing (with new residential housing and commercial property taxed); and charitable and religious services (which would be exempt unless selling goods and services in competition with the private market).[199] See §3.2 for the Panel's proposed treatment of financial supplies. Unlike the *Treasury I* proposal, the Panel proposed a compulsory registration threshold of $100,000 in annual gross receipts.[200]

The Panel accepted that the VAT was regressive but preferred to address this through adjustments to income tax rates and through family and work credits, rather than through alterations to the base or rates.[201] However, as these measures were insufficient to leave the package distributionally neutral, the Panel acknowledged that neutrality might 'require somewhat higher income tax or VAT rates'.[202]

Although the *2005 Tax Advisory Panel* largely accepted the merits of the good VAT, it could not obtain consensus support for adopting one:[203]

> Panel members recognized that lower income tax rates made possible by VAT revenues could create a tax system that is more efficient and could reduce the economic distortions and disincentives created by our income tax. However, the Panel could not reach a consensus on whether to recommend a VAT option.

[198] Ibid., 197. [199] Ibid., 198, 249–52.
[200] Ibid., 250. Entities below the threshold could voluntarily register. [201] Ibid., 193, 252–53.
[202] Ibid., 194. [203] Ibid., 192.

Although noting the opposition of states to VAT reform and the 'major challenge' of coordinating a federal VAT with state sales taxes, the Panel expressed hope that efficiency gains could be achieved if states chose to bring their narrow-based sales taxes in line with the broad-based VAT.[204] The concerns that barred agreement on VAT included the 'compliance and administrative burdens' of the VAT (especially when the tax would be introduced in addition to, rather than in replacement of, the income tax), and crucially that:[205]

> Some members were also concerned that introducing a VAT would lead to higher total tax collections over time and facilitate the development of a larger federal government – in other words, that the VAT would be a "money machine."

The 2005 *Tax Advisory Panel* acknowledged that the 'evidence neither conclusively proves, nor conclusively disproves, the view that supplemental VATs facilitate the growth of government'.[206] Nevertheless, concerns about the VAT fuelling the growth of government – particularly in light of its low visibility[207] and the fact that the VAT would likely never be repealed – seems to have been the main motivation for the Panel not recommending a VAT. The latter concern over the VAT's longevity is an ironic observation, given that the conventional approach considers this longevity one of the VAT's strengths. The reaction to the Panel's report was decidedly lukewarm, with none of its proposals acted upon to date.[208]

1.5 *The current state of play – Post-2005 reform trends*

Since 2007, the financial crisis and economic recession have prompted fiscal measures that have further increased pressure on the federal budget. Deficits over the 2009–2012 fiscal years set new postwar records, exceeding $1 trillion and peaking at more than $1.4 trillion, or 10.1 per cent of GDP, in 2009. Although recent CBO estimates indicate the first deficit below $1 trillion in 2013 ($680 billion) and down to $506 billion in fiscal year 2014, current estimates suggest that if existing laws relating to taxing and spending remain unchanged, public debt will constitute 74 per cent of GDP by the end of the 2014 fiscal year – the highest ratio since 1950.[209]

[204] Ibid., 202.

[205] Ibid., 192. The prospect of replacing payroll tax revenue with VAT revenue was outside the Panel's mandate to consider only reform of the income tax: at 192.

[206] Ibid., 203. The reference to supplemental presumably refers to the VAT as a supplement to the income tax.

[207] Ibid., 192, 203–4. Although the 2005 *Tax Advisory Panel* assumed that the VAT would be separately shown on invoices, it was the difficulty of individual taxpayers being able to calculate their yearly VAT liability (absent retaining and tallying up their invoices) that concerned the Panel (at 204).

[208] See, e.g., Reuven S. Avi-Yonah, 'The report of the President's Advisory Panel on Federal Tax Reform: A Critical Assessment and a Proposal', *SMU Law Review* 59(2) (2006), 551.

[209] These figures might be regarded as optimistic in light of the assumptions underpinning the Congressional Budget Office estimates such as those that assume that the laws will remain

Although much initial focus was placed on stimulus spending and then on the political stalemate over increasing the debt limit to pay for the stimulus, nervous attention has also been directed toward the means through which the outpacing of revenue by spending might be addressed. This discussion has encompassed many reform proposals, including suggestions of VAT reform.[210] Despite this discussion, there have been no serious moves toward a VAT at the official level. For example, President Obama's 'Volcker Task Force' considered a range of tax reform options, but the introduction of a VAT was not within its terms of reference.[211] While the occasional voice in Congress or the Senate expresses support for, or proposes, a VAT,[212] and the occasional reference is made to the US Treasury continuing to

unchanged and that certain tax provisions that ostensibly provide temporary tax relief will expire: United States, Congressional Budget Office, *Historical Budget Data* (CBO, Washington, DC, 2013), Table 1; United States Congressional Budget Office, *An Update to the Budget and Economic Outlook: Fiscal Years 2014 to 2024* (CBO, Washington, DC, 2014), 1–6.

[210] See, e.g., the contributions to the special issues of the *Tax Law Review* from a 'Symposium on Designing a Federal VAT': Part I, *Tax Law Review* 63(2) (2010), 285, and Part II, *Tax Law Review* 63(3) (2010), 517; C. Eugene Steuerle, 'Real Tax Reform Is Always Hard: Some Advice for the Task Force', in W. Elmore (ed.), *Toward Tax Reform: Recommendations for President Obama's Task Force* (Tax Analysts, Arlington VA, 2009), 87, 89; Michael van de Leur, 'A VAT in the United States?', *International VAT Monitor* (September/October 2009), 360; Floyd Norris, 'It's Hard to Worry About a Deficit 10 Years Out', *New York Times* 28 August 2009, B1; The Business Research and Advocacy Group, the Committee for Economic Development proposed reforms to introduce a 10 per cent VAT alongside improvements to the income tax: US Committee for Economic Development (CED), *A New Tax Framework: A Blueprint for Averting a Fiscal Crisis (A Statement by the Research and Policy Committee of the Committee for Economic Development)* (CED, Washington, DC, 2005), 2–3; US House of Representatives, Committee on Ways and Means (113th Cong., 2nd session), 'The Tax Reform Act of 2014: Fixing Our Broken Tax Code So That It Works for American Families and Job Creators – Executive Summary' (2014).

[211] The Economic Recovery Advisory Board stated that it:

> was not asked to recommend a major overarching tax reform, such as the 1986 tax reform, the tax plans proposed by the 2005 Tax Reform Panel, or proposals for introducing a value added tax in addition to or in lieu of the current income tax system. We received many suggestions for broad tax reform, and some members of the PERAB believe that such reform will be an essential component of a strategy to reduce the long-term deficit of the federal government. But consistent with our limited mandate, we did not evaluate competing proposals for overarching tax reform in this report.

The President's Economic Recovery Advisory Board, *The Report on Tax Reform Options: Simplification, Compliance, and Corporate Taxation* (2010): at v.

[212] See, e.g., US Congressional Research Service, Government and Finance Division, Molly Sherlock, *Tax Reform in the 113th Congress: An Overview of Proposals* (CRS Report R43060) (CRS, Washington, DC, 2013); Congressional Research Service, Government and Finance Division, James Bickley, *Tax Reform: An Overview of Proposals in the 112th Congress (CRS Report R41591)* (CRS, Washington, DC, 2012), 3; US National Taxpayer Advocate, 2009 *Annual Report to Congress: Volume Two – Research and Related Studies* (IRS, Department of Treasury, 2009), 42; Alan Schenk and Oliver Oldman, *Value Added Tax: A Comparative Approach* (rev. edn., Cambridge University Press, Cambridge; New York, 2007), 56–58; 'Mrs Pelosi's VAT: The Speaker Proposes a Middle-Class Tax Hike' *Wall Street Journal*, 8 October 2009 (online.wsj.com/article/SB10001424052748703298004574457512007010416.html). The

review the VAT as a potential reform option,[213] there are also many who oppose it.[214] Indeed, despite many academics and experts considering the enactment of VAT as inevitable,[215] the mere suggestion of a VAT from the administration continues to provoke a frenzied and usually hostile response, as was seen by the response to President Obama's refusal to automatically rule out VAT reform in 2010.[216]

Witte observed in 1985 that the 'historic bias to tax reduction' in the US and the resulting deficits that have ensued mean that tax reform remains permanently on the agenda.[217] This bias, and the reality of inadequate revenue to finance the US

Congressional Budget Office lists a 5 per cent VAT as a policy option for deficit reduction: United States, Congressional Budget Office, *Choices for Deficit Reduction* (CBO, Washington, DC, 2012), 19. The House Ways and Means Committee considered submissions from an expert panel on VAT reform at a hearing on consumption tax reform: US House of Representatives, Committee on Ways and Means, 112th Cong., 1st session, *Hearing on Tax Reform and Consumption-Based Tax Systems* (26 July 2011, serial 112–15). This was one of a number of hearings on fundamental tax reform. The House Ways and Means Committee final reform package, *The Tax Reform Act of 2014*, however, did not include a VAT: US House of Representatives, Committee on Ways and Means, 113th Cong., 2nd session, 'The Tax Reform Act of 2014: Fixing Our Broken Tax Code So That It Works for American Families and Job Creators – Executive Summary' (2014).

[213] The National Taxpayer Advocate reports that Treasury considered the VAT in 2002 and 2007: US National Taxpayer Advocate, 2009 *Annual Report to Congress: Volume Two – Research and Related Studies* (IRS, Department of Treasury, 2009), 41.

[214] This included the establishment of an 'Anti-Value Added Tax Caucus (Anti-VAT Caucus)' within Congress chaired by Rep Wally Herger: Committee on House Administration, *112th Congress: Congressional Member Organizations (CMO)* (23 January 2012) (cha.house.gov/sites/republicans.cha.house.gov/files/documents/cmo_cso_docs/cmo_112th_congress.pdf).

[215] Van Brederode, for example, states that:

> It is not unlikely, however, that the US government will be forced to introduce a federal consumption tax, even as soon as within 10 years, to retain the confidence of money markets that it is and will remain able to repay the national debt, which is rapidly expanding due to excessive borrowing to finance the economic stimulus plans and bailouts for failing financial institutions and industries.

Robert F. van Brederode, *Systems of General Sales Taxation: Theory, Policy and Practice* (Kluwer Law International Alphen aan den Rijn, 2009), 1.

[216] CNBC Chief Washington Correspondent John Harwood interviewed President Obama:

> JOHN HARWOOD: If reducing consumption is a good idea, could you see the potential for value-added tax in this country?
>
> PRESIDENT OBAMA: You know – I know that there's been a lot of talk around town lately about the value-added tax – that is something that has worked for some countries. It's something that would be novel – for the United States. And before, you know, I started saying, "This makes sense or that makes sense." I want to get a better picture of what our options are.

CNBC, 'Chief Washington Correspondent John Harwood Interview with President Obama', *Street Signs*, 21 April 2010 (cnbc.com/id/36666434). For an example of the response, see 'Obama: VAT May Be a Revenue Option, Spending Cuts First', *The Huffington Post* (21 June 2010) (huffingtonpost.com/2010/04/21/obama-vat-may-be-a-revenu_n_547237.html).

[217] John F. Witte, *The Politics and Development of the Federal Income Tax* (University of Wisconsin Press, Madison, 1985), xx. For earlier instances of being on the precipice of reform,

state, will ensure that large-scale reform continues to remain on the agenda. However, as the next sections explain, introducing a VAT will be extremely difficult. Even if major reform did include the introduction of a VAT, the VAT itself will most likely reflect this historic bias and other institutionalised features of US tax policy-making.

2 FUTURE PATHWAYS TO REFORM

Much discussion has focused on the question of will or should the US introduce a VAT. However, an examination of the contribution of policy analysts and tax specialists to the question of federal VAT reform demonstrates a gap in existing analyses.

The contribution from policy analysts to this issue is generally to highlight the factors that have blocked VAT reform and then to attempt to identify what factors might be required for the US to overcome these impediments and introduce a VAT.[218] For example, many believe that the 'best prospects for success' in tax reform 'may rest with a future financial crisis'.[219] As noted in Chapter 5, §3.2, a common theme in analyses of tax reform is that crises, such as war or economic depression, often produce the conditions necessary for significant tax reform.[220] The histories of tax reform in Australia and the US generally support this claim.[221] Brownlee observes of the US that:[222]

> [T]he introduction of a new tax regime has never stood alone. Every new regime has always been an integral part of a larger transformation of government that became a necessary part of the resolution of a national emergency.

see Charles E. McLure Jr, 'Value Added Tax: Has the Time Come?' in C. E. Walker and M. A. Bloomfield (eds.), *New Directions in Federal Tax Policy for the 1980s* (Ballinger Publishing Company, Cambridge, MA, 1983), 185.

218 Eccleston identified two major barriers to VAT reform in the US: (1) too few advocates in the Bush administration; and (2) a prevailing mood for tax simplification and for containing, rather than expanding, the existing tax code: Richard Eccleston, *Taxing Reforms* (Edward Elgar, Cheltenham, 2007), ch. 7, 162; Junko Kato, *Regressive Taxation and the Welfare State: Path Dependence and Policy Diffusion* (Cambridge University Press, Cambridge, 2003), ch. 3.

219 W. Elliot Brownlee, *Federal Taxation in America: A Short History* (2nd ed., Cambridge University Press, Cambridge, 2004), 242; William G. Gale and Benjamin H. Harris, 'A Value-Added Tax for the United States: Part of the Solution', *Brookings Institution and Tax Policy Center* (July 2010) (taxpolicycenter.org/publications/url.cfm?ID=1001418); Rudolph Penner, 'Do We Need a Value-Added Tax to Solve Our Long-Run Budget Problems?' *Tax Law Review* 63(2) (2010), 301; Reuven S. Avi-Yonah, 'Summary and Recommendations', *Tax Law Review* 63(2) (2010), 285, 300.

220 See, e.g., Sven Steinmo, *Taxation and Democracy: Swedish, British and American Approaches to Financing the Modern State* (Yale University Press, New Haven, CT, 1993), ch. 2; W. Elliot Brownlee, *Federal Taxation in America: A Short History* (2nd ed., Cambridge University Press, Cambridge, 2004), 2; Fred Block, 'The Ruling Class Does Not Rule', in Fred Block, *Revising State Theory: Essays in Politics and Postindustrialism* (Temple University Press, Philadelphia, 1987), 51, 65–68.

221 See Chapter 5, §4.1 of this book.

222 W. Elliot Brownlee, *Federal Taxation in America: A Short History* (2nd ed., Cambridge University Press, Cambridge, 2004), 243.

Although 9/11 and the 2008 financial crisis were crises that could have triggered reform, no significant revenue reforms, let alone VAT reforms, have followed. *TRA86* shows that crisis is not necessary for reform, but in a political world, where perception is as important as reality, the rhetoric of crisis in support of various reforms will be employed. Thus, in 1985, President Reagan invoked the revolutionary cry that 'taxation without representation is tyranny' in support of reforming a system that was 'unwise, unwanted and unfair'.[223]

In contrast to the public policy approach, the general approach of tax specialists is to focus on prescriptions for designing a US VAT.[224] Sometimes claims made as to the VAT's merits are made in relation to a good VAT, often without adequate consideration of how the factors that have prevented the VAT gaining sufficient political traction would in turn likely impact the realisation of these perceived merits. Thus, for example, Gruber claims in relation to sales taxes generally that:[225]

> A single-rate sales tax could reduce many of the inefficiencies associated with the current tax system...most of the elasticity of the tax base with respect to tax revenue arises because of "holes" in our tax system, such as the non-taxation of income paid in the form of fringe benefits. Such opportunities for tax avoidance would, in principle, disappear with a national sales tax that included expenditures such as employer-provided health insurance.

While many tax analysts are acutely aware of the constraints of the US political system,[226] few have linked a detailed consideration of the history of the US VAT reform debate (outlined in §1) with the likely impact on the design of a US VAT. Furthermore, none have done so by factoring in the broader distinction between the good VAT and real VATs drawn by this book. While both the public policy and tax design lines of inquiry are no doubt important in their own right,[227] this analysis fills

[223] Televised address to the nation on 28 May 1985, quoted in Jeffrey H. Birnbaum and Alan S. Murray, *Showdown at Gucci Gulch: Lawmakers, Lobbyists, and the Unlikely Triumph of Tax Reform* (Random House, New York, 1987), 95.

[224] See, e.g., the contributions to the special issues of the *Tax Law Review* from a 'Symposium on Designing a Federal VAT': Part I, *Tax Law Review* 63(2) (2010), 285, and Part II, (*Tax Law Review* 63(3) (2010), 517.

[225] Jonathon Gruber, *Public Finance and Public Policy* (3rd ed., Worth Publishers, New York, 2011), 755. *Contra* Reuven S. Avi-Yonah, 'Summary and Recommendations', *Tax Law Review* 63(2) (2010), 285, 299; Michael Graetz, '100 Million Unnecessary Returns: A Fresh Start for the U.S. Tax System', *Yale Law Journal* 112 (2002–2003), 261, 287.

[226] See, e.g., Reuven S. Avi-Yonah, 'Summary and Recommendations', *Tax Law Review* 63(2) (2010), 285–300; Rudolph Penner, 'Do We Need a Value-Added Tax to Solve Our Long-Run Budget Problems?' *Tax Law Review* 63(2) (2010), 301; see generally the contributions to Cathy Phillips (ed.), *The VAT Reader: What a Federal ComsumptionTax Would Mean for America* (Tax Analysts, Arlington, VA, 2011).

[227] See, e.g., Avi-Yonah's acknowledgement that a number of the reforms identified during the 'Symposium on Designing a Federal VAT' are unlikely to be adopted. However, he contends that '[n]evertheless, it is important to establish best practices in these areas as a beginning point for future legislative efforts': Reuven S. Avi-Yonah, 'Summary and Recommendations', *Tax Law Review* 63(2) (2010), 285, 299.

the gap between the standard public policy and tax specialist accounts by focusing on how some of the key factors that have blocked VAT reform might impact the design of any VAT that the US might enact.[228] It is not for this book to predict whether the US will enact a VAT or what triggers or crises, if any, might prompt VAT reform. Rather, this book contends that the identification and response to any such crisis will be shaped by the institutional context of US policy-making and that, should reform occur, the same institutionalised features that have provided a stumbling block to reform so far will be crucial in determining whether a VAT is enacted and what the shape of that VAT might be. The features are drawn from the history of US VAT reform, discussed in §1 of this chapter. Exactly how these features will likely impact the three design norms of the good VAT is considered at §3.

2.1 *Structural features of US tax policy-making*

As Chapter 4, §6 discussed, the observation is made within the conventional approach that a federal state is less likely to introduce a VAT.[229] By extension, it might be said that if a federal state is going to introduce a VAT, it is more likely to introduce a real VAT than a good VAT. This section focuses on two major institutional components that will shape a US VAT if one is ever introduced: first, the division of taxing powers between the state and federal governments; and second, the federal institutions of tax policy-making.

2.1.1 Federalism and the states

Given the extensive use of sales taxes at the state and local level, the VAT debate in the US might be seen to be less about procuring support for consumption taxation than about garnering support for a significant shift in consumption taxation to the federal level.[230] As §1 revealed, no policy-maker has viewed the fact that all but five states levy sales taxes[231] as a necessary constitutional[232] or legal impediment to

[228] For a similar attempt in relation to other consumption tax proposals, see Daniel Shaviro, 'Simplifying Assumptions: How Might the Politics of Consumption Tax Reform Affect (Impair) the End Product?' in J. W. Diamond and G. R. Zodrow (eds.), *Fundamental Tax Reform: Issues, Choices, and Implications* (MIT Press, Cambridge, MA; London,, 2008), 75.

[229] See, e.g., Michael Keen and Ben Lockwood, 'The Value Added Tax: Its Causes and Consequences', *Journal of Development Economics* 92(2) (2010), 138, 141, 143.

[230] Approximately 8 per cent of total tax revenues in the US are from general consumption taxes, and this is mostly constituted by state and local sales taxes: OECD, *Revenue Statistics: 1965–2012* (OECD Publishing, Paris, 2013), 121, 273, 314.

[231] US Federation of Tax Administrators, *State Sales Tax Rates and Food and Drug Exemptions* (1 January 2014) (taxadmin.org/fta/rate/sales.pdf).

[232] There is no express constitutional prohibition on the US federal government levying sales taxes. There is some debate as to whether a VAT might constitute a direct tax and therefore be subject to apportionment between states on the basis of population in accordance with the US Constitution (*United States Constitution*, art. I §2 cl 3 and art. I §9 cl 4). This issue depends on the incidence of VAT, as direct taxes are generally not regarded as being forward shifted.

the adoption of a federal VAT.[233] However, all acknowledge that the levying of sales taxes by state and local governments will constitute a significant political and administrative barrier to the adoption of a federal VAT.[234]

The political barrier arises from state administrators perceiving a threat to their sales tax base and mobilising to oppose a federal VAT as a states' rights issue. As one federal Treasury official put it, '[f]orty-five states and the District of Columbia impose general sales or use taxes, a revenue source which they tend to view as belonging exclusively to them'.[235] US states have far greater fiscal autonomy than Australian states.[236] In fact, states have accounted for much growth in postwar taxation in the US, with sales taxes constituting approximately half of this revenue.[237] This decentralization of revenue power is matched at the expenditure level, with states increasing spending over the reform

Consistent with the view of the VAT as a consumption tax by the conventional approach, Schenk and Oldman conclude that there is no significant argument that a VAT would constitute a direct tax: Alan Schenk and Oliver Oldman, *Value Added Tax: A Comparative Approach* (rev. edn., Cambridge University Press, Cambridge; New York, 2007), 8. See generally Erik M. Jensen, 'The Apportionment of 'Direct Taxes': Are Consumption Taxes Constitutional?' *Columbia Law Review* 97 (1997), 2334. See also Chapter 2, §4 of this book.

[233] *Treasury I*, vol. 3, ch. 3, 28; 'The 1969 Task Force First Report on VAT', above n 28, 14.

[234] See, e.g., the 1972 *Advisory Commission's* finding that the existence of state sales taxes provided no necessary 'economic' barrier to the imposition of a federal VAT, but acknowledged that the already expressed opposition by state governors to a federal sales tax would provide a significant political barrier, including to the coordination of federal and state sales taxes: US Advisory Commission on Intergovernmental Relations, *The Value-Added Tax and Alternative Sources of Federal Revenue: An Information Report* (Washington, DC, 1973), 2, 12. For acknowledgement of this fact within the conventional approach, see Michael Keen and Ruud de Mooij, '"Fiscal Devaluation" and Fiscal Consolidation: The VAT in Troubled Times', in Alberto Alesina and Francesco Giavazzi (eds.), *Fiscal Policy After the Financial Crisis* (University of Chicago Press, 2013), 443, 475.

[235] George N. Carlson, *Value-Added Tax: European Experience and Lessons for the United States* (Office of Tax Analysis, Department of Treasury; US Government Printing Office, Washington, DC, 1980), 83–84.

[236] In 2010, Australia had the sixth highest concentration of central government revenues as a portion of total tax revenue in the OECD, and the US had the sixth lowest: OECD, *Consumption Tax Trends 2012: VAT/GST and Excise Rates, Trends and Administration Issues* (OECD Publishing, Paris, 2012), 280, Table 79; Commonwealth of Australia Treasury, *Pocket Guide to the Australian Taxation System* (Treasury, Canberra, 2013), 2.

[237] State and local taxes have almost doubled over the postwar period, from 5.5 per cent of GDP in 1948 to 10.1 per cent in 2010, federal government taxes have ranged from 16.2 per cent of GDP in 1948 to a peak of 20.6 per cent in 2000 to 15.1 per cent in 2010: US Office of Budget and Management, *Budget of the United States Government, Fiscal Year 2013 – Historic Tables* (US Government Printing Office, Washington, DC, 2012), 341, Table 15.1. From 1975 to 2010, state taxes accounted for approximately 20 per cent of total taxation revenue, with taxes from goods and services constituting close to 60 per cent of total state revenues over this same period: OECD, *Revenue Statistics: 1965–2011* (OECD, Paris, 2012), 278–79, 282, 318. In the years following the 2007 economic downturn, state and local sales tax revenues declined and have since rebounded but showed some variability: Cheryl H. Lee, Robert Jesse Willhide and Nancy I. Higgins, 'State Government Finances Summary: 2010' (Governments Division Briefs No G10-ASFIN, US Census Bureau, 2011), 3; Cheryl H. Lee, Robert Jesse Willhide and Edwin Pome, 'State Government Finances Summary Report: 2012' (Governments Division Briefs No G12-CG-ASFIN, US Census Bureau, 2014), 2.

period.[238] States therefore have a key fiscal interest in resisting federal intrusion into this revenue source, which history shows they are willing to defend.

The administrative barriers arise from the challenge of integrating sub-national state and local sales taxes with a federal VAT.[239] Ainsworth, for example, claims that more than 11,000 sub-national taxes would need to be integrated with a VAT.[240] Coordinating a federal VAT is not just an impediment to reform, but a major design issue. The fact that no state has ever introduced an invoice-credit method VAT leads some to conclude that coordinating a federal VAT with state RSTs will be more difficult than coordinating a federal RST with state RSTs.[241] By contrast, Bird and Gendron contend that the Canadian experience of harmonising a federal VAT with disparate provincial sales taxes refutes the widely held view that a federal invoice-credit destination VAT is incompatible with sub-national retail sales taxes:[242]

> Canadian experience shows that the existence or non-existence of subnational retail sales taxes is, in both *technical and economic* terms, a matter of indifference when considering a federal VAT.

This may be so, but the Canadian experience also demonstrates that in *political* terms the existence of sub-national VATs is not a matter of indifference.[243] The Canadian provinces counted among the most powerful opponents to VAT reform.[244]

[238] US state and local expenditures from own sources (excluding federal grant monies) rose from 8.4 per cent of GDP in 1960 to 11.2 per cent in 2010. Federal expenditures rose from 17.8 per cent of GDP in 1960 to 23.8 per cent in 2010: US Office of Budget and Management, *Budget of the United States Government, Fiscal Year 2012 – Historic Tables* (US Government Printing Office, Washington, DC, 2011), 344–45.

[239] The defence of local sales taxes on the basis of states' rights is obviously not an issue; however, local taxes frequently piggyback on state sales taxes, and therefore changes to either may pose potentially significant coordination and administrative issues: Charles E. McLure Jr, 'How to Coordinate State and Local Sales Taxes with a Federal Value Added Tax', *Tax Law Review* 63(3) (2009–2010), 639, 646, 673–78.

[240] Randall Jackson, 'Panelists Discuss How US Could Adopt Add-On VAT', *Tax Notes* (2008), 665. As an indication of the potential problems, McLure claims that accurately identifying the number of local taxes in existence is problematic in itself: Charles E. McLure Jr, 'How to Coordinate State and Local Sales Taxes with a Federal Value Added Tax', *Tax Law Review* 63(3) (2009–2010), 639, 641.

[241] *Treasury I*, vol. 3, ch. 4, 28, 32–33.

[242] Richard M. Bird and Pierre-Pascal Gendron, 'Sales Taxes in Canada: The GST-HST-QST-RST System', *Tax Law Review* 63(3) (2009–2010), 517, 577 (emphasis added). See also Avi-Yonah, who further concludes from the contributions of Cnossen and McLure in the same volume of the *Tax Law Review* that the 'federal VAT can be adopted without regard to whether the States maintain the RST or switch to a VAT': Reuven S. Avi-Yonah, 'Summary and Recommendations', *Tax Law Review* 63(2) (2010), 285, 299. For the contrary view that the coordination difficulties might be too great, see 'Secretary Miller Testimony on the Tax Restructuring Act of 1979', above n 56, 20.

[243] See generally Charles E. McLure Jr, 'How to Coordinate State and Local Sales Taxes with a Federal Value Added Tax', *Tax Law Review* 63(3) (2009–2010), 639.

[244] See generally Neil Brooks, *The Canadian Goods and Services Tax: History, Policy, and Politics* (ATRF, Sydney, 1992). A reminder of the hostility toward the GST and the harmonisation process in Canada occurred in July 2011 when, by referendum, voters in the province of British

Some have expressed optimism at the opportunity that a federal VAT might offer to reform state sales taxes, including a chance to improve the taxation of trade crossing state borders.[245] Others see much greater potential. For example, *Treasury I* predicted that:[246]

> At present, many state taxes fall considerably short of the objective of taxing a broad range of consumption goods at a uniform rate. Exemptions for food, clothing, and services are typical. On the other side of the coin, very few states exclude all capital goods and other business purchases from taxation. A comprehensive Federal sales tax would offer the states an opportunity to 'piggyback' the state taxes on the Federal base. States would enjoy the advantage of the broadly-defined Federal base, but would be free to set their own state tax rates depending on state fiscal needs.

However, one reason why states have expressed opposition to a federal VAT is precisely because of the pressure to conform to the federal tax base.[247] The ability to control the setting of the sales tax base and rates is perceived as a valuable political commodity. In addition, the fact that most states provide exemptions or reduced rates for specific goods and services shows how difficult it is to achieve a broad sales tax base. As *Treasury I* acknowledged:[248]

> Though it may not be an inherent defect, state experience with retail sales taxes, however, demonstrates the difficulties, at least in practice, of applying the tax to all consumer expenditures and of excluding business purchases.

The ability of a federal VAT to wipe the slate clean will be made more difficult by the fact that pre-existing state concessions will increase the political pressure for any federal VAT to duplicate these concessions.[249] The proposals for VAT reform put forward over the reform period, such as those in *Treasury I* (see §1.3.1), show how the institutionalisation of approaches in state sales taxation, including concessions and exemptions, have a path-dependent influence on the design proposals for a federal VAT.

Columbia voted to extinguish the harmonised sales tax (i.e., the combined federal-provincial VAT) and to restore the old provincial RST (alongside the existing federal VAT): for further details and analysis, see the contributions to the 'Policy Forum' in *Canadian Tax Journal* 60(1) (2012), 101–22.

245 Charles E. McLure Jr, 'How to Coordinate State and Local Sales Taxes with a Federal Value Added Tax', *Tax Law Review* 63(3) (2009–2010), 639, 692–93, 702–4.

246 *Treasury I*, vol. 3, ch. 3, 28; Charles E. McLure Jr, 'How to Coordinate State and Local Sales Taxes with a Federal Value Added Tax', *Tax Law Review* 63(3) (2009–2010), 639, 654–56. See also the discussion of the 2005 *Tax Advisory Panel* at §1.4.3 of this chapter.

247 Steve Wells and Tonya Flesher, 'Lessons for Policy Makers from the History of Consumption Taxes', *Accounting Historians Journal* (1999), 103, 108.

248 *Treasury I*, vol. 3, ch. 4, 31–33.

249 Shaviro also points to an additional issue whereby reforms might lead to a push to eliminate federal income tax deductions for the payment by individuals and businesses of state and local taxes: Daniel Shaviro, 'Simplifying Assumptions: How Might the Politics of Consumption Tax Reform Affect (Impair) the End Product?' in J. W. Diamond and G. R. Zodrow (eds.), *Fundamental Tax Reform: Issues, Choices, and Implications* (MIT Press, Cambridge, MA; London, 2008), 75, 114–15.

As this history has shown, proposals for a federal VAT will most likely be framed as a consumption tax. However, some states have experimented with variations of a subtraction-method VAT as a form of business taxation.[250] This might in turn influence perceptions of the VAT as a consumption tax in the federal debate.

2.1.2 Federal institutions of tax policy-making

The labyrinthine structure of the US policy-making process, complete with numerous veto points, presents a minefield for prospective reformers, particularly in the self-interested politics of tax reform. The division between the legislative and executive arms of government marks a clear distinction from the Westminster style of the Australian state, where the Executive dominates the legislative agenda. The President cannot impose a tax bill on Congress; tax bills must originate in the House of Representatives and can be amended in the Senate.[251] However, in practice the President initiates much tax legislation, with the Department of Treasury and specifically the Assistant Secretary for Tax Policy generating many policy proposals.[252] The absence of the Executive from Congress results in weaker party discipline, and as a result members of Congress are relatively autonomous. There also exists a much more extensive issue-focused congressional committee system. In tax policy, considerable influence is exerted by the House Ways and Means Committee[253] and the Senate Finance Committee.[254] The approval of these committees is generally required before tax bills are presented to Congress, and they have extensive 'tax writing' powers.[255] However, even proposals supported by both houses of Congress can be derailed by presidential veto, which can only then be overridden by a two-thirds majority of Congress.[256] As was the case with the enactment of *TRA86*, any effort to introduce a VAT would need to have the support of key actors in these major policy-making institutions.[257]

This institutional structure of policy-making promotes issue-specific policy-making and, specifically in tax policy, provides numerous opportunities for deals

[250] See above, n 11. [251] *United States Constitution*, art. 1 §7 cl 1.

[252] See generally Michael J. Graetz and Deborah H. Schenk, *Federal Income Taxation: Principles and Policies* (6th ed., Foundation Press, New York, 2009), 57–58.

[253] The House Ways and Means Committee was first established in 1789 and is one of oldest congressional committees: Committee on Ways and Means, *Committee History* (waysandmeans.house.gov/About/History.htm).

[254] The origins of the Senate Finance Committee date back to 1816: US Senate Committee on Finance, *History of the Committee on Finance (97th Congress, 1st Session – Senate Document No. 97–5)* (6th ed., US Government Printing Office, Washington, DC, 1981), ch. 2.

[255] See further C. Eugene Steuerle, *Contemporary US Tax Policy* (2nd ed., Urban Institute Press, Washington, DC, 2008), 18–20. The Joint Committee on Taxation provides support and analysis, but lacks direct involvement in the legislative process: Michael J. Graetz and Deborah H. Schenk, *Federal Income Taxation: Principles and Policies* (6th ed., Foundation Press, New York, 2009), 58–59.

[256] *United States Constitution*, art. 1 §7.

[257] Although not labelling it as such, Shaviro uses a type of historical institutionalist analysis of plausible scenarios for consumption tax reform:

to be made, log-rolling to occur and the accretion of concessions and privileges for special interests. Alternatively, it can result in the outright stymieing of reform. The frequency of federal elections also encourages deals to be done to prevent electoral fallout from major reform.[258] This institutional structure helps explain the great number of consumption tax reform proposals, but also the failure of any one proposal to gain sufficient consensus.

TRA86 shows that major reform is not impossible and highlights the importance of bipartisan coalition-building and the need for key institutional protagonists to promote reform. However, it also demonstrates the susceptibility of major reforms to the termitic operation of the legislative system. *TRA86* took 17 months to pass through Congress and demonstrates that frequently the cost of support is erosion from a proposed ideal because support is offered in return for amendments in favour of sectional interests.[259]

It is clear from the VAT proposals put forward over the reform period that one institutionalised feature of US tax legislating that is likely to facilitate exclusions from the VAT base is the practice of leaving much of the details in the regulations.

> With relatively fixed institutions, including not only Congress and the presidency but also political parties and interest groups, the process that leads to major tax legislation tends to involve one or another of a finite set of recognizable scenarios.

Daniel Shaviro, 'Simplifying Assumptions: How Might the Politics of Consumption Tax Reform Affect (Impair) the End Product?' in J. W. Diamond and G. R. Zodrow (eds.), *Fundamental Tax Reform: Issues, Choices, and Implications* (MIT Press, Cambridge, MA; London, 2008), 75, 77, and at 78–79. On this basis, Shaviro is sceptical of the prospect of VAT reform in line with the Graetz model: at 85. Avi-Yonah refers to a potential path to VAT reform as being one where the VAT is championed by a President as the 'high road': Reuven Avi-Yonah, 'The Political Pathway: When Will the US Adopt a VAT?' in C. Phillips (ed.), *The VAT Reader: What a Federal Consumption Tax Would Mean for America* (Tax Analysts, Arlington VA, 2011), 334, 335–36. On the importance of key individuals for tax reform, see generally Cedric Sandford, *Successful Tax Reform: Lessons from an Analysis of Tax Reform in Six Countries* (Fiscal, Bath, 1993), 227–29; C. Eugene Steuerle, *Contemporary US Tax Policy* (Urban Institute Press, Washington, DC, 2004), 253; Louis Eisenstein, *The Ideologies of Taxation* (Ronald Press Co., New York, 1961), 230; W. Elliot Brownlee, *Federal Taxation in America: A Short History* (2nd ed., Cambridge University Press, Cambridge, 2004), 246; Timothy Conlan, Margaret Wrightson and David Beam, *Taxing Choices: The Politics of Tax Reform* (Congressional Quarterly Press, Washington, DC, 1990), 248.

258 Elections for the Presidency are conducted every four years, elections for the House of Representatives every two years and elections for the Senate every two years (with one-third of senators up for reelection every two years after serving a six-year term): see generally *Guide to US Elections* (6th ed., CQ Press, Washington, DC, 2010).

259 Steuerle recounts that at each stage of the political process following *Treasury I*:

> certain constituencies or policymakers were appeased by new giveaways, then estimates revealed significant revenue losses because of those giveaways, and, finally, new packages restored some revenues by scrambling to find new "reforms" that could be substituted for the ones abandoned.

C. Eugene Steuerle, *Contemporary US Tax Policy* (2nd ed., Urban Institute Press, Washington, DC, 2008), 121.

The Ullman and 1989 *ABA Model VAT* proposals adopted 'the American tradition of providing basic rules in the statute and leaving many of the details to regulations'.[260] As was demonstrated in Chapter 6, §2.4, this method of legislative enactment facilitated many of the departures from the good VAT in the Australian GST.

Some place much hope in the potential for new processes to overcome the defects of the existing system.[261] Brownlee exemplifies the approach:[262]

> For dramatic change, administrations must approach tax reform in a comprehensive fashion, articulate the goals of reform in ways which rise above the interests of particular groups, and organize the process of reform to insulate experts from political pressure.

Such cries place great faith in the impartiality and ability of experts and officials to draft reform for the public good, as well as evoking all the fiercely contested normative concepts that the term entails. However, even in the hypothetical scenario one might suppose is necessary for Brownlee's wish to hold, where an administration advised by the Treasury, convinced of the merits of the good VAT, is given free rein to design and introduce one, the very process of translating the VAT into legal language at once starts to expose the limitations of the merits-based explanations of the conventional approach. A US Treasury publication in 1980 noted:[263]

> Terms like "taxable transactions" and "taxable persons" must be defined with the precision necessary for tax purposes. Even if the objective is a broad-based consumption tax, demands for exemptions and preferential rates are inevitable.

These demands must be articulated within the existing institutional structures of policy-making and administration. Even absent these demands, the Australian case study shows the difficulty of translating economic goals (such as the taxation of end consumption) into legislative terms such as 'taxable supply' or 'taxable transaction' that are necessary to trigger liability to pay VAT. The interpretation of these terms depends upon existing private laws of contract and property, as well as the nuances of the legislative schemes, which, as was seen in Chapter 6, are themselves often shaped by pre-existing taxes. In addition, the terms are shaped by the institutionalised approaches of the administrators who apply the laws and the judges who interpret them, alongside the constitutional constraints that inform these choices.

[260] Alan Schenk, 'A Model Value Added Tax Statute for the United States', *International VAT Monitor* (September 1990), 2, 11–12.

[261] C. Eugene Steuerle, *Contemporary US Tax Policy* (2nd ed., Urban Institute Press, Washington, DC, 2008), 261–63.

[262] W. Elliot Brownlee, *Federal Taxation in America: A Short History* (2nd ed., Cambridge University Press, Cambridge, 2004), 248.

[263] George N. Carlson, *Value-Added Tax: European Experience and Lessons for the United States* (Office of Tax Analysis, Department of Treasury; US Government Printing Office, Washington, DC, 1980), 72.

Although no doubt influenced by practices elsewhere,[264] policy-makers will not be able to simply adopt 'off the shelf' reforms but must couch the reforms following the (path-dependent) rules of legislative drafting and, in particular, the drafting approaches used in existing tax legislation. Whether or not the terms are applied in a manner consistent with the end goal of taxing consumption will depend on the institutional context that structures the actions of drafters, administrators and judges. The Australian experience shows that policy learning need not necessarily result in meritorious outcomes, and that the achievement of the goal of taxing final consumption can be haphazard at best. It may be more or less haphazard in the US, but this will depend on the institutional context.

One feature of a VAT that makes it a difficult political sell is the fact that the VAT's characteristic regressivity (absent compensating reforms) immediately brings values into the debate. Policy-makers during the reform period generally acknowledged the conventional preference for addressing the VAT's regressivity through expenditure and/or adjustments to the income tax rather than by introducing erosions to the base. Avi-Yonah expresses a preference for the conventional approach to good VAT design when he concludes that, rather than introducing multiple rates or exemptions that are both complex and inefficient, it is better that '[r]egressivity should be addressed in the spending side of the budget (and progressivity should be left to the income and estate taxes)'.[265] However, if the income tax continues its shift toward a consumption base while the estate tax remains diminished or euthanized, the assumption that these taxes will continue to offer a reliable means of achieving overall progressivity in the tax system is seriously undermined. As §1.3.2 indicated, the latter point motivated the decision by the Treasury to recommend reform of the income tax rather than to introduce a consumption tax in *Treasury I*. It might therefore be of little surprise that most official proposals have preferred to adopt the more visible means by which to address the issue of regressivity by carving out exemptions to the VAT base.[266]

The likelihood of erosion to the VAT base increases when concerns over regressivity are joined by a fear of unleashing the 'money-machine' of VAT reform, which in turn will open the Pandora's box of big government. Whether specious rhetoric or genuine concern, this fear of the growth of government manifests within the structure of the US tax system itself.[267] One instance of this is the bipartisan employment of tax expenditures over spending as a means to finance the state; the

[264] See, e.g., the influence of European VAT definitions such as 'taxable transaction' in the Tax Restructuring Act of 1980, §4001.

[265] Reuven S. Avi-Yonah, 'Summary and Recommendations', *Tax Law Review* 63(2) (2010), 285, 289.

[266] This is true of Ulman's revised proposal, *Treasury I*, the 2005 *Tax Advisory Panel* and the consideration of the likely VAT base throughout the 1970s: see §1 of this chapter.

[267] As Chapter 5, §4.1 of this book explained, by OECD standards the US is a relatively low-tax and low-spending state relative to GDP. See also Peters, who contends that '[g]overnment in the United States is large, but it does not appear to be the ever-increasing Leviathan that its

US has one of the heaviest degrees of reliance on tax expenditures in the OECD.[268] This technique has the aesthetic effect of being seen to commit to lower taxes and the reduction of government rather than increasing spending and the size of the state.[269] The approach fits well within the classical liberal rhetoric of freeing individuals from the pervasive influence of government. Moreover, it offers policy-makers the opportunity to indirectly influence social and economic decisions, an opportunity frequently denied them when attempted through the more direct methods of expenditure and intervention. As a result, it is estimated that tax breaks rather than direct expenditure account for one-quarter to one-third of the benefits and subsidies granted to the public.[270]

Even if reform is the product of a bipartisan consensus among key actors,[271] measures would be required to obtain Democrat support (including measures to address regressivity) alongside measure to appease Republicans by limiting the VAT's revenue-generating capabilities.[272] Shaviro goes so far as to suggest that this requirement alone would make alternative consumption tax proposals that allow for progressive consumption taxation more likely.[273] Whether or not this is so, the important point in relation to the VAT is that it is likely to lead to intense bipartisan pressure for exemptions and special treatment on both sides, therefore increasing the likelihood that the US will enact a decidedly real VAT with many erosions to the base (see §3.1).

2.2 *Interest groups, business and lobbyists*

Interest groups and lobbying are an entrenched part of the US political process, in part as a result of a political system with institutions designed to check the

critics portray it to be': B. Guy Peters, *American Public Policy: Promise and Performance* (6th ed., CQ Press, Washington, DC, 2004), 39.

268 OECD, *OECD Economic Surveys – United States Volume 2010/15* (OECD, 2010), 25–26.

269 C. Eugene Steuerle, *Contemporary US Tax Policy* (2nd ed., Urban Institute Press, Washington, DC, 2008) 5; B. Guy Peters, *American Public Policy: Promise and Performance* (6th ed., CQ Press, Washington, DC, 2004), 42.

270 C. Eugene Steuerle, *Contemporary US Tax Policy* (2nd ed., Urban Institute Press, Washington, DC, 2008), 2. Of course, views of tax expenditures differ, and measuring the precise impact of tax expenditures is fraught with difficulty. See also Christopher Howard, *The Hidden Welfare State: Tax Expenditures and Social Policy in the United States* (Princeton University Press, Princeton, NJ, 1997).

271 Shaviro contends that the remote likelihood of this occurring means that a Republican-led partisan effort would most likely entail the reform by stealth approach discussed above at §1.4.2: Daniel Shaviro, 'Simplifying Assumptions: How Might the Politics of Consumption Tax Reform Affect (Impair) the End Product?' in J. W. Diamond and G. R. Zodrow (eds.), *Fundamental Tax Reform: Issues, Choices, and Implications* (MIT Press, Cambridge, MA; London, 2008), 75, 83–85.

272 For a similar observation, see Martin A. Sullivan, 'Was the VAT a Money Machine for Europe?', *Tax Notes* (2012), 143, 145.

273 Daniel Shaviro, 'Simplifying Assumptions: How Might the Politics of Consumption Tax Reform Affect (Impair) the End Product?' in J. W. Diamond and G. R. Zodrow (eds.), *Fundamental Tax Reform: Issues, Choices, and Implications* (MIT Press, Cambridge, MA; London, 2008), 75, 78.

concentration of power at many turns.[274] It is not simply the structure of federal policy-making institutions, discussed at §2.1, but also the institutionalisation of interest-group influence in US politics that will likely influence VAT reform. For example, political action committees (PAC's), which raise funds for candidates and are formed by groups with varying interests, exert considerable influence over individual candidates, including those on the powerful congressional tax committees. The number of PACs has risen from 608 in 1974 to 5680 in 2014.[275] PACS are just one of a number of institutionalised avenues available for lobbyists to pursue their cause – including promoting or opposing a VAT or lobbying for favourable treatment under a VAT. This section therefore considers what groups might influence the VAT reform process.[276]

Commentators on US tax reform identify 'cycles of reform' whereby 'comprehensive changes' are 'followed by the accretion of numerous special benefits and then another comprehensive reform'.[277] This argument is confirmed by the great number of amendments since the enactment of *TRA86*. Eugene Steurele captures the lament:[278]

> Bills today are introduced, and often enacted, through a process of almost random reactions to pressures from interest groups and lobbyists. . .The problem, of course, is that the modern tax policy process gives lobbyists so much heed that disinterested parties. . .often cannot be heard amidst the din created.

The process can go both ways, however. Campbell cites the Reagan administration's efforts to actively encourage business groups to lobby Congress to pass the 1981 tax cuts as an example of actively encouraging a feedback loop to support government policy and reinforce the power of privileged interests.[279]

[274] Sandford claims that the 'United States is pre-eminent in the strength and influence of the lobbies': Cedric Sandford, *Why Tax Systems Differ: A Comparative Study of the Political Economy of Taxation* (Fiscal Publications, Bath, 2000), 182. See also Jeffrey H. Birnbaum and Alan S. Murray, *Showdown at Gucci Gulch: Lawmakers, Lobbyists, and the Unlikely Triumph of Tax Reform* (Random House, New York, 1987).

[275] US Federal Election Commission, 'PAC Count – 1974 to present' (January 2014) (fec.gov/press/summaries/2011/2011paccount.shtml); Michael J. Graetz and Deborah H. Schenk, *Federal Income Taxation: Principles and Policies* (6th ed., Foundation Press, New York, 2009), 60–61; Cedric Sandford, *Why Tax Systems Differ: A Comparative Study of the Political Economy of Taxation* (Fiscal Publications, Bath, 2000), 182–83.

[276] See also Daniel Shaviro, 'Simplifying Assumptions: How Might the Politics of Consumption Tax Reform Affect (Impair) the End Product?' in J. W. Diamond and G. R. Zodrow (eds.), *Fundamental Tax Reform: Issues, Choices, and Implications* (MIT Press, Cambridge, MA; London, 2008), 75, 77.

[277] B. Guy Peters, *The Politics of Taxation: A Comparative Perspective* (Blackwell, Cambridge, MA, 1991), 298.

[278] C. Eugene Steuerle, *Contemporary US Tax Policy* (2nd ed., Urban Institute Press, Washington, DC, 2008), 258–59.

[279] John L. Campbell, 'The State and Fiscal Sociology', *Annual Review of Sociology* 19 (1993), 163, 175.

The history of VAT reform in the US shows that, unlike what occurred in Australia, no group has consistently and actively promoted VAT reform. By contrast, groups opposing VAT reform range from those concerned with social welfare to those concerned with the growth of government. It is clear that the merits of a VAT to business are not as widely felt as they were in Australia, despite the efforts of some, such as the multinational accountancy firms, to promote these merits.[280] Instead, business and conservative lobbyists remain hopelessly divided on their preferred vehicle for consumption tax reform – promoting everything from flat taxes, X-taxes,[281] USA taxes, retail sales taxes such as the Fair Tax, as well as invoice-credit method VATs.[282] As indicated in the previous section, the institutional features of US policy-making help explain both why there have been so many consumption tax reform proposals and why, as the next section explains, none bar the reform by stealth method get legislated. Moreover, in light of the reform by stealth process, some powerful groups can afford to remain publicly divided on overt consumption tax reform proposals.

2.3 *The VAT as one of many competing proposals and the path-dependent framing of merits*

As a result of the frenetic policy environment outlined in the previous sections, the VAT has been one of a number of consumption tax proposals put forward during the reform period. Although a number of VAT bills have been introduced in

[280] See, e.g., Harley Duncan and Jon Sedon's account of the KPMG LLP's Washington Office (in which the former is Managing Director and the latter is a manager) conducting an:

> initiative to inform the debate over a VAT as a tax reform option in the United States. The project comprises webcasts, publications, speaking engagements, and university instruction, all designed to inform professionals, academics, and policymakers about VAT issues.

Harley Duncan and Jon Sedon, 'Coordinating a Federal VAT with State and Local Sales Taxes', in C. Phillips (ed.), *The VAT Reader: What a Federal Consumption Tax Would Mean for America* (Tax Analysts, Arlington, VA, 2011), 139. Further to these informative and promotional ends, see KPMG, *Views on VAT: An Article Series* (KPMG, Washington, DC, 2011). See Chapter 4, §5.2 of this book for the strategic interest of multinational accounting firms in promoting VAT reform. See also the efforts of one entrepreneur with Vatinfo.org (2014).

[281] The X-tax was developed by David Bradford and is a variation of a Hall-Rabushka two-tier consumption tax model but which, in essence, consists of a progressive wage tax and a cash-flow or VAT-type tax levied on business: David A. Weisbach, 'Does the X-Tax Mark the Spot?' *SMU Law Review* 56(1) (2003), 201; David F. Bradford, 'The X Tax in the World Economy' (CEPS Working Paper No. 93, Center for Economic Policy Studies [Princeton], 2003), 3–5. The influence of the X-tax can be seen in the Growth and Investment Tax Plan proposals of the 2005 *Tax Advisory Panel* outlined at §1.4.3 of this chapter.

[282] See §1.4 of this chapter. See also W. Elliot Brownlee, *Federal Taxation in America: A Short History* (2nd ed., Cambridge University Press, Cambridge, 2004), 228. Wells and Flesher note that '[c]uriously, business and labor groups have not shown a consistent or uniform position toward sales taxes': Steve Wells and Tonya Flesher, 'Lessons for Policy Makers from the History of Consumption Taxes', *Accounting Historians Journal* (1999), 103, 113.

Congress during the reform period, the proposals have generally failed to garner much attention during congressional hearings, let alone invite the type of serious committee deliberations necessary to progress the bills into law. This history has focused primarily on those proposals considered by Congress or the administration, but there have been many more consumption tax proposals put forward by academics and various non-government actors.[283] Given the number of proposals, the recent history of US VAT reform is but a part of a number of proposals geared toward moving the federal US revenue base toward consumption.[284]

In another sign of how the merits of any new policy depend on the failings of what the policy proposes to replace, all these proposals are united by the expression of a gross dissatisfaction with the income tax. Frequently, ideal consumption tax proposals are compared against the actual income tax, and when the latter bears the scars of real-world implementation, the former always comes up trumps. However, official consideration of a VAT has repeatedly acknowledged that the VAT may be no less susceptible to departures from a broad base. Indeed, as was seen in the proposals in *Treasury I* for the special treatment of not-for-profits, charities and religious organisations, the institutionalisation of special treatment in pre-existing taxes like the income tax increases the pressure to replicate them in a VAT. In his testimony before the House Ways and Means Committee on the Ullman VAT, then Treasury Secretary Miller stated that:[285]

> Our current income tax does not apply with full force to all types of saving and investment. For example, home ownership, pensions reserves, and assets eligible for the investment tax credit or the asset depreciation range receive relatively favourable tax treatment. Similarly not all forms of consumption will be taxed the same under any likely value added tax.

This assessment of the VAT's vulnerability has also been informed by the real-world experience of VAT implementation elsewhere.[286] Ultimately, this may work to the disadvantage of the VAT in light of other competing and untried consumption tax proposals, on which there is no direct empirical basis to assess the validity of the claims made of them.

[283] See, e.g., McAffrey's progressive consumption tax proposal: Edward J. McCaffery, *Fair Not Flat: How to Make the Tax System Better and Simpler* (University of Chicago Press, Chicago, 2002); Michael Graetz, *100 Million Unnecessary Returns, A Simple, Fair and Competitive Plan for the United States* (Yale University Press, New Haven, CT, 2008).

[284] See generally Alan Schenk, 'The Plethora of Consumption Tax Proposals: Putting the Value Added Tax, Flat Tax, Retail Sales Tax, and USA Tax into Perspective', *San Diego Law Review* 33(1996), 1281.

[285] Secretary Miller Testimony on the Tax Restructuring Act of 1979, above n 56, 6.

[286] US Advisory Commission on Intergovernmental Relations, *The Value-Added Tax and Alternative Sources of Federal Revenue: An Information Report* (Washington, DC, 1973), 9, 34; *Treasury I*, vol. 3, ch. 2, 11; Jonathon Gruber, *Public Finance and Public Policy* (3rd ed., Worth Publishers, New York, 2011), 761.

In this environment, the merits of a VAT over other reform options are not necessarily apparent, and appeals to the merits of the VAT are not necessarily heard over the din of other competing proposals. In an observation that might come as a surprise to the conventional approach, Graetz contends that alternative consumption tax proposals, such as the flat tax and USA tax, disguise themselves as more politically palatable by 'donning dark glasses and a false moustache' so as to look like the income tax.[287] Brederode makes a similar observation of VAT proposals:[288]

> Interestingly, notwithstanding the dominance of the credit invoice method VAT, all [*sic*] proposals for a federal VAT in the United States are for a subtraction VAT, probably because it offers a closer resemblance to the income tax it is supposed to replace.

This might seem remarkable, given that the proposals seek to displace the very thing they appear to replicate. Hall and Rabushka, the inventors of the flat tax, contend that there may be many 'economically equivalent ways to impose consumption taxes', as Graetz explains:[289]

> Despite their economic similarities, however, all methods are not *politically* equivalent. Politicians want to avoid a sales or value-added tax look as well as any separate statement to consumers of the amount of taxes included in the price of the goods and services they buy. Achieving close association with the income tax apparently is also desirable politically, notwithstanding the decline in the public's support for the income tax. Politicians must believe that both of these features – looking more like an income tax than a sales tax and invisibility to consumers – provide them political cover. They may think a good disguise and a clever label allows them to deny that any federal consumption tax is being suggested.

The reform by stealth approach is the ultimate dark glasses and false moustache, and is therefore the most successful of these acts of subterfuge because it does not even announce itself and, as was detailed at §1.4.2, has occurred at the behest of select groups. Reform by stealth is further facilitated by deliberately obstructive legislative techniques such as 'phase-out' provisions.[290] This obfuscation makes achieving big-bang reform like the introduction of a VAT difficult because, without

[287] Michael J. Graetz, *The Decline (and Fall?) of the Income Tax* (W. W. Norton & Company, New York, 1997), 216. See also Alan Schenk, 'The Plethora of Consumption Tax Proposals: Putting the Value Added Tax, Flat Tax, Retail Sales Tax, and USA Tax into Perspective' *University of Sandiego Law Review* 33 (1996), 1281, 1286.

[288] The quote more accurately should read 'most', given that invoice-credit VATs have been put before Congress: Robert F. van Brederode, *Systems of General Sales Taxation: Theory, Policy and Practice* (Kluwer Law International Alphen aan den Rijn, 2009), 3. See also George R. Zodrow, 'The Sales Tax, the VAT, and Taxes in Between – Or, Is the Only Good NRST a "VAT in Drag"?' *National Tax Journal* 52(3) (1999), 429.

[289] Michael J. Graetz, *The Decline (and Fall?) of the Income Tax* (W. W. Norton & Company, New York, 1997), 216 (original emphasis). Hall and Rabushka quoted in Graetz at 216.

[290] For an explanation of phase-out provisions, see above, n 157.

a reliable base from which to measure the current tax system, it is hard to provide a package that allows for the clear identification of the losses and gains of any proposed reform.

2.4 *Disputes about the merits of the VAT and the path-dependent assessment of merits*

The conventional approach relies on the appeal of the VAT's merits to explain its rise. However, it is clear from the US history that this appeal is not universal. Whereas Australian Treasury officials counted among the most consistent supporters of VAT reform in Australia, the same degree of enthusiasm has not been present in official consideration of the VAT in the US.

Although mostly accepting of the general merits of consumption taxation and, to a lesser extent, the merits intrinsic to the good VAT, such as its neutrality,[291] officials expressed deep scepticism that these merits were ever likely to be realised in the institutional context of US policy-making.[292] US officials have also remained sceptical of the wider benefits claimed of the good VAT, such as its ability to improve broader macro-economic outcomes such as increasing rates of savings, investment and growth,[293] and improving the balance of trade.[294] As Chapters 2 and

[291] See, e.g., *Treasury I*:

> A properly designed consumption-type value-added tax would be neutral with respect to consumption decisions and production methods. If the tax applies to most goods and services at a single rate, with only minimal exceptions for clear and justifiable social or administrative reasons, it would constitute a uniform percentage of consumer expenditure. Consumers would not be given an incentive to consume more of some goods and less of others.

Treasury I, vol. 3, ch. 4, 31. See also US Advisory Commission on Intergovernmental Relations, *The Value-Added Tax and Alternative Sources of Federal revenue: An Information Report* (Washington, DC, 1973), 8.

[292] US Advisory Commission on Intergovernmental Relations, *The Value-Added Tax and Alternative Sources of Federal Revenue: An Information Report* (Washington, DC, 1973), 9, 34. See §1.2.1 of this chapter.

[293] See above, n 84. Alan Schenk, 'Recent Activity in the United States Involving the Value Added Tax' *International VAT Monitor* (1992), 2, 7–8; See also this assessment by Treasury in 1969:

> While arguing from historical precedents often turns out to be a useless form of forecasting, one is entitled to raise the question as to whether there are not very basic factors in the American economy that are determinative of the relationship of consumption and investment which are so strong that tax changes, much more drastic than that being analysed here, have not been able to alter them.

'Treasury Paper for the 1969–1970 Expert Panel 10 Sep 1969', above n 26, 16.

[294] *Treasury I, vol.* 3, ch. 3, 22; 'The 1969 Task Force First Report on VAT', above n 28, 15–16, 17; Secretary Miller Testimony on the Tax Restructuring Act of 1979, above n 56, discussed at §1.2; George N Carlson, *Value-Added Tax: European Experience and Lessons for the United States* (Office of Tax Analysis, Department of Treasury; US Government Printing Office, Washington, DC, 1980), 79–80.

3 indicated, this book is prepared, for the purposes of argument, to concede the merits claimed of the good VAT by the conventional approach. But, should one wish to explore the most potent challenge to these claims, one could do far worse than consider the assessments of the VAT made by US officials. It is perhaps ironic that the similarly unproven suggestion that a VAT might lead to a growth in government has been sufficient to deter nearly all policy-makers, despite the absence of evidence for the claim.[295]

As Chapter 4 discussed, both the strong and the weak articulation of the merits argument under the conventional approach suggest that one factor that contributes to the rise of the VAT is its neutrality toward trade. However, the intuitive appeal of the VAT as a one-size-fits-all solution has not been so strongly apparent to US policy-makers. The US is the world's largest trading nation, with a large domestic economy where imports consistently exceed exports.[296] Although it is not the intention of this book to analyse the ongoing debate about the likely economic impact of a VAT in the US,[297] it is useful to note some trends from the history of US VAT reform that reveal how the structure of the US economy has shaped the political debate on VAT.

Beyond expressing scepticism that the introduction of the VAT would result in a trade advantage for the US, policy-makers have responded that, even if this was the case, the perceived trading advantages in adopting a VAT would come at too great a cost, given the relative significance of exports vis-à-vis domestic consumption. For example, the 1969 *Task Force* on Business Taxation commented that:[298]

> In considering a value-added tax as a measure to deal even in part with the export-import, balance of payments problems, sight must not be lost of the relative size of exports and imports and our domestic economy. Exports and imports are each running currently in the neighbourhood of 40 billion dollars, whereas the value-added tax would be imposed on 350 to 500 billion dollars of base. The Task Force is of the view that the benefits to be derived in the international field are too problematical to justify the introduction of a value-added tax into our domestic economy.

Others express the view that a VAT might dampen domestic consumption. For example, John Harwood, interviewing President Obama in 2010 about the appeal of VAT reform, asked, 'if reducing consumption is a good idea, could you see the

[295] *Treasury I, vol.* 4, ch. 3, 23.

[296] US Exports as a share of GDP have constituted around 10 per cent over the reform period. This is compared to about 20 per cent for Australia: World Bank, *Exports of Goods and Services (% of GDP)* (2012) (data.worldbank.org/indicator/NE.EXP.GNFS.ZS).

[297] See, e.g., Alan Schenk, 'Recent Activity in the United States Involving the Value Added Tax' *International VAT Monitor* (1992), 2, 5–7.

[298] 'The 1969 Task Force First Report on VAT', above n 28, 17. See also Lindholm who contended in 1976 that inertia on VAT reform was due in part to the fact that exports were only about 10 per cent of GNP of US: Richard W. Lindholm, *Value-Added Tax and Other Tax Reforms* (Nelson-Hall, Chicago, 1976), 47.

potential for value-added tax in this country?'[299] Whether or not the perception about dampening domestic consumption is valid, the size of US domestic consumption relative to exports has influenced perceptions of the costs and benefits of VAT reform.

Unlike developing nations, as the world's most powerful trading nation, the US is less likely to be dictated to by the international organisations promoting VAT reform. For Australia, a nation with a small domestic economy that is heavily dependent on exports, the case for the merits of the VAT was compelling for policy-makers, especially given the presence of the WST. Moreover, as a relatively small, trade-exposed economy, Australia is concerned to promote its economic reputation. Validation by benchmarking organisations such as the OECD is one component of this.[300] Unlike lesser trading powers such as Australia, the US is less concerned to seek validation from benchmarking organisations. However, this does not give the US carte blanche to do as it pleases; for example, policy-makers have consistently expressed concern about GATT/WTO rules that allow for the refund of indirect but not direct taxes, but they have not disregarded those rules. However, the fact that policy-makers perceive the renegotiation of these rules as a viable alternative option to VAT reform, even though this has not eventuated, is indicative of the relative imperviousness of US policy-makers to seemingly inevitable global policy trends.[301]

It is not self-evident how this imperviousness to international trends might flow through to the design of a real VAT. US policy-makers have been clearly influenced by good VAT prescriptions and had close involvement with European officials over the reform period.[302] Moreover, US experts have been at the forefront of designing VATs overseas. Nevertheless, policy-makers from Ullman to *Treasury I* have departed from the prescriptions of the good VAT when translating the VAT into a prospective legislative form.[303]

The doubts expressed over the VAT's merits have been influenced by the existing tax system or, in other words, assessments of the VAT's merits have rarely taken place without consideration of existing taxes the VAT might replace. US officials have been at pains to point out that the special position of Europe does not apply to the US – not simply the absence of a need to pursue a common market, but the

[299] CNBC, 'Chief Washington Correspondent John Harwood Interview with President Obama', *Street Signs*, 21 April 2010 (cnbc.com/id/36666434).

[300] These organisations have consistently recommended VAT reform for the US: OECD, *OECD Economic Surveys – United States Volume 2010/15* (OECD, 2010) 26–27; see also IMF, above n 3 and n 4.

[301] See §1.2.1 of this chapter.

[302] Treasury documents show close engagement with European officials over the European VAT reforms and the likely shape of a US VAT: see, e.g., George N. Carlson, *Value-Added Tax: European Experience and Lessons for the United States* (Office of Tax Analysis, Department of Treasury; US Government Printing Office, Washington, DC, 1980) and §1 of this chapter.

[303] See, e.g., the departure in *Treasury I* from setting compulsory VAT registration thresholds: see §1.3.1.

need to replace comparable existing taxes widely perceived as being flawed, such as the turnover tax.[304] The 1972 *Advisory Commission* quoted with approval Professor Harris' observation that the 'U.S. government does not utilize a general turnover tax and, therefore, does not have the chief reason for the adoption of value-added taxation elsewhere...'[305] As Chapter 6 explained, many of the claims made in support of VAT reform in Australia stemmed from arguments about how deficient the existing WST was. However, in the US, comparisons of the VAT have been made against various taxes, including the income tax (particularly the corporate income tax), property taxes, payroll taxes and social security taxes. The VAT's merits vary depending on the comparator used. As *Treasury I* observed:[306]

> Some of this discussion necessarily involves comparing a value added tax with other taxes, such as the personal and corporate income taxes and the social security or payroll tax. This is because revenue generated by a value-added tax could also be raised by one of these other levies, or could permit these other taxes to be reduced.

The choice of comparator impacts the perception of the VAT's merits. For example, when measured against the income tax, the VAT is more strongly rated for its neutrality and simplicity. However, the VAT is viewed as particularly regressive when assessed as a possible replacement for the corporate income tax. By contrast, the VAT is assessed as being largely distributionally neutral when compared against social security taxes.[307]

Whereas there was never any serious doubt expressed over the status of the VAT as a consumption tax in countries with existing sales taxes in place, such as Australia and across the EU, doubt over incidence has in the past been expressed in the context of the reform debate in the US. This is in part a result of the academic debate over whether the VAT is forward shifted (see Chapter 2, §4),

[304] See, e.g., US Advisory Commission on Intergovernmental Relations, *The Value-Added Tax and Alternative Sources of Federal Revenue: An Information Report* (Washington, DC, 1973), 5; *Treasury I*, vol. 3, ch. 3, 28.

[305] US Advisory Commission on Intergovernmental Relations, *The Value-Added Tax and Alternative Sources of Federal revenue: An Information Report* (Washington, DC, 1973), 5.

[306] *Treasury I*, vol. 3, ch. 3, 17.

[307] On the 1979 Ullman VAT, Secretary Miller testified:

> While a value-added tax, by itself, is regressive, one must consider which tax it replaces. The corporate income tax probably is progressive since it falls on income from capital. Therefore, substituting a value added tax for the corporate income tax would make the tax structure less progressive. The social security tax, on the other hand, also is regressive because it is limited to the first $22,900 of wages and applies only to labor income. Accordingly, substituting a value added tax for the social security tax would not make the tax system noticeably less progressive. One regressive tax would be substituted for another.

'Secretary Miller Testimony on the Tax Restructuring Act of 1979', above n 56, 12–14. See also George N. Carlson, *Value-Added Tax: European Experience and Lessons for the United States* (Office of Tax Analysis, Department of Treasury; US Government Printing Office, Washington, DC, 1980), 80.

but, as this history has shown, official consideration over the reform period seems to have become more accepting of the incidence of the VAT being shifted forward to consumers. Doubts over incidence are more a product of uncertainty as to the tax the VAT is likely to replace. Thus, in assessing the likely impact of a VAT on prices, *Treasury I* explained that:[308]

> Economists continue to differ on the shifting pattern of the corporate income tax. Some contend that it is treated like a business cost and reflected in higher product prices. Others argue that it reduces the after-tax return to capital. If the former observation is more accurate, the impact of reducing the corporate income tax would offset the price-increasing effect of the value-added tax. If the payroll tax (at least the employer portion) is reflected as a cost element in output prices, any reduction in this tax would also offset the price-increasing influence of the value-added tax.

The existing tax structure further shaped perceptions of merits in that the lack of federal experience with a sales tax, especially one levied at each point of turnover, was itself regarded as a reason to caution against VAT reform.[309] Australian consumption tax reformers were able to take advantage of the WST by arguing that the GST was replacing an antiquated and unfair federal consumption tax with a more efficient and fair one. Their agenda was never wholesale substitution. In contrast, American reformers, left without a federal consumption tax foil, instead shift focus mostly to the pre-existing income tax and deem it so hopelessly beyond redemption that it needs euthanizing. This constitutes a much more radical shift than simply replacing one bad sales tax with a better one. Even less radical reform proposals, such as the President's Panel's hybrid VAT, face the political challenge of trying to introduce an entirely new tax instrument at the federal level. These proposals, far more ambitious in design than the Australian VAT reforms, must be achieved in a far more fragmented and contested institutional framework.

However, it is also clear that design choices made in relation to possible VATs have been influenced by the institutionalisation of design choices in other taxes. As §1 explained, the favourable treatment under the income tax that is extended to bodies such as private schools, religious and non-profit organisations has been replicated in VAT reform proposals. Adding momentum to these departures from a broad consumption base were the common institutional exemptions in state sales taxes.[310]

This section has highlighted how the factors that have prevented VAT reform will also influence any future paths to VAT reform. The next section examines in

[308] *Treasury I*, vol. 3, ch. 3, 21. §1 of this chapter also highlighted how the uncertainty of US officials in relation to the true incidence of predecessor taxes that a VAT might replace contributed to their scepticism over whether a VAT would improve the US balance of trade.

[309] *Treasury I*, vol. 3, ch. 3, 28.

[310] See, e.g., US Advisory Commission on Intergovernmental Relations, *The Value-Added Tax and Alternative Sources of Federal Revenue: An Information Report* (Washington, DC, 1973), 38.

greater detail how these pathways to reform will influence the shape of any VAT should it become a reality.

3 HOW A POTENTIAL US VAT MIGHT MEASURE UP AGAINST THE THREE NORMS OF GOOD VAT DESIGN

This section considers how, in the event that a VAT is enacted in the US, it is likely to measure up against the three norms of good VAT design; that is, a single-rate VAT on a broad consumption base (norm 1), levied through the invoice-credit method (norm 2) on a destination basis (norm 3).

Australian policy-makers embraced all three norms of good VAT design, but fell short on the realisation – particularly in relation to norm 1. By contrast, it is not necessarily clear that US policy-makers would even embrace all three design norms. Given the preponderance of subtraction-based consumption tax proposals in the US, it is not necessarily guaranteed that a US VAT would be levied through the invoice-credit method.[311] Nor is it necessarily certain that a VAT would be levied on a destination basis, as a number of competing tax proposals adopt features of an origin-based consumption tax.[312] As §2.3 demonstrated, this is in large part because of the path-dependent efforts of US consumption tax reformers to don the 'dark glasses and false moustache' of the income tax to increase the familiarity and appeal of the relevant consumption tax proposal put forward. Even assuming compliance with these two norms, however, it is likely that deviations from the first norm, of levying the VAT on a broad consumption base at a single rate, will be significant. The remainder of this section therefore focuses on the likely departures from the first norm of good VAT design.

The institutional structure of policy-making provides insights into what might be the likely fate of a VAT proposal that survives the legislative process. These institutions will presumably be as effective at generating pressure for special treatment in relation to a VAT that survives the legislative process as they are in relation to the income tax. As Witte observed, consumption taxes like the value-added tax:[313]

[311] See §2.3 of this chapter.

[312] Bradford's X-tax, referred to above, n 281, is able to be levied on an origin or destination basis. Although Bradford views the two bases as being equivalent, his preference appears to have been for an origin-based tax: David F. Bradford, 'The X Tax in the World Economy' (CEPS Working Paper No. 93, Center for Economic Policy Studies [Princeton], 2003), 6–17, 50. The Hall-Rabushka flat tax is an origin-based tax: Alan Schenk and Oliver Oldman, *Value Added Tax: A Comparative Approach* (rev. edn., Cambridge University Press, Cambridge; New York, 2007), 35. While most US states employ destination-based sales taxes, a number of states and localities levy sales taxes on an origin basis: Charles E. McLure Jr, 'How to Coordinate State and Local Sales Taxes with a Federal Value Added Tax' *Tax Law Review* 63(3) (2009–2010), 639, 696.

[313] John F. Witte, *The Politics and Development of the Federal Income Tax* (University of Wisconsin Press, Madison, 1985), 378–79. See also Daniel Shaviro, 'Simplifying Assumptions: How Might the Politics of Consumption Tax Reform Affect (Impair) the End Product?' in

> would undoubtedly not remain simple, but rather products and services would be differentiated for all the reasons income tax provisions expanded and became more complex. Once this differentiation began, intense interest group pressures similar to those that earlier affected tariff and excise legislation would arise. In short, a complex maze of tax devices would be born, with a matching amount of political and administrative time devoted to their maintenance and change.

The practice of building in exclusions to the VAT base at the design stage, as was done in *Treasury I*, and the fate of VATs introduced into Congress, such as the Ullman and Hollings proposals, suggest that Witte's observation is likely to be borne out.

3.1 *Key sources of departures from a broad consumption base norm*

During the reform period of 1960–2010, official estimates of a likely VAT base ranged from approximately 40 to 78 per cent of total consumption expenditure.[314] The upper range of the estimates reflected VATs with only 'principled' exclusions, not the likely exclusions factored into most proposals.[315] Schenk, the reporter for the 1989 *ABA Model VAT* proposals, noted the dilemmas of drafting VAT proposals:[316]

> The Ullman bill introduced in 1980 and the Hollings bill introduced in 1989 were not subjected to Congressional debate, yet they proposed a VAT with a narrower base than the Model Statute. The question is thus whether Congress is more likely to enact a broad-based neutral tax if it begins its deliberations on a US VAT with a proposal such as the Model Statute that has not been subject to the political process rather than proposals like the Ullman-Hollings bills that already include some political compromises.

The quote demonstrates that even during the initial stages of VAT development, design choices are influenced by the anticipated behaviour of key political actors based on an analysis of the likely institutional constraints of reform.

Given that most VATs proposed over the reform period contained built-in exemptions in anticipation of the likely legislative process, even the 40 per cent estimate of these proposals might seem optimistic, given that none progressed seriously through

J. W. Diamond and G. R. Zodrow (eds.), *Fundamental Tax Reform: Issues, Choices, and Implications* (MIT Press, Cambridge, MA; London, 2008), 75, 87–92; US Advisory Commission on Intergovernmental Relations, *The Value-Added Tax and Alternative Sources of Federal Revenue: An Information Report* (Washington, DC, 1973), 9, 34; *Treasury I*, vol. 3, ch. 2, 11; Alan Auerbach and Joel Slemrod, 'The Economic Effects of the Tax Reform Act of 1986', *Journal of Economic Literature* 35 (1997), 589, 628; Steve Wells and Tonya Flesher, 'Lessons for Policy Makers from the History of Consumption Taxes', *Accounting Historians Journal* (1999), 103, 113.

314 *Treasury I*, vol. 3, ch. 3, 18. See §1 of this chapter.

315 Ibid., ch. 2, 16.

316 Alan Schenk, 'A Model Value Added Tax Statute for the United States', *International VAT Monitor* (September 1990), 2, 12.

the legislative process. For example, Ullman's second attempt to introduce a VAT contained many more exclusions from the base than the first effort.[317] These likely exclusions are the product of a legislative process that requires deals to be done with a number of actors with the power to make or break reform efforts.

This history has shown the path-dependent pull of existing taxes at both the federal and state level in shaping the likely VAT base. Policy-makers have acknowledged that taxing supplies given preferential treatment under the income tax will be difficult under a VAT, hence the proposed exclusion of the family home[318] and of religious organisations and private education providers. One could do much worse than to look at state sales tax exemptions to calculate a likely VAT base – both for the reflection they offer on the political deals struck in relation to these taxes but also because imposing new federal taxes on things already exempt from state sales tax is likely to be much more difficult because of the likely pushback from taxpayers who enjoy existing preferences under state sales tax regimes. As §2.1.2 highlighted, concerns over regressivity will most likely be addressed through exclusions to the VAT base, given the need to counter Leviathan paranoia.

The manner of introducing exclusions to the VAT base is likely to be a mix of zero-rating, exemption or exempting supplies by certain providers but allowing credit for the inputs used in their supplies – a unique approach suggested by a number of proposals, including the Ullman and *Treasury I* proposal, and informed by the practice of state sales taxes (§1.3.1). Based on the proposed VATs examined in this history, likely exclusions to the VAT base will consist of food; healthcare; the sale and leasing of residential housing (except perhaps an initial sale of a new home); the activities of religious and charitable organisations; public and private education; state and local government services; agricultural supplies; public transport; and financial supplies.[319] To this might be added the exclusions likely to be won by lobbyists for powerful industry sectors, such as the oil and gas industry which, like the mining industry in Australia, already benefit from many favourable taxation provisions and wield significant political power.[320]

The Australian history showed that it is the treatment of a nation's most powerful economic sectors that can determine the success and shape of VAT

[317] See §1.2 of this chapter.

[318] The US applies one of the most generous income tax treatments to the family home by allowing for the deductibility of interest paid on a home mortgage from other income: IRC §163(h) (2006).

[319] See also Reuven S. Avi-Yonah, 'Summary and Recommendations', *Tax Law Review* 63(2) (2010), 285, 299; Daniel Shaviro, 'Simplifying Assumptions: How Might the Politics of Consumption Tax Reform Affect (Impair) the End Product?' in J. W. Diamond and G. R. Zodrow (eds.), *Fundamental Tax Reform: Issues, Choices, and Implications* (MIT Press, Cambridge, MA; London, 2008), 75, 87–92.

[320] Daniel Shaviro, 'Simplifying Assumptions: How Might the Politics of Consumption Tax Reform Affect (Impair) the End Product?' in J. W. Diamond and G. R. Zodrow (eds.), *Fundamental Tax Reform: Issues, Choices, and Implications* (MIT Press, Cambridge, MA; London, 2008), 75, 91–92.

reform. In 2010, the top four industry sectors in the US, when measured as a percentage of value added to GDP, were real estate (12.7 per cent); professional and business services (including legal and IT services: 12.1 per cent); manufacturing (11.7 per cent – although the contribution of this sector is on a steady decline from 25.3 per cent in 1960); and the finance and insurance sector (8.4 percent, up from 3.7 per cent in 1960).[321] As Chapter 2 explained, the treatment of two of these sectors, real property and financial services, is a frontier issue that is problematic for a good VAT. In response, as Chapter 3 explained, real VATs often exempt transactions within these sectors, meaning that businesses providing these services cannot claim credit for VAT paid on their inputs. This in turn would impact the second largest industry sector – the professional and business services sector that commonly provides services to these sectors. The problematic application of the VAT to three out of four major US industries would both impact the likely realisation of a VAT (because if major industries do not perceive an advantage in reform, they are unlikely to back it and indeed will be more likely to actively oppose it) and the shape of the VAT, should reforms occur. Should a VAT be enacted, it is likely that extensive pressure will be brought to bear by lobbyists for these sectors. The Australian history suggests that the responses to these problems are likely to depend more on local politics than on the merits of the VAT.

The next section explores the potential treatment of one of these hard-to-tax sectors, the financial services sector, and examines whether, unlike most VATs, a US VAT might find an effective method by which to resolve the frontier issue of applying the VAT to financial supplies.

3.2 *Exploring the likely treatment of financial supplies*

In discussing the prospect of VAT reform in the US, Keen and de Mooij observe that one potential advantage offered by the lateness with which the US might come to VAT reform is the opportunity to learn from experience elsewhere, so as to develop a best-practice approach. They identify the treatment of financial services as one area of potential improvement.[322] However, US policy-makers have long considered this issue, and their conclusions are instructive.

The application of an invoice-credit method VAT to financial supplies was considered a number of times throughout the reform period. While most proposals

[321] US Department of Commerce, Bureau of Economic Analysis, 'Value Added by Industry as a Percentage of Gross Domestic Product (Excel spreadsheet covering data from 1947 to 2010) (13 December 2011), available for download at bea.gov/iTable/iTable.cfm?ReqID=5&step=1.

[322] Michael Keen and Ruud de Mooij, '"Fiscal Devaluation" and Fiscal Consolidation: The VAT in Troubled Times', in Alberto Alesina and Francesco Giavazzi (eds.), *Fiscal Policy After the Financial Crisis* (University of Chicago Press, 2013), 443, 475–76.

expressed a desire to tax the value of financial intermediation services,[323] they were generally short on the detail as to how this might occur. The discussion generally concerned the taxation of basic financial transactions, such as borrowing and lending, but not of more complex financial transactions. Professor Carl Shoup during the meetings of the Treasury 1969–1970 *Expert Panel* urged that '[s]ome way should be found to tax the imputed services of banks, so that household recipients of the services would pay a tax and business recipients would be able to credit'.[324] However, the Ullman proposal only went so far as to adopt the European approach to exempt financial services but, unlike the European approach, sought to tax insurance.[325]

Treasury I undertook the most comprehensive consideration of the appropriate treatment of financial supplies under a VAT. *Treasury I* expressed a strong preference to include financial supplies in the VAT base.[326] Like the *A New Tax System Statement* that framed the Australian GST, the report favoured taxing financial services charged for by an explicit fee, such as the rental of safety deposit boxes (meaning financial institutions could obtain credit for inputs used in providing those services and would charge VAT on the services themselves).[327]

On the more intransigent issue of applying the VAT to financial intermediation services charged through a margin spread, the Treasury made some interesting observations about how one might measure the value-add of financial intermediation on a transactional basis, but ultimately provided no proposals for the mechanism to implement a VAT on a transactional basis.

The Treasury expressed a presumption that 'the value added by banks and other financial institutions is basically the difference between what they pay depositors and the amount received from their loans and investments'.[328] This is a relatively uncontroversial proposition about the nature of the value added by financial institutions in relation to their intermediary services.[329] The Treasury then went on to

[323] This is despite a line of argument from some US economists that financial services should not be the subject of a consumption tax base because they are not the product of end consumption: see Chapter 2, §4.2.5.1, n 133 of this book.

[324] 'Summary of 1969–1970 Expert Panel meeting of 4 August 1970', above n 69, 20.

[325] With the base being the difference between the excess of the insurance premium attributable to the insurance coverage over the actuarial cost to the insurer of providing the coverage: Tax Restructuring Act of 1980, §4036.

[326] *Treasury I*, vol. 3, ch. 6, 47, 49.

[327] *Treasury I*, vol. 3, ch. 6, 52. However, the Treasury was ambivalent about the appropriate treatment of brokerage services. Although acknowledging that they were capable of being taxed, the Treasury acknowledged that 'the argument may be raised that taxing them would interfere with the free functioning of capital markets and that these services, such as for the purchase of securities, are not truly a consumption expenditure' (at 53).

[328] Ibid., 49.

[329] Schenk and Oldman infer from this reference that the Treasury implicitly endorsed a subtraction-method approach to the application of a VAT to financial supplies. As the following discussion of *Treasury I* in this section shows, this inference seems incorrect: Alan Schenk and Oliver Oldman, 'Analysis of Tax Treatment of Financial Services under a

say that if depositors/suppliers were registered businesses, the banks could be charged VAT on the interest paid to depositors (and receive credit for the tax paid to these suppliers/depositors) and in turn charge VAT on their '"sales", that is, to the interest received on their loans...'[330] What is interesting about this statement is the issues it raises about valuing the intermediation services of financial institutions. Unlike some other experts, the Treasury seemed to accept the possibility that the retail interest rate paid to depositors and charged to borrowers might be a potentially viable base for the levying of a VAT on financial intermediation.[331] That is, if the VAT is charged on all transactions (on all deposits and loans), when the VAT paid by banks on deposits is subtracted from the VAT charged by banks to lenders on borrowings, the financial institution's margin spread can in effect be reached because the net amount is the margin spread (which is indirectly taxed through applying the VAT to all transactions).[332]

However, the Treasury expressed two reservations in relation to the application of the VAT to depositors. First, even though the Treasury seemed to implicitly assume that the bank would both collect and remit the VAT charged to it by depositors,[333] the Treasury expressed concern about the administrative challenge and confusion that would arise from the need to distinguish between registered depositors (who should charge VAT) and private/unregistered depositors (who should not charge VAT). This gives rise to a similar although distinct issue that arises under an RST, although here the issue is in requiring the bank to determine the status of the supplier (rather than the recipient) in order to determine whether to pay (as opposed to charge) the VAT.[334]

The second reservation related to a concern that retail interest rates do not always reflect the value of the services provided, particularly in relation to depositors. This might be the case, for example, when a depositor receives a lower rate of interest but also a free cheque service with their account (a particular issue for the US which, following the Great Depression, has had a strong history of regulating interest paid on insured deposits).[335]

Consumption Style VAT: A Report of the American Bar Association Section of Taxation Committee on Value Added Tax', *Tax Lawyer* 44(1) (1990–1991), 181, 189–90.

[330] *Treasury I*, vol. 3, ch. 6, 49. The bank both collecting and charging the VAT is an obvious departure from the standard practice under a VAT, which generally requires the supplier (i.e., the depositor) to remit the VAT. Although not stated in the *Treasury I* Report, the mechanism by which to facilitate this would be the reverse-charge mechanism discussed at Chapter 2, §4.2.5.1, n 160 and at Chapter 3, §5.1. See below, n 348.

[331] See, e.g., the discussion of the 1989 *ABA Model VAT* in this section below.

[332] Zee also accepts this proposition: Howell H. Zee, 'VAT Treatment of Financial Services: A Primer on Conceptual Issues and Country Practices', *INTERTAX* 34(10) (2006), 458, 468.

[333] *Treasury I*, vol. 3, ch. 6, 49.

[334] Ibid., 49–50.

[335] See generally Richard A. Posner, *The Crisis of Capitalist Democracy* (Harvard University Press, Cambridge, MA, 2010).

Therefore, as an alternative to charging VAT on deposits and loans, *Treasury I* considered an option to 'apply value-added tax to the interest they [financial institutions] charge their borrowers on new loans'.[336] Under this approach, businesses charged VAT on business loans would receive a credit for the VAT paid and consumers charged VAT on consumption loans would incur the VAT on the interest paid.[337] The Treasury favoured the application of VAT to consumption loans on the basis that 'loans to consumers are essentially a consumption expenditure that enables persons to consume sooner than otherwise'.[338] However, the Treasury perceived that this would lead to complications not, as one might expect, arising from valuation difficulties, but arising from the application of the VAT to loans taken out by taxpayers exempt from paying VAT, such as farmers and government borrowers, or to the application of the VAT to exempt transactions, such as borrowing to fund the purchase of the family home.[339]

This proposal raises a further interesting issue about the valuation of financial supplies. When suggesting that interest charged to borrowers be made subject to VAT, but interest received by depositors not be subject to VAT, the Treasury stated that:[340]

> In itself, this is not a serious matter; the banks would simply be remitting value-added tax on the value added *both* by themselves and their depositors.

Table 7.2 illustrates the idea. The example is based on a 10 per cent VAT levied on a VAT-inclusive basis.

As Table 7.2 demonstrates, the net VAT remitted is the same under either proposal when either (1) applying the VAT to both deposits and borrowings; or (2) applying the VAT just to borrowings. However, in the second alternative, the bank remits the entirety of the VAT, including, as Treasury notes, that VAT corresponding to the value added by the bank *and* by the depositor (and reflected in the interest paid to them by the bank).[341] This is where the conceptual point arises: the Treasury's analysis presupposes that a depositor in a bank is providing a service that generates value-add and therefore should be captured in the VAT base. That is, the Treasury accepts that it is possible to conceive of a VAT chain from the depositor through to the bank; and then from the bank to the borrower. However, this presupposition is by no means universally shared.[342] Chapter 2, §4.2.5.1 highlighted how the manner in which financial institutions charge for the intermediation

[336] *Treasury I*, vol. 3, ch. 6, 50. Charging VAT on existing loans was rejected because the transitional issues involved in charging VAT on existing loans would result in windfall losses to banks.

[337] Ibid., 50. [338] Ibid., 51. [339] Ibid., 50–51. [340] Ibid., 50 (emphasis added).

[341] *Treasury I*, vol. 3, ch. 6, 50.

[342] For an explanation of more fundamental objections to the taxation of borrowers under a consumption tax than those outlined here, see Harry Grubert and Richard Krever, 'VAT and Financial Services: Competing Perspectives on What Should Be Taxed', *Tax Law Review* 65 (2011–2012), 199.

TABLE 7.2 – *Illustration of a VAT chain for financial supplies under* Treasury I[b]

	Depositor →	Bank	Bank →	Borrower	Net VAT remitted
10 per cent VAT applied to borrowing and deposits	Registered depositor remits VAT – D/11 VAT	Bank receives D/11 credit	Bank charges VAT to borrower and remits – B/11 VAT	Net VAT remitted by bank – (B-D)/11	Net VAT remitted B/11
10 per cent VAT on borrowing only	No VAT paid by depositor	No credits to bank	Bank charges VAT to borrower and remits B/11 VAT	Net VAT remitted by bank – B/11	Net VAT remitted B/11

[b] 'D' represents the VAT base of the depositor (i.e., the retail interest rate applied to the amount deposited), and 'B' represents the VAT base for the borrower (i.e., the retail interest rate applied to the borrowing). Thanks to Patrick Emerton for his assistance with this table.

services they provide, that is, through a margin spread across a range of transactions including and extending beyond borrowing and lending, leads some to contend that it is highly artificial to match a specific depositor with a specific lender to complete the supply chain.[343] Others contend that it is only the value added by the bank (in the form of the intermediation services) that is the appropriate object of the VAT, not the value added by the depositor.[344] This is a crucial point of difference, because if it is correct that depositing funds in a bank is not adding value, then the amount of VAT remitted – the burden of which is presumably borne by the borrower – is excessive. If the borrower is not a registered business, and so cannot claim credits for this VAT paid, then the borrower is being over-taxed.[345] This is because the borrower incurs the VAT for the value added by *both* the bank and the depositor (rather than just the value added by the bank). This further illustrates the challenges to good VAT implementation in the area of financial supplies – it seems that the value add of the financial service provider cannot be captured on a transactional basis without first determining the difficult economic question of how the depositor's value-add (if any) should be understood.

Having noted this issue with depositors, the Treasury went on to consider but not commit to three options for the treatment of financial services: first, apply VAT to all interest charged on all new loans; second, apply VAT to interest charged on all new loans but zero-rate interest charged on loans to government, farming and

[343] Arthur Kerrigan, 'The Elusiveness of Neutrality – Why Is It So Difficult to Apply VAT to Financial Services?' *International VAT Monitor* (March/April 2010), 103, 104.

[344] This is the inference in Zee: Howell H. Zee, 'VAT Treatment of Financial Services: A Primer on Conceptual Issues and Country Practices', *INTERTAX* 34(10) (2006), 458, 469–70.

[345] Ibid., 469–70.

housing; or, finally, apply VAT to interest charged on new consumer loans only but exclude interest charged on housing loans.[346] The final two options would require banks to apportion their inputs and entitlement to VAT credits among taxable and non-taxable supplies.[347]

However, *Treasury I* did not directly address the mechanism by which to apply the VAT on a transactional basis. After the difficulty of accurately disaggregating the true value of the bank's value-add on a transactional basis, the means by which to actually levy the VAT on financial transactions through the invoice-credit method is a major issue.[348] Moreover, even if a workable method is found, it still requires the translation of economic terms, such as margin spread, into legislative language, which in turn is influenced by the drafting styles of the jurisdiction.

Other VAT proposals similarly proposed taxing financial services but without identifying the actual means to do so under the invoice-credit method. For example, the 1989 *ABA Model VAT* proposed taxing financial services that do not involve intermediation (such as brokerage, safe deposit boxes and investment advice).[349] The American Bar Association also expressed a desire to tax the value of financial intermediation services, but, tellingly, could not reach agreement on a 'workable method of imposing the tax on financial services involving intermediation'[350] and therefore purposefully left the relevant section incomplete.[351]

[346] *Treasury I*, vol. 3, ch. 6, 52. [347] Ibid.

[348] See, e.g., Auerbach and Gordon, who conclude that:

> Even if the appropriate treatment of financial services under a VAT is clear in an abstract theoretical model, the actual implementation of such a tax on financial services can face many more practical problems than exist in other sectors.

Alan J. Auerbach and Roger H. Gordon, 'Taxation of Financial Services under a VAT', *American Economic Review* 92(2) (2002), 411, 415–16. See further Chapter 2, §4.2.5.1, n 160. However, it is interesting to consider how the Treasury's approach could work. For example, if it were thought desirable to apply the VAT to deposits, this could be done via a reverse-charge mechanism, as is suggested by Zee. However, given the Treasury's willingness to include the value added by both the bank and the depositor in the VAT base, it would not be necessary to include Zee's modification to the reverse-charge mechanism (a type of franking account that offsets the VAT paid by the bank on deposits against the VAT paid by lenders). This is because, unlike Zee, the Treasury appeared willing to include the value added by a depositor in the VAT base and therefore would not regard the VAT paid by a borrower (reflecting both the value added of the bank and of the depositor) as over-taxation. By contrast, Zee's desire that only the value added by the bank be taxed warrants the need for the franking account to offset the overpayment of VAT by the borrower that is a product of the fact that the amount paid reflects the value added by both the bank and the depositor: Howell H. Zee, 'VAT Treatment of Financial Services: A Primer on Conceptual Issues and Country Practices', *INTERTAX* 34(10) (2006), 458, 468–70.

[349] Alan Schenk (Reporter), American Bar Association Section of Taxation, *Value Added Tax: A Model Statute and Commentary (A Report of the Committee on Value Added Tax of the American Bar Association Section of Taxation)* (American Bar Association 1989), 169.

[350] Ibid.

[351] Ibid. Unlike *Treasury I*, the 1989 *ABA Model VAT* did not favour using the retail interest rate as the base to tax financial services. However, later consideration of the issues by the

Although the 2005 *Tax Advisory Panel* favoured taxing financial services, the mechanism for doing so was not through the invoice-credit VAT, but as part of its growth and investment tax plan.[352]

In a recent article on possible approaches for the US to consider in the application of a VAT to financial supplies, Schenk spoke favourably of the Australian approach to financial supplies, specifically the use of the reduced input tax credit (RITC), as an effective second-best approach to the issue beyond actually taxing the supplies:[353]

> There is no indication that the tax authorities and taxpayers in these countries are having any significant problems in administering and complying with these rules under credit-invoice VATs.

Chapter 6, §4.3.3.4 and §4.3.4 outlined the significant problems in the application of the GST (including the RITC) to financial supplies. This apparent misunderstanding of the practical complexities of the Australian financial supply provisions arises from a misunderstanding of the institutional context of the provisions and therefore a misreading of what the provisions actually do. This provides an additional reason to doubt whether the taxation of financial supplies under a VAT in the US could be workable, although there is of course the ironic possibility that the Australian approach might work in the US context by virtue of the fact that it is free of the institutional constraints of the Australian model. However, in a pessimistic reflection of the likelihood of taxing fee-based financial services, Avi-Yonah observes that the taxation of financial supplies is likely to be 'the subject of intense lobbying and therefore less likely to be adopted'.[354] Whatever the outcome, the US approach would be shaped by the institutions of US policy-making, which would produce a unique (or uniquely complex) approach to the issue.

4 CONCLUSION

The US remains the elephant in the room for the conventional approach's merits-based account of the VAT's rise; if the VAT is so good, why, after having considered VAT reform so many times, doesn't the US, as the world's most dynamic industrial

contributors to the proposal came up with no workable alternative measurements or solutions for the financial supplies issue: Alan Schenk and Oliver Oldman, 'Analysis of Tax Treatment of Financial Services under a Consumption Style VAT: A Report of the American Bar Association Section of Taxation Committee on Value Added Tax', *Tax Lawyer* 44(1) (1990–1991), 181, 185–87.

352 US President's Advisory Panel on Federal Tax Reform, *Simple, Fair, and Pro-Growth: Proposals to Fix America's Tax System* (2005), 162–72, 244–49.

353 Alan Schenk, 'Taxation of Financial Services Under a U.S. Value-Added Tax', *Tax Law Review* 63(2) (2010), 409, 439.

354 Reuven S. Avi-Yonah, 'Summary and Recommendations', *Tax Law Review* 63(2) (2010), 285, 299.

economy and home of many at the forefront of exporting the VAT worldwide, have one? The US resistance to VAT reform challenges the underlying presumption in the conventional approach, that the good is self-actualising.

This chapter has employed the method of historical institutionalism to explore the reasons why the VAT has not been self-actualising in the US. The history has shown that VAT reform in the US has been influenced by a range of factors, such as the path-dependent effect of previous taxes, including those taxes would-be reformers seek to replace with a VAT, such as the federal income tax, as well as state sales taxes; the impact of prior policy decisions, such as the enactment of *TRA86* or the ill-fated Ullman VAT proposals; the institutions of the policy-making process within which the VAT is thrown up as one of many reform proposals by individuals and groups with varying and often conflicting interests; and the preferences, choices and behaviour of actors in institutional positions of power who, more often than not, have themselves queried the VAT's merits or the capacity of US policy-making institutions to realise those merits. Not only is the perception of the VAT's intrinsic merits by these actors shaped by historical and institutional constraints, but, even if policy-makers have accepted the VAT's merits, an assessment of the history and institutions of US tax policy by these policy-makers has left them inherently sceptical of the ability of the US to realise the proclaimed merits of the VAT to the extent that no policy-maker has seriously sought to do so. It is revealing to note that US policy-makers have seemed more aware of the divide between the good VAT and real VATs than has the conventional approach.

While the suggestion by some policy-makers that, rather than adopt a VAT, the US could renegotiate GATT rules might indicate US exceptionalism, this book contends that this is but one instance of the phenomenon that every nation is in a sense exceptional and this exceptionalism manifests differently in institutions that in turn shape the receptiveness and response of actors to reform.[355] As the US history demonstrates, VAT reform is shaped by real actors whose perceptions of the VAT's merits and actions in response to these perceptions are profoundly shaped by the history and institutions of the US policy-making process. This point has been implicitly acknowledged by US policy-makers themselves. As the Government Accountability Office notes:[356]

> The choice of tax type is typically heavily influenced by criteria other than administrability. Revenue needs, impact on economic performance, and

[355] See also Martin et al. for a rethink of arguments on US exceptionalism: Isaac William Martin, Ajay K. Mehrotra and Monica Prasad, 'The Thunder of History: The Origins and Development of the New Fiscal Sociology', in I. W. Martin, A. K. Mehrotra and M. Prasad (eds.), *The New Fiscal Sociology: Taxation in Comparative and Historical Perspective* (Cambridge University Press, New York, 2009), 1, 17.

[356] US Government Accountability Office, *Value-Added Taxes: Lessons Learned from Other Countries on Compliance Risks, Administrative Costs, Compliance Burden, and Transition* (GAO-08–566) (Washington, DC, 2008), 46.

> distributional consequences are prominent considerations and have been at the forefront of the debate in the United States about tax reform. Administrability and the details of how a new tax would be implemented often get less attention. However, administrability and design details do matter. The benefits of a new or reformed tax system, in terms of revenue, economic performance, or equity, would be at least partially offset by poor design that unnecessarily increased compliance risks, administrative costs, and compliance burden.

Even in the event that the US adopts a VAT, the fact it does not yet have one despite considering it many times suggests that merits will not be sufficient to account for its introduction or design. Despite the optimism expressed by some policy-makers and commentators that the US will be well positioned to learn from 'best practice' approaches elsewhere, this chapter has shown that should the US enact a VAT, it will be a real VAT informed by the institutions of US policy-making and likely to contain significant departures from the conventional approach's three norms of good VAT design, especially in relation to the first design norm of reaching a broad consumption base. Shaviro reaches a similar conclusion on the likely outcome of alternative consumption tax reform proposals, but contends that:[357]

> The conclusion that seems to be merging is that a well-designed consumption tax, while likely to involve significantly greater tax planning and compliance issues than its advocates might have expected or hoped for, would nonetheless probably be simpler than the current income tax.

Unlike Shaviro, this book is not concerned with promoting one tax base over another, nor is it concerned with assessing the merits claimed of the VAT or determining whether a good VAT is better than a good income tax or whether a real VAT is better than a real income tax. Rather, this book is concerned with explaining the rise of real VATs. This chapter has shown that a merits-based account of the VAT's rise, absent an understanding of the agents, institutions and histories that shape reform outcomes, is entirely insufficient in accounting for real VAT outcomes, as it is in explaining US resistance to VAT reform.

[357] Daniel Shaviro, 'Simplifying Assumptions: How Might the Politics of Consumption Tax Reform Affect (Impair) the End Product?' in J. W. Diamond and G. R. Zodrow (eds.), *Fundamental Tax Reform: Issues, Choices, and Implications* (MIT Press, Cambridge, MA; London, 2008), 75, 76.

8

Conclusions on the rise of the value-added tax

This book has addressed the fact that, despite the rapid rise and growing significance of the value-added tax (VAT), very little is known about how and why the VAT has spread. This book is not anti-VAT. It does not dispute the merits of the good VAT as presented by the conventional approach, nor does it dispute that real VATs have merit. However, the book is a reminder of the importance of separating the descriptive component of explaining the rise of the VAT from a normative commitment to furthering the rise of the VAT. It contends that the explanation by the conventional approach that attributes the VAT's rise to its merits does not adequately account for the rise of the more than 150 real VATs actually in existence. The book has proposed that a better way to understand the rise of the VAT is to look to the manner in which the historical and political context shapes real VAT outcomes – only then can we understand why real VATs end up the way they do.

Chapter 1 introduced the conventional approach, a term used to denote a general body of work by authors, often with shared organisational affiliations, who are united in their support for VAT reform and by a shared conception of what constitutes best-practice VAT design. The conventional approach dominates VAT analysis to the extent that one is hard pressed to find an analysis of worldwide VAT reform outside it.

1 PART I – THE RISE OF THE VALUE-ADDED TAX – THE GAP BETWEEN EXPECTATION AND DELIVERY

Chapter 2 introduced the good VAT, which does not denote a theoretically pure ideal but rather captures, in their own language, the consensus within the conventional approach on what a best-practice VAT should look like based on real-world experience and certain shared normative preferences. Chapter 2 detailed the three design norms necessary to achieve the good VAT, which consist of levying the VAT: (1) on a broad consumption base at a single rate; (2) through the invoice-credit method; and (3) on a destination basis. The associated merits these design norms are said to facilitate include those traditionally related to the evaluation of revenue instruments, such as revenue generation, efficiency, neutrality and to a lesser extent simplicity and equity. The chapter also introduced some frontier issues that test the limits of the good VAT, such as the application of the VAT to real property and cross-border supplies, as well as the increasingly problematic issue of VAT fraud. The book focused on one frontier issue – the taxation of financial supplies – to illustrate the types of issues that arise when the limits of the good VAT are reached.

Chapter 3 explained that, by the conventional approach's own measures, few, if any, of the real VATs that have actually been introduced resemble the good VAT. Real VATs depart in many and varied ways from the three norms of good VAT design. As a result, real VATs fail in varying degrees to realise the merits promised of the good VAT, including in relation to revenue generation, efficiency and neutrality. This is not to say that real VATs are bad, or are not as good as, or are better than, other alternatives, but rather to identify the empirical reality that real VATs depart in various ways from the good VAT. This distinction is significant because, as Part II demonstrated, the conventional approach posits the merits of the good VAT as lying behind the rise of real VATs.

2 PART II – EXPLAINING THE RISE OF THE VALUE-ADDED TAX

Despite acknowledging that few, if any, real VATs realise the merits of the good VAT, the conventional approach generally attributes the rise of the VAT to the merits of the good VAT. Indeed, such is the confidence in the belief of the merits of the good VAT by the conventional approach that many of its proponents treat the history of VAT reform as irrelevant or unproblematic. As Chapter 4 explained, whereas the histories of the VAT's rise are treated as having little or no bearing on the VAT's design and operation, the design of the VAT is presented as having ultimate bearing in explaining the history of the VAT's rise.

This book has not sought to dispute the merits of the good VAT as presented by the conventional approach, nor does it dispute that real VATs have merit. Rather a primary contention of this book is that the explanation by the conventional approach that attributes the VAT's rise to its merits does not adequately account for the rise of the more than 150 VATs actually in existence.

Chapter 4 explained that one might object to an explanation that attributes the spread of a policy instrument to its merits at a fundamental level by reference to the observation by Raymond Geuss that 'neither the good nor the true is self-realising'.[1] If the good were self-realising, then we would live in a state of endless peace with

[1] Raymond Geuss, *Philosophy and Real Politics* (Princeton University Press, Princeton, NJ, 2008), 28.

a healthy environment and enough food and clean water to support us all *and* perhaps a good tax system to match.

More specifically, Chapter 4 demonstrated that an explanation that attributes the VAT's rise to the merits of the good VAT falters when confronted by the fact that in practice no one has a good VAT. Put simply, if real VATs are not the good VAT, then the merits of the good VAT cannot explain their existence. If the explanation then instead rests on the merits of real VATs to explain the VAT's rise, once it is acknowledged that different aspects of the merits of real VATs appeal to different actors in different places in different ways, the explanation is incomplete without an account of the local context of reform. So, in developed countries, the VAT appeals because it does not apply to exports; yet in some developing countries, the VAT appeals because it does apply to exports. When it is acknowledged that no one has a good VAT, or that the merits of real VATs operate in different and sometimes contradictory ways, the empirical account of the conventional approach fails. In essence, the conventional approach is explaining the rise of something that does not exist – there is no one good VAT in practice, just as there is no one meritorious real VAT that appeals to all people in all places at all times. Instead, there are a number of real VATs that appeal for overlapping, different and sometimes contradictory reasons dependent on local context. So, if one still wants to resort to merits-based explanations, at a minimum the merits of real VATs cannot explain the rise of real VATs without taking into account the local histories and context that shape perceptions of merits and which, ironically, the existing merits-based explanations of the conventional approach ignore or downplay.

Chapter 4 demonstrated that the explanations provided by the conventional approach of the VAT's rise lack an adequate account of the policy process. Under the strong version of the explanation, the merits of the VAT (good or real) are presented as solely determinative of its rise. That is, the account assumes that the reasons the VAT appeals to the conventional approach are sufficient to explain why the VAT has risen. Imputed perceptions of rational motivation (policy-makers should implement the good VAT) are mistaken for an actual causal explanation (motivated by the perception of goodness, policy-makers have introduced good VATs). Beyond the occasional reference to the whole of government as an actor, there is insufficient consideration of the intermediating factors necessary to introduce reform such as individual actors in the policy process or the institutions through which reforms take place.

Weak articulations of the merits explanation begin to take into account some of the intermediating factors that influence the introduction of new policies, such as the role of transnational actors, the impact of fashionable trends or yardstick competition. However, the promise of the weak articulations is cut short by the conventional approach treating these factors as mere consequences of the merits of the VAT, good or real. So, international government actors, such as the International Monetary Fund (IMF) and the World Bank, simply become mere messengers of the virtues of the good VAT, and countries converge on fashionable trends not because it is fashion but because the fashion is virtuous or good. There is little discussion, for example, of what deeper forces, if any, underpin the fashionable trend toward VAT reform, or of how key intergovernmental actors have shaped VAT reform or of what has prompted their actions. Moreover, there is virtually no discussion of the role of other transnational actors, such as consultants, private firms and aid and development agencies, in promoting VAT reform. These omissions are particularly striking, given that it is those within the conventional approach who have been at the forefront of VAT reform. In addition, right at the point where the merits matter the most, at the point of a country deciding whether to introduce a VAT, rather than examining this context and deriving some useful insights into how merits are actually perceived and how real VATs come about, the conventional approach circumvents the analysis by simply attributing the VAT's rise back to its general merits.

Chapter 5 brought to light those aspects of the policy process ignored or downplayed by the conventional approach. It considered two prominent yet diverging approaches to policy analysis, public choice and historical institutionalism, to show that either approach would reject outright an account of the rise of the VAT that rests wholly or largely on the merits of the tax. Both approaches highlight the manner in which policy outcomes are constrained by a combination of factors that challenge the very perception of merits, let alone the realisation of those merits. Public choice, for example, shows how the constraints on, and choices of, actors in the tax policy-making process can result in policy outcomes that might be considered politically optimal but decidedly unmeritorious from the perspective of the conventional approach. So, the much-derided features of real VATs, such as their multiple rates or exclusions to the base, might be the politically efficient, if not economically efficient, outcome of the political constraints of the policy-making process. Historical institutionalism emphasises how history and the institutionalisation of past choices influence both the perception of merits and the capacity of actors to realise policy outcomes, whether or not motivated by merits or otherwise.

In recognition of the fact that it is real VATs that have actually risen, the book refocused the inquiry into one that examines how real VATs have come about. To demonstrate the benefits of an alternative approach that takes seriously the role of actors in the reform process, the impact of local institutions and the constraints of history in explaining the rise of these real VATs, the book drew on the historical institutionalist method to examine two case studies – the VAT reform debate in Australia and the US from 1960 to 2010.

3 PART III – CASE STUDIES ON THE REAL-WORLD CHALLENGES OF VAT REFORM

Analysis of the Australian and US case studies not only provided new insights into the VAT reform debate in these jurisdictions, but provided the basis for the development of deeper insights into the rise of VATs generally. The deliberate selection of the case studies was motivated by the fact that both the US and Australia share similar fiscal histories and both offer examples of VAT reform that has been particularly controversial. However, the outcomes in both cases are very different. Although Australia was the last OECD country to adopt the VAT, the Australian GST is considered a modern VAT because it more closely resembles the good VAT than, say, earlier European VATs. By contrast, the US remains the ultimate frontier case study for the conventional approach as the only developed country without a VAT, despite considering VAT reform on many occasions. The Australian VAT has even been held out as a model for the US in the VAT reform debate. The case studies were illustrative of how merits alone do not explain policy outcomes and how, contrary to the inference of the conventional approach, history does matter to explaining the rise of real VATs. Specifically, the use of legal analysis was crucial in revealing a number of new findings in relation to the rise of real VATs. First, the case studies demonstrated the manner in which questions relating to the legal design and implementation of VATs impact both the decision to adopt a VAT and the shape of the real VATs that get adopted. Second, the case study analysis highlighted the ways in which real VATs depart from the good VAT, and the often overlooked political and legal processes that lead to these departures. In doing so, the book addressed a gap in both the explanations given by the conventional approach and those provided by public policy studies of the VAT undertaken to date.

In Australia, policy-makers were clearly motivated by the merits of the good VAT, yet Australia does not have a good VAT. In the US, policy-makers have been less convinced of the merits of the good VAT and the US also does not have a good VAT. Australia has a real VAT, but the US does not. Merits alone do not account for these outcomes.

The case studies demonstrated that even using a narrow definition of institutions as those formal bodies that write and implement law, important insights in relation to VAT reform can be derived. Both case studies revealed, for example, how the constitutional separation of federal taxing powers has influenced the trajectory of federal VAT reform in each jurisdiction. While the exact outcomes that might be produced by these institutions might not be predicted, the institutions that themselves will influence real VATs are readily identifiable and, by virtue of their institutionalisation, cannot be easily ignored.

The Australian history demonstrated that, even when merits were central in the mind of policy-makers, a good VAT is not necessarily the result. The case study pointed to the highly visible impact of institutions such as the constitutional and voting rules that contributed to the exclusion of food in order to pass the *A New Tax System Act* ('*ANTS Act*')[2] through parliament. In addition, by focusing on the

[2] *A New Tax System (Goods and Services Tax) Act* 1999 (Cth).

impact of law on the (in)ability of the Goods and Services Tax (GST) to reach a broad consumption base, the case study also highlighted the less obvious institutional influences, such as local drafting practices and the rules of judicial interpretation, that result in real VATs. Case analysis revealed how the merits of the good VAT favoured by policy-makers are, at best, part of the context in interpreting the *ANTS Act* and, at worst, thoroughly misconstrued, as when Australian judges interpreting and applying the laws introducing the GST deny that the GST is even a consumption tax.

Whereas Australian policy-makers were clearly motivated by the merits of the good VAT, US policy-makers have been more circumspect. In large part, this is because of a belief, informed by the history of prior reforms, that even if the merits of the good VAT are genuine, these merits will not be realised by any VAT that manages to survive passage through the institutions of US policy-making. US policy-makers have been aware that should the US introduce a VAT, it will be a real VAT; this is reflected by the fact that most official policy proposals have factored in exclusions to the base at the design stage in anticipation of the policy process. Chapter 7 explained how the same institutions that have blocked VAT reform will inevitably also profoundly shape a US VAT, should it ever eventuate. The chapter highlighted in particular that balancing the pressure to address the VAT's perceived inequity against fears that the revenue-generating capability of the VAT will trigger the growth of government will most likely result in a real VAT with multiple exclusions to the base. The chapter revealed that the conventional approach's preferred method of dealing with concerns over inequity – through adjusting income taxes or through spending – is severely constrained not merely by a lack of revenue but by past choices relating to other taxes. These include moves to reduce the progressivity of the income tax, to shift the income base to a consumption base by stealth and to reduce the impact of estate and gift taxation. All these moves constrain the ability of these other taxes to compensate for the VAT's perceived inequity and therefore will add to pressure to address concerns over the VAT's incidence through alterations and exclusions to the VAT itself.

The case studies also showed how perceptions of merits are path dependent. That is, the VAT is only as good as the tax that it replaces. In Australia, the case for a VAT was strengthened by the defects of the wholesale sales tax (WST), but in the US, the lack of a federal sales tax has meant that the merits of the VAT have varied depending on the comparator used, which has ranged from the corporate income tax to payroll taxes and property taxes. This in part has meant that the VAT debate in the US has, at times, been as much a debate about business or income taxation as it has been about consumption taxation. The observation that perceptions of merits are the path-dependent product of pre-existing taxes helps explain why real VATs might be perceived as meritorious for different and at times conflicting reasons in different places.

Furthermore, despite the perceived deficiencies of existing taxes often motivating reform, the case studies revealed how new reforms are profoundly influenced by these same pre-existing taxes. This was revealed in the Australian case study when drafting practices in relation to the WST were transferred to the GST, as was shown with the move to legislate through regulations in relation to the drafting of the food and financial supply provisions. In the US, this was demonstrated through the efforts of the many consumption tax proposals to don the 'dark glasses and false moustache'[3] of the income tax so as to garner support for reform. Whereas various actors in both jurisdictions express a desire for root-and-branch tax reform, the very taxes that are the target of these reforms and the administrative practices that accompany them continue to make their presence felt.

Chapter 4 highlighted a belief by those within the conventional approach that an evolutionary imperative underlies the rise of the VAT. The implication is that, with time, countries will inevitably move toward the good VAT because the merits of the good VAT will eventually become compelling to all. However, the Australian experience shows that policy learning need not be such a linear process, nor need it produce results consistent with the good VAT. The Australian case study showed how policy learning variously resulted in one of the prime supporters of consumption tax reform in Australia, Paul Keating, turning to become one of the main opponents of GST reform, motivated not by merits but by the desire to win reelection. In an effort to avoid the mistakes of the political sell of the GST in *Fightback!*,[4] the expedited and secretive development of the *ANTS* package led to unintended outcomes. This was shown when, in eschewing consultation with the welfare sector, the miserly approach in the ANTS package to compensating for the GST's perceived inequity led to later pressure to exclude basic food from the GST base. The commitment by Australian policy-makers to the good VAT also led to some other perverse and unintended consequences, such as the extensive use of domestic zero-rating rather than the use of multiple rates. Policy learning in the US has not necessarily increased support for the VAT over the myriad other consumption tax proposals put forward over the reform period. In fact, learning from the problems of real VATs elsewhere potentially disadvantages VATs against other untested proposals. As has occurred with the income tax, once real VATs start to bear the scars of real-world implementation, perceptions of the merits of these tried and tested taxes diminish against the merits of ideal and as yet untried and untested models.

This book's focus on the frontier issue of the taxation of financial supplies has illustrated the types of issues that arise when the limits of the good VAT are reached. These frontier issues also include the taxation of real property, the levying

[3] Michael J. Graetz, *The Decline (and Fall?) of the Income Tax* (W. W. Norton & Company, New York, 1997), 216.

[4] Liberal and National Parties of Australia, *Fightback! Fairness and Jobs* (Liberal and National Parties, Canberra, 1992).

of VAT on a destination basis in a world with increasingly porous borders and addressing increasingly sophisticated VAT fraud. These issues stretch the limits of the good VAT, just as they stretch the plausibility of the merits-based explanation for the VAT's rise. There is much scope to further build on the new insights developed in this book in relation to the treatment of financial supplies to explore how responses to other frontier issues, perceived often as technical limitations, are similarly shaped by historical and political constraints.

In light of the significant cost of these issues, either to revenue or to business, these frontier issues tend to dominate much VAT analysis. Although policy-makers in Australia were not prepared to push the frontiers and tax financial supplies, despite the calls by the financial sector to do so, policy-makers, learning from the experience of real VATs elsewhere, sought to expand the GST base to include a number of readily taxable ancillary supplies made to financial institutions. However, as Chapter 6 revealed, the cost of doing so was the reduced input tax credit (RITC), which was driven by actors (financial institutions and their suppliers) protecting their own domestic interests by reference to real VATs elsewhere. Whereas the RITC is now seen as a measure to address the bias to self-supply that arises from exempting financial supplies, the history revealed at least two more domestic rationales (increasing competition in the banking sector and extending a level playing field within the sector), neither of which relate to the merits of the VAT. That the RITC, despite its many problems, is variously thrown up as an option in reform discussions elsewhere, including in Europe and the US, shows the distortion inherent in policy learning that examines proposed policy solutions absent sufficient consideration of their context.

As Chapter 5 stressed, institutions are intermediary and not wholly determinative – they mediate broader social, economic and political structures and impact agents' preferences, choices and actions. The conventional approach tends to treat economic structures as determinative in the sense that the VAT has risen because it suits the needs of domestic and global economies. However, the conventional approach fails to take sufficient account of the role of institutions and actors in the policy-making process. This book has taken seriously the call from some historical institutionalists to broaden the focus on actors to include an examination of non-government as well as government actors. Whereas the conventional approach struggles to take into account the indirect influence of international government organisations, the Australian case study showed the importance of the benchmarking provided by these organisations as a catalyst, or at least a selling point, for VAT reform. By contrast, the economic power of the US has meant that policy-makers have been more impervious to the benchmarking of these organisations or to being labelled an outlier, but nevertheless remained clearly influenced by these organisations, given the extensive discussion of the impact of trading rules on VAT reform (under the General Agreement on Tariffs and Trade [GATT] and later the World Trade Organization).

This book focused on the role of business and its representatives in VAT reform. The insights were revealing and underscore the importance of further research in this area. Whereas the conventional approach generally discusses business as the beneficiary of reform, Chapters 4 and 6 highlighted how business and its representatives have been major change agents in VAT reform. A key factor underpinning the VAT's rise has been a perception by business that, consistent with the good VAT, the VAT is not a cost to business other than in compliance. The fragmentation of business support for the VAT in the US, which in part might be the product of a perception that the VAT might be a cost to business, suggests the importance of business support to achieve reform outcomes.

In Australia, business representatives went from division and parochialism in relation to VAT reform to actively promoting it. However, Chapter 6 also highlighted that the support of business need not necessarily result in good VAT outcomes. This was highlighted in business's disregard for the concerns of welfare groups during the design stage (which contributed to the later exclusion of basic food from the GST base). It was further highlighted in showing how business opposition to reform of the GST treatment of financial supplies creates a positive feedback mechanism against reform (for better or worse).

While the close involvement or the dominance of business in tax policy-making is nothing new, the Australian case study revealed the institutionalisation of this influence. The success of business in lobbying for GST reform was rewarded with the promotion of those lobbyists to institutionalised policy-making roles. While all democracies are faced with the dilemma of how to balance accountable and consultative policy-making in the public interest against the risk of capture, the move from business as stakeholders to business as policy-makers is one that gives business a privileged agenda-setting role that is not enjoyed by other interest groups. This results in a prioritisation of tax reform issues that impose a cost to business, such as the input taxation of financial supplies, at the expense of other issues. It also results in other reforms less favourable to business receiving less attention. As Slemrod highlights, what is good for business can be, but is not necessarily, good for tax reform or economic policy.[5]

4 CLEARING THE PATH TO REVEAL REAL TRENDS

This book has revealed the inadequacies of the dominant explanation for the rise of the VAT put forward by the conventional approach. In doing so, it first drew the necessary distinction between the good VAT and real VATs. It demonstrated that, beyond the inherent flaws in a merits-based explanation, the merits imputed to the

[5] Joel Slemrod, 'Is Tax Reform Good for Business? Is a Pro-Business Tax Policy Good for America?' in J. W. Diamond and G. R. Zodrow (eds.), *Fundamental Tax Reform: Issues, Choices, and Implications* (MIT Press, Cambridge, MA; London, 2008), 143–45.

good VAT by the conventional approach cannot explain the rise of real VATs that consistently fail to realise these merits. It further showed that the merits attributed to real VATs cannot explain the VAT's rise without at least taking into account the local context that shapes perceptions of the VAT's merits. In response, the book developed an approach that takes seriously the need to account for this context so as to better explain how real VATs may or may not come to be. In showing the potential of an alternative approach, however, there is much left to do.

As the purpose of the case studies was to demonstrate the potential of an alternative approach to analysing the rise of real VATs, there is scope to apply the approach to other jurisdictions. As Chapter 5 highlighted, useful initial case studies in the developed world might be VAT reform in New Zealand or the member states of the European Union (EU). Another useful line of inquiry would be an examination of the extent to which local institutionalised, and not necessarily meritorious, responses to policy issues, such as the extensive use of exemptions and multiple rating in European VATs, become adopted elsewhere, often due to an inadequate consideration of the policy's original context. There is, however, a pressing need to apply the type of analysis undertaken by this book to VAT reform in developing and transitional countries, given that these countries constitute the vast number of VAT adoptees and have been perhaps most influenced by the conventional approach acting as agents, rather than analysts, of reform. Despite the criticisms of the appropriateness of VAT reform in developing countries,[6] the dominance of the conventional approach in VAT analysis means that few of these criticisms have been sufficiently developed or explored. This includes the interesting defence made by the conventional approach to questions raised about the appropriateness of the VAT in developing counties, which explicitly relies on real VATs rather than the good VAT.[7] Given the dominance of the conventional approach in VAT analysis, examining the role of the conventional approach as an agent of reform is well overdue.

This book raises questions about the state of tax analysis at an international and domestic level. The domination of VAT analysis by people so closely involved in its formation and promotion means that explanations of the VAT's rise are compromised by proximity or an agenda that seeks to promote rather than explain complex histories. The reluctance by authors within the conventional approach to acknowledge their own agency, or that of the organisations to which they are frequently affiliated, is but one instance of the gap in understanding the factors that have contributed to the VAT's rise. No one, for example, has explored how the rise of

6 See, e.g., Scott Riswold, 'VAT in Sub-Saharan Africa – A Critique of IMF VAT Policy', *International VAT Monitor* (March/April 2004), 97; Joseph E. Stiglitz, 'Development-Oriented Tax Policy', in R. H. Gordon (ed.), *Taxation in Developing Countries: Six Case Studies and Policy Implications* (Columbia University Press, New York, 2010), 11.

7 See Chapter 4, §2.1 of this book. As Chapter 4, §4.2 explained, Bird and Gendron begin to do so, but their account is undermined by resting on the VAT's merits.

the VAT might in part have been encouraged by multinational firms or consultants keen to develop a growing market for their technical VAT advisory services.[8] There is a need for independent scholarship to address this gap, particularly in light of the growing influence of business and its representatives in the analysis and promotion of tax reform at a global and domestic level. While the technical expertise of these agents is not disputed and is no doubt beneficial at some level, in order to have genuine and meaningful dialogue on a range of reform issues there is a need for more rather than fewer perspectives. The benefits will accrue not merely to improving understanding of tax reform but to improving the quality of advice. For example, it is clear, at least from the Australian case study, that policy-makers placed too little weight on addressing the VAT's perceived inequity. Similarly, the US case study demonstrated that theoretical and largely unverifiable defences of the VAT on the basis of the lifetime equivalence of income and consumption taxes might satisfy economists but, as *Treasury I* showed, may not necessarily satisfy policy-makers who might be sympathetic to the theoretical argument but are also keenly aware of political constraints. As this book has demonstrated, the conventional approach has been slow to come to the same realisation. Keen, for example, contends that:[9]

> Potentially adverse equity implications of VAT design should not be dismissed with vague references to dealing with them on the spending side: precision is needed as to exactly how, if at all, that can be done, and this has often been lacking – reflecting, once again, a lack of serious academic work.

Yet, as was demonstrated in Chapter 2, §2.2.6 and Chapter 4, §6, it has been the conventional approach's too ready dismissal of these equity implications, or at least a failure to prioritise them, that have contributed to this lack of serious academic work. The greater air of circumspection apparent in this quote is perhaps a result of the persistence of measures frequently incorporated into real VATs to address equity concerns, such as exclusions to the base, despite the conventional approach's dismissal of such measures as ill-conceived.

Indeed, as the conventional approach is increasingly faced with the reality of the more than 150 VATS in existence, it is possible to detect a more sober assessment about the capacity of real VATs to resemble the good VAT in some accounts. Keen

8 See, e.g., Hodge and Bowman, who have documented the large size of the global consulting sector. In 2006, the authors estimated that it employed some 463,000 employees across 123 countries, and attracted total revenues of around US $170 billion per annum. They also note that the 'Big Four' global consulting companies alone (Deloitte, Ernst & Young, KPMG and PricewaterhouseCoopers) had revenues totalling US$71.1 billion as of 2004–2005: Graeme Hodge and Diana Bowman, 'The 'Consultocracy': The Business of Reforming Government', in G. Hodge (ed.), *Privatization and Market Development: Global Movements in Public Policy Ideas* (Edward Elgar, Northampton, MA, 2006), 97, 102.

9 Michael Keen, 'What Do (and Don't) We Know about the Value Added Tax? A Review of Richard M. Bird and Pierre-Pascal Gendron's *The VAT in Developing and Transitional Countries*', *Journal of Economic Literature* 47(1) (2009), 159, 167.

and de Mooij, for example, state that there is clear potential for substantially improving understanding of where the weaknesses of VAT design and implementation lie. The authors then go on to state that the 'difficulty is overcoming the political resistance to such reforms that nonetheless persists. For that, something more than technically compelling arguments are needed.'[10] This book has demonstrated, however, that the capacity of the conventional approach to understand the political resistance to reform is hampered by its own blind adherence to the allure of the VAT's technically compelling arguments. Whereas the conventional approach makes some limited (albeit inadequate) concessions to local constraints in their design norms for the good VAT, the explanations they provide for the VAT's rise do not. This is an omission that is significant in light of the fact that no one has a good VAT, even with these design concessions. Whether this in turn calls for a reevaluation of the advice, as some others suggest, might require further investigation,[11] but it certainly calls for a more transparent explanation of the rise of these real VATs. As this book has demonstrated, by virtue of the status of institutions as enduring and relatively stable, an analysis of institutional constraints can be undertaken in advance even if the exact reform outcomes might not be able to be predicted.

As Chapter 4 highlighted, those who have offered a critique of the merits of the VAT, good or real, are accused by the conventional approach of seeking to tear down meaningful reform without offering anything in its place. Such a defence is not relevant to this book, which seeks to better explain the rise of real VATs rather than to object to the merits of the good VAT. Nevertheless, in offering an alternative explanation, the analysis has shown the importance of taking serious account of the historical and institutional constraints in the formation and implementation of tax policy. Learning from these constraints, whether it be from the impact of the cash economy or from the impact of the domestic rules of legal interpretation, is likely to genuinely advance policy learning. This is arguably a better approach than one which, when forced to confront the failure to realise the good VAT, retreats to an irrelevant defence of the merits of the good VAT for fear of undermining the perceived success of VAT reform, or to an admonishment of policy-makers to try harder to reach the hitherto unrealised ideal of the good VAT.

The reply of the conventional approach to a critique of an explanation of a worldwide phenomenon that states that local histories matter might be to agree

[10] Michael Keen and Ruud de Mooij, '"Fiscal Devaluation" and Fiscal Consolidation: The VAT in Troubled Times', in Alberto Alesina and Francesco Giavazzi (eds.), *Fiscal Policy After the Financial Crisis* (University of Chicago Press, 2013), 443, 476.

[11] See, e.g., Scott Riswold, 'VAT in Sub-Saharan Africa – A Critique of IMF VAT Policy', *International VAT Monitor* (March/April 2004), 97; Joseph E. Stiglitz, 'Development-Oriented Tax Policy', in R. H. Gordon (ed.), *Taxation in Developing Countries: Six Case Studies and Policy Implications* (Columbia University Press, New York, 2010), 11; Richard Bird and Pierre-Pascal Gendron, *The VAT in Developing and Transitional Countries* (Cambridge University Press, New York, 2007), 8, 25.

with the premise but suggest that taking into account local circumstances is a task for local policy-makers and administrators. By contrast, it might be argued that the conventional approach is driven by providing best-practice advice. However, best-practice advice should be informed by a genuine appreciation of political constraints. As Brennan and Buchanan remind us:[12]

> One may, of course, argue that these variants of the orthodox normative approach do not need to incorporate a model of how political processes operate since they are all designed for the purpose of proffering advice to governments, in any shape or form, advice grounded on ethical norms. Nonetheless, there is contained in all of these variants the implicit belief, or faith, that the politicians-bureaucrats, the audience for whom the normative advice is designed, not only have the power to determine governmental-political outcomes, but also are likely to find the ethically based arguments compelling.

The Australian case study showed that as real VATs falter under the weight of administration, cash-flow taxes are again gaining favour among policy-makers as the next best way to tax consumption.[13] Despite being championed in the 1970s, no country has introduced a comprehensive cash-flow tax.[14] As was demonstrated with the analysis of the *Henry Review*'s consideration of such reform, the merits of cash-flow taxes have been informed by unfavourable comparisons to real VATs.[15] However, policy-makers assessing the potential merits of cash-flow taxes, or whatever other variety of reform proposal, ignore at their own peril the institutional constraints that result in real VATs, as these institutions will undoubtedly continue to constrain the realisation of any new policy proposal. The many and varied complexities in real VATs, moreover, might call for a reexamination of the many general benefits claimed for consumption taxes over the income tax. Despite the promise some see in a pure consumption tax, both the good VAT and real VATs show that consumption taxes have their own complexities in practice and are not necessarily as neutral or efficient as their proponents might claim in theory.

[12] James M. Buchanan and Geoffrey Brennan, *The Power to Tax: Analytical Foundations of a Fiscal Constitution* (Cambridge University Press, Cambridge, 1980), 14.

[13] See also the cash-flow tax component in the options put forward under the Growth and Investment Tax Plan by the US President's Advisory Panel on Federal Tax Reform, *Simple, Fair, and Pro-Growth: Proposals to Fix America's Tax System* (2005), 61–62.

[14] See, e.g., US Department of the Treasury, *Blueprints for Basic Tax Reform* (Dept. of the Treasury, Washington, DC, 1977); Institute for Fiscal Studies, *The Structure and Reform of Direct Taxation (Report of a Committee Chaired by Professor J. E. Meade)* (Allen and Unwin, London, 1978). Some countries have taxes with elements of cash-flow taxation (such as with the use of resource-rent taxes), but none have implemented a system-wide cash-flow tax: see John Norregaard and Tehmina S. Khan, 'Tax Policy: Recent Trends and Coming Challenges ' (Working Paper No. WP/07/274, IMF, 2007), 22, 46.

[15] Commonwealth of Australia Treasury, Australia's Future Tax System Review Panel, *Australia's Future Tax System: Report to the Treasurer* (Australia's Future Tax System Review Panel: The Treasury, Canberra, 2009), 279–84.

This book has shown the benefits of an interdisciplinary approach to the analysis of tax policy outcomes. The application of public policy analysis to the rise of the VAT highlighted the limitations of the conventional approach and the benefits of an analytical approach that takes history seriously. However, the book has also shown the benefits to policy analysis that accrue from a focus on technical detail. Chapter 5 illustrated how the deference by public policy analysts to the conventional approach on the technical assessment of the VAT implicitly accepts that real VATs carry the benefits of the good VAT. This is because such analyses fail to take into account the distinction between the good VAT and real VATs revealed by this book. This failure has the dual effect of undermining the explanatory value of these policy accounts and inadvertently reinforcing the flawed merits-based explanations put forward by the conventional approach. This book has shown that policy analysis has as much to gain from extending its focus to technical legal detail as the conventional approach has to gain from absorbing the insights of policy analysis. The analysis speaks to the debate on the transferability of ideas and of policy convergence and reminds us of the need to move beyond simple stories of convergence and explore the complex histories of tax reform that reveal these trends to be anything but straightforward.[16] The book demonstrates that, even when tax policies seemingly converge, scholars and policy-makers should not ignore the local, institutionalised constraints that ultimately determine real-world outcomes. A focus on law shows how ostensibly technical choices can be as much influenced by historical and political constraints as are the more visible and contestable high-profile policy decisions.

Further disentangling real VATs from the good VAT is the appropriate subject of an interdisciplinary approach that draws upon public finance, policy analysis and legal analysis. Such a task is essential to building on the work of this book so as to develop an understanding of the rise of this important revenue instrument that more accurately reflects reality rather than the unrealised hope of the good VAT.

[16] See, e.g., Richard Krever and Rita de la Feria, 'Ending VAT Exemptions: Towards a Post-Modern VAT', in R. de la Feria (ed.), *VAT Exemptions: Consequences and Design Alternatives* (vol. 37, EUCOTAX Series on European Taxation, Kluwer Law International, Alphen aan den Rijn, 2013), 3, 34.

Bibliography

CASES

Alcan (NT) Alumina Pty. Ltd. v. *Commissioner of Territory Revenue* (NT) (2009) 239 CLR 27
ATS Pacific Pty Ltd. v. *Commissioner of Taxation* (2014) 219 FCR 302
AXA Asia Pacific Holdings Ltd. v. *Commissioner of Taxation* (2008) 173 FCR 500
Brady King Pty. Ltd. v. *Commissioner of Taxation* (2008) 69 ATR 271
Capital Duplicators Pty. Ltd. v. *Australian Capital Territory (No. 2)* (1993) 178 CLR 561
CIC Insurance Ltd. v. *Bankstown Football Club Ltd.* (1997) 187 CLR 384
Commissioner of Taxation v. *Unit Trend Services Pty. Ltd.* (2013) 297 ALR 190
Commissioner of Taxation v. *Qantas Airways Ltd.* (2012) 291 ALR 653
Commissioner of Taxation v. *American Express Wholesale Currency Services Pty. Ltd.; Commissioner of Taxation* v. *American Express International Inc.* (2010) 187 FCR 398
Commissioner of Taxation v. *Multiflex Pty. Ltd.* (2011) 197 FCR 580
Taxation v. *Qantas Airways Ltd.* (2012) 291 ALR 653
Commissioner of Taxation v. *Reliance Carpet Co. Pty. Ltd.* (2008) 236 CLR 342
Commissioner of Taxation v. *Ryan* (2000) 201 CLR 109
Gloxinia Investments Pty. Ltd. as trustee for the Gloxinia Unit Trust v. *Commissioner of Taxation* (2009) 183 FCR 420
Ha v. *New South Wales* (1997) 189 CLR 465
HP Mercantile Pty. Ltd. v. *Commissioner of Taxation* (2005) 143 FCR 553
Qantas Airways Ltd. v. *Federal Commissioner of Taxation* (2011) 195 FCR 260
Project Blue Sky Inc. v. *Australian Broadcasting Authority* (1998) 194 CLR 355
Saga Holidays Ltd. v. *Commissioner of Taxation (Cth) and others* (2006) 156 FCR 256
Société Thermale d'Eugénie-les-Bains v. *Ministère de l'Économie, des Finances et de l'Industrie* [2007] 3 CMLR 1003
Sterling Guardian v. *Federal Commissioner of Taxation* (2006) 228 ALR 712
State of South Australia v. *Commonwealth (Uniform Tax Case (No. 1))* (1942) 65 CLR 373
Travelex Ltd. v. *Commissioner of Taxation* (2010) 241 CLR 510
Victoria and New South Wales v. *Commonwealth (Uniform Tax Case (No. 2))* (1957) 99 CLR 575

LEGISLATION AND LEGISLATIVE MATERIALS

Australia

Australian Constitution

A New Tax System (Goods and Services Tax) Amendment Regulation 2012 (No. 1) (Cth)
A New Tax System (Goods and Services Tax Administration) Act 1999 (Cth)
A New Tax System (Goods and Services Tax) Act 1999 (Cth)
A New Tax System (Goods and Services Tax) Regulations 1999 (Cth)
A New Tax System (Indirect Tax and Consequential Amendments) Act (No. 2) 1999 (Cth)
A New Tax System (Luxury Car Tax) Act 1999 (Cth)
A New Tax System (Pay As You Go) Act 1999 (Cth)
A New Tax System (Wine Equalisation Tax) Act 1999 (Cth)
Appropriation (Supplementary Measures) Act (No. 1) 1999 (Cth)
Auditor-General Act 1997 (Cth)
Commonwealth Electoral Act 1918 (Cth)
Explanatory Memorandum, A New Tax System (Goods and Services Tax) Bill 1998 (Cth)
Explanatory Memorandum, Tax Laws Amendment (2008 Measures No. 5) Bill 2008 (Cth)
Explanatory Statement, A New Tax System (Goods and Services Tax) Regulations 1999 (Cth), *Attachment E, Regulation Impact Statement*
Federal Financial Relations Act 2009 (Cth)
Income Tax Assessment Act 1936 (Cth)
Income Tax Assessment Act 1997 (Cth)
Inspector-General of Taxation Act 2003 (Cth)
Minerals Resource Rent Tax Act 2012 (Cth)
Ombudsman Act 1976 (Cth)
Sales Tax Assessment Act 1992 (Cth)
Sales Tax (Exemptions and Classifications) Act 1992 (Cth)
Taxation Administration Act 1953 (Cth)
Tax Laws Amendment Act (2011 Measures No. 9) Act 2012 (Cth)
Tax Laws Amendments (2005 Measures No. 2) Act 2005 (Cth)

Canada

Excise Tax Act, RSC 1985, c E-15 (Can)

European Union

Council Directive 2013/42/EU of 22 July 2013 Amending Directive 2006/112/EC on the Common System of Value Added Tax, as Regards a Quick Reaction Mechanism against VAT Fraud [2013] OJ L201/1

Council Implementing Regulation (EU) 282/2011 of 15 March 2011 Laying Down Implementing Measures for Directive 2006/112/EC on the Common System of Value Added Tax (Recast), OJ L77/1 (2011)

Council Directive 2010/23/EU of 16 March 2010 Amending Directive 2006/112/EC on the Common System of Value Added Tax, as Regards an Optional and Temporary Application of the Reverse Charge Mechanism in Relation to Supplies of Certain Services Susceptible to Fraud [2010] OJ L72/1

Council Directive 2006/112/EC of 28 November 2006 on the Common System of Value Added Tax [2006] OJ L 347/1
First Council Directive 67/227/EEC of 11 April 1967 on the Harmonisation of Legislation of Member States Concerning Turnover Taxes [1967] OJ L 1/14; [1967] OJ Spec Ed 14
Second Council Directive 67/228/EEC of 11 April 1967 on the Harmonisation of Legislation of Member States Concerning Turnover Taxes – Structure and Procedures for Application of the Common System of Value Added Tax [1967] OJ 1/14; [1967] OJ Spec Ed 16
Sixth Council Directive 77/388/EEC of 17 May 1977 on the Harmonization of the Laws of the Member States Relating to Turnover Taxes – Common System of Value Added Tax: Uniform Basis of Assessment [1977] OJ L 145/1
The Treaty Establishing the European Economic Community, as revised (*Official Journal of the European Union*, 2006/C321/E1)
Revision of the Treaty Establishing the European Economic Community, opened for signature 25 March 1957, 298 UNTS 11 (entered into force 1 January 1958)
Council Regulation 904/2010 of 7 October 2010 on Administrative Cooperation and Combating Fraud in the Field of Value Added Tax (Recast) [2010] OJ L268 of 12/10/2010/1, art 18

New Zealand

Goods and Services Tax Act 1985 (NZ)

Singapore

Goods and Services Tax Act (Singapore, cap 117A, rev. edn. 2005)
Goods and Services Tax (General) Regulations (Singapore, cap 117A, rev. edn. 2008)

United States

United States Constitution IRC (2006)
Economic Growth and Tax Relief Reconciliation Act of 2001, Pub. L No. 107–16, 115 Stat. 38 (2001)
Economic Recovery Tax Act of 1981, Pub. L No. 97–34, 95 Stat. 172 (1981)
Job Creation and Worker Assistance Act of 2002, Pub. L No. 107–47, 116 Stat. 21 (2002)
Jobs and Growth Relief Reconciliation Act of 2003, Pub L No. 108–27, 117 Stat. 752 (2003)
Tax Reform Act of 1986, Pub. L No. 99–514, 100 Stat. 2085 (1986)

US Bills

Deficit and Debt Reduction and Social Security Solvency Act of 1999, S 1376, 106th Cong., 1st session (1999)
Fair Tax Act of 2007 HR 25/S 1025, 110th Cong. (2007)
Flat Tax Act of 2003, S 907, 108th Cong., 1st session (2003)
National Health Insurance Act of 2009, HR 15, 111th Cong., 1st session (2005)
National Retail Sales Tax Act of 1996, HR 3039, 104th Cong. (1996)
Revenue Restructuring Act of 1996, HR 4050, 104th Cong. (1996)
Tax Simplification Act of 2003, S 1040, 108th Cong., 1st session (2003)
Comprehensive Tax Restructuring and Simplification Act of 1994, S 2160, 103rd Cong. (1994)
Freedom and Fairness Restoration Act of 1997, HR 1040

Simplified USA Tax Act of 2003, HR 269, 108th Cong. (2003)
Tax Restructuring Act of 1979, HR 5665, 96th Cong. (1979)
Tax Restructuring Act of 1980, HR 7015, 96th Cong., 2nd session (1980)
USA Tax Act of 1995, S 722, 104th Cong, (1995)

ARTICLES/BOOKS/REPORTS

Aaron, Henry J. and Brookings Institution, *The Value-Added Tax: Lessons from Europe* (Brookings Institution, Washington, DC, 1981)

Ackerman, Jonathan and Altshuler, Rosanne, 'Constrained Tax Reform: How Political and Economic Constraints Affect the Formation of Tax Policy Proposals', *National Tax Journal*, 59(1) (2006), 165

Acosta-Ormaechea, Santiago and Yoo, Jiae, 'Tax Composition and Growth: A Broad Cross-Country Perspective' (Working Paper No. WP/12/257, International Monetary Fund, 2012)

Adams, T. S., 'Ideals and Idealism in Taxation', *American Economic Review*, 18(1) (1928), 1

'Professor Adams's Views on Tax Revision', *New York Times*, 13 December 1920, 14

'Fundamental Problems of Federal Income Taxation', *Quarterly Journal of Economics* 35(1) (1921), 527

'The Taxation of Business', *Proceedings of the National Tax Association* (1917), 185

Adema, Willem and Ladaique, Maxime, '*Net Social Expenditure – More Comprehensive Measures of Social Support*' (Social, Employment and Migration Working Paper No. 29, OECD, 2005)

Agha, Ali and Haughton, Jonathan, 'Designing VAT Systems: Some Efficiency Considerations', *Review of Economics and Statistics* 78(2) (1996), 303

Aguolu, Osita, 'VAT in Nigeria – Theory and Practice', *International VAT Monitor* (2009), 296

Ainsworth, Richard, '*VAT Fraud: MTIC & MTEC – The Tradable Services Problem*' (Working Paper No. 10–39, Boston University School of Law, 2010)

'VAT Fraud and Technological Solutions', in C. Philips (ed.), *The VAT Reader: What a Federal Consumption Tax Would Mean for America* (Tax Analysts, Arlington VA, 2011), 204

'VAT Fraud as a Policy Stimulus – Is the US Watching? VAT Withholding, RTVAT, and the Mittler Model' (Working Paper No. 11–08, Boston University School of Law, 2011)

'*VAT Experimentation – New York & Illinois* (Working Paper No. 12–23, Boston University School of Law, 2012)

Aizenman, Joshua and Jinjarak, Yothin, 'The Collection Efficiency of the Value Added Tax: Theory and International Evidence', *Journal of International Trade and Economic Development* 17(3) (2008), 391

Akerlof, George A, 'The Market for "Lemons": Quality, Uncertainty and the Market Mechanism', *Quarterly Journal of Economics* 84(3) (1970), 488

Alvesson, Kerstin, 'Anti-Avoidance Rules in the European Union and a Comparison with Canada and Australia', in M. Lang, P. Melz and E. Kristoffersson (eds.), *Value Added Tax and Direct Taxation: Similarities and Differences* (IBFD, Amsterdam, 2009), 517

Alymer, Sean, 'Big Four to Pass Extra GST Costs to Customers', *Australian Financial Review*, 8 June 1999, 4

'Compensation Too Low' *Australian Financial Review*, 20 April 1999, 8

"Banks Fear Backlash over Tax Exemption", *Sydney Morning Herald*, 10 August 1998, 33

American Bar Association Section of Taxation, Alan Schenk (Reporter), *Value Added Tax: A Model Statute and Commentary (A Report of the Committee on Value Added Tax of the American Bar Association Section of Taxation)* (American Bar Association, 1989)

Andrews, Edmund, 'Bush Tax Cuts Offer Most for Very Rich, Study Finds', *New York Times*, 8 January 2007, 16

Andrews, William, 'A Consumption-Type or Cash-Flow Personal Income Tax', *Harvard Law Review*, 87 (1974), 1113

Annacondia, Fabiola and van der Corput, Walter, 'Overview of General Turnover Taxes and Tax Rates', *International VAT Monitor* (March/April 2013), 2

'Overview of General Turnover Taxes and Tax Rates', *International VAT Monitor*(March/April 2012), 2

'Overview of General Turnover Taxes and Tax Rates', *International VAT Monitor* (March/April 2009), 1

Arbouw, John, 'Dick Warburton: Boardroom Warrior', *Company Director Magazine* 19(1) (1 February 2003), 10

Arnold, Brian J., 'Successful Tax Reform: Lessons from an Analysis of Tax Reform', *Canadian Tax Journal* 12(5) (1994), 1431

'The Process of Tax Policy Formulation in Australia, Canada and New Zealand', *ATF* 7(4) (1990), 379

Atkinson, Anthony B. and Stiglitz, Joseph E., "The Design of Tax Structure: Direct versus Indirect Taxation" *Journal of Public Economics* 6 (1976), 55

Auerbach, Alan J., *'The Choice Between Income and Consumption Taxes: A Primer'* (Paper presented at Conference for Key Issues in Public Finance, New York University, New York, 2006)

Auerbach, Alan J. and Gordon, Roger H., "Taxation of Financial Services under a VAT", *American Economic Review* 92(2) (2002), 411

Auerbach, Alan and Slemrod, Joel, "The Economic Effects of the Tax Reform Act of 1986', *Journal of Economic Literature* 35 (1997), 589

Austen-Smith, David, 'Interest Groups, Campaign Contributions and Probabilistic Voting', *Public Choice* 54 (1991), 123

Australian Associated Press, 'GST Failures the Fault of States: Costello', *CCH Tax and Accounting News Headlines*, 27 June 2006

Australian Bureau of Statistics, 5506.0 – *Taxation Revenue, Australia*, 2011–12 (ABS, Canberra, 2013)

1301.0 – *2012 Year Book Australia* (ABS, Canberra, 2012)

5204.0.55.008 – *Information Paper: The Non-Observed Economy and Australia's GDP* (ABS, Canberra, 2012)

5506.0 – *Taxation Revenue, Australia, 2009–10* (ABS, Canberra, 2011)

8153.0 – *Internet Activity, Australia* (ABS, Canberra, 2010)

5506.0 – *Taxation Revenue, Australia, 2004–05* (ABS, Canberra, 2006)

5302.0 – *Balance of Payments and International Investment Position, Australia, March Quarter 2006* (ABS, Canberra, 2006)

6537.0 – *Government Benefits, Taxes and Household Income 2003–2004* (ABS, Canberra, 2006)

3201.0 – *Population by Age and Sex, Australian States and Territories* (ABS, Canberra, 2006)

1301.0 – *2006 Year Book Australia* (ABS, Canberra, 2006)

1301.0 – *2005 Year Book Australia* (ABS, Canberra, 2005)

Australian Council of Social Service, *Indicators of Inequality Fact Sheet* (ACOSS, 27 March 2011)

Australian Council of Social Service (ACOSS), *Tax Reform Pack* (ACOSS, Strawberry Hills NSW, 1997)

Taxation in Australia: Home Truths and International Comparison (Information Paper 347) (ACOSS, Strawberry Hills NSW, 2003)

Australian Electoral Commission, *Electoral Newsfile 79: Federal Election 1998 Results Guide* (7 December 2007) (aec.gov.au/About_AEC/Publications/Newsfiles/1998/No_79.htm)

Australian Taxation Office (ATO), *Legal Database* (2014) (law.ato.gov.au/atolaw/Browse.htm?Node=0&Ima=CollapseAll)

ATO Continues Clamp-Down on GST Fraud and Those Not Reporting Cash Income (Media Release, 2011/39, 2011)

ATO, *Guide to Luxury Car Tax* (14 February 2014) (ato.gov.au/Business/Luxury-car-tax/)

Australian Taxation Office, *Taxation Statistics: 2011–12* (Australian Taxation Office, Canberra, 2013)

GST Administration Annual Performance Report 2012–13 (ATO, Canberra, 2013)

ATO Consultation Framework (27 October 2014) (ato.gov.au/General/About-consultation/ATO-consultation-framework/#TechAndSpPurposeWorkingGps)

Australian Taxation Office, *Test Case Litigation Program* (10 May 2013) (ato.gov.au/Tax-professionals/Legal-practitioners/In-detail/Litigation-and-case-law/Test-case-litigation-program/)

Australian Taxation Office, *Goods and Services Tax: Tax Invoices*, GSTR 2013/1, 27 March 2013

Australian Taxation Office, *Guide to Wine Equalisation Tax* (13 December 2012) (ato.gov.au/Business/Wine-equalisation-tax/)

Australian Taxation Office, *Public Rulings, Determinations and Bulletins* (2012) (law.ato.gov.au/atolaw/htmlfile.htm?fileid=ldbcontents#rul)

Australian Taxation Office, *Goods and Services Tax: Do the Acquisitions of the Services Provided under the Arrangement Described in Taxpayer Alert TA 2010/1 Form Part of a Reduced Credit Acquisition Made by the Financial Supply Provider under Item 9 of the Table in Subregulation 70–5.02(2) of the A New Tax System (Goods and Services Tax) Regulations 1999?* GSTD 2011/3, 30 November 2011

ATO, *Ruling Compendium*, GSTD 2011/3EC (2011)

Australian Taxation Office, *Taxation statistics: 2008–09* (Australian Taxation Office, Canberra, 2011)

Australian Taxation Office – National Tax Liaison Group, GST Sub-Committee, *Minutes 14 September 2011 – Risk Differentiation Framework (RDF) for Taxpayers* (ATO, Canberra, 2011)

GST Administration Annual Performance Report 2009–2010 (ATO, Canberra, 2010)

Australian Taxation Office – National Tax Liaison Group, GST Sub-Committee, *GST Minutes 1 March 2010 – Item 11 Taxpayer Alert 2010/1 – Financial Supplies Arrangement* (ATO, Canberra, 2010)

Australian Taxation Office, *Taxpayer Alert 2010/1: GST – Interposing an Associated 'Financial Supply Facilitator' to Enhance Claims for Reduced Input Tax Credits for Expenses Incurred in the Course of a Company Takeover*, TA 2010/1, 19 February 2010

Goods and Services Tax: Determining the Extent of Creditable Purpose for Providers of Financial Supplies, GSTR2006/3, 12 April 2006

Goods and Services Tax Ruling: Goods and Services Tax: In the Application of Items 2 and 3 and Paragraph (b) of Item 4 in the Table in Subsection 38–190(1) of the A New Tax System (Goods and Services Tax) Act 1999, GSTR 2004/7, 1 December 2004

Goods and Services Tax: GST and Bovine Colostrum Powder, ATO ID 2004/622, 30 July 2004

Goods and Services Tax: Reduced Credit Acquisitions, GSTR2004/1, 25 February 2004

Goods and Services Tax: Financial Acquisitions Threshold, GSTR 3003/9, 14 May 2003

Goods and Services Tax: GST and Edible Chocolate Body Paint, ATO ID 2004/38, 27 September 2002

Goods and Services Tax: GST Treatment of Financial Supplies and Related Supplies and Acquisitions, GSTR 2002/2, 26 June 2002

Avi-Yonah, Reuven, 'The Political Pathway: When Will the U.S. Adopt a VAT?' in C. Phillips (ed.), *The VAT Reader: What a Federal Consumption Tax Would Mean for America* (Tax Analysts, Arlington VA, 2011), 334

'Summary and Recommendations', *Tax Law Review* 63(2) (2010), 285

'Structuring a US Federal VAT', *International VAT Monitor* (July/August 2009), 275

'Risk, Rents and Regressivity Revisited', *Australian Tax Forum* 24 (2009), 41

'Tax Competition, Tax Arbitrage and the International Tax Regime', *Bulletin for International Taxation* 61(4) (2007), 130

'The Report of the President's Advisory Panel on Federal Tax Reform: A Critical Assessment and a Proposal', *SMU Law Review* 59(2) (2006), 551

'Does Atlas Shrug? The Economic Consequences of Taxing the Rich', *Yale Law Journal* 111(6) (2002), 1391

'Globalization, Tax Competition, and the Fiscal Crisis of the Welfare State', *Harvard Law Review* 113(7) (2000), 1573

Bachrach, Peter and Baratz, Morton S., 'Two Faces of Power', *American Political Science Review* 56(4) (1962), 947

Bachrach, Peter and Baratz, Morton S., 'Decisions and Nondecisions: An Analytical Framework' *The American Political Science Review* 57(3) (1963), 632

Bakker, Carl and Chronican, Phil, 'Financial Services and the GST: A Discussion Paper' (Victoria University Press for the Institute of Policy Studies, Victoria University of Wellington, 1985)

Bankman, Joseph and Griffith, Thomas, 'Is the Debate Between an Income Tax and a Consumption Tax a Debate About Risk? Does It Matter?' *Tax Law Review* 47 (1992), 377

Bankman, Joseph and Weisbach, David A., 'The Superiority of an Ideal Consumption Tax over an Ideal Income Tax', *Stanford Law Review* 58 (2006), 1413

Barnes, Joe, 'The Politics and Ideology of Fundamental Tax Reform', in G. Zodrow and P. Mieszkowski (eds.), *United States Tax Reform in the 21st Century* (Cambridge University Press, Cambridge, 2002), 294

Barrie, JM, *Peter Pan; or, The Boy Who Would Not Grow Up* (Hodder and Stoughton, London, 1928)

Bartlett, Bruce, 'The Trouble with Tax Cuts', *Tax Notes* 85 (1999), 1457

Bates, Robert, 'A Political Scientist Looks at Tax Reform' in M. Gillis (ed.), *Tax Reform in Developing Countries* (Duke University Press, Durham, NC, 1989), 473

Beam, David R., 'If Public Ideas Are So Important Now, Why Are Policy Analysts So Depressed?' *Journal of Policy Analysis and Management* 15(3) (1996), 430

Bean, C., 'Issues in the 1993 Election', *Australian Journal of Political Science* 29 (special issue) (1994), 134

Bean, C. and McAllister, I., 'GST and All That: The Impact of Issues and Leaders in the 1998 Federal Election', *AQ: Journal of Contemporary Analysis* 71(3) (1999), 46

Beito, David, *Taxpayers in Revolt: Tax Resistance During the Great Depression* (University of North Carolina Press, Chapel Hill, 1989)

Bell, Stephen and Wanna, John, *Business-Government Relations in Australia* (Harcourt Brace Jovanovich, Sydney, 1992)

Berg, Bruce L, *Qualitative Research Methods for the Social Sciences* (3rd ed., Allyn and Bacon, Boston, 1998)

Bergevin, Philippe, *A Primer on Federal Consumption Taxes* (Parliamentary Information and Research Service, Library of Parliament, Canada, 2007)

Bird, Richard, 'The Cost and Complexity of Canada's VAT: The GST in International Perspective', *Tax Notes International* 8(1) (1994), 37

Bird, Richard M. and Gendron, Pierre-Pascal, 'Sales Taxes in Canada: The GST-HST-QST-RST System', *Tax Law Review* 63(3) (2009–2010), 517

Bird, Richard and Gendron, Pierre-Pascal, *The VAT in Developing and Transitional Countries* (Cambridge University Press, New York, 2007)

'VAT's in Federal Countries: International Experience and Emerging Possibilities', *Bulletin for International Fiscal Documentation* 55(7) (2001), 293

Bird, Richard, Mintz, Jack and Wilson, Thomas, 'Coordinating Federal and Provincial Sales Taxes: Lessons from the Canadian Experience', *National Tax Journal* (2006), 889

Birnbaum, Jeffrey H. and Murray, Alan S., *Showdown at Gucci Gulch: Lawmakers, Lobbyists, and the Unlikely Triumph of Tax Reform* (Random House, New York, 1987)

Black, Duncan, *The Theory of Committees and Elections* (Cambridge University Press, Cambridge, 1958)

Block, Fred, 'The Ruling Class Does Not Rule' in Block, F. (ed.), *Revising State Theory: Essays in Politics and Postindustrialism* (Temple University Press, Philadelphia, 1987), 51

'Towards a New Understanding of Economic Modernity', in C. Joerges, B. Strath and P. Wagner (eds.), *The Economy as a Polity: The Political Constitution of Contemporary Capitalism* (UCL Press, London, 2005), 3

Blount, Simon, 'The Politics of Taxation: The Introduction of the GST into New Zealand, Canada, Japan and Australia', *Australian Tax Forum* 16(4) (2001), 439

'The 'Fair Go' in Australia: Popular Support for Taxing and Spending', *POLICY* (2000–2001), 13

'Public Opinion and Tax Aversion in Australia', *Journal of Sociology* 36(3) (2000), 275

Blue, Tim, 'Financial Planners Brace for Shake-Up', *The Australian*, 1 June 1999, 22

Blyth, Mark M., '"Any More Bright Ideas?" The Ideational Turn of Comparative Political Economy', *Comparative Politics* 29(2) (1997), 229

Blyth, Mark M, *Great Transformations: Economic Ideas and Institutional Change in the Twentieth Century* (Cambridge University Press, Cambridge, 2002)

Boadway, Robin and Keen, Michael, 'Theoretical Perspectives on the Taxation of Capital Income and Financial Services' in P. Honohan (ed.), *Taxation of Financial Intermediation: Theory and Practice for Emerging Economies* (World Bank; Oxford University Press, Washington, DC, 2003), 31

Board of Taxation, *The Charter of the Board of Taxation* (2012) (taxboard.gov.au/content/Content.aspx?doc=about/charter.htm)

Review of the Application of GST to Cross-Border Transactions: A Report to the Assistant Treasurer (Canberra, 2010)

Review of the Legal Framework for the Administration of the Goods and Services Tax: A Report to the Assistant Treasurer and Minister for Competition Policy and Consumer Affairs (Australian Government, Canberra, 2008)

Scoping Study of Small Business Tax Compliance Costs (Australian Government, Canberra, 2007)

Bodin, Jean-Paul and Koukpaizan, Vincent, 'The Rise of VAT in Africa – Impact and Challenges' *International VAT Monitor* (2009), 178

Bogetic, Zeljko and Hassan, Fareed, 'Determinants of Value-Added Tax Revenue: A Cross-Section Analysis' (Policy Research Working Paper No. WPS 1203, Washington, DC, 1993)

Boreham, Tim, 'Customers Face Hike in Fees', *The Australian*, 22 July 2000, 5

'The Y2K Bug Has a Friend, the GST Slug', *The Australian*, 9 April 1999, 21

'Banks Dealt a Blow on GST Front', *The Australian*, 3 August 1998, 35

'Bankers Charge to Fore in GST Debate', *The Australian*, 20 March 1998, 23

Boskin, Michael J. and McLure, Charles E., *World Tax Reform: Case Studies of Developed and Developing Countries* (ICS Press, San Francisco, 1990)

Bowers, Peter, 'Hawke Had No Choice But to Opt for Damage Control', *Sydney Morning Herald*, 6 July 1985, 1

Bradford, David F, *'The X Tax in the World Economy'* (CEPS Working Paper No. 93, Center for Economic Policy Studies (Princeton), 2003)

Bradford, David F., Auerbach, Alan J. and Shaviro, Daniel N., *Institutional Foundations of Public Finance: Economic and Legal Perspectives* (Harvard University Press, Cambridge, MA, 2008)

Bradshaw, S. and Wallace, M., *Global Inequalities* (Longman, South Melbourne, 1996)

Brammall, Bruce, 'Bank GST Levy', *The Herald-Sun*, 15 August 2000, 1

Brandon, Robert M., Rowe, Jonathan, and Stanton, Thomas H., *Tax Politics: How They Make You Pay and What You Can Do about It* (New York, 1976)

van Brederode, Robert F., 'VAT News: Bahamas – Introduction of VAT", *International VAT Monitor* 24(4) (July/August 2013), 209, 237

'VAT Has Come of Age – Review of Thomas Ecker, *A VAT/GST Model Convention*', *International VAT Monitor* (November/December 2013), 360

Systems of General Sales Taxation: Theory, Policy and Practice (Kluwer Law International Alphen aan den Rijn, 2009)

'Towards a Federal Sales Tax in the United States?' *International VAT Monitor* (March/April 2008), 114

Brinsden, Colin, 'Tax Forum – A GST-Free Zone', *The Australian* (online), 16 September 2011 (theaustralian.com.au/business/breaking-news/tax-forum-a-gst-free-zone/story-e6frg90f-1226138927909)

Bronfenbrenner, M., 'Report on Japanese Taxation by the Shoup Mission; Second Report on Japanese Taxation by the Shoup Mission (Book Review)', *American Economic Review* 41(5) (1951), 983

Brooks, Neil, *The Canadian Goods and Services Tax: History, Policy, and Politics* (ATRF, Sydney, 1992)

'Lessons for Australia from the Canadian Experience with the GST: Don't Do It!' in B. Tran-Nam (ed.), *Tax Reform and the GST: An International Perspective* (Prospect Media, St Leonards, 1998), 109

'The Logic, Policy and Politics of Tax Law: An Overview', in T. Edgar (ed.), *Materials on Canadian Income Tax* (12th ed., 2000)

'An Overview of the Role of the VAT, Fundamental Tax Reform, and a Defence of the Income Tax', in R. Krever and D. White (eds.), *GST in Retrospect and Prospect* (Thomson Brookers, Wellington, 2007), 597

Brooks, Neil and Hwong, Thaddeus, *The Social Benefits and Economic Costs of Taxation: A Comparison of High and Low Tax Countries* (Canadian Centre for Policy Alternatives, Ottawa, 2006)

Brown, Amanda, et al., 'Contrasting VAT – Avoidance Approaches' *International Tax Review* 18 (2004), 18

Brown, Jerome, 'The Tax Debate, Pressure Groups and the 1998 Federal Election', *Policy, Organisation and Society* 18 (1999), 75

Brown, Karen B. and Fellows, Mary Louise (eds.), *Taxing America* (New York University Press, New York, 1996)

Brownlee, W. Elliot, *Funding the Modern American State, 1941–1995: The Rise and Fall of the Era of Easy Finance* (Cambridge University Press, Cambridge, 1996)

Federal Taxation in America: A Short History (Cambridge University Press, 2nd ed., Cambridge, 2004)

Buchanan, James M., 'Public Choice: Politics Without Romance', *Policy* 19(3) (2003), 13

The Limits of Liberty: Between Anarchy and Leviathan (University of Chicago Press, Chicago, 1975)

Buchanan, James M. and Brennan, Geoffrey, *The Power to Tax: Analytical Foundations of a Fiscal Constitution* (Cambridge University Press, Cambridge, 1980)

Buchanan, James M., Tollison, Robert D. and Tullock, Gordon, *Toward a Theory of the Rent-Seeking Society* (Texas A&M University, College Station, 1980)

Buchanan, James M. and Tullock, Gordon, *The Calculus of Consent, Logical Foundations of Constitutional Democracy* (University of Michigan Press, Ann Arbor, 1962)

Buchanan, James M. and Wagner, Richard E., *Democracy in Deficit: The Political Legacy of Lord Keynes* (Free Press, New York, 1977)

Buettner, Thiess and Erbe, Katherine, 'Revenue and Welfare Effects of Financial Sector VAT Exemption', *International Tax and Public Finance* 21 (6) (2014), 1028

Buffini, Fiona, 'Brace for GST Amendments Galore', *Australian Financial Review*, 17–18 July 1999, 4

'Tax Professionals Scaling the Heights', *Australian Financial Review*, 20 May 1999, 31

Burgess, Robin and Stern, Nicholas, 'Taxation and Development', *Journal of Economic Literature* 31(2) (1993), 762

Burnham, Peter, *Research Methods in Politics* (Palgrave Macmillan, 2nd ed., Basingstoke, Hampshire; New York, 2008)

Burns, Lee, 'Consumption Taxation of Supplies of Financial Services in the Asia-Pacific Region', *Asia Pacific Tax Bulletin* 14 (2008), 352

Burrell, Steve, 'Give 'Em All a Good Kicking', *Sydney Morning Herald*, 8 September 2000, 26

Burton, Tom, 'Opposition Support Down Since *FightbackII* Poll', *Australian Financial Review*, 25 January 1993, 3

Campbell, John, 'Institutional Analysis and the Role of Ideas in Political Economy', *Theory and Society* 27(3) (1998), 377

'Ideas, Politics, and Public Policy', *Annual Review of Sociology* 28 (2002), 21

Campbell, John L., 'The State and Fiscal Sociology', *Annual Review of Sociology* 19 (1993), 163

Campbell, Robert M., Paul, Leslie A. and Howlett, Michael (eds.), *The Real Worlds of Canadian Politics* (4th ed., Broadview Press, Peterborough, NH, 2004)

Capoccia, Giovanni and Kelemen, R. Daniel, 'The Study of Critical Junctures: Theory, Narrative, and Counterfactuals in Historical Institutionalism', *World Politics* 59 (2007), 341

Carlson, George N., *Value-Added Tax: European Experience and Lessons for the United States* (Office of Tax Analysis, Department of Treasury; US Government Printing Office, Washington, DC, 1980)

Carlyon, Les, 'Carlyon', *Business Review Weekly*, 27 November 1992, 15

Carr, Mathew, 'Quarterly Payout to Help Small Retailers in "The GST Guide for Business (Liftout)"', *Australian Financial Review*, 9

Caspersen, Erik and Metcalf, Gilbert, 'Is a Value Added Tax Regressive? Annual versus Lifetime Incidence Measures', *National Tax Journal* 47(4) (1994), 731
Cassidy, John, 'Tax Code', *The New Yorker* (6 September 2004), 70
CCH Australia Limited, *GST & Sales Tax Guide (Online Reporter Services)*, looseleaf, CCH, North Ryde, NSW
Central Planning Bureau (CPB), Netherlands Bureau for Economic Policy Analysis, *Study to Quantify and Analyse the VAT Gap in the EU-27 Member States – Final Report (TAXUD/2012/DE/316; FWC No. TAXUD/2010/CC/104)* (Study Commissioned by the European Commission, CPB Netherlands Bureau for Economic Policy Analysis, The Hague, 2013)
Chisholm, A. G., Freebairn, J. W. and Porter, M. G., *A Broad Based Consumption Tax for Australia* (Centre of Policy Studies, Monash University, Clayton, 1990)
Christian, Ernest and Robbins, Gary A., 'Stealth Approach to Tax Reform', *Washington Times*, 1 November 2002
Claus, Iris, et al. (eds.), *Tax Reform in Open Economies: International and Country Perspectives* (Edward Elgar, Cheltenham, 2010)
Cleary, Paul, 'Treasury's Role in the GST "Nightmare on Main Street"', *Australian Financial Review*, 12 July 1999, 1, 19
'Diesel Users Face Tough Penalties, Compliance', *Australian Financial Review*, 24 June 1999, 4
'Input Credit Details Made Regulations (GST: The Fine Print)', *Australian Financial Review*, 24 June 1999, 4
'The McDonald's Amendment', *Australian Financial Review*, 4 June 1999, 41
'Hard-Nosed Democrat Who Saved the GST', *Australian Financial Review*, 20 May 1999, 27
'Tax Avoidance Rules Loosen Up', *Sydney Morning Herald*, 23 April 1999, 2
'No Jobs with Tax: Treasury', *Sydney Morning Herald*, 5 March 1992, 6
Cleary, Paul and Buffini, Fiona, 'GST: Business Hits Delays', *Australian Financial Review*, 25 October 1999, 1, 4
Cleary, Paul and Lewis, Steve, 'Hail the New Powerbrokers', *Australian Financial Review*, 29–30 May 1999, 4
Lewis, Steve and Cleary, Paul, 'Business Tastes a Bitter Defeat', *Australian Financial Review*, 29–30 May 1999, 6
Cnossen, Sijbren, 'VAT Coordination in Common Markets and Federations: Lessons from the European Experience', *Tax Law Review* 63(3) (2010), 583
'A VAT Primer for Lawyers, Economists, and Accountants', *Tax Notes International* 55(4) (2009), 319
'Global Trends and Issues in Value Added Taxation', *International Tax and Public Finance* 5(3) (1998), 399
Value Added Taxes in Central and Eastern Europe: A Survey and Evaluation (European Commission OECD, Paris, 1998)
'VAT Treatment of Immovable Property', in V. Thuronyi (ed.), *Tax Law Design and Drafting: Volume 1* (International Monetary Fund, Washington, DC, 1996), 231
'Administrative and Compliance Costs of the VAT: A Review of the Evidence', *Tax Notes International* 8 (1994), 1649
'VAT and RST: A Comparison', *Canadian Tax Journal* 35(3) (1987), 559
Cohen, G. A., *Karl Marx's Theory of History: A Defence* (expanded ed., Princeton University Press, Princeton, NJ, 2000)
Colebatch, Tim, 'GST "Hole" Now $4b – Tax Office', *The Age*, 17 December 1991, 10

'GST Would Hurt Poor Families, Say Economists', *The Age*, 25 February 1992, 6
Collier, Karen, 'Bank Fees Add to Costs', *The Herald-Sun*, 29 May 2000, 44
Collier, Ruth Berins and Collier, David, *Shaping the Political Arena* (Princeton University Press, Princeton, NJ, 1991)
Colm, Gerhard, 'The Basis of Federal Fiscal Policy', *Taxes – The Tax Magazine* 6(17) (1935), 338
Commonwealth of Australia, *National Taxation Summit: Record of Proceedings*, (Summit held from Monday July 1 to Thursday July 4, 1985, Parliament House, Canberra, Australian Government Publishing Service)
Royal Commission on the Activities of the Federated Ship Painters and Dockers Union, *Interim Report No. 4* (1982)
Royal Commission on the Activities of the Federated Ship Painters and Dockers Union, *Final Report* (1984)
Commonwealth of Australia Government, *GST Distribution Review Final Report* (Australian Govt Pub Service, Canberra, October 2012)
Commonwealth of Australia Parliament, Senate Select Committee on A New Tax System, *Main Report* (Parliament of the Commonwealth of Australia, Canberra, 1999)
Taxation Review Committee (Asprey), Full Report (Australian Government Publishing Service, Canberra, 1975)
Taxation Review Committee (Asprey), Preliminary Report (AGPS, Canberra, 1974)
Commonwealth of Australia Treasury, *Tax Expenditures Statement 2013* (Australian Government, Canberra, 2014)
Australia's Future Tax System Review Panel, *Australia's Future Tax System: Report to the Treasurer* (Australia's Future Tax System Review Panel: The Treasury, Canberra, 2009)
Australia's Future Tax System Review Panel, *Architecture of Australia's Tax and Transfer System* (Commonwealth of Australia Treasury, Canberra, 2008)
Australia's Future Tax System Review Panel, *Consultation Paper* (Commonwealth of Australia Treasury, Canberra, 2008)
Pocket Guide to the Australian Taxation System (Treasury, Canberra, 2013)
Tax Expenditures Statement 2012 (Australian Government, Canberra, 2013)
Budget 2012–2013 – Budget Paper No. 2 (AGPS, Canberra, 2012)
The Low Value Parcel Processing Taskforce Final Report (Commonwealth of Australia Treasury, Canberra, 2012)
Consultation Paper – Minerals Resource Rent Tax Bill 2011 (10 June 2011) (archive.treasury.gov.au/contentitem.asp?ContentID=2070)
Pocket Guide to the Australian Tax System (Australian Government, Canberra, 2011)
Submissions: Exposure Draft – GST Financial Supply Provisions (23 November 2011) (archive.treasury.gov.au/contentitem.asp?ContentID=2234)
Tax Expenditures Statement 2010 (Australian Government, Canberra, 2011)
Implementation of the Recommendations of Treasury's Review of the GST Financial Supply Provisions (Australian Government, Canberra, 2010)
Implementation of the Recommendations of Treasury's Review of the GST Margin Scheme – Discussion Paper (Australian Government, Canberra, 2010)
Mid-Year Economic and Fiscal Outlook (Australian Government, Canberra, 2010)
Tax Expenditures Statement 2009 (Australian Government, Canberra, 2010)
Budget Paper No. 1: Budget Strategy and Outlook 2008–09, Statement 5: Revenue (Australian Government, Canberra, 2009)
Consultation Paper on the Review of the Margin Scheme (Australian Government, Canberra, 12 May 2009)

GST Margin Scheme Review – Consultation Paper (Australian Government, Canberra, 2009)
Review of the GST Financial Supply Provisions – Consultation Paper (Australian Government, Canberra, 2009)
Tax Expenditures Statement 2008 (Australian Government, Canberra, 2009)
Australian Taxation Office/ Treasury Protocol – Tax Policy and Legislation (6 March 2008) (archive.treasury.gov.au/documents/1362/PDF/ATO_Treasury_Protocol.pdf)
Budget Overview (Australian Government, Canberra, 2007)
Pocket Guide to the Australian Tax System (Australian Government, Canberra, 2006)
Annual Report 2000–2001 (Australian Government, Canberra, 2001)
Historical Material: Entity Taxation – Taxing Trusts Like Companies Overview (4 April 2001) (archive.treasury.gov.au/contentitem.asp?ContentID=454)
The Commonwealth Budget Papers 2000 – 2001 (2000), Appendix A (budget.gov.au/2000–01/papers/bp3/html/appa.htm)
The Application of Goods and Services Tax to Financial Services – Consultation Document (Australian Government, Canberra, 1999)
Tax Reform: Not a New Tax, a New Tax System: The Howard Government's Plan for a New Tax System (AGPS, Canberra, 1998)
Reform of the Australian Tax System: Draft White Paper (Australian Govt. Pub. Service, Canberra, 1985)
A Guide to Tax Reform: A Guide to the Government's Draft White Paper on Tax Reform, Presented to the National Taxation Summit Conference, July 1985 (Australian Govt Pub. Service, Canberra, 1985)
Commonwealth Office of Parliamentary Counsel, *Tax Law Improvement Project Building the New Tax Law (Information Paper No. 2)* (April 1995)
Conlan, Timothy, Wrightson, Margaret and Beam, David, *Taxing Choices: The Politics of Tax Reform* (Congressional Quarterly Press, Washington, DC, 1990)
Conrad, Robert and Grozav, Anca, 'Real Property and VAT', in R. Krever (ed.), *VAT in Africa* (Pretoria University Law Press, Pretoria, 2008), 81
Cooper, Graeme, '*The Discrete Charm of the VAT*' (University of Sydney Law School Legal Studies Research Paper No. 07/65, University of Sydney, 2007)
Cooper, Graeme and Vann, Richard, 'A Few Myths About the GST', *University of New South Wales Law Journal* 23 (2000), 252
'Implementing the Goods and Services Tax', *Sydney Law Review* 23 (1999), 337
Coorey, Phillip, 'Taxpayers Lose $60b in Mining Profits Compromise', *Sydney Morning Herald* (online), 16 February 2011 (smh.com.au/national/taxpayers-lose-60b-in-mining-profits-compromise-20110215-1av7f.html)
Corlett, W. J. and Hague, D. C., 'Complementarity and the Excess Burden of Taxation', *Review of Economic Studies* 21 (1953), 21
van der Corput, Walter and Annacondia, Fabiola (eds.), *EU VAT Compass* (IBFD Publications, Amsterdam, 2007)
Council of Australian Governments (COAG), *National Health and Hospitals Network Agreement* (April 2010) (federalfinancialrelations.gov.au/content/related_agreements/NHHN_Agreement.pdf)
Intergovernmental Agreement on the Reform of Commonwealth-State Financial Relations (25 June 1999)
Crawford, Ian, Keen, Michael and Smith, Stephen, 'Value Added Tax and Excises' in Stuart Adam et al. (eds.) for the Institute for Fiscal Studies, *Dimensions of Tax Design: The Mirrlees Review* (Oxford University Press, Oxford, 2010), 275

Creedy, John, 'The GST and Vertical, Horizontal and Reranking Effects of Indirect Taxation in Australia', *Australian Economic Review* 35(4) (20002), 380

'Are Consumption Taxes Regressive?', *Australian Economic Review* 31(2) (1998), 107

and the Melbourne Institute of Applied Economic and Social Research, *Are Consumption Taxes Regressive?* (Melbourne Institute of Applied Economics and Social Research, Melbourne, 1997)

Crum, Robert P., 'Value-Added Taxation: The Roots Run Deep Into Colonial and Early America', *Accounting Historians Journal* 9(2) (1982). 25

Cui, Wei and Wu, Alan, 'China', in Thomas Ecker, Michael Lang and Lejeune, I (eds.), *The Future of Indirect Taxation: Recent Trends in VAT and GST Systems Around the World* (Kluwer Law International, Netherlands, 2012), 159

Cui, Wei, 'Learning to Keep the Consumption Tax Base Broad: Australian and Chinese VAT Design for the Housing Sector', in C. Peacock (ed.), *GST in Australia: Looking Forward from the First Decade* (Lawbook Company, Pyrmont, 2011), 367

'Indirect Taxation of Cross-Border Services in China: (Partial) Switch to Destination-Based Taxation', in M. Lang, P. Melz and E. Kristoffersson (eds.), *Value Added Tax and Direct Taxation: Similarities and Differences* (online book, IBFD, Amsterdam, 2009), Introduction.

Dabner, Justin, 'The Japanese Consumption Tax: Lessons for Australia?', *Journal of Australian Taxation* 5(2) (2002), 185

Dahl, Robert Alan, *Who Governs? Democracy and Power in an American City* (Yale University Press, New Haven, CT, 1961)

A Preface to Democratic Theory (University of Chicago Press, Chicago, 1956)

Daley, John, McGannon, Cassie and Ginnivan, Leah, *Game-Changers: Economic Reform Priorities for Australia* (Grattan Institute, Melbourne, 2012)

Damme, Lauren, Misrahi, Tiffany and Orel, Stephanie, 'Taxation Policy in Developing Countries: What Is the IMF's Involvement?' (Consultancy Project No. DV406 for the Bretton Woods Project, 2008)

Farber, Daniel A. and Frickey, Philip P., *Law and Public Choice: A Critical Introduction* (University of Chicago Press, Chicago, 1991)

Danziger, Sheldon and Gottschalk, Peter, *Uneven Tides: Rising Inequality in America* (Russell Sage Foundation, New York, 1993)

D'Ascenzo, Michael, 'The Australian Approach to GST Administration', in R. Krever and D. White (eds.), *GST in Retrospect and Prospect* (Thomson Brookers, Wellington, 2007), 389

Das-Gupta, Arindam and Gang, Ira N., 'A Comparison of Sales Taxes', *Public Finance* 51(2) (1996), 217

Daunton, Martin, *Just Taxes: The Politics of Taxation in Britain, 1914–1979* (Cambridge University Press, Cambridge, 2002)

Trusting Leviathan: The Politics of Taxation in Britain, 1799–1914 (Cambridge University Press, Cambridge, 2001)

Davidson, Kenneth, 'Editorial – Political Burdens: Myths, Lies and Charades', *Dissent* (19) (2005–2006), 2

Davies, David, *United States Taxes and Tax Policy* (Cambridge University Press, Cambridge, 1986)

Davis, Mark, 'A Snip at $22m to Get Rid of PM', *Sydney Morning Herald* (online), 2 February 2011 (smh.com.au/business/a-snip-at-22m-to-get-rid-of-pm-20110201-1acgj.html)

De la Feria, Rita (ed.), *VAT Exemptions: Consequences and Design Alternatives* (vol. 37, EUCOTAX Series on European Taxation, Kluwer Law International, Alphen aan den Rijn, 2013)

The EU VAT System and the Internal Market (IBFD, Amsterdam, 2009)
De la Feria, Rita and Lockwood, Ben, 'Opting for Opting-In? An Evaluation of the European Commission's Proposals for Reforming VAT on Financial Services', *Fiscal Studies* 31(2) (2010), 171
De la Feria, Rita and Walpole, M., 'Options for Taxing Financial Supplies in Value Added Tax: EU VAT and Australian GST Models Compared', *International and Comparative Law Quarterly* 58(4) (2009), 897
De La Mettrie, Laurent and Murre, Donald, 'The European Financial Transaction Tax: Update', *Derivatives & Financial Instruments* (November/December 2013), 218
Denscombe, Martyn, *The Good Research Guide: for Small-Scale Social Research Projects* (McGraw-Hill/Open University Press, 4th ed., Maidenhead, UK, 2010)
Desai, Mihir A. and Hines, James R. Jr, *'Value-Added Taxes and International Trade: The Evidence'* (Workshop in Law and Economics Working Paper, University of Chicago, Law School, 2002)
Department for International Development (United Kingdom), *DFID Evaluation of Revenue Projects (Evaluation Summary)* (DFID, 2001)
Diamond, John W. and Zodrow, George R. (eds.), *Fundamental Tax Reform: Issues, Choices, and Implications* (MIT Press, Cambridge, MA, 2008)
Diamond, Peter A., 'A Many-Person Ramsey Rule', *Journal of Public Economics* 4 (1975), 335
Diamond, Peter and Mirrlees, Jim, 'Optimal Taxation and Public Production I: Production Efficiency', *American Economic Review* 61(1) (1971), 8
'Optimal Taxation and Public Production II: Tax Rules', (Part 1 of 2)) *American Economic Review* 61(3) (1971), 261
DiMaggio, Paul J. and Powell, Walter W., 'The Iron Cage Revisited: Institutional Isomorphism and Collective Rationality in Organizational Fields', *American Sociological Review* 48(2) (1983), 147
Dirks, Reginald, 'Reform of Swiss VAT – The VAT Act from 2010', *International VAT Monitor* (2009), 481
Disney, Julian and Krever, Rick (eds.), *Restoring Revenue: Issues and Options* (Centre for International and Public Law Taxation Law and Policy Research Institute, Melbourne, 1995)
Dodd, Tim, 'Coalition Will Turn to Crime in Bid to Sell *Fightback!* Package', *Australian Financial Review*, 29 May 1992, 7
Dodson, Louise, 'Push to Reduce GST Avoidance', *Australian Financial Review*, 18 June 1999, 5
'Catholic Doctrine Bone of GST Dissent', *Australian Financial Review*, 7 May 1999, 41
'ACOSS Appeals to Business', *Australian Financial Review*, 30 April 1999, 9
'Focus on Scoring Points', *Australian Financial Review*, 20 April 1999, 9
Dodson, Louise, Lewis, Steve and Cummins, Kath, 'Business Takes Hard Line on GST', *Australian Financial Review*, 25 May 1999, 1, 8
Van Doesum, Ad and van Norden, Gert-Jan, 'The Right to Deduct under EU VAT', *International VAT Monitor* (September/October 2011), 323
Domhoff, G. William, *The Four Networks Theory of Power: A Theoretical Home for Power Structure Research*, Who Rules America? (April 2005) (www2.ucsc.edu/whorulesamerica/theory/four_networks.html)
Douglas, Roger, 'The New Zealand GST Policy Choice and Its Political Implications', in R. Krever and D. White (eds.), *GST in Retrospect and Prospect* (Thomson Brookers, Wellington, 2007), 3
Downing, R. I. and Social Science Research Council of Australia, *Taxation in Australia: Agenda for Reform* (Melbourne University Press, Melbourne, 1964)

Downs, Anthony, *An Economic Theory of Democracy* (Harper and Bros, New York, 1957)

Due, John F., 'VAT Treatment of Farmers and Small Firms', in M. Gillis, C. S. Shoup and G. P. Sicat (eds.), *Value Added Taxation in Developing Countries* (World Bank, Washington, DC, 1990), 58

Due, John F, *Sales Taxation* (University of Illinois Press, Urbana, 1957)

Duff, David, 'The Abolition of Wealth Transfer Taxes: Lessons from Canada, Australia, and New Zealand', *Pittsburgh Tax Review* 3(1) (2005), 1

Duncan, Harley and Sedon, Jon, 'Coordinating a Federal VAT with State and Local Sales Taxes' in C. Phillips (ed.), *The VAT Reader: What a Federal Consumption Tax Would Mean for America* (Tax Analysts, Arlington, VA, 2011), 139

Dye, Thomas, *Understanding Public Policy* (Longman, 13th ed., New York, 2011)

Dynan, Karen E., Skinner, Jonathon and Zeldes, Stephen P., 'Do the Rich Save More?', *Journal of Political Economy* 112(2) (2004), 397

Ebeke, Christian and Ehrhart, Helene, *Does VAT Reduce the Instability of Tax Revenues?* (Centre for Studies and Research on International Development, online paper – E 2011.24, 2011)

Ebrill, Liam, et al., *The Modern VAT* (International Monetary Fund, Washington, DC, 2001)

'The Allure of the Value Added Tax', *Finance and Development* 39(2) (2002), 44

Eccleston, Richard, *Taxing Reforms* (Edward Elgar, Cheltenham, 2007)

The Thirty-Year Problem: The Politics of Australian Tax Reform (ATRF, Sydney, 2004)

'Taxing Times: A Political Retrospective', *Australian Taxation Forum* 17(3) (2002), 287

'The Significance of Business Interest Association in Economic Policy Reform: The Case of Australian Taxation Policy', *Business and Politics* 2(3) (2000), 309

Ecker, Thomas, *A VAT/GST Model Convention* (Doctoral Series 25) (IBFD, Amsterdam, 2013)

Economics References Committee, Commonwealth of Australia Senate, *Competition within the Australian Banking Sector* (2011)

Edgar, Tim, 'Comment: Is the Comprehensive Application of Cash-Flow Taxation Necessary to Integrate Financial Services into an Invoice/Credit VAT?' in R. de la Feria, *VAT Exemptions: Consequences and Design Alternatives* (vol. 37, EUCOTAX Series on European Taxation, Kluwer Law International, Alphen aan den Rijn, 2013), 357

'The Search for Alternatives to the Exempt Treatment of Financial Services under a Value Added Tax', in R. Krever and D. White (eds.), *GST in Retrospect and Prospect* (Thomson Brookers, Wellington, 2007), 131

'Exempt Treatment of Financial Intermediation Services under a Value-Added Tax: An Assessment of Alternatives', *Canadian Tax Journal* 49(5) (2001), 1133

Editorial, 'The Persuasive Mathews Report', *Australian Financial Review*, 30 May 1975, 2

Edlin, Aaron S., Gelman, Andrew and Kaplan, Noah, 'Vote for Charity's Sake', *The Economists' Voice* 5(6) (2008), 1

Edlin, Aaron, Gelman, Andrew and Kaplan, Noah, 'Voting as a Rational Choice', *Rationality and Society* 19(3) (2007), 293

Edmiston, Kelly D. and Fox, William F., 'A Fresh Look at the VAT', in J. Alm, J. Martínez-Vázquez and M. Rider (eds.), *The Challenges of Tax Reform in a Global Economy* (Springer, New York, 2006), 249

Edmundson, Peter, 'GST and Financial Supplies: A Comparative Analysis of Legislative Structure', *Australian Tax Review* 30 (2001), 132

Eichengreen, Barry J, and Lindert, Peter H., *The International Debt Crisis in Historical Perspective* (MIT Press, Cambridge, MA, 1989)

Eisenstein, Louis, *The Ideologies of Taxation* (Ronald Press Company, New York, 1961)
Elster, Jon, *Explaining Social Behavior: More Nuts and Bolts for the Social Sciences* (Cambridge University Press, Cambridge; New York, 2007)
'Rational Choice History: A Case of Excessive Ambition', *American Political Science Review* 94(3) (2000), 685
'Some Unresolved Problems in the Theory of Rational Behaviour', *Acta Sociologica* 36 (1993), 179
Making Sense of Marx (Cambridge University Press, Cambridge, 1985)
Employment Workplace Relations Small Business and Education References Committee, Commonwealth of Australia Senate, *Report of the Inquiry into the GST and a New Tax System* (1999)
Emran, M. Shahe and Stiglitz, Joseph E., 'On Selective Indirect Tax Reform in Developing Countries', *Journal of Public Economics* 89 (2005), 599
Ernst & Young, *Worldwide VAT, GST and Sales Tax Guide* (Ernst & Young, 2014)
European Commission (EC), Directorate-General for Economic and Financial Affairs, Directorate General for Taxation and Customs Union, *Tax Reforms in EU Member States: Tax Policy Challenges for Economic Growth and Fiscal Sustainability – 2013 Report* (EC, Brussels, 2013)
European Commission, *VAT Rates Applied in Member States of the European Union (Situation as at 1 July 2013)* (Brussels, 2013)
Communication from the Commission to the European Parliament and the Council on Concrete Ways to Reinforce the Fight against Tax Fraud and Tax Evasion Including in Relation to Third Countries COM(2012), 351
Communication from the Commission to the European Parliament and the Council on an Action Plan to Strengthen the Fight against Tax Fraud and Tax Evasion COM(2012), 722
'Commission Proposes Green Light for Enhanced Cooperation on Financial Transactions Tax' (Press Release, IP/12/1138, 23 October 2012)
European Commission and PricewaterhouseCoopers, 'Review of Current Practices for Taxation of Financial Instruments, Profits and Remuneration of the Financial Sector' (Working Paper No. 11/09/12, European Commission, 28 June 2012)
Directorate-General Taxation and Customs Union, Indirect Taxation and Tax Administration, VAT and other Turnover Taxes, *Summary Report of the Outcome of the Public Consultation on the Green Paper on the Future of VAT Towards a Simpler, More Robust and Efficient VAT System (1 December 2010 – 31 May 2011)*, taxud.c.1 (2011) 1417007
Communication from the Commission to the European Parliament, the Council, and the European Economic and Social Committee on the future of VAT – Towards a Simpler, More Robust and Efficient VAT System Tailored to the Single Market COM (2011), 851
'Financial Transaction Tax: Making the Financial Sector Pay Its Fair Share' (Press Release IP/11/1085, 28 September 2011)
'Staff Working Paper Accompanying the Document Proposal for a Council Directive on a Common System of Financial Transaction Tax and Amending Directive 2008/7/EC – Impact Assessment: Instruments for the Taxation of the Financial Sector' (SEC(2011) 1102 final, Vol. 1, European Commission, 2011)
Communication from the Commission to the Council, the European Parliament, the European Economic and Social Committee, 'On a Coordinated Strategy to Improve the Fight against VAT Fraud in the European Union' COM (2008) 807
Green Paper on the Future of VAT: Towards a Simpler, More Robust and Efficient VAT System [2010] COM(2010), 695
'Background Paper Requested by the Council Presidency; Subject: Financial and Insurance Services' (TAXUD/2414/08)

Impact Assessment: Accompanying document to the Proposal for a Council Directive Amending Directive 2006/112/EC on the Common System of Value Added Tax, as Regards the Treatment of Insurance and Financial Services, SEC (2007) 1554

'Modernising VAT rules Applied on Financial and Insurance Services – Frequently Asked Questions' (MEMO/07/519, European Commission, 2007)

Proposal for a Council Directive Amending Directive 2006/112/EC on the Common System of Value Added Tax, as Regards the Treatment of Insurance and Financial Services (COM/2007/747, European Commission, 2007)

Proposal for a Council Regulation Laying Down Implementing Measures for Directive 2006/112/EC on the Common System of Value Added Tax, As Regards the Treatment of Insurance and Financial Services COM (2007), 746 final

European Commission, Directorate General Customs and Taxation Union, Indirect Taxation and Tax Administration, VAT and Other Turnover Taxes, *Summary of Results: Public Consultation on Financial and Insurance Services* (European Commission, 2006)

'Consultation Paper on Modernising Value Added Tax Obligations for Financial Services and Insurances' (European Commission, Brussels, 2006)

Value Added Tax: A Study of Methods of Taxing Financial and Insurance Services (EC, Brussels, 1996)

European Economic Community and International Bureau of Fiscal Documentation, *The EEC Reports on Tax Harmonization: The Report of the Fiscal and Financial Committee and the Reports of the Subgroups A, B, and C* (International Bureau of Fiscal Documentation, Amsterdam, 1963)

Evans, Chris, Krever, Richard and Mellor, Peter, *Australia's Future Tax System: The Prospects after Henry* (Thomson Reuters (Professional) Australia, Rozelle, NSW, 2010)

Evans, Michael, 'The Value Added Tax Treatment of Real Property – An Antipodean Context' in R. Krever and D. White (eds.), *GST in Retrospect and Prospect* (Thomson Brookers, Wellington, 2007), 243

Evans, Michael B., 'The GST Treatment of Financial Services in Australia', in C. Peacock (ed.), *GST in Australia: Looking Forward from the First Decade* (Thomson Reuters, Pyrmont, 2011), 133

Evans, Peter B., et al., *Bringing the State Back In* (Cambridge University Press, Cambridge; New York, 1985)

Farr, James, Dryzek, John S. and Leonard, Stephen T., 'Introduction', in J. Farr, J. S. Dryzek and S. T. Leonard (eds.), *Political Science in History: Research Programs and Political Traditions* (Cambridge University Press, Cambridge; New York, 1995), xi

(eds.), *Political Science in History: Research Programs and Political Traditions* (Cambridge University Press, Cambridge; New York, 1995)

Federal Commissioner of Taxation, *Australian Taxation Office – Annual Report 2012–2013* (ATO, Canberra, 2013)

Australian Taxation Office – Annual Report 2011–2012 (ATO, Canberra, 2012)

Australian Taxation Office – Annual Report 2010–2011 (ATO, Canberra, 2011)

Australian Taxation Office – Annual Report 2009–2010 (ATO, Canberra, 2010)

Australian Taxation Office – Annual Report 1999–2000 (Australian Taxation Office, Canberra, 2000)

Australian Taxation Office – Annual Report 1998–1999 (Australian Taxation Office, Canberra, 1999)

Fehily, Ken, 'Residential Premises', in C. Peacock (ed.), *GST in Australia: Looking Forward from the First Decade* (Thomson Reuters, Sydney, 2011), 201

'Comment: Real Property Issues in the GST', in R. Krever and D. White (eds.), *GST in Retrospect and Prospect* (Thomson Brookers, Wellington, 2007), 309

Fehr, Hans, Rosenberg, Christoph B. and Wiegard, Wolfgang, *Welfare Effects of Value-Added Tax Harmonization in Europe: A Computable General Equilibrium Analysis* (Springer-Verlag, Berlin; New York, 1995)

Feldstein, Martin (ed.), *American Economic Policy in the 1980s* (University of Chicago Press, Chicago, 1994)

Fenna, Alan, *Australian Public Policy* (Pearson Education Australia, 2nd ed., Frenchs Forest, NSW, 2004)

Flyvbjerg, Bent, 'Five Misunderstandings About Case-Study Research', *Qualitative Inquiry* 12(2) (2006), 219

Foucault, Michel, and Faubion, James D., *Power* (Allen Lane, London, 2001)

Freebairn, John, 'Changing the Tax Mix', *Australian Economic Review* 40(2) (2007), 194

Freeden, Michael, *Ideologies and Political Theory: A Conceptual Approach* (Oxford University Press, Oxford, 1996)

Fried, Barbara H., 'Fairness and the Consumption Tax', *Stanford Law Review* 44 (1991–1992), 961

Friedman, Jeffrey (ed.), *The Rational Choice Controversy: Economic Models of Politics Reconsidered* (Yale University Press, New Haven, CT, 1996)

Friedman, Thomas, 'New Tax on Goods Is Weighed to Pay for Health Care', *New York Times*, 15 April 1993, A1

Ganghof, Steffen, 'Tax Mixes and the Size of the Welfare State: Causal Mechanisms and Policy Implications', *European Journal of Social Policy* 16(4) (2006), 360

The Politics of Income Taxation: A Comparative Analysis (ECPR Press, Colchester, 2006)

Ganghof, Steffen and Eccleston, Richard, 'Globalisation and the Dilemmas of Income Taxation in Australia', *Australian Journal of Political Science* 39(3) (2004), 519

Gentry, William M., 'Optimal Taxation', in J. J. Cordes, R. D. Ebel and J. Gravelle (eds.), *Encyclopedia of Taxation and Tax Policy* (Urban Institute Press, 2nd ed., Washington, DC, 1999), 281

Geuss, Raymond, *Philosophy and Real Politics* (Princeton University Press, Princeton, NJ, 2008)

Gifford, Adam Jr and Kenney, Roy W., 'Socialism and the Revenue Maximizing Leviathan', *Public Choice* 42 (1984), 101

Gillespie, W. Irwin, *Tax, Borrow, and Spend: Financing Federal Spending in Canada, 1867–1990* (Carleton University Press, Ottawa, Canada, 1991)

Gillies, James, 'Federal Tax Reform in a Pluralistic State: Can It Be Done?' in N. Brooks (ed.), *The Quest for Tax Reform: The Royal Commission on Taxation Twenty Years Later* (Carswell, Toronto, 1988)

Gillis, Malcolm, 'Historical and Contemporary Debate on Consumption Taxes', in G. Zodrow and P. Mieszkowski (eds.), *United States Tax Reform in the 21st Century* (Cambridge University Press, Cambridge, 2002), 284

Gillis, Malcolm, Shoup, Carl S. and Sicat, Gerardo P., 'Lessons for Developing Countries', in M. Gillis, C. S. Shoup and G. P. Sicat (eds.), *Value Added Taxation in Developing Countries (A World Bank Symposium)* (World Bank, Washington, DC, 1990), 219

(eds.), *Value Added Taxation in Developing Countries* (World Bank, Washington, DC, 1990)

Goldfinch, Shaun, *Remaking New Zealand and Australian Economic Policy: Ideas, Institutions, and Policy Communities* (Georgetown University Press, Washington, DC, 2000)

Goldstein, Judith and Keohane, Robert O., *Ideas and Foreign Policy: Beliefs, Institutions, and Political Change* (Cornell University Press, Ithaca, NY, 1993)

Good, David A, *The Politics of Anticipation: Making Canadian Federal Tax Policy* (School of Public Administration, Carleton University, Ottawa, 1980)

Goode, Richard, 'Tax Advice to Developing Countries: An Historical Survey', *World Development* 21(1) 1993), 37

Goodin, Robert E. and Klingemann, Hans-Dieter, *A New Handbook of Political Science* (Oxford University Press, Oxford; New York, 1996)

Goodin, Robert E. and Klingemann, Hans-Dieter, 'Political Science: The Discipline', in R. E. Goodin and H.-D. Klingemann (eds.), *A New Handbook of Political Science* (Oxford University Press, Oxford; New York, 1996), 3

Gordon, Michael, 'Libs' GST: On Sale Again', *Sunday Age*, 19 April 1992, 1

Gottliebsen, Robert, 'Finding a Way Out of the Mess', *Business Review Weekly*, 29 November 1991, 6

Gough, Deborah, 'Australians Value a "Fair Go" Highest', *The Sunday Age*, 12 November 2006, 6

Gould, Andrew C. and Baker, Peter J., 'Democracy and Taxation', *Annual Review of Political Science* 5 (2002), 87

Graetz, Michael J. and Schenk, Deborah H., *Federal Income Taxation: Principles and Policies* (Foundation Press, 6th ed., New York, 2009)

Graetz, Michael, 'Tax Policy Challenges', *Ohio Northern University Law Review* 35 (2009), 1

100 Million Unnecessary Returns, A Simple, Fair and Competitive Plan for the United States (Yale University Press, New Haven, CT, 2008)

Death by a Thousand Cuts: The Fight over Taxing Inherited Wealth (Princeton University Press, Princeton, NJ, 2005)

'100 Million Unnecessary Returns: A Fresh Start for the U.S. Tax System', *Yale Law Journal* 112 (2002–2003), 261

The Decline (and Fall?) of the Income Tax (W. W. Norton, New York, 1997)

Grambeck, Hans-Martin, 'B2C Supplies of Electronic Services from 1 January 2015 from a German Perspective', *International VAT Monitor* (July/August 2013), 215

Grandcolas, Christophe, 'The Occasional Failure in VAT Implementation: Lessons for the Pacific', *Asia-Pacific Tax Bulletin* (2005), 6

Grattan, Michelle, 'Howard Bans GST "Forever"', *The Age*, 3 May 1995, 5

'GST Numbers Game – A Matter of Leadership', *The Age*, 23 November 1991, 2

'Libs Snatch Home Ground Advantage', *The Age*, 22 November 1991, 19

Gray, John and Chapman, Emma, *Evaluation of Revenue Projects Synthesis Report: Volume 1* (United Kingdom Department for International Development, 2001)

Green, Donald P. and Shapiro, Ian, *Pathologies of Rational Choice Theory: A Critique of Applications in Political Science* (Yale University Press, New Haven, CT, 1994)

Groenewegen, P. D., *Australian Taxation Policy* (2nd ed., Longman Cheshire, Melbourne, 1987)

Everyone's Guide to Taxation in Australia (George Allen & Unwin, Sydney, 1985)

Australian Taxation Policy: Survey 1965–1980 (Taxation Institute Research and Education Trust, Sydney, 1981)

'Asprey Observed', *Australian Financial Review*, 19 November 1974, 16

Grofman, Bernard, 'Public Choice, Civic Republicanism, and American Politics: Perspectives of a Reasonable Choice Modeller', *Texas Law Review* 71 (1992–1993), 1541

Gruber, Jonathon, *Public Finance and Public Policy* (Worth Publishers, 3rd ed., New York, 2011)

Grubert, Harry and Krever, Richard, 'VAT and Financial Services: Competing Perspectives on What Should Be Taxed', *Tax Law Review* 65 (2011–2012), 199

Grubert, Harry and Mackie, James, 'Must Financial Services be Taxed Under a Consumption Tax?' *National Tax Journal* 53(1) (2000), 23

Gruen, David and Stevens, Glenn, *Australian Macroeconomic Performance and Policies in the 1990s (Research Paper)* (Reserve Bank of Australia, Canberra, 2000)

Gunn, Jeannie, *We of the Never Never* (Hutchinson of Australia, Richmond, 1908)

Haas, Peter M., 'Introduction: Epistemic Communities and International Policy Coordination', *International Organization* 46(1) (1992), 1

Hall, John A. and Schroeder, Ralph, *An Anatomy of Power: The Social Theory of Michael Mann* (Cambridge University Press, Cambridge; New York, 2006)

Hall, Peter and Taylor, Rosemary C., 'Political Science and the Three New Institutionalisms', *Political Studies* 44 (1996), 936

Hall, Peter A., 'Policy Paradigms, Social Learning and the State', *Comparative Politics* 25 (1993), 275

(ed.), *The Political Power of Economic Ideas: Keynesianism across Nations* (Princeton University Press, Princeton, NJ, 1989)

Governing the Economy (Oxford University Press, New York, 1986)

Hall, Robert E. and Rabushka, Alvin, *The Flat Tax* (Hoover Institution Press, Stanford, CA, 1985)

Hallerberg, Mark and Basinger, Scott, 'Internationalization and Changes in Tax Policy in OECD Countries: The Importance of Domestic Veto Players', *Comparative Political Studies* 31(3) (1998), 321

Hamilton, R. W. and Whalley, J., 'Efficiency and Distributional Effect of the Tax Reform Package', in J. Mintz and J. Whalley (eds.), *The Economic Impacts of Tax Reform, Canadian Tax Paper No.* 84 (Canadian Tax Foundation, Toronto, 1989

Hampton, Jean, 'Free-Rider Problems in the Production of Collective Goods', *Economics and Philosophy* 3(2) (1987), 245

Hansen, Susan B., *The Politics of Taxation: Revenue without Representation* (Praeger, New York, 1983)

Harrison, Graham and Krelove, Russell, 'VAT Refunds: A Review of Country Experience' (Working Paper No. WP/05/218, International Monetary Fund, 2005)

Harrison, John and Stretton, Marilyn, *The GST Debate* (Originally published as *The GST Debate – A Chronology: Background Paper No. 1 1997–1998*; Updated by Marilyn Stretton to February 1999) (AGPS, Canberra, 1999)

Hartcher, Peter, 'Opposition Fears GST Cost Votes', *Sydney Morning Herald*, 14 April 1992, 3

Hatta, Tatsuo, 'The Nakasone-Takeshita Tax Reform: A Critical Evaluation', AEA *Papers and Proceedings* 82(2) (1992), 231

Haupt, Robert, 'Asprey Tax Flop', *Australian Financial Review*, 6 June 1974, 1

Hayes, Terry, 'GST Margin Scheme Restructure Will Not Proceed', *Weekly Tax Bulletin* (28) (29 June 2012), 1059

Head, John G. (ed.) *Fightback!: An Economic Assessment: Papers from a Conference Organised by the Public Sector Management Institute, Monash University* (Australian Tax Research Foundation, Sydney, 1993)

Monash University Centre of Policy Studies and Australian Tax Research Foundation, *Taxation Issues of the 1980s: Papers Presented at a Conference* (Australian Tax Research Foundation, Sydney, 1983)

Headey, Bruce, Warren, Diana and Harding, Glenys, *Families, Incomes and Jobs: A Statistical Report of the HILDA Survey*, Melbourne Institute of Applied Economic and Social Research, University of Melbourne (2006)

Heclo, Hugh, *Modern Social Politics in Britain and Sweden: From Relief to Income Maintenance* (Yale University Press, New Haven, CT, 1974)

Hepworth, Annabel, 'Games Lose, PC buyers Win, and the Net Will Be Widened', *Special GST Guide for Business Liftout, Australian Financial Review*, 28 June 1999, 4

'Banks to Get Input Credits under GST', *Australian Financial Review*, 10 June 1999, 29

Hettich, Walter and Winer, Stanley L., *Democratic Choice and Taxation: A Theoretical and Empirical Analysis* (Cambridge University Press, Cambridge, 1999)

Higgs, Robert, *Crisis and Leviathan: Critical Episodes in the Growth of American Government* (Oxford University Press, New York, 1987)

Hindess, Barry, *Discourses of Power: from Hobbes to Foucault* (Blackwell Publishers, Oxford; Cambridge, MA, 1996)

Hines, J. R., 'Might Fundamental Tax Reform Increase Criminal Activity?', *Economica* 71 (283) (2004), 483

Hobbes, Thomas, *Leviathan* (Cambridge University Press, Cambridge, first published 1651, 1991 ed.)

Hodge, Graeme and Bowman, Diana, 'The 'Consultocracy': The Business of Reforming Government', in G. Hodge (ed.) *Privatization and Market Development: Global Movements in Public Policy Ideas* (Edward Elgar, Northampton, MA, 2006), 97

Hodler, Roland, 'Political Economics', *Australian Economic Review* 41(3) (2008), 330

Hofferbert, Richard I. and Cingranelli, David Louis, 'Public Policy and Administration: Comparative Policy Analysis', in R. E. Goodin and H.-D. Klingemann (eds.), *A New Handbook of Political Science* (Oxford University Press, Oxford; New York, 1998), 593

Hoover, Kenneth R., *Economics as Ideology: Keynes, Laski, Hayek, and the Creation of Contemporary Politics* (Rowman & Littlefield, Lanham, MD, 2003)

Howard, Christopher, *The Hidden Welfare State: Tax Expenditures and Social Policy in the United States* (Princeton University Press, Princeton, NJ, 1997)

Howard, John, 'Taxation Reform', *Australian Tax Forum* 1(1) (1984), 8

Hudson, Phillip, 'No GST Deal for Financial Sector', *The Age* (Melbourne), 9 March 1999, 6

Huizinga, Harry, 'A European VAT on Financial Services?' *Economic Policy* 17(35) (2002), 497

Hunter, F., *Community Power Structure: A Study of Decision Makers* (University of North Carolina Press, Chapel Hill, 1953)

Hutchinson, Andrew, 'GST Anti-Avoidance: Sharper Teeth! – Bigger Bite?' *Weekly Tax Bulletin* (10) (1999)

Hywood, Gregory, 'As Summiteering Gives Way to Bargaining, a Compromise Is On, Says Hawke', *Australian Financial Review*, 3 July 1985, 1

'Power Politics and the Summit', *Australian Financial Review*, 28 June 1985, 1

'Hawke Clear Way for Retreat from Option C', *Australian Financial Review*, 26 June 1985, 8

'Hawke to Shed Light on Form of Tax Review', *Australian Financial Review*, 29 October 1984, 3

'Keating's Brave Defeat: A Comprehensive Retreat on Reform', *Australian Financial Review*, 5 July 1975, 1

Institute for Fiscal Studies (IFS), *A Retrospective Evaluation of Elements of the EU VAT System: Final Report for the European Commission* (IFS, London, 2011)

Institute for Fiscal Studies, *Dimensions of Tax Design: The Mirrlees Review* (Oxford University Press, Oxford, 2010)

The Structure and Reform of Direct Taxation (Report of a Committee Chaired by Professor J. E. Meade) (Allen and Unwin, London, 1978)

International Bureau of Fiscal Documentation (IBFD), *Country Surveys* (2014)

International Monetary Fund (IMF), *Fiscal Monitor (October 2013) – Taxing Times* (IMF, Washington, DC, 2013)

IMF Country Report No. 11/201 – The United States – 2011 Article IV Consultation (IMF, Washington, DC, 2011)

Fiscal Affairs Department: At a Glance (IMF, 2010) International Monetary Fund (IMF), *Fiscal Monitor (November 2010) – Fiscal Exit: From Strategy to Implementation* (IMF, Washington, DC, 2010)

A Fair and Substantial Contribution by the Financial Sector – Final Report for the G-20 (IMF, Washington, DC, 2010)

International Monetary Fund (IMF) Fiscal Affairs Department, 'Should Equity Be a Goal of Economic Policy?' *Finance and Development* (September 1998), 2

International Monetary Fund (IMF) Legal Department, *Tax Law Drafting Samples VAT* (24 January 2006) IMF (imf.org/external/np/leg/tlaw/2003/eng/tlvat.htm)

International Monetary Fund, et al., *Helping Countries Develop: The Role of Fiscal Policy* (IMF, Washington, DC, 2004)

International Tax Dialogue (ITD), *About Us* (itdweb.org/Pages/AboutUs.aspx)

'The Value Added Tax: Experience and Issues' (Background Paper Prepared for the International Tax Dialogue Conference on the VAT, Rome, ITD, 15–16 March 2005)

Inwood, Gregory J, *Understanding Canadian Public Administration* (Pearson, 3rd ed., Prentice Hall, Toronto, 2009)

Ishi, Hiromitsu, *The Japanese Tax System* (Oxford University Press, 2nd ed., Oxford, 1993)

Jack, William, 'The Treatment of Financial Services under a Broad-Based Consumption Tax', *National Tax Journal* 53(4) (2000), 841

Jackson, Randall, 'Panellists Discuss How US Could Adopt Add-On VAT', *Tax Notes* (2008), 665

Jackson, Robert J. and Jackson, Doreen, *Politics in Canada: Culture, Institutions, Behaviour and Public Policy* (3rd ed., Prentice Hall, Scarborough, Ontario, 1994)

James, Kathryn, 'An Examination of Convergence and Resistance in Global Tax Reform Trends', *Theoretical Inquiries in Law* 11(2) (2010), 475

'We of the "Never Ever": The History of the Introduction of a Goods and Services Tax in Australia from 1970 to 2005', in John Tiley (ed.), *Studies in the History of Tax Law: Volume 3* (2009), 139

'We of the "Never Ever": The History of the Introduction of a Goods and Services Tax in Australia', *British Tax Review* (3) (2007), 320

Jeffrey, Michael and Maynard, Russell, 'Australia's GST: What It Means for the Mining Industry', *Australian Mining and Petroleum Law Journal* 18(1) (1999), 54

Jenkins, Glenn P., Jenkins, Hatice and Kuo, Chun-Yan, 'Is the Value-Added Tax Naturally Progressive?' (Queens University, 2006) (ssrn.com/abstract=897677)

Jenkins, Glenn P. and Kuo, Chun-Yan, 'A VAT Revenue Simulation Model for Tax Reform in Developing Countries', *World Development* 28(4) (2000), 763

Jensen, Erik M., 'The Apportionment of 'Direct Taxes': Are Consumption Taxes Constitutional?' *Columbia Law Review* 97 (1997), 2334

Jespersen, Claus Bohn, *Intermediation of Insurance and Financial Services in European VAT* (Kluwer Law International, Alphen aan den Rijn, The Netherlands, 2011)

Johansson, Asa, et al., 'Taxes and Firm Performance: Evidence from the OECD', in I. Claus et al.(eds.), *Tax Reform in Open Economies: International and Country Perspectives* (Edward Elgar, Cheltenham UK, 2010), 15

Johnson, David, Freebairn, John and Scutella, Rosanna, *Evaluation of the Government's Tax Package* (Melbourne Institute of Applied Economic and Social Research, University of Melbourne, Melbourne, 1999)

Jørgensen, Erik and Owens, Jeffrey, 'The Move to VAT', *OECD Observer* (August/September 1995), 21

Kaldor, Nicholas, *An Expenditure Tax* (Allen & Unwin, London, 1955)

Kantowicz, Edward R., 'The Limits of Incrementalism: Carter's Efforts at Tax Reform', *Journal of Policy Analysis and Management* 4(2) (1985), 217

Kato, Junko, *Regressive Taxation and the Welfare State: Path Dependence and Policy Diffusion* (Cambridge University Press, Cambridge, 2003)

Katznelson, Ira and Milner, Helen V., 'American Political Science: The Discipline's State and the State of the Discipline', in I. Katznelson and H. V. Milner(eds.), *Political Science: State of the Discipline* (Norton; American Political Science Association, New York, Washington, DC, 2002) 1

(eds.), *Political Science: State of the Discipline* (W. W. Norton & Company, New York, 2002)

Kay, Adrian, *The Dynamics of Public Policy: Theory and Evidence* (Edward Elgar, Cheltenham, UK, 2006)

Kay, J. A. and King, Mervyn A., *The British Tax System* (Oxford University Press, Oxford; New York, 1978)

Keating, Paul, 'The Government's Taxation Objectives', *Australian Tax Forum* 1(1) (1984), 2

Keen, Michael, 'The Anatomy of VAT' (Working Paper No. WP/13/111, International Monetary Fund, 2013)

'What Do (and Don't) We Know about the Value Added Tax? A Review of Richard M. Bird and Pierre-Pascal Gendron's *The VAT in Developing and Transitional Countries*', *Journal of Economic Literature* 47(1) (2009), 159

'VAT, Tariffs, and Withholding: Border Taxes and Informality in Developing Countries', *Journal of Public Economics* 92 (2008), 1892

'VAT Attacks!' (Working Paper No. WP/07/142, International Monetary Fund, 2007)

Keen, Michael and Hellerstein, Walter, 'Interjurisdictional Issues in the Design of a VAT', *Tax Law Review* 63(2) (2010), 359

Keen, Michael, Krelove, Russell and Norregaard, John, 'The Financial Activities Tax', in Stijn Claessens, Michael Keen and C. Pazarbasioglu (eds.), *Financial Sector Taxation: The IMF's Report to the G-20 and Background Material* (International Monetary Fund, 2010), 118

Keen, Michael and Lockwood, Ben, 'The Value Added Tax: Its Causes and Consequences', *Journal of Development Economics* 92(2) (2010), 138

'Is the VAT a Money Machine?', *National Tax Journal* 59(4) (2006), 905

Keen, Michael and Mintz, J., 'The Optimal Threshold for a Value-Added Tax', *Journal of Public Economics* 88 (2004), 559

Keen, Michael and de Mooij, Ruud, ' "Fiscal Devaluation" and Fiscal Consolidation: The VAT in Troubled Times', in Alberto Alesina and Francesco Giavazzi (eds.), *Fiscal Policy After the Financial Crisis* (University of Chicago Press, 2013), 443

Keen, Michael and Smith, Stephen, 'VAT Fraud and Evasion: What Do We Know and What Can Be Done?' *National Tax Journal* 59(4) (2006), 861

Kehoe, John, 'Tax Office Chases Dodgy GST Claims', *Australian Financial Review*, 19 February 2010, 10

Kelly, Paul, 'Over the Line', *The Australian*, 29 May 1999, 21

The End of Certainty: The Story of the 1980s (Allen & Unwin, St. Leonards, NSW, 1992)

Kelly, Paul and Waldren, Murray, *Future Tense: Australia beyond Election 1998* (Allen & Unwin, St. Leonards, NSW, 1999)

Kelman, Mark, 'On Democracy-Bashing: A Skeptical Look at the Theoretical and "Empirical" Practice of the Public Choice Movement', *Virginia Law Review* 74 (1988), 199

Kerrigan, Arthur, 'The Elusiveness of Neutrality –Why Is It So Difficult to Apply VAT to Financial Services?' *International VAT Monitor* (March/April 2010), 103

Keynes, John Maynard, *The General Theory of Employment, Interest and Money* (MacMillan, London, 1936)

Kindleberger, Charles Poor and Lindert, Peter H., *International Economics* (R. D. Irwin, 6th ed., Homewood, IL, 1978)

King, Anthony, 'Ideas, Institutions and the Policies of Governments: A Comparative Analysis: Part III', *British Journal of Political Science* 3(4) (1973), 409

'Ideas, Institutions and the Policies of Governments: A Comparative Analysis: Parts I and II', *British Journal of Political Science* 3(3) (1973), 291

King, Gary, Keohane, Robert O. and Verba, Sidney, *Designing Social Inquiry: Scientific Inference in Qualitative Research* (Princeton University Press, Princeton, NJ, 1994)

King, John R., 'The Concept of Income', in P. Shome (ed.), *Tax Policy Handbook* (International Monetary Fund, Washington, DC, 1995), 117

King, Ronald F., 'The Supply-Side Reformation: Business Tax Policies in the Ford Administration', in B. J. Firestone and A. Ugrinsky (eds.), *Gerald R. Ford and the Politics of Post-Watergate America* (Greenwood Press, Westport, CT 1993), 245

Kingdon, John W., *Agendas, Alternatives, and Public Policies* (Longman, 2nd ed., New York, 2003)

Kingston, Margo, 'Hewson Gets a Little Trans-Tasman Aid', *The Age*, 29 November 1991, 6

Kitney, Damon, 'Mining Sector's Good News "The GST Guide for Business"', *Australian Financial Review*, 28 June 1999, 14

Kloeden, David, 'Revenue Administration Reforms in Anglophone Africa Since the Early 1990s' (Working Paper WP/11/162, IMF, 2011)

Kneller, Richard, Bleaney Michael F., Gemmell, Norman, 'Fiscal Policy and Growth: Evidence from OECD Countries', *Journal of Public Economics* 74 (1999), 171

Kohler, Alan, 'Tax That Goes against the Tide of History', *Australian Financial Review*, 5–6 June 1999, 27

KPMG, *The 2012 Benchmark Survey on VAT/GST* (KPMG International, 2012)

Views on VAT: An Article Series (KPMG, Washington, DC, 2011)

Driving Indirect Tax Performance: Managing the Global Reform Challenge (KPMG, 2010)

Krever, Richard, *GST Legislation Plus* (Thomson Reuters, Pyrmont, 2014)

'Forfeited Airfare (VAT Case Note – Australia)', *International VAT Monitor* (November/December 2012), 453

'Designing and Drafting VAT Laws for Africa', in R. Krever (ed.), *VAT in Africa* (Pretoria University Law Press, Pretoria, 2008), 9

(ed.), *VAT in Africa* (Pretoria University Law Press, Pretoria, 2008)

'Understanding Chinese VAT Law: Lessons from Abroad', in X. Yang (ed.), *China VAT Law: Reform and Justice* (China Taxation Publishing House, Beijing, 2007)

'TOFA: The Unfinished Agenda', *Australian Tax Review* 35(2) (2006), 91

'The Political Economy of the GST: A Comment on Professor Brooks' Paper', in B. Tran-Nam (ed.), *Tax Reform and the GST: An International Perspective* (Prospect Media, St Leonards, NSW, 1998), 141

Krever, Richard and de la Feria, Rita, 'Ending VAT Exemptions: Towards a Post-Modern VAT', in R. de la Feria (ed.), *VAT Exemptions: Consequences and Design Alternatives* (vol. 37, EUCOTAX Series on European Taxation, Kluwer Law International, Alphen aan den Rijn, 2013), 3

Krever, R. and White, D. (eds.), *GST in Retrospect and Prospect* (Thomson Brookers, Wellington, 2007)

Krever, Richard and Head, John G. (eds.), *Taxation Towards 2000* (Australian Tax Research Foundation, Sydney, 1997)

Krueger, Anne O., 'The Political Economy of the Rent-Seeking Society', *American Economic Review* 64(3) (1974), 291

Kuttner, Robert, 'Beware a Sales Tax in the Name of Simplicity: Taxes on Consumption Would Hurt the Middle Class and the Poor', *Business Week* (3929) (2005), 19–21

Lagan, Bernard, 'Top Consumer Body Questions Fightback Deal', *Sydney Morning Herald*, 16 November 1992, 7

Lamb, Margaret, et al. (eds.), *Taxation: An Interdisciplinary Approach to Research* (Oxford University Press, Oxford, 2005)

Lasswell, Harold Dwight, *Politics, Who Gets What, When, How* (Peter Smith, New York, 1950)

Lauré, Maurice, *La taxe sur law valeur ajoutée* (Paris, 1952)

Lee, Cheryl H., Willhide, Robert Jesse and Pome, Edward, 'State Government Finances Summary Report: 2012' (Governments Division Briefs No. G12-CG-ASFIN, US Census Bureau, 2014)

Lee, Cheryl H., Willhide, Robert Jesse and Higgins, Nancy I., 'State Government Finances Summary: 2010' (Governments Division Briefs No. G10-ASFIN, US Census Bureau, 2011)

Lees, Meg, 'Democrats' Recipe', *Australian Financial Review*, 30 April 1999, 41

van Leeuwen, Hans, 'Bank Racing Tax Deadline', *Australian Financial Review*, 29 October 1999, 54

'Credit Unions Secure Outsourcing Break', *Australian Financial Review*, 29 October 1999, 54

'Credit Unions and Societies under Threat', *Australian Financial Review*, 8 October 1999, 62

'New Headache for Non-Bank Home Lenders', *Australian Financial Review*, 27 April 1999, 4

Leigh, Andrew, 'Political Economy of Tax Reform in Australia', *Public Policy* 1(1) (2006), 1

Lejeune, Ine, Daou-Azzi, Jeanine and Powell, Mark (of PricewaterhouseCoopers), 'The Balance Has Shifted to Consumption Taxes – Lessons Learned and Best Practices for VAT', in M. Lang, P. Melz and E. Kristoffersson (eds.), *Value Added Tax and Direct Taxation: Similarities and Differences* (IBFD, Vienna, 2009), 59

Lemieux, Pierre, 'The Public Choice Revolution', *Regulation* (2004), 22

Levi, Margaret, 'A Logic of Institutional Change', in M. Levi and K. S. Cook (eds.), *The Limits of Rationality* (University of Chicago Press, Chicago, 1990)

Of Rule and Revenue (University of California Press, Berkeley, 1988)

Lewis, Steve, 'Wine Makers Say New Tax Will Damage a Cellars Market', *Australian Financial Review*, 24 June 1999, 4

Lewis, Steve, and Davis, Mark, 'Business Groups at Odds over Scope of Tax', *Australian Financial Review*, 20 May 1999, 5

Lewis, Timothy, *In the Long Run We're All Dead: The Canadian Turn to Fiscal Restraint* (Vancouver, UBC Press, 2003)

Liberal and National Parties of Australia *Fightback! Fairness And Jobs* (Liberal and National Parties, Canberra, 1992)

Fightback!: The Liberal and National Parties' Plan to Rebuild and Reward Australia, 21 November 1991 (Liberal and National Parties, Canberra, 1991)

Fightback! It's Your Australia: The Way to Rebuild and Reward Australia (Liberal and National Parties, Canberra 1991)

Lieberman, Evan S., 'Taxation Data as Indicators of State-Society Relations: Possibilities and Pitfalls in Cross-National Research', *Studies in Comparative International Development* 36(4) (2002), 89

'Payment for Privilege? Race and Space in the Politics of Taxation in Brazil and South Africa' (PhD thesis, University of California, Berkeley, 2000)

Race and Regionalism in the Politics of Taxation in Brazil and South Africa (Cambridge University Press, Cambridge, 2003)

Lindblom, Charles E., *Politics and Markets: The World's Political Economic Systems* (Basic Books, New York, 1977)

Lindert, Peter H., *Growing Public: Social Spending and Economic Growth since the Eighteenth Century* (Cambridge University Press, Cambridge UK; New York, 2004)

'Growing Public: Is the Welfare State Mortal or Exportable?' (Paper, University of California – Davis, Davis, California, 2005)

Lindholm, Richard W., *A New Federal Tax System* (Praeger, New York, 1984)

The Economics of VAT: Preserving Efficiency, Capitalism, and Social Progress (Lexington Books, DC Heath and Company, Toronto, 1980)

Value-Added Tax and Other Tax Reforms (Nelson-Hall, Chicago, 1976)

Lockwood, Ben, 'How Should Financial Intermediation Services Be Taxed?' (Centre for Economic Policy Research (CEPR) Discussion Paper 8122, University of Warwick – Department of Economics, CEPR, revised 30 September 2013)

Lora, Eduardo, *Latin America After a Decade of Reforms* (IADB, Washington, DC, 1997)

Lora, Eduardo, Inter-American Development Bank (IDB), 'Decade of Structural Reforms in Latin America: What Has Been Reformed and How to Measure It' (Working Paper Green Series No. 348, IDB, 1997)

Luce, R. Duncan and Raiffa, Howard, *Games and Decisions* (Wiley, New York, 1957)

Lukes, Steven, *Power: A Radical View* (Palgrave Macmillan, 2nd ed., New York 2005)

Lang, M., Melz, P. and Kristoffersson, E. (eds.), *Value Added Tax and Direct Taxation: Similarities and Differences* (IBFD, Amsterdam, 2009)

Mackie, Gerry, *Democracy Defended* (Cambridge University Press, Cambridge, 2003)

Mahoney, James, 'Strategies of Causal Assessment in Comparative Historical Analysis', in D. Rueschemeyer and J. Mahoney (eds.), *Comparative Historical Analysis in the Social Sciences* (Cambridge University Press, New York, 2002), xix

Mair, Peter, 'Comparative Politics: An Overview', in R. E. Goodin and H.-D. Klingemann (eds.), *A New Handbook of Political Science* (Oxford University Press, Oxford; New York, 1998), 309

Mann, Michael, 'The Sources of Social Power Revisited: A Response to Criticism', in J. A. Hall and R. Schroeder (eds.), *An Anatomy of Power: The Social Theory of Michael Mann* (Cambridge University Press, Cambridge, 2006), 343

The Sources of Social Power (Cambridge University Press, Cambridge; New York, 1986)

Antonelli, Margherita and Oliver, David (PricewaterhouseCoopers), 'Practical Thoughts on the GST' *Weekly Tax Bulletin* (37) (1998), 1069

Marian, Omri Y., 'The Discursive Failure in Comparative Tax Law', *American Journal of Comparative Law* 58 (2010), 415

Marr, David and Wilkinson, Marian, *Dark Victory* (Allen & Unwin, Crow's Nest, NSW, 2003)

Martin, Isaac W., Mehrotra, Ajay K. and Prasad, Monica (eds.), *The New Fiscal Sociology: Taxation in Comparative and Historical Perspective* (Cambridge University Press, New York, 2009)

Martin, Isaac W., Mehrotra, Ajay K. and Prasad, Monica, 'The Thunder of History: The Origins and Development of the New Fiscal Sociology', in I. W. Martin, A. K. Mehrotra and M. Prasad (eds.), *The New Fiscal Sociology: Taxation in Comparative and Historical Perspective* (Cambridge University Press, New York, 2009), 1

Martin, Isaac W., 'Taxing Reforms: The Politics of Consumption Tax in Japan, the United States, Canada and Australia (Book Review)', *Journal of Economic Literature* 47(1) (2009), 192

The Permanent Tax Revolt (Stanford University Press, CA, 2008)

Martin, Peter, 'Australia Awash in Cold, Hard Cash', *The Age* (online), 26 September 2011 (theage.com.au/business/australia-awash-in-cold-hard-cash-20110925-1krty.html)

'Judge Hits Out at Leaky, Expensive GST", *The Age*, 15 September 2011, 3

'GST Rise a Must, Says Tax Expert', *The Age* (online), 1 September 2011 (theage.com.au/national/gst-rise-a-must-says-tax-expert-20110831-1jm09.html#ixzz1ieVi5H9)

Marx, Karl and Engels, Friedrich, *Collected Works* (Lawrence & Wishart, London, 1975), vol. 3 and 5

Matheson, Thornton, 'Taxing Financial Transactions: Issues and Evidence', in Stijn Claessens, M. Keen and C. Pazarbasioglu (eds.), *Financial Sector Taxation: The IMF's Report to the G-20 and Background Material* (IMF, Washington, DC, 2010), 144

Matthews, Kent, 'VAT Evasion and VAT Avoidance: Is There a European Laffer Curve for VAT?' *International Review of Applied Economics* 17(1) (2003), 105

Maynard, Russell, and Jeffery, Michael, 'Australia's GST: What It Means for the Mining Industry', *Australian Mining and Petroleum Law Journal* 18(4) (1999), 54

McAllister, Ian and Bean, Clive, 'Electoral Politics of Economic Reform in Australia: The 1998 Election', *Australian Journal of Political Science* 35(3) (2000), 383

McCaffery, Edward, 'A New Understanding of Tax', *Michigan Law Review* 58 (2004), 807

McCaffery, Edward and Cohen, Linda R., 'Shakedown at Gucci Gulch: A Tale of Death, Money & Taxes' (USC CLEO Research Paper No. C04–14, USC Centre in Law Economics and Organisation, 2004)

Fair Not Flat: How to Make the Tax System Better and Simpler (University of Chicago Press, Chicago, 2002)

McCarthy, Denis, 'The Australian GST – Why It Is the Way It Is and Where To from Here?' in C. Peacock (ed.), *GST in Australia: Looking Forward from the First Decade* (Thomson Reuters, Sydney, 2011), 61

McCathie, Andrew, 'Abrupt End to Reform Dalliance', *Australian Financial Review*, 14 August 1985, 3

'Option C Sinks, Summit Ends with a Whimper', *Australian Financial Review*, 5 July 1985, 3

'Render unto Caesar: Your Guide to Who's at the Tax Summit', *Australian Financial Review*, 28 June 1985, 33

'Keating Uses an Air Sickness Bag: But Only to Explain Details of His Plan', *Australian Financial Review*, 21 June 1985, 8

McIntosh, Phillip, 'Coalition Support Surges After Package', *Sydney Morning Herald*, 27 November 1991, 4

McKenzie, Andrew, 'Industry Fears Impact of GST", *The Australian*, 6 July 1999, 27

McKenzie, David, 'Political Reality Likely to Block Plans for GST, Say Experts', *The Age*, 13 April 1996, 3

McKibbin, Ross, *The Ideologies of Class: Social Relations in Britain, 1880–1950* (Clarendon Press; Oxford University Press, Oxford; New York, 1990)

McLachlan, Miranda, and Gosnell, Peter, "Banks Face $430m Bill", *The Herald-Sun*, 21 January 2000, 4.
McLure, Charles E. Jr, 'How to Coordinate State and Local Sales Taxes with a Federal Value Added Tax', *Tax Law Review* 63(3) (2009–2010), 639
'What Can the United States Learn from the Canadian Sales Tax Debate?' in J. B. Shoven and J. Whalley (eds.), *Canada-U.S. Tax Comparisons* (University of Chicago Press, Chicago London, 1992), 295
McLure, Charles E. Jr, 'Appraising Tax Reform', in M. J. Boskin and C. E. McLure (eds.), *World Tax Reform* (ICS Press, San Francisco, 1990), Chapter 15
The Value-Added Tax: Key to Deficit Reduction? (American Enterprise Institute, Washington, DC, 1987)
'Value Added Tax: Has the Time Come?' in C. E. Walker and M. A. Bloomfield (eds.), *New Directions in Federal Tax Policy for the 1980s* (Ballinger Publishing Company, Cambridge Massachusetts, 1983), 185
McLure, Charles E. Jr and Zodrow, George R., 'Treasury I and the Tax Reform Act of 1986: The Economics and Politics of Tax Reform', *Economic Perspectives* 1(1) (1987), 37
McMahon, Peter and MacIntyre, Everton, *GST and the Financial Markets* (CCH, Sydney, 2001)
McMorran, Ronald T, 'A Comparison between the Sales Tax and a VAT', in P. Shome (ed.), *Tax Policy Handbook* (International Monetary Fund, Washington, DC, 1995), 82
McQuaig, Linda, 'History of Tax Reform Purged of Class Warfare and Drama', *Canadian Tax Journal* 50(6) (2002), 2045
The Quick and the Dead: Brian Mulroney, Big Business and the Seduction of Canada (Viking, Toronto, 1991)
Behind Closed Doors: How the Rich Won Control of Canada's Tax System – And Ended Up Richer (Viking, Markham, Ontario, 1987)
McTaggart, Douglas, *Microeconomics* (Pearson, 6th ed., Frenchs Forest, 2010)
McTaggart, Douglas, Findlay, Christopher and Parkin, Michael, *Economics* (2nd ed., Addison-Wesley, Sydney, 1996)
Mellish, Morgan, 'Bank to Raise Fees to Beat GST', *Sydney Morning Herald*, 26 January 2000, 3
'Banks' GST Bite on Credit Card Users', *The Sydney Morning Herald*, 25 January 2000, 1
Merkx, Madeline, 'New Implementing Measures for the EU Place-of-Supply Change 2015', *International VAT Monitor* (July/August 2013), 222
Messere, Ken, de Kam, Flip and Heady, Christopher, *Tax Policy: Theory and Practice in OECD Countries* (Oxford University Press, Oxford, 2003)
Metcalf, Gilbert E., 'Consumption Taxation', in J. Cordes et al.(eds.), *Encyclopedia of Taxation and Tax Policy* (Urban Institute Press, Washington, DC, 1999), 64
Meyer, John W. and Rowan, Brian, 'Institutionalized Organizations: Formal Structure as Myth and Ceremony', *American Journal of Sociology* 83(2) (1977), 340
Michael Wigney S. C., 'Text, Context and the Interpretation of a "Practical Business Tax"' *Australian Tax Review* 40 (2011), 94
Michaels, Ralf, 'The Functional Method of Comparative Law', in M. Reimann and R. Zimmermann (eds.), *The Oxford Handbook of Comparative Law* (Oxford University Press, Oxford; New York, 2006), 339
Miliband, Ralph, *The State in Capitalist Society* (Weidenfeld & Nicolson, London, 1969)
Mill, John Stuart, *Principles of Political Economy with Some of Their Applications to Social Philosophy* (Longmans, Green and Co., London, first published 1848, 1909 ed.)
Millar, Rebecca, 'The Destination Principle: Past Developments and Future Challenges' in C. Peacock (ed.), *GST in Australia: Looking Forward from the First Decade* (Thomson Reuters, Pyrmont, 2011), 313

'Cross-Border Services', in R. Krever (ed.), *VAT in Africa* (Pretoria University Law Press, Pretoria, 2008), 175

'Cross-Border Services: A Survey of the Issues', in R. Krever and D. White (eds.), *GST in Retrospect and Prospect* (Thomson Brookers, Wellington, NZ, 2007), 317

Miller, Jonathan M., 'A Typology of Legal Transplants: Using Sociology, Legal History and Argentine Examples to Explain the Transplant Process', *American Journal of Comparative Law* 51(4) (2003), 839

Millett, Michael, 'Hewson Caves In on GST", *Sydney Morning Herald*, 9 December 1992, 1

Mills, C. Wright, *The Power Elite* (Oxford University Press, New York, 1956)

Ministry of Finance (Ontario, Canada), *Budget Papers* (Department of Finance, Toronto, 2009)

Mitchell, Alan, 'Inefficiencies Won't Be the End of the World', *Australian Financial Review*, 20 May 1999, 5

Moran, Michael, Rein, Martin and Goodin, Robert E., *The Oxford Handbook of Public Policy* (Oxford University Press, New York, 2006)

Mueller, Dennis, *Public Choice III* (Cambridge University Press, Cambridge, 2003)

Munday, R. J. C. and Legrand, Pierre, *Comparative Legal Studies: Traditions and Transitions* (Cambridge University Press, Cambridge, 2003)

Murphy, Katharine and Preiss, Ben, 'Retailers Told the Enemy Is Within', *The Age* (Melbourne), 1–2

Murphy, Liam and Nagel, Thomas, *The Myth of Ownership: Taxes and Justice* (Oxford University Press, New York, 2002)

Murray Waldren, Plane, Terry and McGregor, Richard, 'Words of War on Publishing Tax', *The Australian*, 1 June 1999, 4

Musgrave, Peggy, 'Consumption Tax Proposals in an International Setting', *International VAT Monitor* (March/April 2001), 56

Musgrave, Richard Abel and Peacock, Alan Turner, *Classics in the Theory of Public Finance* (Macmillan, 1967)

Nash, Kate, *Contemporary Sociology: Globalization, Politics, and Power* (Blackwell Publishing, Malden, MA, 2000)

National Industrial Conference Board Inc., *General Sales or Turnover Taxation* (New York, 1929)

Neary, Ian, *The State and Politics in Japan* (Polity, Oxford, 2002)

Nehring, Holger, 'The Paradoxes of State-Building: Transnational Expertise and the Income Tax Debates in the United States and Germany, c. 1880–1914' in H. Nehring and F. Schui (eds.), *Global Debates About Taxation* (Palgrave Macmillan, Basingstoke, UK; New York, 2007) 97

Nehring, Holger and Schui, Florian, *Global Debates about Taxation* (Palgrave Macmillan, Basingstoke, England; New York, 2007)

Nelken, David, 'Comparative Law and Comparative Legal Studies', in E. Orucu and D. Nelken (eds.), *Comparative Law: A Handbook* (Hart, Portland, 2007) 3

'Legal Culture', in J. M. Smits (ed.), *Elgar Encyclopaedia of Comparative Law* (Edward Elgar, Cheltenham, UK; Northampton, MA, 2006), 372

Comparing Legal Cultures (Dartmouth, Aldershot, Hants, UK; Brookfield, VT, 1997)

Nellor, David, 'The Effect of Value-Added Tax on the Tax Ratio' (Working Paper No. 87/47, International Monetary Fund, Washington, DC, 1987)

Nevile, J. W. and Committee for Economic Development of Australia, *A Goods and Services Tax: Boon or Bane for Australia?* (CEDA, Sydney, 1992)

Neumark, F., *Neumark Committee, 'Report of the Fiscal and Financial Committee on Tax Harmonization'* (IBFD, Amsterdam, 1963)

Newberry, David and Stern, Nicholas, *The Theory of Taxation for Developing Countries* (Oxford University Press for the World Bank, New York, 1987)

Niskanen, William A., *Bureaucracy and Representative Government* (Aldine, Chicago, 1971)

Nørgaard, Asbjørn S., 'Political Science: Witchcraft or Craftsmanship? Standards for Good Research', *World Political Science Review* 4(1) (2008), 1

Norregaard, John and Khan, Tehmina S., 'Tax Policy: Recent Trends and Coming Challenges' (Working Paper No. WP/07/274, International Monetary Fund, 2007)

Norris, Floyd, 'It's Hard to Worry About a Deficit 10 Years Out', *New York Times*, 28 August 2009, B1

North, Douglas C., *Institutions, Institutional Change, and Economic Performance* (Cambridge University Press, Cambridge, 1990)

Oakes, Laurie, 'Mining New Depths of Political Bastardry', *The Daily Telegraph* (online), 29 May 2010 (dailytelegraph.com.au/news/opinion/mining-new-depths-of-political-bastardry/story-e6frezzo-1225872694228)

O'Brien, D. P., *Taxation and the Promotion of Human Happiness: An Essay by George Warde Norman* (Edward Elgar, Cheltenham, 2009)

O'Donoghue, Cathal, Baldini, Massimo and Mantovani, Daniela, 'Modelling the Redistributive Impact of Indirect taxes in Europe: An Application of EUROMOD' (EUROMOD Working Paper No. EM&/01, Department of Economics, University of Cambridge, 2004)

Organisation for Economic Cooperation and Development (OECD), *Consumption Tax Trends 2012: VAT/GST and Excise Rates, Trends and Administration Issues* (OECD Publishing, Paris, 2012)

Economic Surveys – Australia (OECD, Paris, 2012)

Revenue Statistics: 1965–2012 (OECD Publishing, Paris, 2013)

Revenue Statistics: 1965–2011 (OECD Publishing, Paris, 2012)

Consumption Tax Trends 2010: VAT/GST and Excise Rates, Trends and Administration Issues (OECD, Paris, 2011)

Revenue Statistics: 1965–2010 (OECD, Paris, 2011)

OECD Economic Surveys – United States Volume 2010/15 (OECD, Paris, 2010)

Forum on Tax Administration: Compliance Sub-Group, Information Note, Developments in VAT Compliance Management in Selected Countries (OECD, Centre for Tax Policy and Administration, Paris, 2009)

Revenue Statistics: 1965–2008 (OECD, Paris, 2009)

Consumption Tax Trends 2008 – VAT/GST and Excise Rates, Trends and Administration Issues (OECD, Paris, 2008)

Growing Unequal: Income Distribution and Poverty in OECD Countries (OECD, Paris, 2008)

'Consumption Taxes: the Way of the Future? (Policy Brief)',*OECD Observer* (2007), 1

Revenue Statistics: 1965–2006 (OECD, Paris, 2007)

International VAT/GST Guidelines (April 2014) (www.oecd.org/ctp/consumption/international-vat-gst-guidelines.pdf)

International VAT/GST Guidelines (OECD, Paris, 2006)

OECD Economic Surveys: Japan (OECD, Paris, 2006)

Consumption Tax Trends: VAT/GST and Excise Rates, Trends and Administration Issues (OECD, Paris, 2005)

Revenue Statistics: 1965–2004 (OECD, Paris, 2005)

The Application of Consumption Taxes to the International Trade in Services and Intangibles (OECD, Paris, 2005)

Report on Consumption Tax Obstacles to Cross-Border Trade in International Services and Intangibles (OECD, Paris, 2004)

Indirect Tax Treatment of Financial Services and Instruments (OECD, Paris, 1998)

Consumption Tax Trends (OECD, Paris, 1993)

Offe, Claus, 'Political Economy: Sociological Perspectives', in R. E. Goodin and H. D. Klingermann (eds.), *A New Handbook of Political Science* (Oxford University Press, Oxford, 1998)

Office of Speaker Nancy Pelosi, *President Obama's Budget and the House Budget: Questions and Answers, Rebutting Critics* (20 April 2009) <(majorityleader.gov/docUploads/BudgetQA040109FINAL.pdf)

Olding, Robert, 'Interpretation of the GST Act – Towards a Principled Basis?' in C. Peacock (ed.), *GST in Australia: Looking Forward from the First Decade* (Thomson Reuters, Pyrmont, 2011), 77

Olsen, J. G. and March, J. P., 'The New Institutionalism: Organizational Factors in Political Life', *American Political Science Review* 78 (1984), 734

Rediscovering Institutions: The Organizational Basis of Politics (Free Press, New York, 1988)

Olson, Mancur, *The Logic of Collective Action* (1965)

O'Riordan, Bernard, 'Non-Banks' Tax Breakthrough', *Australian Financial Review*, 3 June 1999, 4

Orloff, Ann Shola, *The Politics of Pensions: A Comparative Analysis of Britain, Canada, and the United States, 1880–1940* (University of Wisconsin Press, Madison, 1993)

Orszag, Peter and United States Congressional Budget Office, *Letter from Peter Orszag to Kent Conrad (Chairman, Committee on the Budget) Re: Federal Tax Revenues from 2003 to 2006* (18 May 2007)

Orucu, Esin and Nelken, David, *Comparative Law: A Handbook* (Hart, Oxford, 2007)

Osgood, Russel K., 'The Convergence of the Taxation Systems of the Developed Nations', *Cornell International Law Journal* 25 (1992), 339

Ozdemir, Ali Riza, 'The Effects of Value Added Tax on the Rate of Government Growth: An OECD Panel Study', *World Tax Journal* 4(3) (2012), 259

Pallot, Marie, 'GST and Financial Services in New Zealand', in C. Peacock (ed.), *GST in Australia: Looking Forward from the First Decade* (Thomson Reuters, Pyrmont, 2011), 161

Parsons, D. W., *Public Policy: An Introduction to the Theory and Practice of Policy Analysis* (Edward Elgar, UK; Brookfield, US, 1995)

van den Noord, Paul, and Heady, Christopher, 'Surveillance of Tax Policies: A Synthesis of Findings in Economic Surveys' (Economics Department Working Paper No. 303, Organisation for Economic Cooperation and Development, 2001)

Peacock, Christine, 'Changes to the Australian GST Immovable Property "Margin Scheme"' *International VAT Monitor* (September/October 2006), 327

Pechman, Joseph A., *Who Paid the Taxes, 1966–85?* (Brookings Institution, Washington, DC, 1985)

Penner, Rudolph, 'Do We Need a Value-Added Tax to Solve Our Long-Run Budget Problems?' *Tax Law Review* 63(2) (2010), 301

Peter Bachrach and Baratz, Morton S., *Power and Poverty: Theory and Practice* (Oxford University Press, 1970)

Peters, B. Guy, *Institutional Theory in Political Science: The 'New Institutionalism'* (Continuum, London, 2005)

American Public Policy: Promise and Performance (CQ Press, 6th ed., Washington, DC, 2004)

Institutional Theory in Political Science: The New Institutionalism (Pinter, Washington, DC, 1999)

Comparative Politics: Theory and Methods (Macmillan, Houndmills, UK, 1998)

The Politics of Taxation: A Comparative Perspective (Blackwell, Cambridge, MA, 1991)

Peters, B. Guy, Pierre, Jon and King, Desmond S., 'The Politics of Path Dependency: Political Conflict in Historical Institutionalism',) *Journal of Politics* 67(4) (2005), 1275

Phillips, Cathy (ed.), *The VAT Reader: What a Federal Consumption Tax Would Mean for America* (Tax Analysts, Arlington, VA, 2011)

Picot, Garnett and Myles, John, 'Income Inequality and Low Income in Canada: An International Perspective' (Research Paper, Statistics Canada, Ottawa, 2005)

Pierce, L. C., *Politics of Fiscal Policy Formation* (Goodyear Publishing, Pacific Palisades, 1971)

Pierce, Roger, *Research Methods in Politics: A Practical Guide* (SAGE, Los Angeles; London, 2008)

Pierson, Paul and Skocpol, Theda, *The Transformation of American Politics: Activist Government and the Rise of Conservatism* (Princeton University Press, Princeton, 2007)

'Historical Institutionalism in Contemporary Political Science', in I. Katznelson and H. V. Milner (eds.), *Political Science: State of the Discipline* (Norton American Political Science Association, New York; Washington, DC, 2002), xv

Pierson, Paul, *Politics in Time: History, Institutions, and Social Analysis* (Princeton University Press, Princeton, NJ, 2004)

The New Politics of the Welfare State (Oxford University Press, Oxford; New York, 2001)

'Increasing Returns, Path Dependence, and the Study of Politics', *American Political Science Review* 94(2) (2000), 251

Piketty, Thomas and Saez, Emmanuel, 'Income Inequality in the United States, 1913–1998', *Quarterly Journal of Economics* 118(1) (2003), 1

Poddar, Satya, 'VAT on Financial Services – Searching for a Workable Compromise', in R. Krever and D. White (eds.), *GST in Retrospect and Prospect* (Thomson Brookers, Wellington, 2007), 179

Poddar, Satya and English, Morley, 'Taxation of Financial Services under a Value-Added tax: Applying the Cash-Flow Approach', *National Tax Journal* 50(1) (1997), 89

Pogge, Thomas W., *Realizing Rawls* (Cornell University Press, Ithaca, NY, 1989)

Polanyi, Karl, *The Great Transformation* (Beacon Press, Boston, 1957)

Posner, Richard A., *The Crisis of Capitalist Democracy* (Harvard University Press, Cambridge, MA, 2010)

Poterba, J. M., 'Lifetime Incidence and the Distributional Burden of Excise Taxes', *American Economic Review* 79(2) (1989), 325

Poulantzas, Nicos, *Political Power and Social Classes* (Sheed and Ward, London, 1973)

Prasad, Monica, *The Politics of Free Markets: The Rise of Neoliberal Economic Policies in Britain, France, Germany, and the United States* (University of Chicago Press, Chicago, 2006)

President of the United States (Ronald Reagan), *The President's Tax Proposals to the Congress for Fairness, Simplicity, and Growth* (US Government Printing Office, Washington, DC, 1985)

Presman, L. and Wildavsky, Aaron, *Implementation* (University of California Press, 2nd ed., Berkeley, 1979)

Prest, A. R., *Value Added Taxation: The Experience of the United Kingdom* (American Enterprise Institute for Public Policy Research, Washington, DC; London, 1980)

Prest, A. R., 'The Australian Tax System Reviewed', *Economic Record* 51 (136) (1975), 576
'The Political Economy of Tax Reform', *Economic Papers* (37) (1972), 11
PricewaterhouseCoopers, *The Impact of VAT Compliance on Business* (PriceWaterhouse-Coopers, 2012)
PriceWaterhouseCoopers, *How the EU VAT Exemptions Impact the Banking Sector: Study to Assess Whether Banks Enjoy a Tax Advantage as a Result of the EU VAT Exemption System* (PWC, 2011)
TaxTalk: GST Special Edition (May 2010) (http://pwc.com.au/tax/assets/taxtalk/TaxTalk-SE_May10.pdf)
Shifting the Balance: The Evolution of Indirect Taxes (PricewaterhouseCoopers, 2007)
Productivity Commission, *Economic Structure and Performance of the Australian Retail Industry* (Productivity Commission, Canberra, 2011)
Puchala, Donald J., *Fiscal Harmonization in the European Communities: National Politics and International Cooperation* (Francis Pinter Publishers, London and Dover, 1984)
Pugel, Thomas A. and Lindert, Peter H., *International Economics* (McGraw-Hill, 11th ed., Boston, 2000)
Purohit, Meahesh C., 'Harmonizing Taxation of Interstate Trade under a Sub-National VAT – Lessons from International Experience', *International VAT Monitor* (May/June 2002), 169
Quiggin, John, *Taxing Times: A Guide to Australia's Tax Debate* (UNSW Press, Sydney, 1998)
'Forget the GST and Focus on Real Issues', *Australian Financial Review*, 20 May 1999, 19
Ragin, Charles C., Berg-Schlosser, Dirk and de Meur, Gisele, 'Political Methodology: Qualitative Methods', in R. E. Goodin and H.-D. Klingemann (eds.), *A New Handbook of Political Science* (Oxford University Press, Oxford, 1998)
Ramsey, Frank P., 'A Contribution to the Theory of Taxation', *Economic Journal* 37(1) (1927), 47
Rawls, John, *A Theory of Justice* (Clarendon Press, Oxford, 1972)
Raz, Joseph, 'Problem of Authority: Revisiting the Service Conception', *Minnesota Law Review* 90 (2005–2006), 1003
Reckon Report, *Study to Quantify and Analyse the VAT Gap in the EU-25 Member States* (Reckon LLP, London, 2009)
Reese, Thomas J., *The Politics of Taxation* (Quorum Books, Westport, CT, 1980)
Reimann, Mathias and Zimmermann, Reinhard, *The Oxford Handbook of Comparative Law* (Oxford University Press, Oxford, 2006)
Reinhardt, Sam and Steel, Lee, 'A Brief History of Australia's Tax System', *Economic Roundup* (2006), 1
Rendahl, Pernilla, *Cross-Border Consumption Taxation of Digital Supplies* (IBFD, Amsterdam, 2009)
Reserve Bank of Australia, *Chart Pack – Regions and Industry: Industry Share of Output* (7 December 2011) (rba.gov.au/chart-pack/regions-industry.html)
Semi-Annual Statement on Monetary Policy (RBA, Canberra, 1997)
Review of Business Taxation and John Theodore Ralph (Chairman), *A Tax System Redesigned: More Certain, Equitable and Durable* (Review of Business Taxation Canberra, 1999)
Richardson, Jack, 'Resolving Deadlocks in the Australian Parliament' (Research Paper No. 9 (2000–01), Department of the Parliamentary Library, Commonwealth, 2000)
Richter, Rudolf, 'Democratic Choice and Taxation: A Theoretical and Empirical Analysis (Book Review)', *Public Choice* (2000), 194
Riswold, Scott, 'VAT in Sub-Saharan Africa – A Critique of IMF VAT Policy', *International VAT Monitor* (March/April 2004), 97

Ritzer, George and Goodman, Douglas J., *Sociological Theory* (McGraw-Hill, 6th international ed., Boston, 2004)

Roberts, Alasdair and Rose, Jonathan, 'Selling the Goods and Services Tax: Government Advertising and Public Discourse in Canada', *Canadian Journal of Political Science* 28 (2) (1995), 311

Rodgers, Joan R., Siminski, Peter and Bishop, James, 'Changes in Poverty Rates during the Howard Era', *Australian Economic Review* 42(3) (2009), 300

Romer, Thomas and Rosenthal, Howard, 'Bureaucrats versus Voters: On the Political Economy of Resource Allocation by Direct Democracy', *Quarterly Journal of Economics* 93(4) (1979), 563

'Political Resource Allocation, Controlled Agendas, and the Status Quo', *Public Choice* 33 (4) (1978), 27

Rose, Richard and Karran, Terence, *Taxation by Political Inertia: Financing the Growth of Government in Britain* (Allen & Unwin, London; Boston, 1987)

Rothstein, Bo, 'Political Institutions: An Overview', in R. E. Goodin and H.-D. Klingemann (eds.), *A New Handbook of Political Science* (Oxford University Press, Oxford; New York, 1996), 133

Rovinsky, David, 'Efficiency Considerations in the Canadian and Australian Goods and Services Taxes', *Australasian Canadian Studies* 25(1) (2007), 63

Rowley, Charles Kershaw, Tollison, Robert D. and Tullock, Gordon, *The Political Economy of Rent-Seeking* (Kluwer Academic Publishers, Boston, 1988)

Rueschemeyer, Dietrich and Mahoney, James, *Comparative Historical Analysis in the Social Sciences* (Cambridge University Press, New York, 2002)

'Comparative Historical Analysis: Achievements and Agendas', in D. Rueschemeyer and J. Mahoney (eds.), *Comparative Historical Analysis in the Social Sciences* (Cambridge University Press, New York, 2002), 3

Rybczynski, T. M. (ed.), *The Value-Added Tax: The U.K. Position and the European Experience (Papers read at a Business Economists' Group Conference sponsored by the United Dominions Trust Ltd.* (Basil Blackwell, Oxford, 1972)

Sabatier, Paul A. (ed.), *Theories of the Policy Process* (Westview Press, Boulder, CO, 1999)

Sandford, Cedric, *Why Tax Systems Differ: A Comparative Study of the Political Economy of Taxation* (Fiscal Publications, Bath, 2000)

'Why Have So Many Countries Adopted VAT?' in B. Tran-Nam (ed.), *Tax Reform and the GST: An International Perspective* (Prospect Media, St Leonards, 1998), ch. 5

Successful Tax Reform: Lessons from an Analysis of Tax Reform in Six Countries (Fiscal, Bath, 1993)

Sandford, C. T., et al., *Costs and Benefits of VAT* (Heinemann Educational Books, London, 1981)

Sarker, Nahida Faridy and Tapan, 'Who Really Pays Value Added Tax (VAT) in Developing Countries? Empirical Evidence from Bangladesh', *International Proceedings of Economics Development and Research* 11 (2011), 191

Schenk, Alan, 'Prior US Flirtations with VAT", in C. Phillips (ed.), *The VAT Reader: What a Federal Consumption Tax Would Mean for America* (Tax Analysts, Arlington, VA, 2011), 52

'Financial Services', in R. Krever (ed.), *VAT in Africa* (Pretoria University Press, Pretoria, 2010), 31

'Taxation of Financial Services Under a U.S. Value-Added Tax', *Tax Law Review* 63(2) (2010), 409

'The Plethora of Consumption Tax Proposals: Putting the Value Added Tax, Flat Tax, Retail Sales Tax, and USA Tax into Perspective', *University of San Diego Law Review* 33 (1996), 1281

'Recent Activity in the United States Involving the Value Added Tax', *International VAT Monitor* (1992), 2

'A Model Value Added Tax Statute for the United States', *International VAT Monitor* (September 1990), 2

Schenk, Alan and Members of the International Monetary Fund (IMF) Legal Department, *Value Added Tax Act of the Commonwealth of New Vatopia* (IMF, 2006)

Schenk, Alan and Oldman, Oliver, *Value Added Tax: A Comparative Approach* (Cambridge University Press, rev. edn., Cambridge; New York, 2007)

'Analysis of Tax Treatment of Financial Services under a Consumption Style VAT: A Report of the American Bar Association Section of Taxation Committee on Value Added Tax', *Tax Lawyer* 44(1) (1990–1991), 181

Schmölders, Günter, *Turnover Taxes* (International Bureau of Fiscal Documentation, Amsterdam, 1966)

Schumpeter, Joseph, *Capitalism, Socialism and Democracy* (Harper, New York, 1943)

'The Crisis of the Tax State', in R. Swedberg (ed.), *The Economics and Sociology of Capitalism* (Princeton University Press, Princeton, NJ, first published 1918, 1991 ed.), 99

Seidman, Steven, *Contested Knowledge: Social Theory Today* (Blackwell, 3rd ed., Malden, MA, 2004)

Sewell, William, 'Three Temporalities: Toward an Eventful Sociology', in T. J. McDonald (ed.), *The Historic Turn in the Human Sciences* (University of Michigan Press, Ann Arbor, 1996), 245

Shalizi, Z. and World Bank Group, *Lessons of Tax Reform* (World Bank, Washington, DC, 1991)

Sharkansky, Ira (ed.), *Policy Analysis in Political Science* (Chicago, 1970)

The Politics of Taxing and Spending (Bobbs Merrill, Indianapolis, 1969)

Shaviro, Daniel, 'Simplifying Assumptions: How Might the Politics of Consumption Tax Reform Affect (Impair) the End Product?' in J. W. Diamond and G. R. Zodrow (eds.), *Fundamental Tax Reform: Issues, Choices, and Implications* (MIT Press, Cambridge, MA; London, 2008), 75

'Replacing the Income Tax with a Progressive Consumption Tax', *Tax Notes* (2004), 91

Sheffrin, Steven, 'Perceptions of Fairness in the Crucible of Tax Policy', in J. Slemrod (ed.), *Tax Progressivity and Income Inequality* (Cambridge University Press, Cambridge, 1994), 309

Shepard, Lee, 'Addressing VAT Fraud Problems', *Tax Notes International* 46 (2007), 225

Shibata, Atsuhi, 'VAT News – Japan', *International VAT Monitor* 23(5) (2012), 248

Shome, Parthasarathi (ed.), *Tax Policy Handbook* (Tax Policy Division, Fiscal Affairs Department, International Monetary Fund, Washington, DC, 1995)

Shoup, Carl S., 'Choosing among Types of VATs', in M. Gillis, C. S. Shoup and G. P. Sicat (eds.), *Value Added Taxation in Developing Countries (A World Bank Symposium)* (World Bank, Washington, DC, 1990), 3

'Retrospectives on Tax Missions to Venezuela (1959), Brazil (1964), and Liberia (1970)', in M. Gillis (ed.), *Tax Reform in Developing Countries* (Duke University Press, Durham; London, 1989), 252

The Value-Added Tax (Center of Planning and Economic Research, Athens, 1973)

Public Finance (Aldine Publishing Company, Chicago, 1969)

Shoup Mission, *Second Report on Japanese Taxation* (Japan Tax Association, Tokyo, 1950)

Report on Japanese Taxation (SCAP, Tokyo, 1949)

von Siemens, C. F., *Veredelte Umsatzsteuer ('Improving Sales Tax')* (Siemensstadt, 1921)

Simeon, Richard, 'Studying Public Policy', *Canadian Journal of Political Science* 9(4) (1976), 548

Simms, Marian and Warhurst, John, 'Editors' Introduction: The Nature and Scope of Howard's Victory', in Marian Simms and John Warhurst (eds.), *Howard's Agenda: The 1998 Australian Election* (UQP, St Lucia, 2000), 1

(eds.), *Howard's Agenda: The 1998 Australian Election* (UQP, St Lucia, 2000)

Simson, Stuart, 'Government Ignores Asprey Report', *Australian Financial Review*, 18 September 1974, 7

Skocpol, Theda, 'Bringing the State Back In: Strategies of Analysis in Current Research', in P. B. Evans, D. Rueschemeyer and T. Skocpol (eds.), *Bringing the State Back In* (Cambridge University Press, Cambridge; New York, 1985), 3

States and Social Revolutions: A Comparative Analysis of France, Russia, and China (Cambridge University Press, Cambridge; New York, 1979)

Slemrod, Joel, 'Is Tax Reform Good for Business? Is a Pro-Business Tax Policy Good for America?' in J. W. Diamond and G. R. Zodrow (eds.), *Fundamental Tax Reform: Issues, Choices, and Implications* (MIT Press, Cambridge, MA; London, 2008), 143

'The Role of Misconceptions in Support for Regressive Tax Reform', *National Tax Journal* 59(1) (2006), 57

Does Atlas Shrug? The Economic Consequences of Taxing the Rich (Russell Sage Foundation; Harvard University Press, New York, 2000)

Tax Policy in the Real World (Cambridge University Press, Cambridge; New York, 1999)

'Professional Opinions About Tax Policy: 1994 and 1934', *National Tax Journal* 48(1) (1995), 121

Tax Progressivity and Income Inequality (Cambridge University Press, Cambridge; New York, 1994)

(ed.), *Do Taxes Matter? The Impact of the Tax Reform Act of 1986* (MIT Press, Cambridge, MA, 1990)

'Optimal Taxation and Tax Systems', *Journal of Economic Perspectives* 4(1) (1990), 157

Slemrod, Joel and Bakija, Jon M., *Taxing Ourselves: A Citizen's Guide to the Great Debate over Tax Reform* (MIT Press, Cambridge, MA, 1996)

Smart, Michael and Bird, Richard M., 'The Impact on Investment of Replacing a Retail Sales Tax with a Value-Added Tax: Evidence from Canadian Experience', *National Tax Journal* 62 (2009), 591

Smith, Dan Throop, Webber, James and Cerf, Carol, *What You Should Know About the Value Added Tax* (Dow Jones-Irwin, Homewood, IL, 1973)

Smith, Dan Throop, "VAT" – The Most Neutral Tax', *New York Times*, 28 February 1972, 31

Smith, Harry Edwin, *The United States Federal Internal Tax History from 1861 to 1871* (Houghton Mifflin, Boston, New York, 1914)

Smith, Julie P., *Taxing Popularity: The Story of Taxation in Australia* (ATRF, Canberra, rev. edn., 2004)

Smith, Stephen, 'VAT Fraud and Evasion', in Robert Chote et al.(eds.), *The IFS Green Budget* (Institute for Fiscal Studies, London, 2007), 167

Smits, J. M. and Edward Elgar Publishing, *Elgar Encyclopedia of Comparative Law* (Edward Elgar, Cheltenham, UK; Northampton, MA, 2006)

Soltan, Karol, Uslaner, Eric M. and Haufler, Virginia (eds.), *Institutions and Social Order* (University of Michigan Press, Ann Arbor, 1998)

Sørensen, Peter Birch, 'The Theory of Optimal Taxation: What Is the Policy Relevance?' *International Tax and Public Finance* 14(4) (2007), 383

Spence, M., 'Job Market Signalling', *Quarterly Journal of Economics* 87 (1973), 355

Stacey, Paul, 'New Zealand Zero-Rates Financial Supplies', *Australian GST Journal* 3 (2003), 116

Standing Committee on Economics, Commonwealth of Australia Senate, *Report – Tax Laws Amendment (2008 Measures No. 5) Bill 2008 [provisions]* (2008)

Steinmo, Sven, 'The Evolution of Policy Ideas: Tax Policy in the 20th Century', *British Journal of Politics and International Relations* 5(2) (2003), 206

Taxation and Democracy: Swedish, British and American Approaches to Financing the Modern State (Yale University Press, New Haven, CT, 1993)

Steinmo, Sven, Thelen, Kathleen and Longstreth, Frank (eds.), *Structuring Politics: Historical Institutionalism in Comparative Analysis* (Cambridge University Press, Cambridge, 1992)

Stephens, Robert, 'The Economic and Equity Effects of GST in New Zealand', in R. Krever and D. White (eds.), *GST in Retrospect and Prospect* (Thomson Brookers, Wellington, 2007), 65

Steuerle, C. Eugene, 'Real Tax Reform Is Always Hard: Some Advice for the Task Force', in W. Elmore (ed.), *Toward Tax Reform: Recommendations for President Obama's Task Force* (Tax Analysts, Arlington, VA, 2009), 87

Contemporary US Tax Policy (Urban Institute Press, 2nd ed., Washington, DC, 2008)

Contemporary US Tax Policy (Urban Institute Press, Washington, DC, 2004)

The Tax Decade: How Taxes Came to Dominate the Public Agenda (Urban Institute Press, Washington, DC, 1992)

Stewart, Miranda, 'Introduction: New Research on Tax Law and Political Institutions', *Law in Context* 24(2) (2006), 1

Stewart, Miranda and Jogarajan, Sunita, 'The International Monetary Fund and Tax Reform', *British Tax Review* (2) (2004), 146

Stiglitz, Joseph E,, 'Development-Oriented Tax Policy', in R. H. Gordon (ed.), *Taxation in Developing Countries: Six Case Studies and Policy Implications* (Columbia University Press, New York, 2010), 11

'Don't Trust Technocrats', *The Guardian* (online), 16 July 2003 (guardian.co.uk/politics/2003/jul/16/globalisation.economy)

Economics (W. W. Norton, 2nd ed., New York, 1997)

Stitt, Ross, 'Uncertainties Surrounding Input Tax Credit Entitlement in Australia', in C. Peacock (ed.), *GST in Australia: Looking Forward from the First Decade* (Thomson Reuters, Pyrmont, 2011), 115

'Financial Supplies and Reduced Input Tax Credits – An Australian Perspective' in R. Krever and D. White (eds.), *GST in Retrospect and Prospect* (Thomson Brookers, Wellington, 2007), 205

Stockwin, J. A. A., 'Governance, Democracy and the Political Economy of the Japanese State', in G. D. Hook (ed.), *Contested Governance in Japan* (RoutledgeCurzon, London; New York, 2005), 1

Stoker, Gerry and Marsh, David, *Theory and Methods in Political Science* (Palgrave Macmillan, 2nd ed., New York, 2002)

Stolberg, Sheryl, 'Bush Releases Budget as Plan to Erase Deficit', *New York Times*, 6 February 2007, 19

Studenski, Paul, 'Towards a Theory of Business Taxation', *Journal of Political Economy* 48(5) (1940), 621

Stutchbury, Michael, 'Dr John Backflip Begs Questions of His Economic Blueprint', *Australian Financial Review*, 21 December 1992, 7

Sullivan, Clara K., *The Tax on Value Added* (New York, 1965)

Sullivan, Martin A., 'Was the VAT a Money Machine for Europe?' *Tax Notes* (2012), 14

Surrey, Stanley S., 'The Congress and the Tax Lobbyist: How Special Tax Provisions Get Enacted', *Harvard Law Review* 70 (1957), 1145

Swank, Duane and Steinmo, Sven, 'The New Political Economy of Taxation in Advanced Capitalist Democracies', *American Journal of Political Science* 46(3) (2002), 642

Tadros, Farid, 'Introducing the Value-Added Tax: Considerations for Implementation' (Investment Climate in Practice Note Series No. 4, World Bank, 2009)

Tait, Alan A., *Value-Added Tax: Administrative and Policy Issues* (International Monetary Fund, Washington, DC, 1991)

Value Added Tax: International Practice and Problems (International Monetary Fund, Washington, DC, 1988)

Value Added Tax (McGraw-Hill, London, New York, 1972)

Tax Consultative Committee (Vos Committee), *The Report of the Tax Consultative Committee* (Commonwealth of Australia Treasury, 1998)

Tax Design Review Panel, *Better Tax Design and Implementation: A Report to the Assistant Treasurer and Minister for Competition Policy and Consumer Affairs* (2008)

Tax Foundation (US), *A Value Added Tax for the United States? Selected Viewpoints* (Tax Foundation, Washington, DC, 1979)

Taylor, Lenore, 'No Business of the Democrats', *Australian Financial Review*, 18

Terra, Ben and Kajus, Julie, IBFD, *A Guide to the European VAT Directives* (online) (15 April 2011)

Terra, Ben and Wattel, Peter J., *European Tax Law* (Kluwer Law International, 4th ed., The Hague, 2005)

Thelen, Kathleen, 'Historical Institutionalism in Comparative Politics', *Annual Review of Political Science* 2 (1999), 369

Thelen, Kathleen and Steinmo, Sven, 'Historical Institutionalism in Comparative Politics', in S. Steinmo K. Thelen and F. Longstreth (eds.), *Structuring Politics: Historical Institutionalism in Comparative Analysis* (Cambridge University Press, Cambridge, 1992), 1

Thirsk, Wayne R., *Tax Reform in Developing Countries* (World Bank, Washington, DC, 1997)

'Intellectual Foundations of the VAT in North America and Japan', in L. Eden (ed.), *Retrospectives on Public Finance* (Duke University Press, Durham, NC; London, 1991), 133

Thomson Reuters, 'Business Coalition for Tax Reform – Tax All Food at a Single Rate', *GST News Alert* (26) (1999)

'Senate Tax Reform/GST Inquiries', *Weekly Tax Bulletin* (51) (8 February 1999)

'Democrats Favour "Irish" Model – Zero-Rate Basic Food', *GST News Alert* (2) (21 April 1999)

'GST and Tax Reform: It's a Deal!' *GST News Alert* (29) (31 May 1999)

'GST Debate Sets Records', *GST News Alert* (49) (29 June 1999)

'Small Business Ups Ante over GST without Food', *GST News Alert* (25) (25 May 1999)

'Business Eats Its Words on GST", *GST News Alert* (22) (20 May 1999)

'Business to Urge Income Tax', *GST News Alert* (24) (24 May 1999)

'Tax Advisory Board: Powers and Target Market', *Weekly Tax Bulletin* (53) (13 December 1999)

Thorndike, Joseph, *Early Proposals for an American VAT* (20 June 2009) Tax Analysts (taxhistory.org/thp/readings.nsf/ArtWeb/6F4B8EADA426FDCE852575F600464B81?OpenDocument)

Thorndike, Joseph and Ventry, Dennis Jr (eds.), *Tax Justice: The Ongoing Debate* (Urban Institute Press, Washington, DC, 2002)

Thuronyi, Victor, *Comparative Tax Law* (Kluwer Law International, The Hague, 2003)

Tax Law Design and Drafting (International Monetary Fund, Washington, DC, 1996)

Tingle, Laura, 'Pledges Kept, Says Howard', *The Age*, 22 August 1996, 7

de Tocqueville, Alexis and Reeve, Henry, *Democracy in America* (Collier, New York, rev. edn., 1900)

Toohey, Brian, 'Tax Reform Deluge: Asprey Report Tabled to Trump Mathews Committee', *Australian Financial Review*, 28 May 1975, 1, 18

Townley, Peter G. C. and Malaysian Institute of Economic Research, *Value-Added Taxation: Preferential Treatment of Goods and Services by Zero-Rating and Exemption* (Malaysian Institute of Economic Research, Kuala Lumpur, 1995)

Tran-Nam, Binh, 'Introduction', in B. Tran-Nam (ed.), *Tax Reform and the GST: An International Perspective* (Prospect Media, St Leonards, NSW, 1998), 1

Tran-Nam, Binh (ed.), *Tax Reform and the GST: An International Perspective* (Prospect Media, St Leonards, 1998)

Trebilcock, Michael J., 'The Choice of Governing Instrument: A Retrospective', in P. Eliadis, M. M. Hill and M. Howlett (eds.), *Designing Government* (McGill-Queens University Press, 2005), 51

Trinca, Helen and AAP, 'Delivers the Goods, Serves Business Well', *Sydney Morning Herald* 14 August 1998, 12

Tullock, Gordon, *The Economics of Special Privilege and Rent Seeking* (Kluwer Academic Publishers, Boston, 1989)

Wealth, Poverty, and Politics (Blackwell, New York, 1988)

'Efficient Rent-Seeking', in J. M. Buchanan, R. D. Tollison and G. Tullock (eds.), *Toward a Theory of the Rent-Seeking Society* (Texas A&M University, College Station, 1980), 97

United Nations Conference on Trade and Development (UNCTAD) – Secretariat, *Trade and Development Report, 2012 (UNCTAD/TDR/2012)* (United Nations Publications, Geneva, 2012)

US Advisory Commission on Intergovernmental Relations, *The Value-Added Tax and Alternative Sources of Federal Revenue: An Information Report* (Washington, DC, 1973)

US Committee for Economic Development (CED), *A New Tax Framework: A Blueprint for Averting a Fiscal Crisis (A Statement by the Research and Policy Committee of the Committee for Economic Development)* (CED, Washington, DC, 2005)

US Committee for Economic Development Research and Policy Committee, *A Better Balance in Federal Taxes on Business: A Statement on National Policy* (Committee for Economic Development, New York, 1966)

US Congressional Budget Office, *Historical Budget Data* (CBO, Washington, DC, 2013)

An Update to the Budget and Economic Outlook: Fiscal Years 2014 to 2024 (CBO, Washington, DC, 2014)

The Budget and Economic Outlook: Fiscal Years 2013 to 2023 (CBO, Washington, DC, 2013)

Choices for Deficit Reduction (CBO, Washington, DC, 2012)

US Congressional Research Service, Government and Finance Division, Sherlock, Molly, *Tax Reform in the 113th Congress: An Overview of Proposals (CRS Report R43060)* (CRS, Washington, DC, 2013)

US Congressional Research Service, Government and Finance Division, James Bickley, *Tax Reform: An Overview of Proposals in the 112th Congress (CRS Report R41591)* (CRS, Washington, DC, 2012)

US Department of the Treasury, *General Explanations of the Administration's Fiscal Year 2008 Revenue Proposals* (2007)

Tax Reform for Fairness, Simplicity, and Economic Growth (Office of the Secretary, Department of the Treasury, Washington, DC, 1984)

Blueprints for Basic Tax Reform (Dept. of the Treasury, Washington, DC, 1977)

US Federation of Tax Administrators, *State Sales Tax Rates and Food and Drug Exemptions* (1 January 2014) (taxadmin.org/fta/rate/sales.pdf)

US General Accounting Office, *Value-Added Tax: Administrative Costs Vary With Complexity and Number of Businesses (Report to the Joint Committee on Taxation, U.S. Congress)* (1993)

Value-Added Tax: Issues for U.S. Tax Policymakers (Briefing Report to the Joint Committee on Taxation) (1989)

US Government Accountability Office, *Value-Added Taxes: Lessons Learned from Other Countries on Compliance Risks, Administrative Costs, Compliance Burden, and Transition (GAO-08–566)* (Washington, DC, 2008)

US House of Representatives, Committee on Ways and Means, (112th Cong., 1st session), *Hearing on Tax Reform and Consumption-Based Tax Systems* (26 July 2011, serial 112–15)

Committee on Ways and Means, (113th Cong., 2nd session), 'The Tax Reform Act of 2014: Fixing Our Broken Tax Code So That It Works for American Families and Job Creators – Executive Summary' (2014)

US Joint Committee on Taxation (111th Cong., 1st session), *Description of Revenue Proposals Contained in the President's Fiscal Year 2010 Budget Proposal; Part One: Individual Income Tax and Estate and Gift Tax Provisions JCS-2–09* (US Government Printing Office, Washington, DC, 2009)

Summary of Conference Agreement on HR 3838 (Tax Reform Act of 1986) (JCS-16–86) (US Government Printing Office, Washington, DC, 1986)

US National Taxpayer Advocate, *2009 Annual Report to Congress: Volume Two – Research and Related Studies* (Internal Revenue Service, Department of Treasury, 2009)

US Office of Budget and Management, *Budget of the United States Government, Fiscal Year 2013 – Historic Tables* (US Government Printing Office, Washington, DC, 2012)

Budget of the United States Government, Fiscal Year 2012 – Historic Tables (US Government Printing Office, Washington, DC, 2011)

US President's Advisory Panel on Federal Tax Reform, *Simple, Fair, and Pro-Growth: Proposals to Fix America's Tax System* (2005)

US President's Economic Recovery Advisory Board, *The Report on Tax Reform Options: Simplification, Compliance, and Corporate Taxation* (2010)

US President's Task Force on Business Taxation, *Business Taxation: The Report* (Washington, DC, 1970)

First Report to the President by the Task Force on Business Taxation – The Value-Added Tax (1969)

US Senate Committee on Finance, *History of the Committee on Finance (97th Congress, 1st Session – Senate Document No. 97-5)* (6th ed., US Government Printing Office, Washington, DC, 1981)

US, *The President's Tax Proposals to the Congress for Fairness, Growth, and Simplicity* (Washington, DC, May 1985)

US Research and Policy Committee of the Committee for Economic Development, *A New Tax Framework: A Blueprint for Averting a Fiscal Crisis* (Committee for Economic Development, Washington, DC, 2005)

United Nations Conference on Trade and Development, *The Least Developed Countries Report 2009: The State and Development Governance* (United Nations, Geneva, 2009)

Uren, David, et al., 'Treasury Exposes Mining Tax Flaws: Parkinson Blames Labor's Concessions to Miners for Shortfall in Revenue', *The Australian*, 15 February 2013, 1, 4

'Editor's Note', *Business Review Weekly*, 11 December 1992, 10

Van de Leur, Michael, 'A VAT in the United States?' *International VAT Monitor* (September/October 2009), 360

Ventry, Dennis Jr, 'Equity versus Efficiency and the U.S. Tax System in Historical Perspective', in D. Ventry Jr and J. Thorndike (eds.), *Tax Justice: The Ongoing Debate* (Urban Institute Press, Washington, DC, 2002), 25

Wade, Matt, 'Banks Lift Rates To Recoup GST', *Sydney Morning Herald*, 22 July 2000, 3

'The GST Made Us Do It: Banks Lift Fees', *Sydney Morning Herald*, 17 July 2000, 6

Wagner, Richard E., *Fiscal Sociology and the Theory of Public Finance: An Exploratory Essay* (Edward Elgar, UK, 2007)

Wallace, R. H., 'Taxation Reform: But What Is the Agenda?' *Economic Record* 51(136) (1975), 564

Walpole, Michael, 'The Henry Review's Tax on Financial Services: An Alternative Approach for Australia', *International VAT Monitor* (January/February 2013), 17

Warburton, Dick and Hendy, Peter, *International Comparisons of Australia's Taxes*, (Commonwealth of Australia Treasury, Canberra, 2006)

Warhurst, John, Brown, Jerome and Higgins, Rohan 'Tax Groupings: The Group Politics of Taxation Reform', in Marian Simms and John Warhurst (eds.), *Howard's Agenda: The 1998 Australian Election* (UQP, St Lucia, 2000), 170

Warren, Alvin C., 'Fairness and a Consumption-Type or Cash Flow Personal Income Tax', *Harvard Law Review* 88(5) (1975), 931

Warren, Neil, 'A Review of Studies on the Distributional Impact of Consumption Taxes in OECD Countries' (Social, Employment and Migration Working Paper No. 64, OECD, 2008)

Warren Neil, Harding Ann and Lloyd Rachel, 'GST and the Changing Incidence of Australian Taxes: 1994–95 to 2001–2002', *eJournal of Tax Research* 3(1) (2005), 114

Wasiliev, John, 'The Full Bite of the GST', *Australian Financial Review*, 5–6 June 1999, 29

Watson, Alan, *Legal Transplants: An Approach to Comparative Law* (University of Georgia Press, 2nd ed., Athens, 1993)

Webber, Carolyn and Wildavsky, Aaron, *A History of Taxation and Expenditure in the Western World* (Simon and Schuster, New York, 1986)

Weber, Max, *Economy and Society: An Outline of Interpretive Sociology* (University of California Press, Berkeley, 1978)

Weingast, Barry R., Shepsle, Kenneth A. and Johnsen, Christopher, 'The Political Economy of Benefits and Costs: A Neoclassical Approach to Distributive Politics', *Journal of Political Economy* 89(4) (1981), 642

Weir, Margaret, 'Ideas and Politics: The Acceptance of Keynesianism in Britain and the United States', in P. Hall (ed.), *The Political Power of Economic Ideas* (Princeton University Press, Princeton, NJ, 1989), 53

Weisbach, David, 'The (Non-)Taxation of Risk', *Tax Law Review* 58 (2004), 1

Weisbach, David A., 'Does the X-Tax Mark the Spot?' *SMU Law Review* 56(1) (2003), 201

Wells, Steve and Flesher, Tonya, 'Lessons for Policy Makers from the History of Consumption Taxes', *Accounting Historians Journal* (1999), 103

Wersand, Frédéric and Cazes, Samuel, 'EU VAT and the Conundrum of Financial Investments', *March/April International VAT Monitor* 24(2) (2013), 83

Widerquist, Karl, 'Public Choice and Altruism', *Eastern Economic Journal* 29(3) (2003), 317

Wilensky, Harold, *Rich Democracies: Political Economy, Public Policy and Performance* (University of California Press, Berkeley, 2002)

Williams, David, 'Value-Added Tax', in V. Thuronyi(ed.), *Tax Law Design and Drafting* (International Monetary Fund, Washington, DC, 1996), vol. 1, 164
Williamson, Jeffrey G. and Lindert, Peter H., *American Inequality: A Macroeconomic History* (Academic Press, New York, 1980)
Williamson, K. M., 'The Literature on the Sales Tax', *Quarterly Journal of Economics* 35(4) (1921), 618
Winsor, Hugh and Howard, Ross, 'Wilson to Sell Tax as One-Time Pain for Long-Term Gain', *The Globe and Mail*, 10 August 1989, A1
Witte, John F., *The Politics and Development of the Federal Income Tax* (University of Wisconsin Press, Madison, 1985)
Woellner, Robin, et al., *Australian Taxation Law* (CCH Australia, 20th ed., Sydney, 2010)
Wolf, Redmar, 'Mecsek-Gabona: The Final Step of the ECJ's Doctrine on Reliance on EU Law for Abusive or Fraudulent Ends in the Context of Intra-Community Transactions' *International VAT Monitor* (September/October 2013), 280
Wolfers, Lachlan, 'The Good, the Bad and the Ugly: A Story of the Life Cycle of ANTS', *Taxation in Australia* 34(12) (2000), 626
Woodward, Dennis, *Australia Unsettled: The Legacy of 'Neo-Liberalism'* (Pearson Education Australia, Frenchs Forest, NSW, 2005)
World Bank and International Finance Corporation, *Doing Business 2013: Smarter Regulations for Small and Medium-Size Enterprises* (World Bank; International Finance Corporation, Washington, DC, 2013)
World Bank Group and PricewaterhouseCoopers, *Paying Taxes 2012: The Global Picture* (World Bank, 2012)
Wright, Maurice, *Japan's Fiscal Crisis: The Ministry of Finance and the Politics of Public Spending, 1975–2000* (Oxford University Press, Oxford, 2002)
Wrong, Dennis Hume, *Power, Its Forms, Bases, and Uses* (Harper and Row Publishers, New York, first published 1979, 1995 ed.)
Yan, Wu, 'Putting the 'Value Added' in China's VAT', *Tax Notes International* (2010), 487
Yeates, Clancy, 'Retail Union Calls for GST on All Imports', *The Age* (online), 9 May 2011, (theage.com.au/business/retail-union-calls-for-gst-on-all-imports-20110508-1ee7c.html#ixzz1Qcv7cDG2)
Yesegat, Wollela Abehodie, 'Value Added Tax Administration in Ethiopia: A Reflection of Problems', *eJournal of Tax Research* 6(2) (2008), 145
Yin, Robert K., *Case Study Research: Design and Methods* (SAGE, 2nd ed., California, 1994)
Yoshida, Reiji, 'Showdown over Sales Tax Breaks on the Horizon', *Japan Times* (online), 17 January 2013 (japantimes.co.jp/news/2013/01/17/business/showdown-over-sales-tax-breaks-on-the-horizon/#.USbo1a7AHPM)
Young, Claire, 'Introduction of a Goods and Services Tax: The Canadian Experience', *Australian Tax Forum* 8(3) (1991), 259
Zee, Howell H., 'Further Thoughts on Reforming the VAT: Treatment of Financial Intermediation Services', in R. de la Feria (ed.), *VAT Exemptions: Consequences and Design Alternatives* (vol. 37, EUCOTAX Series on European Taxation, Kluwer Law International, Alphen aan den Rijn, 2013), 345
'VAT Treatment of Financial Services: A Primer on Conceptual Issues and Country Practices', *INTERTAX* 34(10) (2006), 458
'World Trends in Tax Policy: An Economic Perspective', *INTERTAX* 32(8/9) (2004), 352
'Value-Added Tax', in P. Shome (ed.), *Tax Policy Handbook* (Fiscal Affairs Department, International Monetary Fund, Washington, DC, 1995), 86

Zelenak, Lawrence A., 'The Federal Retail Sales Tax That Wasn't: An Actual History and an Alternate History', *Law and Contemporary Problems* 73(1) (2010), 149

Zodrow, George R. and Mieszkowski, Peter M., *United States Tax Reform in the 21st Century* (Cambridge University Press, Cambridge; New York, 2002)

Zodrow, George R., 'The Sales Tax, the VAT, and Taxes in Between – Or, Is the Only Good NRST a "VAT in Drag"?' *National Tax Journal* 52(3) (1999), 429

'A Hollow Victory', *Australian Financial Review*, 14 August 1985, 12

'Excess Profits Tax or Sales Tax', *New York Times*, 30 May 1920, 1, 6

'GST? It's a Piece of Cake', *Sydney Morning Herald*, 4 March 1993, 1.

'Keating Goes for Broke', *Sydney Morning Herald*, 7 November 1992, 26

'Mrs Pelosi's VAT: The Speaker Proposes a Middle-Class Tax Hike', *Wall Street Journal* (8 October 2009) (online.wsj.com/article/SB10001424052748703298004574457512007010416.html)

'Paper Says President Opposes Value-Added Tax as a Danger', *New York Times*, 20 November 1972, 25

'Policy Forum', *Canadian Tax Journal* 60(1) (2012), 101

'The Curious Case of Option C', *Australian Financial Review*, 2 July 1985, 1

'The GST Guide for Business' *Australian Financial Review* 28 June 1999, 7

'Obama: VAT May Be a Revenue Option, Spending Cuts First' *Huffington Post* (21 June 2010) (huffingtonpost.com/2010/04/21/obama-vat-may-be-a-revenu_n_547237.html)

'Bank to Raise Fees to Cover GST Bill', *The Herald-Sun*, 29 October 1999, 9

'Now Heat Is on Bank Fees', *The Herald-Sun*, 28 June 2000, 2

'Banks' GST Fee Shock', *Sunday Herald Sun* (Melbourne), 25 July 1999, 17

'Congress Approves' 08 Budget Blueprint', *New York Times*, 18 May 2007, 18

Guide to US Elections (CQ Press, 6th ed., Washington, DC, 2010)

OTHER

Australian Broadcasting Corporation, 'Never Say Never', 18 May 1998 (abc.net.au/4corners/stories/s12274.htm)

Berkeley, Brenda, 'GST – The View from Treasury' (Speech delivered at GST in Australia: Looking Forward from the First Decade Conference, Melbourne, 17 November 2010)

Bowen, Chris, 'Tax Design Review Panel to Look at Ways to Streamline Process for Changing Tax Laws' (Media Release No. 006, 8 February 2008)

CNBC, 'Chief Washington Correspondent John Harwood Interview with President Obama', *Street Signs*, 21 April 2010 (cnbc.com/id/36666434)

Commonwealth of Australia, *Parliamentary Debates*, House of Representatives, 31 March 1999, 4835 (Simon Crean, Deputy Leader of the Opposition)

Parliamentary Debates, House of Representatives, 31 March 1999, 4837 (Simon Crean, Deputy Leader of the Opposition)

Parliamentary Debates, House of Representatives, 25 February 1981, 133 (John Howard, Treasurer)

Parliamentary Debates, House of Representatives, 24 February 1981, Hansard, 20 (John Howard, Treasurer)

Parliamentary Debates, House of Representatives, 2 December 1998, 1089 (Peter Costello, Treasurer).

Parliamentary Debates, House of Representatives, 2 December 1998, 1091 (Peter Costello, Treasurer).

Parliamentary Debates, Senate, 14 May 1999, 5116 (Brian Harradine)
Parliamentary Debates, Senate, 14 May 1999, 5516 (Brian Harradine)
Commonwealth, *Parliamentary Debates*, Senate, 6 December 1999, 11272 (Rod Kemp)
Parliamentary Debates, Senate, 6 December 1999, 11272 (Peter Cook, Deputy Leader of the Opposition in the Senate)
Coonan, Helen, 'Minister Welcomes David Vos as Inaugural Inspector-General of Taxation' (Press Release, C075/03, 4 August 2003)
Gillard, Julia and Swan, Wayne, MP, 'Review of GST Distribution' (Joint Media Release, No. 028, 30 March 2011)
Treasurer, 'Review of GST Distribution' (Joint Media Release, No. 028, 30 March 2011)
Hawke, Robert, 'Australian Labor Party Policy Speech' (Speech delivered at the ALP Policy Launch, Opera House, Sydney, 13 November 1984)
Henry, Ken, 'Lessons from Tax Reform Past' (Speech delivered at the Committee for Economic Development of Australia, Sydney, 15 October 2009) (taxreview.treasury.gov.au/content/Content.aspx?doc=html/speeches/10.htm)
Howard, John, 'Taxation Policies in the 80s: The Liberal Party View' (Speech delivered at the Taxation Policies in the 80s Conference, Hotel Hilton International, Sydney, 9 July 1980)
Keating, Paul, 'One Nation' (Statement by the Prime Minister, 26 February 1992)
'Reform of the Australian Taxation System: Statement by the Treasurer' (Press Release, 19 September 1985)
Kelly, Paul, 'The Politics of Economic Change in Australia in the 1980s and 1990s' (Speech delivered at the Reserve Bank of Australia: The Australian Economy in the 1990s, H. C. Coombs Centre for Financial Studies, Kirribilli, 24–25 July 2000)
Oakes, Laurie, Interview with Treasurer Peter Costello (2 July 2006)
Sherry, Nick, 'Rudd Government Appoints Expert Tax Design Advisory Panel' (Media Release, No. 072, 2009)
Swan, Wayne, 'Australia's Future Tax System' (Media Release, No. 036, 13 May 2008)
Treasurer Calls for 2011–12 Budget Submissions (Media Release, No. 090, 2011)
The Value-Added Tax: Hearings before the Joint Economics Committee, 92nd Congress, 2nd Session (Government Printing Office, Washington, DC, 1972)
Willesee, Mike, Interview with John Hewson (3 March 1993)

INTERNET RESOURCES

Australian Electoral Commission (AEC), *Members of the 38th Parliament (1996)* (27 January 2011) (aec.gov.au/Elections/federal_elections/1996/members.htm)
Australian Electoral Commission, *Senators of the 38th Parliament* (27 January 2011) (aec.gov.au/Elections/federal_elections/1996/senators.htm)
Australian Taxation Office, *ATO Consultation Framework* (27 October 2014) (ato.gov.au/General/About-consultation/ATO-consultation-framework/)
Legal Database (2014) (law.ato.gov.au/atolaw/browse.htm?ImA=MainMenu)
Board of Taxation, *Board Members* (2012) (taxboard.gov.au/content/Content.aspx?doc=-about/board_members.htm)
Business Council of Australia (2012) (bca.com.au)
Committee on House Administration, *112th Congress: Congressional Member Organizations (CMO)* (23 January 2012) (cha.house.gov/sites/republicans.cha.house.gov/files/documents/cmo_cso_docs/cmo_112th_congress.pdf)

Committee on Ways and Means, *Committee History*, (waysandmeans.house.gov/About/History.htm)

Commonwealth of Australia Government, *ABN Statistics* (2012) (abr.business.gov.au/StatisticalSearchResult.aspx?Postcode=ALL&Year=2011&StateOptions=1,0,0,0,0,0,0,0,0&Options=0,0,1,0)

Commonwealth of Australia Treasury, Submissions to Review of the GST Financial Supply Provisions by the Commonwealth of Australia Treasury, (21 August 2009) (archive.treasury.gov.au/contentitem.asp?ContentID=1603&NavID=)

Deloitte Access Economics (2014) (deloitteaccesseconomics.com.au/)

Deloitte, *Taxation and Investment: South Sudan – Highlights 2014* (2013) (deloitte.com/assets/Dcom-Global/Local%20Assets/Documents/Tax/Taxation%20and%20Investment%20Guides/2013/dttl_tax_highlight_2013_SouthSudan.pdf)

Department of Economics, Rice University, *Curriculum Vitae – George R. Zodrow* (20 September 2010) (economics.rice.edu/~zodrow/)

Inspector-General of Taxation, *Role and Responsibilities of the Inspector-General of Taxation – Summary* (2009) (igt.gov.au/content/role.asp?NavID=4)

International Tax Dialogue, *ITD Web* (2011)(itdweb.org/Pages/Home.aspx)

National Bureau for Economic Research, *Curriculum Vitae of Charles E. McLure Jr* (12 September 2003) (nber.org/vitae/vita371.htm)

OECD, *Global Forum on VAT* (2015) (www.oecd.org/ctp/consumption/vat-global-forum.htm)

Parliament of Australia, Senate, *About the Senate* (12 July 2011) (www.aph.gov.au/About_Parliament/Senate/About_the_Senate)

US Department of Commerce, Bureau of Economic Analysis, *Value Added by Industry as a Percentage of Gross Domestic Product* (13 December 2011) (bea.gov/iTable/iTable.cfm?ReqID=5&step=1)

US Federal Election Commission, 'PAC Count – 1974 to present' (January 2014) (fec.gov/press/summaries/2011/2011paccount.shtml)

US Federation of Tax Administrators, *State Sales Tax Rates and Food and Drug Exemptions* (1 January 2012) (taxadmin.org/fta/rate/sales.pdf)

US Treasury, *History of the US Tax System – Almanac of Policy Issues* (August 2003) (policyalmanac.org/economic/archive/tax_history.shtml)

Vatinfo.org (2014) (vatinfo.org/)

World Bank, *Country and Lending Groups* (2012) (go.worldbank.org/D7SN0B8YU0)

ARCHIVAL MATERIAL

Price Waterhouse, 'Information Guide: Value Added Tax, April 1980 (Supplement to the Information Guide on Value Added Tax'; File: Value Added Tax; Subject Files 1979–1980 of Geoffrey G. Peterson, Deputy Assistant Secretary for Legislative Affairs, 1979–1980, Office of the Secretary, Office of the Deputy Secretary, Office of the Assistant Secretary for Legislative Affairs; General Records, Subject Files; General Records of the Department of Treasury, Record Group 56; National Archives at College Park, MD (NACP)

Statement by Congressman Al Ullman (upon Introduction of HR 7015, the "Tax Restructuring Act of 1980", April 2, 1980'; File: Value Added Tax; Subject Files 1979–1980 of Geoffrey G. Peterson, Deputy Assistant Secretary for Legislative Affairs, 1979–1980, Office of the Secretary, Office of the Deputy Secretary, Office of the Assistant Secretary for Legislative Affairs; General Records, Subject Files; General Records of the Department of Treasury, Record Group 56; NACP

Memorandum from Donald C. Lubick, Assistant Secretary (Tax Policy) to Treasury Secretary Blumenthal, Subject: Value Added Tax, March 15 1979 – Attaching Revised Treasury Staff Paper – Value Added Tax: Economic and Political Considerations'; File: Value Added Tax; Subject Files 1979–1980 of Geoffrey G. Peterson, Deputy Assistant Secretary for Legislative Affairs, 1979–1980, Office of the Secretary, Office of the Deputy Secretary, Office of the Assistant Secretary for Legislative Affairs; General Records, Subject Files; General Records of the Department of Treasury, Record Group 56; NACP

'Value Added Tax: Economic and Political Considerations' (Revised Treasury Staff Paper) Attachment to Memorandum from Donald C. Lubick, Assistant Secretary (Tax Policy) to Treasury Secretary Blumenthal, Subject: Value Added Tax, March 15, 1979; File: Value Added Tax; Subject Files 1979–1980 of Geoffrey G. Peterson, Deputy Assistant Secretary for Legislative Affairs, 1979–1980, Office of the Secretary, Office of the Deputy Secretary, Office of the Assistant Secretary for Legislative Affairs; General Records, Subject Files; General Records of the Department of Treasury, Record Group 56; NACP

'Value Added Tax', an extract from the American Retail Federation position (p. 8); File: Value Added Tax; Subject Files 1979–1980 of Geoffrey G. Peterson, Deputy Assistant Secretary for Legislative Affairs, 1979–1980, Office of the Secretary, Office of the Deputy Secretary, Office of the Assistant Secretary for Legislative Affairs; General Records, Subject Files; General Records of the Department of Treasury, Record Group 56; NACP

Legislative Affairs, 1979–1980, Office of the Secretary, Office of the Deputy Secretary, Office of the Assistant Secretary for Legislative Affairs; General Records, Subject Files; General Records of the Department of Treasury, Record Group 56; NACP

'Summary of Treasury Consultants' Meeting on Value Added Tax', August 4, 1970 (marked MSF 8/6/70)'; File NN3 056–99–002; Meeting Files of Henry Wallich, Senior Consultant, 1969–1970; Folder 4 – August 4, 1970 – Consultants' Meeting; Meeting Files 1969–1970, Office of the Secretary; General Records of the Department of Treasury; Record Group 56; NACP

'Testimony of the Honorable G. William Miller, Secretary of the Treasury, on the 'Tax Restructuring Act of 1979' before the House Ways and Means Committee – released November 8, 1979'; File: Value Added Tax; Subject Files 1979–1980 of Geoffrey G. Peterson, Deputy Assistant Secretary

'A Note on the Consultants' Meeting on Value Added Taxation' from Henry C. Wallich to Secretary Kennedy, August 5, 1970; File NN3 056–99–002; Meeting Files of Henry Wallich, Senior Consultant, 1969–1970; Folder 4 – August 4, 1970 – Consultants' Meeting; Meeting Files 1969–1970, Office of the Secretary; General Records of the Department of Treasury; Record Group 56; NACP

'Task Force on Business Taxation, First Report to the President – The Value-Added Tax, 1 December 1969, Attachment 2 to a Memorandum from William L Horton (White House) to Mr Finch; File – Value Added Taxes [CFOA 327]; Staff Member and Office Files, Robert H. Finch; White House Central Files; Nixon Presidential Materials Project; NACP

'Agenda Item III Value-Added Tax', discussion leader Arnold Harberger, Treasury Consultants' Meeting, October, 11 1969; File WNRC 80–0005; Meeting Files of Henry Wallich, Senior Consultant, 1969–1970, Folder 2 October 11, 1969 – Consultants' Meeting; Meeting Files 1969–1970; Office of the Secretary, General Records of the Department of Treasury, Record Group 56; NACP

'Preliminary Draft Paper prepared by US Treasury on 'Value Added Tax' September 10, 1969', Attachment 1 to Memorandum from Gerard Brannon (Office of the Treasury Secretary) to Henry C. Wallich, Subject: Materials for the Consultants' Meeting on October 11, 20 September 1969; File WNRC 80–0005; Meeting Files of Henry Wallich, Senior consultant, 1969–1970, Folder 2 October 11, 1969 – Consultants' meeting; Meeting files 1969–1970; Office of the Secretary, General Records of the Department of Treasury, Record Group 56; NACP

Robert Gordon, University of Chicago, to Henry Wallich attaching summary of Treasury Consultants' Meeting, Oct 17, 1969, 12; File WNRC 80–0005; Meeting Files of Henry Wallich, Senior Consultant, 1969–1970, Folder 2 October 11, 1969 – Consultants' Meeting; Meeting Files 1969–1970; Office of the Secretary, General Records of the Department of Treasury, Record Group 56; NACP

Index

For EU product safety concerns, contact us at Calle de José Abascal, 56–1°, 28003 Madrid, Spain or eugpsr@cambridge.org.

www.ingramcontent.com/pod-product-compliance
Lightning Source LLC
LaVergne TN
LVHW020326220926
848484LV00001BB/242

* 9 7 8 1 1 0 7 0 4 4 1 2 8 *